Church, Faith and Culture in the Medieval West

General Editor: Brenda Bolton

About the series

In the last generation an important transformation has taken place in the study of the Medieval Church in the Latin West. This new focus has moved away from a narrow concentration on single religious themes to introduce a greater cultural awareness. Recent cross-disciplinary studies on the Church's rules on consanguinity provide a case in point while other research has benefited from theological, political or literary perspectives.

The new Ashgate series *Church, Faith and Culture in the Medieval West* will contain some of the most innovative work from this area of current research and will be drawn not only from more established scholars but also from those who are younger. The series, therefore, will contribute much new work, approaching the subject vertically throughout the period from *c.* 400 to *c.* 1500 or horizontally throughout the whole of Christendom. The series is conceived as primarily monographic but may also include some collected essays on themes of particular relevance and the significance of individuals. The aim will be to draw authors from a range of disciplinary backgrounds, but all will share a commitment to innovation, analysis and historical accuracy.

About the volume

Starting from the premise of the letter as literary artefact, with a potential for ambiguity, irony and textual allusion, this innovative analysis of the correspondence between the Cluniac abbot, Peter the Venerable, and the future saint, Bernard of Clairvaux, challenges the traditional use of these letters as a source for historical and (auto)biographical reconstruction. Applying techniques drawn from modern theories of epistolarity and contemporary literary criticism to letters treated as whole constructs, Knight demonstrates the presence of a range of manipulative strategies and argues for the consequent production of a significant degree of fictionalisation. She traces the emergence of an epistolary sequence which forms a kind of extended narrative, drawing its authority from Augustine and Jerome, and rooted in classical rhetoric. The work raises important implications both for the study of relations between Cluniacs and Cistercians in the first half of the 12th century and for the approach to letter-writing as a whole.

About the author

Dr Gillian R. Knight is Lecturer in the Department of Classics at the University of Reading, UK.

THE CORRESPONDENCE BETWEEN PETER THE
VENERABLE AND BERNARD OF CLAIRVAUX

Church, Faith and Culture in the Medieval West

General Editor: Brenda Bolton

Other titles in the series:

Michelle Still
The Abbot and the Rule
Religious life at St Albans, 1290–1349

Sylvia Schein
Gateway to the Heavenly City
Crusader Jerusalem and the Catholic West (1099–1187)

Brenda Bolton and Anne Duggan
Adrian IV, the English Pope (1154–1159)

Richard Kay
The Council of Bourges, 1225
A documentary history

The Correspondence between Peter the Venerable and Bernard of Clairvaux

A Semantic and Structural Analysis

GILLIAN R. KNIGHT

Ashgate

© Gillian R. Knight, 2002

Gillian R. Knight has asserted her moral right under the Copyright, Designs and Patents Act, 1988, to be identified as the author of this work.

Published by
Ashgate Publishing Limited
Gower House
Croft Road
Aldershot
Hants GU11 3HR
England

Ashgate Publishing Company
131 Main Street
Burlington
Vermont, 05401–5600
USA

Ashgate website: http://www.ashgate.com

British Library Cataloguing in Publication Data

Knight, Gillian R.
   The Correspondence between Peter the Venerable and Bernard of Clairvaux: A Semantic and Structural Analysis. (Church, Faith and Culture in the Medieval West)
   1. Peter, the Venerable, c.1092–1156. 2. Bernard, of Clairvaux, Saint. 3. Christian saints—France—Correspondence. 4. Abbots—France—Correspondence. 5. Latin letters—History and criticism. I. Title.
   271.1'2'022

US Library of Congress Cataloging in Publication Data

Knight, Gillian R.
   The Correspondence between Peter the Venerable and Bernard of Clairvaux: A Semantic and Structural Analysis / Gillian R. Knight.
    p. cm. (Church, Faith and Culture in the Medieval West)
   Includes bibliographical references.
   1. Peter, the Venerable, ca. 1092–1156—Correspondence. 2. Bernard, of Clairvaux, Saint, 1090 or 91–1153—Correspondence. 3. Abbots—France—Correspondence. 4. Latin letters, Medieval and modern—France—History and criticism. I. Title. II. Series.
   BX4705.P473K56 2002
   271'.1022–dc21   2001053477

ISBN 0 7546 0067 X

This book is printed on acid free paper.
Typeset by Owain Hammonds, Ebeneser, Bontgoch, Talybont, Ceredigion SY24 5DP.
Printed and bound in Great Britain by MPG Books Ltd, Bodmin, Cornwall

Contents

Abbreviations   vi
Introduction   ix

1   Letter-writing and Friendship Reconsidered   1

2   Sanctity and Rebuke: the Relationship between Bernard's *Apologia* and Peter's Letter 28   25

3   The Proof of *Caritas*: Peter, Letter 65, Bernard, Ep. 147   53

4   Fraudulent Alms and Monstrous Election: Peter, Letter 29   73

5   Reproach, *Iocus* and Debate: Bernard, Ep. 228; Peter, Letter 111   101

6   The Salt of *Caritas*: Letter 111 Continued   127

7   Bitterness and Sweetness: Bernard, Ep. 387; Peter, Letter 149   155

8   Salvation, Damnation and *Cohabitatio*: Peter, Letter 150   179

9   A New Crusade: Bernard, Ep. 364; Peter, Letter 164   201

10   Duplicity or Simplicity: Peter, Letters 175 and 181; Bernard, Ep. 265   227

11   An Epistolary Closure: Peter, Letter 192   253

Conclusion   279

Bibliography   283
Index   297

Abbreviations

Biblia sacra iuxta vulgatam versionem, ed. R. Weber, B. Fischer, I. Gribomont, H. F. D. Sparks and W. Thiele, 4th ed., prepared by R. Gryson, Stuttgart, 1994.

Gn	Genesis		Na	Nahum
Ex	Exodus		Hab	Habbakuk
Lv	Leviticus		So	Zephaniah
Nm	Numbers		Agg	Haggai
Dt	Deuteronomy		Za	Zechariah
Ios	Joshua		Mal	Malachi
Idc	Judges		I Mcc	I Maccabees
Rt	Ruth		II Mcc	II Maccabees
I Sm	I Samuel		III Esr	I Esdras
II Sm	II Samuel		IV Esr	II Esdras
III Rg	I Kings		Mt	Matthew
IV Rg	II Kings		Mc	Mark
I Par	I Chronicles		Lc	Luke
II Par	II Chronicles		Io	John
I Esr	Ezra		Act	Acts
II Esr	Nehemiah		Rm	Romans
Tb	Tobit		I Cor	I Corinthians
Idt	Judith		II Cor	II Corinthians
Est	Esther		Gal	Galatians
Iob	Job		Eph	Ephesians
Ps	Psalms		Phil	Philippians
Prv	Proverbs		Col	Colossians
Ecl	Ecclesiastes		I Th	I Thessalonians
Ct	Song of Songs		II Th	II Thessalonians
Sap	Wisdom of Solomon		I Tim	I Timothy
Sir	Ecclesiasticus		II Tim	II Timothy
Is	Isaiah		Tit	Titus
Ier	Jeremiah		Phlm	Philemon
Lam	Lamentations		Hbr	Hebrews
Bar	Baruch		Iac	James
Ez	Ezekiel		I Pt	I Peter
Dn	Daniel		II Pt	II Peter
Os	Hosea		I Io	I John
Ioel	Joel		II Io	II John
Am	Amos		III Io	III John

AbD	Obadiah		Iud	Jude
Ion	Jonah		Apc	Revelation
Mi	Micah			

Patrologia Latina	*Patrologiae cursus completus. Series Latina*
CCCM	*Corpus Christianorum Continuatio Mediaevalis*
CCSL	*Corpus Christianorum Series Latina*
CSEL	*Corpus scriptorum ecclesiasticorum latinorum*
RHGF	*Recueil des Historiens des Gaules et de la France*
JL	Jaffé-Löwenfeld

Introduction

Spanning the first half of the twelfth century, the correspondence between Peter the Venerable, abbot of Cluny, and Bernard of Clairvaux, abbot of Clairvaux and Cistercian figure-head, would appear to offer some reflection of the political issues, major and minor, which troubled Western Europe in that period: papal schism; crusading; the Islamic threat; disputed elections within the Church; quarrels over monastic tithes. In particular, it has been read as providing insights into a conflict between two monastic giants, the established, arguably reactionary, institution of Cluny, and the burgeoning adherents of the reforming Cîteaux.[1] This work aims to offer a detailed study of these letters, approached essentially from the perspective of literature, but set within their historical context. Underlying this, however, are deeper questions relating to the validity of their use as historical documentation and, if this validity is accepted, of the types of approach which can most fruitfully be applied to their study. This issue will be explored through a consideration of the parameters imposed through the requirements and expectations of epistolary dialogue, and of the ways in which the latter are open to manipulation.

The two men were close contemporaries. Born in 1092 or 1094 of an influential seigneurial family, [2] Peter the Venerable became first prior of the Cluniac institution of Domène, then abbot of Cluny from 1122 until his death in 1156. From its foundation in 909, Cluny had become head of a vast empire comprising dependent and associated houses throughout Western Europe.[3] Heir to the new and magnificent church, created by his predecessor Hugh, and blessed by the Cluniac Pope, Urban II, Peter also inherited grave financial problems.[4] Bernard, born

---

[1]   A. H. Bredero, *Cluny et Cîteaux au douzième siècle: l'histoire d'une controverse monastique*, Amsterdam-Maarssen; Lille, 1985. The conflict model can be set against a more moderate view of a complex network of monastic relations as offered by Constable (G. Constable, 'Cluny, Cîteaux, La Chartreuse: San Bernardo e la diversità delle forme di vita religiosa nel XII secolo', in *Studi su S. Bernardo di Chiaravalle, nell'ottavo centenario della canonizzazione, Convegno internazionale certosa di Firenze (6–9 Novembre 1974)*, Bibliotheca Cisterciensis 6, Rome, 1975, 93–114.)

[2]   On Peter's background, see G. Constable (ed.), *The Letters of Peter the Venerable* (Harvard Historical Studies 78), 2 vols, Cambridge, Mass., 1967, II, pp. 233–46.

[3]   On the origins and development of Cluny, see G. de Valous, *Le monachisme clunisien des origines au XVe siècle*, 2 vols, Paris, (2nd ed.) 1970; B. Rosenwein, *Rhinoceros bound. Cluny in the tenth century*, Philadelphia, 1982.

[4]   On these problems, see G Duby, 'Un inventaire des profits de la seigneurerie clunisienne', in G. Constable and J. Kritzeck (eds), *Petrus Venerabilis, 1156–1956: studies and texts commemorating the eighth centenary of his death*, Studia Anselmiana 40, Rome, 1956, 128–140; idem, 'Le Budget de Cluny entre 1080 et 1155', in *Hommes et structures du Moyen Âge. Un recueil d'articles*, ed. G. Duby, Paris, 1973, 61–82.

probably in 1091,[5] in the milieu of the military nobility,[6] followed a different monastic path, entering Cîteaux in 1113.[7] Founded in 1098, Cîteaux had initially struggled to survive.[8] Expansion began, however, with the foundation of La Ferté and of Pontigny between 1112 and 1114, and in 1115 Bernard was entrusted with the foundation of Clairvaux. Under his abbacy, lasting until his death three years before that of Peter, in 1153, the Cistercians as a whole gained considerable prestige, culminating in the papal election in 1145 of Eugenius III, Bernard's former disciple, to the extent that the importance of Clairvaux at this period may seem to have outstripped that of Cîteaux itself.[9]

The extant correspondence consists of some twenty-two letters of widely varying lengths, the bulk of them to be found in one or both of the official letter-collections preserved in the name of each man. For convenience, these have been tabulated below, in the (approximately chronological) order in which they will be examined in this work. The texts used here are taken directly from the recently produced and widely used printed editions of Constable[10] and Leclercq,[11] taking cognisance of manuscript variants as given there. Following the practice of these two editors, and in the interests of clarity, the nomenclature of 'letters' and *epistolae* has been adopted respectively.[12]

Author	Letter no.	Edition	Date
Peter	Letter 28	*Letters*, I, pp. 52–101	1127(?)
Peter	Letter 65	*Letters*, I, pp. 194–5	Late 1137
Bernard	Ep. 147 (= letter 74)	*SBO*, VII, pp. 350–51 (*Letters*, I, pp. 207–8)	Feb/May 1138
Peter	Letter 73	*Letters*, I, p. 206	Spring 1138
Bernard	Ep. 148	*SBO*, VII, p. 352	Around 1138
Peter	Letter 29	*Letters*, I, pp. 101–5	Aug/Sept 1138
Bernard	Ep. 149	*SBO*, VII, p. 352	Around 1138

---

[5] A. H. Bredero, 'Saint Bernard, est il né en 1090 ou en 1091?', in *Papauté, monachisme et théories politiques. Etudes d'histoire médiévale offertes à Marcel Pacaut*, ed. P. Guichard, M.-T. Lorcin, J.-M. Poisson and M. Rubellin, 2 vols, Lyon, 1994, I, 229–41.

[6] A. H. Bredero, *Bernard of Clairvaux, between cult and history*, Grand Rapids, Mich., 1996, pp. 11–14.

[7] On Bernard in general, see B. S. James, *Saint Bernard of Clairvaux, an essay in biography*, London, 1957.

[8] J.-B. Auberger, *L'unanimité cistercienne primitive: mythe ou réalité*, Cîteaux-Achel, 1986, pp. 166–82.

[9] On this question, see Bredero, *Bernard of Clairvaux*, pp. 267–75.

[10] Constable, *Letters*, I. A short list of editors' corrections is provided in G. Constable, 'On editing the letters of Peter the Venerable', *Quellen und Forschungen aus italienischen Archiven und Bibliotheken* 54 (1974), 483–508.

[11] Dom J. Leclercq and H. Rochais (eds), *Sancti Bernardi Opera*, 8 vols, VII, Rome, 1974; VIII, Rome, 1977. A short list of editors' corrections is provided in *Recueil d'études sur saint Bernard et ses écrits*, ed. Dom J. Leclercq, 5 vols, IV, Storia e letteratura 167, Rome, 1987, p. 418.

[12] The punctuation of the printed editions has been followed, but for ease of comprehension the spelling has been adjusted in accordance with classical norms.

Bernard	Ep. 228 (= letter 110)	*SBO*, VII, pp.98–100 (*Letters*, I, pp. 272–4)	Late 1143/early 1144
Peter	Letter 111	*Letters*, I, pp. 274–99	Late spring/early summer 1144
Bernard	Ep. 267	*SBO*, VIII, p. 176	Around 1145
Bernard	Ep. 387* (= letter 148)	*SBO*, VIII, pp. 355–6 (*Letters*, I, pp. 362–3)	June/July(?) 1149
Peter	Letter 149	*Letters*, I, pp. 363–6	Sept 1149
Peter	Letter 150	*Letters*, I, pp. 367–71	Mid-Oct 1149
Bernard	Ep. 389* (= letter 152)	*SBO*, VIII, pp. 356–7 (*Letters*, I, pp. 372–3)	Oct(?) 1140
Peter	Letter 145	*Letters*, I, pp. 360–61	Autumn 1149
Bernard	Ep. 364* (= letter 163)	*SBO*, VIII, pp. 318–19 (*Letters*, I, pp. 395–6)	Mar/Apr 1150
Peter	Letter 164	*Letters*, I, pp. 396–8	Apr 1150
Bernard	Ep. 521*	*SBO*, VIII, pp. 483–4	Between May/July 1150
Peter	Letter 175 (= ep. 264)	*Letters*, I, pp. 416–17 (*SBO*, VIII, pp. 173–4)	Autumn 1150
Bernard	Ep. 265 (= letter 177)	*SBO*, VIII, pp. 174–5 (*Letters*, I, p. 418)	Autumn 1150
Peter	Letter 181	*Letters*, I, pp. 423–5	Mar 1151
Peter	Letter 192	*Letters*, I, pp. 443–8	May 1152

* = preserved outside Bernard's official letter-collection

As the above table shows, the correspondence spans a wide period of time, starting with Peter's letter 28, written some four or five years after he became abbot of Cluny, and ending with his letter 192, written four years before his own death and one year before that of Bernard. At the same time, individual letters can be seen to reflect the particular political and ecclesiastical concerns of the period within which they were produced. For example, Peter's letter 65, together with Bernard's ep. 147, written while Bernard himself was in Italy, are set against the background of the papal schism of 1130–38. Other letters take as their starting-point issues such as elections, tithes and crusading. In terms of epistolarity, the ensuing combination of the 'vertical' and the 'horizontal' can be seen to function as a mirror of the epistolary process: treated as an individual construct, the letter emerges as a fixed point on the epistolary continuum, represented here by the epistolary sequence. As a fixed point, it can be seen to have its own centre of gravity and points of reference. As part of a sequence, however, it is set within a framework of momentum and change. In the following study, attempts will be made to situate the letters both horizontally, in terms of contemporary writings and documentation, and vertically, in terms of both sequence and epistolary tradition.[13]

---

[13] To the best of my knowledge, there is as yet no complete translation of Peter's letters, although certain letters appear translated into English in whole or in part in some items of bibliography cited in this work. Bernard's letters have been translated into English by James (B. S. James, trans., *The Letters of St. Bernard of Clairvaux*, London, 1953, reprinted with introduction by B. M. Kienzle, Thrupp, Stroud, 1998). There is also a recent bilingual edition into French by Rochais (H. Rochais, trans., *Bernard de Clairvaux, Lettres*, texte latin des S. Bernardi Opera by J. Leclercq, H. Rochais and Ch. H. Talbot, intro. and notes by M. Duchet-Suchaux, Sources Chrétiennes, 425, Paris, 1997). In what follows all translations, of all Latin texts, are my own. Where appropriate, letters have been translated in full.

The incorporation of these letters into official collections may seem to give rise to difficulties of a more practical nature. Although the processes involved are largely a matter of conjecture, the collection in each case seems to have gone through successive stages.[14] It seems likely that revision of the letters was undertaken at each stage, and that the early collections, at least, were formed under the authors' supervision. It cannot, therefore, be assumed that the version(s) as preserved is/are identical with that which would initially have been received by the addressee. An additional barrier to the recuperation of complete 'authenticity' is the role which may have been played by intermediaries, such as secretaries and messengers.[15] The critical position adopted here, in line with the discussion on epistolarity given above, is that any one version can, in itself, be treated as 'authentic' in representing one fixed point in the epistolary process. At a more pragmatic level, where letters are preserved in the collection of both letter-writer and addressee, permitting a comparison between the two versions, the (relatively few) discrepancies which emerge are generally explicable in terms of subsequent minor adjustments of style rather than substance.[16] Any exceptions to this principle will be discussed as they arise.

As suggested earlier, the approach taken here will centre on the concept of individual letters treated as whole constructs. At the same time, these constructs will be viewed as part of an emerging and dynamic epistolary sequence. The first chapter will focus on the question of generic definition and consider a range of critical approaches, traditional and modern, to letter-writing in general and to these letters specifically. In particular, there will be a consideration of the relationship between letter-writing and concepts of friendship, both classical and Christian. Successive chapters will be organised largely on a chronological basis. Rather than attempting to track thematic developments, they will concentrate on reconstituting groupings of letters and on establishing the presence of a complex pattern of inter- and intratextual allusion,[17] which renders each letter in some sense a response to and/or development of what has gone before. In essence, it will be argued that such letters can be seen to oscillate between the polarities of 'public' and 'private', 'fact' and 'fiction'. Finally, it will be suggested that subsequent inclusion within and exclusion from a collection, viewed here as a form of extended narrative, can be seen to dislocate and distort this emergent sequence.

---

[14] In the case of Peter, Constable proposes two versions, one shorter and one extended, both produced during his lifetime (Constable, *Letters* II, pp. 12–17; 56). In the case of Bernard, Leclercq proposes three versions, one shorter and one extended within his lifetime, with a third and again enlarged version produced shortly after his death (*SBO*, VII, pp. ix–xvi).

[15] On the role of Bernard's secretaries, see Dom J. Leclercq, 'Lettres de S. Bernard: histoire ou littérature?', in *Recueil d'études*, IV, 125–225, pp. 147–52. In relation to this study, the question of authenticity arises principally in relation to two letters, ep. 387 and ep. 389, and will be addressed *in situ*. In the case of Peter, the homogeneity of style and approach may be held to substantiate the claim of Constable, that Peter was responsible for composing most of the letters in his collection (Constable, *Letters*, II, p. 15).

[16] See the comments of Constable (Constable, *Letters*, II, p. 41).

[17] Recognised textual borrowings are shown in footnotes through =. Unless otherwise indicated, these are drawn from the annotations of Constable and Leclercq. The expansions and suggested allusions, however, are my own.

Chapter 1

Letter-writing and Friendship Reconsidered

The primary aim of this chapter is to situate the Peter/Bernard correspondence within the tradition of epistolary writing, as derived from antiquity and assimilated within the early Christian period and throughout the Middle Ages. As stated in the introduction, an underlying concern of this study is a re-evaluation of the value and nature of these letters as historical documentation, through an examination of the parameters surrounding the use of epistolary discourse. The question will be approached initially through a consideration of the relevance and applicability of models and precepts to be found in classical and medieval rhetorical handbooks. This will be set alongside modern critical theory, in particular, contemporary concepts of epistolarity as developed around the notion of the epistolary relationship pertaining to letter-writer and addressee. The second part of the chapter will consider the relationship between the activity of letter-writing and the development of classical and Christian ideals of friendship, focusing on two aspects in particular: the terminology employed to express such ideals, and the enshrinement of the latter in what can be seen as a form of epistolary etiquette. It will start from the premise that epistolary 'friendship' can in itself be viewed as a construct, utilising a range of standard devices and serving a variety of purposes. This will be demonstrated through selected examples drawn from sources both prior to and contemporaneous with the correspondence in question, together with passages taken from letters of Peter and Bernard addressed to other recipients.

Before this is undertaken, it may be helpful to consider briefly both the circumstances surrounding the study of letters in general and the approaches which have been taken to this correspondence in particular. The difficulties, if they can be viewed as such, would seem to reside principally in the question of generic definition. 'Literary' letters, identified here with letters preserved in edited collections, as is generally recognised, straddle the boundary between history and literature.[1] Rooted in a particular set of historical circumstances, they none-the-less draw on a network of conventions and expectations which can be seen as forming part of a literary tradition. Despite this, there would seem to have been a certain reluctance to acknowledge and take seriously the implications of this literary element, as signalled by Hutchinson in his recent, self-proclaimed 'literary' study of the letters of Cicero.[2] This attitude is beginning to change, as a number of recent studies show. As academic disciplines, history and literature have moved much

---

[1]   G. Constable, *Letters and letter-collections*, Typologie des Sources du Moyen Age occidental 17, Turnhout, 1976, pp. 11–12; Leclercq, 'Lettres de S. Bernard', pp. 136–42.

[2]   G. O. Hutchinson, *Cicero's correspondence. A literary study*, Oxford, 1998, pp. 1–3.

closer in recent years, as evinced by the work of such contemporary writers on Cluniac history as Constable, Rosenwein and Iogna-Prat, and, on Cistercian history, of Lekai, Holdsworth, Auberger and Cowdrey. It may be noted, however, that this rapprochement is not necessarily universally perceived. To cite the words of Clanchy in relation to the twelfth-century 'autobiography' of Abelard: 'The historian is trained to search for a single factual narrative in a text like *Historia Calamitatum*, whereas the literary specialist will question – sometimes perversely in the historian's opinion – whether there is a single meaning in the text or any clear dividing line between fact and fiction.'[3]

Overstated in general terms as this view may seem to be, in the case of the correspondence between Peter and Bernard, a confluence of particular factors may seem to lend it a degree of validity. Traditionally, this correspondence has been taken as providing documentary proof of a personal friendship. This view, as Bredero points out, can be traced back to the comments of Clémencet in his introduction of 1773.[4] The most influential expression of this approach, however, was probably that of Leclercq, who prefaced his 1946 discussion with the statement that despite apparent disagreements 'their friendship did not cease to grow; it showed itself in affectionate declarations which make it, in the lives of both, a particular friendship.'[5] A strong challenge to this view was issued some seven years later by Lortz, who argued that the complimentary language should be read as ceremonious rhetoric, bridging deep-seated underlying tensions.[6] Further criticism of the autobiographical approach was launched by Piazzoni, who dismissed the question of a personal relationship as unsuitable for the historiographer.[7] In consequence, perhaps, the brief study of the letters made in 1986 by Torrell and Bouthillier draws attention to the problem of 'penetrating the rhetorical veil'.[8] More

---

[3]   M. T. Clanchy, 'Abelard – knight (miles), courtier (palatinus) and man of war (vir bellator)', in *Medieval Knighthood* V (Papers from the Strawberry Hill Conference 1994), ed. S. Church and R. Harvey, Woodbridge, 1995, 101–18, pp. 101–2.

[4]   Dom C. Clémencet, *Histoire littéraire de S. Bernard, abbé de Clairvaux, et de Pierre Vénérable, abbé de Cluni*, Paris, 1773, p. *v*. See Bredero, *Bernard of Clairvaux*, p. 227.

[5]   'leur amitié n'a cessé de s'accroître; elle s'est manifestée en des protestations affectueuses qui font d'elle, dans la vie de l'un comme de l'autre, une amitié particulière' (Dom J. Leclercq, *Pierre le Vénérable*, Abbaye St. Wandrille, 1946, p. 67).

[6]   'Ihre wechselseitigen Komplimente, Freundschafts- und Liebeserklärungen entflammen sich typisch rhetorisch an den großen Worten der Schrift und scheinen eher – oder doch wenigstens auch! – höfliche, vom Geist christlicher Bruderliebe getragene Überbrückungsversuche der tiefgehenden Spannungen zu sein als Äußerungen einer echten Sympathie' (J. Lortz, 'Einleitung', in *Bernhard von Clairvaux, Mönch und Mystiker*, InternationalerBernhardcongress, Mainz, 1953, Wiesbaden, 1955, p. xxxiv). As will be seen, however, such complimentary language may equally be thought to function as a 'barrier'.

[7]   A. M. Piazzoni, 'Un falso problemo storiografico: Note a proposito della "amicizia" tra Pietro il Venerabile e Bernardo di Clairvaux', *Bullettino dell'Istituto Storico Italiano per il Medio Evo e Archivio Muratoriano* 89 (1980–81), 443–87. Unlike Lortz, Piazzoni acknowledges the possibility that such protestations of friendship may convey a subtle nuancing of irony (ibid., p. 467).

[8]   J. P. Torrell and D. Bouthillier, *Pierre le Vénérable et sa vision du monde. Sa vie, son œuvre. L'homme et le démon*, Spicilegium Sacrum Lovaniense, Études et documents 42, Louvain, 1986, p. 92. In spite of this *caveat*, however, there is an element of autobiographical conclusion, to the effect that Peter's sentiments were 'warmer' than those of Bernard (ibid., p. 101).

recently, Bredero has also strongly espoused this position.[9] In spite of this, however, the autobiographical tendency has continued to make its presence felt,[10] to the extent that casual references to the 'friendship' often appear in scholarly studies.[11]

The recognition that these letters cannot be treated as straightforward factual documents is an important one, which has wider consequences: just as they cannot be seen as giving transparent information about the personal relationship of Peter and Bernard, so they cannot be used to give transparent information about the relationship between Cistercians and Cluniacs. The point has been made explicitly by Constable in relation to the polemical literature of the period, which he argues presents a 'genuine but partial and distorted picture of the realities as the writers saw them'.[12] On the other hand, the minimalist approach which has been applied more recently brings its own problems. The discussion by Bredero, for example, appears to privilege a reconstruction of the historical contexts of the letters above a study of the letters themselves.[13] His characterisation of the rhetoric as 'high-pitched attestations of ... mutual friendship',[14] appears to miss the point that rhetoric is both a tool of manipulation and itself subject to manipulation. To dismiss it as empty verbiage is to risk divorcing the language from the content, the message from the medium.

As suggested earlier, the problems raised by the treatment of these letters can be related to a more general question of generic definition. This seems to encompass various aspects: what are the defining characteristics of a letter; what, if any, clear demarcation can be drawn between 'real' and 'non-real' letters; what critical framework(s) can be applied, with what sorts of structural and stylistic criteria? An influential attempt to deal with these issues was made by Deissman at the turn of the century. In a number of biblical studies he invoked a distinction between the 'letter' and the 'epistle'. In essence, letters were said to be private and natural;

---

[9]   A. H. Bredero, 'Saint Bernard in his relations with Peter the Venerable', in *Bernardus Magister: papers presented at the nonacentenary celebration of the birth of Saint Bernard of Clairvaux, Kalamazoo, Michigan*, ed. John R. Sommerfeldt, Spencer, Mass., 1992, 315–47, p. 316.

[10]   J. Auniord, 'L'ami de Saint Bernard. Quelques textes', *Collectanea Sacri Ordinis Cisterciensis* 18, 1956, 88–99; A. P. Lang, 'The Friendship between Peter the Venerable and Bernard of Clairvaux', in *Bernard of Clairvaux, Studies presented to Dom J. Leclercq*, Washington, 1973, 35–53; D. Grivot, 'Saint Bernard et Pierre le Vénérable', in *Saint Bernard et la recherche de Dieu*. Actes du colloque organisé par l'Institut catholique de Toulouse (25–29 janvier, 1991), *Bulletin de Littérature Ecclésiastique* 93 (1992), fasc. I, 85–99. While accepting that differences existed between the two men, the latter nevertheless concludes with the (otherwise unsubstantiated) hypothesis initiated by Leclercq, that Peter wanted to end his days in Clairvaux: 'Quel mérite!' (ibid., pp. 97–8). McGuire similarly identifies 'marks of real friendship' in their letters (B. P. McGuire, *The difficult saint. Bernard of Clairvaux and his tradition*, Cistercian Studies Series 126, Kalamazoo, 1991, p. 61).

[11]   A recent example of this is a reference by the generally sceptical Holsinger to Peter the Venerable as the 'sometime friend' of Bernard (B. Holsinger, 'The color of salvation', in *The tongue of the Fathers. Gender and ideology in twelfth-century Latin*, ed. D. Townsend and A. Taylor, Philadelphia, 1998, 156–86, p. 163).

[12]   G. Constable, *The reformation of the twelfth century*, Cambridge, 1996, p. 131.

[13]   Bredero, 'Saint Bernard in his relations'; idem, *Bernard of Clairvaux*, pp. 227–48.

[14]   Bredero, 'Saint Bernard in his relations', p. 316.

epistles to be public and conventional. 'Literary' letters were thereby relegated to the category of 'non-real' letters, on the grounds that they were concerned with artistry rather than with direct communication.[15] This rigid demarcation was challenged by Doty in 1969, who argued for a more flexible and inclusive definition to cover all forms of epistolary writing, and for a consequent degree of blurring of the polarities of private/public, natural/conventional.[16]

Doty defines the letter as a literary product, intended for a private or public reader/s. Letter form is said to be distinguished by being sent or intended for sending, from a writer or from writers to an addressee or addressees, containing greetings, conclusion, or other formally stylised components, usually with reference to or clear intent to be a letter.[17] Central to Doty's discussion is the identification of the epistolary situation, the desire of the writer to communicate with someone distant in space or time:[18] as Doty seems to imply,[19] the recognition of this is perhaps already inherent in ancient definitions of the letter as a substitute for dialogue.[20] This facilitates a further blurring, that of the boundary between 'real' and 'non-real' letters. Fictitious letters can be seen to imitate the epistolary situation, and thus to be differentiated only from real letters by the absence of Doty's first category, that of being sent or intended for sending. His redefinition clears the air for a much broader approach to the whole question of letter-writing and provides a working hypothesis for the first two issues raised above. There remains the problem, however, of developing an appropriate critical framework.

The formal model applied to medieval epistolography is generally based on the rules of the *dictamen*, art of prose-writing, as laid down by various letter-writing manuals.[21] These set down a standard five-part format for a letter comprising salutation (*salutatio*), securing of good-will (*benevolentiae captatio*), exposition (*narratio*), petition (*petitio*), conclusion (*conclusio*). The earliest surviving examples of such handbooks include the *Dictaminum radii*, also known as *Flores*

---

[15]   Deissman's approach is encapsulated in the following citation: 'There are so-called letters in which the writer ceases to be naïve, perhaps because he thinks himself a celebrity and casts a side-glance at the public between every word, coquettishly courting the publicity to which his lines may some day attain. "Letters" such as these, epistolary letters, half intended for publication, are bad letters; with their frigidity, affectation, and vain insincerity they show us what a real letter should not be' (G. A. Deissman, *Light from the ancient East. The New Testament illustrated by recently discovered texts of the Graeco-Roman world*, trans. L. R. M. Strachan, London, 1910, p. 221).

[16]   W. Doty, 'The Classification of Epistolary Literature', *The Catholic Biblical Quarterly* 31 (1969), 183–99.

[17]   Ibid., p. 193.

[18]   Ibid.

[19]   Ibid.

[20]   *Aut quid mi iucundius quam, cum coram tecum loqui non possim, aut scribere ad te aut tuas legere litteras?*, 'Or what is more pleasant for me, since I cannot converse with you face to face, than either to write to you or to read your letters?' (Cicero, *Epistulae ad familiares*, 12, 30. 1, ed. D. R. Shackleton Bailey, Bibliotheca scriptorum Graecorum et Romanorum Teubneriana, Stuttgart, 1988).

[21]   On the whole question of the *dictamen*, see M. Camargo, *Ars Dictaminis Ars Dictandi*, Typologie des Sources du Moyen Age occidental 60, Turnhout, 1991.

rhetorici,[22] and *Breviarium de dictamine* of Alberic of Monte Cassino, written around 1087;[23] the *Praecepta dictaminum* of Adalbert of Samaria, dating to between 1111 and 1118;[24] the *Rationes dictandi prosaice* of Hugh of Bologna, dated probably to between 1119 and 1124,[25] and the anonymous *Rationes dictandi*, written about 1135.[26] Alberic utilises a four-part division of speech: introduction (*exordium*); exposition (*narratio*); argumentation (*argumentatio*); conclusion (*conclusio*). At the same time, as Murphy points out,[27] he is concerned to distinguish between introduction (*exordium*) and salutation (*salutatio*), both of which receive a considerable degree of attention.[28] Adalbert focuses exclusively on the proprieties to be observed in the salutation.[29] Hugh names only three parts of a letter: introduction (*exordium*); exposition (*narratio*); conclusion (*conclusio*). However, as Murphy comments,[30] the salutation is specifically named as one of three 'places' for the securing of 'good-will'.[31] The anonymous *Rationes dictandi*, on the other hand, follows the five-part division set out at the beginning of this discussion.[32]

---

[22] *Alberici Casinensis Flores rhetorici*, ed. D. M. Inguanez and H. M. Willard, Miscellanea Cassinense 14, Montecassino, 1938; Alberic of Monte Cassino, *Flowers of rhetoric*, trans. J. M. Miller in *Readings in medieval rhetoric*, ed. J. M. Miller, M. H. Prosser, T. W. Benson, Bloomington, Indiana, 1973, pp. 131–61.

[23] *Albericus, de dictamine* in L. Rockinger (ed.), *Briefsteller und Formelbücher des eilften bis vierzehnten Jahrhunderts*, Quellen und Erörterungen zur bayerischen und deutschen Geschichte 9, Munich, 1863, reprinted in 2 vols, New York, 1961, 1, pp. 29–46 (partial text only); discussed in J. J. Murphy, *Rhetoric in the Middle Ages. A history of rhetorical theory from Saint Augustine to the Renaissance*, Berkeley; Los Angeles; London, 1974, pp. 207–11.

[24] *Adalbertus Samaritanus, Praecepta dictaminum*, ed. F.-J. Schmale, Monumenta Germaniae Historica, Quellen zur Geistesgeschichte des Mittelalters III, Weimar, 1961, pp. 28–74, discussed in Murphy, *Rhetoric*, pp. 212–14.

[25] *Hugonis Bononiensis, Rationes dictandi prosaice*, ed. Rockinger, in *Briefsteller*, 1, pp. 53–94; discussed in Murphy, *Rhetoric*, pp. 214–20.

[26] *Rationes dictandi* (wrongly attributed to Alberic), ed. Rockinger, in *Briefsteller*, I, pp. 9–28; *Anonymous of Bologna: The principles of letter-writing*, trans. J. J. Murphy, in *Three Medieval Rhetorical Arts*, ed. J. J. Murphy, Berkeley; Los Angeles, 1971, pp. 5–25.

[27] Murphy, *Rhetoric*, pp. 206–7.

[28] The 'colours' appropriate to the *exordium* are said to be those *quibus capitur benevolentia*, 'by which good-will is seized' (*Flores rhetorici*, III, 1, p. 36); the salutation should take into consideration *persona mittentis, persona cui mittitur*, 'the person of the sender, the person to whom it is being sent' (ibid., III, 5, p. 38).

[29] *Salutationes, ut diximus, epistolis praeponendae diverse secundum diversitatem personarum sunt adhibendae*, 'The salutations to be placed before letters, as we have said, are to be applied differently according to the difference of persons' (*Praecepta dictaminum*, 3, p. 34).

[30] Murphy, *Rhetoric*, p. 216.

[31] *Benivolentiam quoque in epistolis alio et alio modo tribus in locis captamus. In salutatione videlicet primo, si tria vel iiii ad laudem adiectiva ponamus..* , 'We secure good-will also in letters in different ways in three places. Namely, in the salutation, if we should place three or four flattering adjectives ... ' (*Rationes dictandi prosaice*, IX, p. 57). The other two 'places' are named as introduction and conclusion.

[32] According to Murphy, this five-part division represents a refinement and scaling down of the (six) Ciceronian parts of a speech, as laid down, for example, in the latter's *De inventione*. The *exordium* has become split into *salutatio* and *captatio*, while *petitio* can be seen to have replaced *confirmatio* or 'proof' (Murphy, *Rhetoric*, p. 225).

Various problems stand in the way of applying this five-part model to letters written during the first half of the twelfth century. First, it is arguably somewhat anachronistic. The *ars dictaminis* would flower in France only in the second half of the twelfth century, although the rules were already known.[33] Second, it is not clear how rigorously this pattern was expected to be applied. The anonymous treatise discussed above, for example, suggests that various sections may be omitted, and that the order may be altered and even intermingled.[34] A rigid application of the dictaminal model to the letters of Peter the Venerable, for example, tends to produce a series of negatives which obscures rather than illuminates the particular qualities of his writing. Constable concludes that the letters show a 'disregard' for the demands of both *dictamen* and *cursus* (the related discipline dealing with rhythmic cadences at the end of sentences, replacing the metrical *clausulae* of antiquity),[35] suggesting that Peter fails to organise his letters according to the five-fold division, ignores and even contravenes the accepted metrical patterns of *clausulae*, neglects the etiquette demanded in salutations, and criticises the contemporary desire for brevity.[36] The letters in Peter the Venerable's collection do indeed display a wide variation in both length and structure. None-the-less, the apparent verbosity and fluidity mask underlying principles of organisation which, while not necessarily strictly conforming to these requirements, often display an awareness of them.[37]

The dictaminal model may accordingly be of some value, but its helpfulness is limited. The alternative, to look backwards to antiquity, is also problematic. Among the various rhetorical treatises still extant, letter-writing is poorly represented. Two

---

[33] Constable, *Letters*, II, pp. 31–2. On the spread of the *dictamen*, see A. Boureau, 'The letter-writing norm, a medieval invention', in *Correspondence: models of letter-writing from the Middle Ages to the Nineteenth century*, R. Chartier, A. Boureau and C. Dauphin, trans. C. Woodall, Cambridge, 1997, pp. 24–58.

[34] *Tacetur crebro petitio, cum nihil intendit petere animus dirigentis. perfecta tamen ex [tribus] reliquis manet epistola*, 'The petition is frequently passed over, when the mind of the sender intends to seek nothing. However, the letter remains complete from the remaining [three] parts' (*Rationes dictandi*, X, p. 22); *Potest autem captatio benevolentiae ... habita narratione non incongrue constitui, ut cum per eam recipientis animus fuerit delinitus confestim petitionis ordo sequatur ...*, 'Indeed, the securing of good-will can fittingly be placed enclosing the narration, so that when the mind of the recipient has been soothed by it the petition may follow in swift order ...' (ibid., XI, p. 23).

[35] For a brief description of the three recommended clause endings, *planus*, *tardus* and *velox*, see Camargo, *Ars dictaminis*, p. 26. For a more detailed study see T. Janson, *Prose rhythm in medieval Latin from the 9th to the 13th century*, Studia Latina Stockholmiensia 20, Stockholm, 1975.

[36] Constable, *Letters* II, pp. 35–8. Janson's study, however, proves, on the contrary, that Peter's letters not only regularly employ rhythmic cadences but also conform to the contemporary preference for *velox* and *planus* over *tardus* (Janson, *Prose rhythm*, p. 75, n. 23; p. 113).

[37] Letter 9, for example, to a certain 'Peter the scholar' (possibly Peter Abelard), utilises a copybook five-part structure, but sets it against a secondary structure built up around a series of biblical citations which form the main 'pillars' of the argument to monastic conversion (Peter, letter 9, *Letters*, I, pp. 14–16). For an analysis, see G. R. Knight, 'Rhetoric and stylistics: the personalisation of convention in the letters of Peter the Venerable', unpublished PhD thesis, Reading, 1997, pp. 5–7.

Hellenistic works, one attributed to Demetrius,[38] the other to Libanius,[39] offer a brief survey of letters categorised by 'type'.[40] Both, however, recognise that types can be mixed and combined. In addition, letter-writing forms a section of two more general handbooks, the *De elocutione*, also attributed to Demetrius,[41] and the *Ars rhetorica* of Julius Victor.[42] Unlike the medieval handbooks, those from antiquity do not lay down rules on structure. However, that of Julius Victor may offer something else. A concern with propriety governs all rhetorical treatises, but the recommendations of the *Ars rhetorica* seem to go beyond this and to recognise, or advocate, a form of epistolary 'etiquette'. Victor speaks of the 'grace' of a letter and of its 'manner' or 'measure';[43] he discusses salutations and valedictions in terms of gradations of friendship or rank;[44] he cites the practice of the ancients of writing in their own hand, or at least signing, letters to their dearest.[45] Letters of the period, the fourth and fifth centuries AD, as will be seen, also reflect and exploit the concept of propriety.

Drawing partly on the ancient theorists, a system of classification by function has been drawn up by Stowers, which relates the development of classical and early Christian letters to the branches of classical rhetoric.[46] Rhetoric was divided into three kinds: forensic (or judicial); deliberative (or advising); epideictic (or panegyric). Broadly speaking, accusing and apologetic letters can be assigned to the first category, letters of advice to the second, and letters of praise and blame to the third. At the same time, Stowers argues that this classification is partly undermined by the existence of another category derived from moral philosophy, that of *paraenesis* (or exhortation), which subsumes the divisions of deliberative and epideictic.[47] The paraenetic letter, combining advice and exhortation with praise or blame, forms an important and influential strand of early Christian writing. The importance attached to imitation and tradition in the Middle Ages, together with the

---

[38] *Demetrii [Phalarei] Typoi epistolikoi*, in *Demetrius and Libanius*, ed. V. Weichert, Leipzig, 1910, pp. 1–12. According to Malherbe, this can be dated anywhere between 200 BC and AD 300 (A. J. Malherbe, *Ancient epistolary theory*, Society of Biblical Literature 19, Atlanta, Georgia, 1988, p. 4).

[39] *Libanii sophistae Epistolimaioi characteres*, in Weichert, pp. 13–34. This is variously dated between the fourth and sixth centuries AD (Malherbe, *Epistolary theory*, p. 5).

[40] 'Demetrius' identifies 21 'types'; 'Libanius' has 41 'styles'.

[41] *Demetrius Phalareus, De elocutione*, ed. L. Radermacher, Stuttgart, 1966; trans. G. M. A. Grube, *A Greek critic: Demetrius on style*, Toronto, 1961. Letter-writing is covered in sections 223–35 (Radermacher, pp. 47–9). Suggestions for dating have ranged from the third century BC to the first century AD: according to Malherbe, its sources may go back to the first century BC (Malherbe, *Epistolary theory*, p. 2).

[42] C. Iulius Victor, *Ars Rhetorica*, ed. R. Giomini and M. S. Celentano, Leipzig, 1980. Letter-writing is dealt with in the final sections, 447–8 (ibid., pp. 105–6.) This work is generally accepted as belonging to the fourth century AD (Malherbe, *Epistolary theory*, p. 3).

[43] The grace of a letter must be maintained, *ne recedat ab epistolae gratia*; the manner of a letter must not be destroyed, *ut ne modum epistolae corrumpas* (*Ars rhetorica*, 447, p. 105).

[44] *Praefationes ac subscriptiones litterarum computandae sunt pro discrimine amicitiae aut dignitatis* (ibid, p. 106).

[45] *Observabant veteres carissimis sua manu scribere vel plurimum subscribere* (ibid.).

[46] S. K. Stowers, *Letter Writing in Greco-Roman Antiquity*, Philadelphia, 1986.

[47] Ibid., pp. 51–2.

availability of earlier letter-collections for use as models, points to classical rhetorical theory as a potential source for some stylistic and structural features of certain types of letters.

An alternative critical approach has meanwhile been developing from a different direction, that of the epistolary novel. Here, too, literary critics have pointed to the difficulty of drawing any strict demarcation between 'real' and 'non-real' letters, for example, Versini,[48] and Brownlee.[49] Rosenmeyer, indeed, in the context of Ovidian poetry, goes so far as to declare, 'On the most basic level, all letters are fictions.'[50] The concept of the epistolary situation, the separation of writer and addressee in time and space, and the consequent desire or necessity of creating an epistolary relationship, is at the heart of the model of epistolarity devised by Altman.[51] Exploring the ramifications of this enforced discontinuity, Altman draws attention to the elements of paradoxicality inherent in letter form, in particular, to its duality of function. In its mediating role, according to Altman, the letter can act as bridge, to abolish distance, or barrier, to create it. Its contents can likewise function as portrait or mask, that is, to reveal or to obscure.[52]

Altman's model of epistolarity, building on the work of Doty, provides a flexible corrective to the formalisation of the medieval handbooks on the one hand, and the lack of specificity of the ancient theorists on the other. An individual letter, as Cherewatuk and Wiethaus point out, gains its significance from the use or misuse to which epistolary expectations are put.[53] The blurring of the distinction between 'real' and 'nonreal' letters makes possible the recognition that the letter is a literary artefact, a fixed point in a continuum of communication, the epistolary process. The epistolary relationship can be viewed as an artificial construct, the result of the projection of *personae* for writer and addressee, the letter itself treated as a form of first-person narrative, with analogies to first-person poetry. This recognition paves the way for the application of the tools of contemporary literary criticism: use and abuse of *topoi*; inter- and intratextual allusion; the potential for irony and for a sub-text below the surface narrative. So viewed, the letter-construct may emerge as multi-layered and ambiguous, generating a range of possible readings, corresponding to a variety of potential readership. At the same time, the letter can be seen to have an internal dynamic, resulting from semantic patternings and allusive sequencings.[54]

---

[48]   L. Versini, *Le Roman épistolaire*, Paris, 1979, p. 9.
[49]   Brownlee defines the letter as a 'metalinguistic medium that comments upon the status of language itself' (M. S. Brownlee, *The severed word. Ovid's Heroides and the novela sentimental*, Princeton, New Jersey, 1990, p.70).
[50]   P. A. Rosenmeyer, 'Ovid's *Heroides* and *Tristia*: voices from exile', *Ramus* 26 (i) (1997), 29–56, p. 51.
[51]   J. G. Altman, *Epistolarity: Approaches to a Form*, Columbus, 1982.
[52]   Ibid., p. 186.
[53]   K. Cherewatuk and V. Wiethaus, *Dear Sister: Medieval Women and the Epistolary Genre*, Philadelphia, 1993, p. 4.
[54]   The value of this kind of approach is demonstrated by Kneepkens's recent analysis of Peter's letter 115 to Heloise, which diagnoses the underlying presence of contemporary scriptural exegesis (C. H. Kneepkens, 'There is more in a Biblical quotation than meets the eye: on Peter the Venerable's letter of consolation to Heloise', in *Media Latinitas, a*

An application of this approach to the Peter/Bernard correspondence would seem to suggest that more, rather than less, attention should be paid to the language of compliment and to the 'attestations of friendship', with a view not to recuperating the actual historical relationship between the two men, but to deconstructing their epistolary relationship in terms of its sources and influences. The close connection between letter-writing and friendship in the Middle Ages has been well documented, particularly in recent times. Together with treatises, letters have provided a major source for studies on the development of the concept of Christian friendship; equally, friendship forms a major theme in most studies of correspondence. The relationship has been formalised by Leclercq, who points to the example of Peter of Blois, who wrote both a treatise on Christian friendship and an 'art of letter-writing', to postulate a parallel development of the two 'arts'.[55] The association between letters and friendship seems to go back a long way: the significance attached to letter-writing as a means of maintaining friendship in the Graeco-Roman tradition is stressed both by Stowers[56] and by Hutchinson.[57] The importance of the activity of letter-writing in the formation of the ideal of Christian friendship is likewise stressed by recent studies, such as that of Conybeare.[58]

This importance is reflected in what can be seen as *topoi*, 'commonplaces', current in the twelfth century, but with roots that can be traced back far earlier. A letter is presented as an act of friendship; conversely, failure to write is equated with failure in friendship, while failure to reply is presented as a serious breach of epistolary etiquette. Letters are expected to be read with care. The classical concept of a letter as a substitute for *viva voce* conversation becomes enshrined in the conceit of spiritual presence in physical absence,[59] as found, for example, in New Testament epistles.[60] The presence of the language of friendship cannot, however, be taken as a straightforward indicator of personal intimacy, as recent studies of twelfth-century letters by McLoughlin[61] and Haseldine[62] have shown. Haseldine, in

---

collection of essays to mark the occasion of the retirement of L. J. Engels, ed. R. I. A. Nip, H. van Dijk, E. M. C. van Houts, C. H. Kneepkens and G. A. A. Kortekaas, Instrumenta Patristica 28, Turnhout, 1996, pp. 89–100.

[55] 'Il semble que l'art des belles lettres soit intimement lié à la doctrine de l'amitié, et l'on comprend que l'un et l'autre se soient développés parallèlement' (Dom J. Leclercq, 'L'amitié dans les lettres au Moyen Age', *Revue du Moyen-Age Latin* I (1945), 391–410, p. 400).

[56] Stowers, *Letter writing*, p. 58.

[57] Hutchinson, *Cicero's correspondence*, p. 17.

[58] C. Conybeare, *Paulinus noster: self and symbols in the letters of Paulinus of Nola*, Oxford, 2000.

[59] On the significance of this conceit in early Christian writing, see C. White, 'Friendship in absence – some patristic views', in *Friendship in Medieval Europe*, ed. J. Haseldine, Stroud, 1999, pp. 68–88.

[60] *nam et si corpore absens sum sed spiritu vobiscum sum*, 'for even if I am absent in body, I am present with you in spirit' (Col 2. 5).

[61] J. McLoughlin, '*Amicitia* in practice: John of Salisbury (c. 1120–1180) and his circle', in D. Williams (ed.), *England in the twelfth century* (Proceedings of the 1988 Harlaxton Symposium), Woodbridge, 1990, 165–81.

[62] J. Haseldine, 'Understanding the language of *amicitia*. The friendship circle of Peter of Celle (c. 1115–1183)', *Journal of Medieval History* 20 (1994), 237–60.

particular, demonstrates that at this period such language provided an important tool for communication and negotiation in monastic and ecclesiastical relations.[63] Indeed, it is arguable that the evocation of friendship in this period functions as a kind of ideological coding, embodying and promoting political, religious, social and cultural stances.[64] That such pragmatic applications of friendship language go back a long way is also suggested by the ancient handbooks, which signal, overtly in the case of 'Demetrius',[65] more discreetly in that of 'Libanius',[66] that friendship can be invoked to form the basis for a request.

By the twelfth century, a rich language of friendship was available for exploitation, complete with associated *topoi* and appropriate sources for citation. Modern works on the development of this language and of the concepts it conveys include those of Fiske,[67] McGuire,[68] White[69] and Hyatte.[70] Fiske argues for a fusion of two traditions, the first, or 'practical', derived from Aristotle, through Cicero and Jerome; the second, or 'mystic', coming from Neoplatonism, filtered through Ambrose and Augustine.[71] The practical tradition can be seen to emphasise reciprocity and mutuality, as summed up in the Ciceronian dictum, 'Nothing is more pleasant than the paying-back of kindness, the interchange of favors and duties.'[72] The mystic tradition, on the other hand, lays stress on the union of individual souls with and within the divine. To the first tradition belongs the terminology of obligation and regulation: *ius, lex, foedus*;[73] to the second, the affective imagery

---

[63]   J. Haseldine, 'Friendship and rivalry: the role of *amicitia* in twelfth-century monastic relations', *Journal of Ecclesiastical History* 44 (1993), 390–414, p. 393.

[64]   See, for example, Haseldine, 'The language of *amicitia*', p. 248.

[65]   'The friendly type is the one that seems to be written by a friend to a friend. For it is not restricted to friends. They (those in authority) ... do this ... in the belief that no-one will gainsay them when they write in a friendly manner, but will submit and act in accordance with what they write' (*Typoi epistolikoi* 1, *Demetrius and Libanius*, pp. 3–4). See Stowers, *Letter writing*, pp. 58-9.

[66]   'I have long since valued your holy disposition, and now I expect to obtain this matter, and know well that I will obtain it. For it is right for true friends to obtain their requests, provided that they are good' (*Epistolimaioi Characteres* 3, *Demetrius and Libanius*, p. 22). See Stowers, ibid.

[67]   A. Fiske, *Friends and friendship in the monastic tradition* (Cidoc Cuardeno 51), Cuérnavaca, Mexico, 1970.

[68]   B. P. McGuire, *Friendship and community, the monastic experience 350–1250*, Kalamazoo, 1988.

[69]   C. White, *Christian friendship in the fourth century*, Cambridge, 1992.

[70]   R. Hyatte, *The arts of friendship: the idealisation of friendship in medieval and early Renaissance Literature*, Leiden, 1994.

[71]   Fiske, *Friends and friendship*, 0/13–0/15; 1/1–2/9. On the development from classical to Christian, see J. McEvoy, 'The theory of friendship in the Latin Middle Ages: hermeneutics, contextualization and the transmission and reception of ancient texts and ideas, from AD 350 to c. 1500', in *Friendship in Medieval Europe*, pp. 3–44. On the classical background in general, see D. Konstan, *Friendship in the classical world*, Cambridge, 1997.

[72]   *Nihil est enim remuneratione benevolentiae, nihil vicissitudine studiorum officiorumque iucundius* (Cicero, *Laelius de amicitia*, XIV. 48 in *Cicero, Laelius, on friendship & The dream of Scipio*, ed. with trans. and commentary by J. G. F. Powell, Warminster, England, 1990).

[73]   Cicero talks of the 'laws' which should be held sacred in friendship (e.g. *Laelius*, XII.

which associates friendship with fire, light, water, wound and sweetness, most effectively illustrated perhaps, as Fiske demonstrates,[74] by the correspondence of Alcuin.[75] The flame of affection glows in the heart, but if it burns low it may need rekindling.[76] Its function is to give light, but it can be threatened by overwhelming darkness.[77] Affection is likened to the fountain which waters paradise and promotes fertility.[78] Love itself is a wound, inflicting painful pleasure or pleasant pain;[79] at the same time, it brings with it the sweetness of spiritual nourishment.[80]

Although the two traditions fused into one, it cannot necessarily be assumed that both were always given equal weight or accorded equal validity. Parallel *sententiae*, 'maxims', were often to be found in both classical and biblical sources, for example, the injunction to friendly admonition;[81] the notion that true

---

40; ibid., XIII. 44); Cassian (*c*. AD 360–435) employs a range of synonyms connoting *foedus*, 'treaty', 'compact', in his discussion of true and false friendship (Cassian, *Collatio XVI, de amicitia*, II. 1; III. 2, *CSEL*, 13, ed. M. Petschenig, Vienna 1886, reprinted 1966, pp. 439–40). On Cassian's debt to Cicero, see White, *Christian friendship*, pp. 175–184.

[74] A. Fiske, 'Alcuin and mystical friendship', *Studi Medievali* 2 (2) series 3 (1961), 551–75.

[75] Alcuin (*c*. 735–804) was born into a noble Northumbrian family. After succeeding to the headship of the cathedral school at York, he was invited by Charlemagne to take charge of the palace school at Aachen, a post which he occupied from 782 to 796. From 796 until his death he was resident abbot of the monastery of St. Martin at Tours. On Alcuin's presentation of friendship, see M. D. Garrison, 'Alcuin's world through his letters and verse', unpublished PhD thesis, Cambridge, 1995, esp. pp. 44–52; pp. 142–252.

[76] (*ut*) *flamma caritatis in corde abscondita aliquam fortasse scintillam elicere valeat, ne totum torpescat, quod intus ignescit* ... , '(that) the flame of affection hidden in the heart may perhaps be able to draw out some spark, lest what glows inside be totally dormant ...' (Alcuin, ep. 139, *Alcuini sive Albini epistolae*, ed. E. Dümmler, Monumenta Germaniae Historica Epistolae IV, Aevi Karolini ii, Berlin, 1895, reprinted 1974, p. 220); *Quid proficit sapientia abscondita vel thesaurum invisum, vel caritas muta? Num ignis in silice, nisi excutiatur, flammificat?*, 'What good is hidden wisdom or unseen treasure, or silent affection? Surely fire in flint does not make flame, unless it should be struck?' (idem, ep. 191, ibid., p. 318).

[77] (*ut*) *vix antiquae dilectionis quaelibet scintilla eluceat inter caliginosas terrenorum desideriorum umbras*, '(so that) scarcely any spark of ancient affection shines out amongst the murky shadows of earthly desires' (idem, ep. 209, ibid., p. 347).

[78] *Sicut fons paradisum irrigans quadrivido tramite latum diffunditur in orbem, sic fons caritatis, pectus virtutum floribus pullulans, in quattuor amoris vivos dirivatur* ..., 'As the fountain which waters paradise spreads out into the wide world by a four-fold path, so the fountain of love causing the breast to sprout with the flowers of the virtues is dispersed into the four streams of love ...' (idem, ep. 19, ibid., p. 53).

[79] *quicumque mellifluo caritatis iaculo vulnera omni favo dulciore in corde accipiet* ..., 'whoever receives in the heart the wounds from the honey-flowing dart of affection, sweeter than all honeycomb ...' (idem, ep. 86, ibid., p. 129.) For the 'wound of love', compare also ep. 59 (ibid., p. 102), ep. 159 (ibid., p. 257).

[80] *Accepimus dignitatis vestrae chartam, vere, ut agnovimus, caritatis floribus depictam ac mellifluo spiritalis iucunditatis sapore refertam*, 'I received the letter of your Dignity, truly, as I recognised, painted with the flowers of affection, and filled with the honey-flowing taste of spiritual sweetness' (idem, ep. 60, ibid., p. 103).

[81] *nam et monendi amici saepe sunt et obiurgandi, et haec accipienda amice, cum benevole fiunt*, 'for often friends are to be warned and chided, and this should be received in a friendly

friendship should not be affected by change of fortune;[82] the comparison of friendship with the maturing of wine.[83] At times, however, they may appear to be juxtaposed in such a way that while ostensibly appearing synonymous, the philosophical difference between them is actually being highlighted. For example, in a letter to Hato, bishop of Troyes,[84] which, it has been argued elsewhere, forms part of what comes to constitute a series of 'conversion' letters,[85] Peter the Venerable juxtaposes two definitions of 'friendship'.[86] The first draws on the frequently cited Ciceronian statement, that friendship comprises 'harmony in matters human and divine together with good-will and affection'.[87] The second citation, attributed by Peter to Gregory the Great, declares that friendship cannot be maintained 'between less than two'.[88] Significantly, the definition from the *Laelius* is preceded there by the rider that all affection is

---

manner, provided that it is done kindly' (Cicero, *Laelius*, xxiv, 88); *meliora sunt vulnera diligentis quam fraudulenta odientis oscula*, 'better are the wounds of one who loves than the deceitful kisses of one who hates' (Prv 27. 6).

[82]   *Quamquam Ennius recte* Amicus certus in re incerta cernitur, *tamen haec duo levitatis et infirmitatis plerosque convincunt, aut si in bonis rebus contemnunt, aut in malis deserunt*, 'Although Ennius says rightly "A sure friend is perceived in an unsure time", most people are convicted of fickleness and weakness by these two things, either if they are neglectful in good circumstances, or desert in bad' (Cicero, *Laelius*, xvii, 64); *Non agnoscetur in bonis amicus, nec abscondetur in malis inimicus*, 'A friend will not be recognised in good times, nor an enemy hidden in bad' (Sir 12. 8).

[83]   *veterrima quaeque, ut ea vina quae vetustatem ferunt, esse debent suavissima ...*, 'as those wines which carry age, the oldest should be the sweetest ...' (*Laelius*, xix, 67); *Vinum novum amicus novus veterescat et cum suavitate bibes illud*, 'a new friend is as new wine. It grows old and you will drink it with sweetness' (Sir 9. 15).

[84]   Archdeacon, then dean of Sens, Hato became bishop of Troyes in about 1122. Evidence from charters shows that he was a generous patron towards Cluny. Peter's letter 69 suggests that he came into conflict with the newly appointed Cistercian bishop, Hugh of Auxerre, over the performance of ordinations for the daughter-house of La Charité, technically in Auxerre's diocese. He retired into Cluny in late 1145 or early 1146, as commemorated by a letter from Prior Peter of the Augustinian house of St. John at Sens. See G. Constable, 'The letter from Peter of St John to Hato of Troyes', in *Petrus Venerabilis*, 38–52, pp. 43–44.

[85]   On this correspondence, see G. R. Knight, 'Uses and abuses of *amicitia*: the correspondence between Peter the Venerable and Hato of Troyes', *Reading Medieval Studies* 23 (1997), 35–67.

[86]   Peter the Venerable, letter 81, *Letters*, I, pp. 217–18.

[87]   *qua (definitione) dictum est quod* amicitia nihil sit aliud, quam divinarum humanarumque rerum cum benevolentia et caritate consensio (ibid., p. 217 = Cicero, *Laelius*, vi, 20).

[88]   *Quae consensio ... ad minus quam inter duos haberi non potest* (letter 81, p. 217). If, as Constable suggests, Peter is drawing here on Gregory's *Homilies on Ezechiel*, Peter may seem to have changed the sense of this statement. In the original, it runs: *Non est enim caritas vera, si minus a duobus cubitis habet*, 'For it is not true charity, if it has less than two cubits.' The 'two cubits', reinforced there by the notion of 'double dyeing', seem to refer to love of God and love of neighbour (Gregory the Great, *Homiliae in Hiezechielem prophetam*, II, iv. 3, *CCSL*, 142, ed. M. Adriaen, Turnhout, 1971, p. 259).

between two or a few'.[89] Arguably, the classical view of friendship is being hinted at here to involve an element of social and political exclusivity, the Christian view to encompass a spiritually superior inclusivity.[90]

The same considerations may apply to the terminology associated with friendship and affection. In classical Latin usage this terminology had revolved around three nouns with their associated cognates: *amicitia*; *caritas*, with its associated adjective, *carus*; and *amor*, with its cognate *amare*. As the study of Pétré shows, these terms could be used to convey differing shades of meaning.[91] In the case of the Ciceronian definition of friendship given above, for instance, Pétré draws attention to an inherent distinction between the first two terms, with *amicitia* seemingly being employed to designate the relationship, and *caritas* to denote the accompanying emotion.[92] Elsewhere, as Pétré indicates, Cicero can be seen to distinguish between *caritas* and *amor*.[93] *Caritas* would appear to encompass an element of esteem or regard, and would seem, in consequence, to be more disinterested. It is said, for example, to characterise relationships with superiors: gods, parents, country, men who excel in wisdom or resources. *Amor*, on the other hand, is apparently reserved for equals or inferiors: wives, children, brothers.[94] In addition to the expressions given above, the verb *diligere* appears as a virtual synonym for *amare*, although, like *caritas*, it may seem to denote the accompanying emotion rather than the action.[95]

These terms, *amicitia*, *caritas*, *amor*, together with *dilectio*, a late Latin coinage from *diligere*, were retained in Christian discourse. Their relative importance and

---

[89] *Quanta autem vis amicitiae sit, ex hoc intellegi maxime potest, quod ... ita contracta res est et adducta in angustum, ut omnis caritas aut inter duos aut inter paucos iungeretur*, 'How great is the force of friendship can best be understood from this, that ... as a thing it was so restricted and narrowed that all affection was joined between two or between a few' (*Laelius*, v, 20.) For the view that Cicero is here advocating exclusivity, see the comments of Powell (*Laelius*, p. 88).

[90] On this notion compare E. G. Cassidy, ' "He who has friends can have no friend": classical and Christian perspectives on the limits to friendship', in *Friendship in Medieval Europe*, 45–67, p. 56; also Conybeare, *Paulinus noster*, pp. 79–80.

[91] H. Pétré, *Caritas, étude sur le vocabulaire latin de la charité chrétienne*, Louvain, 1948.

[92] Pétré, *Caritas*, p. 39.

[93] Ibid., p. 32.

[94] *Amicitiae enim caritate et amore cernuntur. Nam cum deorum tum parentum patriaeque cultus eorumque hominum, qui aut sapientia aut opibus excellunt, ad caritatem referri solent. Coniuges autem et liberi et fratres et alii, quos usus familiaritasque coniunxit, quamquam etiam caritate ipsa, tamen amore maxime continentur*, 'Friendships are distinguished by affection and love. For the cultivation of gods, parents, country and of those men who are pre-eminent in wisdom or wealth is accustomed to be ascribed to affection. But wives, children, brothers and others who are joined by experience and familiarity, although they are also contained by affection, are most of all contained by love' (Cicero, *Partitiones oratoriae*, XXV. 88, in *M. Tulli Ciceronis, Rhetorica*, ed. A. S. Wilkins, 2 vols, Oxford; London; New York, 1935, II, p. 86).

[95] *amare autem nihil aliud est, nisi eum ipsum diligere quem ames nulla indigentia, nulla utilitate quaesita ...*, 'to love is nothing other than to show affection towards him whom you love for himself, out of no need, seeking no advantage ...' (Cicero, *Laelius*, XXVII, 100). According to Pétré, *diligere* combines affection with esteem (Pétré, *Caritas*, p. 31).

significance in the Christian writings of late antiquity have been the subject of much debate.[96] While *amicitia* and *caritas* often appear in conjunction,[97] it is not clear that they were simply perceived as being interchangeable. *Caritas*, together to a lesser degree with *dilectio*, seems, as Pétré illustrates, to have derived a new transcendent force through its New Testament equation with the Greek concept of *agape*.[98] According to White, the relationship of *agape/caritas*, unlike that of *philia/amicitia*, did not require reciprocity, and looked towards its perfect fulfilment in heaven.[99] *Amicitia*, redefined in Christian terms, could encompass an element of the divine. None-the-less, White[100] draws attention to the fact that Augustine considers but rejects it in favour of *caritas* to describe the relationship between the members of the Holy Trinity.[101] Conybeare similarly comments on the seeming absence of the expression *amicitia Christi*, as opposed to *caritas Christi*, in this early period.[102] It is arguable that this apparent distinction persisted into medieval writing. Hyatte, indeed, suggests that in the twelfth and early thirteenth centuries the term *amicitia* was totally avoided by certain writers because of its 'worldly connotations'.[103]

Peter the Venerable appears to exploit a hierarchical distinction between the two terms in a letter to his secretary, Peter of Poitiers,[104] written in early 1134 during a

---

[96]   See, for example, White, *Christian friendship*, pp. 53–4; Conybeare, *Paulinus noster*, pp. 64–7.

[97]   For example, *Haec de amicitia beatus Ioseph spiritali narratione disseruit, nosque ad custodiendam sodalitatis perpetuam caritatem ardentius incitavit*, 'The blessed [Abba] Joseph gave this discourse about friendship in spiritual narration, and incited us ardently to maintain the perpetual affection of companionship' (Cassian, *Collatio XVI*, XXVIII, p. 462); *Nec deseras amicum in necessitate ...; quoniam amicitia vitae adiumentum est. Ideo in ea onera nostra portamus sicut Apostolus docuit: dicit enim his quos eiusdem complexa est caritas*, 'Do not desert a friend in need ... ; since friendship is the adjunct of life. Therefore we carry our burdens in it, as the Apostle taught; for he speaks to these whom the affection of the same has embraced' (Ambrose, *De officiis ministrorum*, III, XXII, 129, *Saint Ambrose, Les devoirs*, ed., trans. and annotated by M. Testard, 2 vols, Paris, 1992, II, p. 142).

[98]   Pétré points out that of the eight examples relating to *agape* found in St. Paul's Letter to the Romans, six employ *caritas* and only two *dilectio* (Pétré, *Caritas*, p. 57, n. 2). Most significant, however, as Pétré indicates, in terms of effect and influence, is the eulogy to *caritas* found in I Corinthians 13 (ibid., pp. 57–8). On the New Testament preference for *agape*, see also McEvoy, 'Theory of friendship', pp. 30–32.

[99]   White, *Christian friendship*, pp. 55–6.

[100]   Ibid., p. 54.

[101]   *Spiritus ergo sanctus commune aliquid est patris et filii, quidquid illud est, aut ipsa communio consubstantialis et coaeterna; quae si amicitia convenienter dici potest, dicatur, sed aptius dicitur caritas; et haec quoque substantia quia deus substantia et deus caritas sicut scriptum est*, 'Therefore the Holy Spirit is something common to Father and Son, whatever that is, or the very consubstantial and co-eternal communion; if it can rightly be named friendship, let it be so named, but more fittingly it is named charity; and this is also substance, because God is substance and God is charity, as it has been written' (Augustine, *De Trinitate*, VI, V. 7, *CCSL*, 50, ed. W. J. Mountain, Turnhout, 1968, p. 235).

[102]   Conybeare, *Paulinus noster*, p. 65.

[103]   Hyatte, *Arts of friendship*, p. 48.

[104]   Peter of Poitiers, a monk from the Cluniac house of St Jean d'Angély in Aquitaine, appears to have been espoused by Peter the Venerable early in the papal schism of 1130–38, at a time when Aquitaine was a hotbed of dissent. From then on he seems to have remained

period of separation.[105] Friendship is first defined in terms of union of wills, using a formula employed by Sallust[106] and borrowed by Jerome,[107] *idem velle et nolle*, 'wanting and not wanting the same thing'.[108] This definition is followed by a second, 'union of souls'.[109] A favourite Christian conceit, the latter is to be found, for example, in Augustine;[110] the sentiment, however, can also be paralleled from Cicero.[111] Thus potentially both definitions have both classical and patristic sources. The first is explicitly linked by Peter with *vera amicitia*, 'true friendship'; the second, by implication, with *caritas Dei*, the 'love of God'. The statement which follows sets Christianity against paganism: 'If there could be such great affection of love in those who were ignorant of God ... what wonder if the love of God has united us in Him who makes both one?'[112] Just as Christianity is superior to paganism, so it may seem that (Christian) *caritas* is superior to (pagan) *amicitia*. At the same time, *caritas* can be seen to encompass an element of universality which is absent from *amicitia*, thus reinforcing the notion of inclusivity in opposition to that of exclusivity, as discussed above. In a letter to another addressee, Peter distinguishes between communal *caritas* and particular *amicitia*.[113] As will be seen,

---

with Peter as his notary until the death of the latter in 1156, taking responsibility for the collection of the letters and for their incorporation within a collection. Constable dates the start of their professional collaboration to this period of 1133–34 (Constable, *Letters*, II, pp. 331–43); van den Eynde, however, postulates the earlier date of 1131 (D. van den Eynde, 'Les principaux voyages de Pierre le Vénérable', *Benedictina* 15 (1968), 58–110, pp. 100–104).

[105] Peter the Venerable, letter 58, *Letters*, I, pp. 179–89. The letter is associated with Peter's visit to Aquitaine in 1133, in an attempt to resolve the problems of papal schism (see Constable, *Letters*, II, pp. 338–9). For a fuller discussion, see G. R. Knight, 'The language of retreat and the eremitic ideal in some letters of Peter the Venerable', *Archives d'Histoire Doctrinale et Littéraire* 63 (1996), 7–43, pp. 26–33.

[106] Sallust, *Catilina*, 20, 4, in *C. Sallusti Crispi, Catilina, Iugurtha, historiarum fragmenta selecta*, ed. L. D. Reynolds, Oxford, 1991, p. 17.

[107] Jerome, ep. 130, 12, *CSEL*, 56/1, ed. I. Hilberg, Vienna, 1918, reprinted 1996, p. 192.

[108] *Ita te ... unanimem habebam ... ut in te uno.. illam verae amicitiae diffinitionem expertus sim, idem scilicet velle, et idem nolle ...*, 'I found you ... so much of one mind ... that in you alone ... I experienced that definition of true friendship, namely wanting and not wanting the same thing ...' (Peter, letter 58, p. 183).

[109] *Ita te ... unanimem habebam ... ut non duobus corporibus duae sed una utrique corpori videretur inesse anima*, 'I found you ... so much of one mind ... that there seemed to be not two souls in two bodies but a single soul in each body' (ibid., p. 183).

[110] *Nam ego sensi animam meam et animam illius unam fuisse animam in duobus corporibus ...*, 'For I felt that my soul and his soul had been one soul in two bodies ...' (Augustine, *Confessiones*, IV, VI. 11, *CCSL*, 27, ed. L. Verheijen, Turnhout, 1981, p. 45).

[111] *qui (homo) et se ipse diligit et alterum anquirit, cuius animum ita cum suo misceat, ut efficiat paene unum ex duobus*, 'who (mankind) both loves himself and seeks another, whose soul he may so mingle with his own, as to make almost one from two' (Cicero, *Laelius*, XXI, 81).

[112] *Quod si tantus innescientibus deum esse potuit amoris affectus ... quid mirum si caritas Dei ... in eo nos univit qui facit utraque unum.. ?* (Peter, letter 58, *Letters*, I, p. 183 = Rm 5. 5; Eph 2. 14).

[113] *Cum enim et caritas communis et amicitia singularis nil contra amicum facere suaderent, excessistis amicitiae metas, et nil vos laedentem amicum laesistis*, 'For while both

such potential distinctions may become crucial in his correspondence with Bernard, which will turn on the issue of monastic harmony.

The integral association between friendship and letter-writing discussed above finds expression in a particular epistolary feature noted by Pepin in relation to the correspondence between two eminent contemporaries of Peter and Bernard, the English scholar John of Salisbury,[114] and the French abbot Peter of Celle.[115] Dubbed by Pepin *amicitia iocosa*, 'joking friendship',[116] its hallmark is what can be characterised as a kind of playful banter, marked by elaborate word-play, which often oscillates between the literal and the metaphorical.[117] One example of this, as discussed by Pepin, concerns a running joke on the drinking habits of the English, in particular, their preference for beer over wine.[118] When expressing 'gratitude' for Peter of Celle's *De panibus*, a treatise on the kinds of bread mentioned in scripture, John seems to combine an allusion to this with a subversion of the *topos* of spiritual nourishment: 'For who would not be refreshed by such an abundance of breads ... ?';[119] 'Now ... I am thirsty, and as a devourer of breads will be able to be choked in dryness, unless your Clemency should provide me with wine. This at least is more available to you than *caelia* (Spanish beer), which in vulgar usage is called *cervisia* (Gallic beer) by those of our country.'[120] Elsewhere, the playfulness

---

communal affection and particular friendship urged you to do nothing against a friend, you exceeded the bounds of friendship, and wounded a friend wounding you in nothing' (Peter, letter 102, to Milo, bishop of Thérouanne, *Letters*, I, p. 264).

[114]   John of Salisbury (*c*. 1120–80), noted for his classical learning, studied at Chartres, and at Paris under Abelard. Subsequently he became clerk at Canterbury, first to Theobald of Bec, then to Thomas Becket. His acquaintance with Peter of Celle seems to date from an early period. He probably acted as the latter's clerk in 1147–48, and subsequently lived at Rheims as Peter's guest from 1164 to 1170, after Becket's break with Henry II. He returned to England in 1170, and in 1176 was elected bishop of Chartres.

[115]   Peter of Celle (*c*. 1115–83) held successive abbacies of two important Benedictine monasteries in northern France, Montier-la-Celle near Troyes, and St Remi at Rheims. From there he wielded considerable monastic and political influence, finally becoming bishop of Chartres in succession after John of Salisbury. On his presentation of friendship, see J. P. Haseldine, 'A study of the letters of Abbot Peter of la-Celle (*c*. 1115–83)', unpublished PhD thesis, Cambridge, 1991, pp. 93–100.

[116]   R. E. Pepin, '*Amicitia iocosa*: Peter of Celle and John of Salisbury', *Florilegium* 5 (1983), 140–56.

[117]   The same features have been isolated and defined in relation to the letters of another twelfth-century English scholar and letter-writer, Gilbert Foliot. Morey and Brooke speak of 'a pastiche of elaborate and allusive banter', 'appropriate between old or close friends,' and made 'fashionable' by the rules of letter-writing (*Gilbert Foliot and his letters*, ed. Dom A. Morey and C. N. L. Brooke, Cambridge Studies in Medieval Life and Thought 11, Cambridge, 1965, p. 13). The keywords here, as will be seen, may be 'fashionable' and 'appropriate'. See Haseldine, 'The language of *amicitia*', p. 238.

[118]   Pepin, '*Amicitia iocosa*', pp. 144–5.

[119]   *Quis enim in tanta panum abundantia non reficiatur ...?* (John of Salisbury, ep. 33, *The letters of John of Salisbury*, ed. W. J. Millor and H. E. Butler, revised C. N. L. Brooke, 2 vols, Oxford, 1955–79, reissued Oxford, 1986, 1, p. 56).

[120]   *Iam ego sitio, poteroque vorator panum in siccitate strangulari, nisi clementia vestra mihi vinum provideat. Hoc utique vobis paratius est quam caelia, quae a nostratibus usu vulgari*

can be seen to exploit the conventions of literary etiquette, for example, John's claim that his original salutation, *salutem et seipsum*, 'greetings and himself', has been criticised as unsuitable, on the grounds that he is 'bitter' or 'tasteless',[121] the latter in itself constituting a double play on the 'sweetness' demanded by friendship, and the notion of 'salt' or 'wit'. In fact, as Brooke demonstrates in his introduction, this opening sally merely paves the way for an erudite display of wit.[122]

Significantly, the feature is given what can be seen as formal recognition by Peter of Celle: 'You have mixed jokes with serious matter, but moderated, and without detriment to dignity and modesty. Your witty remarks without teeth are jokes without cheapness.'[123] 'Without teeth' points to an absence of mordant irony; the remark itself may nevertheless be playfully ironic. The origins of this type of epistolary approach may reach back as far as Cicero, who distinguishes between two types of epistolary style, *familiare et iocosum*, the 'familiar and joking', and *severum et grave*, the 'serious and weighty'.[124] This distinction can be linked with the definition of friendship provided in the *Laelius*: according to Cicero, friendship should be *remissior*, 'more cheerful', *liberior*, 'freer', and *dulcior*, 'sweeter'.[125] Many of Cicero's own letters, as Hutchinson's study demonstrates, do indeed display the kind of banter discussed above.[126] Arguably, such a teasing note creates an impression of intimacy and mutuality, which reflects the reciprocity demanded by the friendship tradition.[127] It does not, however, preclude an underlying seriousness of theme.[128] In the case of Cicero, this may be seen in terms of hidden comment on the current political situation. For example, he announces his (enforced) retirement under Julius Caesar through an allusion to the Sicilian tyrant Dionysius.[129] What follows can be seen as depicting his 'conversion' from Stoic

---

cervisia nuncupatur (ibid., p. 57). Brooke draws attention to the punning nature of *caelia* as 'beer' and 'heavenly' (ibid., n. 11). On this letter, see also Haseldine, 'A study', pp. 80–81.

[121] *ait [notarius] enim te sicut* salutem *acceptare oblatam, sic aspernari quod subiungitur* et seipsum, *forte quia amarum, quia insipidum, praesertim domi suae dulcioribus abundanti*, 'for he [my secretary] said that although you accepted the offered "greetings", you scorned the subjoined "and myself", perhaps as bitter, perhaps as tasteless, especially for one who has an abundance of sweeter things in his own home' (John of Salisbury, ep. 112, ibid., p. 183). The last part of this will subsequently be developed through the notion that Peter has preferred a 'new love' to an 'old friendship'.

[122] Brooke, ibid., pp. xlvii–li.

[123] *Miscuisti siquidem iocos seriis, sed temperatos et sine detrimento dignationis et verecundiae. Sales tui sine dente sunt ioci sine vilitate* (Peter of Celle, ep. 69, *Epistolae*, ed. J.-P. Migne, *Patrologia Latina* 202, Paris, 1855, 515A).

[124] Cicero, *Epp. ad Fam.*, 2, 4. 1.

[125] Cicero, *Laelius*, XVIII, 66.

[126] Hutchinson, *Cicero's correspondence*, pp. 172–99.

[127] Compare the comments of Hutchinson: 'Friendship had at least to be presented externally as a warm and close relationship: letters had to sustain or advance friendship by their manner' (ibid., p. 17). The notion is formalised by Garrison in relation to Alcuin through the phrase 'fictions of familiarity' (Garrison, 'Alcuin's world', pp. 48, 142).

[128] Pepin, '*Amicitia iocosa*', p. 149; cf. Hutchinson, *Cicero's correspondence*, p. 192.

[129] *ut Dionysius tyrannus ... sic ego ... amisso regno forensi ludum quasi habere coeperim*, 'like the tyrant Dionysius ... so I ... having lost my forensic kingdom, have begun to keep a kind of school' (Cicero, *Epp. ad Fam.*, 9, 18. 1).

moderation and political involvement to Epicurean 'indulgence' and detachment, expressed in terms which target both himself and the 'gluttony' of his friend.[130]

Elaborate verbal play associated with epistolary etiquette is likewise to be glimpsed in the letters of two influential patristic writers, Augustine[131] and Jerome.[132] Here, too, it can be seen to encompass and/or prepare for a serious element. For example, Augustine introduces a discourse on 'true' and 'false' friendship through a lengthy exploration of the 'debt of affection':

> Perhaps you wonder why I call myself an unequal payer of this debt, although you understand/feel so much about me, inasmuch as you know me like my soul. But this is the very thing which causes me great difficulty in replying to your letter, because I refrain from saying how great you seem in my eyes for the sake of sparing your blushes, and by saying less when you have conferred such praise on me, what will I remain but a debtor? I would not care for this, if ... I knew that you had said those things not from sincere affection but from flattery, which is hostile to friendship. In this way I would not be a debtor, because I would not be due to repay such; but the more I know with how faithful a mind you speak, the more I see with what a debt I am burdened.[133]

Similarly, Jerome follows a 'reproach' for epistolary brevity with a hyperbolic catalogue of hypothetical 'difficulties' experienced by his addressees, the whole dressed up in learned terms.[134] What follows, however, will celebrate Christian

---

[130] *pluris iam pavones confeci quam tu pullos columbinos*, 'I have now polished off more peacocks than you have eaten baby pigeons' (ibid., 9, 18. 3). See Hutchinson, *Cicero's correspondence*, pp. 193–6.

[131] Augustine (AD 354–430) was born at Thagaste, in north Africa. After teaching rhetoric at Rome and Milan he was converted under the aegis of Ambrose, bishop of Milan, to a form of Christianised Neoplatonism, becoming bishop of Hippo in 395. In addition to major theological works, he left behind a large collection of letters and of sermons.

[132] Jerome (*c.* AD 347–420) was born in Dalmatia but went at an early age to Rome, where he studied rhetoric. In 389, after spending time as an anchoritic monk in the East, he founded a monastery at Bethlehem, where he devoted the rest of his life to study and scholarship. In addition to his work on the Latin Vulgate, he also wrote commentaries and polemical works, as well as being a prolific letter-writer.

[133] *Miraris fortasse cur me huius debiti persolutorem imparem dicam, cum tu de me tam multum sentias, qui me tamquam anima mea noveris. Sed hoc ipsum est, quod mihi magnam difficultatem facit respondendi litteris tuis, quia et, quantus mihi videaris, parco dicere propter verecundiam tuam et utique minus dicendo, cum tu in me tantam laudem contuleris, quid nisi debitor remanebo? quod non curarem, si ea ... non ex caritate sincerissima dicta scirem sed adulatione inimica amicitiae. hoc quippe modo nec debitor fierem, quia talia rependere non deberem; sed quanto magis novi, quam fideli animo loqueris, tanto magis video, quanto debito graver* (Augustine to Severus, ep. 110, 2, *CSEL*, 34–2, ed. A. L. Goldbacher, Vienna, 1898, p. 639).

[134] *Quibus hoc primum queror, cur tot interiacentibus spatiis maris atque terrarum tam parvam epistolam miseritis, nisi quod ita merui, qui vobis, ut scribitis, ante non scripsi. cartam defuisse non puto Aegypto ministrante commercia. et si aliqui Ptolomaeus maria clausisset, tamen rex Attalus membranas e Pergamo miserat, ut penuria cartae pellibus pensaretur; unde pergamenarum nomen ad hanc usque diem tradente sibi invicem posteritate servatum est. quid igitur? arbitrer baiulum festinasse? quamvis longae epistolae una nox sufficit. an vos aliqua occupatione detentos? nulla necessitas maior est caritate.*

love, and the cultivation of virginity and chastity. In both these cases, the playfulness can be seen as conforming to the rhetorical requirement of *captatio benevolentiae*, the securing of the reader's good-will.

Close parallels to the gambits discussed above are to be found in letters of Bernard and Peter addressed to other recipients. The examples which follow are directed towards two influential figures, the one prominent in twelfth-century theology, the other in twelfth-century politics, namely, William of St Thierry,[135] and Henry of Blois.[136] In both cases, an epistolary rebuke may be seen to function as a form of displacement, standing in for other, more serious, matters. In the letter from Bernard, the initial 'reproach' is represented as having emanated from William.[137] Bernard's letter opens with a contrast between divine knowledge and human ignorance which leads to what purports to be a verbatim citation of William's own words: 'You however ... declaim so openly not only about your heart but also about mine, saying "That loving more, I am loved less." '[138] Although unsignalled by Leclercq, this surely draws on Paul's declaration to the

---

restant duo, ut aut vos piguerit aut ego non meruerim. e quibus malo vos incessere tarditatis, quam me condemnare non meriti. facilius enim negligentia emendari potest quam amor nasci, 'First I complain, that with so much space of sea and land intervening you sent so small a letter, unless I deserved it for, as you state, not having written first. I do not think that paper was lacking, since Egypt provides merchandise. And if some Ptolemy had closed the seas, none-the-less king Attalus had sent parchment from Pergamum, so that the lack of paper might be compensated for by skins; whence the name of parchment has been kept by posterity to this day, with the handing down of the name. What then? Am I to think that the bearer was in haste? One night suffices a letter, however long. Or that you were detained by some occupation? No necessity is greater than charity. There remain two possibilities, that either you begrudged it or I did not deserve it. Of the two, I prefer to blame you for sloth rather than condemn myself for lack of merit. For negligence can more easily be emended than love be born' (Jerome to Chromatius, Iovinus and Eusebius, ep. 7, 2, *CSEL*, 54, ed. I. Hilberg, Vienna, 1910, reprinted 1996, pp. 27–8).

[135] William of St Thierry (*c.* 1085–1147/48) retired from his post as Benedictine abbot of St. Thierry near Rheims in 1134 or 1135 to become a Cistercian monk. Noted as a contemplative and theologian, he became one of Bernard's biographers. His attacks on the 'heretical' views of Peter Abelard contributed to the latter's condemnation at Sens in 1140 (see P. Zerbi, 'William of Saint Thierry and his dispute with Abelard', in *William, Abbot of St. Thierry. A Colloquium at the Abbey of St. Thierry*, trans. from the French by J. Carfantan, Cistercian Studies Series 94, Kalamazoo, 1987, pp. 181–203). While still abbot of St Thierry, he appears to have encouraged Bernard to produce his *Apologia*, a critical onslaught on monastic excess which brought the latter into conflict with Peter the Venerable. The *Apologia* will be discussed in the following chapter.

[136] Henry of Blois (1129–71), brother to King Stephen of England, was educated at Cluny. He subsequently became abbot of Glastonbury and bishop of Winchester, positions which he held concurrently. His prestige was further enhanced by a period as papal legate. His ecclesiastical manoeuvrings in relation to the archbishopric of York in the 1140s brought him into conflict with Bernard. See Dom D. Knowles, *Saints and scholars, 25 medieval portraits*, Cambridge, 1962, pp. 51–8. For the financial importance of his assistance to Cluny, see Duby, 'Le budget de Cluny', pp. 76–7.

[137] Bernard, ep. 85, *SBO*, VII, pp. 220–23.

[138] *Tu vero ... non solum de tuo, sed et de meo corde tam aperte declamas:* Ut plus amans, *inquiens*, minus diligar (ep. 85, 1).

Corinthians,[139] where it follows the statement that parents should lay up treasures for their sons, rather than vice versa.[140] As will be seen, this allusion may be relevant to the end of the letter.

Bernard first questions the source of William's knowledge through a heavy exploitation of the notion of certainty: 'Perhaps what you say is true, namely that you are loved by me less than you love me; but certainly I am certain that it is not certain to you. How therefore do you affirm as certain that about which it is certain that you are not at all certain? A marvel!'[141] Later, in an apparent volte-face, he will apparently accept and even reinforce the claim, through a form of syllogism: those who are better deserve more love; those who are better are those who love more; therefore William, who is better, is loved less than he should be, while he, Bernard, who is worse, is loved more than he should be.[142] The acceptance, however, is subsequently undermined through elaborate quantitative play, which links capacity to love with the notion of love as a divine gift.[143] The notion of *amicitia iocosa* can be seen to be formalised towards the end of the letter, through Bernard's self-referential drawing to attention of his 'fooling'.[144]

Peter's letter to Henry of Blois, on the other hand, is constructed round an epistolary 'reproach' from himself.[145] This begins with the claim that he has been waiting for *aliquid iocundum*, 'some pleasant message', to arrive from Henry, and is developed through a triad of synonymous clauses which hover between the literal and the metaphorical: 'In vain I hoped that the sun could rise for me from your west; fruitlessly I believed that hurricanes off the sea could brighten the darkness of our day; superfluously I surmised that our cold could be warmed by southern breezes from the flanks of the north wind.'[146] This intricate series of paradoxical

---

[139] *licet plus vos diligens minus diligar* (II Cor 12. 15).

[140] *Nec enim debent filii parentibus thesaurizare sed parentes filiis*, 'For sons should not lay up treasures for parents but parents for sons' (ibid., 12. 14).

[141] *Forte verum est quod dicis, minus scilicet a me amari te quam me diligis; sed certe certus sum certum non esse tibi. Quomodo ergo pro certo affirmas, de quo certum est quia certus minime sis? Mirum!* (ep. 85, 1).

[142] *Verumtamen si meliores magis diligendi sunt, – sunt autem meliores qui magis diligunt -, quid aliud dixerim quam illum plus me diligere, quem meliorem esse non dubio, me vero minus illum quam debeo, quia minus valeo?*, 'But if those who are better are to be loved more, – indeed, those who love more are better -, what other am I to say than that he, whom I do not doubt to be better, loves me more/more than me, while I love him less than I ought, because I am worth less/less able?' (ibid., 3).

[143] *Sed quanto in te ... maior est caritas, tanto minus contemnenda a te nostra possibilitas, quia etsi plus diligis, quoniam plus vales, non tamen plus diligis quam vales. Nos autem, etsi minus diligimus quam debemus, diligimus tamen quantum valemus; tantum autem valemus, quantum (a Deo) accepimus*, 'But the greater ... the affection in you, the less is my ability to be scorned by you, because although you love more, since you are worth more, you do not love more than you are able. I, although I love less than I ought, nevertheless love as much as I can; but I am able only as much as I have received (from God)' (ibid., 4).

[144] *Nunc vero si talia placent, qualia modo nugatus sum ...*, 'But now, if such fooling as I have just engaged in pleases you ...' (ibid.)

[145] Peter, letter 49, *Letters*, I, pp. 148–50.

[146] *frustra a vestro occidente mihi solem oriri sperabam, incassum marinos turbines nostri diei obscura serenare credebam, superfluo a lateribus aquilonis austrinis flatibus frigora nostra posse tepefieri suspicabar* (ibid., p. 149).

adynata, 'impossibilities', can be seen to exploit both the geographical position of *Brittania vis-à-vis Celtica Gallia*[147] and the metaphorical oppositions of heat/cold, light/dark associated with friendship and its failure.[148] As with the example from Bernard, the idea of playfulness is made explicit, this time through an introductory request to be allowed to say something *ludendo*, 'in play'.[149] In what follows this is picked up and exploited through rhetorical questions and hypothetical types of approach drawn from the area of epistolary etiquette, including a rejection of flattery, reminiscent of that seen in Augustine.[150]

Bernard's 'defence' against the charge of failure in friendship turns around the *topos* of incapacity. This is explicitly grafted on to the notion of writing, as he suggests that the root cause of the reproach is a lapse in epistolary etiquette: 'Perhaps it gives you some anxiety that to the more which you have already written to me, I have not yet replied even once? But when could I think that the maturity of your Wisdom could take pleasure in the frequent scribblings of my ignorance?'[151] This, in turn, can be associated with the end of the letter, where it apparently emerges that the real cause of the problem is Bernard's failure to respond to the request to send William a certain 'little preface'. Here too, however, the acceptance of blame is seemingly undercut, first by the suggestion that the omission was due to volition rather than incapacity,[152] and second by a hint that William, addressed here and previously as *pater*, 'father', has the capacity to undertake this work himself, thus 'laying up treasure' for his 'son', rather than demanding the opposite.[153]

---

[147] The presentation of physical hindrances as potential obstacles to the maintenance of the 'fire' and 'sweetness' of *caritas* can perhaps be characterised as a form of metaphorical topography. It finds a parallel, for example, in Alcuin: *Saepius ad nos currat charta exhortationis tuae, nec eam Alpium frigus vel viarum asperitas vel exundatio fluminum ullatenus impediat*, 'May a letter of your exhortation come to me more frequently, and not be hindered by the alpine cold, the harshness of the ways, or the flooding of rivers' (Alcuin, ep. 60, Dümmler, p. 104).

[148] This may also hint at the passing of winter associated with the coming of the divine *sponsus* in Canticles: *Iam enim hiems transiit imber abiit et recessit*, 'For now the winter has passed, the rain has gone and receded' (Ct 2. 11).

[149] *ut aliquid vel ludendo dicere liceat* ... (letter 49, p. 149).

[150] *Sed fortassis et hunc nostrum ludum dignitas vestra non aequo animo acceptabit. Quid igitur faciam? Si seria dixero, gratus non ero. Si allusero, nec sic placebo. Si questus fuero, asper videbor. Si accessero ut laudator, notabor ut adulator. Quid igitur placendi consilium?*, 'But perhaps your Dignity will not calmly accept even this game of mine. What then am I to do? If I speak seriously, I will not find favour. If I am playful, I will not be pleasing. If I complain, I will seem harsh. If I approach as a eulogizer, I will be branded as a flatterer. What then is the counsel of pleasing?' (ibid.).

[151] *Numquid forte scrupulum movet tibi, quod ad plura iam tua ad nos scripta, necdum vel semel rescripsi? Sed quando ego maturitatem sapientiae tuae delectari posse putarem scriptitationibus imperitiae meae?* (ep. 85, 2).

[152] *Praefatiunculam quam tibi mitti iussisti non habui modo ad manum, neque enim adhuc dictaveram, quia nec necessarium esse putabam*, 'I did not have to hand the little preface which you bid be sent to you, for I had not yet composed it, because I did not think it necessary' (ibid., 4).

[153] *Quidquid vel tibi, vel amicis tuis recte vis, qui dedit velle, det et perficere pro bona voluntate..*, 'Whatever you wish rightly for yourself and your friends, may He who has given

In Peter's letter, what follows the epistolary reproach suggests that it masks a second, more serious 'charge': 'Therefore I complain with the boldness of friendship that your Excellency, more quickly than was just, was moved against me a little while ago, and for a most slight cause disturbed the fixed gravity of friendship with fickle ease.'[154] The breakdown of epistolary relations is subsequently hinted to be a symptom, rather than a cause;[155] the epistolary reproach is explicitly revealed to function as a countering and forestalling device.[156] Bernard's letter is primarily concerned with mystic *caritas*, presented as a gift from God which cannot be measured in crude human terms. Peter's letter, on the other hand, takes its stand firmly and squarely on the reciprocity demanded by *amicitia*: Peter's indulgence should, it is suggested, meet with a similar return.[157] In both cases, the linguistic gambits in which the playfulness is enshrined offer the potential for manipulation. The parallel with Augustine and Jerome suggested above has further ramifications. In what follows, it will be argued that not only do these epistolary predecessors offer general stylistic models for Peter and Bernard, but that the correspondence between them plays a significant formative role in the Peter/Bernard correspondence.

In the twelfth-century samples of *amicitia iocosa* discussed above, the self-reflexive formalisation which seems to accompany it, expressed through references to 'joking' in the case of the Peter of Celle/John of Salisbury correspondence, to 'fooling' in Bernard's letter, and to 'playfulness' in Peter's, may suggest that 'joking friendship' should in itself be regarded as a construct. On the one hand, it can be seen to enable the projection of an intimate and well-established epistolary relationship, conforming to or playing itself off against certain expectations of epistolary etiquette; on the other, it would appear to facilitate the introduction of serious issues, and even serve to soften or mask potentially painful criticism. In particular, it can be seen to lend itself to irony and self-irony: such irony, depending on its context, has the ability to function as either Altman's 'bridge' or 'barrier'. As

---

the will also grant the performance, in accordance with good will ...' (ibid.). The use here of *recte*, 'rightly', and *pro bona voluntate*, 'in accordance with good will', might seem to cast doubt upon the purity of William's intentions. It is possible, although by no means certain, that this preface was intended to front Bernard's *Apologia*. See Leclercq, *SBO*, III, Rome, 1963, p. 65.

[154] *Familiari ergo ausu conqueror, excellentiam vestram citius iusto dudum adversum me commotam fuisse, et pro re levissima fixam amicitiae gravitatem mobili facilitate commovisse* (letter 49, p. 149).

[155] *Non ego replico frequentes querelas, quibus aures legatorum nostrorum in Angliam transfretantium implere consuestis*, 'I do not repeat the frequent reproaches with which you were wont to fill the ears of my messengers who came across to England' (ibid., p. 150).

[156] *Sit iste si placet mutuarum finis querelarum*, 'Let that, if you please, be the end of mutual complaints' (ibid.).

[157] *Indulgeo ego prior absque alia poena multa quae in me non iure commissa sunt. Indulgentiam et mihi etiam si non peccavi, postulo*, 'I show indulgence first without penalty in respect of the many injustices committed against me. I demand indulgence for myself also, even if I have not sinned' (ibid.). The causes of offence are shrouded in mystery, but a reference to the Cluniac foundation of La Charité suggests that they may have a 'political' dimension (see Constable, *Letters*, II, p. 131).

such, *amicitia iocosa* would appear to represent a particular refinement of the evocation of 'friendship' in medieval letters in general, with a manipulative potential which can arguably be viewed through the double perspective of tool and weapon. Its presence, in consequence, cannot be held to offer any more straightforward a diagnostic indicator for the nature and quality of actual relationships than does that of the language of friendship discussed above. This recognition is of crucial importance in the consideration of the Peter/Bernard letters, where, as will be seen, seemingly playful banter plays a vital role.

The aim of the survey given above has been to highlight the problems involved in developing and applying a critical system for the study of letters and letter-writing, in particular, the pitfalls associated with the utilisation of an essentially 'autobiographical' approach, which takes at face value the redeployment of conventional but inherently manipulable declarations of 'friendship'. It has been suggested that while models drawn from medieval and antique handbooks have some value, particularly in establishing the existence of certain expectations and requirements of epistolary etiquette current from the classical period onwards, this value is arguably limited, both by considerations of time and place and by their reductionist nature. In distinction to this, it has been argued that the concept of epistolarity, as developed through the work of Doty and Altman, with its concomitant recognition of a self-conscious and artificially constructed epistolary relationship, offers a flexible alternative which facilitates the application of the techniques of modern literary criticism.

In what follows, it will be argued that the application of such techniques to the correspondence between Peter the Venerable and Bernard of Clairvaux demonstrates the presence of a high degree of what can be termed 'fictionalisation'. Specifically, it will be argued that the use of intertextuality reveals a heavy reliance on a preceding patristic correspondence, that of Augustine and Jerome, the influence of which can be seen to shape the portrayal both of the 'personal' relationship between writer and addressee, and of that between their respective monastic orders. It will likewise be suggested that an examination of the contexts from which the biblical citations, with which both sets of letters are studded, are taken shows a network of interlocking allusions which present slander, deceit and hypocrisy as 'enemies' of monastic *caritas*, and which transfer concrete causes of monastic dispute to the realms of friendship and epistolary etiquette. In conjunction with this, rhetorical gambits will be argued to combine with irony and scriptural subversion to create a veil of ambiguity which straddles both private and public spheres. At the same time, since all the evidence suggests that these letters conform with Doty's first category of definition as being sent or intended for sending, attention will also be paid to locating them within their historical context, and to reconstructing the sequences of events of which they may be thought to offer a selective and manipulated reflection.

Chapter 2

Sanctity and Rebuke: the Relationship between Bernard's *Apologia* and Peter's Letter 28

The correspondence between Peter the Venerable and Bernard of Clairvaux opens with Peter's letter 28.[1] Comprising a lengthy treatise, which extends over some fifty printed pages, this letter mounts an aggressive defence of traditional Cluniac practices, presented as a response to Cistercian criticisms relating to lax interpretation of the *Rule* of St Benedict, the cornerstone of western monasticism.[2] At the same time, it can be seen to conform to epistolary expectations through the device of a 'personal' frame, which addresses itself directly to Bernard, and which entwines the language of mystic friendship with that of Christian brotherhood.[3] The substance of the letter has attracted critical attention, both in relation to its depiction of growing hostility between Cluniacs and Cistercians,[4] and to the points

---

[1]   Peter, letter 28, *Letters*, I, pp. 52–101. Sections of the letter are to be found translated in S. R. Maitland, *The Dark Ages, a series of essays*, London, 1844, pp. 373–81; 387–93; 395–7.

[2]   Composed some time in the first half of the sixth century AD, the *Regula* sets out a detailed plan for the organisation of a fully coenobitical monastic community. Manuscripts can be classified into three types, an 'interpolated' text, current from the sixth century, a 'pure' text, preserved in the region of Monte Cassino, and a 'mixed' text, current from the eighth century. Constable draws attention to variants in Peter's citations which can be related to manuscripts emanating from Monte Cassino (Constable, *Letters*, II, p. 40). The edition followed here, as cited by Constable, is that of Hanslik (*Benedicti Regula*, ed. R. Hanslik, *CSEL*, 75, Vienna, 1960).

[3]   At the end of the letter, Peter seems to draw attention to its ambiguous status through an opposition which transforms an apology for excessive length into a justification: *Haec tibi frater carissime epistolarem brevitatem rerum necessitate supergressus scripsi ...*, 'I have written this to you, dearest brother, contravening epistolary brevity through the coercion of the subject-matter ...' (letter 28, p. 101).

[4]   Bredero, *Cluny et Cîteaux*, pp. 122–3. See also E. Vacandard, *Vie de St Bernard, abbé de Clairvaux*, 2 vols, Paris, 1927, I, pp. 99–134; W. Williams, 'Peter the Venerable, a letter to St Bernard', *Downside Review* 56 (1938), 344–53; Dom D. Knowles, 'Cistercians and Cluniacs: the controversy between St Bernard and Peter the Venerable', Friends of Dr. Williams' Library Ninth Lecture, London, 1955, reprinted in *The historian and character and other essays*, Cambridge, 1963, pp. 50–75. Peter ends the letter with the following somewhat cryptic statement: *Nam praeter austeritatem verborum, quae ad partium latentem simultatem designandam posui, reliqua omnia ut edita sunt intellexi*, 'For apart from the harshness of the words, which I have set down to represent the lurking animosity of (a) faction(s), I have understood/ meant the rest as it has been brought forth' (letter 28, p. 101).

of monastic practice which it enumerates.[5] The recent study by Goodrich goes further,[6] pinpointing the concept of monastic charity, prominent both in Cistercian thought[7] and in the writing of Aelred of Rievaulx,[8] apparently undertaken at the request of Bernard,[9] as crucial to its understanding. In what follows, the focus will be on Peter's use of rhetorical strategies and semantic exploitations to create an illusion of 'debate' which will set the tone and lay down the terms of reference for the correspondence to follow. More significantly, it will be argued that the presentation of this 'debate' is heavily dependent on an earlier theological dispute conducted through the letters of Augustine and Jerome,[10] thus introducing an element of 'fictionalisation'. At the same time, it will be suggested that a close examination of Bernard's polemical *Apologia*,[11] framed as a letter to William of St Thierry, reveals a degree of linguistic coincidence which can most convincingly be explained by accepting that Peter is, in fact, taking his cue from Bernard, and that this 'fictionalisation' can be seen to target a corresponding element in Bernard's own work.

The last issue is potentially complicated by problems over the dating of both works. The question of priority between Bernard's *Apologia* and Peter's letter 28 has been the subject of a long debate, as Constable shows.[12] Letter 28 was traditionally

---

The use of *partes*, connoting faction or factions, leaves it unclear whether Peter is attacking the Cistercian 'critics' or warning that this criticism is breeding disharmony. Certainly, as will be seen, 'harshness' is to be found on both sides of the 'debate'.

5   Constable, *Letters*, II, pp. 115–20.

6   W. E. Goodrich, 'The limits of friendship: a disagreement between Saint Bernard and Peter the Venerable on the role of charity in dispensation from the Rule', *Cistercian Studies* 16 (1981), 81–97.

7   The oldest extant version of the *Carta caritatis et unanimitatis*, the document which bound together the Cistercian houses in a relationship of mutual help and obligation, dates from 1119. Its origins, however, probably go back to the foundation of La Ferté (J. de la Croix Bouton and J. B. van Damme, *Les plus anciens textes de Cîteaux, sources, textes et notes historiques*, Cîteaux, Commentarii Cistercienses Studia et Documenta 2, Achel, 1974, pp. 14–17).

8   Aelred (*c.* 1110–67) was born on the borders of England and Scotland and spent a period in the household of King David of Scotland. Subsequently he became a monk at Rievaulx, a new foundation from Clairvaux, and was made abbot there in 1147.

9   Aelred of Rievaulx, *Liber de speculo caritatis*, in *Aelredi Rievallensis Opera Omnia 1, Opera Ascetica*, ed. A. Hoste and C. H Talbot, *CCCM*, 1, Turnhout, 1971, pp. 3–161. See McGuire, *The difficult saint*, pp. 25–6.

10   The letters of Augustine are in *CSEL*, 34/1, 34/2, 44, 57, ed. A. L. Goldbacher, Vienna, 1895–1911; those of Jerome in *CSEL*, 54, 55, 56/1, ed. I. Hilberg, Vienna, 1910–918, reprinted 1996. A translation of the whole correspondence, together with notes and discussions of background material has been produced by White (C. White, *The Correspondence (394–419) between Jerome and Augustine of Hippo*, Studies in Bible and Early Christianity 23, Lewiston, Queenston, Lampeter, 1990).

11   Bernard, *Apologia*, *SBO*, III, Rome, 1963, pp. 81–108. It has been translated into English by Casey ('Cistercians and Cluniacs: St Bernard's *Apologia* to abbot William', intro J. Leclercq, trans. M. Casey, in *The works of Bernard of Clairvaux*, Cistercian Fathers Series 1, Spencer, Mass., 1970, 3–69, pp. 33–69).

12   See Constable, *Letters,* II, pp. 271–3.

dated to 1123/4, following Vacandard, who argued that it was written before the *Apologia*, dated by him to 1124/5.[13] Recent discussions of the *Apologia* locate it towards the end of 1125.[14] While accepting the slightly later date of 1125 for letter 28, van den Eynde[15] and Leclercq[16] suggest that the two works were written at about the same time, but maintain that they were produced independently of one another. Constable, however, argues on internal evidence for a date of 1126/7 for letter 28.[17] If accepted, this would suggest that letter 28 postdated the *Apologia*, a position currently adopted by Bredero.[18] In view of these uncertainties, scholarly opinion, with the notable exception of Bredero, has tended to deny any direct connection between the two works.[19] Even Goodrich confines himself to the cautious statement that 'each seems to have at least anticipated and responded to the position of the other.'[20]

Certainly, neither work acknowledges the other's existence. The *Apologia*, as stated above, is addressed not to Peter but to William of St Thierry, while in letter 28 Peter claims to be responding to a schedule of Cistercian charges. Peter's decision to intervene at this point, and to make Bernard the recipient of the letter could perhaps be explained by the latter's open and hostile letter to Robert,[21] taking as its subject the removal to Cluny of his cousin Robert of Châtillon, and reassigned by van den Eynde from 1119/20 to spring 1125.[22] Vitriolic as that letter is, however, in itself it seems insufficient to have triggered such a specific and lengthy response. Although Bredero assumes a strong link between letter 28 and the *Apologia*, his argument rests on circumstantial factors and is tied into a somewhat idiosyncratic reading which will be discussed in the next chapter. It will be argued here that the coincidence of internal similarities between these two works makes it improbable that they were written in complete isolation. Priority can theoretically be assigned in either direction, but the balance of probabilities suggests that letter 28 should be seen as constituting an indirect response to the *Apologia*.[23] As will be seen, the parallel with Augustine and Jerome adds considerable weight to this argument.

Both letter 28 and the *Apologia* seem to have existed in a number of versions.

---

[13]   Vacandard, *Vie de Saint Bernard*, I, p. 104, n. 2.

[14]   D. van den Eynde, 'Les premiers écrits de saint Bernard' in *Recueil d'études sur saint Bernard et ses écrits*, ed. Dom J. Leclercq, 5 vols, III, Rome, 1969, 343–422, pp. 354–5; Dom J. Leclercq, 'Introduction', in CFS 1, 3–30, p. 3.

[15]   van den Eynde, 'Premiers écrits', pp. 404–5.

[16]   Leclercq, CFS 1, 11–12.

[17]   Constable, *Letters*, II, p. 273.

[18]   Bredero, 'Saint Bernard in his relations', p. 319; idem, *Bernard of Clairvaux*, p. 226, n. 65.

[19]   Indeed, as Bredero points out, Bernard's criticisms have traditionally been associated with the Cluny of Peter's predecessor, Pons of Melgueil (Bredero, *Bernard of Clairvaux*, p. 218). For a resumé, see Constable, *Letters* II, pp. 271–3.

[20]   Goodrich, 'The limits of friendship', p. 83.

[21]   Bernard, ep. 1, *SBO*, VII, pp. 1–11. Originally placed later in the collection, this letter was subsequently placed at its head, seemingly as some kind of manifesto (Leclercq, 'Lettres de S. Bernard', p. 126).

[22]   van den Eynde, 'Premiers écrits', pp. 395–6.

[23]   This is the position adopted by Bredero. His interpretation, as stated above, will be discussed in the next chapter.

Constable distinguishes between an 'original' version or versions of letter 28, which circulated in letterform during Peter's lifetime, and a 'revised' version as included in the letter-collection.[24] The printed text followed here is the 'revised' version taken from the manuscript tradition argued to represent the earlier letter-collection.[25] Leclercq postulates two versions of the *Apologia*, the second containing several additional passages, both produced within a short period by Bernard himself.[26] The printed text as followed here corresponds to the second of these versions. In both cases, any additional insertions will be noted as such.

The *Apologia* divides into three sections. The first is cast as a self-defence against the charge of slandering the Cluniacs.[27] The second constitutes a rebuke for detraction directed towards 'certain Cistercians'.[28] The third, and longest, section is framed as a heavily satirical criticism of monastic excesses, covering the areas of food and drink, clothing, travel and ornamentation.[29] It concludes with a brief warning against monastic transfer.[30] The traditional view, that the attacks in the *Apologia* were directed solely or even primarily against the Cluniacs, has been recently challenged, most notably by Rudolph, who points to the fact that they are only referred to twice by name, and that only in the first section.[31] This overlooks a reference in the third section to Odo, Maiolus, Odilo and Hugh, 'whom they glory in having as the founders and teachers of their Order', and who, Bernard claims, would not have approved of such abuses.[32] The reference is backed by the citation, 'Having food and clothing, we are contented with these',[33] and developed through the comment 'But we have satiety instead of food, and seek not clothing but adornment'.[34] The naming of the Cluniac fathers at this point would suggest that the attacks on excesses of food, drink and clothing should be seen as primarily aimed at the Cluniacs themselves, even if the attack on ornamentation was, as Rudolph argues, intended as a warning to the new ascetic orders and the Cistercians.[35]

The change from 'defence' to 'attack' might at first sight seem unexpected;[36] in

---

[24] Constable, *Letters*, II, p. 67.

[25] Ibid., pp. 83–4.

[26] Leclercq, *SBO*, III, p. 68.

[27] *Apo*, I–IV, pp. 81–9.

[28] Ibid., V–VII, pp. 90–94.

[29] Ibid., VIII–XII. 30, pp. 95–107.

[30] Ibid., XII. 31, pp. 107–8.

[31] C. Rudolph, *The 'things of greater importance': Bernard of Clairvaux's Apologia and the medieval attitude towards art*, Philadelphia, 1990, p. 162.

[32] *Sic denique sancti Odo, Maiolus, Odilo, Hugo, quos se sui utique Ordinis principes et praeceptores habere gloriantur, aut tenuerunt, aut teneri censuerunt?*, 'Was it thus that the saints Odo, Maiolus, Odilo and Hugh, whom they glory that they have as the founders and teachers of their Order, either held or decreed to be held?' (*Apo* IX. 23).

[33] *Habentes victum et vestitum, his contenti sumus* (ibid. = I Tim 6, 8).

[34] *Nobis autem est pro victu satietas, nec vestitum appetimus, sed ornatum* (*Apo* X. 23).

[35] Rudolph, *The 'things'*, pp. 172–91.

[36] Discussing the possibility, raised by Mabillon, that the *Apologia* might have been composed from two initially separate letters, Leclercq rejects it on the evidence of the manuscript tradition (Dom J. Leclercq, 'Pour l'histoire des traités de S. Bernard', in *Recueil d'études sur saint Bernard et ses écrits*, 5 vols, II, Rome, 1966, 101–30, pp. 123–6).

fact, it is prepared for at the start. The *Apologia* opens with a modesty *topos*: Bernard's previous unwillingness or refusal to comply with William's demands to write is ascribed to his fear of 'presuming what he did not know';[37] his change of heart is presented as a result of a 'complaint' that he is engaging in detraction.[38] Into this complaint is incorporated a citation from Jerome: 'by which [complaint] we, the most wretched of men, in rags and narrow girdles, *from the caves*, as he [Jerome] says, are said to judge the world ...'[39] Significantly, the context from which this is taken is one in which Jerome defends himself from criticism by attacking those who have accused him.[40] The Jeromian voice here is matched, as will be seen, by the presence of Augustinian echoes in letter 28.

The three sections of the *Apologia* are carefully tied together by the motif of detraction, and more significantly, through this, by an exploration of the 'right' and 'wrong' sorts of *caritas*. In the first two sections the absence of *caritas* is equated with detraction. Bernard clears himself of this charge, 'I praise and love all [Orders], wherever it is lived piously and justly in the Church. I embrace one in deed, the rest in affection.'[41] He uses it as a warning to the Cistercians, 'By detraction from your brothers, in extolling yourself, you lose humility; in disparaging others, you lose charity.'[42] In the third section, however, *caritas* is linked with abuse of language of another kind, 'justifying' abuses of the *Rule*: 'For

---

[37] *ne praesumerem quod nesciebam* (*Apo* I. 1).

[38] *Quomodo namque silenter audire possum vestram huiuscemodi de nobis querimoniam, qua ... dicimur ... etiam gloriosissimo Ordini vestro derogare, sanctis, qui in eo laudabiliter vivunt, impudenter detrahere, et de umbra nostrae ignobilitatis mundi luminaribus insultare?*, 'For how can I hear in silence your complaint about us, by which ... we are said ... to disparage even your most glorious Order, to engage in detraction against the holy men who live praiseworthily in it, and from the darkness of our unworthiness to insult the luminaries of the world?' (ibid.). As Rudolph points out, the expression 'your Order', as applied here to William of St Thierry, seems to designate traditional Benedictine monasticism (Rudolph, *The 'things'*, p. 162). In view of the specific reference to the Cluniac founders discussed above, however, it seems more difficult to take the opposition of Cluniacs and Cistercians which follows, *sive Cluniacenses, sive Cistercienses*, 'whether Cluniacs, whether Cistercians' (*Apo*, III. 6); *Cisterciensis sum: damno igitur Cluniacenses?*, 'I am a Cistercian: do I therefore condemn Cluniacs?' (*Apo*, IV. 7), as equally non-specific.

[39] *qua [querimonia] scilicet miserrimi hominum, in pannis et semicinctiis,* de cavernis, *ut ille ait, dicimur iudicare mundum* (ibid., I. 1). The original runs: *Pudet dicere: de cavernis cellularum damnamus orbem, si in sacco et cinere volutati de episcopis sententiam ferimus*, 'It is shameful to speak: from the caves of little cells we condemn the world, if, wrapped in sackcloth and ashes, we pass judgement on bishops' (Jerome, ep. 17, 2, *CSEL*, 54, p. 71).

[40] *si [hereticus vocor] ab orthodoxis ... esse orthodixi desierunt ...*, 'if [I am called a heretic] by the orthodox ... they have ceased to be orthodox ...' (Jerome, ep. 17, 2, p. 71); *permittant mihi, quaeso, nihil loqui*, 'let them permit me, I beg, to say nothing' (ibid.); *ecce [carissimi fratres] discedere cupiunt, immo discedunt melius esse dicentes inter feras habitare quam cum talibus Christianis*, 'lo, [my dearest brothers] desire to go away, rather they go away, saying that it is better to live among wild beasts than with such Christians' (ibid., 3, p. 72).

[41] *Laudo enim omnes [Ordines] et diligo, ubicumque pie et iuste vivitur in Ecclesia. Unum opere teneo, ceteros caritate* (*Apo*, IV. 8).

[42] *Detrahendo quippe fratribus, in quo temetipsum extollis, perdis humilitatem; in quo alios deprimis, caritatem ...* (ibid., VII. 13).

moderation is considered to be miserliness, sobriety is believed to be austerity, silence is held to be gloominess. On the other hand, laxness is called discretion, extravagance generosity, loquacity affability, immoderate laughter pleasant cheerfulness ... and when we grant these things mutually, it is called charity.'[43] The wrong sort of *caritas* is therefore equated equally with detraction and with euphemism; the right sort, by implication, with friendly and benevolent rebuke. Thus *caritas* functions both as a weapon, 'That charity destroys charity, this discretion confounds discretion',[44] and as a justification for intervention. Bernard will claim at the end of the *Apologia*, *hoc non est detractio, sed attractio*, 'this is not detraction but attraction'.[45]

Caritas is the dominating feature of Peter the Venerable's letter 28, where it is used as a means of both defence and attack. The letter purports to be a reply to a list of accusations, attributed to 'certain Cistercians', of Cluniac deviations from the *Rule* of St Benedict. A recital of these charges[46] is followed first by a stinging counter-attack,[47] then by a detailed rebuttal,[48] which employs three principal methods: citation of *auctoritates* supported by *exempla*; argument by application of *ratio*; rhetorical devices designed to ridicule the arguments of the opponents. Finally, forming a kind of peroration, there is an aggressive justification based on the single principle of *caritas*.[49] As stated previously, the whole is set within a 'personal' frame, addressed directly to Bernard; the essence of the defence, as observed by Goodrich,[50] that since the *Rule* of St Benedict was founded with *caritas* to ensure the salvation of souls, it should be applied with moderation and discretion to ensure that this is achieved. As will be seen, however, this argument is driven home by a variety of rhetorical devices, including the use of heavy satire.

The main body of the letter creates the illusion that a dialogue, or rather, a legal debate, is taking place. The 'charges' relating to *praevaricatio*, deviation from the *Rule*, are placed directly in the mouth of the Cistercians: 'Accordingly, certain of yours object to ours: "You do not," they say, "follow the Rule whose rectitude you have undertaken to uphold." '[51] Peter casts himself as spokesman on behalf of the Cluniacs, 'we reply as follows to your objections',[52] a role made explicit in revisions of the letter, where the words *ad haec nostri*, 'to this ours [say]', are inserted at the beginning of this section.[53] There is an appeal to 'witnesses', 'let reason, let truth, let the lovers of truth see this, and while we are silent bring forth

---

[43]   *Ecce enim parcitas putatur avaritia, sobrietas austeritas creditur, silentium tristitia reputatur. Econtra remissio discretio dicitur, effusio liberalitas, loquacitas affabilitas, cachinnatio iucunditas.. cumque haec alterutrum impendimus, caritas appellatur* (ibid., VIII. 16).
[44]   *Ista caritas destruit caritatem, haec discretio discretionem confundit* (ibid.).
[45]   Ibid., XII. 31.
[46]   Peter, letter 28, pp. 53–6.
[47]   Ibid., pp. 57–8.
[48]   Ibid., pp. 58–88.
[49]   Ibid., pp. 88–101.
[50]   Goodrich, 'The limits of friendship', p. 87.
[51]   *Obiciunt itaque nostris quidam vestrorum. Non, inquiunt, vos regulam cuius rectitudinem sequi proposuistis, ... sequimini* (letter 28, p. 53).
[52]   *ad ea quae obiecistis taliter respondemus* (ibid., p. 58).
[53]   Ibid., p. 57. See Constable, *Letters*, II, p. 42.

what they feel about it',[54] and a formalisation of the notion of proof, 'so indeed law demands, that the accuser should prove his objection, since proof is always incumbent'.[55] The formal organisation of the letter, reinforced as it is by such quasi-legal terminology,[56] serves to place it in the category of apologetic, with its roots in the language of the law-court.[57]

The fiction of debate is sustained through repeated use of the rhetorical device of *prolepsis*,[58] interspersed with invitations to respond.[59] This technique reaches a climax in the peroration, where it is used to put the Cistercians into a totally false position, even implying at one moment that Peter's argument has left them with nothing to say, 'But we still demand your reply ...';[60] 'but until we hear, what can we reply?'[61] Bernard's *Apologia* similarly makes use of *prolepsis*, most significantly in the second section addressed to the Cistercian dissidents, where it arguably functions to introduce certain criticisms which, while not directly endorsed by Bernard, are none-the-less not directly contradicted by him. For example, ' "But", they say, "how do they keep the Rule, who are clad in furs, who, being healthy, feed on meat and the fat of meat, who allow three or four meals in one day, which the Rule prohibits, who do not perform manual labour, which it orders, who in short change, or increase, or diminish many aspects according to their will?" Rightly: these things cannot be denied ...';[62] ' "What then?", do you say? "Do you urge those labours of the spirit to the extent of condemning the labours of the flesh, which we hold to from the Rule?" By no means; but the one must be performed, and the other not omitted.'[63]

---

[54] *Hoc videat ratio, videat veritas, videant veritatis amatores, et nobis tacentibus quod inde sentiunt proferant* (letter 28, p. 76).

[55] *Sic quippe ius postulat, ut qui aliquem impetit, quod obicit probet, quoniam probatio semper incumbit* (ibid., p. 83).

[56] Cf. *vobis quamvis invitis concedentibus*, 'as you, albeit unwillingly, concede' (ibid., p. 99); *comprobamus*, 'we establish' (ibid.); *nobis ... purgatis, iam pro vobis agite*, 'since we have been cleared, now plead on your own behalf' (ibid.).

[57] See Stowers, *Letter writing*, p. 166.

[58] *Sed forte dicetis* ..., 'but perhaps you will say ...' (letter 28, p. 58); *sed forte adhuc perstatis et dicitis ... Nos econtra* ..., 'but perhaps you still persist and say ... We, on the contrary ...' (ibid., p. 59); *sed forte opponitis* ..., 'but perhaps you object ...' (ibid., p. 77); *sed forte adhuc ad priora recurritis, et dicitis ... Ad quod nos* ..., 'but perhaps you have recourse to the previous argument, and say ... To which we (reply) ...' (ibid., p. 90); *sed forte vos ad ista ... At nos econtra* ..., 'But perhaps you (say) to this ... But we on the contrary ...' (ibid., p. 93); *Respondebitis ... Ad haec nos* ..., 'You will reply ... To this we (say) ...' (ibid., p. 94).

[59] *Dicite ergo* ..., 'Say then ..' (ibid., p. 67); *sed dicite qui haec opponitis* ..., 'but say, you who bring this charge ...' (ibid., p. 71).

[60] *Sed adhuc vestrum responsum poscimus* ... (ibid., p. 95).

[61] *Sed quousque audiamus respondere quid possumus?* (ibid., p. 96).

[62] At, *inquiunt*, quomodo Regulam tenent, qui pelliciis induuntur, sani carnibus seu carnium pinguedine vescuntur, tria vel quattuor pulmentaria una die, quod Regula prohibet, admittunt, opus manuum, quod iubet, non faciunt, multa denique pro libitu suo vel mutant, vel augent, vel minuunt? *Recte: non possunt haec negari* ... (*Apo* V. 11). Bernard goes on to argue that the kingdom of God does not consist in externals; the criticism, however, is left uncontested.

[63] Quid ergo, *inquis?* Siccine illa spiritualia persuades, ut etiam haec, quae ex Regula habemus, corporalia damnes? *Nequaquam; sed illa oportet agere, et ista non omittere* (ibid., VII. 13).

Letter 28 also exploits the device of *prosopopoeia* through a speech placed in the mouth of a personified *caritas*, thereby virtually presented as a witness for the 'defence':

> While she (charity) is saying, 'At that time, the nature of men was stronger to endure labours, inasmuch as the world was more vigorous, but now, with the world growing old and already close to death, whatever is in the world has languished, and therefore many things then necessary have now been made harmful: do what is necessary now, for it is not mine or of this time to so deter novices that while I wish to prove them for a year, condemnation may follow; it is not, I say, mine to fail to supply want of food, drink, clothing and other necessities in accordance with differences of infirmities, places, and times, lest while I do not render to man what is his, he himself may not be able to render to God what is His', they disdain to obey her salutary warnings out of arrogant sanctity.[64]

The dominant metaphor in letter 28 is that of attack and counter-attack.[65] *Caritas* is overtly presented as a means of defence: 'By this same shield of charity we protect ourselves from the blows of those assailing us in all the articles which follow.'[66] Implicitly, it also becomes a means of attack, as the Cistercians are shown to be in need of its protection: 'if you wish to defend the holy men from blame with regard to these matters by any other shield than that of charity, with God's grace helping us,

[64]   *Qua (caritate) dicente,* tunc temporis ad tolerandos labores fortior erat natura hominum utpote saeculo valentiore, nunc vero mundo senescente et iam morti proximo, quicquid in mundo est elanguit, et ideo pleraque tunc necessaria, modo facta sunt contraria, quod nunc necessarium est facite, nam non est meum aut huius temporis sic novicios deterrere ut dum volo per annum probare, sequatur reprobare, non est inquam meum, cibi et potus atque vestitus vel ceterarum rerum indigentiam, pro diversitatibus infirmitatum, regionum ac temporum non supplere, ne dum non reddo homini quod suum est, non possit ipse reddere deo quod eius est, *superba superstitione salutaribus monitis obtemperare dedignantur* (letter 28, p. 97). The version given in the second collection of Peter's letters gives *in mundo* for *immundo*: that version is followed here. See Constable, *Letters* I, p. 97, n. 560.
[65]   By the Cistercians, *ut per ordinem cuncta aggrediamur,* 'so that we may attack everything in order' (letter 28, p. 53); by the Cluniacs, *ut maiora aggrediamur,* 'so that we may attack the greater matters' (ibid., p. 59). Cf. *inde quoque et regulam cuius defensores magis quam observatores videri vultis valde transgredimini,* 'thence also you violently transgress the Rule, whose defenders rather than observers you wish to seem' (ibid., p. 57); *ne magis iniurias verborum verbis ulcisci ... videamur,* 'lest we seem rather to avenge the injuries of words with words' (ibid., p. 58); *istis vos expugnantibus exemplis et testimoniis cinximus,* 'we have encircled you with those assaulting examples and testimonies' (ibid., p. 62). On the language of aggression as characteristic of monastic disputes in the twelfth century, see Dom. J. Leclercq, 'Diversification et identité dans le monachisme', *Studia Monastica* 28 (1986), 51–74.
[66]   *Hoc eodem caritatis scuto ab impugnantium ictibus in cunctis subsequentibus capitulis nos munimus* (letter 28, p. 92). Cf. *Hoc uno nos victos vobis victoribus caedere compellitis, si quae lege caritatis nobis defendimus, ad caritatem non pertinere rationibus certis ostenderitis. In his enim omnibus ... ea solum protectrice tuti, hostibus cunctis inexpugnabiles permanemus,* 'This is the one way in which you can compel us to yield in defeat to you as victors, if you can prove by certain reasons that those things which we defend by the law of charity do not pertain to charity. For in all of these ... safe under her as sole protrectress, we remain impregnable to all enemies' (ibid., p. 93).

you will not be able to defend even yourselves.'[67] In the revised *Apologia*, the attack on gluttony and luxury is pursued through the *topos* of spiritual warfare: 'I ask, what is this freedom from care, in the midst of the flashing spears and flying darts of enemies raging on all sides, to throw down your weapons, as if the war were now over and the Enemy laid low in triumph, and to recline over lengthy meals, or to wallow naked in a soft bed? What is this cowardice, O good soldiers?'[68]

Ostensibly, as stated earlier, the detailed defence against the 'charges' relies on an interplay between *auctoritas* and *ratio*: 'that these matters may be seen not to have been delineated by us through reason, but rather to have been strengthened by canonic authority ...'[69] At times, Peter's use of argument appears to descend into captiousness and equivocation.[70] For example, one of the charges deals with monks who take their vows in one community and then repeat them in another: they must, according to the Cistercians, be held guilty of breaking one set or the other. The charge names three aspects of the broken vows, *stabilitas*, *conversio morum*, *obedientia*, 'stability, (profession of) way of life, obedience', but these are clearly treated as forming a single unity.[71] Peter bases his defence on a provision of the *Rule* which deals with pilgrim monks, not with monks who have moved from one institution to another as alleged in the charge.[72] From this basis, he extrapolates, not perhaps without irony, that it is expedient for such monks to be allowed to promise obedience;[73] as for the monastic way of life, monks are said to reaffirm it daily in

---

[67]   *Si ad ista alio quam caritatis scuto sanctos a culpa defendere volueritis, dei nos gratia iuvante nec vos ipsos defendere praevalebitis* (ibid., p. 96).

[68]   *Rogo quae est haec securitas, inter frendentium undique hostium fulgurantes hastas et circumvolantia spicula, tamquam finito iam bello et triumphato adversario, proicere arma, et aut prandiis incubare longioribus, aut nudum molli volutari in lectulo? Quid hoc ignaviae est, o boni milites?* (*Apo* IX. 21).

[69]   *ut haec non a nobis commentata ratione sed magis canonum auctoritate roborata videantur* ... (letter 28, p. 82). Cf. *Et ut nihil fingere, sed totum divinis auctoritatibus videamur firmare* ..., 'so that we may be seen not to be inventing anything, but to be supporting the whole with divine authorities ...' (ibid., p. 58); *sed et nos requirimus, qua auctoritate ea[s] [pellicias] auferre conamini. Quam cum afferre non potueritis, quod re vera non potestis, nos nostras in medium afferemus rationes* ..., 'but we also ask, by what authority you seek to take them [furs] away. Since you have not been able to bring any, for in fact you cannot, we will bring our reasons into public view ...' (ibid., p. 62).

[70]   Iogna-Prat draws attention to a similar use of disputation techniques in relation to Peter's treatment of heresy (D. Iogna-Prat, *Ordonner et exclure. Cluny et la société chrétienne face à l'hérésie, au judaïsme et à l'islam 1000–1150*, Paris, 1998, pp. 124–52).

[71]   *Nam si prius votum servaverint, secundi rei tenebuntur. Si secundum, prioris noxa constringentur*, 'For if they keep the former vow, they will be held guilty of the second. If the second, they will be bound by guilt for the former' (letter 28, p. 55).

[72]   *Sic enim legimus ibi, ubi* de monachis peregrinis qualiter suscipiantur *tractatur*: Si vero postea *inquit* voluerit stabilitatem suam firmare, non renuatur talis voluntas, 'For thus we read there, where it treats *of how pilgrim monks are to be received*: *If afterwards*, he says, *he wishes to confirm his stability, such a wish should not be refused*' (ibid., p. 76 = *Benedicti Regula*, LXI, 5).

[73]   *Quod si stabilitatem firmare monacho peregrino conceditur, ut in loco quem elegit stabilem se semper esse oportere intelligat, nec ultra inde sibi licere evagari, nihilominus patri monasterii obedientiam illum promittere expedit, ut habeat cui loco Christi obaedire*

the course of confession.[74] This artificial separation of three integral facets, together with its play on 'profession' and 'confession', seems to obscure the fact that the ground of argument has been shifted.[75] Similar in kind is the response to the admonition that the abbot should dine with visitors and pilgrims: 'For does not the abbot make sharers in his own table whomsoever he refreshes with the substance of the monastery?'[76]

Ridicule is also employed, for the accusations which are seen, or rather which are thereby presented, as being weakest. The techniques here borrow from satire and take the form of heavy irony and *reductio ad absurdum*. In response to the charge that the Cluniacs exceed the number of cooked meals allowed by the *Rule*, letter 28 focuses instead on the instructions attaching to the allocation and distribution of bread, and 'invites' the Cistercians to condemn them if they transgress by a hairsbreadth: 'Behold, you who devise calumnies relating to one jot or tittle of the Rule, rise up, attack, you have found something to say, some objection to raise, here plainly you can damn us ... what else are we than condemned by God, excluded from paradise, thrust down in hell as perjurers and sons of perdition?'[77] A similar treatment is given to the requirement to deal in person with the needs of guests: 'Will it (the congregation of Cluny) be damned, if it does not wash the hands and feet of all the guests? It will be necessary, therefore, either for the community to spend all its time in the guest-house, or for the guests to be lodged in the cloister and offices

---

debeat, 'Therefore, if it is granted to a pilgrim monk that he confirm his stability, so that he may realise that he must always remain stable in the place which he has chosen, it is also expedient for him to promise obedience to the father of the monastery, so that he may have one to obey in the place of Christ' (letter 28, p. 77).

[74] *Conversionem vero morum rursum polliceri quid oberit, cum non tantum bis in professione, sed etiam milies in confessione tam deo quam hominibus cotidie morum conversionem et vitae emendationem cum praeteritorum malorum paenitentia promittere debeat?*, 'What will hinder him from again promising way of life, when in penitence for past sins he should promise daily to God and men way of life and emendation of life not only twice in profession but even a thousand times in confession?' (ibid.).

[75] The transition back is effected somewhat disingenuously: *Quod si hoc monacho peregrino non negatur, quare non omni legitime venienti concedetur?*, 'Therefore, if this is not denied to a pilgrim monk, why will it not be conceded to everyone who comes legitimately?' (ibid.). The 'legitimacy' of monastic transfer is, presumably, precisely the point at issue.

[76] *Quoscumque enim abbas substantia monasterii reficit, nonne mensae propriae participes facit?* (ibid., p. 74).

[77] *Ecce qui de iota uno aut uno regulae apice calumnias machinamini, insurgite, irruite, invenistis quid dicatis, quid obiciatis, hic plane nos damnare ... potestis ... quid aliud quam a deo condemnamur, a paradyso excludimur, ut periuri et filii perditionis in inferno retrudimur?* (ibid., p. 65). This seems to draw on two passages from the New Testament: *Amen quippe dico vobis donec transeat caelum et terra iota unum aut unus apex non praeteribit a lege donec omnia fiant*, 'Truly I say to you, until heaven and earth are changed not one jot or tittle will be omitted from the Law' (Mt 5. 18); *facilius est autem caelum et terram praeterire quam de lege unum apicem cadere*, 'it is easier for heaven and earth to perish than for one tittle to be shed from the Law' (Lc 16. 17). The implicit equation of the monastic Rule with the Mosaic law is, as will be seen, of crucial importance to the interpretation of letter 28.

of the brothers.'[78] The latter is prefaced by the following challenge: 'But say, you who bring this objection, whether you speak in play or seriously',[79] and followed by the gibe, 'Does this not seem ridiculous? Would not the insensate themselves abominate such things?'[80] This type of satirical defence can be paralleled from the *Apologia*. In the first section relating to the charge of detraction, Bernard asks: 'Could there not be found for us a path to hell in some way more tolerable, so to speak? If it was so necessary that we descend there, why at least did we not choose that one by which many approach, namely the wide way which leads to death, so that we might cross to grief from joy, and not from grief?'[81]

It is in the peroration of letter 28 that the full force of *caritas* is revealed, in its role as guiding principle, justifying all changes to the *Rule* of St Benedict, and saving the perpetrator from the charge of deviation. The concept is developed through a series of rhetorical figures. Rhetorical questions involving *epanaphora* and *antithesis*, *quid ... /nisi ... caritas?*, 'what ... /except ... charity?', drive home the argument that *caritas* alone possesses the power to waive the authority of tradition within the Church in the interests of salvation.[82] *Polyptoton*

---

[78] *Damnabitur, nisi pedes et manus hospitibus omnibus laverit? Oportebit igitur aut conventum in domo hospitum assidue morari aut hospites in claustro et fratrum officinis hospitari* (letter 28, p. 72).

[79] *Sed dicite qui haec opponitis, utrum ludo an serio hoc dicatis* (ibid., p. 71).

[80] *Nonne haec ridicula videntur? Nonne talia ipsi insensati detestarentur?* (ibid., p. 72).

[81] *Siccine ergo non inveniebatur nobis via, ut ita dicam, utcumque tolerabilior ad infernum? Si ita necesse erat, ut illo descenderemus, cur saltem illam, qua multi incedunt, viam scilicet latam, quae ducit ad mortem, non elegimus, quatenus vel de gaudio, et non de luctu, ad luctum transiremus? (Apo* I. 2 = Mt 7. 13). The statement can be seen to invert the Biblical promise that 'sadness' will be turned into 'joy' (Io 16. 20). On satire in the *Apologia* in general see Leclercq, 'Introduction', CFS 1, pp. 15–23; idem, 'Aspects littéraires de l'œuvre de saint Bernard', *Cahiers de Civilisation Médiévale* 1 (1958), 425–50, pp. 444–50.

[82] *Quid enim coegit regulam de non transferendis episcopis a praecedentibus patribus datam immutari, nisi melius providens ecclesiis caritas? Quid hereticos et criminosos post condignam de criminibus paenitentiam quod primi patres prohibuerant, ecclesiis dei praefecit, nisi multorum saluti consulens caritas? Quid presbiterorum filios episcopari, contra sanctorum apostolicorum antiqua decreta aliquando iussit, nisi earumdem personarum utilitatem ecclesiae utilem esse iudicans caritas? Quid Anglis coniugia indulsit a quibus ceteros inhibuit, nisi novellae eorum fidei timens caritas? Quid multa in hunc modum vetusta praecepta mutavit, quid nova instituit, quid nunc ista nunc illa mandavit, nisi pro moribus, temporibus, locis, nunc generaliter, nunc specialiter, semper tamen humanae saluti sollicite inserviens caritas?,* 'For what compelled the rule given by the earlier fathers concerning the non-translation of bishops to be changed, except charity making better provision for the churches? What placed heretical and guilty men after fitting penitence for their offences in charge of the churches of God, which the first fathers had prohibited, except charity taking thought for the salvation of many? What sometimes ordered the sons of priests to be bishops, against the ancient decrees of the holy apostolic fathers, except charity judging the utility of the same persons to be useful for the Church? What indulged the English with marriages from which it prohibited the rest, except charity fearing for their newly hatched faith? What changed many ancient precepts after this wise, what instituted new ones, what enjoined now these, now those, except charity in accordance with customs, times, places, now generally, now specifically, but always solicitously serving human salvation?' (letter 28, pp. 89–90).

(*caritatis/caritati/caritate/caritatem/caritas*) reinforces the claim that the *Rule* is similarly subject to its dominion.[83] As well as providing a justification for Cluniac practice, *caritas* is turned back against the Cistercians, who are three times accused of failure. They refuse to make good the need of (their) brothers;[84] they are likened to disobedient servants, disobeying the orders of their mistress;[85] their own charge of *praevaricatio* is levelled against them for forcing *caritas* to serve their will, and for neglecting to provide for the care of souls.[86] The peroration ends with the concept of the *regula caritatis*, the rule of charity, which recaps and inverts the notion of *caritas* as the basis of the *Rule*.[87]

---

[83]   *Cum igitur sub iure caritatis omnia canonica mandata immo secundum domini sententiam* universa lex *contineatur* et prophetae, *quis vestrum dicere audebit beati Benedicti regulam caritatis dominio non subiacere? Quomodo enim caritati regula subdita non est, a qua per sanctum illum condita est? Si enim sine caritate condita est, sine deo condita est. Deum vero esse caritatem, Iohannes apostolus dicit:* Deus caritas est ... *Quod ... sequitur ut caritati velut doctrici regula cedat, ac se pro dominantis arbitrio regi permittat*, 'Since therefore all the canonical mandates or rather, according to the judgement of the Lord, *all the Law and the prophets* are contained under the law of charity (= Mt 22. 40), which of you will dare say that the Rule of the blessed Benedict is not subject to the lordship of charity? For how is the Rule not subject to charity, by which it was founded through that holy man? For if it was founded without charity, it was founded without God. That God is charity is stated by the apostle John: *God is charity* ... (= I Io 4. 8). Therefore ... it follows that the Rule should give way to charity as to a teacher, and suffer itself to be ruled in accordance with the judgement of its rule' (letter 28, p. 90).

[84]   *Et quia [caritas] omnia suffert, et omnia sustinet videant utrum eam habeant, qui non solum malorum malitiam ferre nequeunt, sed nec fratrum indigentiam sustinere, vel necessaria ministrando eam supplere cum possint nolunt*, 'And because [charity] *suffers everything, and supports everything* (= I Cor 13. 7), let them see whether they have it, who not only cannot suffer the malice of the evil but cannot support the indigence of the brothers: they refuse to supply it when they could, by administering even the necessities' (letter 28, p. 92).

[85]   *Et sicut contumax et damnandus servus iudicaretur, si dominae aquam afferri praecipienti responderet,* quia heri praecipisti ut ligna de silva succidens domum deferrem, iam ulterius nec aquam deferam, nec aliquid alterius ultra operis agam ... *sic iudicandus est qui magistrae caritati omnia licet diversa et diverso tempore per diversos ad ecclesiae tamen utilitatem cuncta praecipienti oboedire refugit*, 'And just as a servant would be judged contumacious and worthy of condemnation, if he replied to his mistress ordering water to be brought, "Because you ordered me yesterday to chop wood and bring it home from the forest, I will not further bring water, nor do any other work besides ...", so is to be judged he who declines to obey the mistress charity, who orders everything for the utility of the Church, albeit different and at different times through different people' (ibid., pp. 96–7).

[86]   *Praevaricari quippe vos regulam dicimus, quando eius rectitudine non servata, hoc est caritate quae* plenitudo legis *ab apostolo dicitur neglecta, vestrae potius voluntati eam in plerisque inservire cogitis ... Sic certe discretiva caritate relicta, in murmurantibus, fugientibus et languentibus, animarum saluti providere negligitis*, 'We say that you deviate from the Rule, when failing to keep its rectitude, that is, neglecting charity which is said by the Apostle to be the *plenitude of the Law* (= Rm 13. 10), you force it rather to serve your will in many respects ... Thus abandoning the discretion of charity, in respect of those who are grumbling, fleeing and weary, you neglect to provide for the salvations of souls' (letter 28, pp. 99–100).

[87]   *Et haec certissima caritatis regula est, ut quod fratri video esse necessarium non prohibeam ...*, 'This is the most certain rule of charity, that I should not prohibit what I see

The equation of charity with discretion,[88] the right or rather the duty to moderate the requirements of the *Rule* to ensure salvation, is encapsulated in the Augustinian precept,[89] cited twice by Peter in this letter, *Habe caritatem, et fac quicquid vis*, 'Have charity, and do what you will.'[90] As employed by Peter, this precept stands in direct contrast with the attack in Bernard's *Apologia* cited earlier, 'That charity destroys charity, this discretion confounds discretion.'[91] As seen earlier, Bernard equates positive *caritas* with constructive criticism, negative *caritas* with indulgence, which leads to perdition. In this section of letter 28, the Cistercians are made to accuse the Cluniacs of wishing to place their conception of charity above that of St Benedict, founder of the *Rule*.[92] This is countered by an accusation that the Cistercians adapt the meaning of the *Rule* to their own understanding.[93] At the heart of the debate between Peter and Bernard, as Goodrich shows, is a conflict over the interpretation of monastic charity. Goodrich concludes that Bernard's attack in the *Apologia* 'almost seems to be an answer to Peter's main point'.[94] In fact, the centrality of *caritas* to Peter's whole defence seems to make it more probable that he is here adapting Bernard's complaint and placing it in the mouth of the Cistercians.

The peroration of letter 28 also introduces a new technique of argumentation, the use of interlinking logical dilemmas designed to entrap the opponent.[95] The claim

---

to be necessary for my brother ...' (ibid., p. 101); cf. *Super haec omnia matris caritatis regulam in his et in reliquis nos sequi profitemur* ..., 'In these matters and in the rest we profess that we follow the rule of charity, mother over all these ...' (ibid., p. 59).

[88] *Sed et illud quod de tunica et cuculla subsequitur, quam discrete, quam provide, quam caritative dixerit, quantumque a vestrae indiscretionis inhumanitate discordaverit, si nondum perpendistis, tandem animadvertite*, 'But if you have not yet pondered with what discretion, how prudently, how charitably he (Benedict) said what follows about the tunic and the cowl, and how much it was at variance with the inhumanity of your lack of discretion, take heed of it now' (ibid., p. 63); *o homines ... discretionis matris virtutum semitam non sequentes, et ideo a rectitudine deviantes* ..., 'o men ... not following the path of *discretion, mother of the virtues*, and therefore deviating from the right ... ' (ibid., pp. 71–2 = *Benedicti Regula*, LXIV, 19).

[89] *dilige, et quod vis fac*, 'love, and do what you will' (Augustine, *In Ioannis epistolam ad Parthos*, VII, 8, *Commentaire de la première épître de S. Jean*, ed. P. Agaësse, Sources chrétiennes, 75, Paris, 1961, p. 238); *dilige et quicquid vis fac*, 'love, and do whatever you will' (Augustine, *Sermo Frangipane* V. 3, *Sancti Augustini sermones post Maurinos reperti*, ed. G. Morin, *Miscellanea Agostiniana*, 1, Rome, 1930, p. 214). See G. Constable, *Love and do what you will. The Medieval History of an Augustinian precept*, Morton W. Bloomfield Lectures IV, Medieval Institute Publications, Kalamazoo, Mich., 1999.

[90] Letter 28, p. 60; p. 98.

[91] *Apo*, VIII. 16.

[92] *Sed forte vos ad ista*: ... *An fortasse vestram caritatem eius caritati praeponendam esse iudicatis?*, 'But perhaps you will say to that: "... Or perhaps you judge that your charity is to be placed above his charity?" ' (letter 28, p. 93).

[93] *Ergo desinite talia loqui, et non scripturas vestro sensui, sed sensum vestrum scripturis applicate*, 'Therefore cease to say such things, and do not subject the holy writings to your understanding, but your understanding to the holy writings' (ibid., p. 69). That the 'writings' in question are primarily to be identified with the *Rule* is suggested by the fact that this injunction immediately follows a quibble over the wording concerning the readmittance of fugitives.

[94] Goodrich, 'The limits of friendship', p. 89.

[95] The same technique appears in the anonymous *Riposte* to the *Apologia*, attributed by

that since the *Rule* was founded in charity it must be subject to charity is followed by an anticipated objection to the effect that the Cluniacs are bound to their vow of obedience, presented as an attempt on the part of the Cistercians to evade the issue and to force closure.[96] This objection is brushed aside through an equation between *caritas* and *rectitudo*, 'rectitude', 'orthodoxy': 'If we have excluded charity, what we have vowed cannot be called the Rule. For if rectitude is lacking to the Rule, the Rule will not be able to stand fast. The rectitude of the Rule is charity. If, therefore, charity is excluded, rectitude is excluded.'[97] This, in turn, leads into an opposition between *rectitudo* and *tortitudo*, 'injustice', 'prevarication': 'If rectitude is excluded, it remains for prevarication to follow. If prevarication follows, the Rule is necessarily destroyed. Indeed, rectitude and prevarication cannot co-exist.'[98] This sequence (*caritas/rectitudo/tortitudo*) is used to produce a dilemma aimed at the Cistercians: 'You will be obliged either to follow the Rule with rectitude, or prevarication without rectitude, that is, it will be necessary either to maintain the Rule with charity, or an insubstantial nothing without charity. But just as it is impossible for an insubstantial nothing to be held, so it is clear that without charity the Rule can be kept by no one.'[99]

Subsequently, a second anticipated objection, to the effect that if the Cluniacs accept that the *Rule* of St Benedict was founded with *caritas*, they should also accept that it should not be changed,[100] is employed to pave the way for further

---

Wilmart to Hugh of Reading, and tentatively dated to 1127–28 ('Une riposte de l'ancien monachisme au manifeste de Saint Bernard', A. Wilmart (ed.), *Revue Bénédictine* 46 (1934), 269–344; see also C. H. Talbot, 'The Date and Author of the *Riposte*', in *Petrus Venerabilis, 1156–1956: studies and texts commemorating the eighth centenary of his death*, ed. G. Constable and J. Kritzeck, Studia Anselmiana 40, Rome, 1956, 72–80). There it is dubbed *cornutus syllogismus*, a 'horned syllogism', 'forked dilemma', and is aimed at Bernard: *Cornutum syllogismum tibi praetexam ... Aut tu idem es quem superius delusisti, aut non es idem. Si tu es idem, ergo falsum est quicquid de alio dixisti. Si tu non es idem, ergo frivolum est quod hic eundem te esse scripsisti*, 'I will weave a forked dilemma for you ... Either you are the same one whom you mocked above, or you are not the same. If you are the same, whatever you said of another is false. If you are not the same, it is frivolous for you to have written here that you are the same' (*Riposte*, 19, 756–60, p. 329 in Wilmart). This ridicules Bernard's satirical self-identification with a monk suffering from indigestion as a result of over-eating (*Apo*, IX. 22).

[96]   *Sed forte ad priora recurritis, et dicitis:* Quoniam beati Benedicti regulam vos servare vovistis, oportet ut vota reddatis, 'But perhaps you have recourse to the former argument and say: "Since you have vowed to keep the Rule of the blessed Benedict, it is necessary for you to keep your vows" ' (letter 28, p. 90).

[97]   *Si caritatem exclusimus, regula dici non potest quod vovimus. Si enim rectitudo regulae desit, regula iam constare non poterit. Rectitudo autem regulae, caritas est. Si ergo caritas excluditur, rectitudo excluditur* (ibid.).

[98]   *Si rectitudo excluditur, restat ut tortitudo sequatur. Si tortitudo sequitur, necesse est ut regula destruatur. Simul quippe rectum et distortum consistere nequeunt* (ibid.).

[99]   *Aut enim regulam cum rectitudine, aut sine rectitudine tortudinem vos sequi oportebit, id est cum caritate regulam, aut sine caritate nebulam retinere necesse erit. Sed sicut nebulam impossibile est teneri, sic sine caritate patet regulam a nemine posse servari* (ibid.).

[100] *Sed forte vos ad ista:* Sic regulam caritate vos mutasse dicitis, ac si sine illa a sancto illo conditam affirmare velitis ... Si vero hoc sentire ac dicere refugitis, cur quod caritate a tanto

development of this technique. The question is posed by Peter as to whether certain 'holy men' were justified in changing the statutes of their predecessors:[101] the Cistercians are apparently offered three options. The first, to deny that it was permissible, is shown as being productive only of sarcasm: 'If this is conceded, what was thought just is found to be unjust, those who had hitherto been holy will cease to be holy, the Church having followed an error for so long will be judged to have erred, and now, at last, with you preaching, brought back to the path of justice will begin to follow the true way.'[102] The second option, to remain silent, will provoke charges of Pharisaical behaviour.[103] The third way, to agree, would play into the hands of Peter. Consequently, the anticipated response is cast in the form of a *caveat*, that the permissibility of change depends upon the sanctity and authority of those instituting the changes.[104] This, however, is only productive of another impasse. These changes must either have been for the better or for the worse.[105] Accordingly, 'either those who came earlier set up the best, and that best should not have been changed by those who came later, or, if those who changed them acted justly in changing, it is clear that that was not the best'.[106] The dilemma

---

viro institutum fuerat mutare contenditis?, 'But perhaps you will reply to this: "You claim that you have changed the Rule from charity, as if you would wish to affirm that it was founded by that holy man without it ... But if you shrink from feeling and saying this, why do you strive to change what was founded in charity by so great a man?" ' (ibid., p. 93).

[101] *Sed ut quod dicimus manifestius fiat, interrogamus. Sanctis illis quos praedecessorum patrum statuta mutasse supra diximus, licuit ea mutare an non?*, 'But so that what we say may become more clear, we ask: Was it lawful for those holy men, who we said above changed the statutes of the fathers who came before them, to change them or not?' (ibid.).

[102] *Hoc concesso, quod iustum putabatur, iniustum deprehenditur, qui sancti hactenus fuerant, sancti esse cessabunt, ecclesia tanto tempore errorem secuta errasse iudicabitur, et nunc tandem vobis praedicantibus ad semitam iustitiae reducta, vera sequi incipiet* (ibid., p. 94).

[103] *Sed si tacueritis, pharisaeorum vos usos consilio monstrabitis, qui nec fateri veritatem volentes nec eam impugnare valentes, interrogati a domino de Iohannis baptismate utrum* de caelo *esset* an ex hominibus, *silentium elegerunt*, 'But if you keep silent, you will show that you have followed the counsel of the Pharisees, who, neither willing to admit the truth nor able to attack it, questioned by the Lord about the baptism of John, whether it was *from heaven or from men*, chose silence'(ibid. = Mt 21. 25, Mc 11. 30, Lc 20. 4).

[104] *Respondebitis Romanos pontifices tam pro insigni et nota sanctitate qua praediti erant quam pro totius ecclesiae regimine sibi commisso hoc agere potuisse ... nostris autem quia similis sanctitatis et auctoritatis non sunt, similia non licuisse*, 'You will reply that the Roman pontiffs were able to do this by virtue both of the distinguished and noted sanctity with which they were endowed and of the rule over the whole Church which was entrusted to them.. but the same was not permissible to ours, because they are not of similar sanctity and authority ...' (letter 28, p. 94).

[105] *Quod autem de praecedentium decretis subsequentium mutavit auctoritas, aut melius prioribus aut deterius fecit*, 'What, of the decrees of those who came before them, the authority of those succeeding changed, it did either better or worse than those who came before' (ibid., p. 95).

[106] *Aut enim priores optima instituerunt et mutari optima a subsequentibus non debuerunt, aut si mutantes mutando iuste egerunt, patet quia illa optima non fuerunt* (ibid.).

may be aimed at the very origins of Cîteaux, as a break-away formation from the Benedictine abbey of Molesme.[107]

At this point, the notion of dilemma is formalised and *caritas* is given another function: 'This [*caritas*] is the means by which, if you wish to solve this knot, you will be able to, most swiftly, easily and rightly.'[108] The vocabulary of logical argument, reflected in the use of *nodus*, 'knotty problem', and *solvere*, to 'solve a riddle', 'remove a difficulty', is subsequently reinforced by the use of *quaestio*, 'point at issue', 'matter of debate'.[109] In the course of the letter, the Cistercian opponents have been directly branded as Pharisees;[110] they have also been apostrophised as *syllabarum discussores*, 'examiners of syllables', 'cavillers'.[111] The accusation of pharisaical behaviour has also been brought indirectly, through Biblical echoes: they are accused of 'straining out a gnat and swallowing a camel' and of 'paying tithes of mint, anise and cumin', while ignoring the 'weightier matters of the Law'.[112] *Caritas* is accordingly presented as the means of resolving the (false) dilemmas created by the (mis)application of the human intellect, and the Cistercians, taking their stand on the letter rather than the meaning of the 'Law', as defeated by their own choice of weapons.

In the *Apologia*, the Cistercian detractors are similarly labelled as Pharisees. In the first section, Bernard asks what value there is in austerity and self-privation, 'if ... with pharisaical ostentation we despise ... other men ... ';[113] the image is also evoked through self-apostrophe, 'a wretched little man am I, who expend so much

---

[107] The foundation of Cîteaux would appear to have undergone different presentations in successive periods, oscillating between a change from 'bad' to 'good', and one from 'good' to 'better' (H. E. J. Cowdrey, ' "Quidam frater Stephanus nomine, Anglicus natione." The English background of Stephen Harding', *Revue Bénédictine* 101 (3–4) (1991), 322–40; Auberger, *L'unanimité cistercienne*, pp. 42–60). I am endebted to Dr B. Bolton for drawing this article to my attention.

[108] *Hac* [*caritate*] *si hunc nodum solvere volueritis, citissime, facillime, rectissime poteritis* (letter 28, p. 96).

[109] *Sed redeamus ad quaestionis vestrae solutionem. Quam ut lucidius solvere possimus, ipsam rursus quaestionem solutioni sed brevioribus verbis praeponamus ...*, 'But let us return to the solution of your problem. So that we may be able to resolve it more plainly, let us set the problem out again for solution, but in briefer words ...' (ibid., p. 97).

[110] *O pharisaeorum novum genus rursus mundo redditum, qui se a ceteris dividentes, omnibus praeferentes, dicunt quod propheta dicturos eos praedixit,* Noli me tangere (= Io 20. 17), *quoniam mundus ego sum,* 'O new race of Pharisees, given again to the world, who, dividing themselves off from the rest, preferring themselves to all, say what the prophet said that they would say, *Do not touch me,* for I am pure' (ibid., p. 57).

[111] Ibid., p. 67.

[112] *Vere liquantes* culicem *et* camelum glutientes, decimantes mentam et anetum et ciminum, et reliquentes quae sunt graviora legis, iudicium et *iustitiam et veritatem* (ibid., p. 66 = Mt 23. 23–4). Cf. *Et quid est quod dominus ait,* super cathedram Moysi sederunt scribae et pharisei, omnia quaecumque dixerint vobis servate et facite, secundum opera vero eorum nolite facere?, 'And what is it that the Lord says, *the scribes and Pharisees have taken their seat over the seat of Moses: whatever they say to you keep and do, but do not do according to their deeds?*' (ibid., p. 95 = Mt 23. 2–3).

[113] *Si ... pharisaica iactantia ceteros homines ... despicimus, quid nobis prodest tanta in nostro victu parcitas et asperitas ...?* (*Apo* I. 1).

labour and zeal not to be or rather not to seem *like other men* ...'.[114] The allusion is drawn from the parable of the Pharisee and the tax-gatherer, which is explicitly introduced into the second section: 'I say to you therefore, brothers, who even after hearing that parable of the Lord about the Pharisee and the tax-gatherer, presuming on your righteousness, scorn the rest: You say, as it is said, that you alone among men are righteous or holier than the rest, you alone among monks live according to the Rule, while the rest are rather transgressors of the Rule.'[115] Coincidence of language cannot be held to prove priority. It could be argued that Peter's charge of pharisaical behaviour has triggered a similar accusation by Bernard. Equally, however, Bernard's claim here that the Cistercians regard 'the rest' as transgressing the *Rule* might be seen as offering the starting-point for the charge of deviation which is addressed in letter 28.[116] In fact, as will be seen, Peter's development of the concept of pharisaism has implications which reach beyond its use in the *Apologia*, making it likely that Peter is again building on an opening offered by his opponent.

The main argument against postulating a connection between letter 28 and the *Apologia* would seem to be that 28 treats only of standard Cluniac practices, while the *Apologia* focuses on accusations of excessive gluttony and luxury.[117] This is perhaps something of an oversimplification. The *Apologia* does contain hints of more general criticism. For example, as shown earlier, the central section presents the detractors as accusing the Cluniacs of deviations relating to clothing, food and manual work, which recall certain specific accusations found in letter 28.[118] Even in the self-justificatory first section, it is arguable that Bernard hints at the inferiority of the Cluniac way of life to that of the Cistercians. Here, Bernard appears to accept the principle encapsulated in the phrase 'diversity within unity' as discussed by Haseldine and others,[119] that is, the recognition of variety of practice within the unifying structure of the Roman Church, symbolised in the *Apologia* by the

---

[114] *Miser ego homuncio, qui tanto labore et industria studeo non esse vel potius non videre sicut ceteri hominum* ... (ibid., I. 2 = Lc 18. 11).

[115] *Vobis ergo inquam, fratres, qui etiam post auditam illam Domini de Pharisaeo et Publicano parabolam, de vestra iustitia praesumentes, ceteros aspernamini: Dicitis, ut dicitur, solos vos hominum esse iustos aut omnibus sanctiores, solos vos monachorum regulariter vivere, ceteros vero Regulae potius exsistere transgressores* (ibid., V. 10, drawing on Lc 18. 9–14).

[116] In this section of the *Apologia*, the charge of transgression is turned back against the detractors: *Tu ergo cum de horum [corporalium] observatione elatus, aliis eadem non observantibus derogas, nonne te magis transgressorem Regulae indicas, cuius licet minima quaedam tenens, meliora devitas* ..., 'When you, therefore, puffed up with the observation of these [matters of the flesh], disparage others for not observing the same, do you not show yourself rather a trangressor of the Rule, of which, observing certain smallest points, you shun the better ...?' (ibid., VII. 13). Peter likewise turns the charge of deviation back onto the 'detractors'.

[117] Clémencet, *Histoire littéraire*, p. 441; Vacandard, *La vie de saint Bernard*, I, p. 101, n. 2. See Constable, *Letters*, II, p. 271.

[118] *Apo* V. 11.

[119] Haseldine, 'Friendship and rivalry', pp. 390–92. See also, as cited there, P. Meyvaert, 'Diversity within unity: a Gregorian theme', *Heythrop Journal* 4 (1963), 141–62; H. Silvestre, 'Diversi sed non adversi', *Recherches de théologie ancienne et médiévale* 31 (1964), 124–32.

evocation of the 'many-coloured' but 'seamless' tunic of Christ.[120] Goodrich interprets this as conferring 'legitimacy' upon the Cluniac way of life.[121] In fact, what follows may put even this in doubt. Subsequently, Bernard 'justifies' his choice of the Cistercian order over the Cluniac with a citation from I Corinthians: 'All things are allowed, but not all are expedient.'[122] In its original context, the citation continues, 'all things are allowed but not all are edifying':[123] it follows a condemnation of the idolatry of the Gentiles.[124]

In similar vein, Bernard quotes from Psalms to demonstrate that there is a plurality of 'paths of righteousness'.[125] As Goodrich shows, however, 'plurality' does not necessarily connote 'equality'.[126] At the same time, Bernard invokes the New Testament to prove that there is inequality of merit and inequality of reward: 'For although the righteous will shine like the sun in the kingdom of their Father, some will shine more than others, in accordance with the diversity of merits.'[127] Again, in the conclusion condemning monastic transfer, Bernard draws a distinction between 'lesser' and 'greater' blessings: 'For just as these, who have perhaps vowed something greater, are not allowed to come down to what is less, lest they be found apostate, so it is not expedient for all to cross from lesser blessings to greater, lest they be cast down.'[128] This distinction can be related on the one hand to the earlier evocation of 'divisions of graces' to justify the principle of 'diversity

---

[120] *Relinquat [Iesu] videlicet sponsae suae Ecclesia* pignus hereditatis, *ipsam tunicam suam:* tunicam *scilicet* polymitam, *eandemque* inconsutilem, *et* desuper contextam per totum; *sed polymitam ob multorum Ordinum, qui in ea sunt, multimodam distinctionem, inconsutilem vero propter indissolubilis caritatis individuam unitatem* ..., 'Let Him [Jesus] bequeath to his spouse the Church *the pledge of inheritance* (= Eph 1. 14), his very tunic: namely, *the many-coloured tunic* (Gn 37. 23), the same *seamless* and *joined together from above* (Io 19. 23); but many-coloured on account of the manifold distinction of the many Orders which are in it, seamless on account of the indivisible unity of indissoluble charity' (*Apo* III. 6).

[121] Goodrich, 'The limits of friendship', p. 94.

[122] *Quod si quaeris, cur et a pricipio non elegerim, si [Cluniacensem Ordinem] talem sciebam, respondeo: propter id quod rursus ait Apostolus:* Omnia licent, sed non omnia expediunt, 'Therefore if you ask why, if I knew it [the Cluniac order] such, I did not choose it in the beginning, I answer: on account of what the apostle says again: All things are allowed but not all things are expedient' (*Apo* IV. 7 = I Cor 10. 22).

[123] *Omnia licent sed non omnia aedificant* (I Cor 10. 22).

[124] Ibid., 10. 19–21.

[125] *Ponens quippe* semitas *pluraliter, et* iustitia *singulariter, nec diversitatem praetermisit operationum, nec unitatem operantium*, 'Setting down *paths* in the plural, and *righteousness* in the singular, it overlooked neither the diversity of labours nor the unity of those labouring' (*Apo* IV. 8 = Ps 22. 3).

[126] Goodrich, 'The limits of friendship', p. 94.

[127] *Nam etsi fulgebunt iusti sicut sol in regno Patris eorum, alii tamen aliis amplius, pro diversitate meritorum* (*Apo* IV. 9). This conflates Mt 13. 43, *Tunc iusti fulgebunt sicut sol in regno Patris eorum*, 'Then the just will shine as the sun in the kingdom of their Father', with the sentiments of I Cor 15. 41, cited by Bernard immediately previously, *Stella enim ab stella differt in claritate*, 'For star differs from star in brightness.' See Goodrich, 'The limits of friendship', p. 94.

[128] *Sicut enim non licet his, qui maius aliquid forte voverunt, ad id quod minus est descendere, ne apostatentur, sic non omnibus expedit de bonis minoribus ad maiora transire, ne praecipitentur* (*Apo* XII. 30).

within unity',[129] on the other, to the opposition between *spiritualia*, 'spiritual matters', the 'greater' or 'better' part of the *Rule*, and *corporalia*, 'matters of the flesh', the 'lesser' or 'least' part of it.[130] While this may serve to cast a certain ambiguity over the distinction between 'lesser' and 'greater' as used here, it is difficult not to read it as a tactful watering-down of the position adopted in the letter to Robert, where it is forcibly hinted that the Cluniac way may lead to perdition.[131]

The other seeming barrier to reading letter 28 as an indirect riposte to the *Apologia* is its claim to be answering a schedule of charges drawn up by 'certain Cistercians'. In fact, there is no external evidence to corroborate this claim, as Constable acknowledges, suggesting that Peter may be responding to the report of an oral debate.[132] There is, however, another possibility, which he raises, only to dismiss, that the charges were composed by Peter himself as a 'literary device'.[133] Just as Bernard addresses himself to 'certain of our Order',[134] so Peter declares, *Obiciunt itaque nostris quidam vestrorum* ... , 'Accordingly, certain of yours object to ours ...'.[135] The Cistercian 'charges' are characterised by a gradual escalation of insulting terms: in relation to the limit on the readmittance of runaways, 'you scorn that also, like the rest';[136] to manual work, 'you have so cast off manual work ... that ... the obedience, which according to the Rule you promised to show to God, cannot drag out from the lap hands delicate with leisure ...';[137] to the requirement that those

---

[129] *Audi quomodo polymitam*: Divisiones, *ait*, gratiarum sunt, idem autem Spiritus, 'Hear in what way many-coloured: *There are*, he (the apostle) says, *divisions of graces, but the same Spirit*' (*Apo* III. 6 = I Cor 12. 4).

[130] *De corporalibus itaque observantiis patribus calumniam struitis, et quae maiora sunt Regulae, spiritualia scilicet instituta, relinquitis* ..., 'Therefore, you devise calumnies for the fathers relating to the fleshly observances, et abandon what is the greater part of the Rule, namely, the spiritual ordinances ...' (*Apo* VI. 12); *Tu ergo cum de horum [corporalium] observatione elatus, aliis eadem non observantibus derogas, nonne te magis transgressorem Regulae indicas, cuius licet minima quaedam tenens, meliora devitas* ..., 'When you, therefore, puffed up with the observation of these [matters of the flesh], disparage others for not observing the same, do you not show yourself rather a trangressor of the Rule, of which, observing certain smallest points, you shun the better ...?' (ibid., VII. 13).

[131] *Quam multa facta sunt pro unius animulae perditione!* 'How many things were done for the destruction of one little soul!' (Bernard, ep. 1, 5); *et vereor ne ... lugeam miser, non tam cassi laboris damnum quam damnatae sobolis miserabilem casum*, 'and I fear lest I may grieve in wretchedness not so much for the loss of a fruitless labour as for the wretched fall of a damned offspring' (ibid., 10). While it might be argued that Robert is regarded as being 'damned' for his 'apostasy', the heavy sarcasm which follows suggests that he is equally damned for the decline into a sinful way of life: *Salus ergo magis in cultu vestium et ciborum est opulentia quam in sobrio victu vestituque moderato? ... quid moror et ego quod te non sequor?*, 'Does salvation then lie rather in the cultivation of clothing and the richness of foods? ... why do I delay and not follow you as well?' (ibid., 11).

[132] Constable, *Letters*, II, p. 271.

[133] Ibid.

[134] *Unde nunc mihi conveniendi sunt quidam de Ordine nostro..* (*Apo* V. 10).

[135] Letter 28, p. 53.

[136] *Sed vos, sicut cetera, sic et istud quoque contemnitis..* (ibid., p. 54).

[137] *Opus manuum ... ita abiecistis, ut ... (nec) obaedientia quam iuxta regulam deo vos exhibere promisistis, delicatas otio manus de sinu ... extrahere valeat* (ibid.).

who cannot go to Church genuflect where they are, 'although it is not very heavy, you neglect it, using your own laws, in your customary fashion, and scorning those which are common'.[138] The whole schedule of accusations is subsequently characterised as 'invective'.[139] The verbal 'violence' attributed to his opponents can be seen as justifying the 'violence' of Peter's reply.[140] More significantly, it may represent a transposition of the scathing sarcasm found in the *Apologia*.[141]

The most convincing argument for taking letter 28 as a response to the *Apologia* relates to the part of the letter not yet considered, that is, the 'personal' frame which provides its opening and closure. This framework, as will be seen, simultaneously distances Bernard from, and implicates him in, the accusations. More importantly, it utilises gambits which point to the model of an earlier patristic correspondence, that between Augustine and Jerome. The correspondence between Augustine and Jerome comprises seventeen extant letters, written between AD 394/5 and AD 419.[142] The first part is dominated by a theological dispute arising from Jerome's commentary on the Pauline Epistle to the Galatians,[143] namely the correct manner of interpretation to be applied to the passage where St Peter is rebuked by St Paul.[144] Theological arguments are entwined in both sets of letters with gambits drawn from the tradition of friendship writing and from literary etiquette. The difference between the two men is never actually resolved within the correspondence, but Augustine's sixth letter,[145] whilst completely maintaining its intellectual position, presents itself as a closure to dispute, and the matter is not raised again.[146] This

---

[138]   *more vobis solito legibus propriis utentes et communes contemnentes, cum nec istud valde grave sit, tamen negligitis ...* (ibid., p. 55).

[139]   *Tenemus eam [regulam] plane hac ratione [caritate], etiam in omnibus illis propter quae nos eam praevaricari in tota vestra invectione dixistis. Cuius invectionis capitulis singulis licet superius singillatim responderimus ...*, 'We hold to it [the Rule] plainly by this reason [charity], even in all those matters on account of which you have said in your whole invective that we deviate from it. Although we have responded above one by one to each article of this invective ...' (ibid., p. 91).

[140]   Peter's 'violence', however, as Goodrich points out, is rarely acknowledged (Goodrich, 'The limits of friendship', p. 88 and n. 22).

[141]   For example, on inebriation: *Si autem ad vigilias indigestum surgere cogis, non cantum, sed planctum potius extorquebis. Cum vero ad lectum devenero, requisitus incommodum plango, non crapulae peccatum, sed quod manducare non queo*, 'But if you compel him to go to the night office suffering from indigestion, you will extort not a chant, but rather a lament. When indeed I come to bed, if sought again I lament as misfortune not the sin of inebriation, but what I cannot digest' (*Apo*, IX, 21); in the revised version, on the healthy feigning illness: *Sociis in sanguine et caede versantibus, vos aut cibos diligitis delicatos, aut somnos capitis matutinos?*, 'With your comrades engaged in blood and slaughter, do you choose delicate food, or take morning naps?' (ibid., IX. 22).

[142]   See the summary in White, *The correspondence*, pp. 19–34.

[143]   The relevant letters of Augustine are 28, 40, 67, 71, 73, 82; those of Jerome are 102, 105, 112, 115.

[144]   Gal 2. 11–14.

[145]   Augustine, ep. 82, *CSEL*, 34/2, pp. 351–87.

[146]   *Proinde carissimos nostros, qui nostris laboribus sincerissime favent, hoc potius, quanta possumus instantia, doceamus, quo sciant fieri posse, ut inter carissimos aliquid alterutro sermone contra dicatur nec tamen caritas ipsa minuatur nec veritas odium pariat, quae*

correspondence, as White points out, evoked continuing interest,[147] and Peter the Venerable signals his familiarity with it in a letter to the Carthusians, where he asks them to send him a copy to replace one which has been damaged.[148]

Letter 28 opens with an elaborate compliment based on the *topos* of friendship preceding personal acquaintance:[149] 'It is long, dearest brother, since, drinking in with the inmost sense of my heart the scents of your goodly way of life, fragrant with spritual sweetness, beginning to love you before knowing you, to venerate you before beholding you, I have desired to see you, to embrace you, to speak with you about the increase of the soul.'[150] Augustine's first letter to Jerome opens with an opposition between spiritual knowledge and physical ignorance: 'Never has anyone become known to another in appearance as you have become known to me through the quiet joy and bountiful practice of your studies in the Lord ...'.[151] Peter's first compliment, on Bernard's spiritual grace, is followed by a second, on his learning, secular and divine, which adapts a well-known image deriving from Augustine:[152]

---

debetur amicitiae ..., 'Accordingly, let us rather instruct those dearest to us, who favour us most sincerely in our toils, with all the vehemence we can, to know that it is possible between friends for something to be said against the other's speech without charity itself being diminished or the truth which is owed to friendship begetting hatred ...' (ibid., IV. 32, pp. 382–3); *Tamen placeat nobis invicem non tantum caritas, verum etiam libertas amicitiae, ne apud me taceas vel ego apud te, quod in nostris litteris vicissim nos movet, eo scilicet animo, qui oculis dei in fraterna dilectione non displicet. Quod si inter nos fieri posse sine ipsius dilectionis perniciosa offensione non putas, non fiat*, 'However, let us mutually enjoy not only charity, but also freedom in friendship, so that neither I nor you may keep silent about what moves us in one another's letters, namely in that spirit, which does not displease the eyes of God in brotherly affection. If you do not think that this can happen between us without pernicious offense to affection itself, let it not happen' (ibid., V. 36, p. 387).

[147] White, *The Correspondence*, p. 1.

[148] *Mittite et vos nobis si placet maius volumen epistolarum sancti patris Augustini, quod in ipso paene initio continet epistolas eiusdem ad sanctum Ihronimum et sancti Ieronimi ad ipsum. Nam magnam partem nostrarum in quadam oboedientia casu comedit ursus*, 'Send also, if you please, the greater volume of the letters of the holy father Augustine, which contains almost at its start his letters to the holy Jerome, and those of the holy Jerome to him. For by chance in a certain estate a bear has eaten the great part of ours' (Peter the Venerable, letter 24, p. 47). This is cited in evidence by White (White, *The correspondence*, p. 1).

[149] This *topos* can be traced back to Cicero: *Nihil est enim virtute amabilius, nihil quod magis alliciat ad diligendum, quippe cum propter virtutem et probitatem etiam eos quos numquam vidimus quodam modo diligamus*, 'For there is nothing more lovable than virtue, nothing which can attract more to love, seeing that on account of virtue and probity we love, in one sense, even those whom we have never seen' (Cicero, *Laelius*, VIII. 28).

[150] *Diu est frater carissime ex quo bonae conversationis tuae aromata spirituali suavitate fraglantia intimo cordis odoratu hauriens, teque ante diligere quam nosse, ante venerari quam contemplari incipiens, te videre, te amplecti, tecum de animae profectibus loqui desideravi* (Peter, letter 28, p. 52). At a literal level of interpretation, this seems to imply that the two men have not yet met. McGuire puts their first meeting at Pisa, in 1135 (McGuire, *Friendship and community*, p. 253). As will be seen, this seems to be confirmed by letter 65.

[151] *Numquam aeque quisquam facie cuilibet innotuit quam mihi tuorum in Domino studiorum quieta laetitia et vere exercitatio liberalis* (Augustine, ep. 28, I. 1, *CSEL* 34/1, p. 103).

[152] Augustine likens the retention of the liberal arts and moral precepts deriving from the ancients to the gold and silver vessels taken by the Israelites in their flight from Egypt

Bernard is depicted as being so endowed with 'the spoils of the Egyptians and the wealth of the Hebrews' that, while himself remaining 'rich', he can 'supply the lack of others'.[153] Augustine concludes his first letter to Jerome by anticipating the return of the bearer: he will not be able to 'fill up' what in Augustine will still be 'empty' and 'eager' for Jerome's opinions.[154]

Before raising the issue of Galatians, Augustine turns to the question of Jerome's Hebraic translations, declaring that he himself does not dare to 'pass a certain opinion' on the superiority of the Septuagint, while making it very clear that in his view their authority should not be questioned.[155] In the course of praising Bernard's 'riches', Peter casts him as one who can 'pass a certain opinion' on matters that are 'in doubt'.[156] In dealing with Galatians, Augustine will approach the discussion through the terms of 'knot' and 'enquiry' found in Peter's central section: 'I have also read certain writings ... on the letters of the apostle Paul: while you were trying to unknot that one to the Galatians, there came to hand that passage ...';[157] 'it is one question whether a good man should sometimes lie, and another question, or rather, no question, whether the writer of the holy

---

(Augustine, *De doctrina christiana libri quattuor*, II, XL. 60, ed. G. M. Green, *CSEL*, 80, Vienna, 1963, 144–5).

[153] *Novi enim te eruditione saecularium, et quod est longe utilius scientia divinarum litterarum instructum pariter et ornatum, et relicta Aegypto, Aegyptiorum spoliis et Hebraeorum opibus sic ditatum, ut ... aliorum indigentiam ipse dives permanens supplere ... valeas* (Peter, letter 28, p. 53). The addition of the phrase the 'wealth of the Hebrews' may anticipate the implicit equation of the Benedictine Rule with the Mosaic Law to follow.

[154] *Ego enim me fateor tui capaciorem, sed ipsum video fieri pleniorem ... et posteaquam redierit ... cum eius pectoris abs te cumulati particeps fuero, non est impleturus, quod in me adhuc vacuum erit atque avidum sensorum tuorum*, 'For I admit that I am capable of holding more of you, but I see him becoming more full of you ... and after he returns, although I will become a sharer in his heart filled up by you, he will not be able to fill up in me what will still be empty and eager for your opinions' (Augustine, ep. 28, IV. 6, pp. 112–13).

[155] *Omitto enim LXX, de quorum vel consilii vel spiritus maiore concordia, quam si unus homo esset, non audeo in aliquam partem certam ferre sententiam, nisi quod eis praeminentem auctoritatem in hoc munere sine controversia tribuendam existimo ...*, 'For I omit the Seventy, concerning whose concord of counsel or spirit, whether it was greater than if they had been a single man, I do not dare to pass a certain opinion in either direction, except that I think that pre-eminent authority should be attributed to them in this function without dispute ...' (ibid., II. 2, p. 106).

[156] *Novi ... te ... sic ditatum ut.. de dubiis certam ferre sententiam valeas*, 'I know ... you to be ... so endowed ... that you can pass a certain opinion on matters which are in doubt' (letter 28, p. 53). Again, this may take advantage of an opening provided by Bernard. The first section of the *Apologia* ends with what may be read as a variant of the incapacity *topos*: *Et de operibus quidem saepe incerta, et ob hoc periculosa sententia fertur, cum multoties minus iustitiae habeant, qui magis operantur*, 'An opinion passed concerning works is often uncertain, and on this account dangerous, since they often have less righteousness, who work more' (*Apo* IV. 9). The *Apologia* as a whole, however, concludes with the statement, *Haec est nostra de vestro et nostro Ordine sententia*, 'This is my opinion concerning your and our Order' (ibid., XII. 31).

[157] *Legi etiam quaedam scripta ... in epistulas apostoli Pauli, quarum ad Galatas cum enodare velles, venit in manus locus ille ...* (Augustine, ep. 28, III. 3, p. 107).

scriptures should have lied'.[158] Augustine will stress the fallibility of the human intellect, 'The object must be, therefore, that such a man approaches to knowledge of the holy scriptures as ... would rather pass over what he does not understand, than place his mind above that truth'.[159] Subsequently, the matter will apparently be left to Jerome's discretion: 'But I leave this to your understanding. For if you devote more careful consideration to reading, you will see it perhaps much more easily than I.'[160] In the same way, at the end of letter 28, Peter apparently passes the responsibility to Bernard: 'It will be your task, henceforth, if you have a different understanding, to reveal this also to me ...'.[161]

Both Peter and Augustine appear to leave room for disagreement; in both cases, however, it is qualified. In his second letter to Jerome, written after the first one failed to be delivered,[162] Augustine declares: 'I was prompted by that [letter], while I was composing these words, of something which I should not have overlooked in this [letter], that, if your opinion is otherwise and it is better, you should freely forgive my fear.'[163] The notion of 'better' is then qualified by that of truth: 'For if you understand otherwise and you understand truly, for, unless it is true, it cannot be better ...'.[164] The expression *aliter sentire*, to 'feel', 'understand' otherwise, had occurred with negative connotations earlier in Peter's letter: 'From there it is manifest, that when we grant something to a neighbour, *not* in *feigned charity*, which the apostle condemns, but in the true charity, which he himself frequently praises, we follow the Rule of the blessed Benedict without any error, since to understand it differently is nothing other than to err.'[165] Peter's

---

[158] *Alia ... quaestio est, sitne aliquando mentiri viri boni, et alia quaestio est, utrum scriptorem sanctarum scripturarum mentiri opportuerit; immo vero non alia, sed nulla quaestio est* (ibid., p. 108).

[159] *Agendum est igitur, ut ad cognitionem divinarum scripturarum talis homo accedat, qui.. potius(que) id, quod non intelligit, transeat, quam cor suum praeferat illi veritati* (ibid., III. 4, p. 110). This can be compared with the accusation in Peter's letter 28 that the Cistercians are subjecting the Rule to their understanding, rather than their understanding to the Rule (letter 28, p. 69).

[160] *Sed hoc intelligentiae relinquo tuae. Admota enim lectioni diligentiore consideratione, multo id fortasse facilius videbis quam ego* (Augustine, ep. 28, III. 5, p. 111).

[161] *Erit amodo tuum si aliter senseris, et hoc quoque mihi ... revelare ...* (Peter, letter 28, p. 101).

[162] *Scripseram iam hinc aliquando ad te epistulam, quae non perlata est, quia nec perrexit, cui perferendam tradideram ...* (idem, ep. 40, V. 8, *CSEL*, 34/2, p. 78). Subsequently, Augustine will enlarge upon this statement, and attribute the failure to the promotion, followed shortly by the death, of the bearer (Augustine, ep. 71, I. 2, ibid., pp. 249–50).

[163] *Ex qua illud mihi suggestum est, cum ista dictarem, quod in hac quoque praetermittere non debui, ut si alia est sententia tua eademque est melior, timori meo libenter ignoscas* (Augustine, ep. 40, V. 8, pp. 78–9).

[164] *Si enim aliter sentis verumque tu sentis – nam, nisi verum sit, melius esse non potest ...* (ibid.).

[165] *Unde constat, quod quando* non ficta caritate, *quam apostolus damnat, sed vera quam ipse celebriter collaudat, proximo aliquid impendimus, beati Benedicti regulam absque ullo errore sequimur, quoniam aliter de ea sentire, nihil est aliud quam errare* (Peter, letter 28, pp. 90–91). The expression *non ficta caritate* occurs most notably in II Cor 6. 6, where it is set alongside labours, vigils and fasts, as ways of showing oneself a minister of God.

'invitation' to Bernard is similarly pursued through terms which have been negatively applied elsewhere: 'so that, the matter having been carefully investigated (*discussa*), and defined (*definita*) especially through you ...':[166] the Cistercian critics have been labelled as *syllabarum discussores*, 'cavillers',[167] and the authority of Christ has been invoked for rejecting any 'definitive' limit to the forgiveness of sins.[168]

The correspondences with Augustine reach beyond verbal and thematic similarities. The main issue in the Augustine/Jerome correspondence, the interpretation of *Galatians*, can be related to Peter's treatment of the the Cistercian complaints and to the role of Bernard. The relevant passage in Galatians also centres on a type of 'dispute'. St Paul recounts there how he rebuked St Peter at Antioch for giving in to the pressure of certain Jews. Before they came, Peter was eating with the Gentiles; after their arrival he withdrew, 'fearing those who were of the circumcision': his behaviour is characterised as *simulatio*, 'pretence', 'hypocrisy'.[169] Jerome, following Origen, had propounded the view that the 'rebuke' and, indeed, the whole incident, had been a pretence concocted between the two disciples in order to placate both parties, an explanation apparently designed to rescue Paul from a charge of hypocrisy, in rebuking Peter for something of which he himself was guilty.[170] The letters of Augustine evoke a double issue of

---

[166] *ut re diligenter discussa, et per te maxime definita* ... (Peter, letter 28, p. 101).

[167] Ibid., p. 67.

[168] *Ostendant quomodo intelligunt, quod alibi ipse dominus ait: Si dimiseritis unusquisque fratri suo de cordibus vestris,* dimittet et vobis pater vester caelestis *peccata* vestra, *nec definitum numerum remissionis praefecit, sed indefinite posuit, dans intelligi quod quotiens quis fratri indulserit, totiens ei deus indulgeat,* 'Let them show also how they understand, what the Lord himself says elsewhere: If each one of you forgives his brother from his heart, *your heavenly Father will also forgive your* sins, nor did he place any precise number to forgiveness, but set it indefinitely, giving it to be understood that God forgives someone as many times as he has forgiven a brother' (Peter, letter 28, p. 68–9 = Mt 6. 14; Lc 11. 4). This comes in a section which plays heavily on the notion of 'correct' and 'incorrect' understanding: cf. *Verba quoque regulae quae prave vel parum intelligentes ista dicere praesumpsistis* ..., 'The words also of the Rule, which, understanding them badly or too little, you have assumed to say this ...' (letter 28, p. 69).

[169] *Cum autem venisset Cephas Antiocham in faciem ei restiti quia reprehensibilis erat prius enim quam venirent quidam ab Iacobo cum gentibus edebat cum autem venissent subtrahebat et segregabat se timens eos qui ex circumcisione erant et simulationi eius consenserunt ceteri Iudaei,* 'But when Cephas (Peter) had come to Antioch, I opposed him to his face because he was reprehensible. For before certain came from James he was eating with the Gentiles. But when they had come he withdrew himself and set himself apart, fearing those who were of the circumcision. And the rest of the Jews joined in with his pretence' (Gal 2. 11–13).

[170] *Secundo loco quaeris, cur dixerim in commentariis epistulae ad Galatas Paulum id in Petro non potuisse reprehendere, quod ipse fecerat, nec in alio arguere simulationem, cuius ipse tenebatur reus* ..., 'In the second place, you ask, why I said in the commentaries on the letter to the Galatians that Paul could not have rebuked in Peter what he himself had done, nor censure in another a dissimulation of which he himself was held guilty ...'(Jerome, ep. 112, 4, *CSEL*, 55, p. 370). On the significance of the issue as a whole, see the discussion in White, *Correspondence*, pp. 43–7 and bibliography, ibid., pp. 61–4.

deception: *perniciosa simulatio*, the 'pernicious deception', of St. Peter,[171] and *officiosum mendacium*, the 'dutiful lie', attributed by Jerome to St. Paul.[172]

The points at stake in the Augustine/Jerome correspondence are thus seen to be rebuke (of one authority figure by another authority figure); deception or hypocrisy (of one, or perhaps two, authority figures); strict conformity to the 'Law' (represented by the opposition between 'Jews' and 'Gentiles'); judaising (forcing others to conform to standards of which one does not wholly approve or wholly maintain oneself); interpretation of the Scriptures and the critical attitude to be applied to 'holy writings'. All these issues can be found to have their parallel in Peter the Venerable's letter 28. Augustine is rebuking Jerome for bringing the authority of the Scriptures into disrepute, by putting forward a perverse interpretation.[173] Peter rebukes the Cistercian opponents for their perverse understanding and distortion of the *Rule* of St Benedict. In Galatians, St Peter is rebuked for his 'pernicious deception': that is, living as a Gentile but forcing the Gentiles to 'judaise'.[174] In their schedule of charges, the Cistercians are shown as insisting that the Cluniacs adhere to the strict letter of the *Rule*.[175] Subsequently, they themselves are accused of being 'prevaricators'.[176] Most significantly, Bernard himself as addressee is cast in the role of Jerome and St Peter, thus producing an equation of rebukers (Peter the Venerable/Augustine/St Paul) and of those subject to rebuke (Bernard/Jerome/St Peter).

---

[171] *venit in manus locus ille, quo apostolus Petrus a perniciosa simulatione revocatur*, 'there came to hand that passage, in which the apostle Peter is recalled from pernicious hypocrisy' (Augustine, ep. 28, III. 3, p. 107).

[172] *Si enim ad scripturas sanctas admissa fuerint velut officiosa mendacia, quid in eis remanebit auctoritas?*, 'For if, as it were, dutiful lies are admitted to the holy scriptures, what authority will remain in them?' (idem, ep. 40, III. 3, pp. 71–2).

[173] *Ad hanc considerationem coget te pietas, qua cognoscis fluctuare auctoritatem divinarum scripturarum, ut in eis, quod vult quisque credat, quod non vult, non credat, si semel fuerit persuasum aliqua illos viros, per quos nobis ministrata sunt, in scripturis suis officiose potuisse mentiri*, 'Piety will compel you to this attention, by which you recognise that the authority of the divine scriptures is put in doubt, so that each one may believe in them what he wants, and not believe what he does not want, if he is once persuaded that those men, through whom these things were administered to us, were able to lie dutifully in their writings about some matters' (Augustine, ep. 28, III. 5, p. 111).

[174] *Si tu, cum Iudaeus sis, gentiliter et non iudaice vivis, quomodo gentes cogis iudaizare?*, 'If you, although you are a Jew, live as a Gentile and not as a Jew, how do you force the Gentiles to judaise?' (Gal 2. 14).

[175] *Insuper ad augmentum praevaricationis et divinae irritationis coram deo et sanctis eius voto vos astringitis, quod transgredientes reos vos violati voti absque dubio ostenditis*, 'Moreover, to the increase of deviation and divine provocation, in the presence of God and his saints you bind yourself by a vow, transgressing which you show yourselves without doubt guilty of violation of the vow' (Peter, letter 28, p. 53).

[176] *Inde quoque et regulam cuius defensores magis quam observatores videri vultis valde transgredimini ... Cuius manifestissimi praevaricatores esse convincimini, qui colorem humilitati et abiectioni magis competentem abicitis ...*, 'There also you transgress the Rule, of which you want to be seen as the defenders rather than the observers ... You are convicted of being the clearest prevaricators, who cast away the colour more suited to humility and abjection ...' (ibid., p. 57).

The analogy with the correspondence between Augustine and Jerome would suggest that Bernard has provided the trigger to which Peter is responding. Theoretically, this might be equated with his open 'Letter to Robert'; it seems more likely, however, that the real cause of dispute is the more subtle, and consequently more damaging, *Apologia*.[177] Arguably, the stance adopted there, moving from defence to attack, from condemnation of detraction to renewal of criticism, may have laid Bernard open to the charge of hypocrisy. In a letter to William of St Thierry, to whom the *Apologia* is addressed, Bernard claims that he has been requested by William both to defend himself against charges of detraction and to renew the attack on Cluniac excesses.[178] The close association between Bernard and William[179] may point towards a potential application of the concept of *officiosum mendacium*, namely, that the notion of 'complaint' with which the *Apologia* opens[180] might be read as a contrivance, devised between Bernard and William, to enable the former to engage in fresh criticism. In that case, it may well be that we have a 'fiction' answering a 'fiction': fictional charges supplying the pretext for defence in letter 28, replying to a fictional rebuke towards 'certain Cistercians' in the *Apologia*, anticipating and defusing criticism for the attack to follow.[181]

---

[177] The potency of the *Apologia* is demonstrated by the critical exegesis found in the anonymous *Riposte* cited earlier.

[178] *Quod me huiusmodi operam dare iubes, per quod tollendum sit scandalum de regno Dei, libenter accipio; sed quomodo id velis fieri, necdum satis elucet mihi. Nam ... intellexi quidem te velle ut illis, qui de nobis tamquam detractoribus Cluniacensis Ordinis conqueruntur, satisfaciam ... At si post hanc satisfactionem rursus victus eorum ac vestitus superfluitatem, et cetera quae subiungis, quemadmodum iniungis, carpere voluero ... quomodo sine scandalo facere queam, non video,* 'I willingly accept that you order me to take pains of this kind, through which a cause of offence may be removed from the kingdom of God; but it is not yet sufficiently clear to me how you wish it to be done. For.. I have understood that you want me to give satisfaction to those, who complain of us as detractors of the Cluniac Order ... But if, after this satisfaction, I again wish to criticise the superfluity of their food and clothing, and the rest which you enjoin in the way that you enjoin, I do not see how I may do it without scandal' (Bernard, ep. 84[bis], *SBO*, VII, p. 219). The traditional view that this letter furnished the *Apologia* with its preface has been refuted (see Leclercq, *SBO*, III, pp. 63–5).

[179] See A. H. Bredero, 'William of Saint Thierry at the crossroads of the monastic currents of his time', in *William, abbot of St Thierry, a colloquium at the abbey of St Thierry*, trans. J. Carfantan, Cistercian Studies Series 94, Kalamazoo, 1987, 113–37.

[180] *Quomodo namque silenter audire possum vestram huiscemodi de nobis querimoniam ...*, 'For how can I hear in silence your complaint concerning us, namely ...' (*Apo* I, 1).

[181] Both the *Apologia* and letter 28 may appear susceptible to a more formal four-part division of speech, recalling that advocated by Isidore of Seville (Isidore, *Etymologiae*, II. VII. 1–2, *Isidori Hispaliensis Episcopi, Etymologiarum sive originum libri XX*, ed. W. M. Lindsay, 2 vols, Oxford, 1911, reprinted 1985, I): *exordium*, 'introduction' (Bernard's self-condemnation; Peter's compliments); *narratio*, 'narration' (Bernard's statement of diversity within unity; Peter's list of charges); *argumentatio*, 'proof', subdivided into *confirmatio*, 'confirmation' (Bernard's rebuke; Peter's attack) and *refutatio*, 'refutation' (Bernard's criticisms; Peter's rebuttal); *peroratio*, 'peroration' (Bernard's justification; Peter's justification). On Isidore, see H. Lausberg, *Handbook of literary rhetoric, a foundation for literary study*, trans. M. T. Bliss, A. Janson and D. E. Orton, ed. D. E. Orton and R. D. Anderson, foreword G. A. Kennedy, Leiden; Boston; Cologne, 1998, p. 204.

The intertextual borrowing which has been argued for here has important implications for the presentation both of the 'personal' relationship between Peter and Bernard and of the relationship between their respective orders. By adopting the Augustinian voice, Peter can be seen as attempting to usurp the moral high ground. At the same time, by casting both participants in the roles of saints and patristic authorities, a monastic dispute is raised to the level of ideological debate. More than that, it can be argued that the passage from Galatians which lies behind the epistolary exchange between Augustine and Jerome is crucial in shaping the presentation of the later monastic dispute. The implicit equation of the Benedictine *Rule* with the Mosaic Law[182] entails a concomitant identification of the Cistercian critics with 'judaisers', and of the Cluniacs with 'Gentiles'.[183] Certainly, the influence of the epistolary relationship between Augustine and Jerome will continue to be a dominating factor for the next part of the correspondence between Peter and Bernard, as will be seen in the next chapter. This will begin by considering the implications of the Bernard/Peter interchange, in particular, the interpretation given by Bredero, and continue by looking at the next phase, dating to some ten years later.

---

[182] Lekai draws attention in the context of letter 28 to the statement by Orderic Vitalis that Robert of Molesme withdrew with twelve companions, 'which holy men had decided to keep the Rule of St Benedict to the letter, as the Jews the Law of Moses' (Ordericus Vitalis, *Historia ecclesiastica*, VIII, iii, 442, in *The ecclesiastical history of Orderic Vitalis*, ed. and trans. M. Chibnall, 6 vols, 4, Oxford, 1973, p. 322). He does not, however, extrapolate beyond this to Augustine and Jerome (L. J. Lekai, *The Cistercians, ideals and reality*, Kent, Ohio, 1977, p. 24).

[183] Arguably, the *Apologia* also contributes to this characterisation, through Bernard's allusion to the parable of the Pharisee and the tax-collector (*Apo* V. 10), and by the kind of monastic apartheid advocated in its conclusion (ibid., XII. 30). It seems to be Peter, however, who takes it further, through the application of the Augustine/Jerome model which transforms a charge of 'pharisaeism' into one of 'judaising'.

Chapter 3

The Proof of *Caritas*: Peter, Letter 65;
Bernard, Ep. 147

In the previous chapter it was argued that Peter the Venerable's letter 28 should be read as constituting an indirect response to Bernard's *Apologia*. As stated there, this chapter will begin by considering what significance should be attributed to Bernard's intervention and to Peter's reply, before turning to the next phase of the correspondence, dating from 1137 to 1138. Bredero links both works with a troubled period of Cluny's history. The year 1126 saw the brief return to Cluny of Pons of Melgueil, Peter's predecessor but one. The latter had abdicated his position as abbot, whether voluntarily or under compulsion, in 1122, to go to the Holy Land. On his return, he attempted during Peter's absence to reclaim the abbey. Violence ensued, and Pons finally died in prison.[1] According to Bredero, rather than voicing external criticism in the *Apologia*, Bernard should in fact be seen as promoting internal Cluniac moves towards reform.[2] This proposition is intimately bound up with his thesis that Pons's abdication arose from his attempts to implement these moves, and that Peter the Venerable was appointed as a proponent of traditional Cluniac monasticism.[3] As Pacaut has pointed out, however, this contention is unsupported by external evidence.[4]

Equally controversial is Bredero's interpretation of letter 28. This is presented as an attempt to distract attention from these internal problems, by 'scapegoating' Bernard and creating the impression that criticism was restricted to the outside.[5] In keeping with this claim, letter 28 is argued to have been destined primarily for

---

[1]   The traditional view, that Pons, abbot since 1109, was forced to leave Cluny as a bad and wasteful administrator, has been challenged in a number of recent works. Conflict with Calixtus II over papal changes to episcopal exemptions is posulated by Tellenbach (G. Tellenbach, 'La chute de l'abbé Pons de Cluny et sa signification historique', *Annales du Midi* 76 (3–4) (1964), 355–62) and Cowdrey (H. E. J. Cowdrey, 'Abbot Pontius of Cluny', *Studi Gregoriani* 11 (1978), 177–298). Zerbi, on the other hand, stresses episcopal opposition to Cluny, coming to a head in 1119 (P. Zerbi, 'Intorno allo scisma di Ponzio, abbate di Cluny (1122–1126)', in *Tra Milano e Cluny, momenti di vita e cultura ecclesiastica nel secolo XII*, Italia Sacra 28, Rome, 1978, pp. 309–71.) More recently, Wollasch has propounded the thesis of clashing seigneurial interests (J. Wollasch, 'Das Schisma des Abtes Pontius von Cluny', *Francia* 23/1 (1996), 31–52.)
[2]   A. H. Bredero, 'Saint Bernard in his relations', pp. 317–8; idem, *Bernard of Clairvaux*, pp. 218–27.
[3]   See Bredero, *Cluny et Cîteaux*, pp. 27–93; ibid., pp. 277–326.
[4]   M. Pacaut, *L'ordre de Cluny*, Paris, 1986, p. 201.
[5]   Bredero, 'Saint Bernard in his relations', pp. 319, 344; idem, *Bernard of Clairvaux*, pp. 111, 226.

internal consumption.[6] It is certainly the case that in a subsequent letter addressed to Cluniac priors and sub-priors, Peter will show that he expects them to be familiar with the contents of letter 28, thus indicating that the letter must have circulated internally.[7] In view of its polemical nature, however, this is perhaps hardly surprising. It cannot in itself be held to prove that they were its primary recipients. The writings themselves neither directly confirm nor disprove Bredero's interpretation, although both contain what might be read as hints pointing in that direction. The *Apologia* evokes the notion of internal criticism on two occasions: 'Indeed, to those who love the Order I do not fear that I will be troublesome in this matter: rather, they will doubtless accept it as pleasing, if I pursue what they themselves hate';[8] 'others indeed (do these things), because they cannot stand out against the multitude of those contradicting them, who defend these things with outspoken voice as if on behalf of the order; whenever the former begin to restrain or change some things as reason dictates, the latter soon resist them with all their authority'.[9] It could be argued, however, that this is merely another device, aimed at providing justification for Bernard's intervention.

Letter 28 ends with the expression of desire that *scandalum*, 'scandal', 'strife' be averted.[10] In its Biblical sense of 'stumbling-block', 'inducement to sin',[11] it seems to anticipate the warning which follows, that *caritas* is being damaged, and destroyed *robigine invidiae*, by the 'rust', 'ulceration', of jealousy.[12] This could

---

[6]   Idem, 'Saint Bernard in his relations', p. 319; idem, *Bernard of Clairvaux*, p. 111.

[7]   *Si enim de noviciis suscipiendis, si de opere manuum, si de vestibus et quibusdam similibus, a bonis patribus post sanctum Benedictum, mutatum est, non dubia sed certa et rationabili causa factum est. Et causa vel ratio, quia bis a me in duabus epistolis, olim domino abbati Clarevallensi directis, studiose descripta est, hic iterare superfluum iudico*, 'For if with regard to the receiving of novices, manual work, clothing and other similar matters, changes have been made by the good fathers after the holy Benedict, it was done for no dubious, but a certain and reasonable cause. Since the cause or reason has been carefully set out by me twice in two letters directed previously to the lord abbot of Clairvaux, I judge it superfluous to repeat it here' (Peter, letter 161, *Letters*, I, p. 390). The second letter should probably be identified with letter 111. See Constable, *Letters*, II, p. 206, cited by Bredero, 'Saint Bernard in his relations', p. 319, n. 11.

[8]   *Et quidem diligentibus Ordinem in hac re molestum me fore non timeo: quinimmo gratum procul dubio accepturi sunt, si persequimur quod et ipsi oderunt (Apo VII. 15).*

[9]   *alii vero [haec agunt], quia resistere non valent multitudini contradicentium, qui haec utique tamquam pro ordine libera voce defendunt; et quoties isti aliqua, prout ratio dictat, restringere vel mutare incipiunt, illi mox tota eis auctoritate resistunt* (ibid., VIII. 18).

[10]   *(ut) ... eorum qui super hac re scandalum patiuntur dubietas auferatur* ... , '(that) the doubt of those who suffer scandal over this matter may be taken away' (letter 28, p. 101). This concept had been invoked in the *Apologia* on several occasions: *Melius est ut* scandalum *oriatur*, quam veritas relinquatur, 'It is better that *offence* arise, *than that the truth be abandoned*' (*Apo.*, VII. 15 = Gregory the Great, *In Hiezech.*, I, VII. 5, p. 85); *sermonem brevio, praesertim quia utiliora sunt pauca in pace, quam multa cum scandalo. Et utinam haec pauca scripserim sine scandalo!*, 'I shorten the speech, especially since a little in peace is better than much with offence. And would that I may have written this little without offence!' (ibid., XII. 30).

[11]   Mt 18. 7; Rm 14. 13.

[12]   *ut caritas quae ... cotidie laeditur, longe remota omni invidiae robigine confirmetur*, 'so that charity which ... is wounded daily, may be healed, with all ulceration of jealousy far removed' (letter 28, p. 101).

simply refer to the threat towards mutual charity caused by the arrogance of the Cistercians. Alternatively, it might be regarded as a hint that certain Cluniacs are being incited to disaffection. Equally ambiguous is the portrayal of the 'contumacious and damnable servant', accused of interfering with the willing obedience of his fellows: 'Not content to withdraw themselves alone from the rule of charity, they attempt, with all the importunity they can muster, to ally to their transgression others who are desiring to obey her.'[13] Interpreted in terms of the communal monastic family, it suggests that Cistercians are attempting to subvert Cluniacs. Given a narrower frame of reference, within the family of Cluniacs, it might be held to imply that Cluniacs themselves are interfering with the loyalty of their fellow monks.

Irrespective of the roles of conservative and reformer assigned by Bredero to Peter and Pons respectively, the co-incidence of dating makes it likely that Peter saw the *Apologia* as fanning the flames of Cluniac revolt. Indeed, it is possible that letter 28 contains a veiled allusion to these difficulties. Peter claims that he would have preferred to talk to Bernard face to face,[14] but states that this has been prevented by the twin factors of distance and the 'multitudinous bitterness of business and tribulations assailing us'.[15] This statement is explained plausibly by Constable as constituting a reference to the invasion by Pons.[16] The use of *ingruere*, 'to assail', foreshadowing the language of attack which will follow in the main part of the letter, may have here both literal and metaphorical associations, and may indeed implicate Bernard as bearing some responsibility for what took place. This in itself is sufficient to rescue Peter from the charge of 'scapegoating' Bernard. Even if, as Bredero claims, Bernard could not have foreseen exactly what would happen,[17] he could be held guilty of having intervened in the internal affairs of Cluny.

Even if, as seems probable, Cluniacs were envisaged as a secondary audience for letter 28, the analogy with the correspondence between Augustine and Jerome points to Bernard as the primary target. Bredero seems to imply that it was Peter who paved the way for the future resentment between the two orders, by misrepresenting Bernard's intentions.[18] In fact, it is arguable that, by posing as mouthpieces for their respective orders, and through their complementary fictions, Bernard and Peter between them created a myth of Cistercian–Cluniac relations which, in the following decade, would appear to have become 'fact'. Certainly,

---

[13] *Nec contenti a iure caritatis se solum subducere, alios ei parere cupientes qua valent instantia suae tentant transgressioni sociare* (ibid., p. 97).
[14] *Malui quippe vivo sermone secreta cordis mei tibi aperire, quam haec schedulae calamo percurrente committere*, 'I (would have) preferred to open the secrets of my heart to you in living speech, rather than to entrust these matters to a small leaf of paper with a scurrying pen' (ibid., p. 53). This can be compared with the opposition elsewhere of 'living speech' to the 'dead figures' of a letter (Peter, letter 13 to an unidentified Odo, *Letters*, I, p. 19).
[15] *Sed multa terrarum intercapedo, multa negotiorum et tribulationum nobis ingruentium amaritudo, hoc ne contingeret hucusque prohibuerunt* (letter 28, p. 53).
[16] Indeed, it plays an important part in his argument for the later dating of letter 28 (see Constable, *Letters*, II, p. 273).
[17] Bredero, *Bernard of Clairvaux*, p. 225.
[18] Bredero, *Bernard of Clairvaux*, pp. 226–7.

between them, the *Apologia* and letter 28 can be seen to establish the terms of reference for the debate to follow, just as the letters between Augustine and Jerome can be said to determine its tone. The dominating terms would emerge as arrogance, associated with the Cistercians,[19] and jealousy, with the Cluniacs.[20] Oppositions between rich and poor, old and new, Jew and Gentile would figure prominently in the polemics, with tithes and episcopal election supplying the concrete causes of dispute.[21]

The next documented phase of the Peter/Bernard correspondence takes place some ten years later, towards the end of the papal schism of 1130–38 between Innocent II and the so-called antipope Anacletus, a former monk of Cluny.[22] Both

[19]   Arrogance is frequently associated with detraction and hypocrisy in the *Apologia*: *Vae semel, et vae iterum pauperibus superbis!*, 'Woe once, and woe again, to the arrogant poor!' (*Apo* I. 2); *Et quomodo intra praesaepium Domini simulatrix arrogantia se coartat ...*, 'And how does hypocritical arrogance compress itself into the manger of the Lord.. ' (ibid., I. 3); *quippe qui etsi ordinate viventes, superbe tamen loquentes, cives se faciunt Babylonis ...*, '..who, although living according to the Rule, nevertheless, speaking arrogantly, make themselves citizens of Babylon ...' (ibid., V. 10); *Tunicati et elati abhorremus pellicias, tamquam melior non sit pellibus involuta humilitas, quam tunicata superbia ...*, 'Clad in tunics and puffed-up we abhor furs, as if humility wrapped in furs were not better than pride clad in a tunic ...' (ibid., V. 11); *Repleti deinde ventrem faba, mentem superbia, cibos damnamus saginatos ...*, 'Then our bellies filled with beans, our mind with pride, we condemn fatted food ...' (ibid.). Letter 28 represents arrogance as an enemy to *caritas*: *Quod igitur ecclesia Dei ... ratum habuisse cognoscitur, irritum fieri debere quis iudicare audeat, nisi qui se sanctis patribus meliorem tumente superbiae spiritu iudicat?*, 'What therefore the Church of God ... is known to have ratified, who would dare judge should be rendered void, except one who in the swelling spirit of pride judges himself better than the holy fathers?' (letter 28, p. 81); *superba superstitione salutaribus monitis obtemperare dedignantur*, 'they disdain to obey [her] salutary warnings out of arrogant sanctity' (ibid., p. 97); *Hoc namque apud illos quos superbia dividit, non apud illos quos caritas unit contingere solet*, 'For this (wishing to increase one's own prestige at the expense of someone else's) is accustomed to happen among those whom pride divides, not among those whom charity unites' (ibid., p. 93).
[20]   Bernard suggests that offence will be avoided, *si qui accepit iam esse bonus, non invideat melioribus ...*, 'if he who has already accepted to be good, does not envy those who are better ...' (*Apo.*, XII. 30). Peter asks for Bernard's help in removing *invidiae robigo*, 'the ulceration of jealousy' (letter 28, p. 101).
[21]   Traces of this 'debate' exist outside the writings of Bernard and Peter. In addition to the *Riposte* cited in the previous chapter, there is the anonymous *Incipit tractatus abbatis cuiusdam*, a tract in defence of Cluniac observances dating to the first half or middle of the twelfth century (Dom J. Leclercq (ed.), 'Nouvelle réponse de l'ancien monachisme au manifeste de saint Bernard', *Revue Bénédictine* 67 (1957), 77–94) and the Cistercian *Dialogus duorum monachorum* of Idung of Prüfenig (1155), mocking the Cluniacs (Idung of Prüfenig, *Dialogus duorum monachorum*, R. B. C. Huygens (ed.), *Studi Medievali*, 3rd series, 13.1 (1972), 307–8). More recently, the *Ysengrimus*, a mid-twelfth-century Latin beast epic, has been argued by Billy to incorporate within its satirical form both Cistercian and Cluniac propaganda (D. J. Billy, 'The *Ysengrimus* and the Cistercian–Cluniac controversy', *The American Benedictine Review* 43 (1992), 301–28).
[22]   See P. F. Palumbo, *Lo Scisma del MCXXX: i precedenti, la vicenda romana e le ripercussioni europee della lotta tra Anacleto e Innocenzo II, col regesto degli atti di Anacleto II*, Rome, 1942; F.-J. Schmale, *Studien zum Schisma des Jahres 1130*, Forschungen zur kirchlichen Rechtsgeschichte und zum Kirchenrecht 3, Cologne–Graz, 1961.

Peter and Bernard gave their support to Innocent at an early stage. Peter's subsequent activity is more difficult to chart. Although he claims in a letter to Innocent written in 1133 to have spared no pains in 'speaking, writing, ordering, terrifying, soothing' those joined in friendship to Cluny,[23] only two such letters are preserved in his collection, both to Gilo of Tusculum, an errant Cluniac.[24] He is, however, known to have visited Aquitaine, in an attempt to win over the schismatic duke, William X.[25] Bernard, on the other hand, played an active part outside France through this period, undertaking diplomatic missions to Germany, and taking part in the march on Rome.[26]   This phase of the correspondence is represented by Peter's letter 65[27] and Bernard's ep. 147,[28] both written while Bernard was with Innocent in Italy. These letters have been taken traditionally as marking the flowering of a personal friendship.[29] In contrast to the formality of the *Apologia* and letter 28, both are characterised by a degree of seeming fluidity and flexibility, somewhat greater in the case of Peter. Both are distinguished by elaborate 'compliment', and make play with the language of affection, although, again, this is more marked in the case of Peter.[30] Bredero, on the other hand, drawing presumably on Peter's rejection of oral messages as unreliable, concludes that the interchange may have concealed an 'oral altercation'.[31] As will be seen, a close examination of both letters does indeed suggest the presence of a subtle and potentially ambivalent sub-text.

To the venerable and beloved to me lord Bernard, abbot of Clairvaux, brother Peter, humble abbot of the Cluniacs, wishes strength always in the Lord.

How much reverence, how much love for you my soul maintains in its inner chambers, is known to Him whom I venerate and embrace in you. I did this, even while your absence

---

[23]   *Quoscumque mihi et Cluniacensi ecclesiae qualibet amicitia iunctos, reges et principes, nobiles et ignobiles, magnos et pusillos agnovi, hos maiestatis vestrae pedibus subdere per me ipsum sive per alios, loquendo, scribendo, mandando, terrendo, mulcendo, pro posse non distuli*, 'In accordance with my ability, I have not delayed to subdue to the feet of your majesty whomsoever I knew joined in any friendship to myself and to the church of Cluny, kings and princes, noble and ignoble, great and small, by speaking, writing, ordering, terrifying, soothing' (Peter, letter 39, *Letters*, I, p. 132).

[24]   Peter, letter 40, written probably between 1130 and 1133 (*Letters*, I, pp. 134–36); idem, letter 66, dating to 1138, after the death of Anacletus (*Letters*, I, pp. 195–7). Gilo had close links with Gerald of Angoulême, papal legate and vicar in Aquitaine to Anacletus. See Constable, *Letters*, II, p. 293; G. R. Knight, 'Politics and pastoral care: papal schism in some letters of Peter the Venerable', *Revue Bénédictine* 109 (3–4) (1999), 359–90, pp. 364–71.

[25]   According to van den Eynde, there were two visits within this period, in 1131 and 1133/34 (van den Eynde, 'Principaux voyages', pp. 100–109). Peter's (unsuccessful) meeting with William X is described in a letter to Peter of Poitiers associated with the second of these (Peter, letter 58, *Letters*, II, p. 179).

[26]   See Vacandard, *Vie de Saint Bernard*, I, pp. 329–44; 366–91; II, pp. 1–25.

[27]   Peter, letter 65, *Letters*, I, pp. 194–5.

[28]   Bernard, ep. 147, *SBO*, VII, pp. 350–51.

[29]   Leclercq, *Pierre le Vénérable*, p. 70; Auniord, 'L'ami de saint Bernard', pp. 89–90.

[30]   Indeed, Torrell and Bouthillier conclude that Peter must have been 'disappointed' in Bernard's reply (Torrell and Bouthillier, *Pierre le Vénérable*, pp. 93–4).

[31]   Bredero, 'Saint Bernard in his relations', p. 325.

still grudgingly hid from me your corporeal face, because reputation, swifter than the body, already brought in the way it could to the eyes of my mind the face of your blessed soul. But when I at last attained what had long been denied, and the phantasms of dreams vanished as truth took their place, my soul adhered to you, nor could it be torn thereafter from loving you. To such an extent did your affection claim me wholly for itself, did your virtues and ways ravish me, that they left me nothing of myself which was not yours, that they permitted nothing of you not to be mine. There has remained in me constantly since that time – and would that it may remain so in you – mutual affection undertaken for the sake of Christ, which, because it alone never knows how to how to fail, has excellently maintained its custom in me as much as pertains to you. And since I have laid this up in my bosom, hidden it in my treasure, dearer than all gold, brighter than any gem, I wonder, that over so great a time I have not received such proof as I would wish of this affection guarded by you towards me. Indeed I give thanks, that by salutations sent frequently through various people, you have indicated that you have not completely forgotten a friend. But I complain, that thus far you have not given more certain proof through a letter. I have said more certain, because paper cannot change the speech impressed upon it, while the tongue of speakers too often changes the truth which has been enjoined by addition or subtraction. Therefore because, as a chosen fighter ready for the day of war, on behalf of the perils of the church of God you use right and left, and fight *through the arms of righteousness on the right and on the left*, I entrust without fear my messengers, whom I am directing to the lord Pope, to your tried friendship, since you, who assist the causes of strangers, will not be able to fail the business of your own. So that my complaint may be soothed through them, entrust news of your state and return, and of the state of the lord Pope, not only to my legates but also to a letter from yourself. Would that freed, you from the laborious court, and me from dangerous pastoral cure, as I have always hoped, we might be retained by one place, never to be changed, united by one affection, received by one Christ.

The letter shows a heavy reliance on *topoi* associated with friendship writing and epistolary etiquette: conventional as these are, however, association with what has gone earlier may seem to give them a particular force. The letter moves from the evocation of friendship preceding acquaintance,[32] recalling the opening of letter 28,[33] to that of friendship from first knowledge, expressed in terms of the 'glue of affection'.[34] Peter also incorporates the concept of the friend as *alter ego*, 'second self',[35] and of affection as spiritual 'treasure' to be stored up;[36] the latter may recall

---

[32]   *Feci hoc, etiam dum adhuc absentia tua vultum corporis mihi invidens abscondebat ...* (letter 65, p. 194).

[33]   *Diu est ... ex quo ... te(que) ante diligere quam nosse, ante venerari quam contemplari incipiens ...* (letter 28, p. 52).

[34]   *At ubi quod diu negatum fuerat tandem assecutus.. adhaesit anima mea tibi ...* (letter 65, p. 194.) Cf. *Ex quo ... excellentiam sublimitatis tuae mea humilitas agnoscere meruit, tenacissimo dilectionis glutino ... mea anima tibi adhaesit*, 'Since ... my humility has deserved to know the excellence of your sublimity ... my soul has adhered to you with the most tenacious glue of affection' (letter 38, to Peter of Lyons, *Letters*, I, p. 125). Since letter 65 can be dated to 1137, a literal reading would suggest that the first meeting between Peter and Bernard had taken place fairly recently, probably, as McGuire hypothesises, at the council of Pisa in 1135 (McGuire, *Friendship and community*, p. 253).

[35]   *(ut) nihil mihi de me quod tuum non esset [virtutes tuae et mores] relinquerent, nihil tibi de te non meum esse permitterent* (letter 65, p. 194). On this concept in Bernard, see S. M.

the allusion to Bernard's 'treasures' of learning at the start of letter 28.[37] Of the terms available to express the concept of affection, *amicitia* is invoked twice,[38] *amor* twice,[39] *dilectio* once.[40] The term which dominates the letter, however, is *caritas*. Peter declares that he was claimed *caritate tua*, 'by your affection', 'by affection for you';[41] he expresses a wish that *mutua caritas*, 'mutual affection', may remain in Bernard;[42] he 'wonders' that he has not received proof *custoditae caritatis*, 'of the affection guarded' towards him by Bernard;[43] he wishes that they might be united *una caritate*, 'by one affection'.[44]

At a 'personal' level, these statements, associated with expressions of wishing (*utinam*) and reinforced by subjunctives (*maneat/vellem/uniret*), suggesting hopes at present unfulfilled or uncertain of future fulfilment, may serve to cast doubt on the reality of Bernard's *caritas* towards Peter. At another level, they seem to look back towards the role of *caritas* in the *Apologia* and letter 28, suggesting that here Peter is drawing a parallel between 'personal' friendship and communal harmony. The final sentence of this letter was interpreted by Leclercq as 'le secret bien gardé', Peter's desire to retire to Clairvaux.[45] It should, perhaps, be seen rather as indicating a desire, as yet unfulfilled, that Cluniacs and Cistercians should 'dwell' together in a single understanding of charity.[46] Taken in conjunction with the epistolary 'reproach', the absence of a letter from Bernard, the emphasis on physical separation may also look to a gambit employed by Augustine. In his second letter to Jerome, written in 399, some five years after the failure of ep. 28 to be delivered, and taking up the same arguments, Augustine invites Jerome to

---

Kramer, 'The friend as "second self" and the theme of substitution in the letters of Bernard of Clairvaux', *Cistercian Studies Quarterly* 31:1 (1996), 21–33.

[36] *(Cumque) hanc [mutuam caritatem] omni auro cariorem, omni gemma clariorem in sinu meo reposuerim, in thesauris absconderim* ... (letter 65, p. 194).

[37] *Novi ... te ... sic ditatum* ... (letter 28, p. 53).

[38] *Ago ... gratias, quod ... non penitus te amici oblitum signasti* (letter 65, p. 194); *nuntios meos ... expertae amicitiae tuae secure committo* (ibid., p. 195).

[39] *Quantum ... amoris tibi anima mea ... conservet ...; ... nec ab amore tuo ultra divelli [anima mea] potuit* (ibid., p. 194).

[40] *Venerabili et dilectissimo mihi..* (ibid.).

[41] *(Ita) caritas tua totum me sibi deinceps vindicavit* ... (ibid.).

[42] *(et) utinam sic in te maneat ... mutua caritas* ... (ibid.). The insertion *quae [caritas] ... numquam excidere novit*, 'which ... never knows how to fail', points towards the eulogy of *caritas* in *I Corinthians*, where it is said to 'suffer everything' (I Cor 13. 7–8).

[43] *miror quod ... non qualia vellem indicia huius a te mihi custoditae caritatis acceperim* (letter 65, p. 194).

[44] *Utinam ... una caritas uniret* ... (ibid., p. 195).

[45] Leclercq, *Pierre le Vénérable*, pp. 80–81.

[46] This can be linked with the reference at the start of the letter to the love conserved *in penetralibus animae*, in the 'inner chambers of the soul' (letter 65, p. 194). The *topos* of a dwelling-place in the heart can be traced back to Augustine, where it is linked with spiritual insight: *et perge cogitando in pectus meum et cerne, quid illic de te agatur. patebit enim oculo caritatis cubiculum caritatis* ..., 'and proceed in thought into my heart and see what is effected concerning you there. For the resting-chamber of charity will be open to the eye of charity ...' (Augustine, ep. 58, 2, *CSEL*, 34/2, p. 217). See Fiske, *Friends and Friendship*, 2/5.

engage in a 'written conversation', in order to minimise the disjunctive effect of physical absence.[47] This pressure is renewed in a brief letter, written three years later, after Jerome has failed to reply,[48] where 'written conversation' is presented as a second-best alternative to frequent personal contact: 'Would that it had been possible to enjoy you, even if not as a fellow-dweller, at least as a neighbour in the Lord, for frequent and sweet conversation! But since that has not been granted, I ask that you strive to maintain that we be together in Christ, as best we can.. and not to scorn written replies, however rare.'[49] In both cases, Augustine appears to have in mind the unresolved problem of Galatians.

Letter 65 may contain two further echoes of Augustine. The first of these occurs in the *captatio*, where Peter sets up an elaborate opposition between body and soul/mind: *vultus corporis tui*, 'the face of your body'; *beatae animae tuae facies*, 'the face of your blessed soul'; *(fama) velocior corpore*, '(reputation) swifter than the body'; *oculi mentis meae*, 'the eyes of my mind.' This language appears to play on the distinction between corporeal and spiritual perception, a concept crucial to the theological and philosophical writings of Augustine. In particular, the use of *phantasmata*, 'images', 'phantasms',[50] may point towards a passage from the *De Trinitate*. In this passage, Augustine draws a distinction between *phantasiae*, images of corporeal things taken in by the senses, and *ficta phantasmata*, images which are imagined, 'whether otherwise than they are, or, by chance, as they are'.[51] Both types of image are said to be subject to the corrective judgement of truth, that is of spiritual perception.[52] The illustration which follows concerns love based on

---

[47]   *Quare adgredere, quaeso, istam nobiscum litterarium collocutionem, ne multum ad nos disiungendos liceat absentiae corporali* ..., 'Therefore, I beg, undertake this written conversation with me, so that physical absence may not serve to disunite us ...' (Augustine, ep. 40, I. 1, *CSEL*, 34/2, p. 70).

[48]   *Audivi pervenisse in manus tuas litteras meas; sed quod adhuc rescripta non merui, nequaquam imputaverim dilectioni tuae* ...; 'I have heard that my letter has reached your hands; but I would in no way ascribe to your Affection the fact that I have not yet deserved an answer ...' (Augustine, ep. 67, I. 1, ibid., p. 237).

[49]   *O si licuisset etsi non cohabitante saltem vicino te in domino perfrui ad crebrum et dulce colloquium! Sed quia id non est datum, peto, ut hoc ipsum, quod in Christo, quam possimus, simul simus, conservare studeas.. et rescripta quamvis rara non spernere* (idem, ep. 67, II. 3, p. 239).

[50]   *(et) phantasmata somniorum veritate succedente evanuerunt* ... (Peter, letter 65, p. 194).

[51]   *Unde etiam phantasias rerum corporalium per corporis sensum haustas et quodam modo infusas memoriae, ex quibus etiam ea quae non visa sunt ficto phantasmate cogitantur sive aliter quam sunt sive fortuito sicuti sunt* ..., 'Whence also the images of corporeal things drunk in through the sense of the body and in a certain manner infused into the memory, from which also those things which have not been seen are imagined by a fictitious phantasm, whether otherwise than they are or, by chance, as they are ...' (Augustine, *De Trinitate*, IX, VI. 10).

[52]   *aliis omnino regulis supra mentem nostram incommutabiliter manentibus vel approbare apud nosmetipsos vel improbare convincimur cum recte aliquid approbamus aut improbamus*, 'by other rules which remain immutably over our mind we are convinced either to approve within ourselves or to disprove, whenever rightly we approve or disprove something' (ibid.); *Viget et claret desuper iudicium veritatis* ..., 'There flourishes and shines from above the judgement of truth ...' (ibid.).

reputation, for a man who proves on personal experience to be less than he was reputed to be: he is loved not for what he is, but for what he was thought to be, or what he ought to be.[53]

On the surface, Peter seems to be saying the inverse: Bernard proved to be more, or more truly, what Peter believed him to be, and Peter's love is therefore deeper. However, the qualification of *phantasmata* by *somniorum*, 'of dreams', 'of nightmares', and the description of *fama* as *velocior corpore*, 'swifter than the body', may appear to introduce an element of uncertainty. *Phantasmata* can connote devishly inspired delusions.[54] *Fama*, personified in the *Aeneid* as 'an evil, than which none other is swifter',[55] can represent rumour as well as reputation. The statement 'the phantasms of dreams vanished as truth took their place' leaves room for the interpretation that a previously negative impression, fuelled by rumour, has been dispelled by personal knowledge. The opposition here between 'reality' and 'unreality' paves the way for a linguistic nexus which centres on the concept of change and changeability. Peter demands *certiora per litteras indicia*, the 'more certain proof' of a letter; he claims that 'paper cannot change the speech imprinted upon it',[56] while 'the tongue of speakers ... too often changes the truth which has

---

[53] *Nam unde in me fraterni amoris inflammatur ardor cum audio virum aliquem pro fidei pulchritudine et firmitate acriora tormenta tolerasse? Et si mihi digito ostendatur ipse homo, studeo mihi coniungere, notum facere, amicitia colligare ... Quod si mihi inter nostras loquelas fateatur aut incautus aliquo modo sese indicet quod vel de deo credat incongrua ... vel speratae pecuniae cupiditate vel inani aviditate laudis humanae [illa pertulerit], statim amor ille quo in eum ferebar offensus et quasi repercussus atque ab indigno homine ablatus in ea forma permanet ex qua eum talem credens amaveram. Nisi forte ad hoc amo iam ut talis sit cum talem non esse comperero,* 'For whence in me is the ardour of brotherly love enflamed, when I hear that some man has suffered fierce torments for the beauty and stability of the Faith? And if the man himself should be pointed out to me, I am eager to join him to me, to make him known, to bind him in friendship ... Therefore if he should confess to me in our conversations or incautiously in some way betray himself in some way, that he believes unsuitable things about God ... or that [he endured those things] out of desire for money or vain eagerness for human praise, straightaway that love by which I was carried towards him, offended and as if struck back and carried off from that unworthy man, remains on that form from which, believing him such, I had loved him. Unless perhaps I love him for this, that he may be such, when I have learned him not to be such' (ibid., VI. 11).

[54] *Vox senioris nostri, sed imago diaboli. Non subsistamus, sed fugam maturemus: phantasma vult nos pessumdare,* 'It is the voice of our lord, but the image of a devil. Let us not stay here, but hasten flight: a devilish delusion wishes to destroy us' (Hrotswitha of Gandersheim, *Dulcitius*, V, *Hrotsvithae opera*, ed. H. Homeyer, Paderborn, 1970, p. 272). In the context of a Christian martyrdom, the expression may be ironic. Hrotswitha would appear to be placing Christian sentiments into the mouth of pagan soldiers.

[55] *Fama, malum qua non aliud velocius ullum..* (Virgil, *Aeneid*, IV, l.174, in *P. Vergili Maronis opera*, ed. R. A. B. Mynors, Oxford, 1969, reprinted 1972).

[56] *nescit carta impressum mutare sermonem ...* (letter 65, p. 194). The use of *impressus* may point towards an underlying allusion to the role of memory. The analogy of the retention of impressions on the memory as the stamping of imprints with a seal-ring on a block of wax is employed, among others, by Augustine (*de Trinitate*, XI, II, 3). On the history of this analogy, derived from Plato and Aristotle, see J. Coleman, *Ancient and medieval memories*, Cambridge, 1992, pp. 7–8; 19–20). Peter displays familiarity with the image elsewhere, for example, letter 54 (*Letters*, I, p. 175); letter 87 (ibid., p. 227).

been enjoined';[57] he conjures up the image of 'one place never to be changed'.[58] Peter might seem to be hinting that positive, as well as negative, impressions need corroboration. Augustine, too, develops an opposition between mutability and immutability: 'how a man is' changes according to circumstances, but 'how a man should be' is immutable.[59]

The second of these potential echoes again concerns Augustine's correspondence with Jerome. Invoking the language of warfare, Peter presents Bernard as *electus proeliator*, an 'elect champion', of the Church. He is said to use *dextera et laeva*, 'the right (hand) and the left (hand),' and to fight *per arma iustitiae a dexteris et a sinistris*, 'through the arms of righteousness on the right and the left'.[60] Peter seems to be combining three biblical allusions here. The first, taken from Isaiah, conjures up the vengeful Jehovah of the Old Testament.[61] The initial reference to 'right' and 'left' may imply an opposition between weapons of aggression and defense, suggesting that Peter has in mind the 'shield of Faith' and the 'sword of the Spirit', equated there with the 'Word of God', from Ephesians.[62] The subsequent allusion, taken directly from II Corinthians, may, as will be seen, add a less positive nuance. At a literal level of interpretation, Peter seems to be alluding here to Bernard's active role in the papal schism. At a figurative level, the addition of the phrase *paratus in diem belli*, 'ready for the day of war', conjures up the motif of spiritual warfare, and, in particular, of the abbot's spiritual role as leader of his flock on the day of judgement, as set out by Peter in a letter to the

---

[57]   *(cum) loquentium lingua ... iniunctam mutet saepius veritatem* (letter 65, pp. 194–5).

[58]   *nunquam mutandus unus locus ...* (ibid., p. 195).

[59]   *Unde manifestum est aliud unumquemque videre in se quod sibi alius dicenti credat, non tamen videat; aliud autem in ipsa veritate quod alius quoque possit intueri, quorum alterum mutari per tempora, alterum incommutabili aeternitate consistere. Neque enim oculis corporeis multas mentes videndo per similitudinem colligimus generalem vel specialem mentis humanae notitiam, sed intuemur inviolabilem veritatem ex qua perfecte quantum possumus definiamus non qualis sit uniuscuiusque hominis mens, sed qualis esse sempiternis rationibus debeat*, 'Whence it is clear that each one sees something in himself which another may believe him saying, but not see, but something else in truth itself which another may also see: the one can change through circumstances, the other remains steadfast in incommutable eternity. For not by seeing many minds with the eyes of the body do we acquire through similitude general or particular knowledge of the human mind, but we contemplate the inviolable truth from which, perfectly as we can, we may define not how the disposition of each man is, but how it should be by eternal reason' (Augustine, *de Trinitate*, IX, VI. 9).

[60]   Peter, letter 65, p. 195 = II Cor 6. 7.

[61]   *Dominus sicut fortis egredietur sicut vir proeliator suscitabit zelum vociferabitur et clamabit super inimicos suos confortabitur*, 'The Lord will go forth as a strong man, as a fighter He will stir up zeal. He will cry out and shout aloud, He will be strengthened above His enemies' (Is 42. 13). In view of what follows in Peter, it may be noted that *zelus* is not unambiguously positive, but can connote both 'zeal' and 'jealousy'.

[62]   *in omnibus sumentes scutum fidei in quo possitis omnia tela nequissimi ignea exstinguere et galeam salutis assumite et gladium Spiritus quod est verbum Dei*, 'taking in everything the shield of faith, in which you may be able to extinguish all the fiery darts of the most worthless one, assume the helmet of salvation and the sword of the Spirit, which is the Word of God' (Eph 6. 16–17).

Carthusians.[63] It is not clear, however, that these two functions are being presented as mutually compatible. Subsequently Bernard's position *curia laboriosa*, at the 'wearisome papal court', is juxtaposed to Peter's involvement *cura periculosa*, in 'dangerous pastoral cure'. Similarly, Peter sets *alienorum causae*, the 'causes', 'cases', of 'strangers', against *tuorum negotia*, the 'business of your own'. Arguably, this creates a potentially critical opposition between the secular and the spiritual, politics 'abroad' and pastoral care 'at home'.[64]

Significantly, the same citation from II Corinthians is evoked in Augustine's fifth letter to Jerome,[65] written in 404 in answer to a hostile and blocking letter from Jerome.[66] It appears in the context of the hostility consequent on a theological dispute between Jerome and his former 'friend' Rufinus,[67] an enmity which seems, as White suggests,[68] to have functioned as a parallel for the relationship between Jerome and Augustine himself.[69] 'Therefore, who of the wise would not see how patiently, consoled by conscience, you bear the incredible present enmity of one who was once a most familiar friend, and how far you class either what he throws out, or what perhaps is believed by some, among the weapons of the left, which, no less than the weapons of the right, are used to fight the Devil.'[70] In its original

---

[63] *Video draconem de caelo proiectum tertiam partem rutilantium stellarum de summis ad ima cauda trahentem, et adversum sanctae mulieris semen acrius solito proeliantem. Cumque ille peritissimus perdendi artifex multiformibus insidiis caelestia castra infestet, me ignaro, me infirmo, me timido duce, nesciente, non valente, non audente resistere, spem sibi victoriae de Christi militibus glorians repromittit*, 'I see the Dragon cast down from heaven dragging with its tail a third part of the glowing stars from the heights to the depths, and fighting more fiercely than usual against the seed of the holy woman. And when that most skilled contriver of destruction attacks the heavenly camp with multifarious deceits, he boastfully promises himself hope of victory over the soldiers of Christ, with me unaware, infirm, a timid leader, not knowing, unable, not daring to resist' (letter 24, p. 45, modelled on Apc 12. 13–17.) This follows the revised version of the letter-collection, which gives *audente* for *audiente*: see Constable, *Letters*, II, p. 45, 8. On this letter, see Knight, 'The language of retreat', pp. 38–40.

[64] I have argued elsewhere that this opposition characterises Peter's letters written during the schism (Knight, 'Politics and pastoral care', pp. 389–90.)

[65] Augustine, ep. 73, *CSEL*, 34/2, pp. 263–78.

[66] Jerome, ep. 102, *CSEL*, 55, pp. 234–6. This letter will be discussed in the following chapter.

[67] See *Saint Jérôme, Apologie contra Rufin*, ed. and trans. P. Lardet, Sources chrétiennes 303, Paris, 1983, pp. 1–75.

[68] White, *The correspondence*, p. 26.

[69] Jerome had ended his first, aggressive, response to Augustine with the following words: *Misit mihi temeritate solita maledicta sua Calpurnius cognomento Lanarius, quae ad Africam quoque studio eius didici pervenisse. Ad quae breviter ex parte respondi et libelli eius vobis misi exemplaria latius opus, cum opportunum fuerit, primo missurus tempore ...*, 'Calpurnius, surnamed Lanarius, with his customary temerity sent me his imprecations, which, I have learned, by his zeal reached Africa also. I have replied briefly in part and sent you a copy of the book, intending to send the fuller work as soon as is opportune ...' (Jerome, ep. 102, 3, p. 236). As White suggests, this gesture was surely intended as a warning for Augustine (White, *The correspondence*, p. 22).

[70] *Quapropter quis prudentium non videat, etiam tu quam tolerabiliter feras amicissimi quondam et familiarissimi incredibiles nunc inimicitias consolante conscientia et quem ad*

context the citation, beginning 'Let us show ourselves in all things ministers of God ...', continues 'through glory and dishonour, through infamy and good reknown ...'.[71] What follows in Augustine suggests that his commendation of Jerome's 'moderation' is to be understood ironically: 'But I would have preferred him [Rufinus] in some way more gentle than you more armed in that fashion'.[72] The passage as a whole suggests that the 'weapons of the left' are to be equated with invective and detraction. The emphasis placed on the use of 'left' and 'right' by Peter's doubling of the motif may imply that Bernard, too, is being implicated in accusations of detraction.

Such an implication may be read in two ways. At one level, it may reflect Bernard's role in the campaign of negative propaganda waged against the anti-pope Anacletus and his supporters.[73] Linked with the opposition between *curia* and *cura*, this might appear to insinuate that Bernard has been devoting his efforts to political polemic rather than to bringing peace between the monastic orders. More damagingly, it might represent a glance back to Bernard's polemical *Apologia*. The letter as a whole displays a seeming indeterminacy of purpose which may, as Bredero suggests, have led to its being treated as a straightforward declaration of affection.[74] In fact, as the above reading shows, a number of features, the stress on *caritas*, the allusion to detraction, the echoes of Augustine, combine to suggest the presence of a sub-text, which harks back to the *Apologia* and letter 28, and which serves to reintroduce the question of Cluniac–Cistercian relations. The precise sense of this sub-text, however, is, perhaps intentionally, difficult to pin down.[75] The letter might be read as a warning, that *caritas* was founded on a false assessment of Bernard and is at risk; a challenge, that Bernard show himself such as Peter believed him to be and as he ought to be; or as a simple plea for reassurance, that Bernard write and dispel any false rumours or misunderstandings. It seems, in short, that Peter's declaration of *caritas* is not disinterested, but is functioning as a pressurising lever.

It seems likely, as Constable suggests, that Bernard's ep. 147 represents his reply

---

modum, vel quod iactitat vel quod a quibusdam forsitan creditur, in sinistris armis deputes, quibus non minus quam dextris contra diabolum dimicatur? (Augustine, ep. 73, III. 10, p. 278).

[71] *(sed) in omnibus exhibeamus nosmet ipsos Deo ministros.. per gloriam et ignobilitatem per infamiam et bonam famam..* (II Cor 6. 4–8).

[72] *Verum tamen illum maluerim aliquo modo mitiorem quam te isto modo armatiorem* (Augustine, ep. 73, III. 10, p. 278).

[73] See A. Grabois, 'Le schisme de 1130 et la France', *Revue d'Histoire Ecclésiastique* 76 (1981), 594–612; Knight, 'Politics and pastoral care', pp. 364–6.

[74] Bredero, 'Saint Bernard in his relations', p. 324; idem, *Bernard of Clairvaux*, p. 231.

[75] Julius Victor, in his discussion of the need for clarity, makes a partial exception of what he terms the 'secret' letter: *(nisi cum) consulto [consilio] clandestinae litterae fiant, quae tamen ita ceteris occultae esse debent, ut his, ad quos mittuntur, clarae perspicuaeque sint,* '(except when) letters are secret on purpose; they should, however, be secret in regard to others while being clear and transparent to those to whom they are sent' (*Ars rhetorica*, 448). Letter 65 might be viewed as a letter of this type; alternatively, it might be construed as a challenge to Bernard to interpret its 'meaning' in the light of spiritual perception.

to letter 65.[76] Although this is accepted neither by Leclercq,[77] nor Bredero,[78] both of whom postulate a 'missing' letter from Peter, the internal evidence, as will be seen, strongly supports Constable's hypothesis. Written from Italy, ep. 147 can be dated to the early part of 1138, after the death of the anti-pope Anacletus, but before the formal ending of the schism in that year. Like letter 65, this letter presents a surface appearance of reciprocal compliment; beneath the compliment, however, may lurk an equally ambiguous sub-text.

> To the lord and most reverend father, Peter, abbot of Cluny, his Bernard, what his (Bernard wishes)[79]

> May the Light springing from on high visit you, O good man, because you have visited me *in an alien land*, and consoled me *in the place of my exile*. You have done well, showing concern *over the poor and needy*. I was absent, and absent already over a long time, and you, a great man, occupied in great matters, remembered my name. Blessed (be) your holy angel, who suggested it to your pious heart; blessed (be) our God, who persuaded it. Lo, I hold whence to glory among strangers, your letter, and that letter in which you poured out your soul to me. I glory that you have me not only in memory, but also in grace. I glory in the privilege of your love, I am refreshed from the abundance of the sweetness of your heart. Not only so, but I glory also in whatever tribulations I have been held worthy to suffer for the Church. This plainly is *my glory and exulting my head*, the triumph of the Church. For if we have been sharers in the labour, we will be sharers also *in the consolation*. It was needful to work together and to take compassion on the mother, lest she complain of us also, saying: *Those who were near me stood far off, and those who were seeking my life did violence. Thanks to God, who gave* her *the victory, graced* her *in*

---

[76]   See Constable, *Letters*, II, p. 141.

[77]   Leclercq, *SBO*, VII, n. 2. He mentions but apparently does not accept, Constable's hypothesis.

[78]   Bredero, *Bernard of Clairvaux*, p. 232. Previously he had accepted Constable's view (Bredero, 'Saint Bernard in his relations', p. 325). He gives no reason for his change of mind.

[79]   *Domino et patri reverentissimo, Petro Cluniacensi abbati, suus Bernardus: quod suus* (Bernard, ep. 147, *SBO*, VII, p. 350). This is rendered by James as 'the entire devotion of his Bernard' (James, *Letters*, p. 216). Bernard himself suggests elsewhere that this is not a standard salutation formula. Ep. 86, to William of St Thierry, has the salutation *Frater Bernardus de Claravalle: suo illi quod suo*, 'Brother Bernard of Clairvaux: to that one of his what (he wishes) for his'. Bernard goes on to claim that this salutation is modelled on the one he received from William himself, *Hanc mihi tu salutationis formulam tradidisti, scribendo: Suus ille quod suus. Accipe quod tuum est, et agnosce usurpationem unanimitatis esse indicium, et cum quo est mihi commune verbum, animum non distare*, 'You handed down to me this formula of salutation, by writing: "That one of his, what his." Receive therefore what is yours, and recognise the usurpation as being a proof of unanimity, and that there is no distance of mind from one with whom I have a common expression' (Bernard, ep. 86, 1, *SBO*, VII, p. 223). In that letter, Bernard plays heavily on the concept of 'wishing': what William wishes for himself (apparently to retire from the abbacy and, presumably, to enter Clairvaux); what Bernard wishes for him (the same); what God wishes (that William remain where he is and benefit those of whom he is in charge). The salutation as given to Peter also occurs in ep. 178 to Innocent, where Bernard invokes the openness demanded by friendship to justify making known his complaints and desires. On this type of accusative phrase, employing *quicquid* or *quod*, and expressing a wish, see C. D. Lanham, *Salutatio formulas in Latin letters to 1200: syntax, style and theory*, Munich, 1975, p. 10.

labours and brought completion to her labours. Our sadness has been turned into joy and our grief into the lyre. *The winter has passed, the rain has departed and gone, the flowers have appeared in our land, the time for pruning has come.* The useless branch, the rotten limb has been cut off. That wicked man who caused Israel to sin, has been swallowed up by death and borne across into the belly of hell. He had made, in the words of the prophet, a *pact with death*, and had entered into *an alliance with hell.* Therefore, according to Ezekiel, *he has been brought to ruin, and he does not abide to eternity.* Another also, just as the greatest enemy of all, so also the worst, has none-the-less been cut off. And he was one of the friends of the Church, but of those about whom she is accustomed to complain and say: *My friends and my neighbours approached towards me and stood.* We hope for the same judgement swiftly on any similar who remain. The time is near for me to return to my brothers, if the season accompanies, intending to pass through you. Meanwhile I commend myself to your holy prayers. I greet brother Hugh, the chamberlain, and all who are around you, with the rest of the holy multitude.

At first sight the letter can be divided into a 'personal' *captatio*, praising Peter for his letter, and a 'public' narration, celebrating the triumph of the Church and the destruction of Innocent's enemies. Peter's letter is seemingly presented under a dual guise, as a source of consolation, and as a source of glory. As will be seen, however, this may not be quite so straightforward as it appears. The opening sentence combines three biblical allusions, two of them taken from the Old Testament and one from the New Testament.[80] All three can be seen to have potential connotations with the end of schism, thus undermining the barrier between 'private' and 'public'. The first, evoking the 'Light springing from on high', denotes the coming of redemption and peace.[81] The second, 'in an alien land', represents the words of Moses, in exile in Midian, on the birth of a son,[82] while the third, 'in the place of my exile', comes from a context which praises the justice of God.[83] The language of exile and alienation can be paralleled from a letter written by Bernard to the monks of Clairvaux in the previous year, where he simultaneously evokes and denies the memory of his monks as a potential source of 'consolation': *'Sad is my soul* until I return and does not wish to be consoled even unto you. For what consolation is there to me *in the evil time* and *in the place of my exile*? Is it not you in the Lord? Indeed, the sweet memory of you does not desert me wherever I go; but the sweeter the memory, the more troublesome the absence.'[84]

---

[80]   *Visitet te* Oriens ex alto, *o bone vir, quia visitasti me* in terra aliena *et* in loco peregrinationis meae *consolatus es me* (Bernard, ep. 147, 1, p. 350 = Lc 1. 78; Ex 2. 22; Ps 118. 54).

[81]   *per viscera misericordiae Dei nostri in quibus visitavit nos oriens ex alto illuminare his qui in tenebris et in umbra mortis sedent ad dirigendos pedes nostros in viam pacis*, 'through the entrails of the mercy of our God in which the Light springing from on high has visited us to bring light to those who sit in darkness and in the shadow of death, to direct our feet into the way of peace' (Lc 1. 78–9).

[82]   *quae (Seffora) peperit filium quem vocavit Gersam dicens advena fui in terra aliena*, 'who gave birth to a son whom he called Gershom saying, "I have been a stranger in an alien land" ' (Ex 2. 22).

[83]   *Cantabiles mihi erant iustificationes tuae in loco peregrinationis meae*, 'Your justifications were worthy to be sung by me in the place of my exile' (Ps 118. 54).

[84]   Tristis est anima mea usque *dum redeam et non vult consolari usque ad vos. Quae enim est mihi consolatio* in tempore malo *et* in loco peregrinationis meae? *Nonne vos in Domino?*

The same letter may also serve to cast some doubt on Bernard's protestations that he 'glories' in Peter's friendship.[85] *Gloria* can denote either 'glory' or 'vainglory'. It is in the latter sense that Bernard uses it to his monks, through a *praeteritio* which stands in marked contrast to the triumphalist declaration in his letter to Peter: 'But how necessary to the Church of God is or has been in this time the presence of my littleness, I would tell for your consolation, if it were not redolent of vainglory. Now it is better that you learn this through others.'[86] In what follows in ep. 147, the source of 'glory' will be abruptly switched from Peter's letter to Bernard's 'sufferings' on behalf of the Church, and to the the successful ending of the schism.[87] Moreover, the language which surrounds these protestations displays a certain obliquity. The opening *apostrophe*, *o bone vir*, 'O good man', represents a form of address rare in Bernard's surviving letters. Significantly, the only other occurrence in this form is in a subsequent letter to Peter.[88] Traditionally, the address *bone vir* appears to have connoted facetiousness or irony.[89] Bernard may also be drawing on Biblical reminiscences. In Ecclesiasticus, the 'good man' is said to 'pledge help' to his neighbour.[90] The narration which follows, as will be seen, may call into question Peter's loyalty towards the Church, expressed in terms of friendship and neighbourliness. In the Gospels, on the other hand, Christ denies that it is possible for any man to be called good 'except God'.[91]

Minime quidem deserit me, quocumque iero, dulcis memoria vestri; sed quanto memoria dulcior, tanto absentia molestior (Bernard, ep. 144, 1, *SBO*, VII, p. 344 = Mt 26. 38; Ps 76, 3; II Mcc 1. 5; Ps 118. 54).

[85] *En teneo unde glorier apud extraneos, litteras tuas .... Glorior quod habeas me ... in gratia. Glorior privilegio amoris tui ...* (Bernard, ep. 147, p. 350).

[86] *Sed et hac vice quam necessaria Ecclesiae Dei sit vel fuerit praesentia parvitatis nostrae dicerem ad consolationem vestram, si non gloriam redoleret. Nunc autem melius est ut hoc per alios cognoscatis* (Bernard, ep. 144, 3, p. 346).

[87] *Non solum autem, sed et glorior in tribulationibus, si quas habitus sum pro Ecclesia pati. Haec plane gloria mea et exaltans caput meum, Ecclesiae triumphus* (idem, ep. 147, p. 350 = Rm 5. 3; Ps 3. 4).

[88] Bernard, ep. 265, *SBO*, VIII, p. 174. This letter will be discussed in Chapter 10. On the few occasions when Bernard does apply the epithet *bonus* to the addressee, the context seems to be one of sarcastic rebuke or ironic surprise: for example, *Modestiae quidem vestrae erat, o boni fratres, super querimonia vestra priori nostra satisfactione contentos esse debere, et iam ab immeritorum infestatione quiescere. Sed quia prioribus malis peiora iunxistis, et rursus nobis iurgiorum seminaria transmisistis ...*, 'It was due to your moderation, O good brothers, to be content with our first satisfaction concerning your complaint, and to rest from the harrying of the innocent. But because you have added worse evils to the former and again transmitted to us the seedbeds of altercation ...' (Bernard, ep. 68, 1, *SBO*, VII, p. 165: the context is that of monastic transfer); *O bona domina, quid tibi et nobis?*, 'O good lady, what is your concern with us?' (idem, ep. 118, ibid., p. 298).

[89] *Age, tu illuc procede, bone vir, lepidum mancipium meum*, 'Come, come here my dear fellow, my charming purchased slave' (Plautus, *Captivi*, V. ii. i., in *T. Macci Plauti Comoediae*, ed. W. M. Lindsay, 2 vols, Oxford, 1904, reprinted 1946, 1).

[90] *Vir bonus fidem facit proximo suo et qui perdiderit confusionem derelinquet sibi*, 'The good man pledges assistance to his neighbour; he who has lost shame will forsake it towards him' (Sir 29. 19).

[91] *Iesus autem dixit ei quid me dicis bonum nemo bonus nisi Deus* (Mc 10. 18, Mt 19. 17, Lc 18. 19).

There is room for irony, too, in Bernard's depiction of Peter as *homo magnus, occupatus in magnis*, 'a great man, occupied in great matters'. This characterisation serves to create an opposition between Peter and himself, depicted here as *egenus et pauper*, 'poor and needy'.[92] In itself, the antithesis between 'grandeur' and 'humility' is innocuous, representing a standard modesty *topos* of a type common in Bernard's writing.[93] The introduction of the motif of 'poverty', however, may suggest that it has more serious implications. As will be demonstrated in the next chapter, the opposition between 'rich' and 'poor', the material wealth of the Cluniacs in contrast to the poverty of the Cistercians, played an important part in the polemics relating to the giving or withholding of tithes, which raged from 1132 onwards. At the same time, translated into spiritual terms, the concepts are open to inversion: wealth is a barrier to salvation;[94] humility, 'poverty of spirit', ensures it.[95]

The presentation of Peter's letter as a source of glory and consolation may be further undercut by the Biblical contexts from which Bernard's citations are drawn. The citations with which the letter opens celebrate the mercy and power of God. The prophecy of Zacharias, from which the reference to the 'Light springing from on high' is taken, begins 'Blessed is the God of Israel because he has visited and brought redemption for his people ...'.[96] The passage from the Psalms which contains the reference to 'the place of my exile' sets up the motif of divine consolation, contrasting (divine) eloquence with (human) humility.[97] Similarly, the reference to spiritual sweetness, 'I have been refreshed from the abundance of the sweetness of your heart',[98] is adapted from a paean to the magnitude of God.[99] At

---

[92]   *Bene fecisti,* intelligens super egenum et pauperum, 'You have done well, *showing concern over the poor and needy*' (Bernard, ep. 147, 1, p. 350 = Ps 40. 2).

[93]   For example, the·reference to *parvitas nostra* in the letter to Clairvaux (idem, ep. 144, 3).

[94]   *Facilius est enim camelum per foramen acus transire quam divitem intrare in regnum Dei,* 'It is easier for a camel to pass through the eye of the needle than for a rich man to enter into the kingdom of God' (Lc 18. 25).

[95]   *Beati pauperes spiritu quoniam ipsorum est regnum caelorum,* 'Blessed are the poor in spirit for theirs is the kingdom of heaven' (Mt 5. 3; Lc 6. 20).

[96]   *Benedictus Deus Israhel quia visitavit et fecit redemptionem plebi suae* ... (Lc 1. 68).

[97]   *Memor esto verbi tui servo tuo in quo mihi spem dedisti haec me consolata est in humilitate mea quia eloquium tuum vivificavit me ... memor fui iudiciorum tuorum a saeculo Domine et consolatus sum ... cantabiles mihi erant iustificationes tuae in loco peregrinationis meae,* 'Be mindful of your word to your servant in which you gave me hope. This consoled me in my humility because your eloquence restored me to life ... I was mindful of your judgements, Lord, of old and I was consoled ... Your justifications were worthy to be sung by me in the place of my exile' (Ps 118. 49–54).

[98]   *refectus sum de* abundantia suavitatis *pectoris tui* (ep. 147, 1 = Ps 144. 7).

[99]   *Magnus Dominus et laudabilis nimis et magnitudinis eius non est finis generatio et generatio laudabit opera tua et potentiam tuam pronuntiabunt magnificentiam gloriae sanctitatis tuae loquentur et mirabilia tua narrabunt memoriam abundantiae suavitatis tuae eructabunt et iustitia tua exultabunt,* 'Great is the Lord and most praiseworthy and there is no end to his magnitude. Generation and generation will praise your works and proclaim your power. They will speak of the magnificence of the glory of your sanctity and tell your marvels. They will utter the memory of the abundance of your sweetness and they will exult in your righteousness' (Ps 144. 3–7).

one level, this appears to hint at a potential equation between God and Peter; at another, it might be thought to establish the distance between them. Arguably, this distance is made explicit in the narration to follow, as Bernard effects the shift between 'private' and 'public', by removing the notions of 'glory' and 'consolation' from Peter and his letter, and attaching them to God as the ender of papal schism.

Bernard weaves together a range of biblical echoes from contexts which establish Christ as mediator,[100] God as protector,[101] and, subsequently, as bringer of consolation.[102] Just as letter 65 seemed to play with the potential for uncertainty of the subjunctive mode, so Bernard's letter appears to exploit certain syntactical ambiguities. In the final allusion mentioned above, Bernard is adapting a citation from II Corinthians, 'knowing that just as you are sharers in the sufferings, so you will be also of the consolation'.[103] In Bernard's version, a shift from second-person to first-person plural is accompanied by a shift from statement to condition, 'if we have been sharers in the labour, we will be sharers also in the consolation'.[104] The gerundives which follow indicate actions which should have been taken, without necessarily confirming that they were taken, 'It was necessary to work together and to take pity on the mother (Church) ...'.[105] These, in turn, lead into one of a matched pair of citations, which frame the narration, and which invoke failure in friendship: 'Those who were near me stood far off, and those who were seeking my life did violence';[106] 'My friends and my neighbours came against me and stood.'[107]

---

[100] *Iustificati igitur ex fide pacem habeamus ad Deum per Dominum nostrum Iesum Christum per quem et accessum habemus fide in gratiam istam in qua stamus et gloriamur in spe gloriae filiorum Dei non solum autem sed et gloriamur in tribulationibus ...*, 'Therefore, justified from Faith, let us have peace towards God through our Lord Jesus Christ, through whom we have access in the Faith to that grace in which we stand and glory in the hope of the glory of sons of God. Not only that, but we also glory in the tribulations ...' (Rm 5. 1–3).

[101] *Domine quid multiplicati sunt qui tribulant me.. tu autem Domine susceptor meus es gloria mea et exultans caput meum*, 'Lord, why are those who afflict me multiplied? ... But you, Lord, are my protector, my glory and exalting my head' (Ps 3. 2; ibid., 3. 4).

[102] *Benedictus Deus et Pater Domini nostri Iesu Christi Pater misericordiarum et Deus totius consolationis qui consolatur nos in omni tribulatione nostra.. et spes nostra firma pro vobis scientes quoniam sicut socii passionum estis sic eritis et consolationis*, 'Blessed be the God and Father of our Lord Jesus Christ, the father of mercies and God of all consolation, who consoles us in all our tribulation.. and our hope is firm for you, knowing that just as you are companions of the sufferings, so you will also be of the consolation' (II Cor 1. 3–4; ibid., 1. 7).

[103] *scientes quoniam sicut socii passionum estis sic eritis et consolationis* (ibid., 1. 7).

[104] *Nam si socii fuimus laboris, erimus* et consolationis (Bernard, ep. 147, 1, p. 350 = ibid.)

[105] *Collaborandum fuit et compatiendum matri..* (ibid.) In his next major letter to Bernard Peter will employ a string of gerundives to indicate actions which were clearly not taken but which should have been taken by the latter (Peter, letter 29, *Letters*, I, p. 102). This letter will be discussed in the following chapter.

[106] *Qui iuxta me erant de longe steterunt, et vim faciebant qui quaerebant animam meam* (ep. 147, 1, p. 350 = Ps 37. 12–13).

[107] *Amici mei et proximi mei adversum me appropinquaverunt et steterunt* (ep. 147, 2, p. 351 = Ps 37, 12). Bernard might also have in mind the saying from the Gospels, *Qui non est mecum adversum me est*, 'He who is not with me is against me' (Lc 11. 23).

Significantly, each is introduced by a 'complaint', placed in the mouth of the Church, suggesting that they may represent a riposte to the epistolary 'reproach' found in Peter's letter 65, by bringing into question Peter's role during the schism.[108]

Two additional indications may serve to confirm this letter as a reply to Peter's letter 65. Peter depicts Bernard as *electus proeliator*; here, Bernard associates 'glory' with *triumphus*, the 'triumph', 'victory-procession', of the Church. Peter opposes the labour of the papal court to the danger of pastoral cure; Bernard replaces *passiones*, the 'sufferings', of II Corinthians with *labor*, 'labour', 'suffering'. Letter 65, behind a complimentary facade, may hint at a double failure in *caritas*: towards Peter, and towards the cause of Cluniac–Cistercian relations. Bernard's letter can be seen to produce a justification of his concern in external 'politics' which links it with a wider vision of *caritas*. The continuation of the passage from *Romans* from which the claim, 'I glory in tribulations', is drawn links 'tribulation' with salvation through *caritas*.[109] At the same time, the narration comprises a reprise of the invective employed by Bernard and others throughout the schism. The denunciation of *ille iniquus*, 'that wicked man', as having made 'a pact with death' and 'an alliance with hell'[110] reflects the standard equation of the anti-pope Anacletus with Antichrist.[111] The image of a 'fruitless tree', evoked through the claim that 'the useless branch, the rotten limb has been cut off',[112] can be linked, as Stroll has demonstrated,[113] with attacks on Anacletus's Jewish origins. The attribution of the victory to God[114] can be seen as providing its own justification for such detraction.[115]

---

[108] *ne et de nobis quereretur, dicens ...* (ep. 147, 1, p. 350); *sed illis, de quibus solet queri et dicere ...* (ibid., 2, p. 351). Cf. *Sed queror..* (Peter, letter 65, p. 194); *ut querela mea sopiatur ...* (ibid., p. 195).

[109] *scientes quod tribulatio patientiam operatur patientia autem probationem probatio vero spem spes autem non confundit quia caritas Dei diffusa est in cordibus nostris*, 'knowing that tribulation effects patience, patience proving, proving hope, and hope does not confound, because the love of God has been diffused in our hearts' (Rm 5. 4–6).

[110] *Fecerat quippe, secundam Prophetam*, pactum cum morte, et cum inferno foedus inierat (Bernard, ep. 147, 2, p. 351 = Is 28. 15).

[111] Cf. *Nam qui Dei libenter iunguntur ei (Innocentio), qui autem ex adverso stat, aut Antichristi est, aut Antichristus*, 'For those who are God's are joined freely to him (Innocent), he who stands against is either Antichrist's or the Antichrist' (Bernard, ep. 124, 1, *SBO*, VII, p. 305).

[112] *amputatum est sarmentum inutile, putre membrum* (ep. 147, 2, p. 351).

[113] M. Stroll, *The Jewish Pope: ideology and politics in the papal schism of 1130*, Leiden, 1987, p. 166 and n. 37.

[114] Deo autem gratias, qui dedit *ei (ecclesiae)* victoriam.. (ep. 147, 2, p. 351 = I Cor 15. 57).

[115] It is possible that the attacks which follow that on Anacletus target Peter more directly. The 'other' said to have been 'cut off' may refer to Roger of Sicily, Anacletus's chief secular supporter (see Knight, 'Rhetoric and stylistics, pp. 201–2). In a subsequent letter to Roger, Peter will claim to have warned Innocent against trusting in Roger's 'enemies' and the 'troublers' of his and Roger's peace (Peter, letter 90, *Letters*, I, p. 231). Those for whom Bernard invokes the 'same judgement' might be thought to include the Cluniac cardinal Gilo of Tusculum, who did not reappear subscribing to papal bulls until mid-June 1138 (see Constable, *Letters*, II, p. 293).

A Pauline dimension may also underlie Bernard's repeated stress on *gloria* and *gloriari*. In II Corinthians, St Paul plays at some length on the latter: 'if it is necessary to glory it is not expedient';[116] 'For myself, I will glory in nothing except in my infirmities';[117] and again, 'He (the Lord) said to me, "My grace suffices you, for virtue is perfected in infirmity": willingly therefore I will glory in my infirmities, that the virtue of Christ may dwell in me.'[118] If, as Stowers suggests, this section of the Pauline epistle can be read as 'ironic apology',[119] Bernard might be seen as producing an ironic 'defence', couched in terms of compliment, to an ironic 'attack', likewise masquerading as elaborate praise. An adoption of the Pauline voice here by Bernard would seem to be a fitting riposte to Peter's adoption of the Augustinian voice in letter 65. As stated previously, *gloria* can represent either 'glory' or 'vainglory', setting up a potential opposition: Peter's letter is a source of vainglory, labour in the schism a source of salvation. This passage of II Corinthians throws up one final, tantalising possibility. Between the last two verses cited above comes an allusion to an 'angel of Satan', sent as a warning against pride: 'lest the magnitude of the revelations puff me up, I have been given an angel of Satan as a goad to the flesh to box my ears ...'[120] In the *captatio,* Bernard appears to 'bless' Peter's 'angel' for suggesting that he 'visit' him through a letter.[121] It might be thought that this allusion presents Peter as the thorn in Bernard's flesh, meant to bring him down to earth.

Bernard's letter seems to end with the promise of a visit.[122] Here also the language has suggestive, if cryptic, overtones. The phrase *si vita comes fuerit,* 'if the season accompanies', may represent a conflation of two biblical allusions on a similar theme. The first, signalled by Leclercq, concerns the divine visitation to Abraham and the prophecy of a son to his aged wife Sarah.[123] The second, the syntax of which corresponds exactly with that found in Bernard, relates to Elisha's prophecy of a son to *mulier magna,* a 'great woman', of Shunem, whose husband is old.[124] In the second case, the son dies and is miraculously restored to life. In fact,

---

[116] *Si gloriari oportet non expedit quidem* (II Cor 12. 1).

[117] *pro me autem nihil gloriabor nisi in infirmitatibus meis* (ibid., 12. 5).

[118] *Et dixit (Dominus) mihi sufficit tibi gratia mea nam virtus in infirmitate perficitur libenter igitur gloriabor in infirmitatibus meis ut inhabitet in me virtus Christi* (ibid., 12. 9).

[119] Stowers, *Letter-writing,* p. 173. II Corinthians introduces the 'charge' that Paul's letters are 'strong', but his bodily presence 'weak' and his speech 'contemptible' (II Cor 10. 10). In what follows there, the accusation of weakness is seemingly embraced and shown to be a source of strength.

[120] *ne magnitudo revelationum extollat me datus est mihi stimulus carnis meae angelus Satanae ut me colaphizet ...* (ibid., 12. 7).

[121] *Benedictus sanctus angelus tuus, qui pio pectori tuo id suggessit ...* (ep. 147, 1, p. 350).

[122] *Prope est ut revertar ad fratres meos,* si vita comes fuerit, *per vos, sicut intendo, transiturus* (ibid., 2, p. 351 = Gn 18. 10).

[123] *Revertens veniam ad te tempore isto vita comite et habebit filium Sarra uxor tua,* 'Returning I shall come to you at that time when the season accompanies and your wife Sarah shall have a son' (Gn 18. 10).

[124] *In tempore isto et in hac eadem hora si vita comes fuerit habebis in utero filium,* 'At that time and in this hour if the season accompanies you will have a son in your womb' (IV Rg 4. 16).

the theme of a miraculous birth had been signalled at the start of the letter, in a kind of ring composition, through the prophecy relating to the birth of John the Baptist to the barren and aged Elizabeth, and the allusion to a son for Moses in exile. As with Bernard's allegation of 'poverty', the contexts seem to point to the language surrounding the issue of tithes, namely to the contrast between the (venerable) age of Cluny and the (upstart) newness of Cîteaux which, as will be seen, forms a prominent theme in Peter's letters on the subject. Bernard may be building here on the 'wish' expressed at the end of letter 65 that Peter and himself be retained by 'one place never to be changed'. Which of them is to be identified with the miraculous son, for the benefit of which institution, is left, perhaps deliberately, open to doubt.[125] At the same time, II Corinthians may also be of relevance here. St Paul warns the Corinthians that his coming may bring no pleasure: 'I fear lest when I have come I may not find you such as I wish, and may be found by you such as you do not wish, lest perhaps there should be contentions, jealousies, animosities, dissensions, detractions, whisperings, puffings-up, insurrections amongst you ...'[126]

Letter 65 and ep. 147 seem to find a coda in two much briefer letters also dating to the same phase of the correspondence, Peter's letter 73,[127] dated by Constable to spring 1138,[128] and Bernard's ep. 148,[129] dated by Leclercq, following Mabillon, to 'around 1138'.[130] How precisely these letters fit in with those discussed above, however, is a matter for conjecture. Letter 73 presents itself as a cover note for an oral message carried by Archdeacon Gebuin, described as 'most well known to me and to you, most dear to me and to you, as I believe'.[131] This in itself may seem slightly surprising. In a letter to Hato, bishop of Troyes,[132] dated by Constable to mid-March of the same year,[133] Peter appears to cast doubt on Gebuin's integrity, associating him with the 'guile of the fox'.[134] In letter 73, Peter refers to a 'longer', 'recent' letter.[135] He claims that the present letter is 'tongueless', because it 'trusts

---

[125]   Like Sarah and Elizabeth, Cluny is 'old'; like the woman of Shunem it is, or claims to be, 'great.' Like Moses, Bernard is in 'exile'; Moses' son undergoes (enforced) circumcision at the hands of its (Gentile) mother (Ex 4. 25–6).

[126]   *Timeo enim ne forte cum venero non quales volo inveniam vos et ego inveniar a vobis qualem non vultis ne forte contentiones aemulationes animositates dissensiones detractiones susurrationes inflationes seditiones sint inter vos ...* (II Cor 12. 20).

[127]   Peter, letter 73, *Letters*, I, p. 206.

[128]   Constable, *Letters*, II, p. 147.

[129]   Bernard, ep. 148, *SBO*, VII, p. 352.

[130]   Leclercq, *SBO* VII, p. 352, n. 1.

[131]   *Est hic quem loquimur Gebuinus, mihi et vobis notissimus, mihi vobisque ut credo carissimus* (Peter, letter 73, p. 206).

[132]   Idem, letter 70, *Letters*, I, pp. 202–3.

[133]   Constable, *Letters*, II, p. 144.

[134]   *At ego et vultum nubilum in eo et Guarinum fratrem eius cum eo attendens, intellexi dolos in vulpe latentes ...*, 'But I, giving heed to the cloudy visage in him and his brother Gebuin with him, perceived the guile lying hidden in the fox ...' (letter 70, p. 202). Peter goes on to suggest that his real aim is to 'extort' a prebend promised to his brother, and says that he has sent a messenger to report on Gebuin's behaviour.

[135]   *Scripsi nuper longiores, nunc breviores litteras mitto ...*, 'Recently I wrote a longer letter, now I send a shorter one ...' (letter 73, p. 206).

in the tongue of the bearer'.[136] What follows appears to suggest that the previous letter, too, was to be understood in the light of oral information: 'nor was the cause of that (the former letter) any other than to send the reader to the carrier, and to warn him that what it itself kept silent was to be demanded from him'.[137] If, as Constable suggests, and as seems most likely, the previous letter in question is letter 65,[138] this statement may again cause surprise, since in that letter Peter placed the reliability of messengers in doubt.

According to Bredero, this letter is to be taken as an indication that Bernard had not yet replied to letter 65.[139] In fact, nothing compels this interpretation. Internal evidence indicates that Bernard's ep. 147 was written after the death of Anacletus in late January 1138, and before the ending of the schism in May of that year. Letter 73, as indicated above, can be associated with the letter to Hato dated to mid-March. If, as Constable suggests, Bernard's letter was written in the early part of 1138,[140] it seems quite possible that the letter could have been delivered to Peter in time for letter 73 to serve as a reply.[141] If so, it may be that Peter should be seen as attempting in this letter to smooth over any hostility arising from his previous letter, by hinting that it has been 'misunderstood' by Bernard.

Bernard's ep. 148 is more problematical in that, as seen above, it cannot be dated with any precision, nor does it offer any indication as to where it is being written from. Bernard stayed on at the papal *curia* until the end of the schism, leaving it probably in early June.[142] The letter shares certain features with ep. 147, which indeed may seem to stand out more starkly through the brevity of the letter. There is elaborate play on the opposition between grandeur and humility. This begins in the salutation, which offers *humile dilectionis obsequium*, the 'humble obedience of affection'. It continues with Bernard's delight that *tantus*, 'so great a man', has troubled to anticipate *tantillus*, 'so little a man', in the 'blessings of sweetness', that is, a letter.[143] The opposition is reinforced by verbal play on the notion of condescension. Peter is said to 'deem worthy' meeting and conference.[144] Bernard

---

[136] *quae [litterae] idcirco elingues sunt, quia in lingua latoris confidunt* ... (ibid.).

[137] *nec alia fuit causa illarum, quam ut legentem ad portitorem mitterent, et ab eo exigi quod ipsae reticebant monerent* (ibid.).

[138] See Constable, *Letters*, II, p. 73.

[139] Bredero,'Saint Bernard in his relations', p. 325; idem, *Bernard of Clairvaux*, p. 231.

[140] Constable suggests February/March (Constable, *Letters*, I, p. 147).

[141] Citing Peter's letter 112, Constable argues elsewhere that twenty-four days was seen as somewhat on the slow side for a letter to reach Cluny from Rome (Constable, *Letters*, II, p. 29). Zerbi argues that it was possible for a letter to reach Rome from Sens in a little over a month (P. Zerbi, 'Remarques sur l'epistola 98 de Pierre le Vénérable', in *Pierre Abélard–Pierre le Vénérable. Les courants littéraires et artistiques en occident au milieu du XIIe siècle*, Colloques internationaux du Centre National de la Recherche Scientifique 546, Paris, 1975, 215–32, p. 219; ibid., p. 220, n. 27).

[142] G. Constable, 'The disputed election at Langres in 1138', *Traditio* 13 (1957), 119–52, p. 135.

[143] *Lectis litteris vestris, laetatus sum in eis, quod tantillum videlicet tantus in benedictionibus dulcedinis praevenire curastis* (Bernard, ep. 148, p. 352).

[144] *Ceterum videndi nos invicem et colloquendi pariter, quoniam dignum iudicatis* ..., 'But (the opportunity) of seeing one another and of conferring together, since you deem it worthy ...' (ibid.).

proceeds to ask, 'Otherwise, when would my littleness dare this (to burden you), if the humility of your condescension did not grant access to grandeur?'[145] Although, as seen above, the possibility of a visit is again seemingly raised, here what follows renders it open-ended, even, perhaps, cast in doubt, 'when will that opportunity, the suitable place, the right occasion offer itself?'[146]

Again, Leclercq suggests that this answers a 'missing' letter from Peter.[147] Although, in view of the uncertainties, this must remain a possibility, it is not an inevitable conclusion. Rather, the uncertainties attached here to the proposed visit might suggest that it had been 'blocked' by Peter in the oral messages delivered by Gebuin and accompanying letter 73. Such a negative response might serve to explain Bernard's remark that he has returned *paucis vestris pauca*, 'few (words) in return for your few', and that he will 'give more' when he knows that it will not be *onerosum*, 'burdensome' for Peter.[148] This comment would be in keeping not only with the actual nature of letter 73, but also with a supposition that Bernard is hinting that the visit has been spurned as unwelcome. It appears, indeed, that the visit did not take place. Peter was absent from Cluny and in the region of Aquitaine at some time between June and August.[149] Van den Eynde suggests that he was probably involved in business relating to the aftermath of schism, possibly even dealing with the recalcitrant Gilo of Tusculum.[150]

In this chapter, it has been suggested that letter 65 and ep. 147, its principal focus, cannot be read in isolation, but should be seen both in relation to what has gone before, that is, the debate over *caritas* initiated by the previous interchange, and to the particular circumstances under which they were written, in this case, the politics surrounding the papal schism. The aim, as with the chapters to follow, has been not to present any one definitive reading of this phase of the Peter/Bernard correspondence, but rather to demonstrate that it is capable of generating diametrically opposing readings. Indeed, it seems very possible that the degree of subtle ambiguity diagnosed here should in itself be seen as a result of and a reaction against the damaging polemic of what has gone before. At the same time, the fluidity and flexibility consequently imparted to any potential 'meaning' should perhaps also be related to the possibility of multiple readership, encompassing that of inclusion within a future letter-collection. The next chapter will consider epistolary reactions to two concrete causes of dispute, the polemics surrounding the issue of the giving or withholding of tithes, and the contention relating to the episcopal election held at Langres in 1138, a contention coinciding with, and perhaps triggered by, the return of Bernard from Italy and with that of Peter from Aquitaine.

---

[145] *Alioquin quando hoc ipsum auderet nostra pusillitas, nisi daret ad dignitatem accessum vestrae dignationis humilitas?* (ibid.).

[146] *quando se offeret illa opportunitas, quando conveniens locus, quando iusta occasio?* (ibid.).

[147] Leclercq, *SBO*, VII, p. 352, n. 2.

[148] *Haec interim paucis vestris pauca reddidimus, ampliora libenter donaturi, cum ea vobis onerosa non fore cognoverimus* (ep. 148, p. 352).

[149] According to Constable, it was July and August (Constable, *Letters*, II, p. 260; idem, 'Langres', pp. 135–6.) Van den Eynde raises the possibility of a slightly earlier date (van den Eynde, 'Principaux voyages', pp. 108–9).

[150] Van den Eynde, ibid., p. 109. The latter suggestion depends upon the date of Peter's arrival in Aquitaine. Gilo is known to have set out for Rome by the beginning of July (ibid.).

Chapter 4

Fraudulent Alms and Monstrous Election: Peter, Letter 29

The two principal letters discussed in the previous chapter, Peter's letter 65 and Bernard's ep. 147, are set within what appears to be a period of worsening relations between Cluniacs and Cistercians, marked at one end by disputes about tithes, and at the other by a disputed episcopal election in the diocese of Langres. As stated previously, letter 65, written in late 1137, offers no clear statement of its purpose. In consequence, the motivating causes for Peter's covert reopening of the question of Cluniac–Cistercian relations at this point can only be conjectured. Bredero links his suggestion that the letter conceals an 'oral altercation' with Cistercian non-payment of tithes, an issue which had become a bone of contention in the decade post 1130.[1] Receiving tithes had formed one of the accusations against the Cluniacs in letter 28.[2] Cluny itself possessed exemption from paying tithes, first granted in 931,[3] and reconfirmed by subsequent papal privileges.[4] This privilege, however, was apparently not automatically exercised.[5] In 1132, the Cistercians had also been

---

[1] Bredero, 'Saint Bernard in his relations', pp. 325–6; idem, *Bernard of Clairvaux*, pp. 232–3.

[2] *Ecclesiarum parrochialium primitiarum et decimarum possessiones quae ratio vobis contulit, cum haec omnia non ad monachos sed ad clericos canonica sanctione pertineant?*, 'What justification has conferred upon you the possession of the first-fruits and tithes of parish churches, when all these by canonic sanction pertain not to monks but to clerics?' (Peter, letter 28, p. 56). Peter's defence draws a satirical contrast between deserving monks and undeserving clerics: *Qui namque iustius fidelium oblata suscipiunt, monachi qui assidue pro peccatis offerentium intercedunt, an clerici qui nunc ut videmus summo studio temporalia appetentes spiritualia et quae ad animarum salutem pertinent omnino postponunt?*, 'For who more justly receive the offerings of the faithful, the monks who assiduously intercede for the sins of the offerants, or the clerics who now, as we see, seeking the temporal with all their effort, completely neglect the spiritual and what pertains to the salvation of souls?' (ibid., pp. 81–2).

[3] Under Pope John XI = JL 3584 (P. Jaffé, *Regesta pontificum Romanorum*, 2nd ed., F. Kaltenbrunner, P. Ewald and S. Löwenfeld, 2 vols, Leipzig, 1885–88).

[4] JL 3648; JL 3895. See G. Constable, 'Cluniac tithes and the controversy between Gigny and Le Miroir', *Revue Bénédictine* 70 (1960), 591–624, pp. 605–6, reprinted in G. Constable, *Cluniac studies*, Variorum Reprints, London, 1980; idem, *Monastic tithes from their origins to the twelfth century*, Cambridge Studies in Medieval Life and Thought 10, Cambridge, 1964.

[5] So, at least, Peter claims in two letters on the subject to be discussed subsequently (Peter, letter 33 to Innocent, *Letters*, I, pp. 107–9; idem, letter 34 to Haimeric, the papal chancellor, ibid., pp. 109–13.) In the first of these he states that for more than two hundred years, Cluny has paid tithes *indifferenter omnibus*, 'without differentiation to all' (letter 33, p. 108). In the

granted exemption from the payment of tithes by Innocent II.[6] Constable draws attention to the increasing importance of tithes in the monastic economy, particularly that of Cluny.[7] In consequence, conflict could, and did, arise between individual institutions in close proximity, where Cistercians acquired lands from which tithes were paid to the Cluniacs.[8] The most serious of these, the dispute between the Cluniac priory of Gigny and the Cistercian abbey of Le Miroir, flared up in the course of the 1130s. It would culminate, as will be seen in a subsequent chapter, in an attack on the Cistercian institution in 1152, and the imposition of heavy damages on the Cluniacs.

At some time after 1132, Peter the Venerable wrote four letters attacking Cistercian non-payment of tithes. Letter 33, to Innocent II, and letter 34, to Haimeric, cardinal and papal chancellor,[9] are protesting against a decree to take effect within forty days, banning Gigny from holding divine offices, 'on account of their tithes sought from their parish'.[10] Two other letters, 35[11] and 36,[12] are addressed to the generality of the Cistercian abbots. The first of these makes no specific reference to Gigny, only to 'the law-suit of tithes which is now being conducted',[13] but the strong similarity of the language and gambits employed in all three letters suggests a close connection between them. Letter 36, written a year later, talks of the threat to charity 'by reason of those tithes'.[14] The letters cannot be definitively dated, but a probable allusion in letter 34 to the papal schism as still in

---

second, the claim is given rhetorical amplification, together with a satirical twist: *(cum) nos monachis, clericis, canonicis regularibus, et si posset dici saecularibus, monialibus, militibus, raptoribus etiam [decimas] persolvamus*, '(when) we pay [tithes] to monks, clerics, canons regular and, if it could be said, secular, nuns, knights, even robbers' (letter 34, p. 110). The claim appears to be confirmed by Constable (Constable,'Cluniac tithes', p. 606).

[6]   JL 7537. See Constable, 'Cluniac tithes', pp. 606–7; idem, *Monastic tithes*, pp. 241–2.

[7]   Constable, 'Cluniac tithes', p. 595 and n. 4; idem, *Monastic tithes*, pp. 107–9 and n. 5. Constable's claim that Peter estimated tithes as making up one tenth of Cluny's income is based on a statement by the latter which may betray some rhetorical exaggeration. Peter states that Cluny is so surrounded by new institutions *ut, si omnibus decimas indulserimus, iam decimam fere numeri nostri partem perdamus*, 'that, if we indulge tithes to all, we would lose nearly a tenth part of our number' (Peter, letter 33, p. 108). Peter seems to be playing here on the correspondence between *decima pars* and *decimae*, the whole forming part of a pressurising device, to the effect that Cluny will be forced to diminish either in numbers or in number of institutions. On the importance to Cluny of tithes in general see Duby, 'Un inventaire des profits'; Iogna-Prat, *Ordonner et exclure*, pp. 77–9.

[8]   Constable, 'Cluniac tithes', pp. 607–8.

[9]   According to Constable, Haimeric was papal chancellor from 1123 to 1141 (Constable, *Letters*, II, pp. 98–9). Leclercq, however, gives the later date of 1126 (Leclercq, *SBO*, III, p. 111). Schmale comments that Peter's appeal to 'friendship' was 'in vain' (Schmale, *Schisma*, p. 168; see also ibid., pp. 188–9).

[10]   *propter repetitas parrochiae suae decimas suas* (letter 33, p. 108).

[11]   Peter, letter 35, *Letters*, I, pp. 113–16.

[12]   Idem, letter 36, ibid., pp. 116–17.

[13]   *(in) causa ista quae nunc agitur decimarum* (letter 35, p. 116).

[14]   *quam (caritatem) in cordibus nostrorum decimarum illarum occasione periclitari videbam*, 'which I saw to be in danger in the hearts of ours by reason of those tithes' (letter 36, p. 117).

progress puts it before 1138.[15] Constable accordingly proposes a date between 1135 and 1137 for the beginning of the controversy.[16]

The precise sequence of events is difficult to determine. According to Constable, some kind of official tribunal had sat at Rome, to which both sides had been summoned and which had been attended by a messenger from Cluny. The sentence of interdiction had then been passed without further summons.[17] This seems to be based on Peter's letter to Haimeric, where Peter lays stress on the supposed illegality of the action. The sentence is said to have been passed 'without summons, without audience':[18] 'to pass judgement in anticipation on matters which have not been examined, what else is it than to condemn someone in their absence by the decision of an arbitrator alone?'[19] Peter makes no reference to attendance at any previous tribunal, nor is it clear that the charge of illegality is other than a rhetorical ploy.[20] He does, however, defend himself against an accusation of having fraudulently obtained *quaedam litterae*, 'a certain letter' or 'certain letters',[21] interpreted by Constable as 'some papal documents'.[22] Peter goes on to make it clear that this has to do with *capitulum*, an 'article' sent via a messenger, which, according to him, asked the Pope to write to those of Le Miroir, to the effect that the tithes be restored.[23] This seems to leave open the possibility that Peter had put

---

[15] *Novit prudentia vestra ecclesiam dei unguento ... indigere ..., maxime hoc tempore, quando viribus exhaustis, magna pars ipsius membris trementibus nutat ...,* 'Your Prudence knows that the Church of God is in need of a soothing balm ..., especially at this time, when, its strength exhausted, a great part of it totters, with trembling limbs.. ' (letter 34, p. 112).

[16] Constable, 'Cluniac tithes', pp. 615–17.

[17] Ibid., p. 615.

[18] *Iam de sententia super Gigniacenses, absque vocatione absque audientia prolata, quid dicam non invenio,* 'Now I cannot find what to say concerning the sentence passed on the monks of Gigny, brought forth without summons, without audience' (letter 34, p. 112).

[19] *Ante autem de indiscussis sententiam ferre, quid est aliud quam solo arbitrio absentem damnare?* (ibid.); *Quando enim solo arbitrio, sine iudicio, quaelibet ... muliercula suo iure ab apostolica iustitia spoliata est?*, 'For when has ... any worthless woman been deprived by apostolic justice of her right by the decision of an arbitrator alone, without judicial investigation?' (ibid., p. 110).

[20] The language can be paralleled, for example, in a complaint relating to the expulsion of the Cluniac monks of St Paul at Verdun in favour of Premonstratensian canons: *Quodque nec de furibus fit, antequam audiatur (ordo iste) condemnatur, antequam sub iudice de culpa agatur, proscribitur, ante reatum cognitum ut reus addicitur,* 'And what does not happen even in the case of thieves, it (that order) is condemned before being heard, proscribed before blame is established in a court of law, adjudged guilty before guilt is known' (Peter, letter 47 to Matthew of Albano, *Letters*, I, p. 47).

[21] *Sed et illud quod in eadem domini nostri epistola continebatur, quasdam sibi litteras fraudulenter extortas, non parum mihi et his qui audierant stuporem ingessit,* 'But as to the charge which was contained in the same letter of the lord Pope, that (a) certain letter(s) had been fraudulently extorted from him, it caused no little amazement in myself and those who heard it' (letter 34, p. 112.)

[22] Constable, 'Cluniac tithes', p. 615.

[23] *recolo ... me ... capitulum in haec verba transmisisse. Ut monachis de Miratorio.. scribatur, ut decimas reddant,* 'I remember that ... I ... sent an article to this effect, that it should be written to the monks of Le Miroir.. that they should restore the tithes' (letter 34, p. 112).

pressure on Innocent to intervene, and that this action had somehow been turned
back against him, precipitating the papal interdiction.

Three main motifs run through these letters: old versus new, rich versus poor, the
danger of *scandalum*, 'scandal', 'stumbling-block'. They are handled to different
effect in each case, according to the nature of the individual letter and the identity
of the recipient(s). The letter to Innocent mounts a relatively straightforward
'defence', based on Cluny's record, founded in tradition, of receiving and paying
tithes, and spiced with the threat that an adverse judgement will see Peter's
retirement from office.[24] The letter to Haimeric goes further, employing elaborate
imagery, and launching a scathing attack on Cluny's opponents with similar
techniques to those found in letter 28. The first letter to the Cistercians, on the other
hand, is couched more obliquely. It mounts a discreet two-pronged offensive, based
on the weapons of *caritas* and *fama*, the whole being presented under the guise of
the friendly warnings of *amicitia*.[25] Significantly, however, as will be seen, it
contains what can be read as veiled allusions to the *Apologia*.

The opposition between old and new appears in its most developed form in the
letter to Innocent. It is introduced through the standard relationship of papal
father/monastic son, 'Your community.. asks that new sons should not expel old
from a father's love, since although the new should be loved, the old should not be
cast away on account of the new, unless they have deserved it.'[26] This is then
developed through an appeal to the claims of primogeniture, supported by the
exemplum of Esau and Jacob: 'Remember how much honour was shown by the
ancients among the people of God to the first-born, so that if Esau had not sold his
birthright, never would Jacob, albeit holier, be I do not say preferred, but even
compared to him in authority of primogeniture. If, therefore, we are the first-born,
it is right that we should not lose what we have not sold for the benefit of younger
sons.'[27] 'Not selling one's birthright' can perhaps be equated with the Cluniac
'refusal' to take advantage of their privilege of exemption from tithes, by which
they might have been seen to forfeit their right to their 'inheritance'. The reference
to Jacob's greater 'holiness' appears to compliment the Cistercians. At the same
time, the allusion may also serve to evoke the biblical sequel, whereby Jacob, the

---

[24]   *Si aliter res processerit ... aut sua mecum ecclesia retinebit, aut sine me hucusque iuste
possessis carebit*, 'If the matter goes forward otherwise ... either the church (of Cluny) will
retain its possessions with me, or it will be bereft of what its has justly possessed up until
now without me' (letter 34, p. 109).

[25]   These three aspects are brought together at the conclusion: *consulo ut amicus, ut ... vobis
pariter et nobis consulatis, vobis ne infamiam, nobis ne violentiam inferatis, et ne nobis simul
ac vobis caritatem ... auferatis*, 'I counsel as a friend, that ... you take thought for yourselves
and us alike, lest you inflict infamy on yourselves, violence on us, and take away charity ...
from us and yourselves together' (letter 35, p. 116).

[26]   *Rogat ... congregatio vestra, ut ab amore paterno novi filii veteres non expellant,
quoniam etsi novi diligendi non tamen propter novos nisi promuerint sunt veteres abiciendi*
(letter 33, p. 108).

[27]   *Recordamini quantum ab antiquis in populo dei primogenitis deferretur, ut nisi Esau
primogenita vendidisset, nunquam ei licet sanctior Iacob in primogenitorum dignitate non
dico praeferretur, sed nec etiam conferretur. Si ergo primogeniti sumus, dignum est ut quod
non vendidimus, pro iunioribus non perdamus* (ibid., p. 109).

younger son, through deception and disguise, tricks Esau, the elder, out of their father's blessing while the latter is absent, fulfilling their father's bequest.[28]

The same opposition appears in the letter to Haimeric under two guises. The first contrasts the 'many and ancient' privileges of the Cluniacs with the 'singular and new' privilege (of exemption) 'claimed' by the Cistercians.[29] The second comprises a 'threat', that loss of tithes may cause the numbers of the Cluniacs to be drastically reduced: 'through the grace of God, so great is the multiplication of the new crop that if, as they demand, the old are compelled to give way to the new, the former crops must go to ruin'.[30] It seems to be this phrase that Constable has in mind, when he states that the dispute was due to the 'exceptional size of the new harvest', and argues that it probably took place in the harvest season.[31] In fact, the 'new crop' picks up the notion of the rapid gowth of new institutions already signalled in the letter to Innocent, and is surely metaphorical.[32] There may be a third, hidden allusion. The 'storm', that is, the interdiction on Gigny, is said to have arisen *novo ordine*, 'by a new order' or 'by a novel dispensation', which has changed 'day to night' and disturbed the 'calm face of heaven'.[33] The motif of cosmic upheaval is not unfamiliar,[34] but the wording here may conceal the suggestion that the interdiction is the result of Cistercian manipulation.[35]

---

[28]   Gn 27. 1–41.

[29]   *Inde habent Cluniacenses plura et vetera, unde Cistercienses singularia et nova se dicunt habere privilegia* (letter 34, p. 111).

[30]   *tanta est per gratiam dei multiplicatio novae segetis, ut si velut illi exigunt novis veteres coguntur caedere antiquos labores oporteat deperire* (ibid., p. 111).

[31]   Constable, 'Cluniac tithes', p. 616.

[32]   *tanta ... est ... ipsorum (Cisterciensium) et aliorum religiosorum ubique terrarum in circuitu nostro numerositas, ut si omnibus decimas indulserimus, iam decimam fere numeri nostri partem perdamus*, 'so great ... is ... the multitude of themselves (the Cistercians) and of other monks everywhere in the vicinity of our lands, that if we indulge tithes to all, we would lose nearly a tenth part of our number' (letter 33, p. 108).

[33]   *Sed nunc novo ordine de luce tenebrae ortae sunt, dies in noctem mutatus, serena caeli facies in horrendam tempestatem conversa*, 'But now, by a new order, darkness has sprung up from light, day has been turned to night, the bright face of heaven has been turned into dreadful storm' (letter 34, p. 110).

[34]   *Rerum natura mutata est; oriens in occasum conversus est* ..., 'The natural order has been changed; east has been turned into west .. ' (Peter, letter 5 to Hato of Troyes, *Letters*, I, p. 9). In that letter the motif leads into the complaint of loss of friendship. At a deeper level, however, it may also relate to the upheaval of the papal schism (see Knight, 'Uses and abuses of *amicitia*', pp. 39–42).

[35]   In the first part of the letter, the metaphor of the storm has been developed at some length, with Cluny as the 'little ship', Peter as Jonah, and Innocent as the captain: *si propter peccata mea.. tempestas haec contra Christi naviculam quam ... perita manus illius regit insurrexit, ...* tollat me et mittat in mare, *tantum cesset mare a naufragantibus*, 'if, on account of my sins ... this storm has arisen against the little vessel of Christ which ... his skilful hand directs ... *let him take me and cast me into the sea*, provided that *the sea* may cease *from* those suffering shipwreck' (letter 34, p. 110 = Ion 1. 12, with *cesset* replacing *cessabit*.) If Peter is not a disobedient Jonah, as the introduction of *tantum*, 'only', 'provided that', and the replacement of the future *cessabit*, 'will cease', by the subjunctive may seem to suggest, the storm may be due to human rather than divine intervention. In another letter to Hato of

The same motif makes a brief but telling appearance in the letter to the Cistercian abbots: 'I bring forward only this, that new are subject to old, sons to fathers, by the order of justice, and that it is dangerous if what the Church is agreed to have maintained up until now preserving faith and charity, were to be changed.'[36] *Iustitia*, 'justice', has both legal and spiritual connotations. In its sense of 'righteousness', conduct in accordance with divine law, it is a key element in the attainment of salvation, and as such figured prominently in Bernard's *Apologia*.[37] In letter 28 the Cistercians were presented as the proponents of tradition. Here they appear as promoting a change harmful to *caritas*. Throughout this letter, as will be seen, they will be warned, directly and indirectly, that their behaviour is putting their own salvation at risk.

The opposition between rich and poor is not used in the letter to Innocent, but is heavily exploited in the one to Haimeric. Placed initially in the mouth of 'unnamed' opponents, it is seemingly dissociated from the Cistercians:[38] 'Certain people, generous with the property of others, say: "These are poor, those are rich. Therefore the rich should help the poorer." '[39] Peter's next words, *et recte*, 'and rightly', appear to endorse the claim. Subsequently, however, he will undermine it, by subverting scripture to prove that the need of the Cluniacs is greater, and that the action of their opponents is contrary to justice, human and divine. A citation from Ecclesiastes is made to justify Cluny's retention of its tithes, 'But let them pay attention to the words of Solomon: *Where there are many* riches, *there are also many who devour them.*'[40] Taken from a context dealing with the oppression of the poor and the futility of wealth, the original continues by opposing the 'sweet rest' of the labourer to the sleepless 'satiety' of the rich man.[41] Peter transposes this into

---

Troyes, dated to 1138, Peter employs a series of images, culminating in that of a shooting-star, which brightens the night only to leave behind a thicker darkness, to depress the pretensions of an over-zealous and newly appointed Cistercian bishop (Peter, letter 69, *Letters*, I, p. 200). See Constable, *Letters*, II, p. 143.

[36]   *Hoc tantum infero, antiquis modernos, patribus filios, iustitiae ordine subdi, et quod ecclesiam constat salva fide et caritate hactenus tenuisse, periculosum si mutetur existere* (letter 35, p. 115).

[37]   *Apo*, IV. 8–9.

[38]   Clanchy comments that this technique of *denominatio*, the non-naming of opponents, is much used by Peter the Venerable, whom he dubs a 'Ciceronian' (M. T. Clanchy, *Abelard, a medieval life*, Oxford, 1997, p. 320). The technique appears twice more in this letter, in contexts connoting detraction and deception: *(Quod) si quilibet hoc patris nostri auribus insusurravit* ..., 'If anyone has whispered (this) into the ears of our father ...' (letter 35, p. 112); *quia mirum.. videri non debet, si homini tantis totius mundi curis in diversa distracto quilibet sua quaerens subripere potuit* ..., 'because it should not seem ... wonderful, if anyone seeking his own has been able to impose upon a man torn in different directions by such great cares of the whole world ...' (ibid., p. 113). The latter contains an allusion to I Cor 13. 5, where it is said of *caritas*, *non quaerit quae sua sunt*, 'it does not seek its own'.

[39]   *Sed aiunt quidam de alieno munifici:* Hi pauperes sunt, illi divites. Debent ergo divites pauperioribus subvenire (letter 34, p. 111).

[40]   *Sed attendant quod ait Salomon:* Ubi multae *divitiae*, multi et qui comedunt eas (ibid. = Ecl 5. 10, with *divitiae* replacing *opes*).

[41]   *Dulcis est somnus operanti sive parum sive multum comedat saturitas autem divitis non sinit dormire eum*, 'Sweet is sleep for the labourer whether he should eat little or much, but the satiety of the rich man does not allow him to sleep' (Ecl 5. 11).

the 'fullness' of the poor man and the 'beggarly state' of the king who must provide for many thousands.[42] As will be seen, this subversion may be countering alleged subversion of scripture on the part of the Cistercians and their supporters.

Citations from Leviticus[43] and Exodus,[44] to the effect that the law must not discriminate between rich and poor, serve to introduce a section of heavy sarcasm: 'If charity is to be expended upon the poor man, is injury to be inflicted by the poor man? If alms are to be given to him, is rapine to be exercised by him? It is a monstrous kind of pillage, if holy poor men are to labour to extort from the rich, what the wicked rich were accustomed to take away from the poor.'[45] The paradoxical link forged here between 'alms' and 'extortion' is echoed elsewhere in the letter: 'When has an offering pleasing to God been made from the goods of others extorted by violence?';[46] 'what is freely offered to God is one thing, what is violently taken away is another'.[47]

Subsequently, extortion is linked with 'fraud', through the issue of the 'fraudulent letter(s)' supposedly extorted by Peter from Innocent. The *reductio ad absurdum* which follows emphasises the notions of fraud and extortion, while

---

[42] *Et quandoque ditior est pauper in tugurio, quam rex in solio, quia ille, si satur est, iam nullius eget, iste multis milibus dum providere non sufficit, mendicat,* 'And sometimes the poor man in his hut is richer than the king on his throne, since the former, if he is full, now needs nothing, and the latter, while he has not the means to provide for many thousands, goes begging' (letter 34, p. 111). As Constable suggests, the sentiments can be compare to those found in a passage of Augustine: *Plus est enim pauperi videre caelum stellatum, quam diviti tectum inauratum,* 'For it is more for the poor man to see the starry sky than for a rich man to see a gilded roof' (Augustine, *Enarrationes in Psalmos*, CXXVII, 16, ed. D. E. Dekkers and I. Fraipont, 3 vols, *CCSL*, 38–40, Turnhout, 1956, 40, p. 1879). The use of *tugurium*, 'hut' might also, however, point towards a passage from Virgil's *Eclogues*:

en umquam patrios longo post tempore fines,
pauperis et tuguri congestum caespite culmen
post aliquot, mea regna videns, mirabor aristas?
impius haec tam culta novalia miles habebit?
(Virgil, *Eclogues*, I, 67–70).

'Lo, shall I ever, seeing my native territory after a long time and the roof of a poor hut, piled high with turf, my kingdom, wonder at a few ears of corn? Shall an impious soldier possess these so cultivated fields?' The translation follows the interpretation offered by Page (*P. Vergili Maronis, Bucolica et Georgica*, ed. T. E. Page, 1898, reprinted London; Melbourne; Toronto; New York, 1968, p. 101); cf. Clausen (W. Clausen, *A commentary on Virgil's Eclogues*, Oxford, 1994, p. 58). The context, one of forced dispossession in favour of 'foreign soldiers', might appear to lend an added irony to Peter's complaint.

[43] Non *accipies inquit lex aeterna* personam pauperis, nec honores vultum potentis, ' "You will *not* approve", says the eternal law, "*the person of the poor man, nor honour the face of the powerful man*" ' (letter 34, p. 111 = Lv 19. 15).

[44] *Pauperis quoque non misereberis in iudicio,'You will not pity the poor man also in judgement'* (ibid. = Ex 23. 3).

[45] *Si misericordia impendenda est pauperi, nunquid irroganda est iniuria a paupere? Si danda est ei elemosina, nunquid exercenda est ab eo rapina? Monstruosum praedae genus, si laborent divitibus sancti pauperes extorquere, quod pessimi divites pauperibus solebant auferre* (letter 34, p. 111).

[46] *Quando de aliorum bonis violenter extortis grata deo oblatio facta est?* (ibid., p. 110).

[47] *aliud est quod sponte deo offertur, aliud quod violenter aufertur* (ibid., p. 111).

deflecting attention away from the significance of the document on to the circumstances under which it was obtained: 'Whose fraud could this be here, I ask? If the bearer's, it is a wonder that such an insignificant little man could deceive such great judges of the world. If the article's, no less wonderful. For since it is called fraud when falsity is alleged, and truth hidden, out of a desire to deceive, how was a letter "fraudulently extorted", which hid none of the truth in a desire to deceive, and alleged no falsehood?'[48] 'Extortion' and 'deception' are accordingly presented as charges originating from Cluny's opponents, and subsequently turned back against them in connection with alms.

The explanation of this linguistic nexus (alms/fraud/extortion) may be found in the biblical parable of the 'steward of injustice',[49] and the subsequent treatment of it by Augustine. The parable recounts how, threatened with dismissal for wasting his master's goods, the steward is said to have gone round the master's debtors, winning their favour by letting them off a portion of their dues. It concludes with the statement that, 'the lord praised the steward of injustice because he had acted prudently',[50] followed by the admonition, 'make for yourselves friends from the mammon of injustice, so that when you fail they may receive you into the eternal tabernacles'.[51] Exegesis interpreted the parable as a reminder of the need to take thought for the future life; it also linked it with giving alms.[52] Augustine, however, on several occasions warns against interpreting the parable over-literally as an encouragement to bestow alms obtained by fraud.[53] Peter, therefore, is presenting

---

48   *Cuius hic rogo fraus esse potuit? Si cursoris, mirum est, quod tantillus homullulus tantos orbis iudices fallere potuit. Si capituli, neque hoc minus mirum. Nam cum fraus dicatur quando studio fallendi falsitas praetenditur, veritas occultatur, quomodo fraudulenter litterae extortae sunt, quae nihil veritatis studio fallendi occultaverunt, nihil falsitatis praetulerunt?* (ibid., p. 112).

49   Lc 16. 1–12. This parable will be directly cited in letter 192, Peter's final letter to Bernard, again in the context of the conflict over tithes.

50   *et laudavit dominus vilicum iniquitatis quia prudenter fecisset* (Lc 16. 8).

51   *facite vobis amicos de mamona iniquitatis ut cum defeceritis recipiant vos in aeterna tabernacula* (ibid., 16. 9).

52   *Et improperat nobis ipse dominus dicens:* Prudentiores sunt filii tenebrarum quam filii lucis; *quia nos neglegimus futura in caelis nobis praevidere, cum ille in terris prudenter sibi prospexisset ... Mamona aurum est; ut hii, qui pecuniae deserviunt et aurum colunt pro deo, faciant sibi redemptionem peccatorum suorum dispensando pauperibus, ut, cum defecerint de hoc saeculo, recipiantur ab angelis vel a sanctis in aeterna tabernacula,* 'And the Lord himself chides us, saying: *More prudent are the sons of darkness than the sons of light,* because we neglect to provide for the future in heaven, while he had prudently provided for himself on earth ... Mammon is gold; that those who serve money and worship gold as a god, should make for themselves redemption for their sins by expending money on the poor, so that when they die from this world, they may be received by the angels or the saints into the eternal tabernacles' (Epiphanius Latinus, *Interpretatio Evangeliorum*, LI, ed. A. Hamman, *PL supplementum* 3, Paris, 1964, 930–31).

53   In vilico quem Dominus eiecebat de vilicatu, et laudavit eum quod in futurum sibi prospexerit, *non omnia debemus ad imitandum sumere. Non enim aut domino nostro facienda est in aliquo fraus, ut de ipsa fraude elemosinas faciamus ...,* 'In the (story of the) steward, whom the Lord threw out from his stewardship, and praised him because he took thought for himself for the future, we should not take everything to imitate. For fraud must

the supporters of the Cistercians as trying to gain spiritual profit for themselves at the expense of the Cluniacs. The contrast between wealth and poverty reappears in the letter to the Cistercians abbots, where it is attributed to the Cistercians themselves, and linked with the charge of 'superfluity'.[54] Again, the retaining of tithes is linked with violence and injustice.[55]

The third motif found in these letters, that of avoiding *scandalum*, is invoked in relation to the Cluniac refusal to exercise their privilege of exemption from tithes in both the letter to Innocent and the letter to Haimeric, in conjunction with a citation from *Matthew*, 'woe to him through whom scandal comes'.[56] In the latter case, however, the motif is first extended, then turned back against the 'opponents'. Peter claims that the Cluniacs abrogated their privilege, 'lest, being the origin and cause of scandals, they should be judged worthy *that a mill-stone should be hung around* their *necks and they should be sunk in the depths of the sea*'.[57] The image can be seen to pick up and reverse the direction of an earlier depiction of the Cluniacs as *naufragantes*, 'suffering shipwreck' in the present 'storm' over Gigny.[58]

---

not be committed against our Lord in anything(one), so that we may make alms from fraud itself ...' (Augustine, *Quaestiones evangeliorum*, II, XXXIV, 1, ed. A. Mutzenbecker, *CCSL*, 44B, Turnhout, 1980, p. 84); *Hoc quidem male intellegendo rapiunt res alienas, et aliquid inde pauperibus largiuntur, et putant se facere quod praeceptum est ... Nolo sic intelligatis. De iustis laboribus facite eleemosynas; ex eo quod recte habetis date*, 'Understanding this badly, they seize the property of others, and bestow something thence on the poor, and think that they are doing what was ordered ... I do not want you to understand it thus. Give alms from just labours; give from what you rightly have' (Augustine, *Sermones de scripturis veteris et novi testamenti*, CXIII, II. 2, ed. J.-P. Migne, *Patrologia Latina* 38, Paris, 1865, 648–9).

[54] Sed angit nos, *inquiunt aliqui vestrorum*, paupertas, ' "But", say some of yours, "poverty distresses us" ' (letter 35, p. 115); *Sed forte dicitis hanc scandalorum sententiam nostros magis arguere, qui quod eis superfluit, nolunt pauperioribus erogare*, 'But perhaps you say that this pronouncement on stumbling-blocks rather convicts ours, who are unwilling to give to those who are poorer, what is superfluous for them' (ibid.). The third section of the *Apologia* had attacked *vanitates et superfluitates*, the 'vanities and superfluities', to be seen in many monasteries (*Apo* VIII. 16).

[55] Si ditior non vult pauperiori propria tribuere, pauperior debet ditiori sua auferre? Quis magis videtur iniustus, dives parcus, an pauper violentus? Quis maiore dignus est supplicio, retentor propriorum an raptor alienorum?, 'If the richer does not wish to concede his own to the poorer, should the poorer deprive the richer of his property? Who seems the more unjust, the niggardly rich man, or the violent poor man? Who is more deserving of punishment, the one who keeps his own property or the one who seizes what belongs to others?' (letter 35, p. 115).

[56] noluerunt tamen uti hac potestate, scientes scriptum esse, vae illi per quem scandalum venit, 'however, they refused to make use of this privilege, knowing that it is written, *woe to him through whom scandal comes*' (letter 33, p. 108 = Mt 18. 7); *Sed scientes sententiam domini*, vae illi per quem scandalum venit, *nolunt uti potestate concessa*, 'But knowing the pronouncement of the Lord, *woe to him through whom scandal comes*, they refuse to make use of the privilege conceded' (letter 34, p. 111 = ibid.).

[57] ne existentes origo et causa scandalorum, digni iudicentur ut suspendatur mola asinaria in collo *eorum* et demergantur in profundum maris (letter 34, p. 111 = Mt 18. 6).

[58] tantum cesset mare a *naufragantibus* ..., 'provided that *the sea* may cease *from* those suffering shipwreck' (ibid., p. 110 = Ion 1. 12). See above.

Later, the motif of *scandalum* will be directed against those who are putting *caritas* in danger: 'such a scandal is being prepared from there as may indeed begin in our time, but may never be ended in our age'.[59]

The use made of the motif in the letter to the Cistercians is given a more subtle development. Here, the same citations from the Gospels are posed as general questions rather than being applied directly to either party.[60] The citation which follows, taken from I Corinthians, equates the (illicit) keeping of tithes with 'eating food for idols': 'Where is the Apostle's saying, "*I will not eat flesh for ever, lest I scandalise my brother?*"' Surely these words should be yours also, "I will not eat from these tithes for ever, lest I scandalise my brother'?" '[61] The Pauline passage from which this is taken begins by opposing 'knowledge' to charity,[62] and develops into a warning: 'We know that an idol is nothing in the world ... But knowledge is not in all. Some indeed, in their consciousness until now of the idol, eat as if of offerings to idols, and their conscience, since it is infirm, is polluted ... See to it that this freedom of yours does not become a stumbling-block to the weak.'[63] The context is one of Jews and Gentiles, the culminating statement, 'All things are allowed, but not all are expedient. All things are allowed, but not all are edifying',[64] had been employed in the *Apologia*, in a context pointing to the superiority of the Cistercian way.[65] Peter is surely exploiting this claim to 'superior spirituality' and turning it against them. They alone may be able to safely retain the tithes which they condemn others for claiming, but in so doing, they will 'drive to sin' their 'weaker brethren', who will be led to imitate them.[66]

The letter to the Cistercian abbots contains another, concealed reference to *scandalum*, which may serve to reinforce the warning. The dispute over tithes is

---

[59]   *tale inde scandalum praeparatur, quod nostro quidem tempore incipere, sed nostra nunquam aetate valeat terminari* (ibid., p. 111).

[60]   *Et ubi est quod dominus ait,* vae illi per quem scandalum venit? *Et iterum:* Expedit ei ut suspendatur mola asinaria in collo eius, et demergatur in profundum maris, 'And where is what the Lord says, *woe to him through whom scandal comes*? And again: *It is meet for him that a mill-stone be hung around his neck, and that he be sunk in the depths of the sea*' (letter 35, p. 115 = Mt 18. 7; ibid., 18. 6).

[61]   *Ubi est quod ait apostolus,* non manducabo carnem in aeternum, ne fratrem meum scandalizem? *Nonne et haec vox vestra esse deberet, non manducabo ex decimis his in aeternum, ne fratrem meum scandalizem?* (letter 35, p. 115 = I Cor 8. 13).

[62]   *De his autem quae idolis sacrificantur scimus quod omnes scientiam habemus scientia inflat caritas vero aedificat,* 'Concerning the things which are sacrificed to idols we know that we all have knowledge. Knowledge puffs up, but charity edifies' (I Cor 8. 1).

[63]   *Scimus quia nihil est idolum in mundo ... Sed non in omnibus est scientia quidam autem conscientia usque nunc idoli quasi idolothytum manducant et conscientia ipsorum cum sit infirma polluitur ... Videte autem ne forte haec licentia vestra offendiculum fiat infirmibus* (I Cor 8. 4–9).

[64]   *Omnia licent sed non omnia expediunt omnia licent, sed non omnia aedificant* (ibid., 10. 22–3).

[65]   *Apo*, IV. 7.

[66]   On two occasions in the *Apologia* Bernard had alluded to the possibility that his criticism might give rise to *scandalum*, 'offence' (*Apo*, VII. 15; ibid., XII. 30). Peter had ended letter 28 with the demand that the 'stumbling-block' of doubt be 'taken away' (letter 28, p. 101). See Chapter 3, n. 10.

presented as the work of the Devil, through an allusion to the parable of the tares sown among the good wheat by the action *inimicus*, of an 'enemy'.[67] In the parable, the master gives orders that at the time of harvest the tares be collected separately and burnt.[68] In its biblical context, the spiritual significance of this is spelled out: 'Just as the tares are collected and burnt in the fire, so it will be at the end of the world. The Son of Man will send his angels, and they will collect from his kingdom all the scandals and those who work unrighteousness, and they will put them into the furnace of the fire.'[69] Again, therefore, the letter seems to be hinting that the Cistercians are endangering the salvation for which they strive. That this letter caused offence is clear from letter 36, written in the following year.[70] Unsurprisingly, letter 36 is briefer and much more guarded: none-the-less, Peter returns to the attack, by insinuating that they 'mis-read' his letter, which, he insists, was written out of *caritas*.[71] This surely hints at the need to apply *iudicium veritatis*, the 'judgement of truth' as invoked by Augustine,[72] that is, *oculus simplex*, the 'single eye' of the Gospels.[73] The latter had already been invoked by Peter in letter 28.[74] It will emerge as a dominant motif in his second 'open' letter to Bernard.[75]

What part, if any, Bernard played in this controversy over tithes is unclear. The letters discussed above, as Constable points out, can be only loosely dated, between the outer limits of 1132, when the Cistercian privilege of exemption was granted, and Haimeric's last appearance as papal chancellor in 1141.[76] He suggests, however, that Peter's mention in letter 34 of a 'decree' which is endangering charity[77] may refer to a statute emanating from the Council of Pisa in 1135, extending the privilege of exemption to monks and regular canons.[78] A consequent

---

[67]   *et* inimicus *homo semini divino nocturnum* superseminavit zizania, 'and the *hostile* man *sowed tares in the night over* the divine seed' (letter 35, p. 114 = Mt 13. 25).

[68]   Mt 13. 30.

[69]   *Sicut ergo colliguntur zizania et igni comburuntur sic erit in consummatione saeculi mittet Filius hominis angelos suos et colligent de regno eius omnia scandala et eos qui faciunt iniquitatem et mittent eos in caminum ignis* (ibid., 13. 40–42). The passage concludes, *tunc iusti fulgebunt sicut sol in regno Patris eorum*, 'then the righteous will shine as the sun in the kingdom of their Father' (ibid., 13. 43). This may recall the subversion of this citation in the *Apologia*, where it is combined with I Cor 15. 41–2 to make the point that some will be more blessed than others (*Apo* IV. 9).

[70]   *Relatum mihi est a pluribus, quod litterae ... quosdam vestrorum laeserint ...*, 'I have been told by many that the letter.. wounded certain of yours ...' (letter 36, p. 116).

[71]   *Viderint primae illius epistolae lectores quo eam spiritu legerint quo sensum eius interpretati sint ...*, 'Let the readers of that first letter consider in what spirit they read it, in what spirit they interpreted its meaning ...' (letter 36, p. 116).

[72]   Augustine, *De Trinitate*, IX, VI. 10.

[73]   Lc 11. 34; Mt 6. 22.

[74]   *Sed et dominus in aevangelio [inquit]:* Si oculus tuus fuerit simplex, totum corpus tuum lucidum erit, 'But the Lord also [says] in the Gospels: *If your eye is single, your whole body will be light*' (letter 28, p. 60).

[75]   Peter, letter 111, *Letters*, I, pp. 274–99. This letter will be the focus of discussion in the next two chapters.

[76]   Constable, 'Cluniac tithes', p. 616.

[77]   Letter 34, p. 112.

[78]   Constable, 'Cluniac tithes', p. 616 and n. 7.

date for the letters of 1135–37 seems to favour Bredero's contention that this is the issue underlying Peter's letter 65. Bredero concludes that Peter's letter 65 was sent with a view to obtaining Bernard's mediation.[79] The hint there that Bernard is involved with detraction, the 'weapons of the left',[80] might seem, however, to point in the opposite direction, that is, as voicing the concealed reproach that Bernard has the ear of pope and chancellor, and is working against the cause of the Cluniacs. No more will be heard about Gigny and Le Miroir until the 1150s, but as Constable points out, in view of the pro-Cistercian sympathies of Innocent and Haimeric, it is unlikely that the situation was resolved in favour of the Cluniacs.[81]

Although there is room for uncertainty concerning Bernard's part in this affair, there is no doubt about the active role which he played in the next concrete cause of dispute, which broke out on his return from Rome. Langres had been without a bishop since the death of the previous incumbent in 1136, a lacuna seemingly caused by a split in the cathedral chapter.[82] Both Molesme, the mother-house of Cîteaux, and Clairvaux itself fell within its diocese, giving Bernard particular cause for concern.[83] In the late spring of 1138, a delegation from Langres which included their metropolitan archbishop, Peter of Lyons, went to Rome to seek the right to hold a 'free' election.[84] What precisely took place in Rome is known only through the subsequent letter of Bernard, who claimed that they had entered into an undertaking, ratified by Innocent, on the names of two agreed candidates to be put forward for election.[85] In the event, the election fell on a Cluniac monk, probably William of Sabran.[86] Bernard, together with prominent members of the metropolitan chapter of Lyons and support from within the chapter at Langres, mounted a vigorous challenge against the suitability of the bishop-elect, which finally resulted in the holding of a new election, and the appointment of Godfrey of La Roche-Vanneau, Bernard's kinsman and prior of Clairvaux. That, contrary to the Cistercians, the Cluniacs, invoking papal privilege, regarded themselves as exempt

---

[79]   Bredero, *Bernard of Clairvaux*, p. 232.

[80]   Letter 65, p 195. See Chapter 3.

[81]   Constable, 'Cluniac tithes', p. 617.

[82]   The complex issues and events surrounding this episcopal election have been reconstructed by Constable (G. Constable, 'The disputed election at Langres in 1138', *Traditio* 13 (1957), 119–52, reprinted in idem, *Cluniac studies*).

[83]   Constable, ibid., p. 120.

[84]   *Venerunt et cum eo (archiepiscopo Lugdunensi) Robertus, decanus ecclesiae Lingonensis, et Olricus canonicus, quaerentes licere sibi et capitulo Lingonensi eligere sibi episcopum*, 'There came also with him (the archbishop of Lyons) Robert, dean of the church of Langres, and canon Ulric, seeking that it should be allowed to them and to the chapter of Langres to elect a bishop' (Bernard, ep. 164, 1, *SBO*, VII, p. 372). See Constable, *Letters*, II, p. 147; idem, 'Langres', p. 127.

[85]   *prius tamen habita inter nos collatione mutua ac diuturna super facienda electione, et ... duabus [personis] tandem nominatis, a quibus nullus nostrum penitus dissentiret, quamlibet illarum eligi placuisset*, 'having first held amongst us a mutual and and lengthy deliberation about holding the election, and ... having at last named two [persons], from whom none of us completely dissented, whichever of them the election choice should fall on' (Bernard, ep. 164, 1). See Constable, 'Langres', p. 125; pp. 132–3.

[86]   See Constable, 'Langres', appendix A.

from the authority of the diocesan bishop, had been one of the Cistercian 'charges' contained in letter 28.[87]

Peter's letter 29 to Bernard,[88] dating to August or September 1138,[89] can be seen as putting the Cluniac side of the case: there is no preserved response from Bernard. In terms of structure, letter 29 seems to fall somewhere between letter and formal oration. Peter abandons the device of a personal *captatio* drawing on the language of mystic friendship, instead launching directly into a selective and minimal narration of 'events', presented in apparently impersonal terms. This is followed by a section which most closely resembles an argumentation or proof, and which divides into two contrasting parts, the contrast being underscored by repetition and syntax: the actions which should have been taken by Bernard, and the actions which were taken by Peter. These parts can perhaps be seen as corresponding to (positive) confirmation and (negative) refutation. Finally, the letter modulates, via the language of petition, into what is essentially a hortatory peroration. It will be argued that the construction of the letter as a whole works to minimise the issue of the (un)suitability of the Cluniac candidate, first, by redirecting attention onto external hostility, and second, by launching an appeal for monastic unity. The dominating concepts are friendship and enmity, slander and veracity, rumour and trust. As used here, as will be seen, they may be thought to comprise some kind of indirect riposte to the insinuations contained in Bernard's ep. 147.

The narration focuses on the election of the Cluniac candidate and on the investiture performed by Louis VII. Two features, in particular, are emphasised: the legality of the proceedings, and Peter's unwilling involvement. Peter claims to have been presented with the election as a *fait accompli*. The canons of Langres are said to have told him that they had elected the candidate 'harmoniously and canonically, with the entirety of the clergy and people of their Church'.[90] The archbishop of Lyons had 'advised and confirmed it'.[91] Peter himself confirms that the investiture was carried out by the king in person 'in the customary manner', 'as is wont to happen'.[92] Peter himself was met as he was returning from Poitou, 'suspecting no such thing'.[93] They 'pressed him' to give consent 'with all their might'.[94] He 'hesitated', but finally gave way, 'yielding to the importunity of their

---

[87] *Super haec omnia quod omnibus iniustum et contra ecclesiastica decreta esse perspicue patet, et unde ab universis iuste iudicamini, nequaquam relinquere vultis, sed contra totius orbis morem proprium episcopum habere refugitis*, 'Above all these, you refuse to abandon a practice which, it is very clear to all, is unjust and against all the decrees of the Church, and whence you are justly judged by all, but against the custom of the whole world you shrink from submitting to your own Bishop' (letter 28, p. 56). Peter's 'defence' there is that they obey the Pope himself (ibid., pp. 79–80).

[88] Peter, letter 29, *Letters*, I, pp. 101–4.

[89] See Constable, *Letters*, II, p. 121.

[90] *cum universo clero et populo ecclesiae suae, se in episcopum concorditer et canonice eligisse.. dixerunt* (Peter, letter 29, p. 102).

[91] *Lugdunensi metropolitano id consulente et confirmante* ... (ibid.).

[92] *(rex) de regalibus sicut solet fieri manu propria sollemniter investivit* (ibid.).

[93] *Reverenti mihi nuper de Pictavensi pago Lingonenses canonici occurrerunt, et nil tale suspicanti ... (dixerunt)* (ibid.).

[94] *Institerunt toto nisu..* (ibid.).

requests'.[95] His presence at Le Puy where the investiture took place is carefully explained away,[96] as is the arrival of the bishop-elect.[97] This stress on legality can be compared with that found in the propaganda campaign waged after Anacletus's challenge to the election of Innocent at the beginning of the papal schism.[98] Here, it will be used to set up an opposition between the actions of Bernard and 'certain from Lyons', and the general will.[99]

A comparison with the narrative given by Bernard points to certain omissions and glossings-over. Peter presents the investiture as a straightforward sequel to the election; Bernard's account suggests that it was preceded by a failed consecration at Lyons. According to Bernard, who also presents his role as one of reluctant involvement, he was met on his return from Italy by 'a number of religious men', who persuaded him to divert his course through Lyons, 'that, if possible, we might prevent the wicked deed from taking place'.[100] Bernard claims that he persuaded Peter, archbishop of Lyons, to place the matter before a council; meanwhile, the bishop-elect arrived but left again almost immediately, without appearing in the court. The subsequent investiture is presented by Bernard in consequently negative terms: 'Meanwhile, indeed, the fellow who had fled the consecration and annulled the election, hastened to the King. He obtained the investiture of the temporalities – by what merits, let him see.'[101] It is possible, but unlikely, that Peter at Le Puy remained unaware of the rumpus at Lyons.

Peter's letter suggests that the choice of candidate was supported by the entire cathedral chapter at Langres, and that the opposition came solely from Lyons. This is in complete contradiction with Bernard's account, which names Pontius, archdeacon of Langres, and the canon Bonami as appellants to the Pope.[102] Finally, it is clear that the beginnings of the affair go back to the earlier part of 1138. Bernard's account starts with his involvement in the delegation to Rome

---

[95]   *caedens importunitati rogantium..* (ibid.).

[96]   [*regalis curia*] *cui ipse necessitate non voluntate interfui* ..., '[the royal court] at which I was present of necessity, not of choice ...' (ibid.).

[97]   *(rex) visa quae tunc forte ad me venerat persona* ...., '(the King), having seen the person in question who had then come to me by chance ...' (ibid.).

[98]   *Electio meliorum, approbatio plurium, et quod his efficacius est, morum attestatio, Innocentium apud omnes commendant, summum confirmant Pontificem*, 'The election of the better, the approbation of the more, and more powerful than these, the attestation of character, commend Innocent among all, confirm him pope' (Bernard, ep. 124, 2, *SBO*, VII, p. 306). Cf. the characterisation of Innocent's election as *sanior*, 'sounder', 'more healthy' (idem, ep. 126, 13, ibid., p. 318).

[99]   *Cumque ita cleri, populi, metropolitani, ipsius quoque ... principis, in hanc unam sententiam, in hunc unum electum vota convenerint, quosdam Lugdunenses voluntatem vestram a communi omnium proposito ... avertisse ... accepi*, 'While the wishes of the clergy, the metropolitan archbishop, the King himself, came together on this one decision, on this one elect, I have heard that certain from Lyons have turned away your will from the common purpose ...' (letter 29, p. 102).

[100]   *A religiosis viris non paucis.. persuasi sumus divertere per Lugdunum, quatenus, si fieri posset, rem nefariam ne fieret prohiberemus* (Bernard, ep. 164, 2).

[101]   *Interim nempe homo qui et consecrationem fugerat et electionem refutarat festinavit ad Regem. Regalium investituram obtinuit, quibus meritis, ipse viderit* (ibid., 5).

[102]   Ibid.

mentioned earlier. Peter of Lyons is presented as having gone back on the agreement made there.[103] What follows presents him as guilty of a second breach of faith, first ordering, then cancelling, a second election.[104] That Peter was aware of, and to some extent involved in, the original legation is clear from a letter of recommendation to Innocent dating from spring 1138.[105] Letter 29, however, appears to gloss over this prior knowledge, implying that he only became involved at a late stage of the proceedings.

The second section of letter 29 turns the spotlight first on to Bernard, then onto Peter. It opens with an apparent palliative to criticism, which at the same time develops the motif of rumour, previously introduced through the statement that Bernard was swayed *nescio quibus rumoribus*, 'by some rumours or other': 'I do not wonder, nor is it to be wondered at, that hearing bad things displeased a good man.'[106] This paves the way, however, for a string of gerundives which, seemingly impersonal, in fact target actions left undone by Bernard, thus condemning him for precipitate action,[107] and culminating in a double imperative.[108] These unfulfilled and exhorted actions contrast strongly with a rapid fire of first-person verbs representing the action taken by Peter in response to rumour.[109] The key-note of the opening part of this section mounts an opposition between 'friendship' and 'enmity', linked to a further opposition between slander and veracity. Peter commits his reproach to 'the ears of a like-minded friend' in a 'friendly complaint'.[110] 'Personal' relationship is broadened to encompass community, as Bernard is reminded that the bishop-elect is a monk of 'your Cluny', the son of an abbot 'beloved to you'.[111] Those who have attacked the bishop-elect, on the other hand, are presented as having undertaken *iurata bella*, 'sworn wars', and as 'so

---

[103] *Conveni archiepiscopum, reverenter quidem, super pacto quod fecerat et super mandato quod acceperat, et nihil horum negavit*, 'I accosted the archbishop, reverently indeed, over the agreement which he had made and the mandate which he had received, and he denied none of it' (ibid., 3).

[104] *Et intulit quia quicquid hactenus egerit, iam pro nostro deinceps arbitrio se facturum*, 'And he replied that, whatever he had done up until then, henceforth he would act in accordance with my judgement' (ibid.).

[105] *Rogati rogamus, ut paterna pietas ... eam eligendi libertatem ... nobili, magnae, famosae Lingonensi ecclesiae conservari iubeat*, 'Having been asked, we ask that paternal pity ... order that freedom of election ... be conserved to the noble, great, famous church of Langres' (Peter, letter 72, *Letters*, 1, p. 206). See Constable, 'Langres', p. 130.

[106] *Non sane miror, nec mirandum est, si bono viro mala audita displicuerunt* (letter 29, p. 102).

[107] *Sed advertendum fuit ... cogitandum fuit ... attendum fuit ... videndum fuit ...*, 'But attention should have been paid ... thought should have been taken ... heed should have been given.. it should have been considered ...' (ibid.).

[108] *Credite magis ... Credite mihi ...* (ibid., p. 103).

[109] *Conveni ipse hominem ... rogavi, admonui, adiuravi ... dixi ... adieci ... nec dissimulavi ...*, 'I myself accosted the man ... I asked, I admonished, I adjured ... I said ... I added ... nor did I neglect ...' (ibid.).

[110] *(quod) apud unanimis amici aures familiari querela depono ...* (ibid., p. 102).

[111] *Cogitandum fuit ... hunc ... vestrae Cluniacensis ecclesiae monachum, et dilecti vobis abbatis ... filium esse* (ibid.).

great and so open enemies'.[112] They are twice characterised as *maledici*, 'slanderous', and Bernard exhorted to believe 'truthful friends' rather than 'slanderous enemies'.[113] As Peter effects the transition into the second part of the section, the concept of slander modulates into that of *mendacium*, the 'lie', which, set against *fides*, trust, good faith, on the one hand, and *veritas*, truthfulness, on the other, dominates what follows, and underpins the section as a whole.

While both slander and trust form part of the tradition of friendship writing,[114] Peter's exploitation of *mendacium* forms a kind of leit-motif which runs through this section and extends into the next, passing through a series of metaphorical incarnations with potentially significant repercussions. In its introductory form, it is directly linked with a biblical citation: 'Believe me ... who, although I cannot be free from the common lie by which *all men are liars*, nevertheless, be it absent that I should not beware the lie there, where I can beware it'.[115] Originating in the Old Testament,[116] the citation was reused in *Romans*.[117] The Pauline passage, which can be linked, according to Stowers, with the style of the diatribe, takes the form of a dialogue, countering 'real' or anticipated objections from a Jewish opponent.[118] The latter is shown as bringing the Law into disrepute, because of his failure to live by it.[119] The passage ends with what can, perhaps, best be seen as a further example of ironic *apologia*, with St Paul apparently accepting his opponent's criticism, only to turn it back against him through logical absurdity: 'why not, as we are reviled and as certain say us to say, let us do evil that good may come? Their condemnation is just.'[120]

In this passage from Romans, the 'faithfulness' of God is implicitly opposed to the 'faithlessness' of Israel. In both punishing and rewarding the Jews, God will

---

[112]   *tantis tamque manifestis inimicis credere, tantis tamque manifestis hostibus fidem dare, nec vestrum nec aliquorum bonorum est*, 'to believe so great and so open enemies, to give trust to so great and so open enemies, is neither your part nor that of any good men' (ibid.).

[113]   *Credite magis ... amicis veridicis quam inimicis maledicis* (ibid., p. 103).

[114]   *Est enim boni viri ... haec duo tenere in amicitia: primum ne quid fictum sit neve simulatum ...; deinde non solum ab aliquo allatas criminationes repellere, sed ne ipsum quidem esse suspiciosum ...*, 'It is the part of a good man ... to hold to these two principles in friendship: firstly, that there should be nothing feigned or simulated ...; secondly, not only to reject accusations brought by anyone, but not to be himself suspicious ...' (Cicero, *Laelius*, XVIII, 65.) Peter will ask at the end of the letter, *purgetur ista suspicio ...*, 'let that suspicion be purged ...' (letter 29, p. 104).

[115]   *Credite mihi ..., qui etsi a communi mendacio quo* omnis homo mendax est *immunis non possum, absit tamen ut ibi non caveam mendacium, ubi cavere possum* (ibid., p. 103).

[116]   *Ego dixi in excessu meo omnis homo mendax*, 'I said in my aberration of mind, "all men are liars", (Ps 115. 11).

[117]   *Est autem deus verax omnis homo autem mendax sicut scriptum est*, 'For only God is truthful, all men are liars, just as it has been written' (Rm 3. 4).

[118]   S. K. Stowers, *A re-reading of Romans*, New Haven, London, 1994, pp. 159–75. Stowers's reading is supported by Moo (D. J. Moo, *The epistle to the Romans*, New International Commentary on the New Testament, ed. N. Stonehouse, F. Bruce and G. Fee, Grand Rapids; Cambridge, 1996, p. 178 and n. 4).

[119]   Stowers, *A re-reading*, p. 158.

[120]   *(quid) non sicut blasphemamur et sicut aiunt nos quidam dicere faciamus mala ut veniant bona quorum damnatio iusta est* (Rm 3. 8).

remain faithful to his promises.[121] Set within the wider context of salvation and 'judaising', this section of the Pauline epistle mounts an opposition between the 'letter and the spirit' of the Law, couched in terms of 'circumcision of the flesh' and 'circumcision of the heart',[122] and preaches justification through faith rather than through the 'works of the Law'.[123] In relation to letter 29, the evocation of the passage as a whole can be seen to set up a number of significant resonances. The debate between Paul and a judaising opponent evokes the presentation of Cistercians and Cluniacs as 'Jews' and 'Gentiles' in letter 28.[124] The irony with which it ends may suggest that Cluniacs, because of their 'deviation' from the *Rule*, are automatically subject to gross distortion of their motives and actions. In turn, this may serve to deflect attention from the particular charges brought against the bishop-elect, which Peter never reveals. Finally, through scriptural subversion, Peter turns back the accusation against Bernard, by hinting that he is the one who has been found 'faithless'. He has withdrawn his 'faith' from those to whom it was due, and given it to those who do not deserve it.[125] At the same time, the choice of this passage from Romans, with its overtones of ironic *apologia*, may constitute a response to Bernard's ironic defence in ep. 147, drawing on the embracing of abjection found in II Corinthians.[126]

The repetition of *mendacium* in the second half of the statement, 'be it absent

---

[121] *si autem iniquitas nostra iustitiam Dei commendat quid dicemus numquid iniquus Deus qui infert iram secundum hominem dico absit alioquin quomodo iudicabit Deus mundum*, 'But if our iniquity commends the justice of God, what shall we say? Is God unjust, who inflicts his anger? I speak according to man. Be it absent. Otherwise, how shall God judge the world?' (ibid, 3. 5). See Moo, *The epistle*, pp. 179–80.

[122] *Non enim qui in manifesto Iudaeus est neque quae in manifesto in carne circumcisio sed qui in abscondito Iudaeus et circumcisio cordis in spiritu non littera cuius laus non ex hominibus sed ex deo est*, 'For not who manifestly is a Jew nor the circumcision which is manifestly in the flesh, but who is secretly a Jew and circumcision of the heart in the spirit not the letter, whose praise is not from men but from God' (Rm 2. 28–9).

[123] *Ubi est ergo gloriatio exclusa est per quam legem factorum non sed per legem fidei arbitramur enim iustificari hominem per fidem sine operibus legis*, 'Where then is the glorying? It is excluded. Through what law? Of deeds? No, but through the law of faith. For we think that man is justified through faith without the works of the Law' (ibid., 3. 27–8).

[124] Previously in Romans, Paul had launched a charge of *praevaricatio*, 'deviation': *Circumcisio quidem prodest si legem observes si autem praevaricator legis sis circumcisio tua praeputium facta est*, 'Circumcision indeed is of value if you observe the Law, but if you should deviate from the Law, your circumcision has been made a prepuce' (ibid., 2. 25; cf. ibid., 27). This charge had formed the key-stone of the accusations attributed to the Cistercians in letter 28.

[125] *Videndum fuit, si fidem prudentiae vestrae illorum maledicorum verba facere debuerunt*, 'It should have been considered, whether the words of those slanderers should have found faith with your prudence ...' (letter 29, p. 102); *Eapropter ... tantis tamque manifestis hostibus fidem dare, nec vestrum nec aliquorum bonorum est*, 'Therefore ... it is not your place nor that of any good men to give faith to so great and so open enemies ...' (ibid.).

[126] In ep. 147, Bernard, like St Paul, had played heavily on the notion of 'glory'. Peter prefaces his allusion to *Romans* with the statement, *(qui) ... amici apud vos nomine glorior*, '(I who) ... glory in the title of friend in the sight of you' (letter 29, p. 103). *Apud vos* may equally imply 'in your writings'.

that I should not beware the lie, there where I can beware it', may draw on yet another biblical context. The account of Peter's interview with the bishop-elect which follows depicts him in the role of father-confessor, and sets up a hypothetical opposition between faithfulness and faithlessness: 'I said that I wished to approach his conscience not as a faithless revealer of mystery, but as a faithful custodian of those (things) entrusted ...'.[127] *Detector*, 'revealer', can be paralleled in Tertullian, where it denotes Christ, 'the revealer of the Creator',[128] and is linked with the miracle of the healing of the blind man.[129] Here, paradoxically, it is qualified by the adjective *perfidus*, 'faithless'. That the 'faithless revealer' is to be understood as one who plays the role of Satan rather than of Christ is confirmed by the succeeding statement: '[I said that] I did not wish to reveal the wounds of souls to mock, but to heal.'[130] Satan is *illusor*, the 'mocker',[131] Christ is *medicus*, the 'healer'. The clue to Peter's choice of words may lie in a passage from II Thessalonians, which invokes *mysterium iniquitatis*, the 'mystery of iniquity',[132] identified with the figure of the Antichrist, and heralding the second coming,[133] said to be 'according to the operation of Satan, in all power and signs and lying prodigies ...'.[134] The continuation contrasts *caritas veritatis*, the 'charity of truth', with the 'lie', to present the latter as a mechanism leading to damnation: 'and in all seduction of

---

[127] *Dixi me non ut perfidum mysterii detectorem, sed ut fidum commissorum custodem, ad conscientiam eius velle accedere..* (letter 29, ibid.).

[128] *Non tamen confirmator erroris, immo etiam detector creatoris, ut non prius hanc caecitatem hominis illius enubilasset, ne ultra Iesum filium David existimaret. Atquin.. manifestissime confirmavit caeci praedicationem et ipsa remuneratione medicinae et testimonio fidei,* 'He (Christ) is not, however, a confirmer of error, but a revealer of the Creator, that he should not first have removed the cloud of this blindness of that man, so that he should no longer consider Jesus the son of David. But rather.. he manifestly confirmed the truth of the blind man's proclamation, both by the reward of healing and by the testimony to (his) faith' (Tertullian, *Adversus Marcionem*, IV, 36. 10, ed. E. Evans, Oxford Early Christian Texts, 2 vols, Oxford, 1972, 2, p. 470). The context is one of refuting heresy. As will be seen, the language here finds an echo in what follows in Peter's letter.

[129] Mc 10. 46–52; Lc 18. 35–43.

[130] [*Dixi*] *... nolle me patefactis animarum vulneribus illudere sed mederi* (letter 29, p. 103).

[131] *Absit ... ut ille (Sathan) ... in tantum ipse servis eius [salvatoris] et ancillis illudat ...*, 'Be it absent ... that he (Satan) ... should himself so mock His [the Saviour's] servants and maidservants ...' (Peter, letter 111, p. 278).

[132] *Nam mysterium iam operatur iniquitatis ...*, 'For he is already working the mystery of iniquity ...' (II Th 2. 7).

[133] *Ne quis vos seducat ullo modo quoniam nisi venerit discessio primum et revelatus fuerit homo peccati filius perditionis qui adversatur et extollitur supra omne quod dicitur Deus aut quod colitur ita ut in templo Dei sedeat ostendens se quia sit Deus,* 'Let no one lead you astray in any way, since (it will not be) until the schism comes and the man of sin, the son of perdition, who fights against and is extolled above everything which is called God, or which is worshipped, is revealed, so that he sits in the temple of God, showing himself to be God ...' (ibid., 2. 3–4). Cf. *et in fronte eius nomen scriptum mysterium Babylon magna mater fornicationum et abominationum terrae,* 'and on her forehead is written the name, mystery, Babylon, the great mother of the fornications and abominations of the earth' (Apc 17. 5).

[134] *(eum) cuius est adventus secundum operationem Satanae in omni virtute et signis et prodigiis mendacibus* (II Th 2. 9).

iniquity for those who perish because they have not received the charity of the truth in order to be saved. Therefore God sends to them the operation of error so that they may believe the lie, so that all may be judged who have not believed the truth but have consented to iniquity.'[135]

Bernard is seemingly distanced from this evocation of the 'operation of Satan', yet the letter surely implicates him in two ways. In dissociating himself from the desire to be a 'faithless revealer of (the) mystery', Peter sets up an implicit contrast between them. The propaganda campaign waged by Bernard and others throughout the papal schism had denounced and vilified the anti-pope Anacletus as an incarnation of the Antichrist, the 'Beast' of Revelations.[136] Bernard's denunciation of the bishop-elect is more moderate, but, as will be seen, similar linguistic echoes creep in. Peter himself claims to 'beware the lie'. Later in the letter he will suggest, first, that Bernard has allowed his judgement to be 'clouded' by the 'lie', then, through *praeteritio*, that he is at best passively, even perhaps actively, involved in its promulgation.[137] In short, Peter seems to be hinting that the champion of orthodoxy has allowed himself to be 'seduced' by those whose 'right hand is the right hand of iniquity'[138] into performing the harmful work of Satan rather than the healing work of Christ.

The two appearances of *mendacium* which follow further develop the metaphor of concealment and revelation, introduced through the phrase *mysterii detector*. The bishop-elect is reported as having sworn to Peter that he had never 'veiled his heart with the mantle of the lie'.[139] Peter suggests that Bernard himself is in need of enlightenment: 'I would have revealed to clarity how the murky cloud of the lie, dark from the abyss, has tried to eclipse the sharp vision of your mind. I will do it

---

[135] *et in omni seductione iniquitatis his qui pereunt eo quod caritatem veritatis non receperunt ut salvi fierent ideo mittit illis Deus operationem erroris ut credant mendacio ut iudicentur omnes qui non crediderunt veritati sed consenserunt iniquitati* (ibid., 2. 10–12).

[136] *Nam qui Dei sunt libenter iunguntur ei (Innocentio), qui autem ex adverso stat, aut Antichristi est, aut Antichristus*, 'For those who are of God are joined to him (Innocent) freely, but he who stands against him is either of the Antichrist, or Antichrist' (Bernard, ep. 124, 1, *SBO*, VII, p. 305); *Viri mendaces, quos Veritas, sicut et caput eorum Antichristum, destruit* spiritu oris sui ..., 'Lying men, whom, together with their head, Antichrist, Truth destroys *with the breath of* her *mouth* ...' (idem, ep. 127, 1, ibid., p. 320 = II Th 2. 8).

[137] *rogo ... ne naevo mendacii Cluniacensis congregationis corpus deformare non dico velitis, sed nec patiamini* ..., 'I ask ... that you do not, I do not say wish, but allow, the dishonouring of the body of the congregation of Cluny by the stain of the lie ...' (letter 29, p. 103).

[138] *Videndum fuit, si fidem prudentiae vestrae illorum maledicorum verba facere debuerunt, quorum os locutum est vanitatem, impudenter mentiendo, et* dextera eorum dextera iniquitatis, *irreverenter innocentes monachos verberando*, 'It should have been considered whether the words of those slanderers were to convince your Prudence, *whose mouth has spoken vanity*, by lying shamelessly, and *their right hand is the right hand of iniquity*, irreverently beating innocent monks' (ibid., p. 102 = Ps 143. 8; 11).

[139] *numquam se amictu mendacii cor suum mihi velasse [respondit]* (letter 29, p. 103). The wording may present an echo of the widowed Ezekiel's obedience to the divine injunction, *nec amictu ora velabis*, 'you will not veil your face with the mantle' (Ez 24. 17). In the case of the bishop-elect, the death of a 'wife' might be equated with the threatened loss of Langres.

when I can.'[140] 'Dark from the abyss' conjures up the state of the world preceding the creation of light;[141] it also seems to point to Satan and Hell as the source of the 'lie'.[142] *Caligosa.. nubes*, the 'murky cloud', can be linked with Augustine's *De Trinitate*. In the passage dealing with memory and imagination discussed previously in relation to letter 65, 'corporeal' perception is likened to a cloud, while the 'judgement of truth' is said to shine from above. It is said to be 'covered underneath' by this cloud, but not 'envelopped and confounded'.[143] Augustine further develops the analogy: 'But it makes a difference whether, under or in that murk, I am cut off as if from the clear sky, or, as is wont to happen in the highest mountains, enjoying the free air between the two, I perceive both the brightest light above and the thickest cloud below.'[144] Accordingly, Peter seems to be hinting that Bernard's 'spiritual' perception has been impaired by slander and malice. In consequence, he needs to apply *oculus simplex*, the 'single eye', of *caritas*.

In contrast with the first section of the letter, therefore, which is seemingly impersonal and public, the second section can be seen to encompass both public and private, personal and communal. Through its allusions to Augustine on the one hand and to Satan and the Antichrist on the other, it sets up a quasi-private dialogue with Bernard, which contains hidden allusions to letter 65 and ep. 147. It is noticeable that the nature of the accusations against the bishop-elect is never spelled out, by either Peter or Bernard. If the candidate is to be equated with William of Sabran, as Constable suggests, they may relate to an attack on the abbey of Saint-Gilles in 1121, which resulted in a sentence of excommunication. Constable conjectures that William may have repented subsequently and entered the Cluniac priory of St Saturnin-du-Port, from where he would have been put forward as a candidate for the bishopric of Langres.[145] Peter reduces the candidate's denial of the accusations to a single statement.[146] He hints, however, that the source of the accusation is the unnamed 'enemies' of Cluny: 'I know from whom, and why, and how, those words

---

[140]   *quam tenebrosa abysso perspicuam mentis vestrae aciem caligosa mendacii nubes obfundere conata sit, ad liquidum indicassem. Quod cum potero faciam* (letter 29, p. 103).

[141]   *Terra autem erat inanis et vacua et tenebrae super faciem abyssi*, 'The earth, indeed, was empty and void, and there was darkness over the face of the abyss' (Gn 1. 2).

[142]   *bestia quae ascendit de abysso* ..., 'the beast which comes up from the abyss ...' (Apc 11. 7); *et data est illi clavis putei abyssi* ..., 'and he was given the key of the pit of the abyss ...' (ibid., 9. 1).

[143]   *Viget et claret desuper iudicium veritatis.. et si corporalium imaginum quasi quodam nubilo subtexitur, non tamen involvitur atque confunditur* (Augustine, *de Trinitate*, IX, VI, 10).

[144]   *Sed interest utrum ego sub illa vel in illa caligine tamquam a caelo perspicuo secludar, an sicut in altissimis montibus accidere solet inter utrumque aere libero fruens et serenissimam lucem supra et densissimas nebulas subter aspiciam* (ibid., VI, 11). At the end of this section Augustine will use the expression *acies mentis*, 'the sharpness of sight of the mind' (ibid.). This can be linked with Peter's reference here to *perspicua mentis vestrae acies*, 'the sharp vision of your mind' (letter 29, p. 103).

[145]   See Constable, 'Langres', p. 135 and Appendix A.

[146]   *eorum quae dicebantur ita se esse immunem, ut si velim, iniecta omnia securissime sacramento expurget* [*respondit*], '[he replied] that he was so guiltless of what was being said that, if I wished, he would fearlessly purge all the insinuations by the sacrament' (letter 29, p. 103).

which begot scandal in you, arose, were increased and disseminated.'[147] Peter seemingly offers Bernard a choice: to ally himself with these 'enemies', or to prove himself a 'friend' of Cluny.

The petition is lauched in the name of personal friendship and communal charity: 'Meanwhile, I ask your Affection, always to be embraced by me, and beseech through her [charity] who has made us of one mind in the house of God, not to allow.. the body of the Cluniac congregation to be disfigured by the stain of the lie ...'.[148] This image, as Constable indicates, may utilise a passage in Horace's *Satires*, which draws a comparison between character defects of a trivial kind and a scattering of *naevi*, 'blemishes', 'moles', on an otherwise beautiful body.[149] At the same time, the association here with *mendacium* may also look back to letter 28, where Peter claimed that the Cluniacs had been 'cleansed' from the 'stain of trangression' imputed to them by the Cistercians.[150] The image of the 'body' leads directly into a citation from I Corinthians, which ostensibly makes the point that all Cluniacs will share in the defamation of one Cluniac: 'since the very shame of the disgrace which has been charged would compel the ascription of this not to that one man, but to each and every one of us, because when *one limb* suffers, *all the limbs* suffer'.[151] Since, however, the Pauline passage has already established that 'all' embraces 'Jews' and 'Gentiles' alike,[152] this may be read as constituting both a warning and an admonition. The Cistercians, as fellow monks, will also suffer from the defamation; equally, they should suffer in the sufferings of their brothers.

The appeal to monastic unity is reinforced by an echo of *Deuteronomy* which serves to further undermine the opposition between 'Jew' and 'Gentile'. Peter claims to be making this plea because 'no true Israelite' can cause or suffer a name of ill-repute to be spread abroad concerning a 'daughter of Israel', that is, Cluny.[153]

---

[147] *Novi ipse a quibus et quare et qualiter, verba illa quae scandalum vobis pepererunt, exorta, aucta, disseminata fuerunt* (ibid.).

[148] *Interim amplectendam mihi semper dilectionem vestram rogo, et per eam* [caritatem] *quae nos in domo dei unanimes fecit obsecro, ne naevo mendacii Cluniacensis congregationis corpus deformare ... patiamini ...* (ibid.).

[149] *Atqui si vitiis mediocribus ac mea paucis*
   mendosa est natura, alioqui recta, velut si
   egregio inspersos reprehendas corpore naevos ...
'But if my nature is faulty with mediocre and small faults but otherwise upright, as if you were to reprehend scattered moles on a beautiful body ...' (Horace, *Satires*, I, VI. 65–7, *Q. Horati Flacci opera*, ed. D. R. Shackleton Bailey, Bibliotheca Scriptorum Graecorum et Romanorum Teubneriana, 3rd ed., Stuttgart, 1995). In adapting this image, Peter appears to be exploiting the post-classical association between *mendosus*, 'faulty', and *mendax*, 'lying'.

[150] *Nobis ergo transgressionis naevo a vobis obiecto purgatis ...* (letter 28, p. 99).

[151] *quoniam non hoc illi uni asscribere, sed nobis et singulis et omnibus imputare pudor ipse obiectae infamiae compelleret, quia cum dolet* unum membrum, *condolent* omnia membra (letter 29, p. 103 = I Cor. 12. 26). *Condolere* here replaces the original *compati*: both verbs can imply sharing grief as well as pain.

[152] *Etenim in uno Spiritu omnes nos in unum corpus baptizati sumus sive Iudaei sive gentiles sive servi sive liberi ...*, 'For we have all been baptised in one Spirit into one body, whether Jews or Gentiles, whether slaves or free ...' (I Cor 12. 12).

[153] *quia malum nomen diffamari super filiam Israel, nec verus Israhelita facere nec verus Israhelita potest sufferre* (letter 29, p. 103 = Dt 22. 19).

Significantly, cross-referencing suggests that the opposition between Cluniacs and Cistercians is being replaced with an alternative opposition between monks and clerics. The passage in Deuteronomy concerns a false accusation of failed virginity brought against a wife, *virgo Israhel*.[154] Peter's shift in terminology, from *virgo* to *filia*, can be linked back to his earlier attack on 'certain from Lyons'. The citation from the *Psalms* attached to the latter, 'whose mouth has spoken vanity ... and their right hand is the right hand of iniquity',[155] is preceded in the original context by a request to be freed 'from the hand of alien sons',[156] subsequently reformulated as 'sons of alien women'.[157]

Cluny, therefore, is a true 'daughter', the dissident clerics, 'sons' of interlopers. Peter never spells out this opposition but leaves it implicit in the peroration which follows. The piety and education of the bishop-elect is set against the indifferent religion and learning of 'secular clerics', previous incumbents of Langres.[158] A call to trust between fellow-monks counterbalances the earlier condemnation of trust in (slanderous) clerics.[159] The letter closes with an appeal to nature,[160] and with a promise of *dilectio*, which invokes the notion of spiritual profit, and draws a parallel between personal and communal affection: 'Therefore, if a monk is bishop of Langres, he will love Cistercians and other monks, because by loving, he will experience greater profit for himself, and by not loving, greater loss. Nor will our monk dare to do other, than what he sees us do by loving.'[161] In the event, a monk would be bishop of Langres, but not a Cluniac.

---

[154] *adprehendentque senes urbis illius virum et verberabunt illum ... quoniam diffamavit nomen pessimum super virginem Israel ...*, 'the old men of that city shall take the man and beat him ... since he has spread abroad a name of evil repute concerning a virgin of Israel' (Dt 22. 18–19).

[155] quorum os locutum est vanitatem ... *et* dextera eorum dextera iniquitatis ... (letter 29, p. 102 = Ps 143, 8; 11).

[156] *Eripe me ... de manu filiorum alienorum* (Ps 143. 7).

[157] *eripe me ... de manu filiorum alienigenarum* (ibid., 11).

[158] *Quod si Lingonensi ecclesiae multi saeculares clerici, quorum nec multa religio, nec multa scientia eminebat episcopali nomine.. olim principati sunt, quid indecens, si religiosae ecclesiae, religiosus, sapiens, litteratus monachus.. electus est ...?*, 'Therefore if many secular clerics, whose piety and knowledge shone out little in episcopal renown.. formerly governed the church of Langres, what impropriety is there in a pious, wise, lettered monk.. having been elected to a pious church?' (letter 29, pp. 103–4).

[159] *(si) ... monachi monachos, religiosi religiosos, Cistercienses Cluniacenses verentur, et minus de illis de quibus magis confidere deberent confidunt ...*, '(if) ... monks fear monks, men of religion fear men of religion, Cistercians fear Cluniacs, and trust less in those in whom they should trust more ...' (ibid., p. 104). The rhetorical effect of this three-fold antithesis is enhanced by *polyptoton* and alliteration.

[160] *omne animal consimile sibi diligere ... natura ipsa docente discat*, 'let every living thing, taking nature herself as teacher, learn to love its like' (ibid.). Although not noted by Constable, this surely draws on Ecclesiasticus, *Omne animal diligit similem sibi sic et omnis homo proximum sibi*, 'Every living thing loves its like; so every man also loves what is nearest to him' (Sir 13. 19). The appeal to natural order will form a prominent feature of Peter's letter 111.

[161] *Diliget ergo si monachus fuerit Lingonensis episcopus Cistercienses et ceteros monachos, quia diligendo maius sibi lucrum, non diligendo maius sentiet detrimentum. Nec noster*

Although Bernard produced what Constable characterises as a 'barrage of letters' aimed at overturning the election,[162] there is no extant reply to letter 29 from Peter. However, these letters do contain a number of points of verbal contact with letter 29. Most notably, the letters to Innocent and to the Roman cardinals show a return to the verbal violence seen previously in Bernard's ep. 147, and relating there to the schismatics. Here, the violence is directed rather against Cluny, and the 'friends' of Cluny. Bernard, too, invokes the notion of rumour, but in terms which render it prejudicial to the bishop-elect: 'But the shameful and grievous rumour, spreading far and wide and increasing in strength, had filled the city.'[163] In contrast with the anonymity practised in Peter's letter, Bernard specifies the supporters of the bishop-elect and characterises them as *amici Cluniacenses*.[164] Peter the Venerable himself, together with Peter of Lyons, is marked down for particular condemnation. Both men are denounced as 'strong gods of the earth'.[165] The further depiction of them as 'trusting *in their strength*' and 'glorying *in the multitude of their riches*'[166] may seem to recall the opposition between wealth and poverty found previously in Peter's letters concerning tithes.[167] Bernard's letters also evoke the Antichrist: 'They (the multitude of holy men) will accept this (such a yoke) as if forced to bow the knee before Baal, or certainly, in the words of the Prophet, to make a pact with death and to enter into a covenant with hell.'[168]

---

monachus aliud audebit, quam quod nos facere diligendo videbit (ibid.). Peter may be drawing on the Gospels: *Quid enim prodest homini si mundum universum lucretur animae vero suae detrimentum patiatur*, 'For what does it profit a man if he should gain the whole world but suffer the loss of his soul?' (Mt 16. 26). At the same time, the ambiguity between the material and the spiritual inherent in *lucrum*, 'profit', may also point back to the issue of tithes.

[162] Constable, 'Langres', p. 139.

[163] *Sed et rumor pudendus dolendusque passim crebrescens et invalescens civitatem repleverat* (Bernard, ep. 164, 2). Cf. *de quo utinam meliora atque honestiora audivissemus*, 'of whom (the bishop-elect) would that I had heard better and more honourable' (ibid.).

[164] *Et hoc praesumpserunt Lugdunensis, Aeduensis, Matisconensis, amici Cluniacenses*, 'And this presumption was due to the prelates of Lyons, Auton and Macon, Cluniac friends' (Bernard, ep. 166, 1, *SBO*, VII, p. 377).

[165] *Siquidem dii fortes terrae vehementer elevati sunt, Lugdunensis scilicet archiepiscopus, et Cluniacensis abbas*, 'Indeed *there rose up vehemently strong gods of the earth*, namely the archbishop of Lyons and the abbot of Cluny' (idem, ep. 168, 1, *SBO*, VII, p. 380 = Ps 46. 10).

[166] *Hi, confidentes* in virtute sua et in multitudine divitiarum suarum *gloriantes*, adversum me appropinquaverunt et steterunt, 'These, trusting *in their strength and* glorying *in the multitude of their riches, approached me and stood*' (ibid. = Ps 48. 7). The citation had also featured in Bernard's ep. 147.

[167] The attack on wealth and influence is pursued elsewhere: *Ubi nimirum imperabat aurum, iudicabat argentum; leges canonesque silebant, locum ratio et aequitas non habebat*, 'Where gold held too much sway, silver passed judgement; laws and statutes were silent, reason and justice had no place' (Bernard, ep. 166, 1); Si inveni gratiam in oculis *vestris, eripite* inopem de manu fortiorum eius, egenum et pauperum a diripientibus eum, 'If I have found grace in your eyes, snatch *the helpless from the hand of those who are stronger than him, the poor and needy from those who are plundering him*' (idem, ep. 168, 2 = Gn 18. 3; Ps 34. 10).

[168] *Hoc (tale iugum) ita accepturi sunt (multitudo sanctorum), ac si cogantur genua curvare ante Baal, aut certe, iuxta Prophetam*, pactum facere cum morte et cum inferno foedus inire (ep. 166 = Is 28. 15). The same citation appears in ep. 147, attached to Anacletus.

The closest contact with letter 29 is to be found in the imagery contained in Bernard's letter to Dean Falco and the treasurer, Guido, the figureheads of the opposition at Lyons.[169] The letter opens with the metaphor of *plaga*, a 'wound', which needs the care of the 'heavenly doctor'.[170] The church of Lyons is castigated for behaving as *noverca*, a 'stepmother', towards her daughter-church of Langres, in providing her with a monstrous 'son-in-law.'[171] The consequent 'marriage' between church and bishop is represented as a travesty, through biblical allusions which conjur up images of fornication and adultery: 'Am I to call that *an honourable marriage* and *an immaculate marriage-bed*, which has been made of such a one, and in such a way?'[172] The original context promises that God will judge 'fornicators and adulterers'.[173] The motif of fornication is picked up at the end of the letter, through an allusion to the punishment inflicted on a 'man of Israel' and a foreign 'harlot': 'There has been none found ... to put on the zeal of Phineus and to pierce the fornicators with the blade of the tongue.'[174] Although priority between this letter and letter 29 cannot be established with any certainty, Peter's use of Deuteronomy might be seen as reversing the direction of Bernard's biblical allusions. Cluny, not Langres is presented as the 'daughter of Israel', falsely accused of unchastity. In return, it is the clerics who are hinted to be 'foreigners'. In other words, Peter may be indicating that Bernard's concern should be for Cluny rather than for Langres.

As with the letters discussed in the previous chapter, this affair may find a postscript. Bernard's ep. 148 is followed in his letter-collection by a brief letter, absent from that of Peter, and dated to the autumn of 1138.[175] In this letter, Bernard advises Peter to proceed 'more moderately' in the case of the monastery of Saint-Bertin.[176] This Benedictine monastery was engaged in a process to free itself from the authority of Cluny, a dispute which, according to van den Eynde, had lasted for

---

[169] Bernard, ep. 165, *SBO*, VII, pp. 375–6.

[170] *Plaga ... ecclesiae nostrae magna est et multa eget cura, nec modo multa, sed cita, ita ut assidue cum lacrimis Medico caelesti instemus, dicentes:* Domine, descende priusquam moriatur, 'The wound.. of our church is great and needs much care, not only much but swift, so that we treat assiduously with tears with the heavenly doctor, saying: *Lord, come down before* she *dies*' (ibid., p. 375 = Io 4. 49).

[171] *O Lugdunensis pia mater ecclesia! Cuiuscemodi non sponsum, sed monstrum tuae filiae procurasti nunc, non plane matrem te in hoc, sed novercam sensimus*, 'Oh, pious mother church of Lyons! In now procuring no spouse, but a monster of what a kind, for your daughter we have plainly perceived you no mother but a stepmother' (Bernard, ep. 165, p. 376).

[172] *Egone id dixerim* honorabile conubium *et torum immaculatum, quod de tali et taliter factum est?* (ibid. = Hbr 13. 4).

[173] *Honorabile conubium in omnibus et torus immaculatus fornicatores enim et adulteros iudicabit Deus*, '(Let there be) honourable marriage in all and an undefiled marriage-bed, for God will judge fornicators and adulters' (Hbr 13. 4).

[174] *Non est inventus ... qui ... se indueret zelum Phinees et linguae mucrone confoderet fornicantes* (ep. 165, p. 376 = Nm 25. 7–8). The language may find an echo in letter 29, where Peter claims to have scrutinised the conscience of the candidate, presented through the image of *intima parietis*, the 'inmost part of the wall', *acutae interrogationis fossorio*, 'with the mattock of sharp interrogation' (letter 29, p. 103).

[175] Bernard, ep. 149, *SBO*, VII, p. 353.

[176] *De monasterio Sancti Bertini vellem vos moderatius agere quam coepistis* (ibid.).

thirty years.[177] Superficially sympathetic, Bernard's letter warns Peter that he is not in a position to 'claim it without great effort' or to 'hold it in peace'.[178] It ends with the statement, *honesta vobis ... praebetur quiescendi occasio, timor inquietandi*, 'an honourable opportunity for renouncing (the claim) is offered to you, the fear of pressing (it)'.[179] The second half of this statement suggests that *occasio* functions here in a double sense, connoting both 'opportunity' and 'pretext'. The letter can be related to a papal tribunal, to which both Peter and the abbot of Saint-Bertin had been summoned, set for 11 November 1138, in the middle of the wrangle over Langres.[180] Van den Eynde, drawing attention to a papal bull which states that Peter failed to attend at the appointed time,[181] concludes that this failure was in response to Bernard's letter.[182] To this can be added the comments of Bredero, who interprets the letter as a critical response to the criticism contained in letter 29.[183] Bernard's letter may accordingly constitute both a riposte and a veiled threat: if Peter does proceed against Saint-Bertin, he may find himself pitted once again against Bernard.

The material considered in this chapter offers ample evidence that between 1130 and 1140 there were 'real' causes of dispute between Cluniacs and Cistercians, centring primarily on issues of tithes and episcopal election. These issues find their reflection in a flurry of letters from both men, with Peter championing the cause of Gigny, and Bernard setting himself up as protagonist for Langres. In terms of the epistolary relationship, a certain negativity can be perceived. Peter's letter 29 can be characterised as the most overtly critical of his extant letters to Bernard. Written after the end of the papal schism between Innocent II and Anacletus, its apocalyptic overtones may seem to look both backwards and forwards. Peter would seem to be hinting that while the schism in Italy is over, another threatens to break out in the heart of French monasticism. Bernard had been instrumental in resolving the first; it may seem that his intervention at Langres threatens to initiate the second. Against this can be set Bernard's apparent failure to reply, together with the brief but damaging 'demonisation' of Peter in his letter to the Roman cardinals. Letter 29 is followed by a gap of some five years in the epistolary record. When the correspondence resumes in 1143, it is seemingly initiated by Peter. The subject, as will be seen in the next chapter, is once again the question of the relationship between Cluniacs and Cistercians.

---

[177] Van den Eynde, 'Principaux voyages', pp. 70–72.

[178] *Nunc vero, cum nec absque magno labore vindicare vobis praefatum monasterium, nec in pace, ut aiunt, queatis possidere ...* (ep. 149).

[179] Ibid.

[180] Constable reconstructs the following timetable for Langres: the holding of the election in June/July, 1138; the investiture in mid-August/early September; the consecration in mid-September; the new election (probably) in January 1139 (Constable, 'Langres', *passim*).

[181] JL 8016.

[182] Van den Eynde, 'Principaux voyages', p. 72.

[183] Bredero, 'Saint Bernard in his relations', p. 328; idem, *Bernard of Clairvaux*, p. 235.

Chapter 5

Reproach, *Iocus* and Debate: Bernard, Ep. 228; Peter, Letter 111

As stated in the previous chapter, Peter's letter 29, written in 1138, is followed by a seeming epistolary silence which is not broken until late 1143/early 1144, after Peter's return from a visit to Spain. Ep. 228 from Bernard, presenting itself as the reply to a missing letter from Peter,[1] will be followed by Peter's letter 111, a second 'open' letter on the subject of Cluniac–Cistercian relations.[2] Although Zerbi's assertion that the intervening gap represents a period of epistolary 'coolness' cannot be proved, several factors may appear to make it likely.[3] The overt link forged in letter 111 between tithes and Langres as potential threats to *caritas* seems, as he suggests, to signal the public resumption of the correspondence.[4] Bernard's ep. 228 makes references to two failures to reply on the part of Peter. This is taken by Torrell and Bouthillier as evidence of further missing letters.[5] In fact, as will be seen, the surrounding language may suggest that there is no need to look here beyond the earlier letters written by Bernard from Italy during the papal schism.[6] Like letter 28, letter 111 employs the device of a 'public' centre and a 'private' frame. While the first of these seems to offer a far more conciliatory approach than that found previously, the second, developed at considerably greater length than in the earlier letter, may be thought to constitute a challenge to Bernard. In particular, it will be argued in what follows that both ep. 228 and letter 111 draw heavily on the Augustine/Jerome correspondence, specifically the demand by Augustine that Jerome engage in 'debate' and/or write a 'palinode', that is, a public recantation of his interpretation of *Galatians*. The evidence suggests that Bernard should be seen as responding to pressure from Peter contained in the latter's missing letter. As will be seen, Bernard's response can best be construed in a negative fashion.

---

[1] Bernard, ep. 228, *SBO*, VIII, pp. 98–100. This letter appears in Peter's collection as letter 110, *Letters*, I, pp. 272–4. There are a few minor discrepancies, presumably arising at the stage of incorporation into a letter-collection. Whether these changes were made at Clairvaux or at Cluny can only be conjectured. Any potentially significant variations will be noted as they arise.

[2] Peter, letter 111, *Letters*, I, pp. 274–99.

[3] Zerbi, 'Remarques sur l'epistola 98', p. 217, n. 5; idem, ' "In Cluniaco vestra sibi perpetuam mansionem elegit" (Petri Venerabilis Epistola 98): un momento decisivo nella vita di Abelardo dopo il concilio di Sens', in *Tra Milano e Cluny. Momenti di vita e cultura ecclesiastica nel secolo XII*, Italia Sacra 28, Rome, 1978, 373–95, p. 375 and n. 5.

[4] Ibid.

[5] Torrell and Bouthillier, *Pierre le Vénérable et sa vision*, p. 95.

[6] Bernard, ep. 147; idem, ep. 148.

Bernard's ep. 228, together with the 'private' frame of letter 111, will constitute the main subject of this chapter. Before this is undertaken, however, it should be noted that another potential cause of conflict had arisen in the intervening period, namely the condemnation for heresy of Abelard, largely orchestrated by Bernard, and the subsequent intervention of Peter, under whose aegis Abelard would eventually die.[7] Although there is no record of any direct communication on the subject between Peter and Bernard, a letter written by Peter to Innocent II on Abelard's behalf suggests that they came into indirect contact.[8] Scholarly opinion on the significance of this episode is divided. According to Bredero, it should be seen as furthering some kind of rapprochement between the two abbots.[9] Grivot, on the other hand, includes it among his list of events which brought the two men into opposition.[10] Peter's letter to Innocent, couched, as Bredero indicates, in careful and diplomatic terms, has as its cornerstone the report of a 'reconciliation' between Bernard and Abelard.[11] Its language, however, leaves room for some nuances of criticism as to how the latter has been treated.

While the main outline of events can be reconstructed with some confidence, some of the details are open to debate. The Council of Sens, where the condemnation took place, is generally dated to 2 June 1140. As Mews notes, however,[12] Zerbi has more recently espoused 1141, a possibility which he had previously dismissed.[13] Peter's letter 98, itself only susceptible to relative dating, suggests that Abelard arrived at Cluny shortly afterwards. As will be seen, the letter glosses over how and why.[14] Meanwhile, confirmation of the condemnation, and the

---

[7]   Peter Abelard (1079–1142) acquired a reputation as an influential teacher and a proponent of controversial theological views. Born near Nantes, he studied dialectic and theology in the Loire valley and in Paris. His 'autobiographical' *Historia calamitatum* records his seduction of and subsequent marriage to Heloise, resulting in his castration at the instigation of her uncle. His entry as a monk into St Denis was followed by a chequered career which included the enforced burning of his work on the Trinity at Soissons in 1121 and which culminated in the condemnation at Sens. See C. J. Mews, 'Peter Abelard', *Authors of the Middle Ages, historical and religious writers of the Latin West*, gen. ed. P. J. Geary, Aldershot, Hants, 1995, vol. II, no. 5, 1–88; J. Marenbon, *The philosophy of Peter Abelard*, Cambridge, 1997, pp. 7–35.

[8]   Peter, letter 98, *Letters*, I, pp. 258–59.

[9]   Bredero, *Bernard of Clairvaux*, p. 236.

[10]   Grivot, 'Saint Bernard et Pierre le Vénérable', p. 97.

[11]   Bredero, 'Saint Bernard in his relations', p. 330.

[12]   Mews, 'Peter Abelard', p. 18, n. 43.

[13]   P. Zerbi, 'Les différends doctrinaux', in *Bernard de Clairvaux. Histoire, mentalités, spiritualité*, Colloque de Lyon–Cîteaux–Dijon, Sources Chrétiennes 380, Paris, 1992, 429–58, p. 433, n. 11.

[14]   It is not clear whether Peter and Abelard already knew each other personally. Two letters of exhortation to renounce the world and retire to Cluny are addressed by Peter to a certain *magister Petrus*, 'master Peter' (Peter, letter 9, *Letters*, I, 14–16; idem, letter 10, ibid., pp. 16–17). Constable reports the identification with Abelard proposed by Mabillon and Leclercq, but remains sceptical (Constable, *Letters*, II, pp. 101–2). Zerbi similarly refutes it on grounds of dating (Zerbi, 'Remarques', p. 216; 'In Cluniaco', p. 374 and n. 3). Abelard's (possibly subsequent) influence on Peter's writing is argued for both by Kritzeck (J. Kritzeck, 'De l'influence de Pierre Abélard sur Pierre le Vénérable dans ses œuvres sur

passing of sentence on Abelard were sought from Innocent by Bernard.[15] Excommunication and the imposition of perpetual silence were duly pronounced, in a papal bull dated 16 July and addressed jointly to the archbishops of Sens, Rheims, and Bernard of Clairvaux.[16] In a brief letter written at the same time it was enjoined that Abelard and his fellow-heretic, Arnold of Brescia, be 'shut up separately', in 'places of religion, wherever it seems best to you'.[17] Again, there is some argument over whether these documents are to be dated to 1140 or 1141.[18] Underlying this is a deeper question of whether Peter's letter asking permission for Abelard to remain at Cluny was written in ignorance or awareness of the papal decision. The letter praises apostolic justice[19] and reminds Innocent of his previous affection towards Abelard.[20] Zerbi has argued that this could only appear critical, even 'sarcastic', if Innocent were known to have already passed sentence.[21] Clanchy, however, appears to take the opposite view, presenting the intervention as

---

l'Islam', in *Pierre Abélard–Pierre le Vénérable. Les courants littéraires et artistiques en occident au milieu du XIIe siècle*, Colloques Internationaux du Centre National de la Recherche Scientifique 546, Paris, 1975, 205–12) and by Iogna-Prat (Iogna-Prat, *Ordonner et exclure*, p. 106). The latter also refers on several occasions to their 'intimate friendship' (ibid., pp. 15; 147; 193; 321).

[15] According to Zerbi, Bernard despatched a dossier consisting of some eleven or twelve letters relating to the condemnation, addressed to Innocent and to a range of leading ecclesiastical figures (Zerbi, 'In Cluniaco', p. 390 and n. 26). For the view that some of these letters may have been written earlier, see L. N. d'Olwer, 'Sur quelques lettres de S. Bernard, avant ou après le concile de Sens?', in *Mélanges saint Bernard,* XXIVe congrès de l'association bourguignonne des sociétés savantes, Dijon, 1953, 100–108. These arguments were subsequently espoused by Oursel (R. Oursel, *La dispute et la grace: Essai sur la rédemption d'Abélard*, Publications de l'Université de Dijon 19, Paris, 1959, pp. 89–94).

[16] JL 8148. This document appears as ep. 194 in Bernard's letter-collection (ep. 194, *SBO*, VIII, pp. 46–8).

[17] *mandamus quatenus Petrus Abaelardus et Arnaldus de Brixia.. in religiosis locis, ubi vobis melius visum fuerit, separatim faciatis includi* ..., 'we order that ... you should cause Peter Abelard and Arnold of Brixia ... to be shut up separately in places of religion, where it seems best to you' (re-edited by Dom J. Leclercq, 'Les lettres de Guillaume de Saint-Thierry à saint Bernard', *Revue Bénénedictine* 79 (1969), 375–91, p. 379 = JL 8149).

[18] Constable's proposal of 1141, retaining the date of 1140 for the council of Sens, is based on his identification of Bernard's envoy Nicholas with Nicholas of Clairvaux, known to have remained in Rome until 1141 (Constable, *Letters*, II, pp. 317–20). The thesis was initially challenged by Zerbi, who pointed out that the papal letters could have been entrusted to another envoy (Zerbi, 'Remarques', p. 231; idem, "In Cluniaco vestra', p. 394).

[19] *Iustitiam apostolicam quae nulli umquam nec etiam extraneo vel peregrino defuit, sibi non defuturam diximus; misericordiam ipsam ubi ratio postularet, sibi occursuram promisimus*, 'I said that apostolic justice, which has never failed anyone, even stranger or penitential exile, would not be lacking to him; I promised that mercy would meet him, where reason demanded it' (letter 98, p. 258).

[20] *Rogo igitur ... ut ... more quo omnes bonos colitis, et istum dilexistis, scuto defensionis apostolicae protegatis*, 'I ask therefore ... that ... you protect him with the shield of apostolic defence, in the way in which you cultivate all good men, and have also loved him' (ibid., p. 259).

[21] Zerbi, 'Remarques', pp. 218–19; idem, 'In Cluniaco vestra', p. 378.

a means of forestalling the implementation of the papal authorisation relating to Abelard's 'arrest'.[22]

In view of the uncertainties over dating, the question of the precise degree of Peter's knowledge or ignorance must remain unresolved. In general terms, however, it may be noted that Peter's letter appears to sidestep the whole juridical issue of condemnation and appeal, by presenting the entry into Cluny as a *fait accompli*. The letter as a whole is characterised by a kind of studied vagueness. Clanchy draws attention to the fact that the opening suppresses any reference to Sens or Bernard.[23] Abelard is said to have 'passed through' Cluny, coming 'recently from France'.[24] The account of his motivation is filtered through his own mouth by reported speech: 'He replied that, burdened by the persecutions of certain people, who laid upon him the name of heretic, which he deeply abhorred, he had appealed to apostolic majesty and wished to flee to it.'[25] This selective narration of events may be compared with that found at the beginning of letter 29, where Peter claimed to have been met 'unexpectedly' by the canons of Langres as he happened to be returning from Poitou. The reference here to 'certain people' similarly recalls the reference there to 'certain from Lyons'. The end of the letter returns to the device of unnamed opponents, as Innocent is asked to extend his protection over Abelard, 'lest.. he be able to be expelled or removed ... at the insistence of any'.[26]

While the omission of any reference to the Council of Sens can be seen as minimising the gravity of the situation, the references to Abelard's age and weakness,[27] taken together with the demand for protection, may serve to present Abelard as a victim of persecution. The papacy to which Abelard has appealed is designated as *commune refugium*, the 'common refuge'.[28] The image is pursued through the medium of Cluny, as Abelard is likened to a 'sparrow' which has found a 'home', a 'turtle-dove' which has found a 'nest'.[29] Characterised by Clanchy as

---

[22]   Clanchy, *Abelard*, p. 319. Taken in this light, Peter's references to 'justice' and 'affection' may emerge rather as a form of *insinuatio*, 'ingratiation', designed to manipulate Innocent into rescinding his previous instructions. On the notion of *insinuatio*, see P. von Moos, 'Le silence d'Héloïse', in *Pierre Abélard–Pierre le Vénérable. Les courants littéraires et artistiques en occident au milieu du XIIe siècle*, Colloques Internationaux du Centre National de la Recherche Scientifique 546, Paris, 1975, 425–68.

[23]   Clanchy, *Abelard*, p. 320.

[24]   *Magister Petrus ... nuper a Francia veniens, per Cluniacum transitum fecit* (letter 98, p. 258).

[25]   *Gravatum se vexationibus quorumdam, qui sibi quod valde abhorrebat nomen hereticum imponebant, maiestatem apostolicam se appellasse, et ad eam confugere velle respondit* (ibid.).

[26]   *ne (a domo) ... aliquorum instantia aut expelli aut commoveri valeat* (ibid., p. 259).

[27]   *Quod nos senectuti eius, debilitati eius, religioni eius, congruere putantes ...*, 'Thinking that this (withdrawal to Cluny) was appropriate to his age, his weakness, his religion ...' (ibid.); *Rogo ... ut reliquos dies vitae et senectutis suae, qui fortasse non multi sunt, in Cluniaco vestra eum consummare iubeatis*, 'I ask ... that you bid him to complete the remainder of his days, which perhaps are not many, in your Cluny' (ibid.).

[28]   Ibid., p. 258.

[29]   *Rogo ... ego ... rogat ipse ... ne a domo quam velut* passer, *ne a nido quem velut* turtur *invenisse se gaudet.. aut expelli aut commoveri valeat ... scuto defensionis apostolicae*

the 'rhetoric of understatement', this forms a strong contrast, as he suggests, to the animal imagery employed by Bernard.[30] The latter, for example, on a number of occasions represents Abelard as *draco*, a 'dragon', 'serpent'.[31] Elsewhere, he is likened to *coluber*, a 'snake'.[32] Significantly, the reference to Job on which this draws is linked there with the mythical *hydra*.[33] Seen in relation to this, Peter's imagery can be seen to perform two functions: it both removes the element of demonisation and represents an inversion from predator to prey. In a letter to Heloise, written after Abelard's death, Peter will also invoke Job through his depiction of Abelard as 'a man sincere and upright, fearing God and withdrawing from evil'.[34] The overt point of comparison is through *scabies*, his 'scab', 'mange', and his 'bodily ailments'. The sense of *scabies* as 'pruriency', 'lust', together with the recognised metaphor of heresy as leprosy,[35] makes it difficult, however, not to see here an allusion to his other 'trials', above all, perhaps, to his condemnation at Sens.

In keeping with the lack of precision diagnosed earlier, the 'reconciliation' of Abelard with Bernard is presented in terms which obfuscate the detail of what actually took place, and which present the abbot of Cîteaux rather than Peter himself as its moving force.[36] The former is said to have 'come' to Cluny, and to have treated with Peter and with Abelard alike concerning 'peace between himself and the lord of Clairvaux'.[37] The account of the reconciliation is again mediated

---

protegatis, 'I ask.. he himself asks.. that, lest he be able to be either expelled or dislodged ... from the home, which like *the sparrow*, from the nest, which like the turtle-dove, he rejoices to have found, you should protect him with the shield of apostolic defence' (ibid., p. 259 = Ps 83. 4).

[30] Clanchy, *Abelard*, p. 323.

[31] Bernard, ep. 189, 2, *SBO*, VIII, p. 13; cf. idem, ep. 330, ibid., pp. 267–8; idem, ep. 332, ibid., p. 271. The image appears to be drawn from Revelations (Apc 12. 7).

[32] Bernard, ep. 331, *SBO*, VIII, p. 269.

[33] *Egressus est de caverna sua* coluber tortuosus, *et in similitudinem hydrae, uno prius capite succiso, septem pro uno capita produxit*, '*The tortuous snake* has come forth from its hole, and after the likeness of the hydra, when one head has first been cut off, it has brought forth seven heads in the place of one' (ibid. = Iob 26. 13).

[34] *Tali nobiscum*, vir simplex et rectus, timens deum, et recedens a malo, *tali ... conversatione, ultimos vitae suae dies consecrans deo, pausandi gratia, nam plus solito, scabie et quibusdam corporis incommoditatibus gravabatur, a me Cabilonem missus est*, 'Consecrating the last days of his life to God, in such a way of life with us ... as *a man sincere and upright, fearing God and withdrawing from evil*, for the sake of resting I sent him to Chalon-sur-Saône, for he was burdened more than usual with scab and with certain bodily ailments' (Peter, letter 115, *Letters*, I, p. 307 = Iob 1. 1).

[35] See R. I. Moore, *The origins of European dissent*, London, 1977, revised Oxford, 1985, pp. 246–50.

[36] See comments of Zerbi (Zerbi, 'Remarques', pp. 219–220; idem, 'In Cluniaco vestra', p. 379).

[37] *Venit interim dominus Cisterciensis abbas, et de pace ipsius et domini Clarevallensis ... nobiscum et cum ipso pariter egit*, 'There came meanwhile the lord abbot of Cîteaux ... and treated with me and him alike of peace between him and the lord of Clairvaux' (letter 98, p. 258).

through the mouth of Abelard.[38] Peter's role is limited to one of encouragement, that Abelard should go with the abbot of Cîteaux to Bernard, and to a warning that he should undertake to correct any offensive doctrines.[39] Whether Peter was already aware of the papal bulls or not, the preaching here of emendation rather than punishment can be seen to work against their general trend. As Zerbi points out, however, the assurance that this advice was accepted remains ambiguous. The briefly appended statement, *Et factum est ita*, 'And so it was done', could be taken as applying to either or both pieces of advice.[40] Clanchy points out that there is no Cistercian record of any agreement between Bernard and Abelard.[41] Similarly, despite Peter's subsequent assertion to Heloise that Abelard had been 'restored to apostolic grace by [my] letter(s) and my labour',[42] no official document survives rescinding the sentence.[43] This may suggest, as Clanchy concludes, that the business was settled privately and unofficially, with 'mercy' being extended to Abelard himself, but the 'errors' remaining condemned.[44]

In consequence, it is not at all clear that the affair should be read, as Bredero suggests, as having improved the relationship between Peter and Bernard. Indeed, it may be noted that letter 98 can be said to explicitly exclude the notion of any personal contact between Peter and Bernard, since the meeting with Abelard, not attended by Peter, is said to have taken place not at Cluny, but elsewhere.[45] As stated previously, the correspondence reopens with Bernard's ep. 228, dating, according to Constable, to late 1143 or early 1144.[46] As will be

---

[38]   *Ivit, rediit, cum domino [abbati] Clarevallensi, mediante [domino abbati] Cisterciensi sopitis prioribus querelis se pacifice convenisse, reversus rettulit*, 'He went, he returned; returning he reported that with the [lord abbot] of Cîteaux acting as intermediary, he had met peacefully with the lord [abbot] of Clairvaux, the former complaints having been laid to rest' (ibid., p. 259).

[39]   *Addidimus hoc monitis nostris, ut si qua catholicas aures offendentia, aut scripsisset aut dixisset ... et a verbis suis amoveret et a libris abraderet*, 'I added this to my warnings, that if in any way he had either written or said anything offensive to catholic ears ... he should both remove these from his speech and erase them from his books' (ibid.).

[40]   Zerbi, 'Remarques', p. 220; idem, 'In Cluniaco vestro', p. 380.

[41]   Clanchy, *Abelard*, p. 321; cf. Mews, 'Peter Abelard', p. 19.

[42]   *(postquam) litteris et labore meo, apostolicae gratiae redditus est* ... (letter 115, p. 307).

[43]   Clanchy, *Abelard*, p. 324.

[44]   As Clanchy points out, after the death of Bernard the justice of the condemnation was maintained by Geoffrey of Auxerre, his secretary and principal biographer (William of St. Thierry, Arnold of Bonneval, Geoffrey of Auxerre, *Sancti Bernardi vita prima libri V*, III, V. 13–14, ed. J.-P. Migne, *Patrologia Latina* 185-I, Paris, 1859, 310D–312A). See Clanchy, *Abelard*, p. 321.

[45]   Perhaps at Clairvaux or, in view of the shorter distance and the mediating role of abbot Rainald, at Cîteaux. See Zerbi, 'Remarques', p. 227 and n. 24; idem, 'In Cluniaco vestra', p. 389.

[46]   The date can only be established in relation to letter 111, Peter's reply, written, according to Constable, in 'the year following his return from Spain' (Constable, *Letters*, II, p. 172). This trip has been established as having taken place between March and October 1142 (C. J. Bishko, 'Peter the Venerable's journey to Spain', in *Petrus Venerabilis, 1156–1956: studies and texts commemorating the eighth centenary of his death*, ed. G. Constable and J. Kritzeck, Studia Anselmiana 40, Rome, 1956, 163–75). Constable, perhaps following Bishko, dates Peter's return to Cluny to some time in 1143 (Constable, *Letters*, II, p. 80 and Appendix D, p. 262;

seen, the letter presents a jocular façade. The impression, however, may be misleading.[47]

> To the reverent father and lord Peter, by the grace of God abbot of Cluny, brother Bernard, called abbot of Clairvaux: himself, howsoever little he is.

> Does it please you to joke like this? Graciously indeed and in a friendly manner, provided that you play in such a way as not to mock. *Do not wonder at this*. For your so sudden[48] and unexpected favour makes it suspect to me. For it is not long since writing to you I greeted your highness[49] with due reverence, and you replied not a word. Not much before again I had written to you from the city of Rome, and not even then did I receive one iota. Do you wonder now that I have not presumed to inflict my trifles again upon your recent return from Spain? Wherefore if there is blame not to have written for whatsoever cause, it will certainly not be blameless to have refused, not to say scorned, to write back. Behold, justice would act for me in this, because you demand it of me, if I did not prefer to meet returning grace rather than to keep it back from myself, while wishing to excuse myself unprofitably, or to accuse another. But I have said this, so as not to keep closed in my mind what I would not bring forth with my mouth, since true friendship rejects this. However, because charity *believes everything*, let all suspicion be put out of the way. I rejoice that you have grown warm to remember former friendship, and to recall a friend, even wounded. Recalled, I return willingly. Blessed am I who am recalled. I am mindful of no injuries. Behold me, who had been indeed the servant of your Holiness, both now,

---

Bishko, 'Peter's journey', p. 165). This view, however, has been challenged by van den Eynde, who argues that the evidence does not preclude an earlier return date of October 1142, which, he suggests, would have implications for the dating of Peter's subsequent correspondence (van den Eynde, 'Principaux voyages', p. 99). Theoretically, accordingly, it might appear that letter 111 should be redated from 1144 to 1143. In fact, however, Peter himself is rather more vague than Constable would suggest. Although he twice refers to his 'recent' stay in Spain (letter 111, p. 289; ibid., p. 294), this may be seen as constituting a response to Bernard's comment on his 'recent' return, which in itself forms part of a wider pattern of epistolary reproach. Additionally, the dating of letter 111 to 1144 seems to find confirmation in Peter's reference to his visit to Marcigny (*Le cartulaire de Marcigny-sur-Loire (1045–1144). Essai de reconstitution d'un manuscrit disparu*, ed. J. Richard, Analecta Burgundica 4, Dijon, 1957, pp. 101–2, no 171bis). See Constable, *Letters*, II, p. 172; ibid., Appendix D, p. 262.

[47] Bredero concedes that Bernard's letter may have been 'facetious and rhetorical' (Bredero, 'Saint Bernard in his relations', p. 330.) Lang interprets it as Bernard 'struggling ... to maintain his dignity' in response to Peter's jocularity in the missing letter, but goes on to extrapolate that it is an 'expression of friendship' (Lang, 'The friendship', pp. 40–41).

[48] *Subita*, 'sudden', is absent from letter 110. Leclercq suggests that it may have been omitted as being superfluous (Leclercq, 'Lettres de S. Bernard', p. 174). Equally, it might perhaps have been added in the interests of stylistic balance.

[49] *Vestram magnitudinem* appears as *coronam vestram* in letter 110. According to Leclercq, this substitution may be thought to soften the sense of the original, by replacing an allusion to 'grandeur' with one to the monastic 'tonsure' (Leclercq, ibid.). This, however, ignores the fact that *corona* is itself ambiguous, also connoting 'monarchy', 'kingship'. There is also a further possible sense, which may find support from later in the letter. *Corona* can be used to denote the 'crown' of martyrdom. Bernard may subsequently hint, drawing on Jerome, that his days as a 'champion' of Christ are over, and that it is Peter's turn to take up the 'race'.

and before.[50] I give thanks, I am excellently placed, made again your intimate, as you deign to write.[51] If by chance I had grown cold, as you assert, there is no doubt that I grow hot again swiftly,[52] warmed in the entrails of your charity.

And now I have received with ready hands what it has pleased you to write. I read it eagerly, I re-read it willingly, and it pleases often repeated. The joke pleases, I confess. It is pleasing by its pleasantness, and serious by its gravity. In some way or other among the joking, you so dispose your words in judgement that the joke is not redolent of levity, and the authority that is conserved does not diminish the grace of the merriment. Indeed, authority is so conserved that those words of the holy man could rightly be applied to you: *If ever I smiled, they did not believe me.* Come then, I have written back, and, I think, rightly now I demand more than you promised.[53] It is fitting that you should know what is in my power. It has been decreed to me not to go out beyond the monastery, except to the meeting of the abbots at Cîteaux once a year.[54] Here, supported by your prayers and consoled by blessings, for the few *days, in which I now serve, I wait until my exchange comes. May God be merciful to me,*[55] so as not to turn away your[56] *prayer and his mercy from me.* I will sit and I will be silent, if by chance I may make trial of what the holy prophet utters from the plenitude of innermost sweetness, saying: *It is good to wait for the Lord in silence.* I am broken in strength, and I have a lawful discharge, so that now I cannot run about as I was wont. And in case you should seem to be the only one who has been playful, I think that you will not now dare to rebuke me for this silence of mine, and in your fashion to call sleep what, in my view, the holy Isaiah more fittingly and more accurately names the *cultivation of righteousness*, and of which you read in this same prophet, with the Lord saying: *In silence and in hope will be your strength.* Commend me to the prayers of the holy gathering of Cluny, having greeted (it) first from me as the servant of all, if you judge worthy.

---

[50]   *Et nunc*, 'both now', is missing from letter 110, leaving *et ante* to be translated as 'even before.' Its appearance here seems to look forward to the end of the letter, where Bernard depicts himself as *servus omnium*.

[51]   *Gratias ago, optime locatus sum, intimus vobis denuo factus, sicut dignamini scribere* (ep. 228, 1, p. 99). This appears to constitute a reference to the *salutatio* of Peter's missing letter. Peter's letter concerning Langres had similarly been directed *Venerabili et intimo mihi domino Bernardo abbati Clarevallensi* ..., 'To the venerable and intimate to me lord Bernard ...' (letter 29, p. 101). If Bernard's statement here is read as encompassing an oblique allusion to this critical letter, it might be construed as blaming Peter for any ensuing 'coldness'.

[52]   *Velociter*, 'swiftly', is absent from letter 110.

[53]   *Quae*, 'which', appears for *quam*, 'than', in both letter 110 and in certain MSS variants of ep. 228. This alters the sense considerably, from 'more than you promised' to 'the more which you promised'. On the second reading, the 'promise' might appear to foreshadow Peter's letter 111, not included in Bernard's official collection. Once again, the change could have taken place at either place.

[54]   This refers to the Cistercian General Chapter, which met annually on 14 September, the Feast of the Exaltation of the Holy Cross. What follows may suggest that this statement should be construed as a negative response to an 'invitation' contained in Peter's missing letter.

[55]   Constable identifies this allusion to the Old Testament (Constable, *Letters*, I, p. 273, n.d.). The invocation appears twice in the mouth of David in the context of warding off evil, that he should lay hands on his enemy Saul, the 'Lord's anointed' (I Sm 24. 7; ibid., 26. 11). The allusion may relate, as will be seen, to Bernard's disguised refusal to enter into potentially damaging debate with his old opponent.

[56]   *Meam* replaces *vestram* in letter 110, in accordance with the Psalm from which this whole phrase is adapted (Ps 65. 20).

At first sight, Bernard's letter lends itself to reading as a straightfoward example of *amicitia iocosa*, 'playful friendship', as discussed in the first chapter. Bernard's exploitation of epistolary etiquette, equating failure to write with failure in friendship, is presented as countering and turning back an epistolary 'reproach' emanating initially from Peter.[57] As suggested earlier, one characteristic of *amicitia iocosa* is the mock-reproach, indicative of reciprocity and mutual understanding, and functioning as a means of conveying affection. The impression of jocularity is seemingly reinforced by the linguistic play which characterises the letter as a whole. The primary linguistic nexus centres on the notion of joking and playfulness, *iocari*, *iocus* and *ludere*. The opening question, *Itane iocari libet?*, 'Does it please you to joke like this?', is picked up subsequently, *Placet fateor iocus*, 'The joke pleases, I confess', then subjected to further exploitation.[58] *Ludere*, to 'play', is first set against its cognate *illudere*, to 'mock',[59] then picked up towards the close of the letter, 'in case you should seem to be the only one who has been playful ...'.[60] As argued earlier, however, 'playful friendship' can serve as a cover for more serious matters. Equally, epistolary reproach can function as a displacement for other issues. Most significantly, the very notion of 'joking', as will be demonstrated, may take on another dimension through the medium of Augustine.[61]

There appears to be no trace of the letter from Peter to which Bernard claims to be replying. It is not so clear, however, that the two letters of his own which Bernard claims were left unanswered are also missing, as Bredero implies.[62] If, as Constable suggests, and as letter 111 makes very probable, the earlier letter from Rome can be identified with ep. 147, the reply to Peter's letter 65,[63] the other letter might perhaps be identified with the subsequent ep. 148. The same opposition between grandeur and humility as was found there, together with a similar play on worthiness and

---

[57] *Modo miramini quod ... nugas meas denuo ingerere non praesumpsi?*, 'Do you wonder now that ... I have not presumed to inflict my trifles again?' (Bernard, ep. 228, 1, p. 98); *En in quo pro me faceret iustitia, quia id a me flagitatis ...*, 'Behold, justice would act for me in this, because you demand it of me ...' (ibid.); *Si forte tepueram, ut arguitis ...*, 'If by chance I had grown cold, as you assert.. ' (ibid., p. 99).

[58] *inter iocandum*, 'among the joking' (ibid., 2, p. 99); *(ut) iocus levitatem non redoleat ...*, '(that) the joke is not redolent of levity ...' (ibid.).

[59] *sed si ita luditis, ut non illudatis*, 'provided that you play in such a way as not to mock' (ibid., 1, p. 98).

[60] *ne solus videamini mihi lusisse ...* (ibid., 2, p. 99).

[61] In a study of Bernard's ep. 87, to Oger, canon of Mont-Saint-Eloy, Leclercq demonstrates that the exploitation of what he dubs there the 'vocabulary of play' is linked to irony and self-irony. Surprisingly, in view of this, he nevertheless concludes that its presence in ep. 228 to Peter is merely a matter of 'stylistic ornament' (Dom J. Leclercq, 'Le thème de la jonglerie dans les relations entre Saint Bernard, Abélard et Pierre le Vénérable', in *Pierre Abélard–Pierre le Vénérable. Les courants littéraires et artistiques en occident au milieu du XIIe siècle*, Colloques Internationaux du Centre National de la Recherche Scientifique 546, Paris, 1975, 671–84, p. 683). More recently, the theme has been re-examined by Drumbl (J. Drumbl, ' "Ludus iucundus, honestus, gravis, spectabilis." Die Metapher des Theatrum mundi bei Bernhard von Clairvaux', *Aevum* 72: 2 (1998), 361–74).

[62] Bredero, 'Saint Bernard in his relations', p. 330.

[63] Constable, *Letters*, II, p. 173. Peter's 'defence' in letter 111 will be based on the claim that the letter to which Bernard refers was a reply to a letter from himself.

condescension, forms a secondary linguistic nexus here. Bernard signs himself *quantulus est*, 'howsoever little he is'. Peter is referred to as *vestra magnitudo*, 'your Highness', and said to have been greeted by Bernard *debita reverentia*, 'with due reverence'. Peter's joking is said to have been done *dignanter*, 'graciously', but such unexpected *dignatio*, 'condescension', 'favour', is held 'suspect'. Bernard's letter ends with the words *si dignum iudicatis*, 'if you judge worthy'. Ep. 147 and ep. 148 had alluded to the possibility of a visit, the second in terms which rendered it more doubtful. If, as was suggested in a previous chapter, Peter had for some reason 'blocked' this visit, it might seem that through a 'playful' epistolary reproach, Bernard is reminding Peter that he had previously made overtures which had been rejected. As will be seen, this interpretation may find confirmation in other features of this letter.

Bernard's reproach plays with the motifs of wonder and suspicion.[64] On to and around these motifs are grafted biblical allusions, two of them relating to miracles performed in the Gospels. In the first of these, Bernard seemingly identifies himself with Christ, through the injunction 'Do not wonder at this', addressed to the disbelieving Jews.[65] The second, however, reverses the direction. The accusation, 'you replied to me not a word',[66] concerns a woman of Canaan, whose daughter is troubled by a demon. Initially rejected with the words, 'I have only been sent to the sheep of the house of Israel which have been lost',[67] and 'It is not good to take the bread of sons and throw it to dogs',[68] Christ is finally said to relent, in response to her 'great faith'.[69] The latter, in particular, seems to pick up the opposition between 'Jews' and 'Gentiles' signalled previously. Here, however, it would appear to be Bernard who has been spurned as 'unclean'. Two further allusions may serve to suggest that personal *amicitia* is standing in for communal *caritas*. The accusation, 'not even then did I receive one iota',[70] draws on the claim that 'not one jot or tittle will be omitted from the Law until heaven and earth are changed'.[71] Bernard's assertion, taken from I Corinthians, that 'charity believes everything ...',[72] is followed by the claim, 'I am mindful now of no injuries'.[73] *Caritas*, like *amicitia*, is required to remove suspicion. It is also said to 'suffer everything'.[74]

---

[64]   Nolite mirari hoc, '*Do not wonder at this*' (ep. 228, 1, p. 98 = Io 5. 28); *Modo miramini ...?*, 'Do you now wonder ...?' (ibid.); *Nam suspectum id mihi facit ...*, 'for it is rendered suspect to me ...' (ibid.); *iam omnis suspicio de medio fiat ...*, 'now let all suspicion be put out of the way ...' (ibid., p. 99).

[65]   Io 5. 18.

[66]   *(et) non respondistis mihi verbum* (ep. 228, 1, p. 98 = Mt 15. 23).

[67]   *non sum missus nisi ad oves quae perierunt domus Israhel* (Mt 15. 24).

[68]   *non est bonum sumere panem filiorum et mittere canibus* (ibid., 15. 26).

[69]   Ibid., 15. 28.

[70]   *nec tunc quidem vel unum iota recepi* (ep. 228, 1, p. 98).

[71]   *donec transeat caelum et terra iota unum aut unus apex non praeteribit a lege* (Mt 5. 18).

[72]   *(quia) caritas omnia credit ...* (ep. 228, 1 = I Cor 13. 7).

[73]   *Nullarum iam memor sum iniuriarum* (ep. 228, 1). The expression may have a biblical origin. The (wicked) brothers of Joseph fear *ne forte memor sit iniuriae quam passus est*, 'lest by chance he be mindful of the injury which he suffered' (Gn 50. 15). Likewise, Shimei begs King David, *ne(que) memineris iniuriam servi tui*, 'do not be mindful of the injury of your servant' (II Sm 19. 19). Both Joseph and David display their 'magnanimity'.

[74]   *(Caritas) ... omnia suffert, omnia credit ...* (I Cor 13. 7).

At the same time, two concealed Augustinian allusions may point towards the re-introduction of the epistolary model of his correspondence with Jerome. Although taken from letters addressed to recipients other than Jerome, their significance may lie in the twin evocations of 'debate' and 'song'. Bernard's initial question, 'Does it please you to joke like this?',[75] recalls the opening of a letter from Augustine which equates 'joking' with mock-debate: 'Are we having a serious debate, or does it please (you) to joke?'[76] The letter continues by ridiculing the arguments put forward by Augustine's 'opponent' in favour of paganism. The second potential allusion also occurs in the context of 'play'. Bernard claims that Peter's 'joke' is 'by its pleasantness pleasing, and serious by its gravity'.[77] This epigrammatic statement, rendered striking by its chiastic form, and by the implicit word-play on *iocus/iucunditas*, can be paralleled with an oxymoronic word-play found elsewhere in Augustine: 'For your eloquence delights me, since it is gravely sweet and/or sweetly grave.'[78] The Augustinian context is that of an exhortatory letter. Augustine admits to taking pleasure in the praise of his addressee, but warns against the vanity which praise begets. The citation given above is followed by an anecdote concerning the refusal of Themistocles to 'sing to the lyre' at a banquet. When asked what it pleased him to hear, he is said to have replied, 'My praise'.[79]

At the end of his first letter to Jerome, Augustine had invited Jerome to offer friendly criticisms of his writing, a palliative, perhaps, to his own criticism of Jerome.[80] In his second letter, written apparently because the first was never delivered, Augustine starts by asking Jerome to enter into a 'written debate'.[81] Later in the letter, however, it is made clear that critical judgement should be applied first and foremost to Jerome's own writings. Jerome is invited to to 'sing a palinode', that is, to write a recantation of his commentary on Galatians.[82] Accordingly, Jerome is

---

[75] *Itane iocari libet?* (ep. 228, 1, p. 98).

[76] *Seriumne aliquid inter nos agimus, an iocari libet?* (Augustine, ep. 17, 1, *CSEL*, 34/1, p. 39). The opposition is subsequently reinforced by repetition, *nisi iocari potius quam serie agere maluisses?*, 'unless you had preferred to joke rather than to debate seriously?' (ibid., p. 40).

[77] *Est (iocus) enim et iucunditate gratus, et serius gravitate* (Bernard, ep. 228, 2, p. 99.)

[78] *Nam eloquium tuum me delectat, quoniam graviter suave est vel suaviter grave* (Augustine, ep. 231, 2, *CSEL*, 57, p. 505.)

[79] *Viderint graves et periti viri, quid de illo Themistocle sentiant ... qui cum in epulis ... canere fidibus recusasset ... dictum illi est:* Quid ergo audire te delectat? *ad quod ille respondisse fertur:* Laudes meas, 'Let grave and learned men see what they think of this remark of Themistocles ... who, when he had refused at a banquet to sing to the lyre ... it was said to him: "What then does it please you to hear?" To which, he is said to have replied: "My praise" ' (ibid., 3, p. 505).

[80] *Sane idem frater aliqua scripta nostra fert secum. Quibus legendis si dignationem adhibueris, etiam sinceram fraternamque severitatem adhibeas quaeso,* 'The same brother brings with him some of my writings. If you will do the favour of reading them, I ask that you also apply honest and brotherly criticism' (Augustine, ep. 28, IV. 6, *CSEL*, 34/1, p. 113).

[81] *Quare adgredere, quaeso, istam nobiscum litterariam collocutionem ...,* 'Therefore enter, I beg, into that written debate with me ...' (idem, ep. 40, I. 1, *CSEL*, 34/2, p. 70).

[82] *Quare arripe, obsecro te, ingenuam et vere Christianam cum caritate severitatem ad illud opus corrigendum atque emendandum et παλινωδιαν, ut dicitur, cane,* 'Therefore, I beg you, lay hold of a candid severity, truly Christian with charity, to correct and emend that work, and sing a palinode, as it is said' (ibid., IV. 7, pp. 77–8).

seemingly offered two alternatives, which are not really alternatives at all: to enter into a scholarly debate with Augustine, and/or to write a recantation. The introduction of these allusions into Benard's letter suggests that he is looking towards a reopening of the question of Cluniac–Cistercian relations, responding, it may be presumed, to pressure contained in the letter from Peter. The form in which they are introduced, however, may seem to imply that Peter is not interested in a genuine discussion, but only in hearing 'praise' of Cluny, unleavened by any criticism.

The impression of negativity is heightened by what can be seen as a series of blocking manœuvres, borrowed from the Jeromian side of the correspondence. Augustine would appear to have had to wait some while for any response to his demands. Jerome would first write two letters refusing to answer,[83] on the grounds that what he had received was a 'copy of a letter',[84] 'unsigned',[85] and previously disseminated all over Rome and Italy.[86] Although Augustine would eventually seemingly admit to the truth of the latter charge,[87] in view of the fact that in the meantime he continued to press for an answer,[88] it seems difficult to accept White's suggestion that Jerome remained 'unconvinced' of the letter's authorship.[89] It is more likely that Jerome should be seen as exploiting what is presented as a breach of epistolary etiquette to avoid complying with Augustine's request.

Chief among the blocking strategies employed by Jerome is the reduction of 'debate' to some kind of mock-combat or athletic display, an image which, as will be seen, fuses the notions of Christian warfare and Christian as athlete with Virgilian allusion.[90] Jerome requests Augustine to send a 'more genuine' copy, 'so that without any rancour of displeasure, we may engage in the disputation of the scriptures'.[91]

---

[83]   Jerome, ep. 102, *CSEL*, 55, pp. 234–6; idem, ep. 105, ibid., pp. 242–6.

[84]   *sed epistulae cuiusdam quasi ad me scriptae per fratrem nostrum Sisinnium diaconum huc exemplaria pervenerunt ...*, 'but a copy of a certain letter, purporting to be written to me, reached me here through our brother Sisinnius, the deacon ...' (Jerome, ep. 102, 1, p. 235).

[85]   *cuius (epistolae) ad me ... exemplaria pervenerunt absque subscriptione tua ...* (idem, ep. 105, 1, p. 242).

[86]   *satis mirari nequeo, quomodo ipsa epistola et Romae et in Italia haberi a plerisque dicatur et ad me solum non pervenerit, cui soli missa est ...*, 'I cannot wonder enough, how the same letter is said to be held by many at Rome and in Italy, and has failed to reach me alone, to whom alone it was sent ...' (ibid., p. 243).

[87]   *Credant itaque fratres nostri ... me invito factum nec mediocrem de hac re dolorem inesse cordi meo, quod litterae meae prius in multorum manus venerunt, quam ad te, ad quem scriptae sunt, pervenire potuerunt*, 'Let our brothers believe.. that it happened against my will and that there is no little grief in my heart concerning it, that my letter came first into the hands of many before it could reach you, to whom it was written' (Augustine, ep. 82, IV. 32, *CSEL*, 34/2, p. 383). He goes on to claim that it would be 'lengthy' and 'irrelevant' to explain how this happened.

[88]   Augustine, ep. 67, I. 1, *CSEL*, 34/2, p. 237; idem, ep. 71, I. 2, ibid., p. 249.

[89]   White, *The Correspondence*, p. 22.

[90]   The image of Christian as athlete can be traced back to I Cor 9. 24, that of Christian as soldier of Christ to Eph 6. 14–17.

[91]   *Itaque, si tua est epistula, aperte scribe vel mitte exemplaria veriora, ut absque ullo rancore stomachi in scripturarum disputatione versemur ...*, 'Therefore, if the letter is yours, write openly or send a more genuine copy, so that without any rancour of displeasure, we may engage in the disputation of the scriptures' (Jerome, ep. 102, 1, p. 235).

Subsequently, this 'invitation' will be repeated in terms which establish the metaphor more directly, 'Let us play on the field of the scriptures, if it pleases (you), without mutual harm.'[92] Augustine's response can be seen to exploit the association between *ludere* and *illudere*: 'Then indeed there is playing, as it were, on the field without fear of offence, but it is a wonder if we are not mocked.'[93] The underlying irony of both offer and response is brought out through the preceding definition, which has established the avoidance of offence as the unquestioning acceptance of the assertions of a 'more learned friend'.[94] The interchange as a whole can be seen to cast a fresh and potentially challenging light on Bernard's opening comment that Peter's 'playfulness' is acceptable, provided that it is not 'mockery'.

Linked with this image is a recurring opposition between old age and youth. Jerome presents himself as having done good service, and earned an honourable discharge: 'It remains that you should love one who loves you and, a young man, not challenge an old man on the field of the scriptures. I have had my time and run, as much as I could; now, since you are running and covering long distances, leisure is due to me ...';[95] 'I, formerly a soldier, now a veteran, must praise the victories of you and others, not fight again myself with weary body ...'[96] So, too, Bernard presents himself as *fractus.. viribus*, 'broken.. in strength', and claims to have *legitima.. excusatio*, a 'lawful discharge'.[97] The military imagery is reinforced by Bernard's self-identification with Job, 'Here ... for the few *days in which I now serve, I wait until my exchange comes*', invoking the language of military service and hinting at death as the final release.[98]

The old/young opposition in Jerome proves to be not a ploy invoking pathos, but the prelude to a warning. The Virgilian reference which follows, *memento Daretis et Entelli* ..., 'remember Dares and Entellus ...',[99] alludes to the boxing-match

---

[92]   *In scripturarum, si placet, campo sine nostro invicem dolore ludamus* (idem, ep. 115, 1, *CSEL*, 55, p. 397).

[93]   *Tum vero sine ullo timore offensionis tamquam in campo luditur, sed mirum si nobis non illuditur* (Augustine, ep. 82, I. 3, p. 354).

[94]   *nisi forte ille modus est, quo utrumque hoc vitium vel vitii suspicionem caveamus, si cum doctiore amico sic disputemus, ut quicquid dixerit, necesse sit approbare nec quaerendi saltem causa liceat aliquantulum reluctari*, 'unless perhaps that is the way by which we may avoid each of these faults and the suspicion of fault, to dispute in such a manner with a more learned friend, as to necessarily approve whatever he says, and not to struggle against it even a little for the sake of inquiring' (ibid., I. 2, pp. 353–4). This follows a lengthy and critical exegesis of Jerome's own words, in particular, his references to 'childish boasting' and to a 'sword smeared with honey.'

[95]   *Superest ut diligas diligentem te; et in Scripturarum campo, iuvenis senem non provoces. Nos nostra habuimus tempora, et cucurrimus quantum potuimus; nunc te currente et longa spatia transmittente, nobis debetur otium..* (Jerome, ep. 102, 2, p. 236).

[96]   *Ego quondam miles, nunc veteranus et tuas et aliorum debeo laudare victorias, non ipse rursus effeto corpore dimicare ...* (idem, ep. 105, 3, p. 244).

[97]   Bernard, ep. 228, 2, p. 99. The link seems to be reinforced by the claim that he can no longer *discurrere*, 'run about', as he was used to (ibid.).

[98]   *Hic ... paucis* diebus quibus nunc milito, exspecto donec veniat immutatio mea (ibid. = Iob 14. 14).

[99]   Jerome, ep. 102, 2. p. 236 = Virgil, *Aeneid*, V, 368–484. It finds a historical doublet in his second letter, through a reminder that Hannibal's 'youthful exultation' met its match in the endurance of Fabius Maximus (Jerome, ep. 105, 3, p. 244).

depicted in the *Aeneid*.[100] Assigning to Augustine the role of arrogant, younger challenger, it prognosticates its defeat at the hands of Jerome, his elderly opponent. The allusion may suggest that underlying Jerome's use of the image of 'mock-combat' is an echo of the ceremonial *lusus Troiae*, a cross between a military parade and a mock-battle, supposedly first performed at the funeral games of Anchises by Ascanius and the young Trojans.[101] Subsequently, Jerome will employ a further Virgilian reference, this time taken from the *Eclogues*, to rescue himself from the demand that he produce a 'palinode'. Like the elderly shepherd Moeris, he claims that old age has robbed him of his singing-voice.[102] In parenthesis, it may be noted that the verb *ludere* is commonly used by classical writers to denote the act of composing poetry.

The Dares/Entellus allusion is overtly offered by Jerome as a riposte to Augustine's introduction of the palinode ascribed to the Greek lyric poet, Stesichorus:[103] 'in case you should seem to be the only one who has proposed something from the poets ...'.[104] Bernard uses a similar form of words, 'in case you should seem to be the only one who has been playful ...',[105] to introduce not a classical but a biblical reminiscence, which identifies silence with 'the cultivation of righteousness'.[106] In Isaiah, 'the cultivation of righteousness' is said to be silence, the 'work' of righteousness to be peace.[107] In consequence, Bernard's preceding

---

[100] Entellus at first refuses to fight:

> *ille sub haec:* non laudis amor, nec gloria cessit
> pulsa metu; sed enim gelidus tardante senecta
> sanguis hebet, frigentque effetae in corpore vires.

'Upon this, he (Entellus) replied: "Neither love of praise, nor glory has departed, driven out by fear; but the blood is sluggish, stiff with hindering old age, and the strength, worn out in the body, is chilly" ' (Virgil, *Aeneid*, 5, 394–6). Subsequently, Dares has to be rescued from Entellus's 'hail' of blows (ibid., 5, 458–62).

[101] Ibid., 580–603. Jerome will go on to suggest that Augustine should search out 'eloquent and well-born young men' as his disputants (Jerome, ep. 105, 3, p. 244).

[102] *omnia fert aetas, animum quoque. saepe ego longos*
cantando puerum memini me condere soles.
nunc oblita mihi tot carmina, vox quoque Moerim
iam fugit ipsa ...

'Age takes everything away, even the mind; I remember that as a boy I often brought to a close long suns by singing. Now so many songs are forgotten for me; now even the voice itself flees from Moeris' (Jerome, ep. 105, 3, p. 244 = Virgil, *Eclogues*, IX, 51–4).

[103] According to legend, Stesichorus had been blinded after blaming Helen as the cause of the Trojan War. His 'palinode' reversed the account, and sent a phantom there in her place. Jerome has already displayed his erudition by naming the poet, left anonymous by Augustine.

[104] *ne solus mihi de poetis aliquid proposuisse videaris ...* (Jerome, ep. 102, 2, p. 236).

[105] *ne solus videamini mihi lusisse ...* (Bernard, ep. 228, 2, p. 99).

[106] *puto iam non audebitis me de hoc silentio reprehendere et ... appellare soporem quod ... congruentius ac magis proprie sanctus Isaias* cultum iustitiae *nominat ...* , 'I think that you will not now dare to rebuke me for this silence of mine and.. to call sleep what.. the holy Isaiah more fittingly and accurately names *the cultivation of righteousness* ...' (ibid., pp. 99–100 = Is 32. 17).

[107] *et erit opus iustitiae pax et cultus iustitiae silentium et securitas usque in sempiternum*, 'and the work of righteousness will be peace and the cultivation of righteousness silence and security for eternity' (Is 32. 17).

declaration, *Sedebo et silebo* ..., 'I will sit and I will be silent ...',[108] can also be seen as fulfilling the double function of excuse and warning. Like Jerome, age and weakness have rendered him unfit to participate in debate or recantation. Equally, however, he seems to be hinting that the cause of *caritas* between Cluniacs and Cistercians will be better served by silence.

Bernard's commendation of silence may be more barbed than it appears on the surface. In a letter written some eleven or twelve years previously, addressed to the 'abbots gathered at Soissons',[109] he had used the same citation from Isaiah in an overtly provocative context. According to Ceglar this meeting, scheduled for autumn 1132, represents the second in a series of Chapters of the Benedictine abbots of the ecclesiastical province of Rheims, instigated in 1131 by William of St Thierry.[110] Their purpose, the initiation of reforms, had been strongly opposed by Matthew, cardinal-bishop of Albano, former prior of the Cluniac house of St Martin-des-Champs and, for a brief period, grand prior of Cluny itself.[111] Among the recommendations put forward at Rheims had been that of 'silence'.[112] Matthew of Albano's combative and public reply, dated by Ceglar to the end of spring/summer 1132,[113] focuses almost exclusively on this issue, presented, perhaps as a *reductio ad absurdum*, in terms of a demand for 'perpetual silence'.[114] In the letter excusing his absence from Soissons, Bernard had combined the allusion to Isaiah with a reference to Pharisaeism: 'Let those withdraw also from me and you, who call good bad and bad good. Those who call the cultivation of righteousness bad, what good will they consider good? Formerly the Lord spoke one word, and the Pharisees were scandalised. But now the new Pharisees are scandalised not by the word, but by silence.'[115] The reference to the 'new Pharisees', seemingly

---

[108] Bernard, ep. 228, 2, p. 99.

[109] Bernard, ep. 91, *SBO*, VII, pp. 239–41.

[110] S. Ceglar, 'William of Saint-Thierry and his leading role at the first Chapters of the Benedictine abbots (Reims 1131, Soissons 1132)', in *William, abbot of St. Thierry, a colloquium at the abbey of St. Thierry*, trans. J. Carfantan, Cistercian Studies Series 94, Kalamazoo, 1987, 34–112.

[111] Matthew of Albano (*c.* 1085–1135) became grand prior of Cluny at the beginning of Peter's abbacy, a position which, according to Bredero, he retained only until 1123 (Bredero, *Cluny et Cîteaux*, pp. 49 and 71, n. 136). Raised to the status of cardinal and papal legate under Honorius II, he gave his support to Innocent II during the papal schism. Peter the Venerable provides a glowing account of his life and death in his *De miraculis* (*Petri Cluniacensis abbatis De miraculis libri duo*, II, IV–XXIII, ed. D. Bouthillier, *CCCM*, 83, Turnhout, 1988, pp. 103–39).

[112] *In claustro vero silentium a toto conventu teneatur*, 'In the cloister, let silence be maintained by the whole community' (*Acta primi capituli provincialis ordinis S. Benedicti Remis A. D. 1131 habiti*, ed. Ceglar, 'William of Saint Thierry', 51–63, p. 57).

[113] Ibid., p. 36.

[114] *Epistola Matthaei Albanensis Episcopi*, ed. Ceglar, 'William of St Thierry', 65–82, p. 68. According to Ceglar, Bernard's ep. 91 indicates that he already knew this letter (ibid., p. 43, n. 29).

[115] *Recedant etiam a me et a vobis qui dicunt bonum malum et malum bonum. Qui dicunt cultum iustitiae malum, quodnam bonum iam bonum reputaturi sunt? Unum verbum olim locutus est Dominus, et pharisaei scandalizati sunt. At novos nunc pharisaeos non verbum, sed silentium scandalizat* (Bernard, ep. 91, 4, p. 240).

identified with those who claim to be following their fathers by maintaining traditional practices, but who fail to live up to their sanctity and austerity,[116] surely represents the turning back against the Cluniacs of a charge previously levelled against the Cistercians.[117] In ep. 228, the initial allusion is doubled by a direct citation, '*in silence and hope will be your strength*'.[118] The original is prefaced by the divine promise, 'if you return and keep quiet you will be saved', and followed by the rebuke *et noluistis*, 'and you refused'.[119]

As discussed above, accordingly, Bernard's disguised allusions to Augustine's demand for 'debate' and 'palinode', underpinned by blocking techniques borrowed from Jerome, can best be explained in terms of a negative response to pressure emanating from Peter. In the absence of Peter's letter, however, it is difficult to establish the precise nature of that pressure. At some point during the 1130s Peter himself had begun the attempt to promulgate some reforms amongst the Cluniacs.[120] After initial resistance, these would finally culminate in the *Statutes* of 1146.[121] According to Bredero, Peter's approach to Bernard at this period should be read in the light of an attempt to enlist Bernard's help in promoting these reforms.[122] Goodrich, on the other hand, interprets Peter's intention as one of straightforward concern over continuing acrimony between the two orders.[123] The significance attached to Bernard's use of 'silence' suggested above, with its implicit rebuke for

---

[116] *Aut si sanctis et bonae memoriae patribus gloriantur, imitentur certe sanctitatem, quorum indulgentias dispensationesque pro lege defendunt*, 'But if they glory in them as saints and of good memory, let them at least imitate their sanctity, whose indulgences and dispensations they defend as law' (ibid., 3).

[117] This charge, first levelled in Peter's letter 28, is renewed in the letter of Matthew of Albano: *Absit ut illa dominica exprobatio ad vos respiciat quae dicit:* Vae vobis, scribae et pharisaei, qui tulistis clavem scientiae, quia nec intratis nec alios intrare permittitis, 'Be it absent that that reproach of the Lord look towards you, which says: *Woe to you, scribes and Pharisees, who have taken away the key of knowledge, because you neither enter nor permit others to enter*' (*Epistola Matthaei*, p. 70 = Mt 23. 13; Lc 11. 52).

[118] In silentio et in spe erit fortitudo vestra (ep. 228, 2, p. 100 = Is 30. 15).

[119] *quia haec dicit Dominus Deus Sanctus Israhel* si revertamini et quiescatis salvi eritis.. *et noluistis*.. (Is 30. 15).

[120] The traditional date of 1132 for the convening of a chapter general at Cluny, as given by Orderic Vitalis, has been challenged by Ceglar, who argues plausibly that Peter was unlikely to have initiated such a move at a time when Matthew of Albano was engaged in challenging the decisions of the Benedictine abbots. He suggests instead that Peter's statutes were promulgated at some time between 1134 and 1138 (Ceglar, 'William of Saint Thierry', pp. 43–4, n. 37).

[121] Peter the Venerable, *Statuta*, ed. G. Constable, *Corpus Consuetudinum Monasticorum*, 6, Siegburg, 1975, 19–106. Of these, four relate to the issue of silence (ibid., 19–22, pp. 57–60). Moreover, Peter invokes the same citation from Isaiah (ibid., 19, p. 58). For a general account of the statutes, see Dom D. Knowles, 'The reforming decrees of Peter the Venerable', in *Petrus Venerabilis, 1156–1956: studies and texts commemorating the eighth centenary of his death*, ed. G. Constable and J. Kritzeck, Studia Anselmiana 40, Rome, 1956, 1–20.

[122] Bredero, 'Saint Bernard in his relations', pp. 331–3; idem, *Bernard of Clairvaux*, pp. 229 and 238.

[123] Goodrich, 'Limits of friendship', p. 92.

'help' spurned in the past, might seem to lend weight to Bredero's view. The two views are not necessarily mutually exclusive. A demand for intervention at this stage could plausibly be explained in terms of an attempt to smooth the path for future moves which might appear to be bringing Cluniacs and Cistercians closer together. At the same time, it is possible that Bernard's reminder of previous hostility to change could be seen as insinuating that Peter's overtures are driven by self-interest.

Peter's lengthy reply, letter 111, although only half the length of letter 28, again has more in common with a treatise than a letter. As it stands, it can be divided into three broad sections. The first part addresses itself to Bernard and presents itself as a reply to ep. 228.[124] This modulates into the longest section, an exposé of the relationship between Cluniacs and Cistercians, closing with an appeal to Bernard to intervene.[125] The final section combines an exposition of the doctrines of Islam with an invitation to Bernard to write against them.[126] While the first two sections of letter 111 are closely woven together, through allusions to the two brotherhoods, and to the pastoral responsibilities of Peter and Bernard respectively, the third section is seemingly only loosely appended and contains no further overt reference to what appears to be the main subject of the letter. The correspondence between this last section and two further documents by Peter which function as prefaces for the so-called *Collectio toledana*, the translation into Latin of various documents relating to Islam undertaken at Peter's instigation,[127] has brought into question their relationship with the material contained in letter 111. The possibility has even been raised by d'Alverny that the latter should be regarded as a 'compilation of several letters'.[128] This view, although not espoused by d'Alverny herself, and seemingly rejected by Constable as a 'remote possibility',[129] may bear further consideration, as will be seen in the next chapter.

The first two sections can be seen to replicate the device of 'private' frame and 'public' centre initially found in Peter's letter 28. Here, however, the frame is developed at greater length and in greater detail, supplying the letter with *captatio*[130] and *petitio*,[131] and facilitating the development of a parallel between personal *amicitia* and communal *caritas*. The *captatio* of Peter's response moulds itself so closely round the language of Bernard's ep. 228 that McGuire has labelled it an 'exegesis'.[132] In part, this can be seen as a response to Bernard's exploitation of epistolary etiquette in ep. 228. Bernard claimed to have 'read and re-read' Peter's

---

[124] Peter, letter 111, pp. 274–8.

[125] Ibid., pp. 278–94.

[126] Ibid., pp. 294–9.

[127] In addition to the two documents mentioned above, the *Collectio toledana* comprises five translations from Arabic, including one of the Koran. See Iogna-Prat, *Ordonner et exclure*, pp. 337–8.

[128] M.-T. d'Alverny, 'Deux traductions latines du Coran au Moyen Age,' *Archives d'Histoire doctrinale et littéraire du Moyen Age* 16 (1947–8), 69–131, p. 73, n. 2.

[129] Constable, *Letters*, II, p. 275.

[130] Letter 111, pp. 274–7.

[131] Ibid., pp. 293–4.

[132] McGuire, *Friendship and Community*, p. 256.

letter.[133] Peter takes this a stage further, and presents Bernard's letter as a sacred treasure,[134] to be 'stored up', and used like gold and silver in in the work of 'giving alms'.[135] This recalls the reference to the 'spoils of the Egyptians' and the 'wealth of the Hebrews' in Peter's letter 28.[136] Equally, however, it may represent a glance at the implicit equation of withheld tithes with 'fraudulent alms' in his subsequent letters to Haimeric and the Cistercian abbots.[137] Subsequently, Peter will allude directly both to these and to the affair of Langres. At the same time, the implicit linking of Bernard's letter with holy scripture serves as a pretext for verbatim citation and for a close scrutiny of Bernard's words.

While Bernard's ep. 228 operated simultaneously at two levels throughout, with private reproach masking public debate, the division into private frame and public centre in letter 111 seemingly works to produce greater transparency. At the same time, however, the private frame can be seen to match obliquity with obliquity. At the heart of the *captatio* is a verbal wrangle basing itself on the requirements of epistolary etiquette, which interweaves and transposes motifs which can be paralleled in Augustine and Jerome. Subsequently, Peter will drop a clear hint that this epistolary 'quarrel' should be seen as a sustitute for the 'real' causes of dispute. The 'quarrel' is preluded, however, by an apology couched in echoes of Bernard's own language: 'Perhaps your sagacious Sanctity will wonder and, as I fear, impute to sloth or contempt, that I present myself as a tardy replier to so sweet and pleasant a letter from a friend, to which I should have presented myself pleasantly and swiftly.'[138] It concludes with a repetition of Bernard's own question, 'Does it please you to joke like this?',[139] enclosed within a repudiation of 'play'[140] and a transformation of mock-debate into serious discussion, through the same concepts

---

[133] *Legi avide, libenter relego, et placet saepius repetitum*, 'I read it eagerly, I re-read it willingly, and it pleases often repeated' (Bernard, ep. 228, 2, p. 99).

[134] *[Animus] tractus ... sicque tractus est, ut quod nunquam, nisi sacrorum reverentia librorum me fecisse memini, perlectam epistolam mox exosculatus sim*, '[My mind] was attracted.. and so attracted, that, what I never remember having done, except out of reverence for sacred books, as soon as I had read the letter I kissed it' (Peter, letter 111, p. 275). The repetition of *tractus* may point towards the words of the *sponsa*, *trahe me post te*, 'draw me after you' (Ct 1. 3).

[135] *Recondi.. eas et argenteis sive aureis quos.. ad opus eleemosynae mecum ferre soleo, adiunxi*, 'I stored ... it up and added it to the silver and gold which ... I am accustomed to carry with me for the work of alms-giving' (letter 111, p. 275).

[136] Peter, letter 28, p. 53.

[137] Idem, letter 34; letter 35. See the discussion in Chapter 4.

[138] *Quoniam tam dulcibus et iucundis amici litteris, quibus et ipse iocundus et citus occurrere debuissem, tardus rescriptor occurro, mirabitur fortassis sollers sanctitas vestra, et segnitiei vel contemptui ut timeo deputabit* (letter 111, p. 274). Bernard's letter had emphasised 'wonder' and had hinted at *contemptus*, 'scorn', as a potential cause of Peter's previous failure to reply.

[139] *Sed rursum forte dicetis:* Itane iocari libet?, 'But perhaps you will say again, *does it please you to joke like this?*' (ibid., p. 276).

[140] *ut qui notas simultates de multorum cordibus non ludo sed serie excludere satago* ..., 'as one who is striving not in play but in earnest to shut out acknowledged rivalries from the hearts of many ...' (ibid.).

of 'sweetness' and 'pleasantness': 'Therefore, it is sweet to me to always speak with you, and to preserve the honeyed sweetness of charity between us with pleasant words.'[141] *Iucundus*, 'pleasant', 'delightful', while cognate with *iocus*, is primarily associated elsewhere with *caritas* and with the joys of eternity.[142]

In between, Peter takes issue with Bernard's 'reproach' more directly, in a complicated verbal play which dissects Bernard's words and seemingly refutes, at least in part, the charge of failure in friendship. The technique, as will be seen, may be modelled on Augustine. Peter's 'defence' is grounded in the claim that Bernard's 'unanswered letter' was in fact a reply to a letter from himself. In consequence, it did not require a reply.[143] Seemingly straightforward, the justification is heavily laboured, through a series of suppositions and statements which foreground the notion of priority: 'if I had scorned to write back to so great a friend writing first ...';[144] 'It did not pertain to me, therefore, to write back, since I had written first, but it was your responsibility to write back, because I had written first ...'.[145] This modulates into an appropriation of Bernard's own words, 'If that is so, the blame laid on me, deserting me, begins to look towards you, because you wished to blame one who was blameless, and to load the shoulders of an innocent brother with the burden of another, not to say your own.'[146] In similar fashion, Peter claims that justice is on his side,[147] and hints that if he wished, he could lay claim to the appellation of 'wounded friend'.[148]

---

[141] *Unde dulce mihi est semper vobiscum loqui, et melleam inter nos caritatis dulcedinem iocundis sermonibus conservare* (ibid.).

[142] *cui promittitur omnimoda iucunditas aeternorum*, 'to whom is promised all the kinds of pleasure of eternal (things)' (Peter, letter 10 to Innocent II, *Letters*, I, p. 17); *mallem ... vobiscum in domino iucundari*, 'I would prefer to take delight with you in the Lord' (idem, letter 178 to Hugh of Amiens, ibid., p. 420).

[143] At a literal level, this claim seems to offer further evidence that the letter in question is Bernard's ep. 147, written in answer to Peter's letter 65. The second letter is simply dismissed, *Quod vero vice alia idem a me factum dicitis, quia rei memoria menti non inest, responsio deest*, 'As for the fact that you say the same thing was done by me on another occasion, since there is no memory of the event in my mind, the reply is lacking' (letter 111, pp. 275–6.) The claim to 'forgetfulness' echoes Bernard's 'I am mindful of no injuries', a statement subsequently appropriated by Peter. It may offer further confirmation that this letter can be identified with ep. 148.

[144] *si tanto amico primo scribenti rescribere contempsissem* ... (Peter, letter 111, p. 275); cf. *Fateor enim quod primum scribenti vere rescribere debuissem* ..., 'For I admit that I would have been due to write back to one writing first ...' (ibid.).

[145] *Non ergo ad me pertinuit rescribere, qui prior scripseram, sed vestrum fuit rescribere, quia prior scripseram* (ibid.); cf. *sed prout recolere possum ... scripsi ego prior, rescripsistis posterior vos* ... 'but as I can recall, I wrote first, you wrote back second ...' (ibid.).

[146] *Quod si ita est, culpa mihi imposita me deserens, vos incipit intueri, quia inculpabilem culpare, et sarcina aliena ne dicam vestra aggravare humeros fratris innocentis voluistis* (ibid. = ep. 228, 1, p. 98).

[147] *Et ego: Interim iuxta causas praemissas pro me facit iustitia, quia apud me non invenitur culpa*, 'I, too (say): Meanwhile, in consequence of the reasons mentioned above, justice acts for me, because blame is not found in me' (letter 111, p. 276 = ep. 228, 1, p. 98).

[148] *et* laesum *quod de vobis dixistis* amicum *me vocare potuissem, et laesionis vel iniuriarum poenam merito exigerem*, 'I could have called myself the *wounded friend*, as you did of yourself, and deservedly demand punishment for the harm and injuries' (letter 111, p. 276 = ep. 228, 1, p. 99).

Both the motif of *culpa*, 'blame', and that of *amicus laesus*, the 'wounded friend', originate in Jerome's side of the correspondence. It is Augustine, however, who subjects them to a lengthy development designed to wrong-foot his opponent. Jerome challenges Augustine either to deny authorship of the letter or to admit it openly, 'so that whatever I write in my defence, the blame may rest on you, who provoked it, not on me, who was compelled to respond'.[149] The 'wound of friendship', equated here with rebuke,[150] functions initially as a blocking device: 'I did not think that I should rashly believe in a copy of a letter in case, perhaps, if I replied, being wounded, you might justly complain that I should have proved whether the words were yours before writing back.'[151] Augustine uses this statement to set up a logical dilemma, based on the intended nature of Jerome's projected reply.[152] If this were not meant to be wounding, how could Augustine be wounded and justly complain?[153] A possible escape-route is then blocked. If Augustine was considered sufficiently stupid to be wounded by a letter not intended to be wounding, then Jerome had already wounded him by holding this opinion of him.[154] Jerome, however, would not have been so rash as to form this opinion, since he had refused to believe rashly in a copy of a letter.[155] The inescapable conclusion must be that Jerome was proposing to write a wounding reply, once he had certain proof that the letter had come from Augustine.[156]

---

[149]   *ut, si in defensione mei aliqua scripsero, in te culpa sit, qui provocasti, non in me, qui respondere compulsus sum* (Jerome, ep. 105, 4, p. 245).

[150]   This seems to have a biblical origin: *Meliora sunt vulnera diligentis quam fraudulenta odientis oscula*, 'Better are the wounds of one who loves than the deceitful kisses of one who hates' (Prv 27. 6). Augustine had previously cited a parallel passage: Corripiet me iustus in misericordia et increpabit me oleum autem peccatoris non impinguet caput meum, '*The just man will reprove me in mercy and chide me, but let the oil of the sinner not anoint my head*' (Augustine, ep. 28, IV. 6, p. 113 = Ps 140. 5). See Fiske, *Friends and friendship*, 2/7.

[151]   *non temere exemplaribus litterarum credendum putavi, ne forte me respondente laesus iuste expostulares, quod probare ante debuissem tuum esse sermonem et sic rescribere* (Jerome, ep. 102, 1, p. 235). The image will recur in Jerome's next letter, this time in relation to himself: *in hoc laeditur amicitia, in hoc necessitudinis iura violantur*, 'in this (the request for a palinode) friendship is wounded, in this the laws of intimacy are violated' (idem, ep. 105, 4, p. 245).

[152]   Augustine, ep. 73, I. 1–II. 3, pp. 264–5.

[153]   *Quo pacto enim possumus in hac disputatione sine rancore versari, si me laedere paras? aut si non paras, quo modo ego te non laedente abs te laesus iuste expostularem ...?*, 'For how can we engage in this disputation without rancour, if you are preparing to wound me? Or if you are not so preparing, how could I, being wounded by you without you wounding, justly complain ...? (ibid., I. 1, p. 264).

[154]   *Aut si te non sic rescribente [ut laedas] ego propter nimiam stultitiam meam laedi posse putatus sum, hoc ipso laesisti plane, quod de me ita sensisti*, 'Or if I have been thought capable of being wounded through my great stupidity, without your writing in such a way [as to wound], you have plainly wounded me by having this opinion of me' (ibid., I. 2, p. 265).

[155]   *Sed nullo modo tu me, quem numquam talem expertus es, temere talem crederes, qui litterarum mearum exemplaribus, etiam cum stilum meum nosses, temere credere noluisti*, 'But in no way, never having found me such, would you rashly believe me such, since you refused to believe rashly in a copy of my letter, although you recognised the pen to be mine' (ibid.).

[156]   *Restat igitur, ut laedere me rescribendo disponeres, si certo documento meas esse illas litteras nosses*, 'It remains therefore, that you were preparing to wound me in your reply, if you knew for certain that the letter was mine' (ibid., II. 3, p. 265).

The dilemma is resolved, or perhaps side-stepped, through the conciliatory move of accepting responsibility for 'priority' in 'wounding': 'And so, because I do not believe that you would think that I should be wounded unjustly, it remains that I acknowledge my sin, because I wounded you first by that letter, which I cannot deny to be mine.'[157] Subsequently, Augustine uses the same motif both to renew the pressure for dialogue and to warn Jerome that he risks wounding himself.[158] Peter's seeming transposition of the motif of priority may conceal a hint that the 'wound' in question was initially inflicted by Bernard's *Apologia*. At the same time it may serve as a warning that renewed criticism will not go unavenged.

Like Augustine, however, he concludes the 'quarrel' with a display of magnanimity: 'But I am merciful after my fashion, I remit everything even unasked. As you have said, *I am mindful of no injuries*.'[159] In both cases, this mock-dispute can be seen as representing a transposition of the real issue of debate to the realms of letter-writing. Peter indicates as much, by immediately applying the motifs of 'priority' and 'indulgence' to the issue of communal relations: 'For this also pertains to the matter which follows, that.. I first show indulgence to all, do myself beforehand, what I labour that others should do',[160] that is, promote the cause of *caritas*. The *topos* of 'wounded friendship' will recur in the body of the letter, with (private) *amicitia* replaced by (communal) *caritas*.[161]

While the technique seems to be borrowed from Augustine, the language surrounding the deflection of 'blame' may also draw on Jerome. The claim that Bernard has wished to 'blame one who is blameless' is doubled by a reference to loading the shoulders of an innocent brother *sarcina aliena ne dicam vestra*, 'with the burden of another, not to say your own'.[162] *Sarcina*, 'burden', 'baggage', has military connotations, perhaps reflecting and countering Bernard's hint that he has served his time and deserves an honourable discharge. At the same time, the sentiment it conveys, that of imputing one's own failings to others, may recall Jerome's criticism of Augustine through an adaptation of the classical satirist Persius: 'But that is true reprehension between friends, if, not seeing our own bag.. we should scrutinise the wallet of

---

[157] *Atque ita, quia non credo, quod iniuste me laedendum putares, superest, ut agnoscam peccatum meum, quod prior te illis litteris laeserim, quas meas esse negare non possum* (ibid.).

[158] *Laedes autem me, si mihi tacueris errorem meum, quam forte inveneris in factis vel dictis meis. nam si ea in me reprehenderis, quae reprehenda non sunt, te laedis magis quam me ...*, 'But you will wound me, if you keep silent about any error of mine which you may have found in my deeds or words. For if you find fault with those things in me which should not be found fault with, you wound yourself rather than me ...' (ibid., p. 266).

[159] *Sed parco more meo, sed cuncta etiam non rogatus remitto.* Nullarum *ut dixistis* memor sum iniuriarum (letter 111, p. 276). Peter can be seen here both to echo Bernard and to trump him. 'Forgiveness', Peter implies, is his normal practice.

[160] *Nam et hoc ad sequentem materiam pertinet ut ... prior ipse omnibus indulgeam, et quod ut alii faciant laboro, ante ipse faciam* (letter 111, p. 276).

[161] *Laesa caritas* (letter 111, p. 278); *caritatis laesio* (ibid., p. 287).

[162] Letter 111, p. 275.

others.'[163] Jerome may be invoked again as Peter reveals the concrete causes of dispute: 'When will the sincere affection of my heart, ignited towards you, be able to be extinguished or overwhelmed by any rivulets of sinister rumour, when it could neither be extinguished by the many waters of tithes, nor overwhelmed by the force of the rivers of Langres?'[164] 'Sinister rumour', identified with slander, occurs in Jerome's memorial to Marcella: 'It is difficult in a slanderous citizenry and in the City, in which once the people was the world, and the palm of vices was to detract from honest people and to defile what is pure and spotless, not to attract some talk of sinister rumour.'[165] That the target of Jerome's sarcasm was Rome may point back to Bernard's ep. 147, written from Rome, and to Peter's attribution to him in letter 65 of *sinistra arma*, the 'weapons of the left'.[166]

It is arguable, therefore, that just as Bernard's letter adopted the Augustinan voice but employed Jeromian tactics, so Peter's letter counters with Augustinian tactics, overlaid by a hint of the Jeromian sarcasm which will subsequently be turned against those on both sides who inhibit the cause of peace. In the same way, but by different means, he may be seen to counter Bernard's commendation of silence. Silence in Peter's letter figures in negative terms. It is introduced in the context of epistolary excuse: 'I wished to reply what had taken possession of my mind on the following day, but prevented by the daily or rather continual overseer demanding other things, I kept silent.'[167] The use of *exactor*, 'overseer', 'tax-collector', points towards the enslavement of the Israelites in Egypt,[168] an image

---

[163] *Sed illa est vera inter amicos reprehensio, si nostram peram non videntes aliorum.. manticam consideremus* (Jerome, ep. 102, 2, p. 236 = Persius, *Satires*, IV. 23–4, *A. Persi Flacci, Saturarum liber*, ed. D. Bo, Corpus Scriptorum Latinorum Paravianum, Torino, 1969.) The original runs:

> *ut nemo in sese temptat descendere, nemo*
> *sed praecedenti spectatur mantica tergo*

'How no one tries to penetrate into himself, no one, but the wallet on the back going in front is the object of scrutiny.' Jerome's addition of *pera* may draw on the biblical depiction of David arming himself with pebbles before facing Goliath, thus adding another seemingly unequal pairing which results in an unexpected victory (I Sm 17. 40). The phrase *vera reprehensio*, just as the behaviour it describes, seems to represent a perversion of *vera amicitia*, 'true friendship'.

[164] *Quando enim extingui vel obrui poterit sincerus erga vos et ignitus mei pectoris affectus quibuslibet sinistri rumoris rivulis, cum nec aquae multae decimarum potuerint eum extinguere, nec impetus Lingonensium fluminum obruere?* (letter 111, p. 277). The exploitation here of the citation from *Canticles* which directly proceeds it, *Aquae multae non poterunt extinguere caritatem nec flumina obruent illam*, 'Many waters will not be able to extinguish charity, nor will the rivers overwhelm it' (Ct 8. 7), can be paralleled with Peter's letter 38 to Peter, archbishop of Lyons, where the threatening waters are specifically identified with detraction, 'men murmuring evil' (letter 38, *Letters*, I, p. 126).

[165] *Difficile est in maledica civitate et in urbe, in qua orbis quondam populus fuit palmaque vitiorum, si honestis detraherent et pura ac munda macularent, non aliquam sinistri rumoris fabulam trahere* (Jerome, ep. 127, 3, *CSEL*, 56/1, p. 147).

[166] Letter 65, p. 195.

[167] *Rescribere quod animo insederat sequenti die statim volui, sed a cotidiano immo paene continuo exactore alia reposcente prohibitus, conticui* (letter 111, p. 275).

[168] Ex 5. 6.

employed elsewhere by Peter to represent his enforced involvement in worldly affairs at the expense of spiritual withdrawal.[169] The language of subjection, developed at some length,[170] culminates in a citation celebrating his freedom taken, like that of Bernard, from Isaiah: 'At length I burst the importunate chain, and.. *overcame the yoke of burden and the sceptre of the oppressor* by writing secretly.'[171] Significantly, its context in Isaiah is the prophecy of 'peace.'[172] Whereas in Bernard silence was held up as productive of peace, here it is presented as the product of oppression. *Importunum vinculum*, the 'importunate chain', seems to represent an inversion of *vinculum caritatis*, the 'bond of charity'. Subsequently, Satan's sway over the minds of monks, sowing the seeds of hatred and rivalry, will be portrayed as *ius tyrannicum*, the 'rule of tyranny'.[173]

Behind the complimentary façade, through the medium of Augustine and Jerome, Peter would seem to be conducting a 'private' discussion with Bernard. Within this, however, the path for 'public' debate has already been paved, through the establishment of slander and detraction as the primary threat to *caritas* between the Orders. As Peter effects the transition from private to public, through a direct appeal to shared pastoral responsibility, it becomes clear that what is at stake is spiritual salvation: 'But since each of us is called a shepherd, since our extensive

---

[169] *Sed duro Aegyptiorum imperio urgente, qui* manus *meas magis* in cophino *servire, quam scribendi studio vacare docuerunt, qui luteis operibus eas inquinari, non dei sacrificiis mundari hucusque coegerunt, non potui quod volui, eaque de causa hactenus conticui,* 'But pressed by the harsh command of the Egyptians, who have taught my *hands* rather to be enslaved *in the basket* than to be free for the study of writing, who have forced them hitherto to be stained in muddy works rather than to be purified for sacrifices to God, I have not been able to do what I wished, and for that reason I have remained silent until now' (Peter, letter 13, *Letters*, I, p. 19 = Ps 80. 7). On possible irony in this letter, see Knight, 'Language of retreat', pp. 21–6.

[170] *Imperavi mihi plane silentium cui resistere non poteram, durissimus imperator, et cura multiplex infinitarum causarum, non uno tantum, sed multis me diebus silere coegit,* 'A harsh commander, whom I was powerless to resist, I enjoined silence upon myself, and the manifold charge of countless ca(u)ses compelled me to be silent on not only one but many days' (letter 111, p. 275). The first-person verb *imperavi* sits slightly oddly with the other statements, and indeed appears elsewhere in the variant form *imperavit* (ibid., *apparatus*, n. 9). As it stands, it may recall the presentation of Cluny as Peter's 'Empire' found elsewhere. Peter of Poitiers, for example, speaks of Peter's *imperialis ac piissimus vultus*, 'imperial and most pious countenance' (letter 128, p. 326). On the group of letters of which this forms a part, see Knight, 'Language of retreat', pp. 33–7.

[171] *Rupi tandem importunum vinculum, et..* iugum oneris et sceptrum exactoris *furtim scriptitando* superavi (letter 111, p. 275 = Is 9. 4).

[172] *Parvulus enim natus est nobis filius datus est nobis et factus est pricipatus super umerum eius et vocabitur nomen eius Admirabilis consiliarius Deus fortis Pater futuri saeculi Princeps pacis,* 'For a child has been born to us, a son has been given to us, and the sovereignty is upon his shoulder and his name will be called Wonderful counsellor, powerful God, Father of the world to be, Prince of peace' (Is 9. 6).

[173] *(quando) ... mentibus hominum professione caelestium, exemplo splendentium, iure tyrannico [superbus archangelus] principatur,* '(since) ... he [the arrogant archangel] reigns with tyrannical rule in the minds of men heavenly by profession, splendid by example' (letter 111, p. 277).

sheepfolds are packed with a multitude of the sheep of Christ, since each is ordered: *Diligently know the aspect of your flock*, we must see if our flock is known to us, if it is healthy, if it languishes, if it is weak, if it is strong, if, at least, it is alive or dead.'[174] What follows equates failure in *caritas* with spiritual suicide on the one hand and spiritual murder on the other: 'If ... *he who does not love remains in death*, in what death does he remain who hates? If *he who does not love remains in death*, in what death does he remain who commits detraction?'[175]

Conversely, the concluding section of the personal frame functions at the public level of open petition. Peter demonstrates that intervention is within Bernard's power,[176] that he has merited this intervention by his previous efforts,[177] and that its object, the attainment of salvation through brotherly love, is laudable and desirable.[178] At the same time, echoes of Jerome may serve to link it back to the earlier, more 'private' debate. Bernard is called upon to employ his 'sublime eloquence', '(in)flaming with the spirit of God', to drive out 'childish jealousy'.[179] Fiery eloquence, aflame with *caritas*, can be seen to recall and to counteract the 'rivulets of sinister rumour' evoked in the *captatio*. 'Childish boasting', on the other hand, had been the term applied by Jerome to the proposed theological exchange with Augustine.[180] Through the intertext and multi-layering of this private frame,

---

[174] *Sed cum uterque nostrum pastor dicatur, cum ovilia nostra non parva ovium Christi multitudine sint referta, cum utrique praecipiatur:* Diligenter agnosce vultum pecoris tui, videndum est si pecus nostrum nobis notum est, si valet, si languet, si debile, si robustum, si mortuum certe vel vivum (ibid. = I Io 3. 14). Iogna-Prat notes the tendency of Cluny to equate itself with Rome as the head of the (spiritual) order (Iogna-Prat, *Ordonner et exclure*, p. 34; see also ibid., pp. 86–7). In this letter, however, Peter suggests that Cluny and Cîteaux are to be viewed as joint spiritual leaders: *Restat ... ut ... unius nominis et ordinis maximas congregationes nequaquam ultra dissidere patiamini*, 'It remains ... that ... you do not allow the greatest communities of one name and one order to be divided further' (letter 111, p. 293).
[175] *Si ...* in morte manet qui non diligit, *in qua morte manet qui odit? Si* in morte manet qui non diligit, *in qua morte manet qui detrahit?* (ibid., p. 277 = I Io 3. 14). The original continues, *omnis qui odit fratrem suum homicida est et scitis quoniam omnis homicida non habet vitam aeternam in se manentem*, 'Everyone who hates his brother is a murderer and you know that every murderer does not have eternal life remaining in him' (I Io 3. 14). Peter has previously dissociated himself from those brothers who 'hated Joseph in their heart' (letter 111, p. 276).
[176] *Instate ... pro magna illa gratia a deo vobis collata*, 'Strive.. in accordance with that great grace bestowed on you by God' (ibid., pp. 293–4).
[177] *Studui ego semper, ut ... ipsos (nostros fratres) illis (vestris monachis) perfectae unione caritatis ... etiam inviscerarem*, 'I have always been eager ... to root them, the ones (our brothers) in the others (your monks), in the union of perfected charity' (ibid., p. 293).
[178] *Nam qui in lege sua nullum sacrificium sine sale suscipit, nullius munus virtutis sine tali condimento sibi placere ostendit*, 'For He who under His law receives no sacrifice without salt, shows that he is pleased by the gift of no virtue lacking this seasoning' (ibid. p. 294 = Lv 2. 13).
[179] *Expellite sublimi illo et ex spiritu dei flammante eloquio ab eorum cordibus ... puerilem illam aemulationem* (letter 111, p. 294).
[180] *optime novit prudentia tua ... (et) puerilis esse iactantiae ... accusando illustres viros suo nomini famam quaerere*, 'your Prudence knows well.. that it is a characteristic of childish boasting ... to seek reputation for one's own name by accusing famous men' (Jerome, ep. 102, 2, pp. 235–6.); *(Ne) videamur certare pueriliter ...*, '(Lest) we may be seen to compete childishly ...' (idem, ep. 105, 4, p. 245).

Peter can be seen both to signal his awareness of Bernard's blocking of 'public' debate in ep. 228 and to show his disapproval of it. In the central section, meanwhile, it will be argued that he reproduces such a debate single-handed, while at the same time producing a 'palinode' of his own.

Chapter 6

The Salt of *Caritas*: Letter 111
Continued

In the previous chapter, it was argued that the 'private' frame to letter 111, Peter's second 'open' communication dealing with Cluniac–Cistercian relations, constitutes both an acknowledgement and a rebuttal of the blocking tactics employed by Bernard in his ep. 228. Bernard can be seen to have rejected Peter's proposal to engage in dialogue, through reductive rhetoric borrowed from Augustine and Jerome, associating debate with 'mock-combat' and 'palinode' on the one hand, and pretexting age and infirmity as a justification for 'honourable discharge' from spiritual warfare on the other. While Bernard's subversion of the Augustinian voice to serve Jeromian tactics reads as an attempt to assert control and to impose closure, Peter's conflation of Augustinian and Jeromian echoes in the epistolary 'quarrel' can be seen as abolishing distance and neutralising distinction. Whereas Bernard commends 'silence' as the best means of procuring peace, buttressed by a hidden warning that a reopening of the debate would leave the Cluniacs open to a renewal of painful criticism, Peter counters with an analogy which presents silence as a chief weapon in the 'tyranny' of Satan. Satan is said to have set up his stronghold in the heart of monasticism.[1] Mutual rancour is shown to have replaced mutual charity.[2] 'Joking' and 'mockery', key tools in the reduction of debate to 'mock-combat', are transposed through biblical allusion to the prospective victory of Satan.[3] In what follows, Peter will illustrate through heavy satire that silent detraction is as damaging as verbal abuse.

---

[1]   *Et o res plena lamentis.. superbum archangelum de caelis proiectum rursum caelestia occupasse, et qui in aquilone sedem suam stabilire non potuit, in meridiana hoc est in splendidiore caeli parte eam firmasse*, 'And, O matter full of lamentation ... that the proud archangel, cast down from heaven has again occupied the heavenly heights, and that he who not able to establish his seat in the north has established it here in the south, the more splendid part of heaven' (letter 111, p. 277). The language seems to hint at a further analogy between the failure of (papal) schism in northern Italy and the threat of (monastic) schism in the south of France.

[2]   *Cerno aliquos ... a caritate mutua descivisse*, 'I see that some.. have fallen off from mutual charity' (ibid.); *... expulso eo qui habitat in caelis, et cuius locus non in mutuo rancore sed in fraterna pace factus est ...* , 'having expelled Him who dwells in heaven, and whose place was made not in mutual rancour but in brotherly peace ...' (ibid.).

[3]   *Absit ... ut ille qui sic a salvatore enervatus dicitur, ut ipsius etiam* ancillis ligetur, *ut ipsi a servis eius velut avi illudatur, in tantum ipse servis eius et ancillis illudat, eisque ut vilibus mancipiis dominetur*, 'Be it absent, that he who is said to have been so weakened by the Saviour, that he is *bound even for His maidservants*, that he is *mocked by His servants as a bird*, should himself so mock His servants and maidservants, and lord over them like worthless slaves' (ibid., p. 278 = Iob 40. 24).

The bulk of Peter's letter, which will form the main focus of this chapter, comprises a resumption, some twenty years later, of the Cluniac–Cistercian debate, initiated in the second half of the 1120s through Bernard's critical *Apologia* and Peter's polemical letter 28. It has been suggested earlier that the main terms of this debate, arrogance, jealousy, an opposition between Jews (Cistercians) and Gentiles (Cluniacs), were set at this point. Subsequently, Peter's letters regarding tithes had presented, or created, further oppositions: new versus old; poor versus rich. As Goodrich suggests, at the heart of the debate lies an ideological difference concerning the interpretation of *caritas* in relation to dispensation from the monastic *Rule*.[4] In letter 28, *caritas* had functioned principally as a weapon, defensive or aggressive by turns. Here it plays a rather different role, representing both the goal of monastic harmony, and the means by which this goal may be achieved.[5] This shift is in keeping with the change in tone presented by letter 111 as a whole. Whereas letter 28 constituted an *apologia* on behalf of Cluny and the Cluniac way of life, letter 111 has been characterised by Auniord, with justification, as a double *apologia* for both Cluniacs and Cistercians.[6] Whether this shift in approach is to be attributed to a change in purpose, as Bredero argues, will be discussed subsequently.

The key-note in letter 28 had been *praevaricatio*, deviation from the monastic Rule, pursued through 'charge' and 'counter-charge'. Here, the dominating term is *varietas*, diversity of practice,[7] seemingly used, as Haseldine indicates in relation to the subsequent letter 150, to signal the principle of 'diversity within unity',[8] and perhaps taking its cue from the *figura* of the 'many-coloured tunic' in Bernard's *Apologia*.[9] Previously, Peter had vigorously defended Cluniac practice as

---

[4]   Goodrich, 'The limits of friendship', pp. 82–3.

[5]   *Iam si hanc caritatem ... vis frater Cluniacensis, frater Cisterciensis, integram conservare, si per ipsam maximos tibi thesauros in caelo recondere, si reconditos conservare, da totam quam potueris operam, et causas non dico eam fugantes, non dico eam perimentes, sed vel parum eam laedentes a te abige ...,* 'If you wish now, Cluniac brother, Cistercian brother, to keep this charity.. intact, through it to lay up for yourself the greatest treasures in heaven, to keep them once laid up, make all the effort which you can, and drive from yourself the causes which – I do not say, put it to flight, I do not say, destroy it – but harm it even a little ...' (letter 111, p. 293 = Mt 6. 19; Lc 12. 33).

[6]   Auniord, 'L'ami de saint Bernard', p. 93. This contrasts noticeably with the description given by Leclercq, who characterises it as a second *apologia* on behalf of Cluny (Leclercq, *Pierre le Vénérable*, p. 74.)

[7]   Peter plays repeatedly on *varietas* and its cognates: *..sola eos mentium nescio quae occulta et nefanda varietas separat,* 'only some hidden and impious diversity of minds divides them' (letter 111, p. 277); *(Et) ut in duobus [fratribus] nominatis omnium dissidentium varietas comprehendatur ...* , 'so that in the two [brothers] who have been arraigned, the diversity of all in disagreement may be apprehended ...' (ibid., p. 278); *si varia consuetudo, si multiplex rerum infinitarum varietas Christi servos a mutua caritate divellere debet ...,* 'if diversity of custom, if the manifold diversity of countless matters is to tear apart the servants of Christ from mutual charity ...' (ibid.); *si propter varios usus vestri ... animi variati sunt ...,* '..if because of diversity of practice, your minds.. have been diversified ... ' (ibid., pp. 279–80).

[8]   Haseldine, 'Friendship and rivalry', pp. 391–2.

[9]   *Apo*, III. 6. See also Goodrich, 'The limits of friendship', p. 94.

encompassing the *caritas* demanded by the *Rule*, while hinting that the austerity and rigidity of the Cistercians laid them open to the charge of failure in *caritas*.[10] Further, their preference for white clothing over black had been labelled as a sign of perverse novelty and a symbol of arrogance.[11] Here, *varietas consuetudinis*, diversity of custom, and *varietas vestium*, diversity of habit, will be brought forward in turn, then dismissed as grounds for disharmony. The stress will be on unification and peace, supported by a range of citations from the Old Testament: 'If the unconsecrated man was *peaceful with those who hated peace*, will monk strive with monk in impious warfare?';[12] '*Let there be*, therefore, *peace*, O Jerusalem, *in your virtue*, that there may follow *also abundance in your citadels*.'[13] Such citations can be seen to justify the statement by McGuire, that the letter presents an 'eloquent plea for concord'.[14] They may also serve to prepare the way for the introduction of a call to (externally directed) spiritual warfare in the final section of the letter.

As in letter 28, Peter utilises and sustains the fiction of a legal debate, but with a crucial difference. In that letter he had presented himself as spokesman for the Cluniacs. Here, in keeping with the move towards reconciliation and the abolition of distinction, he seemingly aligns himself with Bernard in the role of arbitrator, as both sides are invited to put their case: 'Let ... the matter for dispute come before the public, and whatever just complaint they can bring against each other, be

---

[10]   *Ad ista forte vel verbis vel cogitatu respondetis. Et ubi nos a praeceptis regulae caritatem excludere dicitis? Ubi animarum saluti providere negligitis. Et ubi nos animarum saluti providere negligimus? Ut exempli causa aliqua ponamus, nonne animarum salutem atque idcirco caritatem negligitis, quando fratribus necessaria negatis, quando eos frigore usu pelliciarum negato affligitis, quando hac violentia nam multi vestrum hoc inviti sustinent, eos vel ad murmurationem vel ad fugam compellitis?*, 'Perhaps you reply to this in words or thought: "And when do you say that we exclude charity from the precepts of the Rule?" When you neglect to provide for the salvation of souls. "And when do we neglect to provide for the salvation of souls?" To put something for an example, do you not neglect the salvation of souls and therefore charity, when you deny the brothers what is necessary, when you afflict them with cold by denying them the use of furs, when by this violence, for many of yours bear with this unwillingly, you drive them to murmuring or flight?' (letter 28, pp. 99–100).

[11]   *(unde) et habitum insoliti coloris praetenditis, et ad distinctionem cunctorum totius fere mundi monachorum, inter nigros vos candidos ostentatis*, '(whence) you spread forth a habit of unaccustomed colour, and show yourself white among black, to distinguish yourselves from all the monks of nearly the whole world' (ibid., p. 57).

[12]   *Si laicus homo* cum his qui oderant pacem pacificus *erat, monachus homo cum monacho homine nefando duello certabit?* (letter 111, p. 280 = Ps 119. 7). Peter's repetition here of the seemingly redundant *homo* may point in the direction of a substitute or champion in a judicial combat.

[13]   Fiat *ergo* pax, *o Ihrusalem*, in virtute tua, *ut sequatur* et abundantia in turribus tuis (ibid., p. 285 = Ps 121. 7). Cf. *Sed ne forte inveniamur de illis esse, qui dicunt* pax, pax, et non est pax ..., 'But lest by chance we be found to be of those, who say, *peace, peace, and it is not peace..* ' (ibid. = Ier 6. 14); *Satisfacite igitur paci, filii pacis ... ne ... proferatur.. contra vos dirissima illa prophetae sententia*: Non est pax dicit *deus meus* impiis, 'Satisfy the demands of peace, therefore, sons of peace ... lest ... there be brought against you that most dreadful sentence of the prophet: *There is no peace*, says my God, *to the impious*' (ibid, p. 290 = Is 48. 22).

[14]   McGuire, *Friendship and community*, p. 257.

determined by the judgement of impartial arbitrators.'[15] In fact, Peter will combine the roles of inquisitor and chief prosecutor, but this time, of both sides alike. Devices from forensic oratory are again employed in maintaining this fiction. *Apostrophe* is used freely, with an alternation of addressee and reversal of the order of address bolstering the impression of even-handedness.[16] *Prolepsis*, anticipated objection, is used here more sparingly,[17] but extends into virtual *prosopopoeia* in the conclusion, where, through a technique adopted from satire and favoured by Jerome,[18] the opponents are made to condemn themselves out of their own mouths. The total effect, however, is noticeably different from that found in letter 28: the emphasis is on persuasion, rather than on verbal cleverness, and the logical dilemma has disappeared as an argumentative technique.

The structure of the 'public' section of letter 111 is created by a series of rhetorical 'markers' which serve to move the 'debate' forwards. The subject of the enquiry, the grounds for the breach of *caritas* which has been previously alleged, is established through a triplet of rhetorical questions, which foreground detraction: 'But why do they oppose each other? Why do they detract from each other? Why are they *devoured by one another*?'[19] Each 'proposition' is brought forward and

---

[15]   *Veniat ... materies litis in medium, et si quid iustae querelae adversum se invicem afferre potuerint, aequis decernentibus arbitris terminetur* (letter 111, p. 278). *Lis*, 'dispute', can connote a lawsuit. As the letter proceeds, it will be replaced by a variety of synonyms, *discordia, divortium, scisma, discidium*. Again, this can be seen as pointing to the presentation of schism between the two leading monastic institutions as replicating the papal schism of 1130–38.

[16]   *quid exigis inquam frater Cluniacensis a fratre Cisterciensi, vel econverso?*, 'what, I say, do you demand, Cluniac brother from Cistercian brother, and conversely?' (letter 111, p. 278.) Cf. *cur tibi, o albe monache, nigredo fratris tui non mentis sed vestis execranda videtur? Cur tibi, o niger monache, albedo fratris tui non mentis sed vestis admiranda creditur?*, 'Why, O white monk, does the blackness of your brother, not of mind but of clothing, seem execrable to you? Why, O black monk, is the whiteness of your brother, not of mind but of clothing, believed to be a matter of wonder?' (ibid., p. 286); *Dic, dic inquam tu ... dic o niger monache ... et quod in imis cordis tui contra fratrem adhuc latet, denuda ... Sed tu albe quid proponis?*, 'Speak, speak, I say, speak, O black monk.. and reveal what still lurks in the depths of your heart against (your) brother ... But you, O white, what have you to say?' (ibid., p. 291).

[17]   *Sed dicetis ...* (ibid., p. 280); *dixistis ... Ad quod ego ...* (ibid.); *sed exigis adhuc ...* (ibid., p. 281); *Sed quid obiicis frater?* (ibid.).

[18]   *Nulla illis (eis virginibus viduisque) nisi ventris cura est et quae ventri proxima. istiusmodi hortari solent et dicere: 'mi catella, rebus tuis utere et vive, dum vivis', et: 'numquid filiis tuis servas?'*, 'They (those virgins and widows) have no care except for the stomach and what is nearest to the stomach. They are wont to exhort and say things of this kind: "My little puppy, make use of your property and live, while you are alive", and: "Are you saving (it) for your sons?" ' (Jerome, ep. 22, 29. 5, *CSEL*, 54, p. 188). See D. S. Wiesen, *St. Jerome as a satirist, a study in Christian Latin thought and letters*, Cornell Studies in Classical Philology 34, Ithaca, New York, 1964, p. 78.

[19]   *Sed cur sibi adversantur? Cur sibi detrahunt? Cur* ab invicem consumantur? (letter 111, p. 278). This is adapted from Galatians, *Quod si invicem mordetis et comeditis videte ne ab invicem consumamini*, 'Therefore if you bite and devour one another, see to it that you are not devoured by one another' (Gal 5. 15). It had been similarly employed in Bernard's *Apologia* (*Apo*, IV. 7).

subjected to scrutiny: 'Perhaps the cause of this strife between you is diversity of custom, diverse observation of the monastic way';[20] 'Perhaps those habits of diverse colour present an incentive for discord, and the multiform diversity of clothing begets also a diversity of minds.'[21] Subsequently, each is dismissed through a new technique which may replace the logical dilemma, that of 'false' closure: 'If this (diversity of practice), brothers, was the whole cause of mutual discord, does this not seem to you to be straightway excluded?';[22] 'If this (diversity of habit) was the whole cause of mutual discord, if this alone was the matter of such great dissolution, if, I say, this furnished the sole and whole pretext for monastic schism, now that this has been driven away by so many reasons, will the old scissure of your hearts not be made whole?'[23]

With these two 'pretexts' removed, an ironic self-apostrophe paves the way for the revelation of the 'true' causes, *invidia* and *superbia*: 'But what have I said? How have I departed from my senses? Where is the understanding of my mind? Whence has (my) sharpness of vision been overcast? I thought that I had found the whole matter for scandal; I judged that I had revealed all the lurking-places of hatred.'[24] The juxtaposition of *acies*, 'sharpness of vision', with the notion of 'darkening', 'clouding', recalls Peter's evocation of the Augustinian language of perception in letter 65[25] and letter 29.[26] In what follows, however, this language is

---

[20] *Est fortasse inter vos litis huius causa diversa consuetudo, varia monastici ordinis observatio* (letter 111, p. 278).

[21] *Fortassis enim vestes istae coloris diversi incentivum discordiae praestant, et multiformis varietas vestium varietatem quoque parit et mentium* (ibid., p. 285).

[22] *Si haec (diversa consuetudo) certe, o fratres, tota mutui erat causa discidii, nonne iam vobis prorsus exclusa videtur?* (ibid., p. 285).

[23] *Si tota haec (vestes.. coloris diversi) mutui causa erat discidii, si sola tanti materia divortii, si inquam scismatis monastici haec sola et tota erat occasio, nonne hac tam multis rationibus explosa, cordium vestrorum iam vetus scissura unietur?* (ibid., p. 290). Other 'false' closures include: *Facile pax reformabitur, laesa caritas curabitur, postquam pro talibus vel similibus ortum fuisse tantum cordium discidium cognoscetur*, 'Peace will easily be re-established, wounded charity healed, when it is learned that so great a separation of hearts sprang up for such and similar (reasons)' (ibid., p. 278); *Estne ... hoc totum quod vos carissimi ab invicem dividit?*, 'Is this.. the whole matter which divides you, dearest, from one another?' (ibid., p. 280); *Si haec certe tota est animorum vestrorum indignatio, si haec tota caritatis laesio, facile curabitur ...* , 'If this is the whole provocation of your hearts, if this is the whole wound to charity, it will easily be cured ...' (ibid.); *(Quod) ... nescio quis locus discordiae, quis discidio, quis oblocutioni superesse iam possit*, '(Wherefore) ... I do not know what place for discord, for separation, for obloquy can still remain' (ibid.); *... non superest tibi, ut mihi videtur, causa aliqua indignandi, non odiendi, non obloquendi*, 'there remains to you, so it seems to me, no cause for indignation, for hatred, for obloquy' (ibid., p. 281).

[24] *Sed quid dixi? Quomodo mente excessi? Ubi intellectus animi? Unde acies obscurata videndi? Putabam me omnem scandalorum materiam invenisse; arbitrabar me omnes odiorum latebras detexisse* (ibid., p. 290). The expression *mente excedere* may draw on II Corinthians: *sive enim mente excedimus Deo sive sobrii sumus vobis*, 'For whether we depart from our senses (is) for God, whether we are sober (is) for you' (II Cor 5. 13).

[25] Letter 65, p. 194. See Chapter 3.

[26] Letter 29, p. 103. See Chapter 4.

given a sardonic twist. Augustine's demand for spiritual perception, seeing a man in the light of *iudicium veritatis*, the (immutable) 'judgement of truth', is here translated into the perception of the reality of human sin:[27] 'But now, with (my) eye made clear, the day made bright, and the midday sun now allowing nothing to remain hidden, I see, I see, I say, what may I be allowed to say saving the peace of all good men, but whence I am certain that I will be allowed to say with the peace of all good men ...'[28]

The (self)-betrayal of (Cluniac) envy, 'Who would suffer new to be placed before old, younger before elder, white before black monks?',[29] and (Cistercian) arrogance, 'Blessed are we ... who are commended by a far more laudable institution, because the world proclaims (us) more blessed than other monks ...',[30] facilitates a formulation which finally promises closure, 'See, see, that is the true cause, more hidden, but far more hostile than the others to charity ...'[31] This, in turn, leads into a peroration which links *humilitas*, *superbia*, *invidia* and *caritas* in a downward spiral: 'For where humility withdraws, there, of necessity, pride takes its place. Where pride takes its place, there, at once, jealousy also is added. Where jealousy springs up, straightway charity dies.'[32] Peter himself has carefully not ascribed the causes directly to either side, 'allowing' them to emerge from the mouths of the plaintiffs. However, the placing of pride first in the spiral suggests that indirectly the Cistercians are being blamed for having given the first cause of offence. On the one hand, this looks back to the reference to 'tithes' and 'Langres' carefully inserted into the 'private' *captatio*; on the other it may hint at the *Apologia* as the starting-point of 'debate'. At the same time, the spiral also serves to reinforce the notion of Cluniacs and Cistercians as a single organism, damaging themselves as well as each other.

The 'public' heart of letter 111 can thus be seen to utilise a basic three-fold division: 'false' cause;[33] 'false' cause;[34] 'true' cause, modulating into peroration.[35] The first two divisions can be further divided into four sub-sections, employing a range of contrasting approaches. In the first sub-section, diversity of practice is defended by a survey of differing customs within the Church according to place and time, supported by appeals to *auctoritates* such as Ambrose and Augustine.[36] This culminates in an echo of the *Apologia*. Bernard had further illustrated the concept

---

[27]   Augustine, *De Trinitate*, IX, VI. 10–11.

[28]   *At nunc clarificato oculo, serenata die, et sole meridiano iam nil latere permittente, video, video, inquam quod liceat mihi dicere omnium pace bonorum, unde tamen certus sum, quod licebit mihi omnium pace bonorum ...* (letter 111, p. 291).

[29]   *Quis patiatur novos veteribus, iuniores senioribus, albos nigris monachis anteferri?* (ibid.).

[30]   *Felices nos ... quos longe probabilior institutio commendat, quod beatiores aliis monachis mundus praedicat ...* (ibid.).

[31]   *Ecce, ecce, vera illa occultior, sed longe aliis caritati infestior causa ...* (ibid., p. 291).

[32]   *Ubi enim humilitas recedit, ibi necessario superbia succedit. Ubi superbia succedit, ibi statim et invidia accedit. Ubi invidia oritur, confestim caritas moritur* (ibid., p. 292).

[33]   Letter 111, pp. 278–85.

[34]   Ibid., pp. 285–90.

[35]   Ibid., pp. 290–93.

[36]   Ibid., pp. 278–81.

of diversity within unity through a citation from the *Psalms*, '*He has led me ... on the paths of righteousness on account of his name.*'[37] Subsequently, however, this concept had been developed into a warning, 'But let each one see by whichever (path) he goes, lest by reason of the diversity of paths, he withdraw from the one righteousness ...'[38] Peter utilises the same allusion to justify both sides alike:

> For if you, O Cluniac, knew the Cistercian or you, Cistercian, knew the Cluniac to be going astray in the purpose undertaken, and according to scripture foresaw him making for destruction through the path which seems to men straight, I admit that you would have just cause for correcting and calling back your brother, or, if he refused to hear you, of rebuking and execrating him ... But now, since I see that each of you ... striving through different paths to the same prize, *is so running that you may seize it*, there remains to you, so it seems to me, no cause of indignation, of hatred, of obloquy.[39]

Bernard's warning had been against abuse of *caritas*, that of Peter targets its absence.[40]

The second sub-section, again dealing with diversity of practice, comprises a recapitulation of the points of difference between Cluniacs and Cistercians which made up the bulk of letter 28.[41] Here, however, both sides are shown as being justified. It is introduced by the coupling of the New Testament demand for *oculus simplex*, the 'single eye',[42] identified as *caritas* through the Pauline citation, '*Let all your (deeds) be done in charity*',[43] with the Augustinian precept first invoked in letter 28, '*Have charity, and do what you will.*'[44] The argument depends upon the simple ploy of repetition and alternation. In turn, strict adherence to the monastic *Rule* and dispensation from it are shown equally to be products of 'singleness of eye'.[45] Significantly, however, as Goodrich points out, there is no departure here

---

[37] *Deduxit me super semitas iustitiae propter nomen suum (Apo*, IV. 8 = Ps 22. 3).

[38] *Viderit autem quisque quacumque (semita) incedat, ne pro diversitate semitarum ab una iustitia recedat.. (Apo* IV. 9).

[39] *Si enim tu o Cluniacensis Cisterciensem, aut tu Cisterciensis Cluniacensem in assumpto proposito errare cognosceres, et iuxta scripturam per viam quae videtur hominibus recta ad interitum tendere provideres, iusta fateor tibi esset causa fratrem corrigendi, revocandi, aut si audire te nollet, obiurgandi et detestandi ... At nunc cum ... utrumque vestrum ... videam ... per diversas semitas ad idem bravium tendentes* sic currere ut comprehendatis, *non superest tibi, ut mihi videtur, causa aliqua indignandi, non odiendi, non obloqiendi* (letter 111, p. 281 = I Cor 9. 24).

[40] The Pauline citation given above commences, *Omnes quidem currunt, sed unus accipit bravium ...*, 'All run, but one receives the prize ...' (I Cor 9. 24).

[41] Letter 111, pp. 281–5.

[42] Si oculus tuus fuerit simplex, totum corpus tuum lucidum erit (ibid., p. 281 = Mt 6. 22; Lc 11. 34). This concept had made a brief appearance in letter 28, where it had been glossed as *bona intentio*, 'good intention' (letter 28, p. 60), a definition echoed here in the form of *puritatis intentio*, 'striving after purity' (letter 111, p. 282).

[43] Omnia vestra in caritate fiant (letter 111, p. 281 = I Cor 16. 14).

[44] Habe caritatem, et fac quicquid vis (letter 111, ibid.; letter 28, pp. 60, 98 = Augustine, *In epist. Ioh.*, VIII, 8; ibid., *Serm. Frang.*, V, 3). See Chapter 2.

[45] *Simplici namque oculo tu uteris ... Simplici oculo et tu uteris ...* (letter 111, p. 282). This technique can be paralleled from the *Regula pastoralis* of Gregory the Great. In discussing

from the ideological stance espoused in letter 28, as the evocation of Augustine makes clear.[46] The principle, that the requirements of *caritas* and the aim of saving souls justify changes to the monastic *Rule*, is repeatedly reinforced: 'see, father Benedict himself ... orders the abbot to so temper everything that souls be saved, and murmuring be absent, and you fear for the salvation of those following diverse practices under the same Rule?';[47] 'But now ... let there be subjoined some articles concerning the present inquiry, in which certain things may be shown to have been changed by the single eye, sincere charity, the intention of saving souls.'[48] At the same time, strict adherence to the letter of the *Rule* is justified under the guise of 'laudable devotion'.[49]

The third sub-section, dealing with diversity of habit, makes a dramatic switch to heavy satire, demonstrating silent detraction, followed by arguments from nature, designed to show the unnaturalness of hostility between monkish brethren.[50] The presence in this section of what appear to be Jeromian allusions to some form of theatrical dumb-show suggests that Peter is simultaneously combating Bernard's commendation of 'silence', and offering a riposte to the latter's exploitation of *iocus* and *ludus* in ep. 228. Employing the technique of *attestatio*, 'eye-witness' testimony,[51] Peter depicts encounters between black and white monks in grotesque and parodic terms: of black monks encountering a white monk, 'as if a Chimaera or Centaur, or some exotic monstrosity were being forced upon their eyes, signing

---

ars praedicationis, 'the art of preaching', he first defines the different types of audience: *Aliter namque viri, aliter admonendae sunt feminae. Aliter iuvenes, aliter senes ...*, 'For men are to be admonished in one way, women in another. Young men in one way, old men in another ...' The same formula is used to introduce the subsequent sections, dealing with each category in turn (Gregory the Great, *Regula pastoralis*, III, I. xxiii, *Grégoire le Grand, Règle pastorale*, ed. B. Judic, C. Morel and F. Rommel, 2 vols, Sources chrétiennes 381–2, Paris, 1992, 382, p. 262).

[46]   Goodrich, 'The limits of friendship', p. 88.

[47]   *ecce, ipse ... Benedictus pater, abbatem sic omnia temperare iubet, ut animae salventur, et murmur absit, et saluti sub eadem regula diversa sequentium metuis?* (letter 111, p. 282).

[48]   *Sed iam ... subiungantur aliqua de instanti quaestione capitula, in quibus simplici oculo, sincera caritate, salvandarum animarum intentione, quaedam mutata monstrentur* (ibid.). Cf. *Habes et tu institutionum tuarum eundem Benedictum auctorem, qui ad finem caritatis universa scripta sua redigi praecipit et animarum saluti quoquomodo, isto vel illo ordine inservire*, 'You also have the same Benedict as authority for your dispositions, who orders all his writings to be reduced to the intention of charity, and to serve the salvation of souls howsoever it may be, by this order or that' (ibid., p. 284).

[49]   *Habes tu huius propositi tui Benedictum auctorem, cuius licet scripta ubi caritas iubet ipso teste minime sequi cogaris, sequi tamen quia tanto viro congrua visa sunt, devotione laudibili delectaris*, 'You have Benedict as authority for this way of life of yours, whose writings you delight to follow with laudable devotion, because they seemed fitting to so great a man, although when charity orders, you are not compelled to follow them, as he bears witness' (ibid.).

[50]   Ibid., pp. 285–7.

[51]   *Vidi plurimos nec recordor quotiens ...*, 'I have seen very many, nor do I recall how often ...' (letter 111, p. 285). This technique had also been employed in Bernard's *Apologia*: *Mentior, si non vidi abbatem sexaginta equos, et eo amplius, in suo ducere comitatu*, 'I lie, if I have not seen an abbot leading sixty horses, and more, in his train' (*Apo* XI. 27).

their stupefaction by voice or bodily gesture';[52] of white monks encountering a black monk, 'previously talkative ... suddenly falling silent, and seeking refuge in the remedy of silence, as if from enemies hunting out the secrets of enemies';[53] of both alike, 'I have seen among men of both kinds the silent tongues, the talkative eyes, hands and feet, crying out more clearly by the support of gestures what they did not wish to indicate with their voice, for fear of betraying themselves.'[54]

As suggested above, the emphasis on exaggerated body language in this passage finds parallels in Jerome. In his letter to Rusticus,[55] Jerome warns against adulators who are revealed to be mockers: 'if you look back suddenly, you would catch them making stork-necks behind your back, or waggling donkey-ears with their hands, or sticking out a raging dog-tongue'.[56] In the same context, one Grunnius, 'the Grunter',[57] generally taken as representing Jerome's arch-enemy, Rufinus,[58] is portrayed as a hybrid chimaera, part-lion, part-goat, part-dragon,[59] indulging in ludicrous grimaces to impress his students.[60] The verb *grunnire* in Jerome routinely connotes jealous slander.[61] So, too, Peter will subsequently declare that difference

---

[52]   *velut si Chimaera vel Centaurus, vel portentum aliquod peregrinum oculis ingereretur, voce vel gestu corporis se stupere signantes* (letter 111, p. 286). This evocation of mythological monstrosities may point in several directions. A letter from Jerome, to be discussed subsequently, offers a description of the chimaera (Jerome, ep. 125, 18, *CSEL*, 56/1, p. 138). Earlier in this letter, Peter has directly cited the *Ars poetica* of Horace, which opens with the depiction of a centaur (Horace, *Ars poetica*, 1–2, Shackleton Bailey, p. 310). At the same time, Peter may also be looking back at the *Apologia*. In his satirical condemnation of ornamentation, Bernard had listed various hybrid monsters, including 'monstrous centaurs' (*Apo* XII, 29). Subsequently, in a letter to the prior of Portes, written after the failure of the Second Crusade, and dated to between 1147 and 1150, Bernard would refer to himself as *Chimaera mei saeculi*, the 'Chimaera of my age' (Bernard, ep. 250, 4, *SBO*, VIII, p. 147).
[53]   *loquaces prius ... subito obmutuisse, et velut ab hostibus hostium secreta rimantibus, silentii sibi remedio praecavisse* (letter 111, p. 286).
[54]   *Intuitus sum utriusque generis hominum linguas tacentes, oculos, manus, pedesque loquentes, et quod voce ne proderentur, indicare nolebant, gestuum suffragio clarius inclamasse* (ibid.).
[55]   Jerome, ep. 125, *CSEL*, 56/1, pp. 118–42.
[56]   *si subito respexeris, aut ciconiarum deprendas post te colla curvari aut manu auriculas agitari asini aut aestuantem canis protendi linguam* (ibid., 18, p. 137; cf. Persius, *Satires*, I. 58-60, Bo, pp. 22–3).
[57]   The figure of Grunnius is taken from the satirical and anonymous *Testamentum Porcelli*, in *Petronii Saturae*, ed. F. Bücheler, Berlin, 1922, pp. 268–9. See E. Champlin, 'The testament of the piglet', *Phoenix* 41 (1987), 174–83.
[58]   Wiesen, *St. Jerome as a satirist*, p. 229.
[59]   *prima leo, postrema draco, media ipsa chimaera* (Jerome, ep. 125, 18, p. 138 = Lucretius, *De rerum natura*, V. 905, *T. Lucretius Carus De rerum natura*, ed. J. Martin, Bibliotheca scriptorum Graecorum et Romanorum Teubneriana, Leipzig, 1969).
[60]   *adducto supercilio contractisque naribus ac fronte rugata duobus digitulis concrepabat hoc signo ad audiendum discipulos provocans*, '..raising his eyebrows, wrinkling up his nostrils and furrowing his brow, he would snap two fingers, challenging his pupils to pay attention' (Jerome, ep. 125, 18, pp. 137–8).
[61]   *Non mirum ergo si contra me parvum homunculum immundae sues grunniant, et* pedibus margaritas conculcent, *cum adversus doctissimos viros, et qui gloria invidiam superare*

in habit offers no cause *grunniendi*, 'for grunting', 'for detraction'.[62] Elsewhere in Jerome's writing, the theatrical connotations of such body language are made explicit: 'This witness is to be used also against the women of the Church, who walk with an extended neck, and speak with winks, and applaud with both hands and feet, and, in order to advance with mincing step, do not follow nature as their guide, but hire actors as their teachers.'[63]

The evocation of monstrosity modulates into arguments from nature, contrasting the perversity of man with the simplicity of animals: 'O the malice of men and the innocence of beasts! O the constancy in its origin of the substance created in brute beasts!; O the perversity of nature in the rational being!'[64] The Biblical motif of 'sheep' which preluded the reopening of debate is used simultaneously to reintroduce and to dispel the opposition between Jews and Gentiles: 'He (Christ) does not, I say, separate any from his sheepfold on account of colour, who.. has congregated Jew and Gentile alike in one sheepfold of the Christian faith.'[65] This is

---

debuerant, livor exarserit, 'No wonder, therefore, if the filthy pigs should grunt against me, a little man, and *trample the pearls with their feet*, when malice has flared up against the most learned men, who should have overcome jealousy by (their) glory' (Jerome, *Hebraicae quaestiones in Libro Geneseos, praefatio* 301/302, ed. P. de Lagarde, *CCSL*, 72, Turnhout, 1959 = Mt 7. 6).

62   Letter 111, p. 287.

63   *Abutendum est hoc testimonio et adversum Ecclesiae feminas, quae ambulant collo extento, et nutibus loquuntur oculorum, et plaudunt tam manibus quam pedibus, et ut composito incedant gradu, non naturam sequuntur ducem, sed histriones redimunt praeceptores* (Jerome, *Commentariorum in Esaiam Libri I–XVIII*, II, iii, 16, ed. M. Adriaen, 2 vols, *CCSL*, 73-73A, Turnhout, 1963, 73, p. 54). Jerome is expanding here on Is 3. 16. See Wiesen, *St. Jerome as a satirist*, p. 122 and n. 41.

64   *Et o malitia hominum et o innocentia pecudum. O constans in sua origine, creata in brutis animalibus substantia; o perversa in rationali animante natura* (letter 111, p. 287). The sentiment is derived from classical rhetoric: *Nam neque feris inter se bella sunt, nec, si forent, eadem hominem deceant, placidum proximumque divino genus*, 'For neither do the beasts have wars amongst themselves, nor, if they did, would the same become man, a calm race and nearest to the divine' (Seneca the Elder, *Controversiae*, II, I. 10, *L. Annaeus Seneca Maior, Oratorum et rhetorum sententiae, divisiones, colores*, ed. L. Håkanson, Bibliotheca scriptorum Graecorum et Romanorum Teubneriana, Leipzig, 1989). From here it passed into Christian writing: *Admonendi sunt discordes, ut si aures a mandatis caelestibus declinant, mentis oculos ad consideranda ea quae in infimis versantur, aperiant; quod saepe aves unius eiusdemque generis sese socialiter volando non deserunt, quod gregatim animalia bruta pascuntur*, 'The discordant are to be admonished that, if they turn away their ears from the heavenly commandments, they should open their eyes to consider those things which are carried on in the depths; that often birds of one and the same species do not desert one another, flying in company, that the brute animals feed in herds' (Gregory the Great, *Regula pastoralis*, III. XXII, XLVI, SC, 382, p. 402). On animal rhetoric in general, see *The Minor Declamations ascribed to Quintilian*, ed. with commentary M. Winterbottom, Berlin, 1984, p. 341, n. 15.

65   *Non inquam secernit (pastor ille) quempiam ab ovili suo propter colorem, qui.. in uno Christianae fidei ovili Iudaeum congregavit pariter et gentilem* (letter 111, p. 287). The opposition is reinforced by two Pauline citations: *In Christo Ihesu neque circumcisio aliquid valet, neque praeputium, sed nova creatura*, 'In Christ Jesus neither circumcision is worth anything, nor the prepuce, but a new creature' (ibid. = Gal 6. 15); *Ubi non est gentilis et Iudaeus, circumcisio et praeputium, barbarus et Scytha, servus et liber, sed omnia et in*

followed by an allusion to *multicolor grex*, the 'multicoloured flock' of Jacob,[66] which may counterbalance the reference to Joseph's *polymita tunica*, 'many-coloured tunic', in the *Apologia*.[67] At the same time, however, Peter gives a twist to the concept of natural harmony: 'Indeed, sometimes ram locks horns with ram, sheep pounds sheep with frequent blows, but these or those are not excited to battle by variation in colour, but provoked in some way or other by the rousing of an anger, innate to all living things.'[68] Pointed up by rhetorical antithesis, this statement recalls the classical *topos* of animals fighting for mastery of the herd, hinting, perhaps, that what is really at stake is a struggle for monastic supremacy.[69]

The fourth sub-section reverts to the citing of *auctoritates*.[70] This is preluded by an assertion that white monks are justified in their choice of colour by the 'single eye of conscience',[71] black monks by the weight of tradition.[72] Both, however, are said to be justified by the provision of the *Rule*, that monks should suit the colour and thickness of their clothing to their circumstances.[73] At this point, Cistercians and Cluniacs would appear to be equally vindicated, by *ratio* and *auctoritas* respectively.[74] The mustering of authorities which follows, however, may seem to

---

omnibus Christus, 'Where there is not Gentile and Jew, circumcision and prepuce, barbarian and Scythian, but Christ is everything and in everything' (ibid. = Col 3. 11).

[66]   Letter 111, p. 287 = Gn 30. 32–3.

[67]   *Apo* III. 5. Both Jacob and Joseph were 'favourite sons.' Peter had identified the Cistercians with Jacob in his letter to Innocent concerning tithes (letter 33, p. 109).

[68]   *Et quidem aliquando aries arietem cornibus impetit, ovis ovem crebris pulsibus tundit, sed hos vel has non varietas coloris ad pugnam excitat, sed innata cunctis animalibus ac modo quolibet ira excita provocat* (letter 111, p. 287).

[69]   *cum duo conversis inimica in proelia tauri*
   frontibus incurrunt, pavidi cessere magistri.
   stat pecus omne metu mutum, mussantque iuvencae
   quis nemori imperitet, quem tota armenta sequantur
'(as) when two bulls lock horns for hostile battle, the fearful herdsmen give way. The whole herd stands mute with fear, the heifers low as to which is to rule the grove, which all the flocks are to follow' (Virgil, *Aeneid*, XII, 716–19).

[70]   Letter 111, pp. 287–90.

[71]   *Habes tu idoneum defensorem albedinis tuae, simplicem.. oculum conscientiae tuae ...*, 'You have as a sufficient defender for your whiteness the single ... eye of your conscience ...' (ibid., p. 287).

[72]   *Habes et tu ... probabilem auctorem nigredinis tuae longissimum et a patribus traditum consuetudinis morem ...*, 'You also have ... as a laudable authority for your blackness, the long practice of custom, handed down by the Fathers ...' (ibid., p. 288).

[73]   *Habes uterque utriusque coloris tui inexpugnabilem propugnatricem ipsius communis regulae vocem, quae praecipit ut de vestium colore aut grossitudine non causentur monachi, sed illius coloris aut qualitatis vestibus utantur, quae in provincia qua habitant vel facilius inveniri vel levius comparari potuerint*, 'Both of you of each colour have as an unassailable protectress the voice of the communal Rule, which orders that *monks should not dispute concerning the colour or thickness* of clothing, but should use clothing of that colour or quality, which have been able either to be found more easily or to be procured more lightly *in the province in which* they live' (ibid. = *Benedicti Regula*, LV. 7).

[74]   *Tutatur ergo albedinem tuam ratio supradicta ... Tuetur et nigredinem tuam paterna auctoritas ...*, 'Therefore your whiteness is protected by the aforesaid reason ... Your blackness also is defended by the authority of the Fathers ...' (letter 111, p. 288).

tip the balance. Of these, all but one are shown to favour black as a sign of humility and mourning. Only Jerome condemns the wearing of black and white alike. Significantly, this condemnation is on the grounds of ostentation.[75] This seeming preference is underscored by personal intervention and *attestatio*: 'For, to admit what I feel, it seemed to those great fathers, so it seems to me, that this colour of black which is in question, was more suited to humility, to penitence, to grief';[76] 'I myself saw recently, being in Spain, and wondered, that this ancient custom is still observed by all the Spanish people.'[77] This time, those who wear black are said to be supported by both reason and authority, those who wear white, more moderately, to be 'not condemned'.[78] This nuancing seems to recall, in softened form, the earlier attack in letter 28, hinting perhaps at the arrogance which will be given pride of place in the peroraration.[79]

The balance, however, may be partly restored by the use of a motif new to this letter, that of reforming zeal, which encloses this mustering of authorities: 'because under the habit of the blacks you saw innumerable of this order grown lukewarm from the undertaking, you wished with praiseworthy skill to rouse them to a greater and new fervour of monastic life by this hitherto unaccustomed whiteness of clothing';[80] 'He distinguishes himself in a certain way by such a colour, not from communal charity ..., but from the tepidity of many of this order, known to all.'[81] The accompanying motif of tepidity may be thought to convey a veiled criticism of (some) Cluniacs. Subsequently, however, the notion of 'zeal' will itself come under scrutiny. In the mouth of the (Cistercian) complainant, it will be presented as a cause for self-congratulation: 'We are restorers of lost piety, resuscitators of a dead order, most righteous condemners of languid, luke-warm, sordid monks. We ... have made the tepidity of the old a laughing-stock, and prove the new fervour of ours to excel.'[82] The concluding part of the 'private' frame makes this potential negativity

---

[75]   Vestes *(Hieronymus) ait* pullas aeque ut candidas devita. *Monens eum (Nepotianum) scilicet, ut fastum vel iactantiam caveret ...*, 'He (Jerome) says: "Avoid black and white garments alike", warning him (Nepotianus) namely to beware arrogance and ostentation' (ibid., p. 288 = Jerome, ep. 52, 9, *CSEL*, 54, p. 430).

[76]   *Nam ut quod sentio fatear, visum est ut mihi videtur magnis patribus illis nigrum hunc de quo agitur colorem magis humilitati, magis paenitentiae, magis luctui convenire* (ibid., p. 289).

[77]   *Vidi nuper ipse in Hispaniis constitutus, et admiratus sum, antiquum hunc morem ab Hispaniis adhuc omnibus observari* (letter 111, p. 289).

[78]   *Hac tanta auctoritate vel ratione tibi colorique tuo, niger monache, satisfacio, nec tamen ideo albi albedinem condemno*, 'By this great authority and reason I vindicate you and your colour, black monk; however, I do not therefore condemn the whiteness of the white' (ibid., pp. 289–90).

[79]   Letter 28, p. 57.

[80]   *quia sub nigrorum habitu innumerabiles huius ordinis tepefactos a proposito cernebas, ad maiorem et novum monasticae religionis fervorem, hoc hactenus inusitato vestium candore excitare arte laudabili voluisti* (letter 111, pp. 287–8).

[81]   *Distinguit se quodammodo tali colore non a communi ... caritate, sed a multorum huius ordinis nota omnibus tepiditate* (ibid., p. 290).

[82]   *Nos religionis perditae restauratores, nos emortui ordinis resuscitatores, nos languentium, tepentium, sordentium monachorum iustissimi condemnatores. Nos ... et veterum teporem ostentui fecimus, et novum nostrorum fervorem praecellere approbamus* (ibid., p. 291).

explicit, through the coupling of *livor*, 'jealousy', with *zelus contrarius*, 'contrary zeal', as enemies to *caritas*.[83] Replacing the earlier pairing of *invidia* and *superbia* seen in the peroration,[84] the terminology seems to hark back to the *Rule* of St Benedict, which distinguishes between 'good' zeal, which leads to salvation, and 'bad' zeal, which leads to destruction.[85]

In relation to the ostensible proposition for 'debate', whether Cluniacs and Cistercians have any 'just' cause for dispute, the case would appear to have been comprehensively 'disproved'. The four sub-sections discussed above can be seen as offering negative proof, while the final section, with its self-revelations demonstrating jealousy and arrogance respectively, stands as an incontrovertible indictment which needs no further evidence Conversely, it is arguable that under this guise Peter has succeeded in demonstrating an alternative proposition, that of the validity of 'diversity within unity', through a combination of 'positive' proof supplied by 'singleness of eye' and the Augustinian precept, '*have charity and do what you will*', and 'negative' proof offered by Jeromian satire and arguments from nature. The central portion of letter 111 may also have affinities with the sermon, as certain of the techniques discussed above suggest. If the transitional part of the private frame of 111 is taken into account, a tripartite structure emerges, with prologue,[86] division in two parts, each with its sub-sections of 'proof', and conclusion.[87] At the same time, set within the 'private' frame addressed to Bernard, the central section can be seen to supply the letter as a whole with *narratio* and (displaced) *conclusio*.

Setting aside, for the moment, the final part of the letter dealing with Islam, there remains the question of what conclusions may be drawn about the underlying intentions of letter 111. According to Bredero, the change of tone between this and letter 28 can be explained by a change of purpose. In letter 28, in Bredero's view, Peter had been concerned to defend traditional Cluniac practices against internal efforts to promote reform.[88] In letter 111, Peter is said to be writing with a view to involving Bernard in an attempt to promote Cistercian-type reforms among the

---

[83]   *ut robiginem illam livoris et zeli contrarii quae interiora viscerum latenter rodere solet eraderem modis quibus potui laboravi*, 'I have laboured, in the ways I could, to eradicate that rust of jealousy and contrary zeal, which is accustomed to gnaw secretly at the inmost entrails' (ibid., p. 293). This seems to extend the image at the end of letter 28, where Peter preaches the removal of *invidiae robigo*, 'the rust of jealousy' (letter 28, p. 101).

[84]   Letter 111, p. 292.

[85]   *Sicut est zelus amaritudinis malus, qui separat a deo et ducit ad infernum, ita est zelus bonus, qui separat a vitia (sic) et ducit ad deum et ad vitam aeternam*, 'Just as there is the bad zeal of bitterness, which separates from God and leads to hell, so there is the good zeal, which separates from vice and leads to God and to eternal life' (*Benedicti Regula*, LXXII, 1–2.)

[86]   Letter 111, pp. 227–8.

[87]   This can be compared, for example, with the structure advocated in the *De modo praedicandi* of Alexander of Ashby (*c*. 1200?), as discussed by Murphy. Although the latter appears to postulate a four-part structure comprising prologue, division, proof, conclusion, the category of 'proof' is, in actual fact, subsumed into that of 'division' (Murphy, *Rhetoric in the Middle Ages*, pp. 312–17.)

[88]   Bredero, 'Saint Bernard in his relations', p. 319; idem, *Bernard of Clairvaux*, p. 226.

Cluniacs.[89] The first of these interpretations has been considered in an earlier chapter, where it was argued that in spite of what could be seen as veiled hints of internal dissension, the focus of letter 28, effected through the parallel with Augustine and Jerome, was a rebuttal of the (mis)interpretation of the monastic *Rule* presented in Bernard's *Apologia*.[90] As suggested above, letter 111 shows no signs of retreating from the position adopted there, that *caritas* legitimises, indeed, demands, dispensation from the strict requirements of the *Rule*,[91] encapsulated here in the statement: 'For such things, as you know, are of the number of moveable precepts, and when charity orders, they are to be moved without any fear of transgression.'[92] Indeed, it is arguable that while Peter's argument abolishes the qualitative distinction between the Orders, it serves to maintain and even reinforce the differences.

At the same time, the appearance of the concept of 'tepidity' might be taken as indicating the possibility and perhaps the desirability of certain modifications in Cluniac practice. One occurrence of this motif may be particularly telling. Peter claims in relation to the Cistercian(s), 'so you ... driving out relaxations due rather to delicacy than necessity, strive to recall the tepidity of our times to the way of ancient and primal fervour'.[93] *Delicatus*, 'delicate', may recall the reference to *delicatae otio manus*, 'hands delicate with leisure', included in the Cistercian attack on the Cluniac rejection of manual labour in letter 28.[94] This is the one issue on which Peter shows overt signs of movement. In letter 28, he had offered a challenge: 'If the same end [that ... idleness may not be able to harm the soul] can be achieved by other exercises of good works, does it not seem to you that the Rule is being well kept? ... for many other good works apart from manual work can be found ...'[95] In letter 111, manual work is said to have been set aside *ex parte*, 'in part', and justification is offered on the grounds of being established in the middle of cities and towns, as opposed to 'woods' and 'deserts'.[96] However, a rider is added

---

[89]   Idem, 'Saint Bernard in his relations', pp. 332–3; idem, *Bernard of Clairvaux*, pp. 236–8.

[90]   See Chapter 3.

[91]   See Goodrich, 'The limits of friendship', pp. 87–8.

[92]   *Talia enim ut nosti de numero praeceptorum mobilium sunt, et quando caritas imperat absque aliquo transgressionis timore movenda sunt* (letter 111, p. 285).

[93]   *sic tu ... delicatis magis quam necessariis condescensionibus explosis, ad antiqui et primi fervoris morem, nostrorum temporum teporem revocare contenditis* (ibid., p. 284).

[94]   Letter 28, p. 54.

[95]   *Si ... aliis bonorum operum exercitiis idem [ne animae.. nocere otiositas valeat] potest fieri, non videtur vobis bene regula servari? ... nam multa alia bona opera praeter opus manuum possunt inveniri ...* (letter 28, p. 70).

[96]   *qui hoc opus manuum ex parte postposuisti, quia non in silvis nec in desertis, sed in medio urbium et castrorum constitutus, et undique populis circumsaeptus, nec totiens, et totiens ire ac redire horum causa operum per promiscuam utriusque sexus multitudinem absque aliquo vel plurimo periculo potes, nec insuper opportuna loca ubi talibus exerceri operibus possis, plerumque possides*, 'who have set aside manual labour in part, because, established not in woods or deserts but in the midst of cities and fortifications, and enclosed on all sides by peoples, you cannot continually come and go for the sake of these works through an indiscriminate multitude of both sexes without any and indeed much danger, nor, in addition, do you commonly possess suitable places where you could be exercised in such works' (letter 111, p. 283).

to this: 'But in case idleness, the enemy of religious men, should find a place to harm you, with you being unoccupied, you either work with your hands where and when you can, or where you cannot you compensate for this manual work by a variety of divine works, and thus occupy the whole space of your life with what sacred endeavours you can, so that the worthless spirit does not claim for itself the dwelling of your heart, being empty.'[97] This seems to foreshadow the commendation of manual work in the reforming decrees of 1146.[98] As noted by Lang, these decrees would also address issues of food, clothing and bedding.[99]

That letter 111 was expected to have circulated also amongst the Cluniacs is clear from the reference in Peter's subsequent letter 161, addressed to the Cluniac priors and sub-priors, to 'two letters previously directed to the lord abbot of Clairvaux' in which he had set out the Cluniac position on dispensation.[100] In this letter, which can only be dated between letter 111 and Peter's death in 1156,[101] he launches a scathing attack on Cluniac abuse of food which, as has been pointed out, finds parallels in the satirical writing of Bernard.[102] Certain features of the language, however, may also serve to link it with letter 111. Peter contrasts the behaviour of the Cluniacs unfavourably with that of *scurrae*, 'servants', 'parasites', *mimi*, 'mimes' and *lixae*, 'camp-followers', 'cooks'.[103] 'Parasites' and 'cooks' were stock figures of Roman comedy, while the theatrical connotations of 'mimes' are explicit. Moreover, anyone who does not conform to this dietary licence is said to be stigmatised *sicut ethnicus et publicanus*, 'as a Gentile and tax-gatherer'.[104] This

---

[97]   *Sed ne inimica religiosis otiositas te vacante locum tibi nocendi inveniat, aut ubi et quando potes manibus operaris, aut ubi non potes opus hoc manuum operibus divinis per vices variando compensas, sicque ne domum pectoris tui vacantem nequam spiritus sibi vendicet, quibus potes sacris studiis totum vitae tuae tempus occupas* (ibid.).

[98]   *Statutum est, ut antiquum et sanctum opus manuum, vel in claustris ipsis, aut ubi honeste remoto conspectu saecularium fieri poterit, ex parte saltem aliqua restauretur, ita ut omni tempore praeter festivos dies, quibus operari non licet, quolibet semper fratres utili opere exerceantur*, 'It has been decreed that the ancient and holy manual work, either in the cloisters themselves, or where it can be done honourably removed from the sight of the laity, should be restored at any rate in some part, so that at all times except feast-days, on which it is not allowable to work, the brothers may always be exercised with some useful work' (Peter the Venerable, *Statuta*, 39, p. 73).

[99]   Lang, 'Friendship with Peter the Venerable', pp. 48–9.

[100]   *Et causa vel ratio, quia bis a me in duabus epistolis, olim domino abbati Clarevallensi directis, studiose descripta est, hic iterare superfluum iudico*, 'Since the cause and/or reason has been carefully set out by me twice in two letters directed previously to the lord abbot of Clairvaux, I judge it superfluous to repeat it here' (Peter, letter 161, *Letters*, I, p. 390).

[101]   Constable, *Letters*, II, p. 206.

[102]   J. de la Croix Bouton, 'Bernard et l'ordre de Cluny', *Bernard de Clairvaux, 1953: Commission d'Histoire de l'ordre de Cîteaux*, Paris, 1953, 193–217, pp. 196–7.

[103]   *relatum est mihi ... nullam iam distantiam esse, quantum ad esum carnium pertinet ... inter scurras et monachos. ..Abstinent causa dei ipsi mimi, vel lixae, a carnibus omni sabbato ...*, 'I have been told ... that there is now no difference, as far as pertains to the eating of flesh ... between parasites and monks ...The very mimes and cooks abstain from flesh, for the sake of God, every Sabbath ... ' (letter 161, p. 388).

[104]   *Reputatur [si quis timore dei ductus a tali esu abstinere voluerit] ab eis sicut ethnicus et publicanus, cavendum esse ab illo sicut ab hoste publico praedicant*, '[Whoever led by fear

appears to represent a satirical inversion of the Jewish-Gentile opposition normally attached to Cistercian–Cluniac relationships.

The harshness of the criticism in this letter might suggest that the defence of Cluniac practice in letter 111 should be seen primarily as an exercise in internal reassurance, designed to render changes more acceptable to the Cluniacs. Alternatively, this letter might be seen as offering a palliative to Bernard, in the form of an internal counterpoint to the external validation of Cistercian austerity found in 111. At the same time, however, as noted above, the criticism of dietary abuse is set against a reminder of the defence of dispensation from other areas of the monastic *Rule* mounted previously by Peter in letters 28 and 111.[105] Despite the criticism levelled against Peter by the contemporary chronicler, Orderic Vitalis, to the effect that in his reforms he 'emulated the Cistercians and other followers of novelties',[106] there seems to be room for doubt as to how far the ensuing *Statutes* actually represented a shift away from traditional Cluniac practice.[107] Equally, there is no external evidence that Peter hoped for Bernard's involvement in their implementation.

That letter 111 was intended for and found a wider circulation, encompassing, as Bredero suggests, both Cluniacs and Cistercians,[108] can perhaps find sufficient

---

of God wishes to abstain from such food] is reckoned by them *a Gentile and a tax-gatherer*: they preach that he is to be guarded against as a public enemy' (ibid., p. 389 = Mt 18. 17).

[105] *Si enim de noviciis suscipiendis, si de opere manuum, si de vestibus et quibusdam similibus, a bonis patribus post sanctum Benedictum, (capitulum) mutatum est, non dubia sed certa et rationabili causa factum est*, 'For if in regard to the acceptance of novices, to manual work, to clothing and certain similar matters, it (the article) was changed by good fathers after the holy Benedict, it was done for no dubious but certain and reasonable cause' (ibid., p. 390). See Constable, *Letters*, II, p. 206; Bredero, 'Saint Bernard in his relations', pp. 332–3.

[106] *Austerus autem praeceptor Salomonis oblitus praecepti, ne transgrediaris terminos antiquos quos posuerunt patres tui. Cistercienses aliosque novorum sectatores emulatus rudibus ausis institit, et ab inceptis desistere ad praesens erubuit*, 'But the harsh preceptor forgot the precept of Solomon, *Do not pass over the ancient bounds which your fathers have set down*. Emulating the Cistercians and other followers of novelties, he insisted upon the new attempts, and was ashamed for the present to desist from his undertakings' (Orderic Vitalis, *Historia ecclesiastica*, XIII. 13, Chibnall, 6, p. 426).

[107] Bredero cites Knowles to the effect that Peter's reforms can be viewed as constituting an approach to the Cistercian way of life (Bredero, 'Saint Bernard in his relations', p. 332; Knowles, *The historian and character*, pp. 69–72). In fact, however, Knowles also claims there that 'Peter remain(ed) a Cluniac ... at heart.' Constable, following Leclercq, notes that these reforms encompassed the alleviation of 'excessive harshness' as well as the raising of standards of 'strictness' (G. Constable, 'The monastic policy of Peter the Venerable', in *Pierre Abélard–Pierre le Vénérable. Les courants littéraires et artistiques en occident au milieu du XIIe siècle*, Colloques Internationaux du Centre National de la Recherche Scientifique 546, Paris, 1975, 119–42, p. 124). Goodrich similarly invokes Leclercq to the effect that Peter 'did not depart from Cluniac principles' (Goodrich, 'The limits of friendship', p. 82; Dom J. Leclerq, 'Pierre le Vénérable et les limites du programme clunisien', *Collectanea Ordinis Cisterciensium Reformatorum* 18 (1956), 84–7).

[108] Bredero, *Bernard of Clairvaux*, p. 238. Peter's statement that he read out Bernard's letter to 'all those round about', in order to 'rouse them to a greater affection', can be taken as a hint to Bernard that he should do the same (letter 111, p. 275).

explanation in the stated purpose of doing away with mutual detraction. The letter may itself hint at a pressing cause for promoting reconciliation. Although the dispute between Gigny and Le Miroir would not break into open violence until 1151–52, it seems unlikely that the resentment over the withholding of tithes had simply gone away. That Peter has this resentment in mind is suggested both by the direct reference to tithes and by his denunciation of the 'sworn wars' of those from certain 'sheepfolds'.[109] It may also lurk behind the warning addressed to both sides alike that the loss of *caritas* entails a threat to the spiritual treasure 'laid up in heaven.'[110] The language here can be seen to combine two biblical allusions, to Tobit, 'Prayer is good with fasting and alms rather than to lay up the treasures of gold',[111] and to the advice of the Gospels, to store up treasure in heaven rather than on earth.[112] Such a reminder might seem to be equally applicable to both sides of the dispute.

Whatever secondary audiences are envisaged for this letter, the setting of the 'public' centre within a 'private' frame ensures that the the primary audience and target is presented as being Bernard. At the end of this frame, Peter will claim, 'I have sent a gem of salt to a gem-like friend, the corporeal use of which I once heard to be useful to you, and the spiritual meaning of which I have thought to be necessary beyond writings.'[113] The 'gift' to which this refers may have a double application, with a significance which oscillates between the literal and the figurative. At one level, it seems likely that, as Leclercq suggests, it refers to a sal-gem, acquired during Peter's recent visit to Spain, and designed to improve Bernard's 'health'.[114] The notion of a symbolic gift occurs also in relation to Peter of Lyons, where it comprises a gold ring set with a 'precious and unknown stone',

---

[109] *Cerno aliquos tam de nostris ovilibus quam de vestris adversum se invicem iurata bella suscepisse* ..., 'I see that some both from your sheepfolds and from ours have undertaken sworn wars against each other ...' (letter 111, p. 277).

[110] *Iam si hanc caritatem ... vis frater Cluniacensis, frater Cisterciensis, integram conservare, si per ipsam maximos tibi thesauros in caelo recondere, si reconditos conservare* ..., 'If you wish now, Cluniac brother, Cistercian brother, to keep this charity ... intact, through it to lay up for yourself the greatest treasures in heaven, to keep them once laid up ... ' (ibid., p. 293).

[111] *Bona est oratio cum ieiunio et eleemosyna magis quam thesauros auri condere* (Tb 12. 8).

[112] *Nolite thesaurizare vobis thesauros in terra ubi aerugo et tinea demolitur ubi fures effodiunt et furantur Thesaurizate autem vobis thesauros in caelo*, 'Do not store up for yourselves treasures on earth where rust and worm destroy them, where thieves dig them out and steal them. But store up for yourselves treasures in heaven.. ' (Mt 6. 19–20). Cf. Mt 19. 21; Mc 10. 21.

[113] *Misi gemmeo amico salis gemmam, cuius corporalem usum vobis utilem olim audivi, et cuius spiritualem intellectum supra scriptis necessarium esse putavi* (letter 111, p. 294).

[114] Leclercq, *Pierre le Vénérable*, p. 74. This interpretation is supported by a reference found in Peter's *Contra Petrobrusianos* to a quasi-miraculous rock-salt mountain seen by him in Eastern Spain (*Contra Petrobrusianos hereticos*, 184, ed. J. Fearns, *CCCM*, 10, Turnhout, 1968, pp. 109–10). I am endebted to Professor Winterbottom for drawing my attention to mention of a salt-mine in Spain by Aulus Gellius, citing Cato (Gellius, *Noctes Atticae*, 2. 22. 29, ed. P. K. Marshall, 2 vols, Oxford, 1968, revised 1990, 1, pp. 113–14).

said to stop the flow of blood, which is also presented as a symbol of Peter's affection.[115] At the same time, the 'sal-gem' may be read figuratively as the contents of this letter, the purpose of which is reiterated to be *caritas*.[116] In Christian terms, 'salt', as spelled out here, symbolises brotherly love, without which salvation cannot be acquired.[117] In a tradition dating from classical antiquity, however, 'salt' may also connote wit and humour.[118] The resulting equation of *amicitia iocosa* with *caritas* can be seen both to reinforce the parallel between private 'friendship' and communal affection and to constitute a final response to the ironic notion of mock-debate.

The final section of letter 111, relating to Islam, raises questions of a different sort. It comprises what may be read as a justification of Peter's initiative in having organised a translation of the Koran and associated writings into Latin,[119] a summary of the life and doctrines of Mohammed, presented in terms which emphasise both his idolatrous (pagan) background and his heretical (Christian) inheritance,[120] and an 'invitation' to Bernard to undertake a written refutation of

---

[115] *Ad haec cum praesentibus litteris mitto anulum aureum in signum amoris, pretiosi et ignoti generis lapidem continentem, atque in se aliquid quod sit pretiosius ipso habentem. Nam omnem sanguinis fluxum exsiccare dicitur*, 'To this end with the present letter I am sending a golden ring as a sign of love, containing a stone of a precious and unknown kind, and having in itself something more precious than itself. For it is said to dry up all flow of blood' (Peter, letter 54, *Letters*, I, p. 175). The sal-gem can also be compared with the gift by John of Salisbury to Peter of Celle of a silver salt-cellar, the symbolic significance of which is spelled out in detail (John of Salisbury, ep. 34, Brooke, I, pp. 60–61).

[116] *Haec (caritas) mihi tota et sola causa scribendi fuit..*, 'This (charity) has been my total and sole reason for writing to you ...' (letter 111, p. 276); *Causa mihi scribendi ut superius professus sum, teste conscientia, sola vere caritas fuit ...*, 'My sole cause for writing to you, as I professed above, has been, as (my) conscience bears witness, truly charity ...' (ibid., p. 293).

[117] *Nam quamlibet multos et pretiosos apparatus virtutum suarum aeterni regis mensae, sui sine fraterni amoris sale intulerint, ut insulsi reiicientur, si hoc sale eos condierint, epulae iam placentes cum offerentibus admittentur*, 'For however many and precious the preparations of their virtues they bring to the table of the eternal King, without the salt of their brotherly love they will be rejected as tasteless; if they season them with this salt, the banquets, now pleasing, will be admitted with their offerants' (ibid., p. 294 = Iob 6. 6; Mc 9. 49).

[118] *Sale vero et facetiis Caesar ... vicit omnes ...*, 'In wit indeed and drollery Caesar ... conquered all ...' (Cicero, *De officiis*, I, 37. 133, *M. Tulli Ciceronis, scripta quae manserunt omnia*, ed. C. Atzert, Bibliotheca Scriptorum Graecorum et Romanorum Teubneriana, fasc. 48, Leipzig, 1963, reprinted 1985.) Peter of Celle similarly refers to the *sales*, 'witty (remarks)' of John of Salisbury (Peter of Celle, ep. 69, *PL*, 202, 515A).

[119] Chief amongst these is the apologetic *Risalâ* of al-Kindî, a Christian *apologia* against Islam dating from the ninth or tenth century. According to d'Alverny, this is the text promised by Peter to Bernard at the end of letter 111 (d'Alverny, 'Deux traductions', p. 95).

[120] *(Et quia) inter barbaros barbarus, inter idolatras et ipse idolatra habitabat ...*, '(And because) he lived as a barbarian among the barbarians, an idolator himself among idolators ...' (letter 111, p. 295); *Inter ista omnium paene antiquarum haeresum faeces quas diabolo imbuente sorbuerat revomens ...*, 'Vomiting up amongst this the dregs of almost all the old heresies, which he had swallowed down, imbued by the Devil ...' (ibid., p. 297). On this oscillation between paganism and heresy see J.-P. Torrell, 'La notion de prophétie et la méthode apologétique dans le *Contra Saracenos* de Pierre le Vénérable', *Studia Monastica* 17 (1975), 257–82, p. 278; idem, 'Une spiritualité de combat. Pierre le Vénérable et la lutte contre Satan', *Revue Thomiste* 84 (1984), 47–81, pp. 72–8.

Islam. In the event, this work would be written by Peter himself, in the form of the *Contra Sarracenos*.[121] Peter's motivation in initiating this translation, together with his attitude towards crusading, has generated considerable discussion.[122] The consensus of critical opinion, as Iogna-Prat points out,[123] has tended to favour the view that 'peaceful debate', based on reason and understanding, is being offered as an alternative to the violence of physical warfare.[124] More recently, however, the straightforward opposition between 'debate' and 'warfare' has been challenged, notably by Brolis, who has argued that the approaches should be seen as complementary rather than mutually exclusive,[125] by Torrell, who has diagnosed an inherent contradiction in Peter's writing between dialogue and polemic,[126] and by Iogna-Prat, who argues that Peter is utilising the model of (oppositional) 'debate' to conduct a 'war of ideas'.[127]

The notion of 'spiritual warfare', conducted against Satan and his enemies, is, as will be seen, crucial to understanding the place and function of this section in

---

[121] Peter the Venerable, *Contra sectam Sarracenorum*, ed. R. Glei, in *Petrus Venerabilis Schriften zum Islam*, Corpus Islamo-Christianum, Series Latina, 1, Altenberge, 1985, 30–225.

[122] Peter stresses that it is intended to remedy 'ignorance', while at the same time seemingly admitting that it will not, or may not, assist in conversion: *Qui (Petrus) epistolam immo libellum multis ut credo propter ignotarum rerum notitiam perutilem futurum perfecit,* 'Who (Peter of Poitiers) brought to completion a letter, or rather, a little book which, so I believe, will be useful to many, on account of its making known matters (previously) unknown' (letter 111, p. 294); *Nec ignoro equidem, quoniam scriptura ista quae perditis illis in propria lingua prodesse non potuit, in Latinam versa minus proderit. Sed proderit fortassis aliquibus Latinis, quos et de ignotis instruet* ..., 'For my part, I am aware that that writing, which could not be of advantage to those wretches in its own tongue, turned into Latin will be of less help. But perhaps it will be of advantage to some of Latin Christendom, whom it will instruct about matters which are unknown ...' (ibid., p. 295). The last statement seems to refer principally to the apologetic *Risalâ*.

[123] Iogna-Prat, *Ordonner et exclure*, p. 332. A significant exception, as he notes, is Berry, who argues that Peter was 'consistently sympathetic' to the notion of crusade (V. Berry, 'Peter the Venerable and the Crusades', in *Petrus Venerabilis, 1156–1956: studies and texts commemorating the eighth centenary of his death*, ed. G. Constable and J. Kritzeck, Studia Anselmiana 40, Rome, 1956, 141–62, pp. 141–2).

[124] This view has been dubbed by Brolis the 'eirenic hypothesis' (M.-T. Brolis, 'La Crociata di Pietro il Venerabile: guerra di arma o guerra di idee?', *Aevum* 61 (2) (1987), 327–54, p. 328.) The term can be traced back to d'Alverny, who contrasts 'l'irénisme' of Peter's writing with 'les invectives coutumières' of writers against heresy (M.-T. d'Alverny, 'Pierre le Vénérable et la légende de Mahomet', in *À Cluny, Congrès scientifique: fêtes et cérémonies liturgiques en l'honneur des saints Abbés Odon et Odilon, 9–11 juillet 1949*, Dijon, 1950, 161–70, p. 170.) Kritzeck similarly cites the claim in the *Contra Sarracenos*, *Aggredior ... vos, non ... odio sed amore*, 'I approach you ... not. in hatred but in love' (*Contra Sarracenos*, I, 24, p. 62), as proof of Peter's pacific approach (J. Kritzeck, *Peter the Venerable and Islam*, Princeton Oriental Studies 23, Princeton, New Jersey, 1964, p. 47) According to Kedar, however, the statement may rather represent a 'rhetorical formulation', possibly modelled on Islamic precedent (B. J. Kedar, *Crusade and mission. European approaches towards Muslims*, Princeton, 1984, pp. 101–2).

[125] Brolis, 'La crociata', pp. 353–4.

[126] Torrell, 'La notion de prophétie', pp. 278–9.

[127] Iogna-Prat, *Ordonner et exclure*, pp. 332–59.

letter 111. As suggested in the previous chapter, this is not as straightforward as it might appear. Letter 111 replicates material found in two other documents written by Peter, and used as prefaces for the translations, *Epistola de translatione sua*,[128] also addressed to Bernard, and *Summa totius haeresis Sarracenorum*.[129] There is some argument as to which came first. Kritzeck,[130] following d'Alverny,[131] has argued for the priority of letter 111, a view followed also by Glei.[132] Constable, on the other hand, argues that the relevant section of letter 111 was concocted out of pre-existing material.[133] As stated previously, however, the latter appears to reject the possibility that within letter 111 it represents a later insertion.[134] Although it may seem unlikely, this possibility cannot be completely ruled out. As Constable himself points out, the concluding part of the 'private' frame could easily provide the letter with an overall conclusion.[135] The statement with which the final section is introduced, 'I have also sent my new translation ...',[136] creates an impression that what follows is only loosely appended.[137] More than that, it might seem to contravene letter-writing etiquette, through the introduction of a new and seemingly unrelated subject.[138] As will be seen, however, this impression is only partly justified.

A close inspection reveals that the section has already been heralded in the body of the letter. The third sub-section of the central portion contains a passage on heresy, bridging the gap between satire and arguments from nature. This concludes with what is surely a reference to Islam, presented as the most recent in a long line of heresies which have threatened Christian unity: 'But succeeding to these, the whirlwind from Africa has striven suddenly to disturb everything, and because he (Satan) knows that faith has prevailed, he endeavours to recoup his former losses by damaging charity.'[139] The digression is introduced by a rhetorical exclamation, 'O wicked and pertinacious plan of the evil angel cast down by God ...',[140] which

---

[128] *Epistola de translatione sua*, ed. R. Glei, in *Petrus Venerabilis Schriften zum Islam*, Corpus Islamo-Christianum, Series Latina, 1, Altenberge, 1985, 22–8.

[129] *Summa totius haeresis Sarracenorum*, ed. R. Glei, in *Petrus Venerabilis Schriften zum Islam*, Corpus Islamo-Christianum, Series Latina, 1, Altenberge, 1985, 2–22. For a comparison of these documents with letter 111, see Constable, *Letters*, II, appendix F.

[130] J. Kritzeck, 'Peter the Venerable and the Toledan Collection' in *Petrus Venerabilis, 1156-1956: studies and texts commemorating the eighth centenary of his death*, ed. G. Constable and J. Kritzeck, Studia Anselmiana 40, Rome, 1956, 176–201, p. 179, n. 12; idem, *Peter the Venerable and Islam*, pp. 28–30.

[131] D'Alverny, 'Deux traductions latines', pp. 73–4.

[132] Glei, *Petrus Venerabilis Schriften*, p. XIX.

[133] Constable, *Letters* II, pp. 276–7.

[134] Constable, ibid., pp. 275–6.

[135] Ibid., pp. 277–8.

[136] *Misi et novam translationem nostram* ... (letter 111, p. 294).

[137] Constable concludes that it is an 'afterthought' (Constable, *Letters*, II, p. 278).

[138] Constable, *Letters and letter-collections*, pp. 18–20.

[139] *Sed his succedens Africus turbo, omnia subito turbare contendit, et quia fidem praevaluisse cognoscit, laesione caritatis pristina damna recompensare molitur* (letter 111, p. 286).

[140] *(Et) o pessimi angeli et a deo proiecti pravum et pertinax consilium* ... (ibid.).

forms part of a wider pattern of such exclamations.[141] The transition back is achieved through a form of *praeteritio*, 'But passing over lamentation, to bring back my pen to those matters which I had started ...',[142] paralleling the device used to introduce the final part of the 'private' frame.[143] In relation to the question of insertion, this argument can work in either direction. Rather than proving the authenticity of the final section, it might be argued that the passage was inserted subsequently in order to facilitate such a preparation. Indeed, it could be excised without difficulty. The sub-section would then pass smoothly from a citation from Proverbs, which concludes the theme of gesticulation,[144] to an apostrophe of white and black, prefacing the argument to come.[145] As it stands, however, internal disharmony is aligned with external threat.

At the same time, certain features of the final section, replicated in the *Epistola de translatione sua*, seem to acquire a particular resonance in the context of letter 111 as a whole. The 'invitation' to Bernard to undertake this refutation of Islam is couched in terms reminiscent of Augustine. Peter draws a distinction between volition and ability: '(If), therefore, with God breathing upon you, the will to labour in these matters is present to your Reverence – for, through His grace, the ability will not be able to be lacking – write back ...'[146] Augustine similarly hints that Jerome has the ability to reply but lacks the will.[147] It may seem, accordingly, that the request is being given in the form of a challenge, that Bernard break his self-imposed 'silence', and make use of his divinely given abilities in the cause of the Church. In similar vein, Peter declares, '(Even) if those in error may not be able to be converted as a result of this, a learned man and a teacher, if he has zeal for righteousness, must not neglect to take thought at least for the weak of the Church,

---

[141] *(Et) o res plena lamentis ... superbum archangelum de caelis proiectum rursum caelestia occupasse ... ,* 'O matter full of lamentation.. that the proud archangel cast down from heaven should again have occupied the heavenly (heights) ...' (ibid., p. 277); *(Et) o malitia hominum et o innocentia pecudum,* 'O the malice of men and the innocence of beasts' (ibid., p. 287); *(Et) o infelix nimiumque deflenda iactura, si.. te.. inanem in conspectu summi iudicis draco veternus effecerit,* 'O unhappy and most lamentable loss, if.. the ancient serpent makes you.. void in the sight of the high judge' (ibid., pp. 291–2).

[142] *Sed ut deploratione omissa, ad ea quae coeperam stilum reducam* ... (ibid., p. 286).

[143] *Iam tandem ad vos mi carissime, cui praesens epistola mittitur, stilus recurrat ...,* 'Now, at last, let my pen return to you, my dearest, to whom the present letter is sent ...' (ibid., p. 293).

[144] *Annuit oculis, terit pede, digito loquitur.. , 'He winks with his eyes, rubs with his foot, speaks with his finger ...'* (ibid., p. 286 = Prv 6. 13–14).

[145] *Cur ... o albe monache ...? Cur ... o niger monache ...?,* 'Why ... O white monk ...? Why ... O black monk ...?' (ibid.).

[146] *Si igitur reverentiae vestrae in his laborandi deo aspirante voluntas affuerit, nam facultas per eius (Dei) gratiam deesse non poterit, rescribite* ... (ibid., pp. 298–9). Cf. *Epistola,* 6, Glei, p. 28.

[147] *Unde agnosco, a me dominum potius deprecandum, ut tuae voluntati det facultatem mittendi, quod rescripseris, nam rescribendi iam dedit, quia, cum volueris, facillime poteris,* 'Whence I recognise that I should rather pray to the Lord that he may give to your will the ability to send what you will have written. For he has already given you the ability of replying, because when you will it, you will very easily be able to' (Augustine, ep. 67, I. 1, p. 237).

who are wont to be scandalised, or secretly moved by even slight causes.'[148] 'Zeal for righteousness' seems to recall both the earlier emphasis on the reforming zeal of the Cistercians, and the subsequent warning against 'contrary zeal'. It may seem, accordingly, that preaching against heresy is being commended as a means of exercising 'good zeal', and presented as an extension of *caritas*.[149]

The key image of this section, as also of the *Epistola*, is the presentation of the proposed refutation of Islam as *Christianum armarium*.[150] Rendered by Iogna-Prat as 'l'armoire-arsenal',[151] this expression may, in fact, encompass three shades of meaning. It is to be a 'chest', designed to hold spiritual treasure; an 'archive', for the information of future generations; an 'arsenal', containing the weapons necessary for spiritual warfare. Peter spells out its significance in terms which ally warfare with adornment, claiming that in the 'Republic of the heavenly King', some things are made 'for protection', some 'for adornment', some 'for both'.[152] The biblical allusions which follow seem to fall into the last category, suggesting that the same designation should also be applied to the envisaged work. Solomon, although a 'peacemaker', is said to have made 'arms for protection',[153] David, to have prepared 'adornment' for the Temple.[154] The first reference should probably be linked with 'golden shields',[155] the second, with ornaments made from the spoils of

---

[148] *Quod si hinc errantes converti non possint, saltem infirmis ecclesiae, qui scandalizari vel occulte moveri levibus etiam ex causis solent, consulere et providere doctus vel doctor si zelum habet iustitiae non debet negligere* (letter 111, p. 298). Cf. *Epistola*, 5, Glei, pp. 26–8.
[149] The use of *scandalizare* may also recall the request at the end of letter 28, that Bernard intervene, to remove the 'doubt' of 'those who suffer scandal' and to restore mutual *caritas* (Peter, letter 28, p. 101).
[150] *Nam ... responsionem ... condignam, sicut contra alias, ita et contra hanc heresim Christianum armarium habere deceret*, 'For ... it would be becoming to have a worthy ... refutation as a Christian armoury against this heresy also, as against the rest' (letter 111, p. 298). The use of *decere*, 'to be fitting', forshadows the concept of *decus*, 'embellishment', 'adornment', to follow. Cf. *Epistola*, 4, Glei, p. 26.
[151] Iogna-Prat, *Ordonner et exclure*, p. 337.
[152] [*quilibet causatus fuerit*] *noverit in re publica magni regis quaedam fieri ad tutelam, quaedam fieri ad decorem, quaedam etiam ad utrumque*, 'let him [any objector] know that in the Republic of the great King, some things are made for protection, some for adornment, some also for both' (letter 111, p. 298).
[153] *Nam ad tutelam facta sunt a Salomone pacifico arma, licet tempore suo minus necessaria* ..., 'For arms were made by the peacemaker Solomon for protection, although not at all necessary in their own time ...' (ibid.).
[154] *praeparati sunt a David sumptus, parata et ornamenta, templi divini constructioni et ornatui deputata. Sed nec illa eius tempore alicui usui profecerunt* ..., 'expenses were prepared beforehand by David, embellishments were also prepared, destined for the construction and adornment of the divine temple. But nor did these serve any use in his time ...' (ibid.). What follows re-inforces the notion of an 'archive': *Manserunt itaque ista aliquanto tempore otiosa, sed incumbente necessitate apparuerunt quae diu vacaverant fructuosa*, 'And so those things remained without use for some time, but when necessity pressed what had long lain idle appeared fruitful' (ibid.).
[155] *Fecit quoque rex Salomon ducenta scuta de auro puro sescentos auri siclos dedit in laminas scuti unius*, 'King Solomon also made two hundred shields from pure gold: he gave six hundred shekels of gold for the layers of one shield' (II Rg 10. 16).

war.[156] These allusions may serve to set up a correspondence between (external) warfare and (internal) peace, a significance of crucial importance to letter 111.

Both warfare and adornment will be invoked in the invitation to Bernard: '..it is your part and the part of all learned men to assail, destroy, trample under foot, with all zeal, word and writing, *every knowledge which raises itself above the height of God*';[157] 'write back ... so that through your mouth filled with His praise the spirit of kindness may reply to the spirit of wickedness, and the treasures of His Church may be supplemented with the riches of your wisdom'.[158] As it appears here, the second of these may be thought to look back to the 'private' frame, where Bernard's friendship is said to be '*above* all *gold and silver*',[159] and he himself is depicted as *gemmeus amicus*, a 'gemlike friend'.[160] Cumulatively, these verbal echoes may seem to work to undermine the apparent division in subject-matter within the letter as a whole. The call to spiritual warfare in the final section can thus be seen as forming a counterpart to the plea for monastic peace contained in the rest of the letter, with legitimate warfare against an external enemy being set against *nefandum duellum*, the internecine warfare of monks.

This opposition may be underlined by the proposed exchange of respective treatises, absent from the *Epistola*, with which letter 111 ends.[161] Interpreted by

---

[156] *Ipse Selemith et fratres eius super thesauros sanctorum quae sanctificavit David rex et principes ... de bellis et manubiis proeliorum quae consecraverant ad instaurationem et supellectilem templi Domini*, 'Shelomoth himself and his brothers were over the treasures of the sacred things sanctified by King David and the chiefs ... which they had consecrated from the wars and the spoils of battles for the renewal and adornment of the Temple of the Lord' (I Par 26. 26–7; cf. III Rg 7. 51).

[157] *..vestrum est et omnium doctorum virorum* omnem scientiam extollentem se adversus altitudinem dei *omni studio, verbo, et scripto impugnare, destruere, conculcare* (letter 111, p. 298 = II Cor 10. 5). Cf. *Epistola*, 4, Glei, p. 26. As noted by Constable, Peter has reversed the positions of *scientia* and *altitudo*. This may represent a hidden allusion to *caritas*. According to *I Corinthians*, *Scientia inflat caritas vero aedificat*, 'Knowledge puffs up, but charity edifies' (I Cor 8. 1).

[158] *rescribite ... ut per os vestrum ipsius laude repletum, spiritui nequitiae spiritus benignus respondeat, et thesauros ecclesiae suae gazis vestrae sapientiae suppleat* (letter 111, p. 299). Cf. *Epistola*, 6, Glei, p. 28. The wording may combine the *spiritalia nequitiae*, 'spiritual (forces) of wickedness' of Ephesians, where spiritual warfare is set against the struggle with flesh and blood (Eph 6. 12), with the 'kindly spirit of wisdom' invoked in Wisdom (Sap 1. 6).

[159] *Nam* super *omne* aurum et argentum *vestra* mihi gratia bona, *vestra caritas est pretiosa*, 'For your *grace* is *good* to me, your charity is precious to me, *above* all *gold and silver*' (letter 111, p. 275 = Prv 22. 1). This citation may also glance towards the disputed tithes, since the original begins, *Melius est nomen bonum quam divitiae multae*, 'Better is a good name than many riches' (Prv 22. 1).

[160] Letter 111, p. 294.

[161] *Mittite si placet ... epistolam illam vestram quibusdam Carnotensibus monachis ... respondentem de regulae praeceptis, et de diversis monastici ordinis usibus ...*, 'Please send ... that letter of yours to certain monks of Chartres ... replying on the precepts of the Rule, and on the differing usages of the monastic order' (ibid., p. 299); *Misissem et ego nostram eruditae dilectioni vestrae, quam contra hereticorum Provincialium quaedam capitula ... scripsi ... Mittetur autem postquam eam ex aliquo exemplari rescripsero*, 'I also would have sent to your learned Affection that one of mine, which I wrote ... against certain articles of the heretics of Provence ... It will be sent, when I have had it recopied from some copy' (ibid.).

Leclercq as a reciprocal sharing of their intellectual and theological work,[162] the proposal may, in fact, provide both an echo of Augustine's request for 'helpful criticism',[163] and a hint of the direction in which Bernard's critical intellect would be better employed. The first of these, Bernard's *De praecepto et dispensatione*,[164] dealing with the interpretation of the monastic *Rule* shows, as Goodrich points out,[165] little real movement on the question of dispensation.[166] The second, Peter's *Contra Petrobrusianos*, on the other hand, had been directed against heresy.[167] The verbal and thematic links signalled above can not be held to provide conclusive evidence that this section was originally included within letter 111, but they may seem to cast some doubt on the genuineness of the 'invitation', both here and within the *Epistola*. According to Iogna-Prat, *Contra Sarracenos* together with *Contra Petrobrusianos* and *Adversus Iudaeos* can be seen to constitute a three-fold defence of the Church, following a traditional double pattern of *dilatatio*, 'propagation', that is, struggle against external enemies, and *purgatio*, 'purification', from internal dissension.[168] At the end of the *Summa*, Peter proclaims his (reluctant) intention of writing the refutation himself, in the absence of one who would do it 'better'.[169] This statement can be interpreted as furnishing Peter with a justification for

---

[162] Leclercq, *Pierre le Vénérable*, pp. 74–5.

[163] Augustine, ep. 28, IV. 6. Peter similarly invites (constructive) 'criticism': he would have sent it *ut hanc legeretis, et si quid supplendum esset, aliquo vestro tractatu vel epistola suppleretis*, 'so that you might read it, and supply whatever supplement might be needed by a tract or letter of your own' (letter 111, p. 299).

[164] Bernard of Clairvaux, *Liber de praecepto et dispensatione*, in *Sancti Bernardi Opera*, ed. Dom J. Leclercq and H. M. Rochais, 8 vols, III, Rome, 1963, 253–94. It has been translated by Greenia (Bernard of Clairvaux, *On precept and dispensation*, trans. C. Greenia, in *The works of Bernard of Clairvaux*, Cistercian Fathers Series I, Spencer Massachusetts, 1970, 105–50).

[165] Goodrich, 'The limits of friendship', pp. 91–2.

[166] Although Bernard seems to concede in this work that monastic rules are subject to the demands of *caritas*, the admission is hedged around with *caveats* which stress their essentially immutable nature: *Quamdiu ergo caritati militant, immobiliter fixa sunt mutarique omnino, ne ab ipsis quidem praepositis, sine offensa possunt*, 'As long, therefore, as they do service to charity, they are immutably fixed and not even by those who have been placed in charge can they be at all changed without sin' (Bernard, *De praecepto et dispensatione*, II. 5, p. 257); *Tenent ergo fixam firmamque immobilitatem, etiam apud praelatos, quae ex stabilii necessario sunt, sed quatenus caritati deserviunt*, 'Therefore they hold a fixed and firm immobility, even in the case of those in charge, issuing from immovable indispensability, but so long as they zealously serve charity' (ibid.). Significantly, he later defines 'singleness of eye' as requiring both purity of intention and right action, the latter being subsequently attributed to *scientia*, 'knowledge': *Ego vero, ut interior oculus vere simplex sit, duo illi esse arbitror necessaria: caritatem in intentione et in electione veritatem*, 'I indeed consider that two things are required for the inner eye to be truly single: charity in intention and truth in choice' (ibid., XIV. 36, p. 279).

[167] Peter the Venerable, *Contra Petrobrusianos hereticos*, ed. J. Fearns, *CCCM*, 10, Turnhout, 1968.

[168] Iogna-Prat, *Ordonner et exclure*, p. 32.

[169] *Quod quia ... non est qui faciat (exspectavi enim diu, et non fuit qui aperiret os et zelo sanctae Christianitatis moveret pennam et ganniret), ego ipse ... id aggredi domino*

undertaking the work, through a form of modesty *topos* with a sting in its tail which targets Bernard's 'refusal'.[170]

There is no trace of any written reply from Bernard to letter 111. However, a brief and enigmatic letter, dating probably to the following year and found only in Bernard's letter-collection, may offer some kind of indirect response.[171]

> To the abbot of Cluny
>
> Your son, brother Galcher, has become also ours, according to that rule: *everything mine is yours, and yours mine.* Let him not be less of the household, because communal, but if (an)other grace should have any power, let him be more of the household and more welcome, as to me, because he is yours, so to you, because he is ours.

The Galcher referred to here, probably the nephew of the cellarer of Clairvaux, is generally held to have transferred from the Cluniacs to the Cistercians.[172] The letter is interpreted by Bredero as an expression of 'religious courtesy', presumably in terms of informing Peter of the change.[173] Certain features of the language, however, might suggest that it may equally be interpreted as a challenge to Peter to display the 'singleness of eye' which he had advocated in letter 111, by demonstrating his approval of the move. The citation, taken from the Gospels, represents Christ's prayer to God: 'I ask for them. Not for the world I ask, but for these (mankind), whom you have given to me because they are yours. All that is mine is yours and yours mine ...'[174] The borrowing may hint at a potential equation of Peter with God, a notion which, it was argued, was previously introduced in Bernard's ep. 147.[175] There Bernard had claimed to 'glory' that Peter held him in 'grace',[176] a claim which had subsequently been undercut by the demonstration of

---

adiuvante proposui. Semper tamen a quocumque altero melius quam a me deterius hoc fieri gratum haberem, 'Therefore because ... there is no one to do it (for I waited long, and *there was none to open his mouth and stir a wing and chirp* from zeal for holy Christendom), I have proposed to undertake it with God's help. But ever would I hold worthy of gratitude that it be done better by any other than worse by me' (*Summa*, 18, Glei, pp. 20–22). Although not noted by Glei, the section in brackets draws on Isaiah 10. 14, which develops an extended image of nestlings. Peter seems to be exploiting the ambiguity between *penna* as 'wing' and 'pen', and *gannire* as to 'chirp' or 'snarl', 'mock'.

[170] Cf. d' Alverny, 'Deux traductions', p. 76; Iogna-Prat, *Ordonner et exclure*, p. 342; Glei, *Summa*, p. 249, n. 85.

[171] Bernard, ep. 267, *SBO*, VIII, p. 176. Leclercq dates this to 'around 1145' (Leclercq, ibid.).

[172] One 'Galcher, nephew of (our) Galcher' is similarly commended to Peter in Bernard's ep. 521, dated to 1150 (*SBO*, VIII, p. 484). See Constable, *Letters*, II, pp. 200–201.

[173] Bredero, 'Saint Bernard in his relations', p. 333. Monastic transfer had been an issue since the removal of Robert from Clairvaux to Cluny. It had appeared as one of the Cistercian charges in letter 28, where such monks had been characterised as 'trangressors and prevaricators of their profession' (letter 28, p. 54).

[174] *Ego pro eis rogo non pro mundo rogo sed pro his quos dedisti mihi quia tui sunt et mea omnia tua sunt et tua mea sunt..* (Jn 17. 9–10).

[175] See Chapter 3.

[176] *Glorior quod me habeas, non modo in memoria, sed et in gratia* (Bernard, ep. 147, 1.) 'Grace' had also played a part in ep. 228, 'justice would act for me.. if I did not prefer to meet

God as true giver of 'glory'. This may underlie the reference to *alia gratia*, '(an)other grace', that is, Bernard's. The biblical verse cited here continues with the notion of *clarificatio*, 'glorification', 'and I am glorified in them'.[177]

Clarificatio, however, also connotes the idea of 'clarification', and it was in this sense that Peter had employed its cognate, *clarificare*, in letter 111: 'But now, with (my) eye made clear ... I see, I see ...'.[178] Foreshadowing the revelation of pride and jealousy as 'true' causes for hostility, it had combined the Augustinian demand for 'enlightenment' with a Biblical condemnation of hypocrisy, 'I saw *the mote in the eye of a brother*, but I could not see the huge *beam*, and strong oak, *in* my and his *eye*.'[179] This had been followed with an echo of Jeromian irony, 'For he who is indignant will, as Jerome says, be admitting (the truth of) the word with regard to himself.'[180] The context from which the latter is drawn can be described as one of ironic *apologia*. Jerome's critics are labelled *maledici*, 'slanderers', and their anger translated into proof that they recognise themselves in his satirical portraits.[181] An allusion here to *clarificatio*, accordingly, lays itself open to a double interpretation. Bernard would seem to be hinting that the enlightenment which Peter desires can be achieved through 'sharing' brothers. At the same time, Peter's challenge may be being turned back against himself. Protest about Galcher's move to Clairvaux will only brand him as guilty of hypocrisy.

This phase of the correspondence is sometimes held to have brought the two abbots closer together.[182] Although this idea may find a reflection in the more conciliatory approach apparently adopted here by Peter towards Cistercian ideals and practices, the potential for irony found both in Bernard's ep. 228 and in the 'personal' sections of Peter's 111 may equally be interpreted in terms of jockeying for the moral 'high ground'. The evocation in both letters of Jerome and Augustine suggests that pressure is being put upon Bernard to retract the negative impression created by his *Apologia*. Whether this should be related to impending Cluniac

---

returning grace ...' (idem, ep. 228. 1). The allusion had been picked up and its direction reversed by Peter in letter 111, where Bernard's 'grace', 'friendship', had been set above earthly treasure (letter 111, p. 275).

[177]   *et clarificatus sum in eis* (Jn 17. 10).

[178]   *At nunc clarificato oculo ... video, video ...* (letter 111, p. 291).

[179]   *Cernebam* festucam in oculo fratris, *sed* trabem *permaximam, et quercum praevalidam* in *meo vel ipsius* oculo *videre non poteram* (letter 111, p. 291 = Mt 7. 3; Lc 6. 41). It is possible that Peter's treatment of this image encompasses a warning about damnation together with a reminder of 'paternal' suffering. The addition of *quercus*, 'oak', may recall the death of Absalom, hanging from an oak-tree 'between heaven and earth' (II Sm 18. 9), and the grief which it caused to his father, David (ibid., 33).

[180]   *Nam qui indignabitur de se ut ait Hieronymus, dictum fatebitur* (letter 111, p. 291 = Jerome, ep. 52, 17, *CSEL*, 54, p. 441).

[181]   *Qui mihi irasci voluerit, prius ipse de se, quod talis sit, confitetur*, 'He who wishes to be angry with me, first admits of himself that he is such' (Jerome, ibid.). The statement is preceded by the same image of 'mote' and 'beam'.

[182]   Auniord, 'L'ami de saint Bernard', p. 93; Torrell and Bouthillier, *Pierre le Vénérable et sa vision*, p. 95. Bredero, however, characterises Peter's letter as one of 'wishful thinking' (*Bernard of Clairvaux*, p. 237), and Bernard's failure to reply in terms of absence of 'sympathy' (ibid., p. 238).

reforms, as Bredero suggests, is less certain. Letter 111 does contain what may be read as hints of movement in relation to the question of manual work, but in essence it reiterates the position relating to the dispensatory role of *caritas* laid out previously in letter 28. The *Statutes* of 1146 would target certain areas of 'excess', notably in food and clothing, but, as stated previously, there is some argument as to how far these decrees should be seen as indicating a move towards Cistercian practice. Letter 111 in no way presents Cistercianism as superior in terms of spiritual well-being. At the same time, the emphasis attached to the motif of (spiritual) 'treasure' may point towards disputes over material possessions as posing the real threat to salvation on both sides.

The final section of letter 111, whether integral or a subsequent addition, can be seen to fulfil a particular function in relation to the letter as a whole. As a unity, letter 111 presents Islam and monastic dissension as parallel threats to the harmony of the Church, the one external, the other internal. Within this context, the 'invitation' to Bernard to write against heresy allows for two possibilities, that the envisaged work against Islam is being presented as complementary to the recantatory 'palinode' vindicating Cluny, or that it is offered as an alternative direction in which to exercise his talents on behalf of the Church. Its significance, however, may, at least in retrospect, extend further. Iogna-Prat and others draw attention to the reservations expressed by Peter elsewhere with regard to the involvement of monks in armed conflict.[183] Following the fall of Edessa in late 1144, Bernard would become heavily involved in preparations for the Second Crusade, which he would preach at Vézelay and elsewhere in 1146. As it stands within the collection, without apparent response from Bernard, letter 111 seems to present a double indictment of Bernard: failure to intervene in the Cluniac–Cistercian 'debate' and failure to direct his intellectual energies against the threat of Islam. To these may be added a third indictment, the preference for involvement in the terrain of 'physical' warfare over that of 'spiritual' warfare as chosen by Peter himself.

---

[183] In reply to the proposal of Abbot Theobald of Sens to take the way to Jerusalem, Peter warns: *Videndum est, ne vanae laudis amor praecordia tangat, et militarem se ac bellicosum, contra propositum et ordinem, monachus et abbas ostentet*, 'Care must be taken, that love of vainglory does not touch the heart, and that a monk and abbot does not show himself martial and warlike, against his undertaking and order' (Peter, letter 144, *Letters*, I, p. 359). See Iogna-Prat, *Ordonner et exclure*, pp. 332–5; Brolis, 'La Crociata', pp. 349–53; P. Lamma, *Momenti di storiografia Cluniacense*, Instituto Storico Italiano per il Medio Evo: Studi Storici 42–4, Rome, 1961, pp. 139–51.

Chapter 7

Bitterness and Sweetness: Bernard, Ep. 387; Peter, Letter 149

As discussed previously, Peter's letter 111, attempting to reopen the Cluniac–Cistercian debate, remains seemingly without response from Bernard. While in terms of the subsequent letter-collection this can be seen as enhancing the moral status of Peter, and in consequence of Cluny, for having made unrequited overtures, as regards the eliciting of some kind of actual and immediate response it should, perhaps, rather be viewed as a failure. Peter will return to the attack in 1149, some five years later, with a third 'open' letter which again centres on the issue of communal *caritas*, this time presented in relation to the notion of *cohabitatio*, 'dwelling together'.[1] Whereas the two previous letters, 28 and 111, employed the device of a 'personal' frame, letter 150 is preceded by a separate letter,[2] which ostensibly addresses itself to a 'personal' communication from Bernard.[3] A closer inspection, however, suggests that in this letter Peter is already paving the way for the 'open' letter to follow. This may indicate that Peter has chosen to vary his tactics, through an apparent separation of 'private' from 'public'. Once again, however, the separation may prove to be misleading. Letter 150 will form the focus of the following chapter. This chapter will concentrate on the 'private' letters which precede it.

Peter's letter 150 forms part of a group of letters which reveals the presence of a new and potentially significant factor in the Cluniac–Cistercian debate, in the role played by Nicholas of Clairvaux. Originally a Benedictine monk at Montiéramey, Nicholas had been known to Peter in his capacity as chaplain to Bishop Hato of Troyes.[4] Shortly after the retirement of the latter into Cluny, probably in 1145 or 1146,[5] Nicholas seems to have moved to Clairvaux, where he became one of Bernard's secretaries.[6] Ep. 387, the seemingly conciliatory letter from Bernard which is presented as having triggered this phase of the correspondence, purports

---

[1]   Peter, letter 150, *Letters*, I, pp. 367–71.

[2]   Idem, letter 149, ibid., pp. 363–6.

[3]   Bernard, ep. 387, *SBO*, VIII, pp. 355–6. This appears as letter 148 in Peter's collection (*Letters*, I, pp. 362–3). It is absent, however, from Bernard's official collection.

[4]   A letter from Peter to Nicholas, dating to 1141, starts from the basis of reciprocity in friendship and presses Nicholas to ensure that Hato visits Cluny (Peter, letter 87, *Letters*, I, p. 227).

[5]   See G. Constable, 'The letter from Peter of St John to Hato of Troyes', in *Petrus Venerabilis, 1156–1956: studies and texts commemorating the eighth centenary of his death*, ed. G. Constable and J. Kritzeck, Studia Anselmiana 40, Rome, 1956, 38–52, p. 44.

[6]   Constable, *Letters*, II, p. 320 and n. 21.

to have been written in response to a 'reproach' from Nicholas.[7] Letter 149, Peter's response, confirms that the letter had been delivered by Nicholas in person, and hints that Nicholas has been entrusted by him with confidential information to be given by word of mouth.[8] Letter 150 is seemingly accompanied by a letter to Nicholas, asking him to intervene with Bernard on behalf of its contents.[9] Bernard's reply, to this or to the previous letter, is given a subscription by Nicholas himself.[10] Nicholas's background, with, as it were, a foot in both the Cluniac and Cistercian camps might seem, as Bredero suggests, to have rendered him ideally fitted for an intermediary.[11] If so, this would seem to have somewhat misfired. Some time after May 1152, Nicholas would leave Bernard's service and Clairvaux in disgrace, accused of falsely sending out letters under Bernard's name and seal.[12] In fact, as will be seen, the nature of Nicholas's 'intervention' may lay itself open to a certain degree of suspicion.

Although Peter's letter 150 was clearly sent separately from the 'private' 149, presumably delivered by Nicholas on his return, it seems likely that all the letters which form part of this group were written within a few months of each other. The year is fixed as 1149 through a reference in Bernard's reply to the election of Henry of France as bishop of Beauvais.[13] Letter 149 asks for mention of Peter

---

[7]   *Haec dico, quia Nicolaus meus ... in spiritu vehementi commotus, commovit me, asserens se vidisse epistolam nostram directam ad vos, in qua voces amaritudinis claudebantur*, 'I say this, because my Nicholas ... disturbed in vehemence of spirit has disturbed me, claiming that he saw my letter directed to you, in which were enclosed words of bitterness' (Bernard, ep. 387, p. 355).

[8]   *De electione Gratianopolitana ... quid sentiam, in ore carissimi mei, vestrique fidelis Nicholai vobis retegendum diligenter reposui*, 'I have placed my feelings concerning the election at Grenoble ... in the mouth of my dearest and your faithful Nicholas, to be revealed to you carefully' (Peter, letter 149, p. 366).

[9]   *Lege illi (domino Clarevallensi) eam (epistolam) intente et studiose, et quantum poteris exhortare, ut quod ... scripsi, ad effectum perducatur*, 'Read it (the letter) to him (the lord of Clairvaux) attentively and studiously, and exhort him to the best of your ability that what ... I have written be brought to effect' (idem, letter 151, pp. 372).

[10]   *Ego Nicolaus vester saluto vos in aeternum, et ultra, et domesticam illam familiam, quae lateri et spiritui vestro adhaeret*, 'I, your Nicholas, greet you in eternity and beyond, and that domestic household, which clings to your side and spirit' (Bernard, ep. 389 in *SBO*, VIII, p. 357). This appears in Peter's collection as letter 152 (*Letters*, I, pp. 372–3).

[11]   Bredero, 'Saint Bernard in his relations', pp. 338–41; idem, *Bernard of Clairvaux*, pp. 239–45.

[12]   *Nicolaus ille exiit a nobis; exiit autem foeda post se relinquens vestigia ... Quis possit dicere ad quam multas personas sub nomine meo, me ignorante, quae voluit scripsit?*, 'That Nicholas has gone from us; but he has gone leaving foul traces behind him ... Who could say to how many people he has written what he wanted, under my name, (but) unbeknownst to me?' (Bernard, ep. 298, *SBO*, VIII, p. 214). The fixing of May 1152 as the proposed *terminus post quem* for Nicholas's departure depends upon the dating of letter 193, the final letter in Peter's collection (Constable, *Letters*, II, appendix P, pp. 326–7). On Nicholas's subsequent career under the patronage of Count Henry I of Champagne, see J. F. Benton, 'The court of Champagne as a literary centre', *Speculum* 36 (1961), 551–91, pp. 555–7, reprinted in Benton, *Culture, power and personality*, ed. T. N. Bisson, London, 1991, 3–43, pp. 7–9.

[13]   *Salutat vos Belvacensis electus, ut vester: vester est enim*, 'The (bishop) elect of

and Cluny to be made in 'the great gathering of holy men who have come together at Cîteaux'.[14] This must refer to the annual Cistercian chapter general, which appears to have normally convened on 14 September, the feast of the the Exaltation of the Holy Cross.[15] The use of the perfect tense here may seem to suggest that the letter is expected to be delivered at Cîteaux itself. Letter 150 refers to a meeting to be held on 1 November: 'I wrote this.. in haste, so that I could send it in haste, before, on the appointed day, which, so I have heard, is to be on the Feast of All Saints, certain of the abbots of your order meet with you ...'.[16] This wording, with its anticipatory present subjunctive points to another (extraordinary) meeting, to be held at Clairvaux rather than Cîteaux, as Constable implies.[17]

The two 'private' letters which preface the 'public' statement of 150, ep. 387 from Bernard, and letter 149 from Peter, have provoked disquiet in several commentators. Torrell and Bouthillier characterise Bernard's letter as 'astonishingly warm' by comparison with his preceding letters, and diagnose the tone of Peter's reply as one of 'unease'.[18] Bredero, on the other hand, notes Bernard's use of 'grandiloquent titles', interpreted by him as a sign of embarassment, and reads mockery into Peter's reply.[19] Leclercq draws attention to the fact that the letter from Bernard was not included in his official register, concluding that it may have revealed too much about Bernard's methods of composition, and the role of his secretaries.[20] His suggestion in regard to ep. 389,

---

Beauvais greets you as yours: for he is yours' (Bernard, ep. 389, p. 357). On the date of this election, generally accepted as end of summer/autumn 1149, see Constable, *Letters*, II, pp. 195–6. Previously, Bouton had postulated an earlier date of 1148 for letter 150, on the grounds that the greeting to Henry contained in 151, the accompanying letter to Nicholas, implied that the election had not yet taken place (J. de la Croix Bouton, 'Negotia ordinis', in *Bernard de Clairvaux*, Commission d'Histoire de l'ordre de Cîteaux 3, Paris, 1953, 147-182, p. 156.) It is not clear, however, exactly when Henry left Clairvaux. Moreover, the date of 1149 seems to find support both from the placing of letter 150 within the letter-collection and from the reference in a subsequent letter from Nicholas, explicitly post-dating the election, to the 'two letters which you sent this year to the lord abbot and myself', most plausibly identified, as Constable suggests, with letters 150 and 151 (letter 153, *Letters*, I, p. 373).

[14] *rogo ... ut ... in hoc tanto sanctorum virorum qui Cistercii convenerunt conventu, mei ... memoriam faciatis ...*, 'I ask ... that ... you make mention of me.. in this great assembly of holy men who have come together at Cîteaux ...' (Peter, letter 149, p. 366).

[15] J.-B. Mahn, *L'ordre cistercien et son gouvernement des origines au milieu du XIIIᵉ siècle (1098–1265)*, Paris, 1945, 2nd ed. Paris, 1951, p. 174.

[16] *Scripsi hoc ... festinanter, ut festinantius mittere possem, antequam ad diem indictam, quae sicut audivi in festo omnium sanctorum futura est, quidam abbatum vestri ordinis tecum conveniant ...* (Peter, letter 150, p. 371). Cf. *Insta ei, quia propter brevitatem temporis instandum est, ut in hoc proximo omnium sanctorum festo, fiat quod opto ...*, 'Urge him (Bernard), since there is need of urgency because of the shortness of the time, that on this next Feast of All Saints, what I hope may be done ...' (idem, letter 151, p. 372).

[17] Constable, *Letters*, II, p. 199.

[18] Torrell and Bouthillier, *Pierre le Vénérable et sa vision*, p. 96.

[19] Bredero, 'Saint Bernard in his relations', p. 337. Subsequently, the letters are referred to as 'rather amusing' (idem, *Bernard of Clairvaux*, p. 240).

[20] Leclercq, 'Lettres de S. Bernard', p. 148.

Bernard's reply, that it may have been composed by Nicholas himself,[21] has been extended by Torrell and Bouthillier to encompass the possibility that Nicholas was also involved in the composition of this first letter.[22] As an examination of ep. 387 will show, if the latter hypothesis is correct, its ramifications with regard to the role being played by Nicholas are both intriguing and potentially disquieting. Written in a lower register and more delicately nuanced than any of Bernard's previous communications with Peter, it may emerge as less categorically positive than it might at first appear.

> To the most reverent father and dearest friend, Peter, by the grace of God abbot of Cluny, brother Bernard, called abbot of Clairvaux: greetings in the true Saviour.
>
> Would that, just as the present letter, so I were able to send you my mind! Without doubt, you would read then most clearly, what the finger of God has written in my heart concerning your love, what it has impressed on my innermost marrow. What then? Do I begin again to commend myself to you? Be it absent! My soul was glued to yours long since, and equality of affection made equal minds from unequal persons. For what would my humility have to do with your sublimity, if condescension had not bowed down grandeur? Thence it came about that my humility and your sublimity were mingled on both sides, that neither could I be humble without you, nor you be sublime without me. I say this because my Nicholas, or rather, yours also, being disturbed in vehemence of spirit, has disturbed me, claiming that he saw my letter directed to you, in which were enclosed words of bitterness. Believe one who loves, that neither has there sprung up in my heart, not has there been extorted from my mouth, anything which might provoke the ears of your Beatitude. The multitude of business is to blame, because while my secretaries do not well retain my meaning, they sharpen their style immoderately, nor am I able to see, what I have ordered to be written. Be merciful this time, because whatever may be the case concerning others, I will see your (letters) and trust only my own eyes and ears. That common son will tell you the rest more plainly and more fully face to face. You will hear him as if me, who loves you *not in word or tongue, but in deed and truth*. Greet for us that holy multitude of yours, and pray that they may pray for their servant.

Bernard's missive presents itself as an attempt to overcome and dispel feared epistolary offence.[23] The parallel with ep. 228 and letter 111, where, it was argued, an epistolary quarrel functioned as a displacement for more serious matters of dispute, would seem to suggest that more weighty matters lie concealed behind this also. At the same time, the crediting of Nicholas with having drawn attention to the lapse could perhaps be viewed as some kind of ploy. In one of his letters to Peter of Celle, John of Salisbury similarly cites his secretary as having pointed out the inappropriateness of his intended salutation, *salutem et seipsum*, '(sends) greetings and himself': 'While I was writing this, the premised address of my salutation moved my secretary to smile. Asked the cause of this, he warned me, as an absurd greeter, to speak more advisedly and to refrain from mixing the bitter and tasteless

---

[21]   Ibid., p. 149. Nicholas is said there to have excelled in imitating the style of others (ibid., p. 149 and n. 78).

[22]   Torrell and Bouthillier, *Pierre le Vénérable et sa vision*, p. 97.

[23]   The letter to which this refers would appear, as Constable suggests, to be missing (Constable, *Letters*, II, p. 197).

with the sweet ...'.[24] The 'bitter and tasteless' is subsequently identified with John himself, as self-castigation modulates into reproach, Peter of Celle being said to have preferred a 'new love' to an 'old friend'.[25] The whole forms part of a witty and erudite display relating to *amicitia iocosa*.[26] Its use here, however, can be read as a ploy of a different and more significant sort, aimed at recommending *Nicolaus meus, immo et vester*, 'my Nicholas, or rather, yours also', as a white monk who also owes allegiance to Peter and the Cluniacs, and as a bearer of accompanying oral messages.

The letter can be seen to encompass the five-parts laid down by the medieval handbooks. The *captatio* draws on two principal *topoi* associated with friendship: the image of the friend imprinted in the heart, and friendship as spiritual union. At a surface level of interpretation, these function as assurances of affection. An image imprinted by human agency can fade, as a letter written by Peter to Nicholas when he was still in the service of Hato of Troyes had made explicit: 'I grieve that the lord (Hato) of Troyes.. has in some way become invisible. For he has absented himself for so long, that when.. he represents himself again, I am much afraid that I may not recognise him without an inscription, and that because the image of the beloved rather the affection itself has been effaced from my heart ... I may blush when he presents himself.'[27] That drawn by God, the master-writer, may be presumed to be indelible.[28] At the same time, however, as will be seen, the surrounding language leaves room for ambiguities.

---

[24] *Cum haec scriberem, notario risum movit praemissa salutationis inscriptio, cuius causam inquisitus, ridiculum me salutatorem monuit loqui consultius et, ne amara vel insipida dulcibus misceam, temperare* ... (John of Salisbury, ep. 112, Brooke, I, p. 183). *Insipidus*, 'tasteless', seems to play on the idea of *sal*, 'salt', 'good sense', 'wit'.

[25] *Quod autem [tuum iudicium] nunc declino, tibi imputandum qui, faciem personae attendens, amorem novum amicitiae veteri praetulisti*, 'That I now shun [your judgement] is to be ascribed to you who, directing your attention to the appearance of the person, have preferred a new love to an old friendship' (ibid., p. 184).

[26] For a discussion of this letter, which heavily exploits classical allusion, see Mynors, in Brooke, I, pp. xlvii–l.

[27] *Dominum Trecensem episcopum ... nescio quomodo factum invisibilem doleo ... Tanto enim iam tempore se absentavit, ut cum ... se ... repraesentaverit, vereor multum ne illum sine indice non cognoscam, et deleta de corde meo non dilectione sed dilecti imagine ... cum occurrerit erubescam*, (Peter, letter 87, p. 227). Drawing on the analogy of memory as an image printed upon wax (see Coleman, *Ancient and medieval memories*, pp. 7–8; 19–20), Peter's statement here may also point towards its development into the concept of artificial memory, as found in the anonymous *Ad Herennium*, incorrectly attributed to Cicero: *Locos, quos sumpserimus, egregie commeditari oportebit, ut perpetuo nobis haerere possint: nam imagines, sicuti litterae, delentur, ubi nihil utimur; loci, tamquam cera, remanere debent*, 'It will be necessary to impress the places which we have chosen extremely well, so that they may be able to remain attached to us forever: for the images, like the letters, are destroyed when we make no use of them; the places, as if the wax, must remain' (*Ad C. Herennium de ratione dicendi*, III, 18. 31, *M. Tulli Ciceronis scripta quae manserunt omnia*, fasc. 1, ed. F. Marx, Bibliotheca Scriptorum Graecorum et Romanorum Teubneriana, Leipzig, 1964, p. 97).

[28] The image of affection imprinted in the heart by the finger of God occurs in a very similar form in a letter to the former countess Ermengarde (Bernard, ep. 116, *SBO*, VII, p. 296). Like the letter to William of St Thierry discussed in Chapter 1, this letter develops

The *narratio* serves to distance Bernard from *scriptores nostri*, 'my secretaries', on the one hand, and the ensuing *voces amaritudinis*, 'words of bitterness', on the other. The conflation of the language of orality (speaking, hearing) with the language of textuality (seeing, reading) serves to introduce two potentially significant oppositions, between words and feelings,[29] and between meaning and expression.[30] These oppositions find parallels from earlier stages of the correspondence. Bernard's previous epistolary reproach had been justified on the grounds of the openness demanded by friendship: 'I have said this, so as not to keep closed in my mind what I would not bring forth with my mouth ...'.[31] Here, the claim that there is no hidden cause of resentment seemingly lends weight to the denial that the words were ever spoken, paving the way for the disavowal of both meaning and expression. In contrast, Peter, at the end of his combative letter 28, had seemingly laid claim to the meaning, but disclaimed the words: 'I have written this ... in which, in the words of others, I have expressed my meaning also. For apart from the harshness of the words ... I have understood everything as it was brought forth.'[32]

The juxtaposition of 'sharpen' with *stilus*, 'pen', 'style', seems to recall the notion of the pen as a weapon, as deployed in the Jerome/Augustine correspondence. Jerome had claimed there: 'But if the friend who attacked me first with the sword has been driven back by the pen, let it be a mark of your humanity and justice to upbraid the accuser rather than the respondent.'[33] Taken by White to refer to Jerome's counter-attack on Rufinus,[34] it may also represent a disguised warning to Augustine. Augustine's letter demanding a recantation had previously been characterised by Jerome as *litum melle gladium*, 'a sword smeared with honey'.[35] There may be a further reminiscence of this correspondence in the

---

elaborate play around the idea of loving less or more: *Intra ergo cor tuum et inspice meum, et vel tantum mihi tribuere amoris erga te, quantum tibi erga me inesse sentis, ne si nos quidem minus, te vero amplius amare praesumpseris, eo te nobis praeferre puteris, quo et vincere nos caritate putaveris*, 'Therefore enter your heart and inspect mine, and attribute to me at least as much love towards you, as you feel there is in you towards me, in case, if you presume that I love less but you love more, you therefore be thought to place yourself above me, because you think that you outdo me in affection' (ibid.).

[29] *nec in corde meo.. nec ab ore meo* ..., 'neither in my heart ... nor from my mouth ...' (Bernard, ep. 387, p. 355).

[30] *(quia) dum (scriptores nostri) non bene retinent sensum nostrum, ultra modum acuunt stilum suum* ..., 'while (they) do not well retain my meaning, they sharpen their style immoderately' (ibid.).

[31] *hoc dixi, ne quid clausum retinerem in mente, quod ore non promerem* ... (Bernard, ep. 228. 1).

[32] *Haec ... scripsi, in quibus aliorum verbis meum quoque intellectum expressi. Nam praeter austeritatem verborum ... reliqua omnia ut edita sunt intellexi* (Peter, letter 28, p. 101). The statement will be further discussed in the next chapter.

[33] *Sin autem amicus qui me primus gladio petiit, stilo repulsus est, sit humanitatis tuae atque iustitiae accusantem reprehendere, non respondentem* (Jerome, ep. 115, *CSEL*, 55, p. 397).

[34] White, *The correspondence*, p. 143, n. 3.

[35] Jerome, ep. 105, 2, *CSEL*, 55, p. 243.

conclusion of the letter, which offers Nicholas as mediator, through the *topos* of the friend as *alter ego*: 'You will hear him as if me ...'.[36] Augustine had introduced the notion of a friend as intermediary in similar terms: 'and before (his) return, when he (Alypius) saw you there, I saw (you), but with his eyes'.[37] At the same time, the stress on the language of perception may also recall the need for spiritual perception expressed in Peter's letter 111.

In retrospect, Bernard's letter can be seen to draw a parallel and contrast between the concept of the mind as a 'living letter', written by God and therefore incorruptible, and a concrete, written letter, produced through human agency and therefore liable to corruption. The result may be to cast doubt on the value of written communication. At the same time, through the concept of the *alter ego*, it seems to offer the possibiity of some kind of oral interaction.[38] The echoes suggested above may point towards the presence of a sub-text which evokes the earlier notions of 'debate' and 'palinode'. Such an interpretation appears to find support from several partially concealed Biblical allusions. The expression *digitus Dei*, the 'finger of God',[39] as signalled by Leclercq,[40] recalls the story of Christ casting out the demon of dumbness.[41] Accused of working through Satan, Jesus ripostes: 'But if I cast out demons in the finger of God, assuredly the kingdom of God is come upon you.'[42] In letter 111, as discussed previously, Peter had presented the discord between Cluniacs and Cistercians as the work of Satan, and silence as the yoke of the oppressor. Here, the allusion may seem to hold out the promise that the demon of discord has been cast out, the silence broken. Peter's reply will apparently acknowledge the allusion, but to ambivalent effect. Unlike the dumb man in the Gospels who was rendered able to speak,[43] he will claim that Bernard's letter, which 'should have made him eloquent', has rendered him 'dumb'.[44]

While the promise of oral intercourse seemingly held out in this letter may function to cancel out the preference for 'silence' expressed in the earlier ep. 228,

---

[36] *Ipsum tamquam me audietis..* (Bernard, ep. 387, p. 356).

[37] *et ante reditum, cum te ille (Alypius) ibi videbat, ego videbam, sed oculis eius* (Augustine, ep. 28, I. 1, *CSEL*, 34/1, p. 104). It is followed there by the *topos* of 'two souls in one body'.

[38] In letter 65, Peter had seemingly challenged the validity of oral messages: *Certiora dixi, quia nescit carta impressum mutare sermonem, cum loquentium lingua addendo vel demendo iniunctam mutet saepius veritatem*, 'I have said more certain, because paper cannot change the speech impressed upon it, while the tongue of speakers too often changes the truth which has been enjoined by addition or subtraction' (Peter, letter 65, pp. 194–5). The concept of the *alter ego* might be seen to counter this.

[39] *Sine dubio tunc clarissime legeretis quid in corde meo de amore vestro digitus Dei scripserit ...*, 'Without doubt, you would then read most clearly what the finger of God has written in my heart concering your love ...' (ep. 387, p. 355).

[40] Leclercq, *SBO*, VIII, p. 355.

[41] *Et erat eiciens daemonium et illud erat mutum ...*, 'And he (Jesus) was casting out a demon and it was dumb ...' (Lc 11. 14).

[42] *Porro si in digito Dei eicio daemonia profecto praevenit in vos regnum Dei* (Lc 11. 20).

[43] *et cum eiecisset daemonium locutus est mutus ...*, 'and when he had cast out the demon, the dumb man spoke ...' (Lc 11. 14).

[44] *(Quia) litterae vestrae, quae me eloquentem facere debuerant, mutum fecerunt* (Peter, letter 149, p. 263).

another lurking biblical allusion seems to further undercut the need for any written 'proof'. The concept of the 'living letter' is modelled on II Corinthians, the source of Bernard's question, 'Do I begin again to recommend myself to you? Be it absent!'[45] Paul similarly asks: 'Do I begin again to commend myself, or do I need, as some do, letters of recommendation to you or from you?'[46] He continues, 'You are my letter, written in my heart, which is known and read by all men. Since you are manifestly a letter of Christ administered by me, and written not in ink, but in the spirit of the living God, not on tablets of stone but on the fleshly tablets of the heart.'[47] In the Pauline passage, the addressees, in that case the Church in Corinth, are presented as a living letter of commendation. By analogy, Peter should function as a living testimony of Bernard's *caritas* in the eyes of the Cluniacs. 'Proof', if any is needed, can be supplied by Nicholas, who carries, as it were, Bernard's 'heart'.

The letter from Bernard gives no overt indication of what the preceding 'words of bitterness' might have been. Peter's reply, however, appears to tackle the issue more directly, giving what purports to be a verbatim citation, 'As for the rest, the source from which your Prudence thought me to have been moved was this. On behalf of the business of a certain English abbot, which is well known to you, your letter contained: "As if, it says, judgement has been overturned, and justice has perished from the world, and there is no one to snatch *the helpless from the hand of those who are stronger than him, the needy and pauper from those who are plundering him*." '[48] According to Constable, nothing is known about this affair.[49] The language, however, might be thought to point towards some connection with the disputed election at York, said by Dimier to have once again revealed the 'latent hostility between the Cluniac and Cistercian orders'.[50] Beginning in 1140, with the death of Thurstan, the ensuing election of William FitzHerbert as archbishop of York had been challenged on the grounds of simony by the Cistercian abbots of Rievaulx and Fountains.[51] Despite Bernard's intervention,[52] the consecration had

---

[45] *Incipio me iterum apud vos commendare? Absit!* (ep. 387, p. 355). See Leclercq, *SBO*, VIII, p. 355.
[46] *Incipimus iterum nosmet ipsos commendare aut numquid egemus sicut quidam commendaticiis epistolis ad vos aut ex vobis* (II Cor, 3. 1).
[47] *Epistola nostra vos estis scripta in cordibus nostris quae scitur et legitur ab omnibus hominibus manifestati quoniam epistola estis Christi ministrata a nobis et scripta non atramento sed Spiritu Dei vivi non in tabulis lapideis sed in tabulis cordis carnalibus* (ibid., 2–3).
[48] *De reliquo unde me motum prudentia vestra putavit, hoc fuit. Pro negotio quod vobis bene notum est, cuiusdam Anglici abbatis, continebant litterae vestrae: Quasi* inquiunt *subversum sit iudicium, et de orbe perierit iustitia, et non sit qui eripiat* inopem de manu fortiorum eius, egenum et pauperem a diripientibus eum (letter 149, p. 365 = Ps 34. 10).
[49] Constable, *Letters*, II, p. 198.
[50] Dom A. Dimier, 'Outrances et roueries de saint Bernard', in *Pierre Abélard–Pierre le Vénérable. Les courants littéraires et artistiques en occident au milieu du XIIe siècle*, Colloques Internationaux du Centre National de la Recherche Scientifique 546, Paris, 1975, 655–70, p. 660.
[51] The classic account is that offered by Knowles (Dom D. Knowles, 'The case of St William of York', *Cambridge Historical Journal* 5(2) (1936), 162–77; 212–14, reprinted in Knowles, *The historian and character and other essays*, Cambridge, 1963, 76–97). See also

taken place in 1143, only to be overturned in 1147 by Eugenius III. The contested election had meanwhile brought Bernard into conflict with Henry of Blois, bishop of Winchester and influential patron of Cluny.[53] William's place was filled by the English Henry Murdach, former monk of Clairvaux, and recently appointed abbot of Fountains.[54]

Whatever the precise circumstances surrounding the citation as given by Peter, the language in which it is couched in itself points to the issue of Cluniac–Cistercian relations. The two antitheses which it employs, between weakness and strength, poverty and plunder, recalls the rich/poor propaganda attributed by Peter to the Cistercians and their supporters in the course of the dispute over tithes. More significantly, the same citation had been employed by Bernard in a letter addressed to the papal Curia in the course of the disputed election at Langres, where it had been linked with (in)justice: '*If I have found grace in* your *eyes,* snatch *the helpless from the hand of those who are stronger than him, the poor*

C. H. Talbot, 'New documents in the case of Saint William of York', *The Cambridge Historical Journal* 10(1) (1950), 1–15; D. Baker, '*Viri religiosi* and the York election dispute', *Studies in Church History* 7, ed. G. J. Cuming and D. Baker, London, 1971, 87–100; D. Baker, 'San Bernardo e l'elezione di York', *Studi su S. Bernardo di Chiaravalle, nell' ottavo centenario della canonizzazione, Convegno internazionale certosa di Firenze (6–9 Novembre 1974)*, Bibliotheca Cisterciensis 6, Rome, 1975, 115–80.

[52]   In a letter addressed to the papal Curia in 1143, Bernard had invoked the judgement of God: *Quod si contra conscientias suas coegerit eos Romana curia curvare genua ante Baal, videat Deus et iudicet; videat curia illa caelestis, in qua nulla poterit ambitione subverti iudicium,* 'Therefore, if, against their consciences, the Roman curia compels them to bow the knee before Baal, let God see and judge; let that heavenly court see, in which no judgement will be able to be subverted by any canvassing' (Bernard, ep. 236, 2, *SBO*, VIII, p. 112 = III Reg 19. 18). What follows there balances demonisation against laudation: *Et ecce audierunt filii incircumcisorum; subsannant Romanam curiam ...,* 'And lo, the sons of the uncircumcision have heard; they mock the Roman Curia ... ' (ibid.); *si non compatimini pauperibus abbatibus, quos a finibus terrae vocatio apostolica Romam traxit ...,* 'if you do not take pity on the poor abbots, whom the apostolic summons has dragged to Rome from the ends of the earth ...' (ibid.) The notion of the pen as a weapon had been invoked against William FitzHerbert in a subsequent letter to Eugenius: *Contra idolum illud Eboracense iterato stilus dirigitur, ea scilicet necessitate, quod saepenumero hoc telo impetitum a nobis, necdum confossum est,* 'The pen is directed once more against that idol of York, in the necessity that, attacked with this weapon by me again and again, he has not yet been pierced ' (Bernard, ep. 239, ibid., p. 120).

[53]   A letter to Lucius II, the short-lived predecessor of Eugenius, targets Henry in language which recalls his earlier attacks on Gerald of Angoulême, the supporter of the anti-pope Anacletus: *Ecce enim ... inimicus homo ille, praeambulus Satanae,* filius perditionis, *adversator iuris et legum, ille, ille posuit* in caelum os suum *et iudicium ab ore apostolici, dictante aequitate ... repudiavit, reprobavit ... contempsit, et erexit simulacrum illud ...,* 'For lo ... *that enemy,* the one who walks before Satan, *the son of perdition,* the adversary of justice and the laws, that man, that man has *set his mouth in heaven* and repudiated, rejected ... scorned the judgement from the apostolic mouth, dictated by justice.. and has erected that idol ...' (Bernard, ep. 520, *SBO*, VIII, pp. 481 = Mt 13. 28; Io 17. 12; Ps 72. 9).

[54]   It might be conjectured that the remark attributed to Bernard by Peter was associated with an attack on Fountains, launched after the suspension of William in 1146 (Knowles, 'The case of St William', p. 173 and n. 50). According to Baker, this furnished the pretext for his deposition (Baker, 'San Bernardo', p. 152 and n. 239).

and needy from those who are plundering him.'[55] It had been doubled there with another citation: 'while the impious man is haughty, the poor man is destroyed'.[56] Moreover, it was in this letter that Peter the Venerable, together with Peter, archbishop of Lyons, had been 'demonised' as 'powerful gods of the earth', 'glorying in their riches'.[57] The language attributed by Peter to Bernard in letter 149 would therefore appear to have associations with public detraction specifically targeting himself and, through him, the Cluniacs.

Peter's reply, accordingly, may be seen as presenting the epistolary offence from which Bernard is distancing himself as one of renewed criticism and attack. It may also serve there to cast doubt on his portrayal in ep. 387 as a 'living letter' of commendation. The overtures contained in the present letter from Bernard may seem, in themselves, to constitute a retraction. However, a closer reading reveals a potential for ambiguity which may be seen as working against its overtly positive message. The apparent levelling of distinction, introduced by the statement 'equality of affection made equal minds from unequal persons',[58] in fact paves the way for an elaborate word-play on 'humility' and 'sublimity'[59] which can be paralleled from previous letters.[60] Indeed, the ambiguity between the spiritual and the material, by which Bernard's 'humility' can be translated into a claim of spiritual superiority, and Peter's 'sublimity' into a criticism of the wealth and power of the Cluniacs, may be accentuated here by the accompanying play on 'mind' and 'person'. At the same time, the formulation of what in itself is a standard friendship

---

[55]   Si inveni gratiam in oculis *vestris, eripite* inopem de manu fortiorum eius, egenum et pauperum a diripientibus eum (Bernard, ep. 168, 2, *SBO*, VII, p. 381 = Gn 18. 3; Ps 34. 10).

[56]   *Placet tibi ... quod*, dum superbit impius, incenditur pauper, *et ille pauper, qui pro tuo servitio, cum non haberet censum quem effunderet, sanguini non pepercit?*, 'Does it please you ... that *while the impious man is haughty, the poor man is destroyed*, and that poor man who, since he did not have property to expend, did not spare his blood in your service?' (ibid. = Ps 9. 23 (2)).

[57]   *Siquidem* Dii fortes terrae vehementer elevati sunt, *Lugdunensis scilicet archiepiscopus, et Cluniacensis abbas. Hi, confidentes* in virtute sua et in multitudine divitiarum suarum *gloriantes*, adversus me appropinquaverunt et steterunt, 'Indeed, *the powerful gods of the earth have risen up*, namely the archbishop of Lyons and the abbot of Cluny. These, *trusting in their strength* and glorying *in the multitude of their riches, approached against me and stood*' (Bernard, ep. 168, 1, p. 380 = Ps 46. 10; Ps 48. 7; Ps 37. 12).

[58]   *de personis imparibus pares animos fecit parilitas caritatis* (Bernard, ep. 387, p. 355).

[59]   *Quid enim meae humilitati cum vestra sublimitate, si non inclinasset dignatio dignationem? Ex tunc factum est, ut utrimque permiscerentur, et mea humilitas, et sublimitas vestra, ut nec ego sine vobis humilis, nec vos sine me sublimis esse possetis*, 'For what would my humility have to do with your sublimity, if condescension had not bowed down grandeur? Thence it came about that my humility and your sublimity were mingled on both sides, that neither could I be humble without you, nor you be sublime without me' (ibid.). The sentiment can be paralleled from Peter, but the impact of the wording is very different: *Ita caritas tua ... me ... sibi ... vindicavit, ita virtutes tuae ... rapuerunt, ut nihil mihi de me quod tuum non esset relinquerent, nihil tibi de te non meum esse permitterent*, 'To such an extent did your affection ... claim me for itself, did your virtues ... ravish (me), that they left me nothing of myself which was not yours, that they permitted nothing of you not to be mine' (Peter, letter 65, p. 194).

[60]   Bernard, ep. 147; ep. 148. See Chapter 3.

topos,[61] 'My soul was glued to yours long since ...',[62] points, as indicated by Leclercq,[63] towards two biblical contexts, the affection of Jonathan for David,[64] and the 'love' of the Canaanite, Shechem, for Dinah, daughter of Jacob and Leah.[65]

Both of these allusions are capable of carrying a deeper, 'public', significance, which may seem to take on a particular resonance in the light of the demand for *cohabitatio* contained in Peter's letter 150 to follow. The love of Jonathan for David is evoked in the *De speculo caritatis* of Aelred of Rievaulx, where it is presented as an *exemplum* of 'rational affection', springing from the contemplation of another's virtue.[66] Hyatte draws attention in this context to its wider typological dimension, that of prefiguring the first Christian community.[67] The relevant verse in Acts links the bonding of soul and heart with community of property.[68] The connection may seem to be reinforced through the *exemplum* which Aelred appends to it, that of Jesus' love for the wealthy young man of the Gospels.[69] Told there to sell his possessions and give the money to the poor, the latter is said to go away 'grieving'.[70] Bernard's letter closes with the claim to love 'not in word or tongue, but in deed and truth'.[71] Drawn from I John, it is expressed there in the form of an exhortation, preceded by the words, 'He who has worldly substance, and sees that his brother has need, and closes off his entrails from him, how does the charity of

---

[61]   This had first been introduced by Peter into letter 65: *adhaesit anima mea tibi, nec ab amore tuo ultra divelli potuit*, 'my soul adhered to you, nor could it be torn thereafter from loving you' (letter 65, p. 194).

[62]   *Iam pridem conglutinata est anima mea animae vestrae ...* (ep. 387, p. 355).

[63]   Leclercq, *SBO*, VIII, p. 355.

[64]   *Et factum est cum complesset loqui ad Saul anima Ionathan colligata est animae David et dilexit eum Ionathan quasi animam suam*, 'It came about, when he had finished speaking to Saul, that the soul of Jonathan was bound to the soul of David, and Jonathan loved him as his own soul' (I Sm 18. 1).

[65]   *Et conglutinata est anima eius cum ea tristemque blanditiis delinivit*, 'And his soul was glued to her and he soothed her sorrow with blandishments' (Gn 34. 3).

[66]   *Hic [rationalis] affectus inter David et Ionathan sacratissimi amoris primitias consecravit, ac socialis vinculum gratiae ne paterna quoque auctoritate solvendum, foedere gratissimae caritatis innexuit*, 'This [rational] affection consecrated the first-fruits of most sacred love between David and Jonathan, and tied the bond of companionable friendship, not to be loosed even by paternal authority, by the compact of most pleasing charity' (Aelred of Rievaulx, *De speculo caritatis*, III. 33, Hoste and Talbot, p. 120).

[67]   R. Hyatte, *The arts of friendship*, p. 60.

[68]   *Multitudinis autem credentium erat cor et anima una nec quisquam eorum quae possidebant aliquid suum esse dicebant sed erant illis omnia communia*, 'The heart and soul of the multitude of believers was one, nor did any of them say anything they possessed to be his, but all things were to them in common' (Act 4. 32).

[69]   *Hunc ipse Iesus mire misericors misericorditer in se transformans affectum*, intuitus *adolescentem qui ei suas virtutes prodiderat, ut ait evangelista;* dilexit eum, 'Jesus himself, wonderfully merciful mercifully transforming this affection in himself, *gazed upon* the young man who had disclosed his virtues; as the evangelist says, *he loved him*' (Aelred, *De speculo caritatis*, III. 33, Hoste and Talbot, p. 121 = Mc 10. 21).

[70]   *Qui contristus in verbo abiit maerens*, 'He, saddened at the word, went away grieving' (Mc 10. 22).

[71]   *qui vos diligit* non verbo neque lingua, sed opere et veritate (ep. 387 = I Io 3. 18).

God remain in him?'[72] That the demand has a particular application here is suggested by Peter's reply, which will introduce the question of a disputed legacy.

More overtly negative would be an allusion to Genesis. Shechem's 'love' is preceded by lust and rape,[73] and followed by betrayal and revenge. Shechem seeks Dinah in marriage, and his people accept 'circumcision', only to be murdered in punishment for the rape. The story is rich in suggestive elements. There is an opposition between Gentiles (the 'uncircumcised') and Jews (the 'circumcised'); there is projected intermarriage and interdwelling of different 'races'; the motivating factors are shown to be desire for expansion in terms of inhabitants[74] and property.[75] The result is the destruction of one party. The manner of its introduction precludes a straightforward one-to-one application. The earlier correspondence would suggest the identification of the Cluniacs with the (Gentile) followers of Shechem, and the Cistercians with the (Jewish) sons of Jacob. The voicing, however, seems to identify Bernard with Shechem, suggesting a potential, possibly ironic, reversal of roles. From the first perspective, the adoption of 'circumcision' might be thought to glance at the Cluniac adoption of Cistercian-type reforms. From the second, the story can be read as a warning against the welcoming-in of enemies who portray themselves as friends. In the light of this allusion, the statement discussed earlier, 'neither could I be humble without you, nor you sublime without me', may appear to lay itself open to contradictory readings: that Bernard and Peter (Cistercians and Cluniacs) are interdependent, materially and/or spiritually; that such interdependence is potentially beneficial, tempering and ameliorating, or potentially harmful, adulterating and contaminating.[76] This may

---

[72]   *Qui habuerit substantiam mundi et viderit fratrem suum necesse habere et clauserit viscera sua ab eo quomodo caritas Dei manet in eo?* (I Io 3. 17). Figuratively, *viscera* can connote both 'heart' and 'property', 'means'.

[73]   *Quam cum vidisset Sychem filius Emor Evei princeps terrae illius adamavit et rapuit et dormivit cum illa vi opprimens virginem*, 'When Shechem the son of Hamor the Hivite, prince of that land, had seen her, he lusted after her and ravished and slept with her, overwhelming the virgin with force' (Gn 34. 2).

[74]   *Negotientur in terra et exerceant eam quae spatiosa et lata cultoribus indiget*, 'Let them (the sons of Jacob) do business in the land, and work it, since it is spacious and broad, and lacks cultivators' (ibid., 34. 21).

[75]   *(et) substantia eorum et pecora et cuncta quae possident nostra erunt*, '(and) their substance and their herds and everything which they (the sons of Jacob) possess will be ours' (ibid., 34. 23).

[76]   Elsewhere in Bernard's writings 'betrayal' is explicitly associated with relaxation of discipline: *Sed tamen deprehendimus interdum forte nonnullos, qui colloquantur hostibus et paciscantur foedus cum morte, hoc est, moliantur, quod in eis est, imminuere Ordinis disciplinam, intepescere fervorem, turbare pacem, laedere caritatem ... Optimum certe castrum tulisti Christo, si inimicis eius tradideris Claram Vallem*, 'But sometimes by chance we discover some of the kind to parley with the enemy and *to make a pact with death*, that is, to strive as is in them to weaken the discipline of the Order, to make the fervour lukewarm, to disturb the peace, to wound the charity ... You have robbed Christ of an outstanding fortress, if you betray Clairvaux to His enemies' (Bernard of Clairvaux, *Sermones per annum, In dedicatione ecclesiae*, 3. 3, *SBO*, 5, ed. J. Leclercq and H. Rochais, Rome, 1968, p. 381 = Is 28. 15).

suggest that an allusion to Genesis can be read as pre-emptive, a warning against hasty 'intermarriage', and/or against impurity of motives.

There is room for ironic reversal, too, in the formulation of Bernard's distancing gambit. Here again the language may draw on two Biblical sources. The letter claims that Nicholas, being himself *commotus*, 'disturbed', *commovit*, 'disturbed' Bernard *in spiritu vehementi*, 'in vehemence of spirit'. On the one hand, this may be thought to look towards Acts, with the gift of tongues bestowed at Pentecost at the coming *spiritus vehemens*, of a 'strong wind'.[77] Such an allusion would appear to look towards the breaking of 'silence' promised earlier by the reference to 'the finger of God'. At the same time, as signalled by Leclercq, it also points to a passage from the *Psalms*.[78] There, it is the (Gentile) 'kings' who are said to be *commoti*,[79] while it is God who will 'crush' the ships of Tarshish in 'vehemence of spirit'.[80] As before, the straightforward opposition between 'Jews' and 'Gentiles' breaks down, this time through the application of both expressions to Bernard and Nicholas. Beneath this, however, may lie a hint that the 'vehemence' projected onto Nicholas should be seen as representing a transference of the 'vehemence' likely to have been experienced by Peter, with its concomitant threat of 'divine' vengeance. In this context, it may be significant, as Bredero points out,[81] that elsewhere in Bernard's writings Clairvaux is presented in terms of a 'fortress', guarded by a 'heavenly watch', and thus equated with the 'earthly Jerusalem'.[82] The citation from Psalms is enclosed there by praise of Sion as divinely protected refuge and haven.[83]

---

[77]   *Et factus est repente de caelo sonus tamquam advenientis spiritus vehementis et replevit totam domum ubi erant sedentes ... et repleti sunt omnes Spiritu Sancto et coeperunt loqui aliis linguis prout Spiritus Sanctus dabat eloqui illis*, 'And there was made suddenly from heaven a sound as of the coming of a strong wind and filled the whole house where they were sitting ... and they were all filled with the Holy Spirit and began to speak in other tongues, just as the Holy Spirit gave them to speak' (Act 2. 2–4). Allusions to Pentecost will similarly occur in ep. 398, Bernard's response to Peter's letter 149.

[78]   Leclercq, *SBO*, VIII, p. 355.

[79]   *Quoniam ecce reges congregati sunt convenerunt in unum ipsi videntes sic admirati sunt conturbati sunt commoti sunt*, 'Since, lo, the kings have congregated, they have come together. Seeing, so they have wondered, they have been disordered, they have been disturbed' (Ps 47. 5–6).

[80]   *In spiritu vehementi conteres naves Tharsis* (ibid., 47. 8). The same citation is applied by Bernard to Innocent's crushing of the schismatics: *Et hoc ego dixerim, non ut apostolicum reprehendam rigorem et zelum igne Dei succensum contra schismaticos, qui* in spiritu vehementi *conterat naves Tharsis ...*, 'I have not said this in order to reprehend apostolic rigour and the zeal kindled by the fire of God against the schismatics to crush *the ships of Tarsus in vehemence of spirit ...*' (Bernard, ep. 213, *SBO*, VIII, p. 73).

[81]   Bredero, *Bernard of Clairvaux*, pp. 267–75.

[82]   *Dicas forsitan:* Cetera quidem evidentia sunt; sed quis angelicas sese vidisse excubias gloriatur? *Etsi tu forte non vides, est tamen qui videt, ipse qui mittit. Quis ille? Nimirum qui loquitur per Prophetam:* Super muros tuos, Ierusalem, constitui custodes, 'Perhaps you may say: "The rest is indeed manifest, but who boasts that he has seen an angelic watch?" Although you, perhaps, do not see, there is one who sees, He who sends. Who is that one? Without doubt, He who speaks through the Prophet: *Over your walls, Jerusalem, I have set guards*' (Bernard, *Sermones in dedicatione ecclesiae*, 4. 1, *SBO*, 5, p. 383 = Is 62. 6).

[83]   *Magnus Dominus et laudabilis nimis in civitate Dei nostri in monte sancto eius fundatur*

It is arguable that the distancing gambit as a whole, excusing Bernard on the grounds that his secretaries are left to do the writing, and that he does even not see the finished result, leaves him open to a charge of breaching epistolary etiquette. Julius Victor notes that the 'ancients' took heed to write to their 'dearest' with their own hand, or at least to 'subscribe their name'.[84] The offence may seem to be compounded by the reference to the pressure of 'business'. This might be seen as undercutting the concept of a letter as an act of friendship, or, at the least, as relegating friendship to second place. Indeed, the letter does not state that Bernard will in future compose his own letters to Peter, merely that he will undertake to 'see' and 'hear' the finished result. The concept of Nicholas as *alter ego* may help to mitigate this breach, but not altogether to cancel it out. Letter 149, Peter's reply, may be read as taking advantage of this apparent lapse.

The exegetical technique previously applied to Bernard's writing in letter 111 is here taken a step further. The first two-thirds of letter 149 are built around a detailed examination of Bernard's own words. Peter's opening claim to have found 'much' in 'little' is susceptible to irony from several directions.[85] It simultaneously reproaches Bernard for his brevity and reinstates the value of a letter, seemingly denied by him. At the same time, it may serve to signal awareness of the latent sub-text discussed above. There may be a further ramification if, as suggested earlier, Nicholas had some hand in the composition of Bernard's letter and Peter was aware of the fact. Peter will consider in turn the salutation, which will furnish the pretext for an epistolary 'rebuke', the *captatio*, which will be exploited for ironic potential, and the narration, which will be attached to the citation claimed to emanate from Bernard's previous letter. At the beginning of the letter, in seemingly playful fashion, Peter sets Bernard up as a 'grave' and 'religious' man.[86] A subsequent echo

---

exultatione universae terrae montes Sion latera aquilonis civitas regis magni Deus in domibus eius cognoscitur cum suscipiet eam, 'Great is the Lord and most worthy of praise. In the city of our God, on his holy mountain, is founded with the exultation of all the earth the mountains of Sion, the flanks of the north wind, the city of the great King. God is known in its houses when he will defend it' (Ps 47. 2–4); *Sicut audivimus sic vidimus in civitate Domini virtutum in civitate Dei nostri Deus fundavit in aeternum*, 'As we have heard so we have seen, in the city of the Lord of virtues, in the city of our God. God has founded it for eternity' (ibid., 47. 9).

[84]   *Observabant veteres carissimis sua manu scribere vel plurimum subscribere* (Julius Victor, *Ars rhetorica*, 448). Jerome had used the pretext of an 'unsigned letter' as one of his blocking tactics towards Augustine. On the significance of the autograph in general and of Nicholas of Clairvaux's use of it in particular see D. Ganz, ' "Mind in character": ancient and medieval ideas about the status of the autograph as an expression of personality', in *Of the making of books. Medieval manuscripts, their scribes and readers, essays presented to M. B. Parkes*, ed. P. R. Robinson and R. Zim, Aldershot, 1997, 280–99, p. 289.

[85]   *Tanta in illis (litteris) licet brevibus legi, ut si ad respondendum me effundere conarer, magis taciturnus quam loquax viderer*, 'I read so much in it, although brief, that if I tried to pour myself out in response, I would seem taciturn rather than loquacious' (letter 149, p. 363); *Brevis est epistola, sed multa respondendi materia*, 'The letter is brief, but there is much matter for reply' (ibid., p. 364).

[86]   *Sed gravi homini, sed religioso loquor. Agendum est ergo prout gravitas postulat, prout religio etsi non mea, tamen vestra efflagitat*, 'But I am speaking to a grave man, a religious man. Accordingly I must act as gravity demands, as religion demands – but yours rather than mine' (ibid.).

will similarly establish Bernard as a 'truthful' man.[87] As will be seen, both of these attributions of gravity and truthfulness will be employed to ironise on Bernard's 'own' words.

The structure of this exegesis can be seen to follow a form of ring-composition, which apparently sets the present letter from Bernard against the previous letter for which it is apologising. While the present letter is said to have rendered Peter 'dumb',[88] the earlier one is said to have found him not only 'dumb', but also 'deaf': 'you should know.. that I was moved by it just as the prophet says of himself ...: *But as if a deaf man, I did not hear and as if a dumb man not opening his mouth.*'[89] Echoing the use in Bernard's letter of *commotus* and *commovit*, the latter might seem to function as reassurance, that Peter's ears were 'closed' to any possible offence. This may be undercut, however, by the allusion contained in the first statement. As stated earlier, the casting-out of the 'demon' gave the dumb man back his speech. The continuing 'dumbness' of Peter might seem to indicate that the second letter has failed to work the miracle desired. In a similar vein, the sweetness said to emanate from this letter might be thought to wipe out the earlier 'words of bitterness': 'I have received ... a letter ... extending the sweetest love and honour more than is due to me'.[90] 'Sweetness' will indeed constitute a major motif in this letter. Here, however, it forms the prelude to an epistolary rebuke, as Peter will dissect, and in one case reject, the 'titles' bestowed upon him in Bernard's salutation. Jerome's image of a 'sword smeared with honey' may again come to mind, reinforced, perhaps, by the inherent ambiguity of *praetendere*, to 'extend', to 'allege'.

The epistolary rebuke is heralded in terms which seem to hark back to the 'sal-gem' of letter 111 with its dual significance of 'wit' and 'brotherly love':[91] 'Bear, I ask, with my insipidity if I say anything other than I ought. For it is a mark of true friendship not only to receive the wit of a friend, but to season or to put up with what is tasteless.'[92] In letter 111, Peter had warned that offerings to God not 'seasoned' with the salt of brotherly love would be rejected as 'tasteless'.[93] The allusion may pick up the only part of Bernard's salutation not directly cited by Peter, that is, its conclusion, *in vero salutari salutem*, 'salvation in the true Saviour'. This particular 'wish' occurs in only one other surviving letter of

---

[87] *Ego de his aliud sentire non possum, quam quod ... a tanto, a tam veraci, a tam sancto homine dictum teneo*, 'I cannot understand otherwise from this than what ... I hold said by so great, so truthful, so holy a man' (ibid., p. 365).

[88] Letter 149, p. 363.

[89] *sciatis prorsus inde me ita motum esse, sicut de se dicit propheta* ...: Ego autem tamquam surdus non audiebam, et sicut mutus non aperiens os suum (ibid., p. 365 = Ps 37. 14).

[90] *Accepi ... litteras amorem dulcissimum et honorem plus quam mihi debitum praetendentes* (letter 149, p. 364).

[91] Letter 111, p. 294. See Chapter 6.

[92] *Fer rogo insulsum, si quod secus dixero quam oporteat. Verae enim amicitiae est non solum salsa amici suscipere, sed et insulsa aut condire aut tolerare* (letter 149, p. 364).

[93] *Nam quamlibet multos et pretiosos apparatus virtutum suarum aeterni regis mensae, sui sine fraterni amoris sale intulerint, ut insulsi reiicientur* ..., 'For however many and precious the preparations of their virtues they bring to the table of the eternal king, without the salt of brotherly love they will be rejected as tasteless ...' (Peter, letter 111, p. 294).

Bernard.[94] There it is glossed by Leclercq[95] as drawing on Mary's words at the annunciation, 'and my spirit has exulted in God my saviour'.[96] The addition of *verus*, 'true', 'genuine', however, may suggest that it is also looking towards another source, perhaps the warning contained in I John, 'And we know that the Son of God has come and has given us the sense to understand the true God and to be in His true son. This is the true God and eternal life. Little sons, guard yourselves from idols.'[97] It is possible that Peter acknowledges this warning by implication through his own citation, which wishes Bernard *post deum et in deo quod est*, 'what is in the power of God and in God'.

Bernard's salutation had addressed Peter as 'most reverent father' and 'dearest friend'. Peter rejects the first appellation, but accepts the second in a form of words which seems to play on Bernard's opposition of heart and mouth: 'I do not know myself to be *most reverent*, I deny that I am *father* in respect of you, your *friend* and *dearest* I not only profess myself with my mouth, but also recognise myself in my heart.'[98] This is followed by a seeming digression, as Peter cites a lengthy passage from a letter to himself, written by Guigo, former prior of La Chartreuse,[99] rebuking Peter for calling him *pater*.[100] In fact, this digression can be seen to fulfil several functions. The epistolary relationship between Peter and Guigo becomes a prism, through which the epistolary relationship between Peter and Bernard can be viewed. This can be seen as offering an alternative to the earlier use of Augustine and Jerome, softening the rebuke and creating a greater degree of reciprocity. There, Peter had identified himself with the line of rebukers, St Paul and Augustine. Here, he presents himself as the middle term, first as the object of rebuke, then as its transmitter to Bernard. In addition, however, this epistolary rebuke may be seen as serving as a displacement for the 'real' cause of rebuke, the 'words of bitterness'. At another level, it may also pave the way for the introduction at the end of the letter of the disputed election at Grenoble, to be discussed subsequently.

---

94   Bernard, ep. 390, to Eskil, bishop of Lund, *SBO*, VIII, pp. 358–9.

95   Leclerq, ibid., p. 358.

96   *et exultavit spiritus meus in Deo salutari meo* (Lc 1. 47).

97   *Et scimus quoniam Filius Dei venit et dedit nobis sensum ut cognoscamus verum Deum et simus in vero Filio eius hic est verus Deus et vita aeterna filioli custodite vos a simulacris* (I Io 5. 20–21). In the letter to Eskil, Bernard may seem to be hinting that salvation lies not in him but in God: *Et si ego [gratiam] retribuere non potero, non est mortuus retributor meus, quia* Dominus retribuet pro me. *Dominus, inquam, in quo et pro quo tanta nos devotione complecteris, tanta stringis affectione*, 'And if I am not able to requite grace, my requitor is not dead, because *the Lord will requite grace for me*. The Lord, I say, in whom and for whom you embrace me with such great devotion, you bind me with such great affection' (Bernard, ep. 390, 1, p. 358 = Ps 137. 8).

98   *Nam* reverentissimum *me esse ignoro*, patrem *quantum ad te me esse nego*, amicum *et* carissimum *tuum me non solum ore profiteor, sed et corde agnosco* (letter 149, p. 364).

99   Guigo of Le Chatel (1083/4–1137) had been the fifth prior of La Grande Chartreuse. His letters have been edited by Greshake (*Epistulae Cartusianae, Frühe Kartäuserbriefe*, ed. G. Greshake, Fontes Christiani 10, Freiburg, 1992, pp. 104–57).

100   Both this letter of Guigo and the letter from Peter which provoked it are included in Peter's letter-collection (Peter, letter 24, *Letters*, I, pp. 44–7; Guigo, ep. 7 = letter 25, ibid., pp. 47–8).

The words of Guigo cited here may carry their own significance: '(Whence) we seek.. that you should so think about your own edification, as not to inflate our weakness with dangerous elation.'[101] The opposition of 'edification' and 'elation' recalls I Corinthians, where knowledge is said to 'inflate', but charity to 'edify'.[102] The prohibition on the title *pater*, imposed by Guigo and Peter alike, can be traced back to the Gospels, where it forms part of an attack on the scribes and the Pharisees: 'Do not allow yourselves to be called Rabbi ... and do not name for yourself a father on earth, for you have one Father who is in heaven.'[103] Read here as a rejection on Peter's part of the pharisaical role it may seem to mirror the inversion of 'Jews' and 'Gentiles' introduced into Bernard's ep. 387, whilst also cancelling out any potential equation of Peter with God. In keeping with the address of *pater*, Bernard's letter had subscribed him as *puer*, 'boy', 'servant', a ploy which may recall but invert the old/young gambit found in Jerome.[104] Later in this letter, Peter will seemingly counter this with a reminder of their co-evality: 'We began to love in Christ when still young men: shall we now, as old men, or nearly, doubt of so sacred, so lengthy, an affection?'[105]

As Peter turns his attention to the *captatio* of ep. 387, the two friendship *topoi*, the image imprinted on the heart and spiritual union, are isolated and given separate treatment.[106] The first is followed by a triplet of biblical citations, each introduced by *vere*, 'truly', and connoting a triad of mystical sweetness, 'perfumed ointment',[107] 'dew',[108] 'milk and honey'.[109] Again, Peter seems to be offering them in opposition to Bernard's preceding 'words of bitterness'. An admonition may lurk behind them, however. The first two citations comprise successive verses of the same Psalm, where they are preceded by the statement: 'See, how good and how pleasant (it is) for brothers to dwell together.'[110] Foreshadowing the demand in letter

---

[101] *(Unde) petimus ... ut ... ita de propria cogitetis aedificatione, ut infirmitatem nostram periculosa non infletis elatione* (letter 149, p. 364).

[102] *Scientia inflat caritas vero aedificat* (I Cor 8. 1). This concept will also come into play in letter 150.

[103] *Vos autem nolite vocari rabbi.. et patrem nolite vocare vobis super terram unus enim est Pater vester qui in caelis est* (Mt 23, 8–9).

[104] Jerome, ep. 102, 2; idem, ep. 105, 3.

[105] *Adhuc iuvenes amare in Christo nos coepimus, et iam senes aut fere de amore tam sacro, tam diuturno dubitabimus?* (letter 149, p. 365).

[106] Utinam *inquis* sicut praesentem epistolam, ita vobis mentem meam mittere possem ... (ibid., p. 364 = ep. 387, p. 355); Iam pridem *ais* conglutinata est anima mea animae vestrae ... (ibid., p. 365 = ep. 387, p. 355).

[107] *Vere haec verba salvo maioris mysterii sacramento*, sicut unguentum in capite, quod descendit de barba Aaron in oram vestimenti eius, 'Truly, these words, saving the sacrament of the greater mystery, are *as ointment on the head, which flows down from the beard of Aaron onto the border of his garment*' (letter 149, p. 364 = Ps 132. 2).

[108] *Vere ista* sicut ros Hermon qui descendit in montem Sion, 'Truly, they are *as the dew of Hermon which comes down onto the mountain of Sion*' (letter 149, pp. 364-365 = Ps 132. 3).

[109] *Vere etiam sic* stillant montes dulcedinem, et colles fluunt lac et mel, 'Truly, also, *so the mountains distil sweetness, and the hills flow with milk and honey*' (letter 149, p. 365 = Ioel 3. 18).

[110] *Ecce quam bonum et quam iucundum habitare fratres in unum* (Ps 132, 1).

150 for *cohabitatio*, this might also be seen as constituting a counter to the Shechem/Dinah allusion discussed earlier. The third, taken from *Joel*, denotes the sanctification of Jerusalem, where it is preceded by the words 'and Jerusalem will be holy and strangers will not pass through it further'.[111] This allusion may seem to pick up and restore to Clairvaux the idea of the 'earthly Jerusalem' discussed earlier, partly displaced in Bernard's letter through the notion of the 'Gentile kings' and the 'ships of Tarshish'. At the same time, it may anticipate the Pauline abolition of distinctions, which will be invoked in letter 150.[112]

The second *topos*, cited verbatim with its accompanying word-play on 'humility' and 'sublimity', is prefaced by a second triplet of biblical citations, which plays on Bernard's opposition between 'mouth' and 'heart'. In contradistinction to the positive formulation employed in the earlier triad, these citations work by *litotes*, *non.. nisi*, 'not.. if not', and distancing. Peter claims to know that the words were brought forth not from 'any mouth', but from the mouth of one who 'does not know how to speak except *from a pure heart and a good conscience and unfeigned love*'.[113] Bernard is said to be 'not of the number of those who *have spoken vain things to their neighbour*',[114] 'not of those, whose *guileful lips have spoken in heart and heart*'.[115] These citations pave the way for what may perhaps emerge as a form of logical dilemma, couched in a series of rhetorical questions, and redeploying Bernard's conflation of textuality and orality:

> Therefore, whenever it pleases your Sanctity to write to me, I receive, read, embrace your writings, not carelessly, not cursorily, but studiously, affectionately. For who would not read carefully, not embrace with much affection, both those words which I have set out above, and those which follow? ... Therefore, are words of this kind to be read carelessly? Must they not hold the eyes of the reader fixed, snatch the heart, unite the minds? See for yourself, my dearest, who wrote this, what you understand from this. I cannot understand otherwise, than what the letter sounds, what I hold said by so great, so truthful, so holy a man.[116]

---

[111]   *et erit Hierusalem sancta et alieni non transibunt per eam amplius* (Ioel 3. 17).

[112]   *cum iuxta apostolum* neque circumcisio valeat aliquid, neque praeputium, sed nova creatura, 'since in the words of the Apostle, *neither circumcision counts nor uncircumcision, but a new creature*' (Peter, letter 150, p. 368 = Gal 3. 28). The verse from *Joel* finds a doublet in *Isaiah* with added detail: *quia non adiciet ultra et pertranseat per te incircumcisus et immundus*, 'because there will not approach further and pass through you the uncircumcised and unclean' (Is 52. 1).

[113]   *Non enim a qualicumque ore prolata scio, sed ab illius, qui loqui non novit, nisi* de corde puro et conscientia bona et *amore* non ficto (letter 149, p. 365 = I Tim 1. 5). The context from which this citation is drawn establishes charity as the main point of the 'Law', and condemns 'false teachers'.

[114]   *Novi ... non esse te de illorum numero, qui ...* vana locuti sunt ad proximum suum (ibid. = Ps 11. 3).

[115]   *(Novi) non esse te de illis, quorum* labia dolosa in corde et corde locuti sunt (ibid. = Ps 11. 3).

[116]   *Idcirco quotienscumque placet sanctitati vestrae scribere mihi, non negligenter, non transitorie, sed studiose, affectuose scripta tua suscipio, lego, amplector. Quis enim non sollicite legeret, non multo cum affectu amplecteretur, et ea quae praemisi, et illa quae sequuntur? ... Huiusmodi ergo verba negligenter legenda sunt? Numquid non debent oculos*

If, as Peter claims, Bernard is a 'truthful' man, his words must always be believed. The words in question, however, represent the elaborate word-play on humility/sublimity discussed earlier. Peter's letter has already demonstrated their inappropiateness through his rejection of the title of *pater*. If Bernard meant what he was saying, he is seemingly guilty of dangerous flattery, which may cast doubt on his wisdom. If he did not mean what he was saying, he would forfeit his reputation for 'veracity'. Moreover, the words might then lend themselves to being viewed as sarcastic and critical. Peter seemingly offers a way of escape, through the playfulness of *amicitia iocosa*: '*Believe one who loves*, to use your words, *that neither in my heart has it sprung up, nor has it been it extorted from my mouth*, that I should ever have doubted your words in any way, provided that they were expressed seriously.'[117] In fact, however, this way has already been blocked, since Bernard was established at the start of the letter as a 'grave' man. In consequence, he would not be 'playful'. The dilemma is left unformulated and unresolved. What follows, relating to the 'words of bitterness', may seem to cast doubts on Bernard's veracity: when and how is he to be believed?

At this point, Peter's declaration of 'deafness' and 'dumbness' can be seen to take on a fresh significance. The Biblical citation through which this is expressed, '*But as if a deaf man, I did not hear and as if a dumb man, not opening his mouth*', is taken from a context which highlights enmity and betrayal.[118] It is preceded there by the verse: 'My friends and my neighbours approached against me and stood, and those who were near me stood far off, and those who were seeking my soul did violence.'[119] The first part of this had been attached to Bernard's demonisation of Peter and the archbishop of Lyons during the dispute over Langres, as mentioned earlier,[120] the second, to the failure of the papal Curia to take action over the affair.[121] Moreover, both parts had been employed to frame the *narratio* of Bernard's ep. 147, written to Peter during the papal schism, in a context which can be read as critical of Peter's failure to display his *amicitia* towards a strife-torn and beleagured Church.[122] Peter similarly follows his first citation with a second, drawn from the succeeding verse: 'And again: *I was made as a man not hearing, and not having refutations in his mouth*.'[123] It may seem that Peter is turning Bernard's own words against him, in a reminder of past detraction.

---

legentis fixos tenere, cor rapere, animos unire? Videris mi carissime, qui haec scripsisti, quid de his sentias. Ego de his aliud sentire non possum, quam quod littera sonat, quam quod a tanto, a tam veraci, a tam sancto homine dictum teneo (letter 149, p. 365).

[117] Credite amanti *ut verbis vestris utar* quia nec in corde meo ortum est, nec ab ore meo extortum est, *ut de verbis vestris quolibet modo si tamen serio expromptis aliquando dubitaverim* (ibid. = Bernard, ep. 387, p. 355).

[118] Letter 149, p. 365 = Ps 37. 14.

[119] *Amici mei et proximi mei adversum me appropinquaverunt, et steterunt, et qui iuxta me erant, de longe steterunt, et vim faciebant qui quaerebant animam meam* (Ps 37. 12).

[120] Bernard, ep. 168, 1, p. 380.

[121] Idem, ep. 168, 2, p. 381.

[122] Idem, ep.147, 1, *SBO*, VII, p. 350; ibid., 2, p. 351. See Chapter 3.

[123] *Et rursum:* Factus sum sicut homo non audiens, et non habens in ore suo redargutiones (letter 149, p. 366 = Ps 37. 15). An associated verse evokes the same motifs of vainspeaking and deception from which Peter had seemingly dissociated Bernard previously: *Et qui inquirebant mala mihi, locuti sunt vanitates, et dolos tota die meditabantur*, 'Those who

The exegesis concludes with an apparent acceptance of Bernard's assurances, presented as a response to Bernard's petition, and functioning as a display of 'magnanimity':[124] 'I am merciful, therefore, and grant pardon concerning an easy matter. It is not a grave labour with me – I speak in humility – even in grave offences, to forgive one who begs, to grant pardon to one who demands it. Therefore, if it is no labour to forgive even in grave matters, how much less is it in light or none?'[125] The word-play may conceal a deeper significance. In letter 150, Peter will draw a contrast between the things which are 'grave', 'heavy' – fasting, poverty, manual work – and the things which are 'light',[126] identified there with *caritas*.[127] A 'light' offence is, accordingly, one associated with failure in charity. In a single move Peter may seem to be hinting both that Bernard has offended against charity and that he himself is acting in accordance with it. The claim may find concrete 'proof' in what follows, a section dealing with two matters which at first seem to be only loosely appended.

The first of these concerns the legacy of one Baro, a sub-deacon of the Church of Rome, who would appear to have first bequeathed his property to Cluny, then transferred it on his deathbed to Clairvaux and Cîteaux.[128] Peter presents his compliance with these wishes as a personal act of 'favour': 'I wish you to know that.. in this the grace of the abbot of Cluny has conferred more on you than the will of Baro.'[129] He displays his familiarity with legal *auctoritates*, seemingly to suggest he is acting in conformity with 'natural justice' rather than legal requirement.[130]

---

were seeking after evils for me spoke vanities and meditated on deceit the whole day' (Ps 37. 13).

[124] *Ego quidem in istis offensus non sum. Sed etsi offensus essem, multum satisfactum est, quando dixisti*: Multitudo negotiorum in culpa est ..., 'I indeed was not offended in that. But even if I had been offended, much amends was made when you said: "The multitude of business is to blame ..." ' (letter 149, p. 366 = ep. 387, pp. 355–6). In view of the potential breach of epistolary etiquette suggested earlier, this remark may, in itself, be slightly ironic.

[125] *Parco igitur, et de facili veniam tribuo. Non est apud me, quod humiliter dico, etiam in offensis gravibus, labor gravis, ut ignoscam oranti, dem veniam postulanti. Quod si in gravibus ignoscere labor non est, quanto minor in levibus aut nullis est?* (letter 149, p. 366). Peter had concluded the epistolary quarrel in letter 111 with the words, 'But I am merciful after my fashion, I remit everything even unasked' (letter 111, p. 276).

[126] *Doleo ... et miseris quibusdam ... condolui ... quod ... quae gravia sunt faciunt, quae levia facere nolunt*, 'I grieve ... and have grieved ... for certain wretches ... that ... they do the things which are heavy, (but) refuse to do the things which are light' (Peter, letter 150, p. 367).

[127] *Servas ... gravia Christi mandata ... et non vis levia servare ut diligas*, 'You ... keep the heavy mandates of Christ ... and you refuse to keep the light, that you should love' (ibid.).

[128] See Constable, *Letters*, II, p. 198.

[129] *Volo tamen vos scire, quia.. plus vobis in his contulit gratia Cluniacensis abbatis, quam testamentum Baronis* (letter 149, p. 366). The use of *gratia* may hark back to previous uses by Bernard in ep. 147 and ep. 267.

[130] *Scio quidem, nec adeo expers sum divinarum vel humanarum legum, ut nesciam quod per posterius testamentum et legatum, et fidei commissum, causa mortis rata sunt. Sed lego tamen alibi*: Nihil tam *iuri* naturali conveniens est, quam voluntatem domini volentis rem suam in alium transferre, ratam haberi, 'I know indeed, nor am I so inexperienced in divine and human laws as not to know, that for posterity a deed of gift, both bequeathed and entrusted to good faith, is ratified by reason of death. But I also read elsewhere: *Nothing is*

Equally, he appears to insinuate that the validity of this death-bed disposition is suspect. The mention of a 'will' is qualified by the words 'which he (Baro) is said to have made when dying'.[131] Peter claims that his action was taken in accordance with what was written to him 'by certain persons who said that this had been enjoined on them by him (Baro)'.[132] In contrast to this hearsay, 'trustworthy witnesses' are said to be available to confirm that the property had previously been entrusted to Cluny as a gift.[133] The gambit can be read in several ways. At one level, it forms a riposte to the hint contained in the letter from Bernard that true *caritas* requires material support.[134] At another, it can be read a demonstration of (communal) charity, paralleling the earlier demonstration of (personal) charity. As such, it may set up a challenge. Reciprocity demands that the favour should be returned, and a reciprocal favour will be demanded in the next letter.

The second appended matter concerns a disputed election at Grenoble. Peter claims to have placed his opinion concerning this affair 'against which our Carthusians are acting' into the mouth of Nicholas.[135] The details of this election are not totally clear, but have been partially reconstructed by Bouton.[136] On the elevation of Bishop Hugh II of Grenoble to the archbishopric of Vienne in 1148,[137] a certain Noel from the Carthusian monastery of Portes was elected to succeed him. The election was broken by Eugenius III, but a delegation from Portes succeeded

---

[131] *(De testamento) ... quod ... moriens fecisse dicitur ...* (letter 149, p. 366).

so in harmony with natural justice, *as for the wishes of an owner wishing to convey his property to another, to be made ratified*' (letter 149, p. 366 = *Digesta*, XLI, I, 9. 3 in *Corpus iuris civilis*, ed. T. Mommsen and P. Krüger, 3 vols, Berlin, 1954, I, p. 691). The 'deed of gift' would appear to refer to the previous deposition of the property at Cluny, 'natural justice' to the death-bed disposition. The use of the latter may recall Peter's previous appeal to nature in letter 111 (letter 111, p. 287).

[132] *factum est quod a quibusdam personis qui sibi hoc ab eo iniunctum esse dicebant mihi scriptum est* (ibid.).

[133] *sicut testes praemissi fatentur, quicquid Cluniaci deposuerat, totum Cluniaco dederat, nisi forte eum recipere contingeret, antequam praesentem vitam finiret,* 'as the previously mentioned witnesses bear witness, whatever he had entrusted at Cluny, he had given the whole to Cluny, unless, perhaps, he should chance to take it back before he finished the present life' (ibid.) Cf. *sicut quidam ut puto testes veridici astruunt ...,* 'as certain, so I think, truthful witnesses assert ...* (ibid.); *sed quod iuxta illorum testimonium meum esse credebam vobis vestrisque concessi,* 'but I have conceded to you and yours what, according to their testimony, I believed to be mine' (ibid.).

[134] The connection seems to be pointed up, perhaps ironically, by Peter's previous declaration, *Facilius mihi possent auri mille talenta surripi, quam haec quolibet casu a corde avelli,* 'More easily could one thousands talents of gold be purloined from me, than this be torn by any occurrence from my heart' (letter 149, p. 365).

[135] *De electione Gratianopolitana, contra quam nostri Cartusienses agunt, quid sentiam, in ore ... Nicholai vobis retegendum diligenter reposui,* 'I have placed my feelings concerning the election at Grenoble against which our Cartusians are acting in the mouth of ... Nicholas, to be revealed to you carefully' (ibid., p. 366).

[136] Bouton, 'Bernard et l'ordre de Cluny', pp. 212–13.

[137] Bouton dates this to 1149 ('Bernard et l'ordre de Cluny', p. 212). Constable and Bredero, however, date it to 1148 (Constable, *Letters*, II, p. 198; Bredero, *Bernard of Clairvaux*, p. 190).

in getting this decision overturned, only to be challenged in turn by Anthelm, prior of La Grande Chartreuse. In the event, the election apparently went to the Carthusian, Othmar, whose exact dates, according to Constable, are not known, but who was followed, from at least 1151, by another Carthusian, Geoffrey.[138] At some point within this period, Bernard seems to have been approached by the prior of Portes, apparently complaining about the breaking of the election. His response survives in the form of a carefully worded letter,[139] which exculpates him from any responsibility in the decision and seems to lend support the rejected candidate, without, however, committing himself to any direct intervention.[140] Although Bernard's letter to Peter makes no mention of it, it seems likely that this was one of the oral messages carried by Nicholas, presumably with a view to sounding out Peter's attitude.[141]

---

[138]   Constable, *Letters*, II, pp. 198–9. Bouton, however, fixes the date of Othmar's accession as 1150 (Bouton, 'Bernard et l'ordre de Cluny', p. 213). According to Bligny, La Grande Chartreuse resented the intrusion of Portes into what it saw as its own area of influence (B. Bligny, 'Les Chartreux dans la société occidentale du XIIe siècle', *Cahiers d'Histoire* 20 (1975), 137–66, p. 153).

[139]   Bernard, ep. 250, *SBO*, VIII, pp. 145–7. Leclercq, following Vacandard, dates this letter to between 1147 and 1150. Two reasons for the possible rejection of Noel are hinted at here. The first is newness of conversion: *Veritus quippe ... linguas obtrectatorum, vetuit (dominus Papa) festinatam novi eremitae promotionem, ne ... lingua maliloqua dicere posset hunc esse, quem semper optaverat, eremi fructum*, 'Fearing indeed ... the tongues of detractors, he (the lord Pope) forbade the hurried promotion of a new hermit, in case ... a slanderous tongue might be able to say that this was the fruit of hermitage for which he had always hoped' (ep. 250, 2, p. 146). The second is a disreputable past: *Quid enim si iuvenis aliqua olim iuveniliter egisse memoratur? ... Consepultus est iterum Christo* per *eremi* baptismum: *ego olim sepulta vitia retractabo?*, 'What if as a young man he is remembered once to have done some things after the manner of youth? ... He has been buried again for Christ *through the baptism* of solitude: shall I re-examine faults once they have been buried?' (ibid. = Rm 6. 4).

[140]   *Nam quod ad me pertinet, mihi decretum est, ubi opportune possem, non solum non impedire, sed etiam totis viribus, et ambabus, ut dicitur, trahere manibus, ubi* de gratia, quae in eo est, *Deo fructificare valeret. Quis dabit mihi homines litteratos et sanctos, in ecclesiis Dei praeesse pastores, si non in omnibus, certe in pluribus, certe in aliquibus saltem?*, 'For, as pertains to me, it has been decreed to me, where I fittingly might, not only not to hinder, but also with all my strength, and with both hands, as it is said, to draw (him) where he might be able to bear fruit for God, from the grace which is in him. Who will grant to me that learned and holy men be in charge as bishops in the churches of God, if not in all at any rate in many, at any rate, at least, in some?' (ibid., 2 = II Tim 1. 6). As Bouton points out, this can be construed as a favourable response (Bouton, 'Bernard et l'ordre de Cluny', p. 213). At the same time, however, it seems sufficiently generalised to leave Bernard room for manoeuvre.

[141]   According to Bouton, Peter shared the opinion of Anthelm, and it was on his advice that Bernard consequently shifted his support away from the rejected candidate (Bouton, 'Bernard et l'ordre de Cluny', p. 213). In fact, a letter from Peter to Eugenius seems less clear-cut. In this letter, dated by Constable to between 1149 and 1151, Peter presents the situation among the Carthusians as one of two divided camps, with La Grande Chartreuse ranged against Portes. Peter suppresses the causes of the opposition through the device of *praeteritio: Dicunt hi, non debere electum episcopari, et causas quasdam quas non est nunc meum dicere, praetendunt*, 'These say that the elect should not be bishop, and allege certain reasons, which it is not now my place to say' (Peter, letter 158, pp. 378–79). Instead, he gives

As discussed above, ep. 387 displays a potentially ambivalent sub-text which can be seen as qualifying the apparently complimentary façade. Arguably, it both opens up the possibility for oral contact and casts doubt on the validity of written communication. Letter 149, Peter's reply, presents a similarly smooth and favourable surface, beneath which lurks the potential for irony and challenge. Into this equation must come the personage of Nicholas, whose intervention is presented as the *raison d'être* for the renewal of contact. The effect of this intervention would appear to be to place Nicholas in a good light, anxious to promote monastic harmony, and eager to demonstrate his continuing loyalty to Peter and the Cluniacs. If, as Torrell and Bouthillier suggest, Nicholas is to be seen as partly responsible for drafting this letter, even, perhaps, wholly responsible for its composition, it seems permissible to speculate on his motivation. In view of the charges of fraud subsequently brought against him by Bernard, the intervention might be viewed as a ploy to ensure Peter's gratitude and support for the future. More cynically, it could be viewed as an attempt to stir up trouble while apparently trying to dispel it. In terms of the correspondence, however, it would seem that, regardless of the intentions of Bernard or Nicholas, this epistolary overture can be seen as having offered Peter the opportunity of reopening the Cluniac–Cistercian 'debate' in the form of letter 150, the subject of the next chapter.

---

a voice to those who disapprove of Carthusian involvement in litigation: *Econverso alii: Quid inquiunt ad vos ista? Cartusiensis ordinis institutio est mala si qua noverint his ad quos spectat nota facere, non autem et litigare ...*, 'Conversely, (the) others say: "What is that to you? The custom of the Carthusian Order is to make known whatever evils it may know of to those whom it concerns, not also to go to law ..." ' (ibid., p. 379).

Chapter 8

Salvation, Damnation and *Cohabitatio*: Peter, Letter 150

As stated previously, Peter's letter 149 to Bernard, dateable by its reference to the Cistercian chapter general to some time preceding 14 September 1149, is closely followed by 150, his third 'open' letter and the focus of this chapter.[1] The reference in the latter to a meeting to be held, probably at Clairvaux, on 1 November, may suggest that this letter should be dated to October of the same year.[2] It was suggested in the previous chapter that letter 149 should be seen as standing in the same relationship to letter 150 as do the 'private' frames of letters 28 and 111. The division here, however, would seem to suggest a change in tactics, creating an apparent distinction between 'private' and 'public'. This hypothesis may seem to find confirmation in certain distinctive features of letter 150. Although addressed to Bernard, it is characterised as *capitulum*, a 'chapter',[3] and Bernard is called upon directly to present its contents to the meeting of Cistercian abbots.[4] Bernard himself, as will be seen, is addressed throughout the letter in his role of *pastor* and spiritual mentor for the Cistercians rather than as personal 'friend' of Peter. The letter itself is notably briefer and narrower in scope than its predecessors, confining itself to one 'proposition', that Cistercians should welcome Cluniacs into their monasteries on an equal footing. While 'dramatic' devices such as *apostrophe* and anticipated objections appear fleetingly,[5] there is no attempt to create and sustain the illusion of dialogue or debate.

The ambiance of urgent exhortation which takes its place, implying perhaps that the time for debate is long gone, begins in the *captatio*. This takes as its starting-point a biblical citation, in this case a moralising *sententia* taken from Job: *Breves dies hominis sunt*, 'Short are the days of man.'[6] This type of *captatio*, while not

---

[1]   Letter 150, *Letters*, I, pp. 367–71.

[2]   Constable, *Letters*, II, p. 199.

[3]   Letter 28 is similarly characterised as *opusculum*, a 'little work', 'literary work' (Peter, letter 28, p. 89). None-the-less, the fiction of a 'letter' is maintained there by the reference at the end to having transgressed 'epistolary brevity' (letter 28, p. 101). Letter 111 is specifically presented as an *epistola: Iam tandem ad vos ... cui praesens epistola mittitur, stilus recurrat ...* , 'Now at last ... let the pen return to you, to whom the present letter is sent ... ' (idem, letter 111, p. 293).

[4]   *(ut) cum illis inter cetera de hoc meo capitulo tractans, eos in hanc sententiam ... adducas ...,* '(so that) treating with them among the rest of this my chapter ... you may persuade them to this opinion ...' (letter 150, p. 371).

[5]   *quicumque talis es ...,* 'you, whoever are such ... (letter 150, p. 367); *Sed interrogas ...,* 'But you ask ... ' (ibid.).

[6]   Letter 150, p. 367 = Iob 14. 5.

uncommon in general terms,[7] stands in marked contrast to Peter's previous letters to Bernard,[8] and paves the way for a kind of patchwork of allusions which point to the coming of death and the need for swift action. The citation from Job is complemented by one from Proverbs, highlighting man's ignorance of the future,[9] and completed by an admonition from Ecclesiastes to accomplish the tasks at hand.[10] In between come two seeming echoes of Horace's *Epistles*. The statement 'Their footsteps are never backwards'[11] may recall the fable of the 'cautious fox' and the 'sick lion', comprising a warning against courting destruction through improvidence.[12] The image of 'flowing water'[13] may likewise conjur up an admonition to amendment of life.[14] Cumulatively, these allusions produce a moralising, almost sermonising, effect, with perhaps an edge of satire deriving from the Horatian overlay.[15] At the same time, the stress on haste finds a literal

---

[7]   See Constable, *Letters*, II, p. 30. Citations are used to open other letters of Peter, for example, letter 13 (*Letters*, I, p. 19); letter 14 (ibid., p. 21).

[8]   Letters 28 and 65 start with gambits drawn from friendship, 73, 111 and 149 with gambits drawn from epistolarity. Letter 29, on the other hand, dispenses with a *captatio* altogether and goes straight into narrative.

[9]   *Eapropter ... non est periculosa procrastinatio sustinenda ... quia nescit homo ut scriptura clamat* quid superventura pariat dies, 'Therefore ... dangerous procrastination is not to be endured ... because, as scripture proclaims, man does not know *what the day to follow after may bring forth*' (letter 150, p. 367 = Prv 27. 1). The citation is preceded there by the words: *Ne glorieris in crastinum ignorans* ..., 'Do not boast for tomorrow, ignorant ... ' (Prv 27. 1).

[10]   *Obtemperandum est ei et alibi dicenti:* Quodcumque potest manus tua facere, instanter operare, 'It (scripture) must be obeyed, saying also elsewhere: *Work pressingly at whatever your hand can do*' (letter 150, p. 367 = Ecl 9. 10.) The verse continues there: *quia nec opus nec ratio nec scientia erunt apud inferos quo tu properas*, 'because there will be neither work nor reason nor knowledge among the dead whither you hasten' (Ecl 9. 10).

[11]   *Vestigia eorum nulla retrorsum* (letter 150, p. 367).

[12]   *olim quod vulpes aegroto cauta leoni*
        respondit referam: quia me vestigia terrent,
        omnia te adversum spectantia, nulla retrorsum
'I would reply what once the cautious fox replied to the sick lion: "Because the footsteps terrify me, all pointing towards you, none back" ' (Horace, *Epistles*, I, 1. 73–5, ed. D. R. Shackleton Bailey, *Q. Horati Flacci opera*, Bibliotheca Scriptorum Graecorum et Romanorum Teubneriana, 3rd ed., Stuttgart, 1995, p. 253).

[13]   *Labitur miser homo more fluentis aquae* ..., 'Wretched man slips away in the manner of flowing water ...' (letter 150, p. 367).

[14]   *Incipe. qui recte vivendi prorogat horam*
        rusticus exspectat dum defluat amnis. at ille
        labitur et labetur in omne volubilis aevum
'Begin! Who puts off the hour for living rightly is a rustic waiting for the river to stop flowing: it flows and will flow, rolling for all time' (Horace, *Epistles*, I, 2. 41–3, Shackleton Bailey, p. 256).

[15]   The effect can be compared with that found in a letter to Hato of Troyes: *In tales poeta ironice invehitur dicens:* O cives, cives, quaerenda pecunia primum est, virtus post nummos. *Et alibi non iam deridens, sed quod verum est pronuntians, ait:* Vilius est argentum auro, virtutibus aurum, 'Against such the poet inveighs, saying in mockery: *O citizens, citizens, money is to be sought first, virtue after money.* And elsewhere, not now mocking but saying what is true:

counterpart at the end of the letter, as Peter claims: 'I wrote this to you, my beloved, in haste, so that I could send it in haste ...'.[16]

The warning note, pointing to the uncertainty of life and the inescapability of death, is partly redressed by a clutch of citations drawn from the New Testament, and directed towards Bernard. The keynote to these, the promise of eternal life, has already been set through the citation invoked in the salutation, wishing Bernard 'the salvation which God has promised to those who love him'.[17] As this salutation indicates, salvation and charity are inseparable. Bernard is seemingly set apart from those to whom the reminder is directed: 'I do not say this, venerable and dearest brother, to challenge you, whose manifold and holy works are known to me and to the world, as if idle to work, or to set the brand of any tardiness upon one hastening by many labours to the heavenly and eternal.'[18] None-the-less, an element of caution may be invoked here, too: 'For it is foolish to say to those running in the stadium, run. But it is not foolish to say, *so run that you may seize hold.*'[19] According to the Pauline context, 'all run, but only one wins the prize'.[20] In what follows, the nature of both 'folly' and 'wisdom' will be brought into question.

The *captatio*, accordingly, can be seen to comprise a two-pronged attack of promise and warning. The 'prize' is salvation, but eternal damnation lies in wait for those who fail the test. As in letters 28 and 111, Bernard is both distanced from and implicated in what will follow. Peter reminds him: 'You have run so far, with the Lord greatly aiding *your steps*, but you must not cease, until with a secure mind you dare to say, *I have finished the course, I have kept the faith.*'[21] This development of

---

Cheaper is silver than gold, gold than virtues' (Peter, letter 6, *Letters*, I, p. 12 = Horace, *Epistles*, I, 1. 52–3, Shackleton Bailey, p. 253). There it forms part of an attack on worldly values and on the devaluation of *amicitia*. See Knight, 'Uses and abuses of *amicitia*', pp. 42–5.

[16] *Scripsi hoc tibi mi dilectissime festinanter, ut festinantius mittere possem* ... (letter 150, p. 371). The 'endearment' preludes the request which plays on Bernard's influence within the Cistercian Order. As such, it may also offer an echo of *Hebrews: Confidimus autem de vobis dilectissimi meliora et viciniora saluti, tametsi ita loquimur,* 'But, beloved, we trust in better things from you and more allied to salvation, although we speak thus ...' (Hbr 6. 9).

[17] *salutem quam repromisit Deus diligentibus se* (letter 150, p. 367 = Iac 1. 12). The preceding part of the biblical reference links salvation to beatitude and trials: *Beatus vir qui suffert tentationem quia cum probatus fuerit accipiet coronam vitae ...,* 'Blessed is the man who undergoes testing, for when he has been proved he will receive the crown of life ...' (Iac 1. 12).

[18] *Non hoc venerande et carissime frater dico, ut te cuius multiplicia et sancta opera mihi ac mundo nota sunt, velut otiosum ad operandum provocem, vel tarditatis alicuius ad caelestia et aeterna multis sudoribus festinanti notam imponam* (letter 150, p. 367).

[19] *Stultum est enim currentibus in stadio dicere, currite. Sed non est stultum dicere,* sic currite, ut comprehendatis (ibid. = I Cor 9. 24).

[20] *Nescitis quod hi in stadio currunt omnes quidem currunt sed unus accipit brabium,* 'Do you not know that of those in the stadium, all run but only one wins the prize?' (I Cor 9. 24).

[21] *Cucurristi hactenus multum iuvante domino gressus tuos, sed non est cessandum, quousque secura mente dicere audeas,* cursum consummavi, fidem servavi (letter 150, p. 367 = Ps 16. 5; II Tim 4. 7). The latter continues with the promise: *In reliquo reposita est mihi iustitiae corona quam reddet mihi in illa die iustus iudex ...,* 'Henceforth there is laid up for me the crown of righteousness, which the righteous judge will bestow on me on that day ...' (II Tim 4. 8).

the image of the athlete of Christ may carry a 'private' message, recalling Bernard's use of a Jeromian blocking manœuvre in ep. 228. Jerome had justified his refusal to 'engage' with Augustine on the grounds that he had 'had his time' and 'run his race'.[22] In similar vein, Bernard had claimed to have a 'lawful discharge', and to be unable to 'run around' as he was wont.[23] Through Peter's adoption of the Pauline voice it may seem that Bernard is once again being challenged to intervention. At the same time, the 'private' message may be counterpointed by a 'public' one. The imagery of race and prize had also been invoked in letter 111 in the context of justifying Cluniac 'discretion', in juxtaposition to Cistercian reforming zeal: 'You also use the single eye, who moderate the mandates of the Rule and Order so that ... he who with panting course cannot seize the prize set before him, is taught at least by slow steps to attain it ...'.[24]

The message contained in the salutation, that salvation is dependent upon *caritas*, is subsequently made overt in a form of doubled *captatio* which works through reversal of expectation. Peter claims to 'suffer with ... certain wretches'.[25] Characterised in what follows as 'a spectacle ... for the world, for the angels and for men',[26] 'fools for Christ',[27] such 'wretches' should surely be destined for heaven and in consequence in no need of Peter's 'sympathy'.[28] What follows, however, sets up a double opposition, *gravis/levis*, 'heavy'/'light',[29] *durus/mollis*,

---

[22]   Jerome, ep. 102, 2.

[23]   Bernard, ep. 228, 2. The assertion had been supported by a citation from *Job*, taken from the same context as that from which the opening gambit of letter 150 is drawn: *Hic ... paucis diebus quibus nunc milito, exspecto donec veniat immutatio mea*, 'Here.. for the few *days in which I now serve, I wait until my exchange comes*' (Bernard, ibid., = Iob 14. 14).

[24]   *Simplici oculo et tu uteris, qui ita et regulae et ordinis mandata moderaris, ut ... qui anhelis cursibus propositum brabium comprehendere non valet, lento saltem pede ad illud pertingere doceatur..* (letter 111, p. 284).

[25]   *Doleo, immo ab antiquo dolui, et miseris quibusdam ... condolui ...*, 'I grieve, or rather, I have grieved of old, and have suffered with.. certain wretches ...' (letter 150, p. 367). Peter may be drawing on Hebrews, where a high priest is said to be set up *qui condolere possit his qui ignorant et errant quoniam et ipse circumdatus est infirmitate*, 'who may be able to suffer with those who are ignorant and in error, since he himself is also encompassed by infirmity ...' (Hbr 5. 2).

[26]   spectaculum facti mundo et angelis et hominibus ... (letter 150, p. 367 = I Cor 4. 9). This image is exploited by Bernard in a letter to Oger, canon of Mont-Saint-Éloi (Bernard, ep. 87, 12, *SBO*, VII, p. 231). Drumbl argues that it is used there to probe the gap between 'reality' and 'appearance' (J. Drumbl, '*Ludus iucundus, honestus, gravis, spectabilis*. Die Metapher des *Theatrum Mundi* bei Bernhard von Clairvaux', *Aevum* 72:2 (1998), 361–74).

[27]   stulti propter Christum ... (letter 150, p. 367 = I Cor 4. 10).

[28]   On the image of the 'holy fool' see D. Mollat and A. Derville, 'Folie de la Croix', in *Dictionnaire de spiritualité ascétique et mystique, doctrine et histoire*, founded M. Viller, F. Cavallera, J. de Guibert, continuation A. Rayez, C. Baumgartner, 16 vols, 5, fasc. 35–6, Paris, 1964, col. 635–50; T. Spidlík and F. Vandenbroucke, 'Fous pour le Christ', ibid., col. 752–70; G. Oury, 'Idiota', ibid., 7.2, fasc. 48–9, Paris, 1970, col. 1242–8.

[29]   *quae gravia sunt faciunt, quae levia facere nolunt*, 'they do what is grave, they refuse to do what is light' (letter 150, p. 367); *Audivimus ... mandata ipsius:* Et mandata eius gravia non sunt, 'We have heard ... his commands: *And His commands are not heavy*' (ibid. = I Io 5. 3). The latter is prefaced there by the words: *Haec enim est caritas Dei ut mandata eius custodiamus ...*, 'For this is the love of God, that we should keep his commandments ...' (I Io 5. 3).

'harsh'/'soft',[30] as physical deprivation is set against spiritual enrichment. The accusation of perversity of behaviour through the wilful rejection of 'spiritual nourishment', 'refusing to refresh yourself with the sweet milk and honey of charity, do you not dread to become reprobate?',[31] may seem to be reinforced and confirmed through perversity of language. *Mollis via*, the 'soft way', which Peter commends,[32] might be expected to lead to perdition rather than to salvation.[33] Here, however, the sin lies rather in its rejection. Peter's language seems to hint that the objects of his sympathy can be seen as doubly wretched, 'wretched' by choice in this world, 'wretched' in that they are endangering the salvation which they are pursuing through lack of *caritas*: 'What profit is there to destroy yourself with tortures, and to advance to no profit of torture through the absence of charity?'[34] The words may also put into doubt the nature of their 'folly'. 'Fools for Christ' in their own eyes, their absence of charity may mark their foolishness as human error rather than divine wisdom.

The introductory *apostrophe*, 'You keep, whoever are such ...', apparently leaves the identity of the addressee open.[35] Several features, however, may point towards the Cistercian 'zealots' as being the primary target. The passage of I Corinthians from which the opening citations are drawn pits, in seeming irony, 'we' against 'you': 'We are fools for Christ, but you are prudent in Christ. We are infirm, but you are strong ...'.[36] In letter 28, the Cistercians had been accused of being able, but unwilling, to show charity towards brethren in need.[37] In letter 111, the allusion to race and prize in the context of Cluniac dispensation had been doubled with an opposition between 'bread' and 'milk': '(you) who so moderate the commands of the Rule and the Order that he who cannot be nourished with bread is at least nourished with milk, lest he lose his life ...'.[38] Moreover, it was Bernard himself, in his *Apologia*, who had introduced the notion of 'double jeopardy', combined with

---

[30] Propter verba labiorum *eius, custodis vias duras.. et propter verba eorundem labiorum eius non vis custodire viam mollem ...?*, '*Because of the words of* His *lips, you keep the harsh ways..* and because of the words of the same lips, do you refuse to keep the soft way ...?' (letter 150, p. 368 = Ps 16. 4).

[31] *et dulci caritatis lacte vel melle te ipsum refovere nolendo, reprobus fieri non perhorrescis?* (letter 150, p. 368). The allusion may also recall the evocation of milk and honey in letter 149 (letter 149, p. 365).

[32] *non vis custodire viam mollem, per eam leniter et placide incedendo?*, 'do you refuse to keep to the soft way, going along it gently and calmly?' (letter 150, p. 368).

[33] In the Gospels, it is *lata porta*, the 'wide gate', and *spatiosa via*, the 'broad way' which lead to destruction (Mt 7. 13; cf. Lc 13. 24).

[34] *Quid prodest tormentis te ipsum absumere, et ad nullum tormentorum profectum absente caritate proficere?* (ibid.), This draws on I Corinthians: *et si tradidero corpus meum ut ardeam caritatem autem non habuero nihil mihi prodest*, 'and if I hand over my body so that I burn but do not have charity, it profits me nothing' (I Cor 13. 3).

[35] *Servas quicumque talis es ...* (letter 150, p. 367).

[36] *Nos stulti propter Christum vos autem prudentes in Christo nos infirmi vos autem fortes ...*, (I Cor 4. 10).

[37] *nonne animarum salutem atque idcirco caritatem negligitis ...?*, 'Do you not neglect the salvation of souls and therefore charity ...?' (letter 28, pp. 99–100).

[38] *(qui) ita et regulae et ordinis mandata moderaris, ut qui pane non potest lacte saltem ne vitam perdat alatur ...* (letter 111, p. 284).

a subverted allusion to the way to perdition: 'A wretched little man am I, who expend so much labour and zeal not to be, or rather not to seem *like other men*, only to receive less, or rather to be punished more heavily, than any other of men. Could there not be found for us a way to hell more tolerable, so to speak ...?'[39]

That failure in *caritas* is not confined to the Cistercians, however, may be indicated as Peter returns his attention to Bernard, who is invoked in his capacity as spiritual healer: 'You, dearest, will be able to succour this great danger of the brothers, to cure this so noxious disease of souls ...'.[40] The metaphor of 'sickness' appears in the Benedictine Rule, where the abbot's role is said to be to that of applying 'healing' to the 'diseased actions' of a 'restless or disobedient flock'.[41] In the Gospels, however, in response to the complaints of the scribes and the Pharisees, the need for healing is associated with the 'publicans and sinners'.[42] Within the correspondence, the image of failure in *caritas* as a deadly disease had first been introduced into letter 111, in language which may hint that it was being set against reform: 'why do I worry about the lassitude of my flock, when I know that it is already dead?'[43] It had been further exploited there in the context of Peter's claim, borrowed from Jerome, that indignation would constitute an admission of guilt: 'The healthy part of the body does not shrink from the hand of the healer, but that which withdraws itself trembling from the fingers of the one who is touching shows clearly that disease lurks within.'[44] In what follows, forming a kind of two-part *narratio*, Peter will first trace the root cause of the 'disease', lack of spiritual perception, then offer a 'remedy', *cohabitatio*.[45]

The first part of this is dominated by an opposition between flesh and spirit. Lack of spiritual perception is demonstrated through a brief reprise of the centaur and

---

[39]   *Miser ego homuncio, qui tanto labore et industria studeo non esse vel potius non videri* sicut ceteri hominum, *minus tamen accepturus, immo gravius puniendus, quam quilibet hominum. Siccine ergo non inveniebatur nobis via, ut ita dicam, utcumque tolerabilior ad infernum ...? (Apo,* 1. 2 = Lc 18. 11).

[40]   *Huic tanto fratrum periculo tu subvenire, huic tam noxio animarum morbo, tu carissime mederi poteris* ... (letter 150, p. 368).

[41]   *si inquieto vel inoboedienti gregi pastoris fuerit omnis diligentia attributa et morbidis earum actibus universa fuerit cura exhibita* ..., 'if, on a restless and disobedient flock, every care has been bestowed, and every healing given to their diseased actions ...' (*Benedicti Regula,* LXVIII, II. 8).

[42]   *Hoc audito Iesus ait illis (scribis et Pharisaeis) non necesse habent sani medicum sed qui male habent,* 'Hearing this, Jesus said to them (the scribes and the Pharisees): "Those who are well have no need of a doctor, but those who are ill" ' (Mc 2. 17; Lc 5. 31; Mt 9. 12).

[43]   *quid ego de languore pecudis meae sollicitor, cum eam iam mortuam esse cognoscam?* (letter 111, p. 277). *Languor* may, perhaps, be connected with *tepor,* the 'tepidity', said to have aroused Cistercian 'zeal'.

[44]   *Non refugit manum medentis pars sospes corporis, sed quae se palpantis digitis tremens subducit, pestem sine dubio intrinsecus latere ostendit* (ibid., p. 291).

[45]   *Sint omnibus omnia communia, non tantum substantia, sed et ipsa habitacula. Unientur paulatim hoc remedio corda discissa* ..., 'Let everything be common to all, not only substance, but also the very dwellings. Sundered hearts will be united little by little by this remedy ...' (letter 150, p. 371).

chimaera imagery of letter 111,[46] black and white viewing each other *quasi monstrum*, 'as if a monstrosity', *velut informe prodigium*, 'as a misshapen prodigy'.[47] To this is opposed the view taken by *oculi rationabiles*, the 'eyes of reason', *oculi spirituales*, the 'eyes of the spirit'.[48] Harking back to the role of *oculus simplex*, the 'single eye' of letter 111,[49] the language may also recall Augustine's insistence that physical perception be filtered through reason and the 'judgement of truth'.[50] Central to this section is a citation from I Corinthians: 'The man of the flesh does not perceive those things which are of the Spirit of God.'[51] The Pauline distinction there between *animalis homo*, the 'man of the flesh', and *spiritalis homo*, the 'man of the spirit',[52] is echoed in Peter's distinction between *spiritualium oculus*, the 'eye of spiritual men', and *carnalium oculus*, the 'eye of fleshly men'.[53] Linked with this is a second Pauline citation, evoking but abolishing the opposition between Jews and Gentiles: 'They (the eyes of the spirit) see, understand, recognise, that in the servants of God variation in colour, diversity of practice, division of dwellings make no difference, since in the words of the Apostle *neither circumcision counts, nor uncircumcision, but a new creature.*'[54] Peter will go on to claim that he does not ask for a change of habit or customs, for 'whites to become blacks, or blacks white'.[55] What Peter is preaching is a 'new creature', a 'spiritual man', who will transcend 'fleshly' differences. At the same time, the section as a whole may serve to recall the distinction between 'circumcision of the flesh' and 'circumcision of the heart' found in Romans.[56]

---

[46]   Letter 111, pp. 285–6.

[47]   *Aspicit albus nigrum, et miratur quasi monstrum. Intuetur niger album, et miratur velut informe prodigium*, 'White beholds black, and wonders as if at a monstrosity. Black looks upon white, and wonders as if at a misshapen prodigy' (letter 150, p. 368).

[48]   *Non illa (nova instituta) sic intuentur oculi rationabiles, non illa sic contemplantur oculi spirituales*, 'Not thus do the eyes of reason look upon these things (novel practices), not thus do the eyes of the spirit behold these things' (ibid.).

[49]   Letter 111, pp. 282–4.

[50]   Augustine, *De Trinitate*, IX. VI. 9.

[51]   *Recordaris scriptum esse:* Animalis autem homo non percipit ea quae sunt Spiritus Dei, 'You remember that it is written ...' (letter 150, p. 368 = I Cor 2. 14).

[52]   *Spiritalis autem iudicat omnia et ipse a nemine iudicatur*, 'But the man of the spirit judges everything and is himself judged by no one' (I Cor 2. 15).

[53]   *Nec ignoras alium esse spiritualium oculum, alium carnalium*, 'You are well aware that the eye of spiritual men is one, the eye of fleshly men another' (letter 150, p. 368).

[54]   [*Oculi spirituales*] *vident, intelligunt, agnoscunt, nihil in servis dei differre colorem varium, nihil usum diversum, nihil divisa habitacula, cum iuxta apostolum* neque circumcisio valeat aliquid, neque praeputium, sed nova creatura (ibid. = Gal 6. 15). This citation is doubled by a second, which itself conflates two passages: *Quia* non est Iudaeus *vel* Graecus, non est masculus neque femina, non barbarus et Scytha, non servus et liber, sed omnia et in omnibus Christus, 'Because *there is not Jew* nor *Greek, there is not male nor female, not barbarian and Scythian, not servile and free, but everything and in everything Christ*' (ibid. = Gal 3. 28; Col 3. 11).

[55]   *Non dico ut color uniatur, hoc est ut de albo niger, vel de nigro albus fiat* (letter 150, p. 368).

[56]   *Non enim qui in manifesto Iudaeus est neque quae in manifesto in carne circumcisio, sed qui in abscondito Iudaeus et circumcisio cordis in spiritu non littera*, 'For not who is openly

Again, Bernard is seemingly set apart from those who lack spiritual insight. I Corinthians attributes 'folly', to the 'man of the flesh'.[57] In what precedes, Bernard has been accredited with 'wisdom': 'Your Wisdom knows, *the number of fools is infinite*, the number of wise finite and small.'[58] In itself, this may constitute a warning. The first half of the verse of Ecclesiastes from which this citation is taken runs: 'The perverse are corrected with difficulty ...'.[59] The continuation associates the possession of 'wisdom' with labour and suffering.[60] The message is made explicit, through a reminder of Bernard's pastoral responsibilities, as he is urged to use *ars*, his 'knowledge', 'skill', in the service of saving souls.[61] At the same time, the sense of *stultus* as 'holy fool' evoked just previously may add another layering which renders the warning a doublet of the earlier reminder of 'race' and 'prize'. Those who become 'fools for Christ' are many. Those who achieve true 'wisdom' and attain it are few. As the Pauline epistles make clear, 'wisdom' is also relative. The opposition between *homo animalis* and *homo spiritalis* is set within the context of a wider opposition between the 'wisdom of God', said to be hidden,[62] and the learned words of 'human wisdom'.[63] Elsewhere, there are frequent reminders that the 'wisdom of this world is folly before God'.[64] Moreover, in the absence of *caritas*, *scientia*, 'knowledge', is said to be nothing.[65]

---

a Jew, nor circumcision which is manifest in the flesh, but who is a Jew in secret, and circumcision of the heart in the spirit not the letter' (Rm 2. 28–9).

[57] *(Ea quae sunt Spiritus Dei) stultitia est enim illi (animali homini) et non potest intellegere quia spiritaliter examinatur*, 'For it (those things which are of the Spirit of God) is foolishness to him and he cannot understand, because it is examined spiritually' (I Cor 2. 14).

[58] *Novit sapientia tua*, stultorum esse infinitum numerum, *sapientum finitum et parvum* (letter 150, p. 368 = Ecl 1. 15).

[59] *Perversi difficile corriguntur* ... (Ecl 1. 15).

[60] *Dedique cor meum ut scirem prudentiam atque doctrinam erroresque et stultitiam et agnovi quod in his quoque esset labor et afflictio spiritus eo quod in multa sapientia multa sit indignatio et qui addit scientiam addat et laborem*, 'I gave my heart that I should learn prudence and learning and errors and foolishness, and I recognised that in these things also there was labour and affliction of the spirit, because in much learning there is much cause for indignation, and he who adds knowledge adds also labour' (ibid., 17–18).

[61] *Ars inquam tibi necessaria est, si hoc opus tam laudabile, tam salutiferum, tam deo gratum implere volueris*, 'Knowledge, I say, is necessary for you, if you wish to fulfil this work, so laudable, so health-giving, so pleasing to God' (letter 150, p. 368). The 'knowledge', 'skill', in question has previously been defined as *ars* ... *artium, regimen animarum*, the 'skill ... of skills, guidance of souls' (ibid. = Gregory the Great, *Regula pastoralis* I, I. 4-5, Judic, p. 128).

[62] *Sed loquimur Dei sapientiam in mysterio quae abscondita est* ..., 'But we speak the wisdom of God which is hidden in mystery ...' (I Cor 2. 7).

[63] *Quae et loquimur non in doctis humanae sapientiae verbis sed in doctrina Spiritus* ..., 'We say this also not in the learned words of human wisdom but in the teaching of the Spirit ...' (ibid., 2. 13).

[64] *Sapientia enim huius mundi stultitia est apud Deum* (I Cor 3. 19). Cf. I Cor, 1. 20.

[65] *(et) si ... noverim mysteria omnia et omnem scientiam ... caritatem autem non habuero nihil sum*, '(and) if ... I know all mysteries and all knowledge ... but do not have charity, I am nothing' (I Cor 13. 2).

At the end of this section, providing a closure to the invocation of spiritual perception, and prefacing the offering of a remedy, Peter returns to the notion of the 'few' and the 'many': 'But, because not all are such, and those of the sort to whom it may be given to see this are rarely found, good will must be shown ... to those who are lesser, and, according to him who says: *I have become all things to all men, so as to* gain *all*, in proportion to their practice, the practice must be administered for them by way of accommodation.'[66] The language here may point back towards the earlier correspondence. *Condescendere*, to 'show good will', can also imply to 'stoop down', 'condescend'. The phrase *mos est dispensative gerendus* may also recall the meaning of *morem gerere*, rendered here as 'to humour'. *Inferiores*, 'those who are lesser', will subsequently be replaced by *infirmi*,[67] and *pusilli*, 'weak'.[68] This potential for double meaning may be thought to evoke the arrogance previously attributed to the Cistercians in regard to their 'weaker' (Cluniac) brethren.[69] Here, the primary target for irony might appear to be Bernard, previously set apart by his 'wisdom'.

In particular, the passage may look back to the whole issue of 'judaising', forcing others to conform to the strict letter of the 'Law', and its equation with the monastic *Rule*, raised, it was argued, by the Augustine/Jerome overlay in letter 28. *Dispensative*, 'by way of accommodation', is a term invoked by Jerome in relation to the disputed passage from Galatians.[70] Jerome's explanation, that Paul's rebuke of Peter was a 'pretence', concocted to placate Jews and Gentiles alike, had been dubbed by Augustine *officiosum mendacium*, a 'dutiful lie'.[71] Jerome, perhaps taking exception to this, rechristens it *honesta dispensatio*, an 'honourable accommodation'.[72] Subsequently the term *dispensative* is applied to the practice of the Jewish Law: 'From this it is apparent that he who is under the Law not by way

---

[66] *Sed quia non omnes tales sunt, et raro inveniuntur quibus hoc cernere detur, condescendum est ... inferioribus, eisque iuxta illum qui ait:* Omnibus omnia factus sum, ut omnes *lucri*facerem, *iuxta eorum morem, mos est dispensative gerendus* (letter 150, p. 368 = I Cor 9. 22).

[67] *Obstruatur igitur tali caritatis obice* os loquentium *talia, ne dicam* iniqua, *consulatur infirmis, quorum se* medicum *Christus dixit,* 'Therefore let the *mouth of those speaking* such words, not to say *iniquities*, be obstructed with such a barrier of charity, let care be taken for the weak, whose *doctor* Christ proclaimed himself' (letter 150, p. 369 = Ps 62. 12; Mt 9. 12).

[68] *Caveatur pusillorum scandalum ...*, 'Let a stumbling-block for the weak be avoided ...' (ibid. = Mt 18. 6; Mc 9. 41).

[69] *At vos sancti, vos singulares, vos in universo orbe vere monachi, aliis omnibus falsis et perditis ...*, 'But you holy, you singular, you alone truly monks in the whole world, with all others false and corrupt ...' (letter 28, p. 57); *Felices nos, inquis.. quod beatiores aliis monachis mundus praedicat ....*,' "Blessed are we," you say, "that the world peaches us more blessed than other monks ..." ' (letter 111, p. 291).

[70] Gal 2. 11–14.

[71] Augustine, ep. 28, III. 4, *CSEL*, 34/1, p. 110; idem, ep. 40, III. 3, *CSEL*, 34/2, p. 71.

[72] *Ego, immo alii ante me exposuerunt causam, quam putaverant, non officiosum mendacium defendentes, sicut tu scribis, sed docentes honestam dispensationem ...*, 'I, or rather, others before me, expounded the reason, as they had conceived it, not defending a dutiful lie, as you write, but teaching an honourable accommodation ...' (Jerome, ep. 112, 11, *CSEL*, 54, p. 380).

of accommodation, as our forefathers wanted, but truly, as you understand it, does not have the Holy Spirit.'[73] The Pauline citation, '*I have become all things to all men..* ', may also look towards the Augustine/Jerome correspondence. Drawn from I Corinthians, it is followed there by two more specific claims. The first of these, 'I have become as if a Jew to the Jews, so that I might gain them',[74] is explained by Augustine in terms of *compassio misericors*, 'merciful sympathy'.[75] The same explanation is subsequently applied to the second, 'I have become weak to the weak ...':[76] 'When he said: *Who is weak and I am not weak?*, he wanted it to be understood that he had suffered with another's infirmity, rather than that he had pretended to it.'[77]

The use here of *condolere*, to 'suffer with', 'share the pain', may add a further dimension to Peter's earlier declaration that he 'felt pity for', 'suffered with', 'certain wretches'. These 'wretches', it was suggested, could be identified with Cistercian zealots. If the statement *mos est dispensative gerendus* is taken in the sense 'practice (of the *Rule*) is to be administered by way of dispensation',[78] it seems to look back to the position Peter upheld in both letter 28 and letter 111, that charity demands discretion in the application of the *Rule*, in order to ensure the salvation of those who are weaker. Accordingly, Peter can be seen to have set up, not without irony, a demand for reciprocity. By 'suffering with' Cistercians he has become 'as if a Jew to the Jews'. Bernard's *sapientia* requires that he become 'weak to the weak'. Later in the letter, this will be given a concrete application, as Peter demands that not only should Cluniacs be admitted into Cistercian institutions, but that 'every kindness should be shown ...'.[79]

---

[73]   *Ex quo apparet, qui sub lege est non dispensative, ut nostri voluere maiores, sed vere, ut tu intelligis, eum spiritum sanctum non habere* (ibid., 14, p. 384). The statement forms part of a virulent rejection of the validity of Jewish ritual. See White, *The correspondence*, p. 27; ibid. p. 46.

[74]   *Et factus sum Iudaeis tamquam Iudaeus ut Iudaeos lucrarer* (I Cor 9. 20).

[75]   *Neque enim a me docendus es, quomodo intelligatur, quod idem dicit:* factus sum Iudaeis tamquam Iudaeus, ut Iudaeos lucrifacerem, *et cetera, quae ibi dicuntur compassione misericordi, non simulatione fallaci*, 'For you do not need to be taught by me, how what he says should be understood: *I have become a Jew to the Jews so that I might gain them*, and the rest, which is said there from merciful sympathy, not from deceitful pretence' (Augustine, ep. 40, IV. 4, p. 73). In what follows Augustine spells out the notion of 'shared suffering': *Fit enim tamquam aegrotus, qui ministrat aegroto, non cum se febres habere mentitur, sed cum animo condolentis cogitat, quemadmodum sibi serviri vellet, si ipse aegrotaret*, 'He who ministers to the sick, becomes as if sick, not by pretending that he has fever, but by thinking with the mind of one sharing the pain, of how he would wish to be served, if he himself were sick' (ibid.).

[76]   *Factus sum infirmis infirmus ut infirmos lucri facerem*, 'I have become weak to the weak to gain the weak' (I Cor 9. 22).

[77]   *Non enim et cum diceret:* quis infirmatur et ego non infirmor?, *infirmitatem alterius simulasse potius quam condoluisse volebat intelligi* (Augustine, ep. 40, IV. 6, p. 77 = II Cor 11. 29).

[78]   Subsequently, *mos* will be given this sense overtly, as Peter will discuss the 'fears' of the Cistercians that visiting Cluniacs may be deterred *mos tam asper*, by 'such harsh practice' (letter 150, p. 369).

[79]   *Credo quod haec verba* (omnis ei exhibeatur humanitas) *magis aliquid humanitatis exhiberi praecipiunt hospiti quam civi ...*, 'I believe that these words (*every kindness is to be*

At the beginning of this section, Peter had postulated three pretexts for disunity, adding diversity of dwelling to the pretexts offered in letter 111, diversity of habit and diversity of custom.[80] This opens the way for the proposition of a remedy in the section which follows. Unity of dwelling becomes the leit-motif, expressed in terms of petition: 'Let the dwellings at least be united, let there be cohabitation, undiscriminating in diversity of colour and practice ...'.[81] At a literal level, this is interpreted in the letter in terms of a plea for visiting Cluniac monks to be received into Cistercian institutions on the same basis as Cistercians.[82] Figuratively, however, it may represent the *topos* of 'dwelling' within the heart of a friend,[83] first introduced into letter 111, where white and black alike had been asked to 'close the door of the heart' against whatever threatened *caritas*, and to keep *caritas* itself as *cohabitatrix aeterna*, an 'eternal co–inhabitant'.[84] Peter's claim here to have admitted all the Cistercians into Cluniac cloisters fifteen years previously may also acquire a figurative significance.[85] It was probably at the Council of Pisa, held in

---

shown to him) order that some kindness should be shown rather to the guest than to the citizen ...' (ibid., p. 370 = *Benedicti Regula*, LIII. 9).

[80] *Color varius, habitacula diversa, usus dissimiles obviant dilectioni, contraria sunt unitati*, 'Variation in colour, diversity of dwellings, dissimilarity of practices hinder affection, are contrary to unity' (letter 150, p. 368).

[81] *Uniantur saltem habitacula, sit indifferens diversorum colorum et usuum cohabitatio ...* (letter 150, p. 369). Cf. *quando et suscepti et suscipientis commune fuerit habitaculum vel hospitium*, 'when the dwelling and hospitality of received and receiver are common' (ibid.); *Sit commune utrisque habitaculum ...*, 'Let the habitation of both be common ...' (ibid.); *Instruatur utraque species fratrum ... frequenti cohabitatione ...*, 'Let both species of brother be instructed ... by frequent cohabitation ...' (ibid., p. 371); *Sint omnibus omnia communia, non tantum substantia, sed et ipsa habitacula*, 'Let eveything be common to all, not only substance, but the dwellings themselves' (ibid.).

[82] *Fiet hoc (ut expellatur contraria caritati iniquitas) vel ex toto vel ex plurima ... si quando antiqui ordinis monachi ad novorum fratrum monasteria vel habitacula venerint, ab ecclesia, a claustro, a dormitorio, a refectorio, seu ab officinis reliquis exclusi non fuerint*, 'This (that harshness contrary to charity may be expelled) will happen, either wholly or for the most part.. if, whenever monks of the old order come to the monasteries or habitations of new brothers., they are not excluded from the church, from the cloister, from the dormitory, from the refectory, or from the rest of the monastic outhouses ...' (ibid.).

[83] See Fiske, *Friends and friendship*, 2/5.

[84] *et causas ... vel parum eam (caritatem) laedentes a te abige, si expulsae redire voluerint, firmi pectoris redeuntibus ostium claude, et cohabitatricem aeternam totis sanctae animae tuae amplexibus retine*, 'and drive away from you the causes ... which damage charity even a little: if, once expelled, they wish to return, shut the door of a firm heart against them, and embrace (her) as an eternal coinhabitant of your holy soul with all your might' (letter 111, p. 293). This may find a parallel in a letter of Augustine to Pammachius: *Patebit enim oculo caritatis cubiculum caritatis, quod claudimus adversus nugas tumultuosas saeculi ...*, 'For there will be open to the eye of charity the dwelling-place of charity, which we close against the tumultuous nonsense of the world' (Augustine, ep. 58, 2, *CSEL*, 34/2, pp. 217–18).

[85] *Admisi ante quindecim annos universos vestri ordinis fratres, et recipi praecepi, praeter Cluniacense claustrum, in omnia claustra nostra*, 'Fifteen years ago I admitted the universality of the brothers of your order, and ordered them to be received into all our cloisters, except the cloister at Cluny' (letter 150, p. 370–71). In fact, as Constable points out, there is no external corroboration of this decree (Peter the Venerable, *Statuta*, p. 21, n. 2).

1135, that he had first met Bernard. In the salutation to letter 111, he had similarly addressed Bernard as the 'indivisible guest of my heart'.[86]

The section will be built around the evocation and dismissal of alterity, the construction of the 'other'. This is introduced through a series of oppositions, placed through virtual *prosopopoeia* in the mouth *advenientis fratris*, 'of an arriving brother', whose words identify him as a Cluniac: '*The old will recede from his mouth*, which he had been accustomed to say, accustomed to repeat: "Am I a Jew? I thought I was a Christian, and I am regarded as a Gentile. I believed myself a monk, and I am rejected as a publican. I judged myself a fellow-citizen, and I am expelled as a Samaritan. Truly, now, I recognise that *Jews do not associate with Samaritans*."'[87] The subsequent characterisation of the utterance as *maledica verba*, 'slander', apparently puts the Cluniacs in the wrong and offers them up for condemnation.[88] The avowed purpose of Peter's intervention, that 'scandal', a 'stumbling-block', be taken away,[89] may, however, rebound on the Cistercians. They will be confronted with the biblical warning, that whoever 'scandalises', 'drives to sin', 'one of the weak', would be better drowned with a millstone around his neck,[90] doubled with a reminder that Christ declared himself a 'doctor' for the 'weak'.[91] The biblical context of the latter, a reproach by the Pharisees that he consorted with 'publicans and sinners', may call to mind the encounter with the Pharisee at the Temple, in which the Pharisee congratulates himself on his superiority to 'the rest of men', while the publican asks for mercy on his sins.[92] The moral of the story is delivered there in the words: 'Everyone who exalts himself will be humbled, and he who humbles himself will be exalted.'[93] The admission of

---

[86]   *Singulari veneratione colendo, totis caritatis brachiis amplectendo, individuo cordis mei hospiti, domino Bernardo Clarevallis abbati* ..., 'To the indivisible guest of my heart, Bernard, the lord abbot of Clairvaux, to be cherished in singular veneration, to be embraced in all the might of charity ...' (letter 111, p. 274).

[87]   Recedent vetera de ore *eius, quae dicere, quae frequentare consueverat. Numquid ego Iudaeus sum? Christianum me esse putabam, et pro Ethnico reputor. Monachum me credebam, et ut publicanus abiicior. Concivem me aestimabam, et ut Samaritanus expellor. Vere nunc agnovi, quia* non coutuntur Iudaei Samaritanis (letter 150, p. 369 = I Sm 2. 3; Io 4. 9).

[88]   *Et quis potest cuncta similia istis.. maledica verba referre? Obstruatur igitur tali caritatis obice* os loquentium *talia, ne dicam* iniqua ..., 'And who can call to mind all the slanderous words, not to say *iniquities*, similar to these? Therefore, let the *mouth of those speaking* such things, let me not say *iniquities*, be blocked with such a barrier of charity ...' (ibid. = Ps 62. 12).

[89]   *Auferetur ab advenientis fratris corde scandalum, ori ne detrahat imponetur silentium* ..., 'Scandal will be taken away from the heart of the arriving brother, silence will be imposed on his mouth so that he does not engage in detraction ...' (ibid.).

[90]   *Caveatur pusillorum scandalum, timeatur* mola asinaria, *quae non caventes mergit* in profundum maris, 'Let a stumbling-block for the weak be avoided, let the *mill-stone* be feared, which sinks those who do not avoid it *in the depths of the sea*' (ibid. = Mt 18. 6, Mc 9. 41).

[91]   *consulatur infirmis, quorum se medicum Christus dixit*, 'let thought be taken for the weak, whose doctor Christ declared himself' (ibid., = Mt 9. 12, Mc 2. 17, Lc 5. 31).

[92]   Lc 18. 10–13.

[93]   *quia omnis qui se exaltat humiliabitur et qui se humiliat exaltabitur* (ibid., 18. 14).

Cluniac 'weakness', accordingly, may function as a pretext to level a counter-accusation of exclusivity and arrogance against the Cistercians.

The second grouping of oppositions can also be seen to wrong-foot the Cistercians. Peter invokes *attestatio*, eye-witness affirmation, to suggest that 'certain' Cistercians are afraid that visiting Cluniacs would be deterred *austeritate consuetudinum*, 'by the harshness of the practices'.[94] The statement in itself can be viewed as pointing to a form of detraction.[95] Seemingly, the onus is placed upon the Cluniacs, through a citation from the monastic *Rule*: '*Let* those who wish to enter *be content with the practice of the place which they find*',[96] an injunction repeated at the end of this section.[97] In between, however, this admonition may be undermined by a form of dilemma. Peter interprets the injunction found in the Benedictine *Rule*, '*After this, let all kindness be shown to him*',[98] in terms of dispensation: 'I believe that these words order that some kindness should be shown rather to the guest than to the citizen, to the stranger than to the native, to the foreigner than to the inhabitant.'[99] If the Cluniacs are to be regarded as *alieni*, 'strangers', special dispensation should be accordingly be shown to them. To regard them as such, however, would be to admit to arrogance.

Subsequently, Peter draws on Galatians to undercut the distinction: 'For if it was

---

[94]   *Non timeatur illud, quod nuper apud Claremvallem a quibusdam fratribus ... audivi, timere se, ne ... advenientes monachi ... tam austeritate consuetudinum, quam insolita ciborum asperitate deterriti, inusitata hospitia perhorrescant ...*, 'Let there not be feared what I heard recently at Clairvaux from certain brothers.. that they feared lest ... arriving monks, deterred both by the harshness of the customs and by the unaccustomed roughness of the food, should have a horror of a hospitality to which they were unused ...' (letter 150, p. 369).

[95]   It seems to recall both the attack on Cluniac indulgence contained in the *Apologia* and the invective of letter 28, which presented the Cluniacs as having hands 'delicate from leisure' (letter 28, p. 54).

[96]   Sint contenti *qui ingredi voluerint* consuetudine loci quam invenerint (letter 150, p. 369 = *Benedicti Regula*, LXI. 2). There may be another hidden point here. This section of the *Rule* goes on to add that if the 'pilgrim-monk' finds fault with anything 'reasonably, and with the humility of charity', the abbot should take note, 'in case the Lord has sent him for this very purpose' (*Benedicti Regula*, LXI. 4). The latter statement may draw on Hebrews: *Caritas fraternitatis maneat hospitalitatem nolite oblivisci per hanc enim latuerunt quidam angelis hospitio receptis*, 'Let the charity of brotherhood remain. Do not forget hospitality. For through this some have entertained angels unawares' (Hbr 13. 1–2).

[97]   *Habeant tantum monachi quamdiu hospites fuerint monachorum claustra communia, sint contenti, si sic vestris placuerit, vestro cotidiano cibo, ordine, institutis*, 'Let only monks, as long as they are guests of monks, have communal cloisters; let them be content, if so it pleases yours, with your daily food, regulation, ordinances' (letter 150, p. 370). The *caveat* here, 'if so it pleases yours', may hint again that the Cistercians are lacking in *caritas* even towards their own.

[98]   *Nam post adorationem, post orationem, post lectionem, de susceptis hospitibus [regula] subdit:* Post haec, omnis ei exhibeatur humanitas, 'For after deferential salutation, after prayer, after divine reading, it (the *Rule*) appends in relation to guests who have been received: *After this, let all kindness be shown to him*' (ibid. = *Benedicti Regula*, LIII. 9).

[99]   *Credo quod haec verba magis aliquid humanitatis exhiberi hospiti quam civi, advenae quam indigenae, peregrino quam colono* (letter 150, p. 370).

rightly ordered, *let us work good to all, but especially to those who are of the household of the faith*, good is to be shown to all clerics and laity, but especially to those of the household of the same monastic order. In those words of his the Apostle set domestics of the faith, that is, Christians, above Jews and Gentiles; on the same basis, I set monks even above other Christians.'[100] The Cistercians are caught both ways. If, as they ought, they regard the Cluniacs as *domestici*, 'domestics of the faith', they are bound to give them special treatment. If they persist in treating them as *alieni*, 'strangers', the same consideration is equally due. The source of this dilemma appears to be the monastic *Rule* itself, which draws on the same passage from Galatians to require that 'fitting honour is to be shown to all, *especially to those of the household of the faith* and to those from foreign parts'.[101] Again, then, Peter seems to be laying the primary responsibility for the maintenance of *caritas* upon the Cistercians through the notion of dispensation.[102]

The language of petition, which has run through this section, now modulates into an open demand for reciprocity, in a conclusion which is again addressed directly to Bernard: 'Put before them the words of the Lord, saying, *whatever you wish men to do to you, do you* the same *to them*.'[103] This commandment is found in two New Testament contexts. In Matthew, it is preceded by the injunction, 'Ask and it will be given to you, seek and you will find, knock and it will be opened to you', thus reinforcing the demand for cohabitation.[104] In Luke, it is followed by the instruction 'love your enemies'.[105] Again, Peter may be creating a form of dilemma. Subsequently he will remind Bernard of the Biblical requirement to 'serve one another': 'If they wish to be served, let they themselves also serve their brothers, so that they may fulfil what is said, *serve one another* from charity.'[106] Taken from

---

[100] *Si enim iure praeceptum est,* operemur bonum ad omnes, maxime autem ad domesticos fidei, *operandum est bonum ad omnes clericos vel laicos, maxime autem ad eiusdem monastici ordinis domesticos. Praetulit tunc in illis verbis suis apostolus Iudaeis et Ethnicis fidei domesticos, id est Christianos, praefero ego a quodam simili ipsis etiam aliis Christianis monachos* (ibid. = Gal 6. 10).

[101] *Et omnibus congruus honor exhibeatur,* maxime domesticis fidei *et peregrinis (Benedicti Regula,* LIII. 2 = Gal 6. 10).

[102] *Non est igitur deterius providendum a monachis iuxta congruam proposito humanitatem hospiti monacho in claustro, quam hospiti clerico vel laico, in exteriore hospitio. Sed non his diutius immoror,* 'Therefore no worse provision is to be made by monks according to the kindness befitting their undertaking for the guest monk in the cloister than for the guest cleric or lay-person in the external lodging. But I will spend no longer on this' (letter 150, p. 370).

[103] *Propone eis verba domini dicentis,* quaecumque vultis ut faciant vobis homines, et vos *eadem* facite illis (letter 150, p. 371 = Mt 7. 12; Lc 6. 31).

[104] *Petite et dabitur vobis quaerite et invenietis pulsate et aperietur vobis* (Mt 7. 7).

[105] *Verumtamen diligite inimicos vestros et benefacite et mutuum date,* 'But love your enemies and do good to them and lend to them' (Lc 6. 35). The motif of 'lending' will be picked up subsequently through *debitum caritatis,* the 'debt/due of charity.'

[106] *Si sibi serviri volunt, ipsi quoque fratribus.. deserviant, ut impleant quod dicitur, ex caritate* servite invicem (letter 150, p. 371 = Gal 5. 13). There may also be an ironic allusion here to 'judaising.' The passage from which the injunction is taken begins, *Ego autem fratres si circumcisionem adhuc praedico quid adhuc persecutionem patior ergo evacuatum est scandalum crucis,* 'But I, brothers, if I still preach circumcision, why do I still suffer persecution? Therefore the stumbling-block of the cross is made void' (Gal 5. 11). This

Galatians, this continues there: 'For the whole Law is fulfilled in one saying, you will love your neighbour as yourself.'[107] If the Cistercians choose to regard the Cluniacs as enemies, they are manifestly in the wrong. If, as they should, they regard them as 'neighbours', they cannot escape their obligation to *caritas*.

This last citation is paired with one taken from Matthew which similarly plays on the notion of servitude: 'If they (the Cistercians) wish to demand the debt of servitude from the mandate of charity from others, let them pay the requital, by the example of Him who says: *I did not come to be waited upon, but to wait upon.*'[108] Servitude had first been introduced into the *apostrophe* of 'certain wretches' through another Pauline citation: '*You castigate your body and reduce it to servitude, lest by chance* you be found *reprobate* ...'.[109] Its continuation there introduces the notion of hypocrisy: 'lest by chance I myself be proved false when I have preached to others'.[110] In similar vein, the citation from *Matthew* is preceded there by a reminder of the need for humility: 'but whoever wishes to become greater among you, let him be your attendant, and whoever wishes to be first among you will be your servant'.[111] At the same time, the language of debt and requital may recall the notion of 'profit', 'gain', contained in the Pauline *lucrifacere*,[112] and attached by Peter to his earlier demand for dispensation.[113] Peter may seem to be hinting that the Cistercians can ensure their own spiritual profit by 'gaining' the Cluniacs through a practical demonstration of *caritas*.

As with letter 111, Bredero relates this letter to Peter's desire for further reform among the Cluniacs.[114] Again, the letter itself gives no overt indication of this. Indeed, as has been seen, it is arguable that it maintains the same position seen previously, that dispensation is justified by *caritas*. In addition, although it seems to promulgate the abolition of internal distinction, the letter does not argue for removal of external differences. Just as letter 111 can be read as a double

---

seems to represent an attack on the 'judaisers': *Quicumque volunt placere in carne hi cogunt vos circumcidi tantum ut crucis Christi persecutionem non patiantur neque enim qui circumciduntur legem custodiunt sed volunt vos circumcidi ut in carne vestra glorientur*, 'Whosoever wish to please in the flesh force you to be circumcised, only so that they may not suffer the persecution of the cross of Christ. For neither do those who are circumcised keep the law, but they wish you to be circumcised, so that they may glory in your flesh' (Gal 6. 12–13).

[107] *Omnis enim lex in uno sermone impletur diliges proximum tuum sicut te ipsum* (Gal 5. 14).

[108] *Si servitutis debitum ex caritatis mandato ab aliis exigunt, reddant vicem illius exemplo qui dicit:* Non veni ministrari, sed ministrare (letter 150, p. 371 = Mt 20. 28).

[109] Castigas corpus tuum et in servitutem redigis, ne forte reprobus *inveniaris* ... (ibid., p. 368 = I Cor 9. 27).

[110] *Sed castigo corpus meum et in servitutem redigo ne forte cum aliis praedicaverim ipse reprobus efficiar*, 'But I castigate my body and reduce it to servitude, lest by chance I myself be proved false when I have preached to others' (I Cor 9. 27).

[111] *sed quicumque voluerit inter vos maior fieri sit vester minister et qui voluerit inter vos primus esse erit vester servus* (Mt 20. 26–7).

[112] I Cor 9. 21; ibid., 9. 22.

[113] Omnibus omnia factus sum, ut omnes *lucri*facerem ... (letter 150, p. 368 = I Cor 9. 22). In the original, the verse runs: *ut omnes facerem salvos*, 'that I might render all saved'.

[114] Bredero, 'Saint Bernard in his relations', p. 333.

apologia, so the statement, 'I do not say either that the old practices should be transformed into the new or the new into the old',[115] might be read as a double reassurance, that both sides should keep to the way they have chosen. It is followed, however, by a somewhat ambiguous *praeteritio*: 'I say nothing of these, although I could with justice say this in part. I fear that, if I were to express my feelings on the matter, with one side perhaps being offended, I would both pour out my words in vain and exasperate with displeasing words those whom I desire to be placated towards one another.'[116]

The studied vagueness of this statement is arguably compounded by linguistic ambiguity. The use of *pars* to indicate both 'part' and 'party' might suggest that *ex parte* could also be translated as 'from one party', *altera pars* as 'the other party'.[117] A similarly ambiguous usage appears at the end of letter 28, where Peter had employed the plural form to imply either 'a party' or 'parties', in a context which might seem to refer either to the Cluniacs or to the Cistercians or to both.[118] If the ambiguity here is intentional, the words might be thought to carry a double message, levelling criticism both at the Cistercian zealots and at Cluniac opponents of reform. The latter suspicion may appear to be fuelled by what looks like a hint that his efforts at promoting *caritas* have met with internal opposition: 'neither was I concerned about mixing white and black in our places, nor did I take heed of those who were concerned, although many were insistent with me that it should not happen'.[119] At the same time, this can be seen to strengthen the petition. Peter's action has been taken at some personal cost. Consequently, it should be met by reciprocity, however difficult the undertaking for Bernard.

In this letter, as in the accompanying letter of recommendation to Nicholas, Peter insinuates that Bernard shares his opinion,[120] although it remains unclear whether this relates to the specific proposition or to the general undertaking of restoring *caritas*. The insinuation, however, could be viewed as a manipulative ploy. In this letter, in particular, the wording is such as to apparently leave Bernard little option: 'I have written this ... so that ... you may bring them (certain of the abbots of your

---

[115] *Non dico ut vel antiqui usus in novos, vel novi transferantur in antiquos* (letter 150, pp. 368–9).

[116] *Nihil horum dico, licet hoc ex parte iure dicere possem. Vereor ne si quod inde sentio dicerem, forte altera parte offensa, et verba in irritum funderem, et quos in invicem placari desidero, verbis non placentibus irritarem* (ibid., p. 369).

[117] The ambiguity seems to be pointed up by the surrounding word-play on *irritus*, 'vain' and *irritare*, to 'irritate'.

[118] *Nam praeter austeritatem verborum, quae ad partium latentem simultatem designandum posui, reliqua omnia ut edita sunt intellexi*, 'For apart from the harshness of the words, which I have cited in order to express the lurking animosity of (a) faction(s), I have understood all the rest as it was brought forth' (letter 28, p. 101). The ambiguity there is compounded by the potential sense of *simultas* as 'jealousy' and of *intellegere* as 'to mean'.

[119] *nec de albo vel nigro colore simul in locis nostris admixto curavi, nec curantes cum multi mihi ne id fieret instarent, audivi* (letter 150, p. 371).

[120] *Insta ei ... ut ... fiat quod opto, et si quos forte obviantes invenerit, in meam quae ut puto et sua est sententiam transire compellat*, 'Press upon him ... that ... what I hope for may happen, and (that) if by chance he finds any opponents, he may compel them to go over to this opinion of mine which, so I think, is also his' (letter 151, p. 372).

order) into this opinion which, so I think, is not only mine but also yours, and publish everywhere that by all the brothers of your order it be held from this time forward, it be held everywhere.'[121] As discussed in the previous chapter, there is no corroborating evidence that Bernard shared any such view. Indeed, the sub-text of ep. 387 might be held to suggest the opposite, at least as far as the proposition of *cohabitatio* is concerned. It is not clear, either, that the absence in ep. 389,[122] the next preserved communication from Bernard, of any direct reference to the request contained here should be taken, as Constable suggests, as evidence that this letter was written before letter 150 had been received.[123] The alternative explanation put forward by Bredero, that it represents a refusal on Bernard's part to enter into discussion, may find some support from certain features of ep. 389 itself.[124]

> To the dearest father and lord Peter, by the grace of God abbot of Cluny, brother Bernard, called abbot of Clairvaux: greetings and prayers.
>
> I saw your letter in a little moment, but with no little affection. I was occupied by such great occupation, as you either know, or you can know, dearest Father. However, I dragged myself away, and escaped from the prayers and responses of all, and shut myself up with that Nicolas, whom your soul loves. I read and re-read the sweetness, and great sweetness, which emanated from your letter. That letter diffused your affection, and moved mine. I grieved, because although I was affected, I was not able to write back. For much *malice of the day* called me away. For there had come together a great multitude *from* almost *every nation which is under heaven*. It behoved me to answer to all, because, as my sins demand, *I was born into the world for this*, to be confounded and burned by many and manifold solicitudes. Meanwhile, I write this little scrap of my soul; but *when I receive the opportune time*, I will compose a letter more carefully than now, which may open up the affection of one who loves more clearly. What you announced to me concerning the will of Baro, in truth I declare to you that I have received not as owed, but as given. I rejoice that I have learned the truth concerning the affair at Grenoble. As to that,[125] be assured that my heart kindled at the words of the common son, which he brought back to me on your part. *I am ready and I am not disturbed* to do your will, wherever I am able. In the assembly of the Cistercians, you as special lord and father and dearest friend, were remembered, and yours both alive and dead. The elect of Beauvais greets you as your own: for he is yours. I your Nicolas greet you in eternity, and beyond, and that familiar household, which adheres to your side and spirit.

---

[121] *Scripsi hoc tibi ... ut ... eos (quosdam abbatum vestri ordinis) in hanc sententiam, quae sicut aestimo non solum mea sed et tua est, adducas, et ut a cunctis vestri ordinis fratribus amodo teneatur, ubique teneatur, ubique promulges* (letter 150, p. 371).

[122] Bernard, ep. 389, *SBO*, VIII, pp. 356–7. The text is drawn from Peter's letter 152.

[123] Constable, *Letters*, II, p. 201. The date of the letter can be only loosely fixed from its references to Henry of France and to the Cistercian chapter-general. Constable postulates October. In fact, if the letter also contains references, as he himself suggests, to the meeting held on 1 November, a slightly later date would seem more plausible (ibid., p. 202).

[124] Bredero, 'Saint Bernard in his relations', p. 338. His more recent discussion seemingly relocates ep. 389 to mid-September. He does not, however, offer any reasons for this (Bredero, *Bernard of Clairvaux*, pp. 241–2).

[125] Despite the claim to be following Constable's text, Leclercq rather oddly has *illum* for *illud* here (*Letters*, I, p. 373).

At first reading, this letter seems to refer unambiguously to Peter' letter 149. The mention of 'sweetness' can be seen as echoing Peter's three citations connoting mystical sweetness. In addition, the will of Baro and the election at Grenoble were discussed or mentioned there, and the mention of commemoration at the Cistercian chapter general is in accordance with Peter's own request.[126] Bernard's claim to have 'shut himself up with Nicholas', together with the allusion to the delivery of an oral message by the latter,[127] seems to point to the intended delivery of that letter at Cîteaux, and to identify the 'occupation' as that of the chapter-general itself. The deployment of tenses, however, may suggest a certain telescoping of the time-scale. The letter moves from a string of verbs in the perfect[128] to more imprecise imperfects,[129] and thence to an unexpected epistolary present, *scribo*, 'I write'. In between comes a reference to the cause of the delay in replying, *Convenerat ... multitudo magna*, 'A great multitude ... had gathered.' Other features may combine to suggest, as Constable postulates, that this gathering refers not to the one at Cîteaux, but to the special meeting held seemingly at Clairvaux itself some six weeks later.[130]

In retrospect, the language of the opening can be seen to have overtones of beleaguerment. *Occupare* and *occupatio* can indicate forcible seizure, investment;[131] *abripere* and *eripere*, forcible removal, rescue.[132] *Includere*, to 'shut up', can be used both of monastic reclusion and of imprisonment.[133] While this could be explained in relation to the meeting at Cîteaux, it would seem to fit more happily with the idea of being 'under siege' at Clairvaux itself. It may be, then, that the letter blurs the details of two separate meetings. If so, it might equally well be held to blur the reception of two separate letters. Certainly, the declaration, '*I am ready and I am not disturbed* to do your will, wherever I am able',[134] might seem to recall the injunction in letter 150 to bring the Cistercian abbots to assent to Peter's request and to promulgate that it be held 'everywhere'. Letter 149 contains no such direct request, although it might, of course, be held to have formed a part of the accompanying oral messages.

---

[126] *In fine rogo ... et supplico ... ut in hoc tanto sanctorum virorum qui Cistercii convenerunt conventu, mei utique vestri memoriam faciatis, meque totumque Cluniacensis congregationis corpus eorum intente orationibus commendetis*, 'Finally, I ask ... and supplicate ... that in this great gathering of holy men who have come together at Cîteaux you make remembrance of me as yours, and commend me and the whole body of the Cluniac congregation intently to their prayers' (letter 149, p. 366).

[127] *Illum autem scitote, quia multum incaluit cor meum ad verba communis filii, quae ex parte vestra retulit mihi* (ep. 389, p. 357). This is rendered in James as 'I must tell you that my heart glowed at the words of our common son which you in part related to me', and glossed with a reference to 'Guy, Prior of the Grande Chartreuse' (James, *The letters*, p. 379). The 'common son' is, however, surely Nicholas.

[128] *Abripui ... eripui ... inclusi ... legi ... relegi ...* (ep. 389, pp. 356–7).

[129] *Dolebam ... valebam ... avocabat ... oportebat ...* (ibid., p. 357).

[130] Constable, *Letters*, II, p. 202.

[131] *Occupatus eram tanta occupatione ...* (ep. 389, p. 356).

[132] *Abripui tamen me, et eripui votis et responsionibus omnium ...* (ibid.).

[133] *et inclusi me cum Nicolao illo ...* (ibid., pp. 356–7).

[134] Paratus sum et non sum turbatus *ad faciendam vestram, ubicumque potuero, voluntatem* (ep. 389, p. 357 = Ps 118. 60).

Further indications that this letter may constitute some kind of response to the proposal contained in letter 150 may come from the central section. Three separate Biblical allusions, each with potentially suggestive overtones, are conflated and slightly subverted in the process. The letter claims that Bernard was called away 'by the great *malice of the day*'.[135] In the Gospels, the disciples are instructed: 'Do not be worried for the morrow, for the morrow will be anxious for itself. Its own evil suffices the day.'[136] Letter 150 had turned on the premise of taking thought for the 'morrow'. 'Procrastination' had been condemned,[137] and mankind warned that he did not know what 'the day to follow after' would bring forth.[138] The description of the gathering can be seen to draw on events at Pentecost, but with a redistribution of motifs. The 'great multitude' which had 'gathered' is said to have been drawn, '*from* almost *every nation, which is under heaven*'.[139] In Acts, this phrase is attached to the depiction of the Jews as 'holy men, dwelling in Jerusalem'.[140] While an allusion to Jerusalem could point to Cîteaux, as discussed previously in relation to ep. 387 and letter 149 it seems more likely to be a reference to Clairvaux. In Acts, it is the multitude which is 'confounded', hearing the disciples speaking in tongues,[141] after the fiery descent of the Holy Spirit.[142] Here, it is Bernard who is 'confounded' and 'burned' by 'many and manifold sollicitudes'.[143] Peter's letter 111 had called upon Bernard to drive out childish jealousy 'with that sublime eloquence, flaming from the Holy Spirit'.[144]

The reference to being 'confounded' and 'burned' is preceded by a third allusion taken from the Gospels. The letter claims *in hoc natus sum in mundum* ..., 'I was born into the world for this ...'. Those were the words of Jesus appearing before Pilate. The citation there continues, 'to bear witness to the truth. Everyone who is

---

[135] *Nempe multa* diei malitia *avocabat* (ibid. = Mt 6. 34).

[136] *Nolite ergo esse solliciti in crastinum crastinus enim dies sollicitus erit sibi ipse sufficit diei malitia sua* (Mt 6. 34).

[137] *non est periculosa procrastinatio sustinenda* ... (letter 150, p. 367).

[138] *quia nescit homo* ... quid superventura pariat dies (ibid. = Prv 27. 1).

[139] *Convenerat enim multitudo magna fere* ex omni natione, quae sub caelo *est* (ep. 389, p. 357 = Act 2. 5).

[140] *Erant autem in Hierusalem habitantes Iudaei viri religiosi ex omni natione quae sub caelo sunt* (Act 2. 5).

[141] *Facta autem hac voce convenit multitudo et mente confusa est quoniam audiebat unusquisque lingua sua illos loquentes*, 'When this sound was made a multitude came together and was confounded in mind, since each one heard them speaking in his own tongue' (Act 2. 6).

[142] *Apparuerunt illis dispertitae linguae tamquam ignis seditque supra singulos eorum et repleti sunt omnes Spiritu Sancto et coeperunt loqui aliis linguis prout Spiritus Sanctus dabat eloqui illis*, 'There appeared to them divided tongues as of fire, and it sat over each of them. And they were all filled with the Holy Spirit, and they began to speak in other tongues, as the Holy Spirit gave them to speak' (ibid., 2. 3–4).

[143] *ut multis et multiplicibus sollicitudinibus confundar et urar* (ep. 389, p. 357).

[144] *Expellite sublimi illo et ex spiritu dei flammante eloquio* ... *puerilem illam aemulationem* ... (Peter, letter 111, p. 294).

of the truth hears my voice.'[145] In this letter, Bernard claims to have 'learned the truth' from Peter.[146] Furthermore, the statement from the *Psalms*, 'I am ready and I am not disturbed ...', points to the continuation 'to keep your mandates'.[147] It continues there, 'The snares of sinners encompassed me, and I did not forget your Law.'[148] The restrictive addition to Bernard's statement, 'wherever I will (have) be(en) able to', has already been doubled by the proposal to compose another letter more carefully, 'when I (will have) receive(d) the opportune time'.[149] This phrase, also taken from the Psalms, is followed there by the words, 'I will proclaim (your) ordinances.'[150] At face value, these allusions might appear to provide a covert justification for failure to implement the proposal contained in letter 150. Their use, however, is sufficiently oblique to leave the exact application uncertain. There seem to be two main lines of possible interpretation: that Bernard was forced to use his eloquence in other matters, and was unable to raise the issue at all; that the issue was raised, but that his eloquence was unable to carry the day. The first might seem to find support in the *caveat*, that he will do Peter's will, *ubicumque potuero*, 'wherever I will have been able to'. The initial result of the Pentecostal experience, however, might seem to favour the second. The bystanders are said to have been filled with wonder, understanding the utterances, but not the meaning of the event,[151] while some mocked, 'They are filled with new wine.'[152] Either way, it seems to turn on a declaration of 'incapacity', which might in itself recall the blocking manœuvres found earlier in ep. 228.

At the same time, these allusions may lend the letter scope for potential irony. The claim in the Psalms, *ego iustitias iudicabo*, 'I will proclaim (your) ordinances',[153] could also be translated as 'I will judge of your ordinances.' Pilate's response to Jesus was 'What is truth?'[154] The biblical phrases associated with the promise 'I am ready and I am not disturbed', 'to keep your mandates',[155] and 'I did not forget your Law',[156] can again be seen as pointing to the identification of Peter with God, and as conveying a certain ironic distancing. In this context, it may be noted that the letter either ignores, or contravenes, the epistolary rebuke contained in letter 149. Peter is twice addressed as *pater*, 'father', although the contravention is arguably softened by the juxtaposition of terms of endearment, *carissimus*, 'dearest',[157] and

---

[145] *Ego in hoc natus sum et ad hoc veni in mundum ut testimonium perhibeam veritati omnis qui est ex veritate audit meam vocem*, 'I was born for this and I have come into the world for this, to bear witness to the truth. Everyone who is of the truth hears my voice' (Io 18. 37).
[146] *Gaudeo quia ... veritatem cognovi* (ep. 389, p. 357).
[147] *Paratus sum et non sum turbatus ut custodiam mandata tua* (Ps 118. 60).
[148] *Funes peccatorum circumplexi sunt me et legem tuam non sum oblitus* (ibid., 118. 61).
[149] *sed* cum accepero tempus *ego accuratius ... dictabo epistolam ...* (ep. 389 = Ps 74. 3).
[150] *Cum accepero tempus ego iustitias iudicabo* (Ps 74. 3).
[151] *Stupebant autem omnes et mirantur ad invicem dicentes quidnam hoc vult esse*, 'But all were stupefied and wondered, saying to one another, "What does this mean?" ' (Act 2. 12).
[152] *Alii autem irridentes dicebant quia musto pleni sunt isti* (ibid., 13).
[153] Ps 74. 3.
[154] *Dicit ei Pilatus quid est veritas* (Io 18. 38).
[155] Ps 118. 60.
[156] Ibid., 118. 61.
[157] *Carissimo patri ...* (ep. 389, p. 356).

amantissimus, 'most beloved',[158] echoing the appellations of *amicus* and *carissimus* which Peter had there declared to be acceptable.[159] The letter also plays on the notion of *affectus*, 'affection', 'disposition'. Bernard claims to have grieved, because although 'affected', he was unable 'to reply',[160] that is, he could not put his desires into practice. Peter had specifically asked in letter 151, the accompanying letter to Nicholas, for his wish to be brought *ad effectum*, 'to effect'.[161]

The subscription by Nicholas, 'I, your Nicholas, greet you *in eternity and beyond*',[162] has given rise to the surmise of Leclercq mentioned in the previous chapter, that the letter as a whole was composed by Nicholas himself.[163] The act of subscription does indeed present intriguing possibilities. Serving in general terms as proof of authenticity,[164] it might seem that the notion is here being stretched further, to encompass a concealed claim to authorship. Equally, however, its presence could be related to the fact, as discussed in the previous chapter, that ep. 387, the previous letter from Bernard, had apparently been delivered by Nicholas in person. It seems possible that Nicholas's intervention in both cases can be seen as being designed to re-activate his own contact with Cluny and Peter. Significantly, the words 'in eternity and beyond' come from a passage of Micah which encompasses a vision of peace: 'And He will judge among many peoples and chide the strong peoples even far off, and they will cut up their swords into ploughshares and their spears into mattocks. People will not take up the sword against people and they will not learn to wage war any more.'[165] As with ep. 387, this positive note may seem to counterbalance the potential negativity diagnosed above, and to leave the way open for further negotiation.

On the surface, Peter's third 'open' letter, 150, furthers the conciliatory approach seen in letter 111. A glance beneath this, however, may suggest that the letter is actually more uncompromising and hard-hitting than its predecessor. Although detraction is attributed openly only to the Cluniacs, the resurrection of the opposition between 'Jews' and 'Gentiles', taken together with the allusions to pharisaeism and the disguised call for dispensation, may seem to lay the responsibility for its continuation firmly at the door of Cistercian arrogance and failure in charity. In particular, the echoes and reprises of letters 28 and 111, in association with Pauline warnings about the uncertain nature of salvation and the fallibility of human wisdom, and the Old Testament allusions to impending death and damnation, may serve to target Bernard for his failure to respond and to take action more swiftly. At the same time, as has been seen, the letter may contain veiled hints that Peter is under internal pressure and needs some external validation.

---

[158] *amantissime Pater* (ibid.).

[159] Letter 149, p. 364.

[160] *Dolebam, quia sicut afficiebar, non valebam rescribere* (ep. 389, p. 357).

[161] *et quantum poteris exhortare ut.. ad effectum perducatur* (Peter, letter 151).

[162] *Ego Nicolaus vester saluto vos* in aeternum et ultra.. (ep. 389 = Mi 4. 5).

[163] Leclercq, 'Lettres de S. Bernard', p. 149.

[164] Ganz, ' "Mind in character" ', pp. 283–5.

[165] *Et iudicabit inter populos multos et corripiet gentes fortes usque in longinquum et concident gladios suos in vomeres et hastas suas in ligones non sumet gens adversus gentem gladium et non discent ultra belligare* (Mi 4. 3).

As mentioned previously, the suggestions here and elsewhere of Bernard's present willingness to cooperate may be deceptive. They lend themselves to viewing as further pressurising devices. Alternatively, they may be thought to have emanated from Nicholas rather than from Bernard himself. In terms of establishing dialogue, it would seem that the letter should be viewed as a failure. It remains either without any preserved response, or, if, as argued above, ep. 389 is to be regarded as constituting a cryptic reply, with an essentially negative response. The seeming absence of any evidence for significant changes in Cistercian practice, as signalled by Constable, may equally seem to brand it a failure in practical terms.[166]

---

[166] Constable, *Letters*, II, p. 199. See, as cited there, J.-H. Pignot, *Histoire de l'ordre de Cluny depuis la fondation de l'abbaye jusqu'à la mort de Pierre-le-Vénérable*, 3 vols, Autun, 1868, III, p. 485, n. 1; *Statuta capitulorum generalium ordinis Cisterciensis ab anno 1116*, ed. J.-M. Canivez, 8 vols, I, Bibliothèque de la Revue d'Histoire Ecclésiastique 9, Louvain, 1933, 45–9; 56–9.

Chapter 9

A New Crusade: Bernard, Ep. 364; Peter, Letter 164

The group of letters discussed in the previous two chapters, all concerned in some way with the 'domestic' matter of Cluniac–Cistercian relations,[1] is flanked in Peter's letter-collection by three letters which address themselves to what can be described as 'political' issues, episcopal election and crusade. The first of these, relating to the election of Henry of France in 1149 as bishop of Beauvais, presents itself as a reply to a request by Bernard for advice.[2] The other two letters, traditionally associated with the Second Crusade of 1147–48, but now accepted as relating to the subsequent attempts to launch a new crusade, comprise an appeal for assistance by Bernard[3] and Peter's response.[4] In consequence, they are dated by Constable to March/April 1150.[5] There has been a move among recent critics of the Peter/Bernard correspondence to differentiate between 'internal' issues concerning monastic policy, on which the two men were clearly divided, and 'external' issues affecting the monastic order as a whole. Piazzoni, who prefers to talk of moments of 'collaboration' and 'alliance' rather than friendship, cites the election at Beauvais as an example of shared concern to promote the status of monasticism by the choice of a monk over a cleric, regardless of his monastic persuasion.[6] Lang speaks of their 'mutual sympathy' for the Second Crusade.[7] The consequent tendency to treat letters on issues such as these in isolation from those relating to Cluniac–Cistercian relations obsures the fact that echoes from the earlier debate may appear to disturb the apparently harmonious surface of these exchanges.

As stated above, Peter's letter 145, the first of the letters in question here, concerns the episcopal election at Beauvais. Its date can only be established in relation to the date of the election, generally set to autumn or late summer 1149.[8] The uncertainty brings into question its relationship with the group discussed previously. The earliest of these, Bernard's ep. 387, is dated by Constable to

---

[1]   Ep. 387 from Bernard, letters 149 and 150 from Peter, together with 151, Peter's accompanying letter of recommendation to Nicholas and ep. 389, Bernard's reply.

[2]   Peter, letter 145, *Letters*, I, pp. 360–61.

[3]   Bernard, ep. 364, *SBO*, VIII, pp. 318–19. The text is drawn from Peter's letter 163 (*Letters*, I, pp. 395–6).

[4]   Peter, letter 164, *Letters*, I, pp. 396–8.

[5]   See Constable, *Letters*, II, pp. 207–8.

[6]   Piazzoni, 'Un falso problema', pp. 471–5.

[7]   Lang, 'The friendship', p. 52. Piazzoni, however, offers a more nuanced treatment of this issue (Piazzoni, 'Un falso problema', 470–71.)

[8]   See Constable, *Letters*, II, pp. 195–6.

June/July of that year.[9] Since, however, it can only be dated in relation to letter 149, Peter's reply, apparently destined for the meeting of the chapter general at Cîteaux on 14 September and delivered through the personage of Nicholas, there seems in theory no reason why it might not date from as late as the end of August. The latest, Bernard's ep. 389, tentatively assigned by Constable to October,[10] contains a greeting from *Belvacensis electus*, 'the (bishop)-elect of Beauvais'.[11] If, as suggested previously, this letter contains concealed references to the meeting at Clairvaux on 1 November, it may, in fact, date from somewhat later. The apparent absence of any written request from Bernard makes it seemingly impossible to decide at which point within the group letter 145 should be set.[12] At the same time, its proximity to these letters might in itself seem to suggest that it cannot be completely dissociated from the issues which they raise.

Henry of France, brother of Louis VII, had entered Clairvaux in 1146[13] or 1147.[14] As Piazzoni points out, there is no evidence that Peter had any close acquaintance with Henry.[15] Letter 145 is marked by rhetorical elaboration and seeming eulogy, leading to its characterisation by him as a favourable response.[16] Beneath the surface, however, as will be seen, may run a concealed vein of mockery, and a certain sardonic detachment.

> To the venerable brother lord Bernard, abbot of Clairvaux, to be recalled and named with honour, brother Peter, humble abbot of the Cluniacs, greetings and the affection of sincere charity.
>
> It has pleased your Sanctity to consult my humility as to my opinion about the election of brother Henry, your son, whether you should give assent or not. But you indeed, full of the spirit of the counsel and the fear of God, do not need my counsel over this, nor is it necessary for you to borrow from one of such as I am what, from the grace bestowed on you by God, you are able and accustomed to lend in abundance to others. But because you wish to hear my opinion on the matter, I (will) tell you briefly. If merit of life is sought, it is great. For how is it not great, when he has made himself so little from being so great, when he has trampled under the foot of hardy humility the pride, so to speak, of royal blood, when he has exchanged the luxuries and delights of the world, flowing from a plenteous horn, for innumerable torments and a thousand deaths, when he has mocked the world smiling at him from all sides, when *denying himself and*

---

9   Constable, *Letters*, II, p. 197.
10   Ibid., p. 201.
11   *Salutat vos Belvacensis electus, ut vester: vester est enim*, 'The elect of Beauvais greets you as yours: for he is yours' (ep. 389, *SBO*, VIII, p. 357).
12   The position of letter 145 within Peter's collection might seem to suggest that it pre-dates ep. 387. If the election can be assigned to late summer, there is a possibility, although unlikely, that the request was contained in the missing letter referred to in ep. 387. More probably, it might have been conveyed orally, perhaps by Nicholas himself. No firm conclusions can be drawn, however.
13   A. Luchaire, *Études sur les actes de Louis VII, histoire des institutions monarchiques de la Fance sous les premiers capétiens (mémoires et documents)*, Paris, 1885, p. 162, no. 197, n. 1.
14   M. Colker, 'Anecdota mediaevalia', *Traditio* 17 (1961), 469–82, p. 479.
15   Piazzoni, 'Un falso problema', pp. 471–2.
16   Ibid., p. 472.

lifting his cross, he has followed Christ? If a harmonious election [is sought], not one from the clergy and people of Beauvais is said to dissent. If the assent of the archbishop and the fellow-bishops, the prayers of all these have, so I have learned, been offered to you en masse for the confirmation of so holy a labour. If, in addition, the will of the lord Pope, a letter from him directed to the lord of Rheims, as I have heard, bears witness of how much this has pleased him. What therefore remains, venerable man, except for you to subject your will to the will of God, which is seen to declare itself by so many proofs, and not further to permit that church to labour, or in coming and returning to expend its means in vain? But if you lack confidence in his skill, as one who is less proved in such matters, powerful is God, who has given great things to him already, to perform even greater. Therefore, as far as it is permitted to see, there must be no further procrastination, no further delay, but when the great personages of your parts come, who, so I have been told, are due to come shortly for this reason, receive them eagerly, hear them kindly, and speedily fulfil their so long held desire, their demand which has been sought again and again, for the sake of Him who fulfils the desire of His own in good things, because so it is righteous.

The opening of the letter sets up an antithesis between Peter's humility and Bernard's sanctity.[17] In itself, this may seem to echo and invert the opposition between (Bernard's) humility and (Peter's) grandeur which has been noted previously in a number of Bernard's letters.[18] What follows, containing potential echoes of two biblical passages, may serve to confirm the presence of a further inversion. The statement that Bernard is 'full of the spirit of the counsel and the fear of God'[19] seems to recall the prophecy of the coming of Christ in Isaiah: 'The spirit of God will rest upon Him, the spirit of wisdom and understanding, the spirit of counsel and fortitude, the spirit of knowledge and piety, and the spirit of the fear of God will fill Him ...'.[20] The subsequent claim that he is 'able' and 'accustomed' to 'lend in abundance to others' from the 'grace' bestowed on him by God,[21] may point to a passage from James, 'If anyone of you needs wisdom, let him demand it from God, who gives to all in abundance ...'.[22] Several of Bernard's previous letters had played on the notion of 'grace' in contexts which

---

[17] *Placuit sanctitati vestrae humilitatem meam consulere* ... (letter 145, p. 360).

[18] *Egenus et pauper/homo magnus, occupatus in magnis* (ep. 147, *SBO*, VII, p. 350); *tantillus/tantus, nostra pusillitas/vestra dignatio* (ep. 148, ibid., p. 352); *vestra magnitudo/ nugae meae* (ep. 228, *SBO*, VIII, p. 98); *mea humilitas/sublimitas vestra* (ep. 387, ibid., p. 355).

[19] *At vos quidem plenus spiritu consilii et timoris dei* ... (letter 145, p. 360).

[20] *Et requiescet super eum spiritus Domini spiritus sapientiae et intellectus spiritus consilii et fortitudinis spiritus scientiae et pietatis et replebit eum spiritus timoris Domini* ... (Is 11. 2–3). The continuation there, *non secundum visionem oculorum iudicabit neque secundum auditum aurium arguet* ..., 'not according to the vision of the eyes will he judge, nor according to the hearing of the ears will he reprove ...' (ibid.), might also point towards the play of sight and hearing in Bernard's ep. 387, and Peter's call for spiritual perception in letter 150.

[21] *(quod) ex collata vobis a deo gratia aliis affluenter nostis et soletis accommodare* (letter 145, p. 360).

[22] *Si quis autem vestrum indiget sapientiam postulet a Deo qui dat omnibus affluenter* ... (Iac 1. 5).

hinted at a potential equation between Peter and God.[23] Here, the disclaimer that Bernard does not 'need to borrow from one such' as Peter[24] may seem both to dispel this equation and to replace it with a new one, that of Bernard with Christ. At the same time, the use of *mutuare*, 'to borrow', may also look towards the biblical rebuke: 'And if you give a loan to those from whom you hope to receive, what grace is there for you?'[25]

The language of financial transaction may have further ramifications. At one level it seems to reflect the parable of the talents,[26] with its injunction to make use of what one has been given by God,[27] thus reinforcing the notion of rebuke. At another it can perhaps be linked with the ambivalent role of the notion of 'profit', oscillating between the material and the spiritual, which has run throughout Peter's side of the correspondence as a whole. Beginning in letter 28, in relation to the Cluniac possession of tithes and property,[28] it had recurred in the image of 'fraudulent alms' as employed in the letters relating to tithes.[29] More importantly in this context, it had also been used in relation to the disputed election of Langres: 'Therefore if a monk is bishop of Langres he will love Cistercian and other monks, because by showing love he will experience greater profit for himself, by not

---

[23]   *Glorior quod habeas me ... in gratia*, 'I glory that you hold me.. in grace' (ep. 147, 1, p. 350); *nisi mallem occurrere gratiae redeunti ...* , 'if I did not prefer to meet returning grace ...' (ep. 228, 1, p. 98); *si est quod possit alia gratia ...*, 'if (an)other grace has any power ...' (ep. 267, *SBO*, VIII, p. 176).

[24]   *meo super hoc consilio non egetis, nec necesse vobis est, ab aliquo talium qualis ego sum mutuare ...* (letter 145, p. 360).

[25]   *Et si mutuum dederitis his a quibus speratis recipere quae gratia est vobis?* (Lc 6. 34). The continuation there runs, *Nam et peccatores peccatoribus faenerantur ut recipiant aequalia*, 'For even sinners lend on interest to sinners, that they may receive an equal amount' (ibid.).

[26]   *Abiit autem qui quinque talenta acceperat et operatus est in eis et lucratus est alia quinque similiter qui duo acceperat lucratus est alia duo qui autem unum acceperat abiens fodit in terra et abscondit pecuniam domini sui*, 'He who had received five talents went away and laboured on them and acquired another five; likewise, he who had received two acquired another two. But he who had received one, going away dug in the ground and hid the money of his master' (Mt 25. 16–18).

[27]   *Respondens ei dominus eius dixit ei serve male et piger ... oportuit ergo te mittere pecuniam meam nummulariis et veniens ego recepissem utique quod meum est cum usura*, 'His master replied to him: "Bad and idle servant ... you should therefore have sent my money to the money-changers, and coming I would assuredly have received at least what is mine with interest" ' (ibid., 25. 26–7).

[28]   *eandem tamen terram et terrena dona ab eisdem hominibus quibus ea dederat suscipit, et ut ita loquamur suis sumptibus caeleste regnum emi permittit, nec inde lucrum suum sed hominum salutem requirit, atque eam ut proprium quaestum amplectitur*, 'He (God) receives the same land and earthly gifts from the same men to whom he had given them, and, so to speak, permits the heavenly kingdom to be bought at his own expense, nor does he seek from there His profit, but the salvation of men, and embraces it as His own profit' (letter 28, p. 83).

[29]   *Contuli ego dum ex caritate rogaverunt quasdam eis decimas, sed aliud est quod sponte deo offertur, aliud quod violenter aufertur*, 'I bestowed on them certain tithes while they asked from charity, but what is freely offered to God is one thing, what is violently snatched away is another' (letter 34, p. 111).

showing love greater loss.'[30] In the light of this it seems reasonable to interpret the statement that Bernard is 'accustomed' to lend his counsel as a sly dig at his interference and rejection of Peter's 'counsel' on that occasion. At the same time, the concept of spiritual profit as salvation may have importance for what follows.

The *narratio* is couched in rhetorical terms, which border on the declamatory. A tricolon of conditional statements relating to the election set out the necessary requirements for validity, unanimity of electors, approval of episcopal overlord and peers, papal validation.[31] To all of these Peter returns a seemingly favourable response. It may be noted, however, that in each case the response is qualified by a phrase which indicates that the opinion is based on hearsay rather than personal knowledge.[32] It may also be remembered that according to Peter's account, these conditions had all been fulfilled in the case of the Cluniac bishop-elect challenged by Bernard.[33] That Peter has the Langres affair in mind may be suggested by his recommendation that Bernard 'subject his will' to the 'will of God'.[34] The same argument had been invoked by Bernard in a letter to Louis VII, after the deposition of the Cluniac candidate and the election of his kinsman and prior of Clairvaux, Godfrey of La Roche-Vanneau: 'But there is One who in a certain manner extorts the assent of those who are unwilling, and who, as He wishes, compels even the adverse wills of men to be subservient to His judgement.'[35] Seemingly directed against his own unwillingness to lose *baculus imbecillitatis meae*, 'the staff of my weakness', it had been followed by a warning to Louis not to set himself up against the will of God.[36]

---

[30] *Diliget ergo si monachus fuerit Lingonensis episcopus Cistercienses et ceteros monachos, quia diligendo maius sibi lucrum, non diligendo maius sentiet detrimentum* (letter 29, p. 104).

[31] *Si concors electio [quaeritur] ... si metropolitani et coepiscorum assensus ... si insuper domini papae voluntas ...* (letter 145, p. 360). The repeated use of *si* to preface what would otherwise be straightforward declarations of fact may be compared with Bernard's use of an open condition, neither confirming nor denying, in relation to the papal schism: 'if we have been sharers in the labour, we will be sharers also in the consolation' (ep. 147, 1, p. 350).

[32] *nec unus dissentire dicitur*, 'not one is said to dissent' (letter 145, p. 360); *ut comperi*, 'so I have learned' (ibid.); *ut audivi*, 'as I have heard' (ibid.).

[33] *Lingonenses canonici ... unum ex fratribus nostris, cum universo clero et populo ecclesiae suae, se in episcopum concorditer et canonice elegisse, Lugdunensi metropolitano id consulente et confirmante dixerunt*, 'the canons of Langres ... said that they had elected one of our brothers as bishop, harmoniously and canonically, with the entirety of the clergy and people of their Church, on the advice and confirmation of the archbishop of Lyons' (letter 29, p. 102). The only element missing from this, papal validation, is arguably replaced there by royal approval.

[34] *Quid ergo restat, vir venerande, nisi ut voluntati dei ... vestram subiiciatis ...?* (ibid.). The address *vir venerande*, 'venerable man', may recall Bernard's probably ironic *o bone vir*, 'O good man' found in the letter relating to schism (ep. 147, 1, p. 350).

[35] *Sed est qui nolentium quodammodo extorquet assensum, et suo arbitrio etiam adversas hominum voluntates, prout vult, subservire compellit* (Bernard, ep. 170, 1, *SBO*, VII, p. 383).

[36] *Sed acquiesco aliter disponenti, cum quo utique aut iudicibus, aut viribus contendere, nec cautum mihi omnino, nec possibile est, sed nec regi. Siquidem* terribilis *est etiam* apud reges terrae, 'But I acquiesce to One disposing otherwise, with whom it is neither prudent for me nor possible to contend in judgement or strength, nor even for a king. Indeed, He is *terrible among the kings of the earth*' (ibid., 2, p. 384 = Ps 75. 13).

The remaining necessary condition, merit of the candidate, has already been demonstrated at greater length and with considerable rhetorical flourishing. Again Peter may seem to distance himself from personal knowledge. Instead, the totality of merit is made to depend, through a quintet of synonymous phrases expressed through the standard tropes applied to 'conversion', on his rejection of worldly pleasures in favour of poverty and self-denial, that is, becoming a monk at Clairvaux.[37] The injunction of Christ alluded to here, 'If anyone wishes to follow after me, let him deny himself and lift up his cross and follow me',[38] was at the heart of the monastic ideal.[39] In the present situation, however, such praise may acquire ironic overtones. Letters of conversion to the monastic way of life frequently dwell on the futility and vanity of ecclesiastical pomp.[40] Henry is said to have 'exchanged' the world for the cloister. The Biblical injunction to take up one's cross is followed there by the warning: 'For what does it profit a man, if he should acquire the whole world, but suffer the loss of his soul? Or what exchange will a man give for his soul?'[41] The allusion may have further ramifications here. It is preceded in the Gospels by a rebuke to St Peter for attempting to avert Christ's prophesy of persecution, death and final resurrection, 'Get thee behind me, Satan.'[42] On one level, this might be thought applicable to the role Peter the Venerable is being asked to play, that of endorsing the election and its consequences for Henry's spiritual well-being. At another, it might perhaps be seen as hinting that Bernard himself has exchanged the role of Christ for that of Satan.

The explanation hypothesised for Bernard's hesitation, lack of confidence in Henry's *scientia*, 'skill' because he has not yet been 'proved', may also be more pointed than it first appears.[43] According to Constable, before his entry into

---

[37]   *Quomodo enim non magnum est, cum de tanto tantillum se fecerit, cum regii sanguinis ut sic loquar superbiam, tam robustae humilitatis pede calcaverit, cum luxus et pleno cornu fluentes mundi delicias, tormentis innumeris et mille mortibus commutaverit, cum undique arridentem mundum irriserit, cum* abnegans semetipsum et tollens crucem suam *Christum morientem* secutus fuerit? (letter 145, p. 360 = Mt 16. 24).

[38]   *si quis vult post me venire abneget semet ipsum et tollat crucem suam et sequatur me* (Mt 16. 24).

[39]   *Haec (paupertas et humilitas) in Christo tuo cuius crucem portas, cuius sepulcrum inhabitas, cuius in te resurrectionem exspectas, specialiter effulserunt ...,* 'These (poverty and humility) shone out especially in your Christ, whose cross you bear, whose tomb you inhabit, whose resurrection you await for yourself ...' (Peter, letter 20 to 'the hermit Gilbert', *Letters*, I, p. 34).

[40]   *Quod utique de Iohanne baptista filio sacerdotis Zachariae (aevangelium) dicens, ostendit eum in ordine vicis suae more patrio et sacerdotium habere potuisse, et illud tamen cum fastu, luxu, et deliciis, vilitate, ieuniis, solitudine commutasse,* 'Saying this about John the Baptist, son of the priest Zacharias, it (the Gospel) shows that he could have held the priesthood in the order of his turn by right of his father, but that he exchanged it, with its haughtiness, luxury and delights, for worthlessness, fasting and solitude' (Peter, letter 86 to Hato of Troyes, *Letters*, I, p. 225). See Dom J. Leclercq, 'Lettres de vocation à la vie monastique', *Studia Anselmiana* 37, Analecta Monastica III, Rome, 1955, 169–97.

[41]   *Quid enim prodest homini si mundum universum lucretur animae vero suae detrimentum patiatur aut quam dabit homo commutationem pro anima sua* (Mt 16. 26).

[42]   *Qui (Iesus) conversus dixit Petro vade post me Satana* (Mt 16. 23).

[43]   *Quod si de scientia veluti minus talia experti diffiditis, potens est deus qui ei iam dedit magna etiam praestare maiora,* 'But if you lack confidence in his skill, as one who is less

Clairvaux, Henry had held multiple royal appointments, as abbot of Notre-Dame at Poissy, St Mellon at Pontoise, St Denis de la Châtre, St Spire at Corbeil, Notre-Dame at Étampes. He had also been treasurer of St Martin at Tours, archdeacon of Beauce in Orléans and possibly of Notre-Dame at Paris.[44] On the other hand, in terms of the cloister he could indeed be presented as unproved, having entered Clairvaux at most three years previously. Bernard himself, in another context, shows an awareness of the scandal which might be provoked by an untimely promotion. In his letter relating to the disputed election at Grenoble, as discussed in a previous chapter, Bernard posits newness of monastic conversion as a possible reason for the rejection by Eugenius III of Noel, Carthusian bishop-elect: 'Fearing indeed, in my judgement, the tongues of detractors, he (the lord Pope) forbade the hurried promotion of a new hermit, in case.. a slanderous tongue might be able to say that this was the fruit of hermitage for which he had always hoped.'[45]

The concluding exhortation appears to reinforce the earlier demand that Bernard 'subdue his will to the will of God'. The adjuration, 'speedily ... fulfil their so long held desire.. for the sake of Him *who fulfils the desire* of His own *in good things*, because so it is righteous' may combine two biblical allusions.[46] In the light of Peter's earlier laudation of Henry's withdrawal to the cloister, the first of these, drawn from the Psalms,[47] may acquire a certain ambiguity. The additional statement, 'because so it is righteous', may point towards a New Testament injunction, 'Masters, perform what is righteous and fair to your servants, knowing that you also have a Master in heaven.'[48] The appearance in this citation of *praestare*, to 'perform', 'discharge', may add another nuance to the earlier assurance, 'powerful is God, who has given great things to him already, to perform even greater'.[49] In view of Henry's previous royal appointments, it seems permissible to speculate that Peter is insinuating that in this matter Bernard is following the will not of God but of Louis VII. Such an insinuation might be thought to acquire particular irony from the fact that in the case of Langres it had been Louis who had been threatened with divine displeasure if he refused to confirm the Cistercian candidate.

Lang, displaying an unwonted scepticism as regards Bernard's motives, raises the possibility that the request may have been intended to elicit a letter of

---

proved in such matters, powerful is God, who has given great things to him already, to give even greater' (letter 145, p. 361). It may be noted that *praestare* can also connote to 'lend' and to 'stand surety for.'

[44] Constable, *Letters*, II, p. 196.

[45] *Veritus quippe, ut aestimo, linguas obtrectarorum, vetuit (dominus Papa) festinatam novi eremitae promotionem, ne ... lingua maliloqua dicere posset hunc esse, quem semper optaverat, eremi fructum* (Bernard, ep. 250, 2, *SBO*, VIII, p. 146). On this letter, see Chapter 7.

[46] *tam diuturnum desiderium eorum ... causa eius* qui replet in bonis desiderium *suorum, celeriter quia sic iustum est adimplete* (letter 145, p. 146).

[47] *qui (Dominus) replet in bonis desiderium tuum ...*, 'who (the Lord) fulfils your desire in good things ...' (Ps 102. 3).

[48] *Domini quod iustum est et aequum servis praestate scientes quoniam et vos Dominum habetis in caelo* (Col 4. 1).

[49] *potens est deus qui ei iam magna dedit etiam praestare maiora* (letter 145, p. 361).

recommendation.[50] Piazzoni, while taking a more positive view of Peter's reply, similarly suggests that Bernard already knew Peter to be favourably disposed.[51] The evidence for this, as the latter implies, comes from a brief letter from Nicholas, dated by Constable to late 1149/early 1150:[52] 'Your Sublimity should know that your letter contributed much to the advancement of brother Henry, and was most willingly listened to by the archbishops and bishops of France ...'[53] The reference in Peter's own letter to the imminent arrival of 'the great personages of your parts ...',[54] might also be read as dropping a hint in this direction.[55] At the same time, it may be noticed that Henry's appointment appears to have led to difficulties, as acknowledged by Bernard in a subsequent letter to Hugh, cardinal-bishop of Ostia, where he seemingly dissociates himself from any capacity to intervene.[56] The dry irony diagnosed above does not, however, constitute evidence that Peter actually disapproved of the election or of the candidate. Rather, it can be related to the previous occurrences at Langres. In addition, the circumstantial association of this letter with Peter's overtures relating to monastic relations might also suggest a veiled reproach on his part that Bernard would be better occupied in focusing on this rather than on matters of external politics.

The lurking presence of such a reproach may seem to become more manifest in the letters on both sides concerning the launching of a new crusade. As stated previously, Bernard's ep. 364 dates to the spring of 1150. The Second Crusade, launched with high hopes at Vézelay on 31 March 1146, had ended with disastrous defeats in Asia Minor, and an ignominious withdrawal from Damascus. Bernard had figured in contemporary accounts as a driving force for its inception.[57] Not

---

[50]   Lang, 'The friendship', pp. 42–4. According to Bredero, the request was designed to prevent 'incidents' and 'misunderstandings' (Bredero, *Bernard of Clairvaux*, pp. 238–9, n. 93).

[51]   Piazzoni, 'Un falso problema', p. 472, n. 119.

[52]   Constable, *Letters*, II, p. 202. This letter appears as letter 153 in Peter's collection.

[53]   *Illud autem non lateat sublimitatem vestram, quia litterae vestrae multum addiderunt promotioni fratris Henrici, et libentissime auditae sunt, ab archiepiscopis et episcopis Franciae* ... (letter 153, *Letters*, I, p. 373).

[54]   *cum ad vos magnae partium vestrarum personae ... venerint* ... (letter 145, p. 361).

[55]   Peter's letter-collection preserves an elaborately worded reply from Henry himself. The latter seemingly reproaches Peter for his intervention, but ends with the request to be associated with Cluny *specialis et uterinus monachus, ne dicam episcopus*, 'as an intimate monk, son of one mother, let me not say bishop' (letter 146, *Letters*, I, p. 362).

[56]   *Sui iuris (dominus Belvacensis) est: iam non est in mea potestate, sed in civitate vita eius et conversatio. Si secus quam debet, vel decet, interdum agit, dolere possum; sed emendare, prout volo, non valeo*, 'He (the lord bishop of Beauvais) is his own master: he is not now subject to my control, but his life and conduct is in the diocese. If he sometimes acts other than he should, or than is fitting, I can grieve; but I cannot correct, as I (would) wish' (Bernard, ep. 307, 1, *SBO*, VIII, p. 226). For the identification, see Leclercq, ibid., p. 226, n. 11.

[57]   The classic account of Bernard's involvement is that of Seguin (A. Seguin, 'Bernard et la seconde Croisade', in *Bernard de Clairvaux*, Commission d'histoire de l'ordre de Cîteaux 3, Paris, 1953, 379–409). More recently, the sources have been re-examined by Rowe (J. G. Rowe, 'The origins of the Second Crusade: Pope Eugenius III, Bernard of Clairvaux and Louis VII of France, in *The Second Crusade and the Cistercians*, ed. M. Gervers, New York, 1992, pp. 79–89) and Ferzoco (G. Ferzoco, 'The origin of the Second Crusade', ibid., pp. 91–9).

surprisingly, he seems also to have borne the brunt of the criticism for its failure.[58] None-the-less, together with Suger, abbot of St Denis,[59] he was to play a prominent part in the attempt to organise a new crusade in 1150, after the death in battle of Raymond of Antioch and the ensuing siege of Antioch itself. An initial meeting held at Laon in April 1150, attended by Louis VII, bishops, archbishops and leading nobles, was followed by the convening of an assembly at Chartres, to be held on 8 May.[60] Letters from both Suger and Bernard requesting the presence of Peter at this assembly appear in Peter's letter-collection, together with his reply to each.[61] In both cases Peter excuses himself from attending, on the grounds of ill-health and a prior commitment. In the light of the previous correspondence, however, the exchange with Bernard can be seen to contain certain features on both sides which render it more pointed and may cast doubt on its seemingly harmonious nature.

> To the most beloved father Peter, by the grace of God abbot of Cluny, brother Bernard of Clairvaux: greetings, and what prayers he can in the Lord.
>
> I think that the exceedingly heavy and wretched groan of the Eastern Church has reached your ears, or rather, even the inmost chambers of your heart. It is fitting indeed that in accordance with your magnitude you should display great sympathy of compassion for the same, your mother and the mother of all the faithful, especially when she is so vehemently afflicted, so gravely in danger. It is fitting, I say, that zeal for the house of God should devour you the more, the greater the place that you hold in it by His authority. But if we harden our entrails, if we make our hearts obdurate, if we esteem this wound lightly, and do not grieve over calamity, where is our charity to God, where is our love for our neighbours? Rather, if we do not strive with all the solicitude we can to apply some counsel and remedy to such great evils and such great dangers, how are we not convicted of ingratitude towards Him who hides us on the day of evils in his tabernacle, more justly and vigorously to be punished from there, inasmuch as negligent both of divine glory and brotherly safety? I have considered that these matters should be suggested to you, both in confidence and in familiarity, on account namely of the grace with which your Excellence dignifies my unworthiness.
>
> For our fathers, the bishops of France, together with the lord King and the great men of the realm, are to come on the third Sunday after Easter to Chartres, and to discuss concerning these tidings: would that we may deserve to have your presence there. For

---

[58] See G. Constable, 'The Second Crusade as seen by contemporaries', *Traditio* 9 (1953), 213–79, pp. 266–7; E. Siberry, *Criticism of crusading 1095–1274*, Oxford, 1985, esp. pp. 78 and 191.

[59] Suger (1081–1151), abbot of St Denis, a leading royal abbey north of Paris, from 1122 until his death, also acted as counsellor to Louis VI and Louis VII. Best known for his architectural innovations, his policy of expanding St Denis brought him into conflict with the institution of Argenteuil, now home to Heloise, and led to her removal, together with her fellow-nuns, to Abelard's Paraclete.

[60] See Berry, 'Peter the Venerable and the Crusades', pp. 159–62; B. Bolton, 'The Cistercians and the aftermath of the Second Crusade' in *The Second Crusade and the Cistercians*, ed. M. Gervers, New York, 1992, pp. 131–40; J. Phillips, *Defenders of the Holy Land*, Oxford, 1996, pp. 100–18.

[61] Suger, ep. 18 (*Oeuvres complètes de Suger*, ed. A. Lecoy de la Marche, Société de l'histoire de la France, Paris, 1867, pp. 268–9) = letter 165 (*Letters*, I, pp. 398–9). Peter's reply is letter 166 (ibid., pp. 399–400).

since it is agreed that this cause needs the great counsels of great men of all kinds, you will offer an obedience pleasing indeed to God, if you do not consider His business alien to you, but prove the zeal of your charity in opportune times, in tribulation. For you know, dearest father, you know, that a friend is proved in necessity. I am confident, indeed, that your presence will offer a great increase to this cause, both by reason of the authority of the holy church of Cluny, of which by the disposition of God you are in charge, and especially in accordance with the wisdom and grace which He himself has bestowed on you, for the advantage namely of (your) neighbours, and His honour. May He now think fit to inspire you, that you may not regard it as a burden to come and to bestow your greatly desired presence on His servants, to be gathered in His name, and for the zeal of His name.

The letter is cast in terms of a formal summons, the language declamatory.[62] Certain aspects of the rhetoric find parallels elsewhere. The evocation of the 'groan' of the Eastern Church[63] can be matched from an earlier letter to Suger, where it is said to 'cry out.. wretchedly'.[64] A letter to Eugenius written after the assembly at Chartres has a similarly arresting opening.[65] Both these letters present tepidity in terms of disloyalty to the Church,[66] while the letter to Eugenius heavily exploits the notion of 'zeal'.[67] In the letter to Peter, however, the call for zeal and friendship is doubled by a stress on the notions of 'charity' and 'neighbourliness'. In addition, the surrounding language seems to contain echoes of earlier word-

---

[62]   It may be noted that Suger's letter, while couched in equally formal terms, concludes, unlike Bernard's, with an approach that combines summons with appeal: *celsitudinem vestram.. interesse et invitamus et summonemus, et suppliciter efflagitamus*, 'we invite and summon and in supplication ask urgently that your Highness ... be present ...' (Suger, ep. 18, p. 269).

[63]   *Gravem nimis ac miserabilem Orientalis Ecclesiae gemitum ad aures vestras ... arbitror pervenisse*, 'I think that the exceedingly heavy and wretched groan of the Eastern Church has reached your ears ...' (ep. 364, 1, p. 318). The addition here of *ad ipsa etiam penetralia cordis*, 'even the inmost chambers of your heart', may point back towards Peter's evocation of the heart as *cubiculum caritatis*, the 'dwelling-place of charity', in letter 111 and again, by implication in letter 150. See Chapter 8.

[64]   *Ipsa enim iam Orientalis Ecclesia (tam) miserabiliter clamat ...*, 'For the Eastern Church itself cries out (so) wretchedly ...'(Bernard, ep. 380, *SBO*, VIII, p. 344). This brief letter, excusing Bernard from attendance at an earlier meeting, is dated by Phillips to early 1150 (Phillips, *Defenders*, p. 106).

[65]   *Non est leve verbum quod sonuit: triste satis et grave est*, 'It is no light tidings which have sounded: they are sad enough and grave' (Bernard, ep. 256, 1, *SBO*, VIII, p. 163).

[66]   *(ut) quisquis non toto compatitur affectu, Ecclesiae filius non esse probetur*, '(so that) whoever is not totally held by compassion is proved to be no son of the Church' (ep. 380, p. 344); *Tu ergo, amice Sponsi, amicum te in necessitate probato*, 'You, therefore, friend of the Spouse, do you prove yourself a friend in need' (ep. 256, 3, p. 164).

[67]   *Cuius locum (Petri) tenetis, zelum neglegere non debetis*, 'You must not neglect the zeal of him whose place (St Peter's) you hold' (ep. 256, 2, p. 164). Cf. *Bene fecistis iustissimum zelum nostrae Gallicanae Ecclesiae collaudando et corroborando ...*, 'You have done well, praising and strengthening the most righteous zeal of our Church in France ...' (ibid., 1, p. 163); *(sed) quicquid habes virium, quicquid zeli, quicquid sollicitudinis, quicquid potestatis, impendes*, 'you will expend whatever strength, whatever zeal, whatever sollicitude, whatever power you have' (ibid., 3, p. 164).

play. The repetition of *dignum*, 'it is fitting',[68] may recall earlier exploitations of *dignatio*, 'condescension'.[69] In each case, it is accompanied by play on the notion of superiority of status,[70] paving the way for a familiar opposition, between Bernard's 'humility' and Peter's 'grandeur', as Bernard justifies his temerity 'on account ... of the grace with which your Excellence dignifies my unworthiness'.[71] The use of *gratia*, hovering between 'grace' and 'friendship', may recall its ambiguous appearances elsewhere, as discussed in relation to letter 145. Here it is prefigured by *ingratus*, conveying the sense of 'ingratitude' towards God,[72] and followed by a reminder that God is the source of 'grace',[73] thus setting up a demand for reciprocity.

In the letter to Peter, the idea of tepidity is specifically linked both with loss of salvation and with failure in *caritas*. A triad of hypothetical clauses, representing hardness of heart, draws on Jeremiah: 'if we harden our entrails, if we make our hearts obdurate, if we esteem this blow lightly and do not grieve *over calamity ...*'[74] In the original, this runs, 'I have been destroyed and afflicted over the calamity of the daughter of my people and numbness has taken hold of me.'[75] It is preceded there by the statement: 'The harvest has passed, the summer is finished and we have not been saved.'[76] Bernard's triad culminates in a double question: 'where is our charity towards God, where is our love for (our) neighbours?'[77] In what follows, the threat to salvation is spelled out clearly, in a doublet equating love of God with

---

[68]   *Dignum quippe est ... dignum, inquam ...* (ep. 364, 1, p. 318).

[69]   *Alioquin, quando hoc ipsum auderet nostra pusillitas, nisi daret ad dignitatem accessum vestrae dignationis humilitas?*, 'Otherwise, when would my littleness dare this, if the humility of your condescension did not grant access to grandeur?' (Bernard, ep. 148, p. 352); *Nam suspectum id mihi facit vestra ipsa tam subita et inopinata dignatio*, 'For your so sudden and unexpected condescension makes it suspect to me' (idem, ep. 228, 1, p. 98).

[70]   *Dignum ... est ut* secundum magnitudinem *vestram, magnum exhibeatis ... compassionis affectum ...*, 'It is fitting that in accordance with your magnitude you should display great ... sympathy of compassion ...' (ep. 364, 1 = Nm 14. 19); *Dignum ... ut tanto amplius comedat vos zelus ... quanto ampliorem in ea (domo Dei) locum ... tenetis ...*, 'It is fitting.. that zeal should devour you the more.. the greater the place that you hold in it (the house of God)' (ep. 364, 1, p. 318). The phrase *secundum magnitudinem vestram* may hint at another equation of Peter with God. The original runs: *Dimitte obsecro peccatum populi tui huius secundum magnitudinem misericordiae tuae*, 'Dismiss, I beseech you, the sin of your people according to the magnitude of your mercy' (Nm 14. 19).

[71]   *ob gratiam utique qua nostram indignitatem excellentia vestra dignatur* (ep. 364, 1, p. 319).

[72]   *quomodo non ingrati esse convincimur ...?*, 'how are we not convicted of ingratitude ...?' (ibid., p. 318).

[73]   *tum maxime pro sapientia et gratia quam vobis ipse donavit*, 'and especially in accordance with the wisdom and grace which He himself has bestowed upon you' (ibid., 2, p. 319).

[74]   *si duramus viscera, si obduramus corda, si plagam hanc parvipendimus, nec dolemus* super contritione ...' (ep. 364, 1 = Ier 8. 21).

[75]   *Super contritionem filiae populi mei contritus sum et contristatus stupor obtinuit me* (Ier 8. 21).

[76]   *Transiit messis finita est aestas et nos salvati non sumus* (ibid., 8. 20).

[77]   *ubi nostra in Deum caritas, ubi dilectio proximorum?* (ep. 364, 1, p. 318).

fraternal affection: 'more justly and vigorously to be punished ... inasmuch as negligent of both divine glory and brotherly safety'.[78] Subsequently, charity is attached to zeal, in a promise which picks up the notion of 'grace' and which can be seen as counterbalancing the previous threat: 'you will offer an obedience pleasing indeed to God, if ... you prove the zeal of your charity ...'[79]

Bernard's demand for intervention in the Holy Land is grafted on to the 'new' commandments, 'Love God',[80] and 'Love your neighbour as yourself.'[81] The implications are driven home by the glimpse of an opposition between near/far, own/other. Finding salvation is made dependent upon a second condition, 'if you do not consider His business alien to you'.[82] *Alienus*, 'other', 'another's', sets up an implicit contrast with *proprius*, 'own'. Explicitly, however, it is set against *proximus*, 'nearest', 'neighbour', used both in the phrase seen above, and again towards the end of the letter, where Peter's wisdom and grace are said to have been bestowed *ad utilitatem ... proximorum*, 'for the advantage ... of neighbours'. The significance of its repetition here may lie in its biblical associations. In Luke, the command 'love your neighbour as yourself' is shown as the way to achieve 'eternal life'.[83] Followed by the question, 'Who is my neighbour?',[84] the answer is supplied there through the parable of the Good Samaritan, namely, a 'stranger' and a 'foreigner'.[85] Peter's letters had restricted the demand for *caritas*, together with the threat of loss of salvation consequent upon its failure, to relations between Cistercians and Cluniacs. Bernard's use of it here can be seen to encompass a far wider reach, the totality of Eastern Christendom.

In terms of the correspondence, the opposition own/other had first been introduced by Peter in the context of papal schism. Letter 65 had set 'the causes of strangers' against the 'business of your own'.[86] Ep. 147, Bernard's reply, had stressed the need to prove oneself a 'friend' to the Church.[87] The reminder here that

---

[78] *iustius ... et vehementius puniendi, utpote tam divinae gloriae quam fraternae salutis neglegentes* (ibid.). *Salus* connotes both 'safety' and 'salvation'.
[79] *gratum profecto obsequium praestabitis Deo, si ... caritatis vestrae zelum probaveritis ...* (ibid., 2, p. 319). In letter 111, Peter had also played on the notion of 'zeal'. The Cistercians had seemingly been praised for their eagerness to reform 'tepidity'. At the same time, there had also been a warning against *zelus contrarius*, 'contrary zeal', hostile to *caritas* (letter 111, p. 293).
[80] *et diliges Dominum Deum tuum* ... (Mc 12. 30; Lc 10. 27).
[81] *diliges proximum tuum tamquam te ipsum* (Mc 12. 31; Lc 10. 27).
[82] *si negotium eius a vobis non duxeritis alienum* ... (ep. 364, 2, p. 319).
[83] *Magister quid faciendo vitam aeternam possidebo?*, 'Master, by doing what shall I possess eternal life?' (Lc 10. 25).
[84] *Et quis est meus proximus?* (ibid., 10. 29).
[85] Ibid., 10. 30–37.
[86] *quoniam qui alienorum causis assistis, tuorum negotiis desse non poteris*, 'since you, who assist the causes of strangers, will not be able to fail the business of your own' (letter 65, p. 195).
[87] *Collaborandum fuit et compatiendum matri, ne et de nobis quereretur, dicens:* Qui iuxta me erant de longe steterunt, et vim faciebant qui quaerebant animam meam, 'It was needful to work together and to take compassion on the Mother, lest she complain of us also, saying: *Those who were near me stood far off, and those who were seeking my life did violence*' (ep. 147, 1 = Ps 37. 12–13).

'a friend is proved in need'[88] seems to draw on the Old Testament maxim that 'a friend will not be recognised in good times, nor an enemy be hidden in bad'.[89] Two further Biblical allusions may present an extension of the opposition. In the New Testament, 'zeal for the house of the Lord' is applied to the action of Christ driving the money-changers out of the Temple.[90] Here, by extension, it may be seen as an injunction to drive the infidels out of the holy places. The expression originates, however, in Psalms, where it is followed by the words, 'the reproaches of those upbraiding you have fallen upon me',[91] and preceded by the verse, 'I am made a stranger to my brothers and a foreigner to the sons of my mother'.[92] The encouragement to offer an 'obedience pleasing to God' seems, as Leclercq suggests,[93] to be modelled on a warning in John: 'I have said this so that you may not be driven to sin. They will make you outside the synagogues. But there comes an hour when everyone who kills you would think that he offers a service to God.'[94] The motif of alienation and persecution lends itself to reading at several levels. Bernard can claim to have 'suffered' already on behalf of the Church. It may seem that Peter is being called upon to do the same. At a further remove, it might also suggest that if Cluniacs wish to be accepted by Cistercians as 'uterine brothers', they must show themselves worthy followers of Christ.

The sub-text contained in Bernard's letter can, accordingly, be construed as a challenge, that Peter first display in concrete terms the *caritas* which he is constantly demanding from Bernard. At first sight, Peter's refusal of the invitation appears unexceptionable. A comparison of letter 164 with letter 166, his answer to Suger on the same subject, shows the same two basic elements, a profession of Christian outrage,[95] and an apology for absence, based on illness and a pre-arranged

---

[88]   *Nostis ... quoniam amicus in necessitate probatur* (ep. 364, 2, p. 319).

[89]   *Non agnoscetur in bonis amicus et non abscondetur in malis inimicus* (Sir 12. 8). The connection is pointed up by the preceding challenge to Peter to prove his zeal *in opportunitatibus, in tribulatione*, 'in opportune times, in tribulation' (Ps 9. 10).

[90]   *Recordati vero sunt discipuli eius quia scriptum est zelus domus tuae comedit me*, 'His disciples indeed remembered that it was written "zeal for your house devours me" ' (Io 2. 17).

[91]   *(quoniam) zelus domus tuae comedit me et opprobria exprobantium tibi ceciderunt super me* (Ps 68. 10).

[92]   *Extraneus factus sum fratribus meis et peregrinus filiis matris meae*. (ibid., 68. 9).

[93]   Leclercq, *SBO*, VIII, p. 319, n. 7.

[94]   *Haec locutus sum vobis ut non scandalizemini absque synagogis facient vos sed venit hora ut omnis qui interficit vos arbitretur obsequium se praestare Deo* (Io 16. 1–2).

[95]   *Nonne [res quae agitur] maxima omnium est, providere, satagere, ne* sanctum *detur* canibus, *ne loca in quibus* steterunt pedes *operantis* salutem in medio terrae *rursum pedibus iniquorum proterantur, ne regia Iherusalem a prophetis, ab apostolis, ab ipso omnium salvatore dedicata, ne nobilis illa totius Syriae metropolis Antiochia, iterum blasphemis et nefandis hominibus subiiciantur, ne ipsa salutaris crux iam ab impiis ut dicitur obsessa, ut olim a Cosrohe capiatur, ne ipsum* sepulchrum *domini, quod hactenus iuxta prophetam* gloriosum *toto in orbe fuerat, fortassis ut illi minari solent radicitus avellatur?*, 'Surely [the matter in question] is greatest of all, to take thought, to strive, that *what is holy* be not given *to the dogs*, that the places in which *stood the feet* of the one working *salvation in the midst of the earth* be not again trampled by the feet of the ungodly, that royal Jerusalem, consecrated by the prophets, by the apostles, by the saviour of all himself, that noble Antioch,

214 The Correspondence between Peter the Venerable and Bernard of Clairvaux

meeting at Cluny.[96] The extended length and rhetorical elaboration of letter 164 can be partly explained in terms of epistolary etiquette, that is, of suiting letter to recipient. At the same time, however, it may be possible to glimpse a sub-text which can be seen both as deflecting the challenge from Bernard and as mounting a challenge of its own. Letter 164 starts with an allusion to Bernard's repetition of *dignum*. His letter is said to have moved Peter much, *ut dignum erat*, 'as was fitting'.[97] Bernard's threefold condition, representing the inappropriate reaction of 'hard-heartedness', and culminating in a double question, invoking love of God and love of neighbour, is answered by a triplet of rhetorical questions, which further develop the notion of affect. 'What Christian', asks Peter, 'would not be moved ...?': by 'so lamentable a report' that the Templars, the king of Jerusalem, the Holy Cross, have been besieged in the city of Antioch;[98] that the Holy Land, recently saved from the 'yoke of impiety' again risks subjection 'to the impious and blasphemers';[99] that 'so health-giving a way of penitent sinners' may be closed off by an 'obstructing barrier of vile Saracens'.[100]

---

that metropolis of all Syria, be not again subjected to blasphemous and evil men, that the salvation-bearing cross itself, besieged already as it is said by the impious, be not captured, as once by Chosroes, that the very *sepulchre* of the Lord, which up to now, in accordance with the prophet, had been *glorious* in all the world, be not perhaps, as they are wont to threaten, torn from its roots?' (Peter, letter 166, pp. 399-400 = Mt 7. 6; Ps 131. 7; Ps 73. 12; Is 11. 10). This passage is cited by Phillips as being among the 'strongest expressions' of concern for the fate of the holy places in the East (Phillips, *Defenders*, pp. 106–7). I am endebted to Professor Malcolm Barber for an elucidation of the allusion to Chosroes: a Persian ruler in the time of Heraclius, he captured Jerusalem in 614 and is said to have carried off the Holy Cross, which was subsequently recovered and re-established in 630.

[96] *Quae iter hoc meum impediunt, multa sunt. Sed inter alia, specialia duo sunt. Unum, multiplex incommodum corporis mei ... Aliud, conventus magnus priorum, quos antequam de istis quae mandastis aliquid scirem ... Cluniacum ea die qua conventus vester apud Carnotum indictus est, venire praeceperam*, 'As to the matters which hinder my journey, they are many. But among the rest, there are two in particular. One, the manifold ailments of my body ... The other, a great assembly of priors, whom, before I knew anything of the matters which you have announced.. I had commanded to come to Cluny on that day on which your assembly has been fixed at Chartres' (letter 166, p. 400).

[97] *Litterae quas mihi sanctitas vestra misit ... moverunt me, et multum ut dignum erat moverunt*, 'The letter which your Sanctity sent to me ... moved me, and moved me much, as was fitting' (letter 164, p. 397).

[98] *Quem ... Christianum.. fama tam lamentabilis non moveret, qua.. divulgatum est, Fratres Templi, regem Iherosolimitanum, ipsam ... dominicam ac salvatricem crucem, in urbe Antiochena ... obsessos ...?* 'What.. Christian.. would not be moved by so lamentable a report, by which ... it has been spread abroad that the Brothers of the Temple, the King of Jerusalem, the very ... salvation-bringing cross of the Lord.. have been besieged in the city of Antioch?' (ibid.).

[99] *Quem non moveat ... ne ... terra illa sancta, a iugo impiorum.. ante non multum temporis eruta, rursum impiis et blasphemiis subdatur?* , 'Who would not be moved ... lest ... that holy land, plucked not long before from the yoke of the impious ... be subjected again to the impious and blasphemers?' (ibid.).

[100] *Quem non moveat, si tam salubris peccatorum paenitentium via.. nequam Sarracenorum obice obstante claudatur?*, 'Who would not be moved, if so health-giving a way of penitent sinners.. be closed off by an obstructing barrier of vile Saracens?' (ibid.).

Thus far Peter may be seen to have displayed a degree of Christian indignation which, if anything, outstrips that found in the letter from Bernard, so clearing himself of the charge of tepidity. What follows, however, reveals a certain ambiguity which may suggest that Peter is in less than full agreement as to the action which should be taken. Crucial to the structure of this letter are two images which seem to be borrowed from Bernard's invitation, those of 'wound'[101] and 'remedy'.[102] The first of these seemingly refers to events at Antioch, the second, as spelled out subsequently in the letter to Eugenius, to armed intervention. Peter develops each image in turn, at some length and in some detail: 'Be it absent, be it absent, I say, that heavenly anger so rage against His own Christians, against the *people of acquisition*, that to a wound newly inflicted, and still fresh, another wound be added, so piercing that by its magnitude it may seem to be now not cleansing but mortal.'[103] At first sight, the 'newly-inflicted wound' would appear to be that inflicted by the Saracen blockade. A closer look, however, suggests that Peter may be alluding to the disasters which befell the Second Crusade.[104] The failure seems to have been commonly explained in terms of divine punishment for human sin.[105] One late source records a sermon preached by Bernard in which the disaster was attributed in part to the arrogance of the Crusaders.[106] Although this account may be apocryphal, the issue of sin and punishment is briefly touched on in the second book of Bernard's *De consideratione*,[107] written, according to Bredero, in 1149.[108]

---

[101] *si plagam hanc parvipendimus* ..., 'if we esteem this wound lightly ...' (ep. 364, 1, p. 318).

[102] *si non satagimus ... consilium aliquod et remedium tantis malis tantisque periculis adhibere* ..., 'if we do not strive ... to apply some counsel and remedy to such great evils and such great dangers ...' (ibid.).

[103] *Absit, absit inquam quod adeo in Christianos suos, in* populum acquisitionis, *caelestis ira desaeviat, ut noviter inflicto, et adhuc calenti vulneri, tam acre denuo vulnus addatur, quod sui magnitudine iam non videatur esse purgatorium, sed peremptorium* (letter 164, p. 397 = I Pt 2. 9).

[104] This identification may be re-inforced by what immediately follows, where what has happened is presented as *tantum periculum, immo tanta clades populi Christiani*, 'so great a danger, or rather so great a disaster of the Christian people' (letter 164, p. 397).

[105] See Siberry, *Criticism of the crusaders*, p. 77 and n. 46; Bolton, 'The Cistercians and the aftermath', p. 135.

[106] G. Constable, 'A report of a lost sermon by St Bernard on the failure of the Second Crusade', in *Studies in Medieval Cistercian History presented to J. F. O'Sullivan*, Cistercian Studies Series 13, Spencer, Mass., 1971, pp. 49–54.

[107] *incidimus ... tempus grave ... cum Dominus scilicet, provocatus peccatis nostris, ante tempus quodammodo visus sit iudicasse orbem terrae, in aequitate quidem, sed misericordiae suae oblitus*, 'we have fallen upon ... a grave time ... since the Lord, provoked by our sins, has seemed in a certain manner to have judged the world before the appointed time, in justice indeed, but forgetful of his mercy' (Bernard of Clairvaux, *De consideratione ad Eugenium Papam*, II, 1. 1, in *Sancti Bernardi Opera*, ed. J. Leclercq, H. M. Rochais, 8 vol., III, Rome, 1963, 393–493, p. 410). This *apologia* goes on to hint at the possibility of a further crusade and presents Bernard as a 'shield' to deflect the 'poisoned darts' of the 'blasphemers'.

[108] Bredero, *Bernard of Clairvaux*, p. 148.

That Peter has this explanation in mind is suggested not only by his apotropaic evocation of *caelestis ira*, 'divine wrath', but also by the reference to *populus acquisitionis*, the 'people of acquisition'. Taken from I Peter, this phrase forms part of a string of apparently complimentary phrases that mark out the addressees as God's elect.[109] It is followed there, however, by an admonition: 'I beg you, dearest, to abstain as strangers and foreigners from the desires of the flesh which fight against the soul, keeping a good way of life among the Gentiles, so that whereas they detract from you as evil-doers, from looking upon (your) good works, they may glorify God on the day of visitation.'[110] Peter has already invoked divine aid as a potential force for protection. Those under siege are said to be doomed to capture, 'unless the hand of the Lord swiftly brings succour *with outstretched arm* ...'[111] The last phrase comes from an Old Testament context which promises both aid and justice. God will bring his people out of exile, but will weed out 'transgressors and the impious', and not allow them to reach 'the land of Israel'.[112] Serving as a reminder that divine rather than human intervention will save the day, it may also point to the need for repentance and contrition to avert further annihilation.[113]

Peter's presentation of a further wound as *acer*, 'piercing', 'sharp', *peremptorius*, 'mortal', 'deadly',[114] as opposed to *purgatorius*, 'cleansing', 'purgatorial', may reflect and invert an aspect of crusading propaganda. That these terms play on an oscillation between the physical and the spiritual is suggested by the preceding characterisation of pilgrimage as *salubris*, 'health-bringing', 'salvation-giving', the latter sense finding reinforcement in the statement that it has saved many 'from the dead', and restored them 'to heaven'.[115] The latter is qualified, however, by a potential restriction: *ut dignum est credere*, 'as it is fitting

---

[109] *Vos autem genus electum regale sacerdotium gens sancta populus acquisitionis ut virtutes adnuntietis eius qui de tenebris vos vocavit in admirabile lumen suum*, 'You indeed are a chosen people, a royal priesthood, a holy race, a people of acquisition, so that you may report His virtues who has called you from the darkness into His admirable light' (I Pt 2. 9).

[110] *Carissimi obsecro tamquam advenas et peregrinos abstinere vos a carnalibus desideriis quae militant adversus animam conversationem vestram inter gentes habentes bonam ut in eo quod detractant de vobis tamquam de malefactoribus ex bonis operibus considerantes glorificent Deum in die visitationis* (ibid., 2. 11–12).

[111] *(ac) nisi manus domini in brachio extento cito succurrat, omnes in brevi captandos*, '(and) all soon to be captured, unless the hand of the Lord swiftly brings succour *with outstretched arm*' (letter 164, p. 397 = Ez 20. 33; 34).

[112] *et eligam de vobis transgressores et impios.. et terram Israhel non ingredientur*, 'and I will weed out from you the transgressors and the impious.. and they will not enter the land of Israel' (Ez 20. 38).

[113] The idea of 'wound added to wound' may also draw upon Job: *Concidit me vulnere super vulnere ...*, 'He (God) destroys me with wound upon wound ...' (Iob 16. 15). It continues there, *Saccum consui super cutem meam et operui cinere cornu meum*, 'I have sewn sackcloth upon my skin and covered my strength with ashes' (ibid., 16. 16).

[114] Cf. *Ubi est mors stimulus tuus stimulus autem mortis peccatum est*, 'Where, death, is your sting? The sting of death is sin' (I Cor 15. 55–6).

[115] *tam salubris peccatorum paenitentium via, quae ut dignum est credere, innumera peregrinantium milia.. inferis abstulit, caelo restituit ...*, 'so health-bringing a way of penitent sinners, which, so it is fitting to believe, has snatched away countless thousands of pilgrims ... from the dead, restored to heaven ...' (letter 164, p. 397).

to believe'. In part this may reflect the reservations towards pilgrimage expressed by Peter elsewhere.[116] At the same time, the general tendency to blur crusading and pilgrimage may serve to give its presence here a sharper edge.[117] Ep. 363, Bernard's so-called circular letter of 1146 preaching the Second Crusade, had presented it as *remedium salutare*, a 'salvation-bringing remedy', sent by God to enable the purging of sins.[118] After its failure, Cistercian apologists continued to emphasise this aspect.[119] It may seem, accordingly, that Peter's reference here to a second wound, rather than simply anticipating a further onslaught from the Saracens, may conceal a warning relating to the launching of a new crusade.

The ambiguity introduced here in relation to the nature of the 'wound', hovering as it does between the physical and the spiritual, is pursued into the next section of the letter, where the issue of a 'remedy' is explored through an analogy between the human body and the Church which has its roots in various Pauline utterances.[120] The second image is introduced by bridging rhetoric, which transforms the notion of 'affect' into 'effect': 'He would not be truly to be counted among the limbs of the body of Christ, who would not be moved from the inmost entrails of the heart by so great a danger, or rather, disaster of the people of Christ. I do not say who would not be moved to feel compassion only, which is light for all, but to assist in accordance with his strength, and to undergo also what is heavy.'[121] This apparent declaration of willingness to undergo suffering can be seen as constituting a response to Bernard's demand that he put his *caritas* into practice. At the same time, the opposition

---

[116] *Maius est vero deo perpetuo in humilitate et paupertate servire, quam cum superbia et luxu Ihrosolimitanum iter conficere. Unde si bonum est Ihrusalem* ubi steterunt pedes *domini visitare, longe melius est, caelo ubi ipse* facie ad faciem *conspicitur, inhiare,* 'It is a greater thing to serve God uninterruptedly in humility and poverty, than to accomplish the journey to Jerusalem in pride and pomp. Therefore if it is good to visit Jerusalem *where the feet* of the Lord *stood*, it is far better to gape after heaven, where he himself is seen *face to face'* (Peter, letter 51, *Letters*, I, p. 152 = Ps 131. 7; I Cor 13. 12). See Iogna Prat, *Ordonner et exclure*, pp. 333–5.

[117] See Phillips, *Defenders*, pp. 73–99.

[118] *Miseratur enim populum suum Deus, et lapsis graviter providet remedium salutare,* 'For God takes pity on His people, and provides a salvation-giving remedy for those who are gravely fallen' (Bernard, ep. 363, 3, *SBO*, VIII, pp. 313); *Necessitatem se habere aut facit, aut simulat, ut militantibus sibi stipendia reddat, indulgentiam delictorum et gloriam sempiternam,* 'He either causes himself to have, or pretends to have need, so that he may render wages to those who serve him, the indulgence of sins and eternal glory' (ibid., 4, p. 314). On the textual history of this letter and the possible involvement of Nicholas in its drafting, see Dom J. Leclercq, 'L'encyclique de saint Bernard en faveur de la croisade', *Revue Bénédictine* 81 (1971), 282–308.

[119] John of Casamare, for example, lays claim in a letter to Bernard to visionary knowledge that the dead have been translated into the place of the fallen angels (John of Casamare, ep. 386, 3, *Sancti Bernardi opera omnia, Patrologia Latina*, 182, ed. D. J. Mabillon, J.-P. Migne, Paris, 1859, pp. 590–91.) See Siberry, *Criticism of crusading*, p. 78.

[120] Rm 12. 5; Eph 5. 30; I Cor 12. 27.

[121] *Non esset vere reputandus inter* membra corporis Christi, *quem ex intimis praecordiorum visceribus non moveret tantum periculum, immo tanta clades populi Christani. Non dico quem non moveret ad compatiendum tantum, quod omnibus leve est, sed ad subveniendum pro viribus, et ad subeundum etiam quicquid grave est* (letter 164, p. 397 = Rm 12. 4, 5).

between 'lightness' and 'heaviness' may seem to hark back to letter 150, which had levelled the accusation against 'certain' brothers that they followed what was 'heavy' but rejected what was 'light', namely, the requirements of *caritas*.[122]

What follows can be seen to focus on the question of the nature of the form this assistance is to take: 'For if in the human body, hand does not hesitate to assist hand, foot foot, any limb any limb, if it is wounded, and considers its wound not as another's but as its own, how much more in the sacred body of Christ, which is His Church, must brother run to and succour brother, neighbour neighbour, with all his force, with all his strength, above all in greater dangers?'[123] The *polyptoton* employed here, *manus manui, pes pedi, membrum quodlibet membro cuilibet*, seems, as Constable indicates, to recall the Old Testament demand of 'an eye for an eye'.[124] The choice of verbs, however, *subvenire, succurrere*, connoting both 'helping' and 'healing', may point towards the Pauline requirement for mutuality in suffering and joy,[125] thus conflating two potentially conflicting ideologies, the vengeful Jehovah of the Old Testament, and the compassionate Christ of the New. In similar vein, the threat of a new and 'deadly' wound is counterbalanced by a stress on spiritual rebirth and renewal, 'The one spirit, quickening all the limbs, does this in the human flesh, the one Holy Spirit, which quickens all its limbs, does the same in the body of the Church. He is not, therefore, quickened by the spirit of Christ, who does not feel the wounds of the body of Christ.'[126]

The language of 'quickening', 'restoring to life', *vivificare, vegetare*, may point towards a hidden Old Testament allusion, which evokes the annulling of divine wrath. God's promise of future mercy in Genesis is expressed in the words: 'I will remember my pact with you and with every living soul which quickens the flesh, and there will no further be the waters of the flood to destroy all flesh.'[127] Taken together, these two sections of Peter's letter can be seen to set physical 'wound' against spiritual 'wound', physical 'remedy' against spiritual 'remedy'. In his subsequent letter to Eugenius, Bernard will present the happenings in the Holy Land as a second crucifixion, recalling Peter's allusion to the 'wounds of Christ'.

---

[122] Letter 150, p. 367.

[123] *Si enim in corpore humano manus manui, pes pedi, membrum quodlibet membro cuilibet, si laesum fuerit subvenire non dissimulat, eiusque laesionem non alienam, sed propriam reputat, quanto magis in sacro corpore Christi, quod est eius ecclesia, toto nisu, tota virtute, frater fratri, proximus proximo, maxime in maioribus periculis, occurrere et succurrere debet?* (letter 164, p. 397 = Ex 21. 24, Dt 19. 21).

[124] *reddet animam pro anima oculum pro oculo dentem pro dente manum pro manu pedem pro pede adustionem pro adustione livorem pro livore*, 'he will give life for life, eye for eye, tooth for tooth, hand for hand, foot for foot, burning for burning, wound for wound' (Ex 21. 23–5; cf. Dt 19. 21).

[125] *Et si quid patitur unum membrum compatiuntur omnia membra sive gloriatur unum membrum congaudent omnia membra*, 'If one limb suffers, all the limbs share the suffering; if one rejoices, all rejoice' (I Cor 12. 26).

[126] *Facit hoc in carne humana, unus universa membra vivificans spiritus, facit hoc idem in corpore ecclesiae, unus qui eius universa membra vivificat spiritus sanctus. Non ergo vegetatur spiritu Christi, qui non sentit vulnera corporis Christi* (letter 164, p. 397).

[127] *Et recordabor foederis mei vobiscum et cum omni anima vivente quae carnem vegetat et non erunt ultra aquae diluvii ad delendam universam carnem* (Gn 9. 15).

Bernard's 'remedy' will call for violence, the unsheathing of both spiritual and temporal 'sword'.[128] Peter's words, on the contrary, lend themselves to construing as a reminder of the priority of searching for and applying a spiritual remedy, the purging out of sin, for a spiritual wound, the loss of salvation threatened by the wrath of God. Once again, as in letter 65, they may seem to represent a setting of pastoral responsibility against political involvement, a notion which may find confirmation in the wording of the subsequent excuse. Further echoes from previous letters can be seen to support the view that Peter is both acknowledging and countering Bernard's challenge. Letter 29 relating to Langres had overtly invoked the Pauline *dictum* 'when *one limb* suffers, *all the limbs* suffer', in a context which called upon Cistercians to support Cluniacs against clerical 'violence'.[129] In the salutation of this letter, Bernard's role as spiritual leader is invoked through his appellation as 'the venerable and outstandingly bright lamp of the Church of God, to be embraced in all the might of charity'.[130] The luminary metaphor had first appeared in letter 111, where Bernard had been portrayed as a 'shining star', bestowed by divine providence as a light for monks and Latin Church alike.[131] There, the complimentary language had functioned essentially as a

---

[128] *Exserendus est nunc uterque gladius in passione Domini, Christo denuo patiente, ubi et altera vice passus est*, 'Both swords must now be drawn in the passion of the Lord, with Christ suffering afresh, where he suffered in another turn' (Bernard, ep. 256, 1, p. 163). See Bredero, *Bernard of Clairvaux*, pp. 145–59. On the doctrine of the two swords, symbolising spiritual and secular power, see also B. Jacqueline, *Épiscopat et papauté chez saint Bernard de Clairvaux*, Sainte-Marguerite d'Elle, 1975, pp. 119–24. As Iogna-Prat points out (Iogna-Prat, *Ordonner et exclure*, p. 333), in a subsequent letter to Bernard Peter will seemingly repudiate this doctrine, by setting the 'sword of the king' against the 'rod of the shepherd' (Peter, letter 192, p. 446). This letter will be discussed in Chapter 11.

[129] *(quia) cum dolet* unum membrum, *condolent* omnia membra (letter 29, p. 103 = I Cor 12. 26). See Chapter 4.

[130] *Venerabili et praeclarae ecclesiae Dei lucernae, totisque caritatis brachiis amplectendo, domino Bernardo abbati Claraevallis* ... (letter 164, p. 396). This may draw on Psalms: *Lucerna pedibus meis verbum tuum et lumen semitis meis*, 'Your word is a lamp for my feet and a light to my paths' (Ps 118. 105). Ep. 364 from Bernard had three times employed the expression *hoc verbum*, 'this word', in contexts which seem to combine a reference to the news from the Holy Land with the sense of 'just cause', 'just case.' The reference here to *brachia*, the 'might', 'violence', of charity, foreshadows the invocation of God's assistance *in brachio extento*, 'in outstretched arm.' Its juxtaposition to the notion of 'embrace' may seem to prefigure the two faces of charity subsequently explored in Peter's letter, vengeance and compassion.

[131] *Restat ut vos quem lacteam fortemque columnam cui innititur, monastici ordinis aedificio summa providentia praeparavit, et velut rutilum sidus exemplo verboque non solum monachis, sed et toti Latinae ecclesiae nostro tempore insigniter lucem donavit ... totam quam potueritis huic divino operi detis operam, et unius nominis et ordinis maximas congregationes nequaquam ultra dissidere patiamini*, 'It remains that you, whom highest providence has prepared as a strong and milky pillar for the edifice of the monastic order, on which it rests, and, as if a shining star by word and example, has notably bestowed as a light not only for monks, but also for the whole Latin Church in our time.. devote all the effort you can to this divine work and not allow the greatest communities of one name and one order to be divided further' (letter 111, p. 293). The image seems to draw on the New Testament reminder that a lamp is not kindled for its light to be hidden (Mt 5. 15; Mc 4. 21; Lc 8. 16, 11. 33).

pressurising device, while at the same time leaving room for irony. The Cistercians had previously been presented as congratulating themselves on the fact that their 'sun' outshone the 'star' of others.[132]

As Bernard had used one part of the opposition own/other, so Peter introduces one half of the related opposition near/far, tied in to a further opposition between East and West, which also reveals a potential for ironic distancing:

> Therefore, it is clearly shown that both you and certain other men of your parts are of the pre-eminent limbs of His body, who are so moved, so distressed, by the wound to His body. The truth of what I say is apparent most of all from the fact that although you are placed in the furthest West, or rather, on almost the very shore of the Western Ocean, with so much space of land intervening, you hasten with all the eagerness you can to succour the Christian people labouring in the East.[133]

The reference to *praecipua membra*, 'outstanding limbs', may conflate and subvert two Pauline references. In Romans the 'limbs' are said to perform different functions.[134] In I Corinthians, the 'weaker' and 'more insignificant' limbs are said to be more necessary and to be given greater honour.[135] The statement is followed by a reminder of domestic responsibility. Peter's declaration of his willingness to go even to Jerusalem is qualified by an unfulfilled condition, 'if the needs of the Church entrusted to me allowed ...'[136] A second *caveat* follows. Peter would willingly attend an alternative meeting, 'unless again an unavoidable cause blocked

---

[132] *Felices nos, inquis ... quorum dies aliorum lucernam, quorum sol aliorum sidus obscurat,* ' "Blessed are we", you say ... "whose daylight obscures the lamp of others, whose sun, the star of others" ' (letter 111, p. 291).

[133] *Monstratur igitur aperte, esse tam vos quam quosdam alios vestrarum partium viros de praecipuis membris corporis eius, quos adeo movet, quos adeo agit, laesio corporis eius. Apparet inde maxime, verum esse quod dico, quod cum in ultimo occidente, immo in ipso paene occidui oceani littore positus sitis, tot interiectis terrarum spatiis, laboranti in oriente Christiano nomini, summo quantoque potestis studio succurrere festinatis* (letter 164, pp. 397–8).

[134] *Sicut enim in uno corpore multa membra habemus omnia autem membra non eundem actum habent ita multi unum corpus sumus in Christo singuli autem alter alterius membra habentes autem donationes secundum gratiam quae data est nobis differentes,* 'For just as in one body we have many limbs but all the limbs do not have the same employment, so, being many, we are one body in Christ, each being limbs one of the other, but having different gifts according to the grace which has been bestowed on us' (Rm 12. 4–6).

[135] *sed multo magis quae videntur membra corporis infirmiora esse necessariora sunt et quae putamus ignobiliora membra esse corporis his honorem abundantiorem circumdamus et quae inhonesta sunt nostra abundantiorem honestatem habent ...,* 'but much rather, the limbs of the body which seem to be weaker are more necessary, and to those limbs of the body which we consider to be more insignificant we give more abundant honour, and those of ours which are inglorious have more abundant respect ...' (I Cor 12. 22–3).

[136] *Non enim tantum usque Carnotum hac tanta de causa venirem, sed nec usque ad ipsam.. Iherusalem, si necessitates commissae mihi ecclesiae paterentur, ire ullomodo dubitarem,* 'For not only would I come to Chartres for this so great a cause, but if the needs of the church entrusted to me allowed, I would not hesitate in any way to go to Jerusalem ... itself' (letter 164, p. 398).

me ...'[137] If, as conjectured by Berry, the meeting of Cluniac priors which forms the basis of Peter's excuse for absence was to discuss proposed reforms,[138] Peter could lay claim both to be promoting domestic harmony, and to be working for penitence and spiritual improvement.

The matter did not, however, rest here. The meeting at Chartres may have achieved less than Bernard had hoped. In addition to Peter, several other prominent figures seem to have been missing.[139] Moreover, shortly beforehand a letter from Eugenius directed to Suger had presented the losses of the Second Crusade as an ongoing cause of fear and grief.[140] At some time between 8 May and 15 July, Bernard made another epistolary overture to Peter, requesting his presence at a further meeting, to be held at Compiègne.[141] Although still marked by rhetorical declamation, this second letter from Bernard can be seen to display marked differences from that sent previously, both in terms of what is included and what is omitted. Impersonal narration has replaced the proliferation of personal verb and pronoun forms, making God rather than man the focus of attention. There is an accompanying absence of ambiguous word-plays on 'grandeur' and 'condescension', no direct challenge in the names of charity and zeal, no overt appeal to the concept of 'neighbourliness'. As will be seen, the apparent change in tone may again betray the hand of Nicholas.

Ep. 521 opens with what can be read as a disguised call to action: 'A great and grave business of the Lord has appeared in the whole world.'[142] This is followed by a lengthy description of the threat to the holy places, forming a patchwork of biblical allusions which can be compared with Peter's earlier protestation of

---

[137] *Si tamen contingeret alio tempore conventum alium vel in vestris vel in nostris partibus celebrari, nisi rursum inevitabilis causa obstaret, sciat reverentia vestra me libentissime iturum* ..., 'But if it befell that another assembly be proclaimed at another time either in your parts or mine, unless again an unavoidable cause blocked me, your Reverence should know that I would most willingly go ...' (ibid.). Such qualifications are absent from Peter's more straightforward declaration to Suger: *Huic ergo tam sancto, tamque necessario tractatui ... libentissime.. interfuissem, si ullo modo potuissem*, 'I would most willingly ... have been present at this so holy and so necessary discussion, if in any way I had been able' (letter 166, p. 400).

[138] Berry, 'Peter the Venerable and the Crusades', p. 159.

[139] Letters of excuse are preserved from Humbert, archbishop of Lyons (Suger, ep. 108, in *Recueil des Historiens des Gaules et de la France. Rerum Gallicarum et Francicarum scriptores*, ed. M. Bouquet et al., 24 vols, Paris, 1738–1904, new ed. L. Delisle, Paris, 1869–1904, 15, ed. M Brial, pp. 523–4) and Geoffrey, archbishop of Bordeaux (Suger, ep. 109, ibid., p. 524). See Bolton, 'The Cistercians and the aftermath', pp. 133–5.

[140] *Gravem namque Christiani nominis iacturam, quam nostris temporibus Ecclesia Dei sustinuit, et recentem adhuc effusionem sanguinis tantorum virorum ad memoriam revocantes, grandi timore concutimur, et maeror inconsolabilis renovatur*, 'For recalling to memory the heavy loss of the Christian people, which the Church of God has suffered in our time, and the still fresh pouring out of the blood of such great men, we are shaken by great fear and inconsolable grief is renewed' (Eugenius III, ep. 65, in Brial, *RHGF*, 15, p. 457). See Bolton, 'The Cistercians and the aftermath', pp. 135–6.

[141] Bernard, ep. 521, *SBO*, VIII, pp. 483–4. In this letter Bernard claims that at Chartres *aut parum aut nihil factum est*, 'either little or nothing was done' (ibid., p. 484).

[142] *Negotium Domini grande et grave apparuit in universa terra* (ibid., p. 483).

outrage to Suger: 'The time is near that the *flowering and seemly couch*, on which the virginal *flower* of Mary was placed for preservation in linen cloths and spices, be snatched away from the earth, that *His sepulchre* be no longer *glorious* but ignominious, to the perpetual ignominy of the Christian faith. They threaten to contaminate the places, distinguished by the utterances of the prophets, the miracles of the Saviour, consecrated by the blood and life of Christ.'[143] The challenge, when it comes, is launched in the names of God and Christ: '*From heaven* looks down *the Lord, to see whether there is any understanding or seeking* Him, whether there is any *to grieve for* His *vicissitude* ...';[144] 'The Son of God has recourse to you ....'[145]

The latter statements are set around a castigation of the tepidity of the temporal powers, which might be construed as offering a response to Peter's reservations, even as comprising a justification on the part of Bernard himself: 'The hearts of the princes have grown luke-warm. They carry *a sword without purpose*: it is sheathed in the hides of dead beasts, consecrated to rust.'[146] If the secular powers will not draw their sword voluntarily, it would seem that the spiritual powers must intervene. At the same time, the reference here to *mortui animales*, 'dead beasts', and *robigo*, 'rust', 'blight', may also seem to convey a hidden warning, that spiritual indifference will lead to spiritual blight.[147] The blurring of the line between spiritual and temporal responsibility seems to be reinforced by the words attributed to Christ, said to turn to Peter as to 'one of His greatest princes of His house.'[148] The allusion to the parable of the talents

---

[143] *Prope est ut auferatur de terra* lectulus floridus et decorus, *in quo virgineus* flos *Mariae linteis et aromatibus conditus est, ut iam non sit* sepulchrum eius gloriosum, *sed ignominiosum ad perpetuam ignominiam fidei christianae. Minantur contaminare loca, prophetarum oraculis, Salvatoris miraculis insignita, consecrata Christi sanguine et conversatione* (ibid. = Ct 1. 15; Is 11. 1; Is 11. 10). Other biblical allusions have gone before: *Grande plane, qui a* rex caeli *perdit terram suam,* terram hereditatis suae, *terram* ubi steterunt pedes eius. *Agitant manus suas inimici eius* super montem filiae Sion, collem Ierusalem, 'Great plainly, because *the King of heaven* is losing his land, *the land of his inheritance*, the land *where His feet stood. His enemies shake their hands over the mount of the daughter of Sion, the hill of Jerusalem*' (ep. 521, p. 483 = Dn 4. 34; Is 19. 25; Ps 131. 7; Is 10. 32).

[144] *De caelo* respicit *Dominus ut videat si est intelligens aut requirens* eum, si sit qui *doleat* vicem *eius* ... (ep. 521, p. 483 = Ps 13, 2–3; I Sm 22. 8).

[145] *Recurrit et ad vos Filius Dei* ... (ep. 521, p. 483).

[146] *Intepuerunt corda principum;* sine causa gladium *portant: pellibus mortuorum animalium reconditus est, robigini consecratus* (ibid. = Rm 13. 4). According to Brolis, Bernard's letter is fuelled by bitterness (Brolis, 'La Crociata', p. 348). This view may seem to find support from the negative inversion of Romans: *Dei enim minister est tibi in bonum si autem male feceris time non enim sine causa gladium portat Dei enim minister est vindex in iram ei qui malum agit*, 'For he is a minister of God to you for good. But if you do evil, be afraid. For not without cause does he carry a sword. For he is a minister of God as an avenger for anger to him who does evil' (Rm 13. 4). The preceding verse brings its relevance here sharply home: *Nam principes non sunt timori boni operis sed mali*, 'For princes are a source of fear not for the good deed but for the bad' (ibid., 13. 3).

[147] Cf. the warning in Deuteronomy, that the Lord will send pestilence on the disobedient *aere corrupto et robigine*, 'with corrupt air and blight' (Dt 28. 22).

[148] *tamquam ad unum de maximis principibus suis domus suae* (ep. 521, p. 484 = Ps 104. 21).

which follows, 'For that *noble man* who *has gone away to a distant region* has entrusted much of his substance to you, both interior and exterior ...',[149] may counter Peter's portrayal of Bernard as an 'outstanding light of the Church'. Equally, it might be thought to comprise a more subtle resumption of the previous grandeur play. The potential ambiguity of *substantia*, 'essence', 'property', suggests that Peter is being reminded that he possesses both spiritual and material wealth which he should use in the cause of Christ.

At the same time, the letter is given a framework which seems to impart a less formal and more conciliatory tone than was found in its predecessor. The salutation addresses Peter as *amicus carissimus*, 'dearest friend', rather than *amantissimus pater*, 'most beloved father', in conformance with the wishes expressed in Peter's letter 149.[150] The letter closes with a recommendation of 'your Galcher, the nephew of our Galcher, or rather, also yours',[151] presumably the bearer and the same Galcher referred to in ep. 267, as a monk who had transferred from Cluny to Clairvaux. To this is appended a greeting from Nicholas, 'Our Nicholas greets you as yours: for he is yours',[152] which seems to recall the subscription found in ep. 389, and to raise the possibility that Nicholas has also had some hand in the composition of this letter.[153] It is noticeable also that the request for Peter's presence combines summons with appeal, 'where (at Compiègne) we both supplicate and demand the presence of your Sublimity'.[154] Despite the greater circumspection of approach, there may be none-the-less, as Brolis diagnoses, a hint of reproach for Peter's previous absence.[155] Not only is his presence at Chartres said to have been 'much sought and expected',[156] but this summons is reinforced by the words: 'Thus it is necessary, thus necessity demands, and great necessity.'[157] Necessity had been invoked by Peter as a reason for absence; the needs had been those of Cluny.

There is no written record of any reply to this letter from Peter. In practice, his response would probably have been irrelevant, since it seems likely that the meeting at Compiègne never took place.[158] The three principal letters discussed in

---

[149] Homo *enim iste* nobilis *qui* abiit in regionem longinquam *multum vobis tam interioris quam exterioris substantantiae suae commisit* ... (ep. 521, p. 484 = Lc 19. 12, cf. Mt 25. 14).

[150] *Nam* reverentissimum *me esse ignoro*, patrem *quantum ad te me esse nego*, amicum *et* carissimum *tuum me non solum ore profiteor, sed et corde agnosco*, 'For I do not know myself to be *most reverent*, I deny that I am *father* in respect of you, your *friend* and *dearest* I not only profess myself with my mouth, but also recognise in my heart' (letter 149, p. 364).

[151] *De cetero Gaucherium vestrum, nepotem Gaucherii nostri, immo et vestri, vestrae gratiae commendamus* ... (ep. 521, p. 484).

[152] *Salutat vos Nicholaus noster ut vester: vester est enim* (ibid.).

[153] *Ego Nicolaus vester saluto vos in aeternum, et ultra* ..., 'I your Nicholas greet you in eternity and beyond ...' (ep. 389, p. 357). See Chapter 8.

[154] *ubi (apud regium Compendium) vestram interesse sublimitatem et supplicamus et exigimus* (ep. 521, p. 484).

[155] Brolis, 'La Crociata', p. 348.

[156] *Ibi (in Carnotensi conventu) multum et expetita et expectata est praesentia vestra* (ep. 521, p. 484).

[157] *Sic oportet fieri, sic exigit necessitas, et necessitas magna* (ibid.).

[158] Phillips, *Defenders*, p. 108; Bolton, 'The Cistercians and the aftermath', p. 138. Among other factors contributing to render the enthusiasm for a new crusade short-lived and

this chapter, letter 145 from Peter, ep. 364 from Bernard and Peter's reply, letter 164, share a high degree of formality and rhetorical display. The first of these appears to offer an enthusiastic endorsement of the election of Henry of France. Bernard's letter presents a stirring call to action on behalf of the Holy Land, while Peter's response combines a declaration of outrage with a carefully worded excuse for absence. Beneath the surface, however, all three reveal the potential for an ironic sub-text. The endorsement is undercut by a reminder of the spiritual cost of temporal advancement, and by what may be read as hints that Bernard is under political pressure from above. Bernard's appeal masks a challenge to a broader interpretation of the concept of *caritas*, encompassing the interests of the Church as a whole, while Peter can be seen to mount a counter-challenge, which foregrounds the need for spiritual remedy and warns against further provocation of divine wrath.

Embedded as these letters are in a specific set of circumstances, relating to a broader range of issues enshrined in a very particular correspondence, the warnings and ambiguities diagnosed here must be treated with circumspection. In consequence of this, it seems unwise to extrapolate generalisations from their sub-texts, that Peter, for example, was actually against the election of Henry or opposed to the crusading ideal in general terms. Letter 145 can be seen as conveying a discreet reproach that Bernard is devoting his energies to matters other than domestic harmony, the subject of Peter's letters 149 and 150. Equally, the nature of Bernard's approach in ep. 364 may be construed both as a riposte to Peter's attempt there to reopen the Cluniac–Cistercian debate and to his dry detachment regarding the election. On the other hand, Peter's letter 164 might seem to lend credence to the view, discussed previously in relation to letter 111, that military intervention is not the business of the Church and churchmen, but should rather be left to the temporal authorities and the laity.[159] At the same time, ep. 521, Bernard's second

---

ineffectual, Phillips suggests low morale, fatigue and lack of money (Phillips, ibid., pp. 108–11.) Despite the efforts of Bernard to stir others to action, the Cistercians as a whole seem to have been antipathetic to the proposed undertaking (Phillips, ibid., pp. 111–12; Bolton, 'The Cistercians and the aftermath', pp. 138–9). Suger, the other leading light, would die early in 1151. In the meantime, his efforts on behalf of the Holy Land would appear to have been confined to funding the Templars (Berry, 'Peter the Venerable', p. 162; Phillips, *Defenders*, p. 111).

[159] This seems to find support in a letter addressed to Roger of Sicily, dating, according to Phillips, to around 1150 (Phillips, *Defenders*, pp. 112–14). In this letter, Peter seemingly calls upon Roger to assume the role of avenger, by punishing the treachery of the Greeks, seen in certain quarters as responsible for the failure of the Second Crusade. His declaration of willingness to suffer in the cause is again qualified by a reminder of his monastic status: *Ut enim iuxta quod in mente mea video loquar, si necesse esset quantum ad monachum pertinere potest, non recusarem mori, si mortem tantorum, tam nobilium, immo paene totius Galliae et Germaniae miserabili fraude exstinctum florem, iustitia Dei per aliquem suorum dignaretur ulcisci*, 'For to speak according to what I see in my mind, if it were necessary, as far as can pertain to a monk, I would not refuse to die, if the justice of God saw fit to avenge through one of His the death of such great, so noble men, or rather the virtual extinction of the flower of the whole of France and Germany by such wretched deceit' (Peter, letter 162, *Letters*, I, p. 395). The 'death' invoked by Peter may accordingly seem to be figurative,

and more conciliatory letter regarding the proposed crusade, seems to offer a glimpse of Nicholas of Clairvaux in his role as potential go-between. Nicholas himself will be central to the next phase of the correspondence, which will focus on the question of a proposed visit to Cluny.

---

explicable in terms of mortification and self-denial rather than literal death in battle. On the (remote) possibility that the new crusade was to be aimed at Byzantium, see Phillips, *Defenders*, pp. 112–18.

Chapter 10

Duplicity or Simplicity: Peter, Letters 175 and 181; Bernard, Ep. 265

As stated at the end of the previous chapter, the next phase of the correspondence, dating between autumn 1150 and spring 1151, is dominated by the proposed visit to Cluny of Nicholas of Clairvaux. This visit, repeatedly postponed, would seem to have become something of a *cause célèbre*. First mooted in Peter's letter 175,[1] it is seemingly blocked in Bernard's ep. 265,[2] on the grounds of (Nicholas's) illness and absence. The request is renewed in Peter's letter 181, more openly combative and fuelled by heavy irony.[3] While Peter's letters to Bernard constitute an appeal to communal charity, underpinned by the concept of salvation, Bernard's preserved response can best be characterised in terms of a blocking manœuvre of the type seen previously. The outcome of the request is not known. According to Constable, Bernard is unlikely to have felt able to refuse.[4] Bredero, however, is, perhaps rightly, more cautious.[5] As will be seen, there may be reason to conclude that the epistolary struggle for 'possession' of Nicholas, initially a Benedictine, now a Cistercian, functions as a microcosm for the whole debate on the nature of *caritas*, with one crucial difference. Here, each in turn appears to acknowledge the superiority of the other's way of life. The underlying sub-text, however, may suggest that these acknowledgements should be viewed rather as manipulative ploys than as evidence of reciprocal 'conversion'.

The antecedents to the request seem to go some way back. Letter 153 in Peter's collection is a brief note from Nicholas, forming a pendant to the group which includes letters 149 and 150.[6] Dated by Constable to late 1149/early 1150,[7] it holds out the expectation of a face-to-face meeting in the near future.[8] There is no clear evidence as to whether or not this meeting took place. In letter 176 to Nicholas, written to accompany 175 to Bernard in the later part of 1150, Peter claims to have put off sending for Nicholas.[9] In both letters, he summons him for a visit, seemingly

---

[1]   Peter, letter 175, *Letters*, I, pp. 416–17 = Bernard, ep. 264, *SBO*, VIII, pp. 173–4.

[2]   Bernard, ep. 265, *SBO*, VIII, pp. 174–5 = Peter, letter 177, *Letters*, II, p. 418.

[3]   Peter, letter 181, *Letters*, I, pp. 423–5.

[4]   Constable, *Letters*, II, p. 325.

[5]   Bredero, *Bernard of Clairvaux*, p. 244.

[6]   Nicholas of Clairvaux, ep. 54 (*Nicolai Claraevallensis Epistolae*, ed. J.-P. Migne, *Patrologia Latina*, 196, Paris, 1880, 1650) = letter 153 (*Letters*, I, p. 373).

[7]   Constable, *Letters*, II, p. 202.

[8]   *In brevi sicut puto visurus faciem vestram* ..., 'Being about to see your face shortly, so I think ...' (Nicholas, letter 153).

[9]   *Distuli diu mandare hoc* [*ut venias*], *cum id tamen in animo fixum haberem, non quia dissimulabam, sed quia tempus congruum expectabam*, 'I have put off ordering this [that you

to take place at Christmas.[10] That this visit did not happen, already suggested by the negative response contained in Bernard's ep. 265, is seemingly confirmed by the complaint lamenting the passage of time contained in a letter from Nicholas written in early 1151:[11] '*Year ... has been added to year, festivals have glided away*, and a day has been given me in return for the year in respect of which which I have not seen ... (my) beloved.'[12] Peter will comply with the plea contained in this letter, that Nicholas be summoned for Easter 1151,[13] in his second letter to Bernard. At the same time, he will also write separately to the prior[14] and cellarer[15] of Clairvaux, as requested by Nicholas, asking them to support the request.

The underlying motivation behind the episode as a whole is open to debate. Bredero opts for an essentially political reading. The interpretation which he offers, that Peter was hoping to improve his relations with Bernard[16] and, in particular, to use Nicholas as an intermediary to win the latter's support for his reforms,[17] seems to rely on certain gambits in Peter's own letters which might equally be classed as pressurising devices. At the other end of the spectrum, McGuire opts for a purely personal and more controversial reading, asserting that Peter may have been 'in love' with Nicholas 'in the modern sense'.[18] He does not offer any substantiating evidence for this view, which may be influenced by the liberal use in Nicholas's letters to Peter of quasi-erotic language, such as the address of 'beloved' seen

---

come] for a long time, although I had it fixed in mind, not because I was hesitating, but because I was waiting for a suitable time' (Peter, letter 176, *Letters*, I, p. 417).

[10]   Peter asks for Nicholas to stay *usque ad octavas domini* ..., 'until the octave of the Lord ...' (letter 175, p. 417). This is rendered, surely incorrectly, by Bredero as 'no later than the octave of Easter' (Bredero, *Bernard of Clairvaux*, p. 243). In the accompanying letter to Nicholas, Peter pleads travel outside Cluny as reason for the delay, but states that he is now forced to stay at Cluny *usque ad Christum natum*, 'until the Lord's birthday' (Peter, letter 176). Moreover, it is clear from the correspondence which follows that the Easter proposal follows subsequently. In his previous discussion Bredero had assigned the visit to 'before Christmas' (Bredero, 'Saint Bernard in his relations', p. 338).

[11]   Nicholas of Clairvaux, ep. 55 (*PL*, 196, 1650) = letter 179 (*Letters*, I, pp. 420–22).

[12]   *Additus est ... annus ad annum, evolutae sunt sollemnitates, et dies pro anno datus est mihi, ex quo non vidi ... dilectum* (Nicholas, letter 179, p. 421 = Is 29. 1). Constable points out elsewhere that a 'year' for Nicholas ran from Easter to Easter (Constable, *Letters*, II, p. 202). This might suggest that Nicholas had been expecting an Easter visit in 1150 which did not take place. At the same time, the 'day' might be held to refer to Nicholas's delivery of Bernard's ep. 387, probably in the latter part of 1149. Nicholas did not deliver the subsequent ep. 364, said by Peter to have been brought by the abbot of Fontanel (Peter, letter 164, p. 398). It seems equally unlikely that he delivered the following ep. 521, as it contains his greetings.

[13]   *scribe patri meo ... et priori nostro, et Gaucherio tuo.. ut in sancto Pascha mittant me ad te* ..., 'write to my Father ... and to our Prior, and to your Galcher ... that they send me to you at the holy week of Easter ...' (Nicholas, letter 179, p. 422).

[14]   Peter, letter 183, *Letters*, I, p. 427.

[15]   Idem, letter 184, ibid.

[16]   Bredero, *Bernard of Clairvaux*, p. 243. Cf. idem, 'Saint Bernard in his relations', p. 338.

[17]   Bredero, *Bernard of Clairvaux*, p. 247. Cf. idem, 'Saint Bernard in his relations', p. 346.

[18]   McGuire, *Friendship and community*, p. 485, n. 117.

above.[19] Such language, drawn from *Canticles* and elsewhere, was however, as McGuire himself notes, a common feature of friendship writing in the twelfth century.[20] There is also a third player in the game to be taken into consideration. It was suggested in previous chapters that Nicholas may have been manipulating Bernard's letters to Peter for his own ends.[21] As Constable notes,[22] the letter from Nicholas which appears to initiate the request seems to offer further hints of intrigue and deceit, suggesting that he may be exploiting the situation in his own interests.

As noted previously, Peter's acquaintance with Nicholas extended back to the period when, as a 'black' monk, he was chaplain to Hato, bishop of Troyes. In a letter written some four or five years before Hato's withdrawal into Cluny, Peter had expressed affection for Nicholas through the *topos* of a dwelling-place in the heart.[23] In letter 151, written to accompany letter 150 to Bernard, he had repeated his protestations of affection, linked this time with the notion of Nicholas's 'change of colour', through his entry into Clairvaux: 'I loved you as long as you were ours by colour, but now too, as far as concerns me, I love you no less, having changed, so I think, your colour not your heart.'[24] This play on colour can be related to the demand contained in letter 150, that black and white monks learn to dwell in one another's hearts, but it also preludes what could be read as a claim to loyalty: 'I would have preferred you mine rather than another's, but because you are everywhere God's, I count you also everywhere mine.'[25] Certainly, it is followed there by an overt demand for reciprocal action,[26] translated into concrete terms as a

---

[19] Cf: Indica mihi quem diligit anima mea, quando veniam et *ap*parebo ante faciem *tuam* ...?, '*Tell me, whom my soul loves, when shall I come and appear before* your *face* ...?' (Nicholas, letter 179, p. 421 = Ct 1. 6; Ps 41. 3).

[20] McGuire, *Friendship and community*, p. 232.

[21] See Chapters 7 and 8.

[22] Constable, *Letters*, II, p. 218.

[23] *Quoniam ex quo te agnovi, bonum et remotum in corde meo tibi semper hospitium reservo* ..., 'Since, from the time that I have known you, I have always kept a good and separate lodging in my heart for you ...' (Peter, letter 87, *Letters*, I, p. 227).

[24] *Dilexi te quamdiu noster colore fuisti, sed et nunc quantum ad me, colore ut puto non corde mutato, non minus te diligo* (Peter, letter 151, *Letters*, I, p. 372). This may represent an adaptation of the Horatian dictum, *caelum non animum mutant, qui trans mare currunt*, 'they change climate not disposition, who run across the sea' (Horace, *Epistles*, I, xi, 27), to be used subsequently to Nicholas in its proper form (Peter, letter 193, *Letters*, I, p. 449).

[25] *Maluissem te meum quam alterius, sed quia ubique dei es, meum quoque te ubique reputo* (Peter, letter 151). Both Bernard's and Peter's letters play with the notion of Nicholas as a joint son: *Nicholaus meus, immo et vester*, 'My Nicholas, or rather, yours also' (Bernard, ep. 387); *Salutat vos Nicholaus noster ut vester: vester est enim*, 'Our Nicholas greets you as yours: for he is yours' (Bernard, ep. 521); *Si meus es ut dico* ..., 'If you are mine, as I say ...' (Peter, letter 176.) Nicholas himself will subsequently repeat the claim in arguably stronger form: *tuus fui, tuus sum, tuus ero quamdiu fuero in visceribus Ihesu Christi*, 'I was yours, I am yours, I will be yours, as long as I am in the bowels of Jesus Christ' (Nicholas, letter 179, p. 422).

[26] *Redde ergo vicem, ut vere te diligentem diligas, quia nec ipse totus suis viribus mundus, ab hoc me proposito avocare potest, nec te quicquam a simili proposito avocet*, 'Make return, therefore, so that you love one who truly loves you, and because the whole world itself with all its forces cannot summon me away from this undertaking, let nothing summon you away from a similar undertaking' (Peter, letter 151, p. 372).

request for Nicholas to encourage Bernard to put into effect the contents of Peter's letter 150.[27] All of these factors may have some bearing on the form taken by the epistolary tug-of-war to follow.

Bredero draws attention to the fact that letter 175, Peter's first written approach to Bernard on the subject, was also included in Bernard's official letter-collection, one of only three not written by Bernard himself to be so.[28] The inclusion of this letter there may be explicable by the surface of highly worked compliment which it presents. Underneath, however, may lurk a degree of self-reflexive irony, which only emerges in the light of what has preceded.

> To the strong and splendid pillar of the monastic order, or rather of the whole Church of God, the lord Bernard abbot of Clairvaux, brother Peter, humble abbot of the Cluniacs, the salvation *which God has promised to those who love Him.*
>
> If it were allowed, if the ordering of God did not thwart it, if his way were *in the power of man*, I would have preferred to cleave to your dearest[29] Beatitude in indissoluble intertwining than to rule or reign elsewhere among mortals. What then? Should not dwelling with you, pleasing not only to men but to the angels themselves, be preferred by me to all earthly kingdoms? If I call you their fellow-citizen, although hope has not yet passed to fact, through the grace of merciful God I will not be a liar. If, plainly, it had been granted to me to be with you here to the last breath, perhaps it would be granted henceforth to be also in perpetuity where you would be. For whither *would I be running*, except *after you*, drawn by you *by the odour of your unguents*? Because this is not granted always, would that it were granted often. And because that is not so, would that at least I may frequently see those sent by you. And because this happens rarely, I wish that your Sanctity may soon visit one who loves him through his Nicholas, to stay with me until the octave of the Lord('s birth), upon whom, so it seems to me, your spirit rests in part, and mine in full. I will see you, holy brother, in him, I will hear you through him, and I will convey through him certain things which I desire to make known privately to your Wisdom. I commend to your holy spirit, and to the holy men serving almighty God under your guidance myself and mine, with all the force,[30] all the devotion in my power.

Superficially, this letter has much in common with the loosely structured letter 65, opening with a lyrical and effusive declaration of affection and passing, via a disguised form of epistolary reproach based on infrequency of contact, to petition and *envoi*. In fact, the apparent looseness of structure is deceptive. The presence of Nicholas as *alter ego* for Bernard, a conceit initially exploited in Bernard's ep. 387,[31] is presented here as a natural corollary to the (frustrated) desire expressed at the start for Bernard's physical presence. The shifting syntax reinforces the sense of

---

[27]   *Scribo epistolam domino Clarevallensi, quam per te illi praesentari volo* ..., 'I am writing a letter to the lord of Clairvaux, which I wish to be presented to him through you ...' (ibid.).
[28]   Bredero, *Bernard of Clairvaux*, p. 276.
[29]   As it appears here, *carissim(a)e* could be treated as either vocative or dative. In Leclercq it appears as *carissimae*, agreeing unambiguously with *beatitudini tuae* (Bernard, ep. 264, *SBO*, VIII, p. 173, l. 9).
[30]   As found in Bernard's collection, *precibus*, 'prayers', replaces *viribus*, 'force' (Bernard, ep. 264, p. 174).
[31]   Bernard, ep. 387, *SBO*, VIII, p. 356. See Chapter 7.

inevitability, as imperfect and pluperfect subjunctives, representing present and past unfulfilled conditions (*liceret/maluissem/datum fuisset/daretur*) make way for expressions of desire, which move from the unfulfilled present (*daretur*) to the present subjunctive of remote possibility (*videam*), and which culminate via indirect command (*visitet*) in statements employing the future indicative which translate desire into seeming certainty (*videbo/audiam/mandabo*). At the same time, the opening phrase *si liceret* ..., 'if it were allowed ...', together with the later statement, *quod quia ... non datur* ..., 'because this ... is not granted ...', and indeed the passage as a whole, may be modelled on a gambit employed by Augustine to Jerome: 'O, if (only) it had been allowed to enjoy you, even if not as a fellow-dweller, at least as a neighbour in the Lord, for frequent and sweet conversation! But because that has not been granted, I ask that you should take pains to conserve this, that we should be together in Christ, as we may be able.. and not to scorn epistolary replies, however rare.'[32]

In addition to manipulation through syntactical means, the letter can be seen to put pressure on Bernard to comply with the request through significant echoes of the previous correspondence, which again evoke the Jewish/Gentile opposition. This starts with the salutation. The depiction of Bernard as *fortis ac splendida ... columna*, a 'strong and splendid pillar', is taken from letter 111,[33] where its use had left room for a touch of glancing irony, as Bernard appeared to displace St Benedict, previously characterised as the one *cui inniteris*, 'on whom you rest'.[34] In itself, the image also points to a crucial Pauline passage, justifying the mission to the Gentiles: 'But on the contrary, when they had seen that the gospel of the uncircumcision has been entrusted to me, as that of the circumcision to Peter ... and when they had learned of the grace which has been given to me, James and Cephas (Peter) and John, who were seen to be pillars, gave to me and Barnabas the right hands of fellowship, that we [should go] to the Gentiles, they to the people of the circumcision.'[35] Drawn from Galatians, this passage precedes the 'rebuke' of St Peter by St Paul for submitting to the pressure of the 'judaisers'. The interpretation of this passage had been the subject of the Augustine/Jerome debate, and in turn had

[32] *O si licuisset etsi non cohabitante saltem vicino te in domine perfrui ad crebrum et dulce colloquium! Sed quia id non est datum, peto, ut hoc ipsum, quod in Christo, quam possimus, simul simus, conservare studeas ... et rescripta quamvis rara non spernere* (Augustine, ep. 67, II. 3, *CSEL*, 34/2, p. 239).

[33] *(Restat ut) vos quem lacteam fortemque columnam cui innititur, monastici ordinis aedificio summa providentia praeparavit* ..., '(It remains that) you, whom highest providence has prepared as a strong and milky pillar for the edifice of the monastic order, on which it rests ...' (Peter, letter 111, p. 293). It had been combined there with a second image of Bernard as a luminary for the Church, used as the salutation for Peter's letter 164 (see Chapter 9).

[34] *Ecce ipse cui inniteris Benedictus pater..* (letter 111, p. 282). In letter 28, the Cistercians had been presented as accusing the Cluniacs of placing their concept of *caritas* above that of St. Benedict (Peter, letter 28, p. 93).

[35] *Sed e contra cum vidissent quod creditum est mihi evangelium praeputii sicut Petro circumcisionis ... et cum cognovissent gratiam quae data est mihi Iacobus et Cephas et Iohannes qui videbantur columnae esse dextras dederunt mihi et Barnabae societatis ut nos in gentes ipsi autem in circumcisionem* (Gal 2. 7–9).

underlain Peter's own combative letter 28. If Peter the Venerable, like St Paul with whom he had implicitly identified himself there, has the 'apostolate' of the 'uncircumcision', Bernard, like St Peter with his mission to the 'circumcised', should extend the hand of fellowship.[36]

The direct citation which forms the second part of the salutation, linking salvation with love of God, had also been employed in the salutation of letter 150.[37] There it had been followed by, and set against, a clutch of allusions, biblical and otherwise, pointing towards the inescapability of death. Here, too, Peter seems in what follows to conflate two partial citations from the Old Testament, both relating to the threat of future judgement, the first of which is signalled by Constable,[38] the second by Leclercq.[39] The phrase *in hominis potestate*, 'in the power of man', looks to Job: 'For it is not further in the power of a man to come to God into judgement.'[40] The warning from Jeremiah that 'man's way is not his own'[41] is followed there by the plea that God be merciful in judgement.[42] In letter 150, the reminder had seemingly been directed principally against the Cistercians, developed through the warning that physical and spiritual austerity, in the absence of *caritas*, is not enough to achieve salvation. In this letter, however, Peter's words will seemingly take another turn, as he will appear to equate the Cistercian way, and Clairvaux in particular, with the path to sure salvation.

This is achieved through an opposition between the spiritual and the temporal which lends itself by implication to being extended to one between Clairvaux and Cluny. Cohabitation with Bernard, *grata ... angelis ipsis*, 'pleasing ... to the angels themselves', would, or should, be preferable *regnis omnibus terrenis*, 'to all earthly kingdoms'.[43] The second half of the opposition is doubled by the preceding use of

---

[36]   The passage from *Galatians* cited above ends with the verse, *tantum ut pauperum memores essemus quod etiam sollicitus fui hoc ipsum facere*, 'provided only that we be mindful of the poor, which I have been also sollicitous to do' (Gal 2. 10). In a letter written to Pope Eugenius over the period of Peter the Venerable's visit to Italy between November 1151 and March 1152, Bernard will state: *Nam, si nescitis, iste est qui manus suas extendit ad pauperes Ordinis nostri ...*, 'For, if you do not know it, he is that one who stretches out his hands to the poor of our Order ...' (Bernard, ep. 277, SBO, *VIII*, p. 189).

[37]   *salutem* quam repromisit deus diligentibus se (Peter, letter 150, p. 367; idem, letter 175, p. 416 = *Iac* 1. 12).

[38]   Constable, *Letters*, I, p. 416, n. b.

[39]   Leclercq, *SBO*, VIII, p. 173, n. 8.

[40]   *Neque enim est ultra in hominis potestate est ut veniat ad Deum in iudicium* (Iob 34. 23). The preceding verse warns *Non sunt tenebrae et non est umbra mortis ut abscondantur ibi qui operantur iniquitatem*, 'There is no darkness and no shadow of death, that those who work inquity may be concealed there' (ibid., 40. 22).

[41]   *Scio Domine quia non est hominis via eius nec viri est ut ambulet et dirigat gressus suos*, 'I know, Lord, that a man's way is not his own, not is it a man's to walk and direct his steps' (Ier 10. 23).

[42]   *Corripe me Domine verumtamen in iudicio et non in furore tuo ne forte ad nihilum redigas me*, 'Correct me, Lord, but in judgement and not in your fury, lest perhaps you reduce me to nothing' (ibid., 10. 24).

[43]   *Nonne regnis omnibus terrenis praeferri a me deberet grata non solum hominibus, sed et angelis ipsis cohabitatio tua?* (letter 175, p. 416).

two verbs connoting kingship, *principari* and *regnare*.[44] In Bernard's ep. 521, in an analogy with the temporal powers, Peter had been characterised as being among *maximi principes*, the 'greatest princes' of God's house.[45] The adoption of temporal imagery for depicting Cluny is, moreover, sometimes glimpsed in Peter's own writings. In a playful letter to his secretary Peter of Poitiers, dated by Constable to 1139/1141,[46] Peter adapts the language of Horace: '*now I am pleased not by* turbulent *Rome*, but *by peaceful Tibur* ...'[47] *Turbida*, 'turbulent', replaces *regia*, 'regal', 'royal', of the original.[48] Peter of Poitiers replies in similar vein: 'You should know that the whole of Cluny, your most glorious city, daily and unanimously also longs for your imperial and most goodly countenance.'[49] On the other side of the fence, as discussed in an earlier chapter,[50] the equation of the Cistercian monasteries in general, and of Clairvaux in particular, with the earthly Jerusalem was, as Bredero points out, a feature of Bernard's writing.[51]

At one level, this seems to represent a playful acknowledgement of Bernard's frequent epistolary play on Peter's 'sublimity', as discussed in previous chapters. What follows, however, hints at a more serious meaning. *Cohabitatio*, co-inhabitation with Bernard, would, it is implied, have ensured for Peter eternal salvation, 'to be also in perpetuity where you would be'.[52] This is reinforced by an adaptation of Canticles, which casts Bernard in the role of divine *sponsus*, 'bridegroom', Peter in that of earthly *sponsa*, 'bride': 'For *whither would I be running* except *after you*, drawn by you *by the odour of your unguents?*'[53] The use

---

[44] *maluissem carissim(a)e beatitudini tuae nexu indissolubili adhaerere, quam vel principari inter mortales alicubi, vel regnare* (ibid.).

[45] Bernard, ep. 521, *SBO*, VIII, p. 484. See Chapter 9.

[46] Constable, *Letters*, II, p. 183.

[47] iam non mihi *turbida* Roma, *sed* vacuum Tibur placet ... (Peter, letter 124, *Letters*, I, pp. 317–18 = Horace, *Epistles*, I, vii, 44–5).

[48] *mihi iam non regia Roma,*
       sed vacuum Tibur placet aut imbelle Tarentum
                          (Horace, ibid.)

[49] *Sciatis etiam Cluniacum, urbem vestram clarissimam totam unanimiter imperialem ac piissimum vultum vestrum cotidie desiderare* (Peter of Poitiers, letter 128, *Letters*, I, pp. 325–6).

[50] See Chapter 7.

[51] Bredero, *Bernard of Clairvaux*, pp. 267–75. As Bredero points out, Bernard's ep. 64, written to Alexander, bishop of Lincoln, seeking permission for one Philip to remain at Clairvaux, makes this identification explicit: *Philippus vester, volens proficisci Ierosolymam, compendium viae invenit, et cito pervenit quo volebat. ... Et si vultis scire, Clarevallis est. Ipsa est Ierusalem, ei quae in caelis est, tota mentis devotione, et conversationis imitatione, et cognatione quadam spiritus sociata*, 'Your Philip, wishing to set out for Jerusalem, has found a short-cut for the journey, and swiftly come where he wished. ... And, if you wish to know, it is Clairvaux. It itself is (a) Jerusalem, allied to that one which is in heaven by all devotion of mind, and by imitation of way of life, and by a certain affinity of the spirit' (Bernard, ep. 64. 1–2, *SBO*, VII, pp. 157–8).

[52] *daretur fortassis post hac, ubi et esses etiam perpetuo esse*, 'it would be granted perhaps hereafter, to be also in perpetuity where you would be' (letter 175, p. 416).

[53] *Quo enim* currerem *nisi* post te, *tractus* odore unguentorum tuorum *a te?* (ibid., p. 417 = Ct 1. 3).

of the unfulfilled present in both cases points in the opposite direction, that Peter is at risk of eternal damnation. What follows, however, may suggest that this apparent self-abnegation should in fact be viewed as a pressurising manœuvre. The claim that Peter's 'whole spirit' and Bernard's spirit 'in part' 'rests upon' Nicholas[54] seems to connote the *topos* of spiritual respite in a friend,[55] and to suggest that Peter's need for this is greater than Bernard's. At the same time it recalls the passing of Elijah, and the coming to Jericho of Elisha.[56] Significantly, Jericho appears elsewhere in the Old Testament as the first 'alien' city to be taken by the Israelites. In the ensuing slaughter, the household of Rahab the 'harlot' alone is said to have been spared, because she had received the 'envoys of the Israelites'.[57] If Cluny is to be equated with Jericho, as Clairvaux with Jerusalem, Peter seems to be suggesting that Cluny is ripe for conversion, or, at least, for infiltration by an emissary.

At the same time, there may also be a concealed reproach. The notion of *cohabitatio*, 'co-inhabitation', together with the depiction of Bernard as *concivis*, a 'fellow-citizen' of the angels,[58] seems to hark back to the sardonic complaint in letter 150 of an (unnamed) Cluniac, that he had believed himself a 'fellow-citizen', and had found himself expelled 'as a Samaritan'.[59] Its coupling here with an unfulfilled condition, 'I would have preferred ...', may hint that Peter's request there, that Cluniacs be received on an equal basis with Cistercians, and/or that Cluniacs and Cistercians dwell in one another's heart, has not yet been brought to fruition, and that neither literally nor figuratively are Cluniacs regarded as 'fellow-citizens' of Cistercians. At the same time, Peter's *caveat*, 'through the grace of merciful God I will not be a liar', seems to recall the statement in Romans, 'All men are liars.'[60] Thus the approach lends itself to being viewed as a mixture of flattery with an undercurrent of warning. By apparently accepting the proposition of the

---

[54]	*in quo (Nicholao) vester.. ex parte, et meus ex toto spiritus requiescit* (ibid., p. 417).

[55]	The same *topos* is employed, for example, in a letter to Peter of Poitiers, in which Peter the Venerable claims that their private conversations represented a 'hermitage', and the 'tabernacle of the Lord': *Fatigatus litibus hominum ... hic quiescebam ...*, 'Wearied by the disputes of men ... I would find repose here ...' (Peter, letter 58, *Letters*, I, pp. 182–3).

[56]	*Videntes autem filii prophetarum qui erant in Hiericho de contra dixerunt requievit spiritus Heliae super Heliseum et venientes in occursum eius adoraverunt eum proni in terram*, 'But seeing (him), the sons of the prophets, who were over in Jericho, said, "The spirit of Elijah has rested on Elisha", and coming to meet him, they honoured him, prone on the ground' (4 Rg 2. 15).

[57]	*sola Raab meretrix vivat cum universis qui cum ea in domo sunt abscondit enim nuntios quos direximus*, 'let only Rahab, the harlot, live with all who are with her in her household. For she hid the envoys whom we sent' (Ios 6. 17).

[58]	*Concivem te illorum (angelorum) si dixero, licet nondum spes in rem transierit, per misericordis dei gratiam mendax non ero* (letter 175, p. 416). This may draw on Ephesians: *Ergo iam non estis hospites et advenae sed estis cives sanctorum et domestici Dei*, 'Therefore you are not now guests and strangers, but you are (fellow) citizens of the saints and of the household of God' (Eph 2. 19).

[59]	*Concivem me aestimabam, et ut Samaritanus expellor* (letter 150, p. 369).

[60]	*Omnis autem homo mendax* (Rm 3. 4.) This phrase, coming from a context which attacks judaising, had first been invoked in relation to Langres (Peter, letter 29, p. 103). See Chapter 4.

spiritual superiority of Bernard (and the Cistercians), it may seem that Peter has presented him with an impossible dilemma. If the Cistercians alone are certain of salvation, they are under the obligation of proselytising to the Cluniacs. Translated into concrete terms, Bernard must send Nicholas, his *alter ego* and envoy, to Cluny. If they (he) fail(s) to do so, they (he) will be guilty of a failure in *caritas*, and their (his) salvation will be in doubt. Since it was Bernard's own letter which had introduced the concept of the *alter ego*, he may seem to be trapped in a dilemma of his making.

Whereas the letter from Peter forms a seamless whole, presenting the visit as a desirable, indeed inescapable, consequence of Bernard's own equation of Clairvaux with the heavenly Jerusalem, and of the Cistercian way with the swiftest and surest path to salvation, ep. 265, Bernard's response, employs a different tactic which effectively separates the request from what precedes it and reduces it, surely in irony, to *petitiuncula*, a 'little petition'. The bulk of the letter, by contrast, seemingly matches compliment with compliment, but the language offers an underlying potential for obliquity which can be read as providing a commentary on the ambivalence of the original.

> What do you do, o good man? You praise a sinner, you beatify a wretch! It remains for you to pray that I be not led into error. I am led, indeed, if delighted by such great commendation, I begin not to know myself. That had nearly happened to me on seeing the letter of your beatitude and of my beatification. How blessed I would now be, if I could be made blessed by your words! However, I would call myself blessed, but by your favour, not by praise of myself. Blessed, that I am loved by you, that I love you. Although I think that this morsel, sweet to me as it is, must be liquified and not, as they say, be admitted with full mouthfuls. Do you wonder why this is? Indeed, I do not see in myself whence I have deserved to be loved so much, especially by so great a man. But I know that the wish to be loved more than is just is missing from the just man. Who may grant me to be able to imitate as well as to admire the mark of such great humility? Who may bestow on me to enjoy your holy and desired presence, I do not say always, I do not say often, but at least once in a year? I think that I would not be returning void of any recompense. Not, I say, in vain would I be contemplating the pattern of virtue, the text-book of monastic discipline, the mirror of sanctity, and, what until now I admit that I have learned from Christ too little, not to no purpose would I be perceiving with clear-sighted faith how you also are *gentle and humble of heart*. But if I proceed to do to you what I complain of your having done to me, even if I should speak the truth, I will not be in harmony with the law of truth, in which it is read: *What* you do not wish *to be done to you, do not* do to another. And so let me now respond to your little petition, with which you concluded your letter. He whom you bid to be sent to you is now not with me, but with the lord of Auxerre, and so weak that he is said not to be able to come as far as me yet without serious harm.

This letter appears in virtually identical form in both letter-collections, but there is one potentially significant difference. The version in Bernard's collection, as seen above, starts abruptly without any formal salutation. In Peter's collection, however, it is prefaced by the following: 'To the lord and sweetest father Peter, by the grace of God abbot of the Cluniacs, brother Bernard, called abbot of Clairvaux, salvation from him who *commands the salvation of Jacob.*'[61] Whilst this salutation might in theory have been added at Cluny, it may seem more probable that it was subsequently excised at Clairvaux.[62] Peter's salutation had linked salvation with *caritas*. In answering it by this citation from Psalms,[63] Bernard may seem to be deflecting the suggestion that he himself is a source of grace. At the same time, the hint that Bernard himself is to be equated with Jacob may also look back towards the Jewish/Gentile opposition and to the issue of judaising. In a letter to Innocent, written during the papal schism and protesting about the loss of tithes, Peter had aligned the Cluniacs with Esau, robbed of his birthright, and the Cistercians with Jacob, characterised there as *sanctior*, 'more holy'.[64] In New Testament terms, on the other hand, *Iacobus* can be identified with the apostle James. In Galatians, it is the arrival of judaisers associated with the latter which causes St Peter to withdraw from eating with the Gentiles.[65] Bernard's salutation, accordingly, may simultaneously acknowledge and rebut the manipulatory implications of Peter's sub-text as discussed above. The form of address which follows, *o bone vir*, 'O good man', replicates that found previously in ep. 147.[66] As there, it might be considered to import facetious or ironic overtones.[67]

What follows can be seen to contain three primary linguistic nexuses. The first centres around the concept of 'beatitude' and 'beatification' (*beatificas/beatitudinis tuae/beatificationis meae/beatus/beari/beatum*). At one level, this can be regarded as a form of concealed epistolary rebuke. As a challenge to Peter's *Beatitudo tua*, it offers a riposte to the latter's reproof in letter 149.[68] It may, however, have a deeper significance. The part of the citation suppressed by Peter in his salutation had defined *beatus vir*, the 'blessed man', as one who undergoes temptation in the hope of salvation.[69] Arguably the 'temptation', 'trials', in question here are those

---

[61]   *Domino et patri dulcissimo Petro dei gratia Cluniacensium abbati, frater Bernardus Claraevallis vocatus abbas, salutem ab eo* qui mandat salutes Iacob (Peter, letter 177, p. 418 = Ps 43. 5).

[62]   Constable, for example, comments of Bernard's ep. 228, which appears as letter 110 in Peter's collection: 'The versions of Bernard's Letter 110 in his own letter collection and that of Peter the Venerable show that it was revised by Bernard before it was included in his collection. This is confirmed by the quotation from Letter 110 in Letter 111' (Constable, *Letters*, II, p. 44, n. 182).

[63]   *Tu es ipse rex meus et deus meus qui mandas salutes Iacob*, 'You yourself are my King and my God, who commands the salvation of Jacob' (Ps 43. 5). As in Peter's letter, the citation plays on the ambiguity of salvation and greeting.

[64]   Peter, letter 33, p. 109. See Chapter 4.

[65]   *Prius enim quam venirent quidam ab Iacobo cum gentibus edebat cum autem venissent subtrahebat et segregabat se timens eos qui ex circumcisione erant*, 'For, before certain from James came, he (Peter) was eating with the Gentiles. But when they had come, he withdrew and separated himself, fearing those who were of the circumcision' (Gal 2. 12).

[66]   Bernard, ep. 147, 1, *SBO*, VII, p. 350.

[67]   Like letter 175, Peter's preceding letter 65 had contained complimentary material of a somewhat ambivalent nature. See Chapter 3.

[68]   *Nam* reverentissimum *me esse ignoro*, patrem *quantum ad te me esse nego* ... (Peter, letter 149, p. 364).

[69]   *Beatus vir qui suffert temptationem quia cum probatus fuerit accipiet coronam vitae* ..., 'Blessed is the man who suffers temptation, because when he has been proved he will receive the crown of life ...' (Iac 1. 12).

represented by the association with Cluny consequent upon the demands of *caritas*. At the same time, it may also point towards a hidden allusion to Galatians, which again evokes the issue of 'circumcision'. The passage in question asserts: 'You know that I preached the gospel to you long since through the infirmity of the flesh, and you did not scorn nor reject your temptation in my flesh, but you received me as an angel of God, as Jesus Christ. Where is your beatitude? For I bear witness to you that if it were possible, you would have plucked out your eyes and given them to me. Therefore am I made an enemy to you speaking the truth?'[70] The sense here might be held to work by ironic inversion. Like Paul, Bernard can lay claim to having preached 'long since'. His gospel, however, had been that of the 'circumcision'. Rejected by Peter and the Cluniacs, he now finds himself seemingly 'beatified', treated as a 'fellow-citizen' of the angels, and equated with the heavenly *sponsus*.

The second nexus can be seen as representing a subversion of the *topos* of spiritual nourishment. Bernard declares that this *bucella*, 'morsel', 'mouthful', must not be gulped down *plenis buccis*, with 'full cheeks', 'copious mouthfuls', but subjected to some process of mastication.[71] On the surface, this functions as a declaration of the 'sweetness' of Peter's subject-matter which can be paralleled with Peter's earlier praise of the 'honey and milk' of Bernard's ep. 387.[72] The terminology, however, serves to introduce potential overtones and undertones. At first sight, the statement seems to connote self-directed mockery, the necessity for Bernard to control his 'greed'. The addition, however, of the words *ut aiunt*, 'as they say', suggests that Bernard is drawing here on a proverbial saying. Analogy with other proverbial uses of *bucca* might point towards a warning against biting off more than one can chew.[73] This finds some confirmation in the presence of *liquare*, which can imply both to 'make liquid' and to 'strain', 'clarify'. The second of these may seem to introduce some element of doubt as to the validity or desirability of this particular form of nourishment. Again, this may find some kind of parallel earlier in the correspondence, this time in Bernard's ep. 228, where Bernard claims that such unexpected 'favour' (Peter's missing letter) is an object of 'suspicion'.[74] At the same time, the statement as a whole may recall and subvert the

---

[70] *Scitis autem quia per infirmitatem carnis evangelizavi vobis iam pridem et temptationem vestram in carne mea non sprevistis neque respuistis sed sicut angelum Dei excepistis me sicut Christum Iesum ubi est beatitudo vestra testimonium enim perhibeo vobis quia si fieri posset oculos vestros eruissetis et dedissetis mihi ergo inimicus vobis factus sum verum dicens vobis* (Gal 4. 13–16). The context is one of rejection. In what follows, Paul apparently lays the blame at the door of judaisers, who seek to trouble the Gentile faith: *Aemulantur vos non bene sed excludere vos volunt ut illos aemulemini*, 'They emulate you not well, but they wish to exclude you, so that you may emulate them' (Gal 4. 17).

[71] *Quamquam et hanc mihi, dulcem licet, bucellam liquandam arbitror, nec omnino plenis, ut aiunt, buccis admittendam* (ep. 265, p. 174).

[72] Peter, letter 149, p. 365.

[73] *Gratis equo oblato non debes pandere buccas* = 'Don't look a gift-horse in the mouth' (see H. Walther, *Lateinische Sprichwörter und Sentenzen des Mittelalters*, 6 vols, Göttingen, 1963–1969, 10451); *Saepe inter buccam casus contingit et offam* = 'There's many a slip 'twixt cup and lip' (ibid., 27143).

[74] *Nam suspectum id mihi facit vestra ipsa tam subita et inopinata dignatio*, 'For your so sudden and unexpected favour makes it suspect to me' (Bernard, ep. 228, 1).

accusation brought in the Gospels against the Pharisees and used by Peter against his opponents in letter 28, that of 'straining out a gnat and swallowing a camel'.[75]

Bucella, on the other hand, is found in several potentially significant Biblical contexts associated with hospitality. Of these, two, coming from the Old Testament, are seemingly positive, one, from the New Testament, overtly negative. The first concerns the divine visitation to Abraham of God and two angels. Abraham offers refreshment with the words, 'I will place a mouthful of bread: strengthen your heart, after you will pass on.'[76] The second concerns Boaz and Ruth. The latter is instructed, 'Come hither and eat the bread, and dip your morsel in the vinegar.'[77] In the first case the invitation is the prelude to the promise of a miraculous son to the aged Sarah, in the second it forms the prelude to a marriage. As argued previously, both the promise of a 'son' and the issue of a 'marriage' have already figured in Bernard's side of the correspondence. Ep. 147, written in 1138, had promised a visit 'if the season accompanies'.[78] The phrasing recalls both the promise to Sarah and the similar prophecy of Elisha to the woman of Shunem.[79] The visit, however, would appear never to have taken place. The claim in ep. 387, written as recently as 1149, that 'my soul was glued to yours long since'[80] may recall the projected intermarriage between the Canaanite Shechem and the Israelite Dinah, which led to betrayal and disaster.[81] The overtly negative instance of *bucella* comes at the Last Supper, where Christ hands his dipped bread to Judas Iscariot as a mark of impending betrayal.[82]

The latent theme of hospitality diagnosed above may point towards another lurking biblical allusion with angelic connotations: 'Let the charity of brotherhood remain. Do not forget hospitality, for through this certain have entertained angels unawares.'[83] Cumulatively, the allusions may represent a concealed response to Peter's expressed desire for the presence of Bernard through the visit of Nicholas. Bernard's approach as a whole may also look back towards a letter of Augustine which, it was argued previously, had furnished him with the means of introducing a covert allusion to the notion of a recantatory palinode into ep. 228.[84] In that letter, while Augustine had claimed to find pleasure in the praise of his addressee, he had stressed that the pleasure was dependent on its nature and its source, thus implicitly

---

[75]   Mt 23. 24. See Peter, letter 28, p. 66.

[76]   *Ponam bucellam panis et confortate cor vestrum postea transibitis* (Gn 18. 5). The visit to Abraham is followed by one to Lot, who, alone with his family, is allowed to escape the destruction of Sodom (ibid., 19. 15).

[77]   *Veni huc et comede panem et intingue bucellam tuam in aceto* (Rt 2. 14).

[78]   *si vita comes fuerit* (Bernard, ep. 147, 2, *SBO*, VII, p. 351).

[79]   IV Rg 4. 16. See Chapter 3.

[80]   *Iam pridem conglutinata est anima mea animae vestrae..* (Bernard, ep. 387, *SBO*, VIII, p. 355).

[81]   Gn 34. 3. See Chapter 7.

[82]   *Et post bucellam tunc introivit in illum Satanas*, 'And after the mouthful there entered into him Satan' (Jn 13. 27).

[83]   *Caritas fraternitatis maneat hospitalitatem nolite oblivisci per hanc enim latuerunt quidam angelis hospitio receptis* (Hbr 13. 2).

[84]   See Chapter 5.

rejecting flattery and insincerity.[85] The careful balance of positive and negative allusions in Bernard's treatment of the theme seems to match obliquity with obliquity and to introduce a note of doubt and distrust. The consequent ambiguity may work at two levels, displaying an elegantly worded scepticism with regard to Peter's motives, and indicating the need for a careful scrutiny of the implications of the invitation to Cluny extended through the concept of Nicholas as *alter ego*.

The third nexus, built around the twin themes of humility and imitation, is set into a section which adopts, but inverts, the syntactical means by which Peter presented the requested visit as both inevitable and certain of fulfilment. Using the same pattern of decreasing frequency (*semper/saepe/semel*), but omitting Peter's crucial *in proximo*, 'soon', remote futures (*det/tribuat*) are succeeded by unfulfilled presents (*reverterer/conspicerem/perciperem*), which seem to deny the possibility of the eye-witness experience which Bernard is evoking. The characterisation of Peter through a synonymous triplet as a role model for monastic discipline[86] culminates in his presentation as a teacher of spiritual humility.[87] The biblical citation incorporated in the last is taken from a context which points back to the wider issue of Cluniac–Cistercian approaches to monasticism: 'Take my yoke upon you and learn from me that I am gentle and humble of heart and you will find rest for your souls. For my yoke is sweet and my burden is light.'[88] Peter in letter 150 had commiserated with those 'wretches' who followed what was 'heavy', but rejected what was 'light'.[89] Moreover, the statement that Bernard would perceive this *fide oculata*, 'with clear-sighted faith', both conveys the notion of *attestatio*, and harks back to Peter's demand in letter 111 for *oculus simplex*, the 'single eye'.[90]

The seeming eulogy of Peter can, accordingly, be translated into a seeming eulogy of Cluny, or, more moderately, into a seeming acknowledgement that a visit to Cluny would enable Bernard to see the virtues of the Cluniac way of life. The syntactical pattern within which this acknowledgement is enclosed, however, casting doubt on the possibility of its fulfilment, might equally appear to bring into

---

[85] *Nam eloquium tuum me delectat, quoniam graviter suave est vel suaviter grave; meis autem laudibus cum profecto nec omnibus delecter nec ab omnibus sed eis, qualibus me dignum esse arbitratus es, et ab eis, qualis es, id est qui propter Christum diligunt servos eius, etiam laudibus meis me delectatum in litteris tuis negare non possum,* 'For your eloquence delights me, since it is gravely sweet and/or sweetly grave. Indeed, while certainly I am delighted neither by all praise of myself nor [by praise of myself] from all, but by that such as you have thought me worthy of, and from those such as you are, that is, who because of Christ love His servants, I cannot deny that in your letter I have been delighted even by praise of myself' (Augustine, ep. 231, 2, *CSEL*, 57, p. 505).

[86] *Non ... frustra conspicerem virtutis exemplar, disciplinae summam, speculum sanctitatis* ... (Bernard, ep. 265, p. 174).

[87] *quodque minus usque adhuc a Christo didicisse me fateor, non incassum ... perciperem* ..., 'and, what until now I admit that I have learned from Christ too little, not to no purpose ... would I be perceiving ...' (ibid.).

[88] *Tollite iugum meum super vos et discite a me quia mitis sum et humilis corde et invenietis requiem animabus vestris iugum enim meum suave est et onus meum leve est* (Mt 11. 29–30).

[89] Letter 150, p. 367. See Chapter 8.

[90] Letter 111, p. 281. See Chapter 6.

question the validity of the experience. Moreover, the eulogy may, in itself, be seen as comprising a blocking manœuvre in relation to Peter's request. The notion of imitation seems to look back to the letter of Augustine discussed above. There, Augustine claims that praise rightly directed benefits the giver rather than the receiver, since it shows the recognition of a suitable model for imitation.[91] Bernard's linking of imitation with humility, 'Who may grant me to be able to imitate as well as to admire the mark of such great humility?',[92] suggests that Peter's letter of praise is, paradoxically, proof of his spiritual superiority. By apparently choosing to accept its sincerity, Bernard has, in fact, undercut the pretext for Nicholas's visit, that only through this can Peter (and the Cluniacs) attain salvation. At the same time, he has imitated Peter stylistically, through a tissue of elaborate compliment which functions as ironic self-depreciation, thus turning the tables on his addressee.

Up until this point, Nicholas himself has not been mentioned. Bernard has seemingly chosen to take Peter's gambit of the *alter ego* at face value, and arrogated the invitation to himself. There may, however, be hidden allusions. Bernard's doubts, as to whether he merits 'such great affection' from 'so great a man',[93] are followed by a *sententia* which may derive from Cicero. On the surface, the statement 'the wish to be loved more than is just is missing from the just man'[94] is applied to Bernard. It might equally, however, be thought to apply to Peter. According to Cicero's *Laelius*, it is an unreasonable desire for the presence of a friend which is said to reveal one who is *parum iustus*, 'too little just'.[95] Peter's compliments have been directed towards Bernard. The object of his pressing request, however, is Nicholas. Further hints may tie in with the earlier allusions to treachery and betrayal, through the citation from Tobit, 'Do not do to another what

---

[91]   *Etenim cum laudantur boni, non laudatis sed laudantibus prodest. Nam illis, quantum ad ipsos attinet, quod boni sunt, sufficit; sed eis, quibus expedit imitari bonos, gratulandum est, cum ab eis laudantur boni, quoniam sic indicant eos sibi placere, quos veraciter laudant*, 'For when good men are praised, it benefits not those who have been praised but those who are praising. For it suffices the former, as far as pertains to them, that they are good; but the latter, for whom it is expedient to imitate good men, are to be congratulated, whenever good men are praised by them, since in this way they show that they are pleased by those whom they truly praise' (Augustine, ep. 231, 4, p. 506).

[92]   *Quis mihi det tantae humilitatis insigne tam imitari posse quam admirari?* (Bernard, ep. 265; *det* appears as *tribuat* in Peter's version.) *Admirari*, to 'wonder at', 'admire', is not always unambiguously positive. As Torrell and Bouthillier point out, what provokes wonder does not necessarily inspire belief or admiration (J.-P. Torrell and D. Bouthillier, '*Miraculum*. Une catégorie fondamentale chez Pierre le Vénérable', *Revue Thomiste* 80 (1980), 357–86, 549–66, pp. 369–70).

[93]   *Nempe non video in me unde tantum diligi meruerim, praesertim a tanto* (Bernard, ep. 265, p. 174).

[94]   *Scio ... quia plus iusto velle diligi, minus est a iusto* (Bernard, ep. 265).

[95]   *Quas (magnas res) qui impedire vult eo quod desiderium non facile ferat, is et infirmus est mollisque natura, et ob eam causam in amicitia parum iustus*, 'He who wishes to obstruct these (great matters) on the grounds that he finds it difficult to bear the grief of absence, is weak and unmanly by nature, and by reason of this too little just/reasonable in friendship' (Cicero, *Laelius*, XX. 75).

you do not wish to be done to you.'[96] This citation occurs in two places in the *Rule* of St. Benedict. The first concerns the prohibition on admitting monks from other institutions without the permission of their abbot,[97] the second, the discipline to be applied to any monk who, among other things, 'presumes to take action without the Abbot's instruction'.[98] According to Bernard, Nicholas's infirmity is the main obstacle to the visit. *Infirmus*, 'weak', can connote bodily weakness and moral instability, *incommodum*, 'damage', 'detriment', with which it is coupled, could be applied to both physical and spiritual harm.

Bernard may seem, accordingly, to be hinting at the dangers of letting Nicholas go to Cluny, with its less rigid adherence to monastic discipline, the 'sweet yoke' and 'light burden'. Whether this suspicion should be seen as being directed towards Peter or Nicholas, or indeed towards both, is open to question. Peter's earlier letter 151 to Nicholas, cited earlier in this chapter, might be read as an attempt to lure Nicholas back to Cluny. Equally, as will be seen, Nicholas's subsequent letter to Peter offers hints, perhaps again to be read as manipulative devices, that his Cistercian fervour may be waning. At the same time, it is possible that what is at issue is a wider question of who commands Nicholas's loyalty, as suggested by Bernard's use of *iubetis*, 'you bid'.[99] The other ground on which the refusal is based, that of Nicholas's absence, may be relevant here. Nicholas himself will claim that his stay with the Cistercian bishop, Hugh of Auxerre,[100] was at the request of Peter, and on Cluniac business.[101] Further, the case in question is said to relate to the abbot

---

[96]   *Quod tibi non vis* fieri, *alii* ne *feceris* (ep. 265, p. 175 = Tb 4. 16). The same injunction, as Constable signals, is to be found in a positive form in the Gospels: *Omnia ergo quaecumque vultis ut faciant vobis homines et vos facite eis*, 'Everything therefore which you wish men to do to you, do you also to them' (Mt 7. 12; Lc 6. 31).

[97]   *Benedicti Regula*, LXI. 14.

[98]   Ibid., LXX. 7.

[99]   *Is quem mitti vobis iubetis*.. (ep. 265, p. 175). In letter 175, Peter had used the expression *volo*, 'I wish', 'I will.' In 176, the accompanying letter to Nicholas, the wording is stronger. Peter both commands Nicholas's presence, *mando ... et omnino volo ...*, 'I command.. and altogether will ...', and claims to have commanded it from Bernard, *nil rogans velut pro imperio mandavi ...*, 'not at all asking, I commanded as by virtue of authority ...' (Peter, letter 176).

[100]   In 1138, Peter seems to have become involved in some kind of skirmish with the then newly elected Hugh of Auxerre, who had objected to ordinations at La Charité being performed by Hato of Troyes, on the grounds that it was in Auxerre's diocese (see Constable, *Letters*, II, p. 143). In a letter to the latter, Peter dismissively represents this new fervour in a series of metaphors, culminating in the image of *coruscus splendor*, a 'dazzling brightness', which lights up the night, only to vanish and leave behind 'thicker darkness' (Peter, letter 69, *Letters*, I, p. 200). He goes on to threaten that Cluny has papal privileges old and new, which, if challenged, carry the penalty of excommunication and which will, if necessary, be brought out and used (ibid.). That a messenger is subsequently said to have returned with news of peace suggests that Hugh is being presented as having backed down. Nicholas had been in Hato's service at that time.

[101]   *Cuius autem culpa est, quod tamdiu fraudatus sum desiderio meo? Mea non est, tam propter infirmitatem, quam propter occupationem, quae mihi a te fuit iniuncta*, 'Whose blame is it, that I have for so long been cheated of my desire? Not mine, both because of my illness and because of the business, which was laid on me by you' (Nicholas, letter 179, *Letters*, I, p. 421–2).

of Vézelay, at that time Pontius, brother of Peter the Venerable.[102] This may suggest that, although at Clairvaux, Nicholas is perceived by Bernard as acting in the interests, and doing the work, of Peter.

The hidden text which emerges from this letter of Bernard suggests that Bredero is correct in diagnosing an unwillingness on Bernard's part to authorise such a visit.[103] His other contention, however, that this unwillingness stemmed from a reluctance to become embroiled in Cluniac affairs, is more difficult to substantiate.[104] Indeed, there is evidence to suggest that Bernard may have chosen to go to Cluny for a Christmas visit in Nicholas's place, a move which might be seen as taking advantage of Peter's gambit of the *alter ego*. The evidence comes from two sources. In 181, Peter's next letter to Bernard, written some time before Easter 1151, Peter refers to a recent conversation held at Cluny, at which the question of Nicholas's visit was again blocked.[105] The letter from Nicholas cited above contains what looks like a further allusion. Nicholas expresses a sense of loss that he did not see 'those two great luminaries at the same time, and in the firmament of heaven, namely in that place, which the Lord chose from all the places of the world, for his name to be there'.[106] This may combine a reference to creation with one to the nativity. In Genesis, God is said to have placed 'luminaries' 'in the firmament of heaven'.[107] Subsequently the sun and the moon are described as *duo magna luminaria*, 'two great luminaries'.[108] According to Luke, the circumcision of

---

[102] *In causa fuit causa fratris tui, domini mei Vizeliacensis abbatis, ad quam ex praecepto tuo oportuit me* pugnare ad bestias *ut* non praevaleret homo, 'The cause was the case of your brother, my lord abbot of Vézelay, for which on your order I had *to fight with the beasts*, that *the man should not prevail*' (Nicholas, letter 179, p. 421 = I Cor 15. 32; II Par 14. 11). According to Constable, this probably relates to a dispute between Pontius and the bishop of Autun, for which Hugh of Auxerre had been appointed as mediator by Eugenius in 1146 (see Constable, *Letters*, II, p. 218).

[103] Bredero, *Bernard of Clairvaux*, p. 243.

[104] Bredero, 'St. Bernard in his relations', pp. 341–2, 346; idem, *Bernard of Clairvaux*, p. 247.

[105] *Sed recolo, quid mihi nuper sanctitas tua Cluniaci constituta dixerit: Ad quid vultis Nicholaum?*, 'But I recollect what your Sanctity recently said to me, being halted at Cluny: "For what purpose do you wish Nicholas?"' (Peter, letter 181, p. 424).

[106] *Quis mihi recompensabit, quod non vidi pariter duo illa magna luminaria, et in firmamento caeli, videlicet loco illo quem elegit dominus ex omnibus locis terrarum, ut esset nomen suum ibi?* (Nicholas, letter 179, p. 421).

[107] *Dixit autem Deus fiant luminaria in firmamento caeli ...*, 'God said, "Let there be luminaries in the firmament of heaven ..."' (Gn 1. 14).

[108] Ibid., 1. 16. There they are characterised as *luminare maius*, the 'greater luminary', or sun, and *luminare minus*, the 'lesser luminary', or moon. In his *Apologia* Bernard had amplified the statement from I Corinthians, 'One is the brightness of the sun, another the brightness of the moon, another the brightness of the stars, for star differs from star in brightness. So also is the resurrection of the dead' (I Cor 15. 41), to claim that while the 'righteous' would all shine 'as the sun', some would shine more than others, 'in accordance with the diversity of (their) merits' (*Apo*, IV. 9). A distorted version of this had, in turn, been placed in the mouth of the Cistercians in Peter's letter 111: *Felices nos ..., quorum sol aliorum sidus obscurat*, 'Blessed are we ..., whose sun eclipses the star of others' (Peter, letter 111, p. 291). Nicholas's use of *pariter*, 'at the same time', 'in like degree', may seem to wipe out this distinction.

Jesus, on the eighth day in accordance with Jewish custom, was followed by his naming, presumably at Bethlehem, preceding the dedication at Jerusalem.[109] Since Nicholas had been invited to stay at Cluny until the 'octave of Christmas', the remark may be self-referential. Nicholas has gone, as it were, from birthplace (Cluny) to deathplace (Clairvaux).

The purpose of Bernard's visit can only be conjectured, but it seems probable, as Constable suggests, that it concerned the ongoing dispute over tithes between Gigny and Le Miroir.[110] According to Peter's next letter to Bernard, it did not, however, resolve the Nicholas affair. This would rear its head again early in 1151, this time initiated by an overture from Nicholas. As Constable suggests, it is in this letter, asking for an Easter visit, that certain, almost conspiratorial, manœuvrings on Nicholas' part might be thought to emerge.[111] The letter hints that Nicholas had been kept in ignorance of the previous invitation.[112] It asks Peter to write to Bernard through his own messenger,[113] rather, presumably, than through the one from Clairvaux, and requests a private copy of the letter.[114] Peter's brief response, sent as Nicholas had requested through the original messenger,[115] makes it clear that he will comply, at least, with the first request.[116] There is no reference there to the second request. However, a longer reply to Nicholas, which presumably accompanied the letter to Bernard, states: 'I have written to him concerning you what you yourself will see.'[117] This could imply that Bernard will show Nicholas the letter, or, less probably, allude to a copy. Nicholas's letter to Peter turns around the traditional motif of the Paschal friend, that is, the association between Easter and the joys of friendship.[118] This might serve to explain the veiled allusions to

---

[109] *Et postquam consummati sunt dies octo ut circumcideretur vocatum est nomen eius Iesus ...*, 'And after the eight days were finished that he be circumcised His name was called Jesus ...' (Lc 2. 21).

[110] See Constable, *Letters*, II, p. 229. This affair will form the focus of the next chapter.

[111] Ibid., p. 218.

[112] *Irascor occupationibus meis, quibus factum est non ut non vellem, sed ut non possem, et etiam ut nescirem*, 'I am angry with my occupations, by which it came about not that I did not wish, but that I was unable, and even that I remained in ignorance' (Nicholas, letter 179, p. 421).

[113] *scribe patri meo per nuntium tuum* ... (ibid., p. 422).

[114] *Rescriptum autem litterarum illarum quas mittes, mitte mihi secreto* ..., 'Send me privately a copy of that letter which you (will) send ...' (ibid.). Constable interprets this as copies of all the letters, that is, including the letters to the prior and Galcher (Constable, *Letters*, II, p. 218). Although this is a possibility, the use of the singular in *rescriptum* suggests that the reference is to the letter to Bernard alone. In technical terms, *rescriptum* implies an 'imperial rescript', replying to a petition.

[115] *Per praesentium latorem communica mihi de verbis illis caelestibus et dulcibus* ..., 'Through the bearer of the present, communicate to me from those heavenly and sweet words ...' (Nicholas, letter 179, p. 422).

[116] *Mittam e vestigio proprium [cursorem], qui nil negligere de iniunctis audeat* ..., 'I will send (my) own [courier] forthwith, who would not dare to neglect any of what is enjoined on him ...' (Peter, letter 180, *Letters*, I, p. 423).

[117] *Scripsi ei de te quod ipse videbis* (Peter, letter 182, *Letters*, I, p. 426).

[118] The motif can be traced back to Gregory the Great, who presents St Benedict as replying to the invitation *Surge, et sumamus cibum, quia hodie Pascha est*, 'Rise up, and let us take

244 The Correspondence between Peter the Venerable and Bernard of Clairvaux

death,[119] martyrdom,[120] Christ's passion[121] and resurrection,[122] with which the letter is studded. On the other hand, these might also be read, as suggested earlier, as hinting that Nicholas is facing 'spiritual death' at Clairvaux, and that he is seeking 'salvation' through Peter and Cluny.[123]

If the previous letter from Peter to Bernard could be reduced by the latter, albeit in irony, to *petitiuncula*, 181, his second extant letter on the subject, can be viewed as a full-blown petition. In terms of outward structure it seemingly fulfils the requirements of the latter, by demonstrating that the request is deserved, desirable, and within the power of Bernard to grant. Indeed, there are two overt pointers, as Peter recounts his earlier fear, that he would again be disappointed *petitis*, 'in (his) requests',[124] and goes on to demand Nicholas's presence *quando post haec petiero*, 'whenever after this I will seek (him)'.[125] It

---

food, because today it is Easter', *scio quod Pascha est, quia videre te merui*, 'I know that it is Easter, because I have deserved to see you' (Gregory the Great, *Dialogues*, II, I, *Gregorii Magni, Dialogi libri IV*, ed. U. Moricca, Istituto Storico Italiano Fonti per la Storia D'Italia, Rome, 1924, pp. 77–8). See Constable, *Letters*, I, p. 422, n. k.

[119] tristis est anima mea usque ad *te*, '*my soul is sad unto* you' (Nicholas, letter 179, p. 421= Mt 26. 38; Mc 14. 34). The biblical context is the impending betrayal of Christ: *te* has replaced *mortem*.

[120] *oportuit me* pugnare ad bestias, 'I had to *fight with the beasts*' (ibid. = I Cor 15. 32). The original runs, *Si secundum hominem ad bestias pugnavi Ephesi quid mihi prodest si mortui non resurgunt*, 'If, according to man, I have fought with the beasts at Ephesus, what does it profit me, if the dead do not rise again?' (I Cor 15. 32).

[121] *(quia)* desiderio desideravi hoc pascha manducare tecum, '(because) I have longed with longing to eat with you this Passover' (letter 179, p. 422 = Lc 22. 15). The biblical context is that of the Last Supper.

[122] *Ita ... fiat, ut aliquot diebus liceat mihi ... etsi non satiari, saltem refocilari praesentia tua*, 'So ... may it happen, that for some days I may be allowed ... if not to be sated, at least to be revivified by your presence' (ibid.).

[123] Most telling in this respect is a citation from Psalms: *O vocem amoris, vocem cui vicem ego rependere non possum* omnibus diebus vitae meae, 'O voice of love, voice which I cannot repay *with all the days of my life*' (ibid. = Ps 26. 4). The original context addresses God as *illuminatio mea et salus mea*, 'my illumination and my salvation' (Ps 26. 1). It continues there with a reference to enemies and tribulation, leading to the plea, *Unam petii a Domino hanc requiram ut inhabitem in domo Domini omnes dies vitae meae*, 'One thing have I sought from the Lord, this will I seek, that I may dwell in the house of the Lord all the days of my life' (ibid., 26. 4).

[124] *Fortassis ut iam bis, ita et nunc tertio petitis frustrareris*, 'Perhaps, as twice already, you would be disappointed in your requests now also a third time' (Peter, letter 181, p. 424). It is tempting to identify this letter with the third request, with the two failed requests being represented by letter 175 and by an oral request made during Bernard's visit to Cluny. This might seem to be reinforced by Peter's statement at the beginning of the letter, that he has asked *nunc scripto nunc verbo*, 'now in writing, now in conversation.' The seeming problem with this interpretation, that the thought is said to have occurred in the course of that visit, might perhaps be resolved by taking the question from Bernard said to have prompted it, *Ad quid vultis Nicholaum?*, 'For what purpose do you wish for Nicholas?', as representing in itself a refusal.

[125] *Nec nunc tantum, sed et quando post haec petiero [ut Nicholaum mittas]*, 'And not only now, but whenever after this I will seek (that you send Nicholas)' (ibid., p. 425).

will be argued here, however, that certain factors in the letter work to undermine the notion of petition both semantically and structurally. The letter sets up a duality of terminology. *Amicitia*, with its roots in the practical tradition of obligation, reciprocity and mutual benefit,[126] is set alongside *dilectio*, love of God and love of other.[127] These resonances are explored and exploited through the language of profit and loss, hovering ambiguously between the material and the spiritual, the literal and the figurative. At the same time, the overall framework incorporates passages of heavy irony and elements of what can be seen as subverted confession, as Peter admits to 'duplicity', then demands that this admission *prosit*, 'be of advantage', to him.

The duality is established at the start of the letter. The salutation draws yet again on James, wishing Bernard the salvation which God has promised *diligentibus se*, 'to those who love Him'.[128] The *captatio* which follows, however, makes use of an adapted citation from the Old Testament, with *propheta*, 'prophet', of the original being replaced by *amicus*, 'friend': 'If it permissible to complain about a friend, and so great a one, I complain, and say to him what was said to a certain person by certain people, "*Father, even if* a friend *had bidden you a great matter, certainly you should have done it*." '[129] The point of this reference to the visit of Naaman to Elisha may reside principally in Naaman's confusion of the material and the spiritual. Seeking a cure for his leprosy, he at first rejects the command to bathe in the river Jordan.[130] Subsequently, he tries to press material recompense upon the prophet, only to be refused. The citation may work in tandem with a hidden Ciceronian allusion, which takes its cue from Bernard's reference to the 'just man'. The Ciceronian condemnation discussed earlier forms part of a wider embargo on making unreasonable and injudicious claims on friendship: 'For warnings/orders can rightly be given in friendships, lest a certain immoderate indulgence should, as often happens, hinder the great benefits of friends ... And in every case consideration must be given both to what you demand from a friend, and to what

---

[126] See Chapter 1.

[127] *Nos ergo diligamus quoniam Deus prior dilexit nos si quis dixerit quoniam diligo Deum et fratrem suum oderit mendax est qui enim non diligit fratrem suum quem vidit Deum quem non vidit quomodo potest diligere*, 'Let us therefore love, since God first loved us. If anyone says, "I love God", and hates his brother, he is a liar. For how can he who does not love his brother, whom he has seen, love God, whom he has not seen?' (I Io 4. 19–20).

[128] *salutem* quam repromisit Deus diligentibus se (letter 181, p. 423 = Iac 1. 12).

[129] *Si de amico et tanto licet conqueri, queror, et ei quod a quibusdam cuidam dictum est, dico*. Pater et si rem grandem dixisset tibi *amicus,* certe facere debueras (ibid. = 4 Rg 5. 13). In what follows, Peter seemingly admits that the matter is *grandis*, 'great.' He denies, however, that *iter*, the 'way', is great. The language here may point back towards letter 150, with its distinction between *via dura* and *via mollis*, the 'harsh' way and the 'soft' way, suggesting that the matter in question is the attainment of salvation through the application of *caritas* (Peter, letter 150, pp. 367–8).

[130] *Iratus Naaman recedebat dicens putabam quod egrederetur ad me et stans invocaret nomen Domini Dei sui et tangeret manu sua locum leprae et curaret me*, 'Naaman withdrew angrily, saying: "I thought that he would come out to me and standing invoke the name of the Lord his God, and touch the place of the leprosy with his hand and cure me"' (4 Rg 5. 11).

you allow to be obtained from you.'[131] At the end of the letter, Peter will declare his intention of taking care 'not to demand anything which should rightly be denied, or which might damage you, not to say myself, in any respect'.[132] In between, as will be seen, Peter has demonstrated that *magnae utilitates*, great 'benefits', 'advantages' will accrue from his request.

As the letter progresses, it can be seen to play on the associations of *amicitia* and *dilectio*. Peter claims that 'to love what a friend loves' is the greatest proof of 'true friendship'.[133] The juxtaposition here of *amicitia* and *amare* may point towards the derivation of *amicitia* from *amor* given in the *Laelius*.[134] The sentiment, however, recalls that of Gregory the Great: 'The proof of affection (*dilectio*) is the display of performance.'[135] The statement is followed by an appeal to reciprocity: 'Since others are accustomed to repay service with service, kindness with kindness, would I not seem ungrateful beyond all measure, if without charge, without expense, I were to deny at least requital alone to one who loves?'[136] Nominally, this refers to the debt which Peter owes to Nicholas, earned by his services to Bernard and to himself.[137] Subsequently, the notion of reciprocity will be translated into terms of the relationship between himself and Bernard: 'May it [my confession], I say, be of advantage. But for what? That for my sake you should remove anything from your granaries? That you should withdraw anything from your cellars? That you should in any way diminish the treasures of gold and silver, even if they were present?'[138] At face value, this seems to represent an ironic allusion to previous (and probably ongoing) disputes over tithes. Unlike these, Peter's demand for Nicholas' presence

---

[131] *Recte enim praecipi potest in amicitiis, ne intemperata quaedam benevolentia, quod persaepe fit, impediat magnas utilitates amicorum.. . Atque in omni re considerandum est et quid postules ab amico, et quid patiare a te impetrari* (Cicero, *Laelius*, XX, 75).

[132] *Nam cavebo si potero, ne quid postulem quod iure negandum sit, vel quod tibi ne dicam mihi in aliquo obsit* (letter 181, p. 425).

[133] *Et quae maior probatio verae amicitiae, quam amare quod amicus amat?* (ibid., p. 423).

[134] *Amor enim, ex quo amicitia nominata est* ..., 'For love, from which friendship has been named ...' (Cicero, *Laelius*, VIII, 26).

[135] *Probatio dilectionis, exhibitio est operis* (Gregory the Great, *Homiliae in Evangelia*, II, xxx, I, ed. R. Étaix, *CCSL*, 141, Turnhout, 1999, p. 256). This is cited directly by Peter in a letter to Hato of Troyes (Peter, letter 5, *Letters*, I, p. 10).

[136] *Cumque alii obsequia obsequiis, beneficia beneficiis soleant rependere, nonne ultra omnem modum ingratus viderer, si absque sumptibus, si absque expensis, solam saltem gratiam amanti negarem?* (letter 181, p. 423). The language of gratitude (*ingratus/gratia*), together with *obsequium*, 'service', 'obedience', may recall the pressure exerted against Peter to support the plans for a new crusade. In Bernard's ep. 364, Peter had been called upon to perform *gratum ... obsequium ... Deo*, 'a service ... pleasing ... to God', after being warned of the dangers of being found *ingratus* (Bernard, ep. 364, 2, *SBO*, VIII, p. 319). See Chapter 9.

[137] *Causa tui [diligo], quia tibi obsequitur, causa sui, quia a tempore domini Trecensis episcopi, multis hoc meritis promeretur*, '[I love him] for your sake, because he serves you, for his sake, because from the time of the lord bishop of Troyes, he earned this by many services' (letter 181, p. 423).

[138] *Dico prosit [quod confessus sum.] Sed ad quid? Ut horreis tuis aliquid mei causa demas? Ut cellariis aliquid subtrahas? Ut de argenti aurique thesauris, etiam si adessent, quicquam imminuas?* (ibid., pp. 424–5).

will inflict no material loss upon Bernard. Indeed, what follows may point towards material gain, in the form of new recruits for Clairvaux.

At the same time, the references to 'grain' and 'treasure' may hint at an underlying figurative significance.[139] Not only will Nicholas's temporary absence inflict no spiritual loss, it may even, as Peter goes on to suggest, bring spiritual gain. Before this has come a cluster of terms relating to *dilectio*: 'But you ask the reason? Does it not suffice to see one who is beloved? He is yours indeed, but he is beloved to me. Or does it not please you, if I love what is yours? Does it not please you, that him, whom you, as I think, love more tenderly than many of yours, I myself love more affectionately?'[140] Several biblical allusions may be embedded here. The expression 'to love tenderly' is used of the affection felt by Jacob for his youngest son.[141] The context, the request by Joseph, his 'uterine brother', that Benjamin be sent to him in exile in Egypt may recall Peter's characterisation elsewhere of his role at Cluny as one of 'enslavement' to the Egyptians.[142] The claim to 'love what is yours' seems to represent an extension of the *alter ego* gambit, but it may also recall I Corinthians, with its injunction, 'Let no one seek what is his own, but what is of another.'[143] Subsequently, this is expanded into the statement, 'not seeking what is useful for me but what is useful for many, that they may be saved'.[144] If the previous nexus around *amicitia* emphasised service and requital, the stress here can be seen to be rather on renunciation and selflessness, with salvation as the goal.

The notion of profit is made explicit in the central section surrounding Nicholas's visit, where *otiosus*, 'profitless', 'fruitless', is set against *lucrosus*,

[139] In a letter to Theobald, abbot of St Columba, warning against undertaking crusade for the wrong motives, Peter uses the metaphor of the dispersal of stored-up grain to represent loss of salvation: *Stultus est, et vere fatua virgo, qui quod aedificat destruit, qui fructus quos collegerat spargit, qui fruges quibus aeterna ne deficiat pascitur vita, iam in arca congregatas, ventis furentibus et undique irruentibus prodit*, 'Stupid is he, and truly a foolish virgin, who destroys what he is building up, who scatters the fruits which he has collected, who exposes the grain with which eternal life is nourished so that it does not fail, already stored in the coffer, to the raging winds, rushing in from all sides' (Peter, letter 144, p. 359). In letter 111, Peter equates Bernard's letter with gold and silver for almsgiving (letter 111, p. 275).

[140] *Sed quaeris causam? Numquid non illa sufficit videre dilectum? Tuus quidem est, sed dilectus mihi est. An non placet tibi si diligo quae tua sunt? An non placet tibi, ut eum quem tu ut arbitror, multis tuorum tenerius diligis, ipse affectuosius diligam?* (letter 181, p. 423). Cf. *Diligo eum causa tui, diligo et causa sui*, 'I love him for your sake, I love him also for his sake' (ibid.).

[141] *Et nos respondimus tibi domino meo est nobis pater senex et puer parvulus qui in senecta illius natus est cuius uterinus frater est mortuus et ipsum solum habet mater sua pater vero tenere diligit eum*, 'And we replied to you, my lord, "We have an aged father and a young boy, who was born in his old age, whose uterine brother is dead, and his mother has only him, but his father loves him tenderly" ' (Gn 44. 20).

[142] *Sed duro Aegyptiorum imperio urgente, qui* manus *meas.. in cophino* servire *..., qui luteis operibus eas inquinari ... coegerunt ...*, '(But) hard-pressed by the harsh command of the Egyptians, who ... have forced my *hands ... to serve in basket-making* ..., to be stained in the works of mud ...' (Peter, letter 13, p. 19 = Ps 80. 7).

[143] *Nemo quod suum est quaerat sed quod alterius* (I Cor 10. 24).

[144] *non quaerens quod mihi est utile sed quod multis ut salvi fiant* (ibid., 10. 33).

'profitable', 'lucrative'. The first of these is introduced through heavy irony, as 'profitlessness' is seemingly equated with the furtherance of salvation and the promotion of monastic harmony: 'If to speak and confer about God, about divine matters, about causes in the highest degree useful to the soul is fruitless, the coming of Nicholas to me is fruitless. If to insert love for your person into the hearts of ours, to commend to all what is of your Order, to unite in short your universality to the body of our congregation with the glue of charity is fruitless, the coming of Nicholas to us is fruitless.'[145] What follows equates 'fruitlessness' with 'play' in a triplet which seems to look back to the blocking role played by *iocus* in Bernard's ep. 228:[146] 'This is the sportiveness, fruitlessness and vanity of Nicholas['s presence] among us.'[147] In contrast, the notion of profit is expressed in language which points towards increased recruitment for Clairvaux and the Cistercians: 'That thing is more profitable for yours than for me, because, after you, venerable man, there is no intermediary through whom they be able to plead among us more efficaciously to persuade, no hook with which they will be able to fish more copiously in any Cluniac sea or river.'[148] As with *amare* and *amicitia* earlier, Peter seems to be playing here with the etymology of friendship. Isidore of Seville had linked *amicus*, 'friend', with *hamus*, 'hook'.[149]

The role seemingly allocated to Nicholas here has already been prepared for in two ways. Peter's initial appeal to the principle of reciprocity, 'Indeed, I am accustomed not only to yield to one who asks, but even to obey one who orders',[150] has been given a concrete application which proves that Bernard has already 'profited' at Peter's expense: 'Why then, my dearest, is one at least not conceded to me for a month, when, drawn by love for you, I have conceded to you Peter, Robert,

---

[145] *Si de deo, si de divinis, si de summae utilibus animae causis loqui vel conferre otiosum est, Nicholai ad nos otiosus adventus est. Si amorem personae tuae cordibus nostrorum inserire, si quae vestri ordinis sunt omnibus commendare, si tandem universitatem vestram corpori congregationis nostrae caritatis glutino unire otiosum est, Nicholai ad nos otiosus est* (letter 181, p. 424).

[146] See Chapter 5.

[147] *Haec sunt ludicra, otiosa vel vana Nicholai apud nos* (letter 181, p. 424).

[148] *Est istud magis lucrosum vestris quam nobis, quia nullo post te venerande vir ... interprete efficacius ad persuadendum apud nos perorare poterunt, nec copiosius hamo aliquo in mari vel flumine Cluniacensi piscari* (ibid.). The metaphor of fishing looks back to the Gospels: *Et ait illis venite post me et faciam vos fieri piscatores hominum*, 'And He said to them, "Come after me, and I will cause you to become fishers of men" ' (Mt 4. 19). The statement here can be compared with that found in the letter from prior Peter of the Augustinian abbey of St John at Sens, celebrating the withdrawal to Cluny of Hato: *O quales et quanti pisces ad hoc litus aliquotiens tracti sunt ... quam plurimi proceres his retibus conclusi ad Cluniacense litus applicati sunt*, 'O, of what kind and how great have fish so often been dragged to this shore ... how many leading men, shut up in these nets, have been brought to land on the Cluniac shore!' (G. Constable, 'The letter from Peter of St John to Hato of Troyes', in *Petrus Venerabilis, 1156–1956: studies and texts commemorating the eighth centenary of his death*, ed. G. Constable and J. Kritzeck, Studia Anselmiana 40, Rome, 1956, 38–52, p. 51, reprinted in Constable, *Cluniac Studies*).

[149] *Amicus ab hamo, id est, a catena caritatis*, 'Friend from hook, that is, from the fetter of charity' (Isidore of Seville, *Etymologiae*, X. 5, Lindsay, I).

[150] *Soleo quippe non solum roganti cedere, sed et imperanti obaedire* (letter 181, p. 423).

very near to you in blood, Garnerius, certain others, not for a month, but in perpetuity?'[151] Nicholas's '*heart*' is said to '*utter the good news* of you and yours'. Further, he is said to '*ask for those things which are for the peace* of Jerusalem'.[152] The first of these, taken from Psalms, in its full form conflates the language of textuality and orality, in a manner reminiscent of Bernard's ep. 387:[153] 'My heart has uttered the good word; I speak my works for the King; my tongue is the pen of a swiftly writing scribe.'[154] The second, taken from the Gospels, forms part of a warning not to undertake what one cannot carry through. The example given there is that of a king who sues for peace, rather than engage with the overwhelming forces of his opponent,[155] the moral drawn, that anyone who wishes to follow Christ must be prepared to give up everything.[156] The addition by Peter of 'Jerusalem', previously, it was suggested, to be identified with Clairvaux, might suggest that the warning can be taken in two directions, that a refusal to send Nicholas will be tantamount to a declaration of 'war', and that, to truly follow Christ, Bernard must be prepared to 'give up' Nicholas.

The final section of the letter takes what seems to be a surprising twist, as Peter admits to previous 'duplicity' at Cluny,[157] said to lie in his denial that he wanted

---

[151] *Cur ergo mi carissime unus saltem mihi per mensem non conceditur, cum ego Petrum, cum Robertum, tibi sanguine proximos, cum Garnerium, cum quosdam alios tractus amore tui, tibi non mense uno sed perpetuo concesserim?* (ibid., p. 424). See Constable, *Letters* II, p. 219. The principle of reciprocity is subsequently formalised in a manner that recalls the Ciceronian demand for justice in friendship discussed above and counters Bernard's use of it in ep. 265: *Nec me paenitet amico cessisse, cui et adhuc in pluribus paratus sum cedere. Sed iustum est ut ipse vicem reddat, iustum ut semper sibi cedenti, et ipse aliquando cedat,* 'I do not repent of having yielded to a friend, to whom I am prepared to yield in still more. But it is just that he himself make return, it is just that to one always yielding to him, he himself should sometimes yield' (letter 181, p. 424).

[152] *Eructuat cor* eius semper nobis de vobis vestrisque verbum bonum, *quaerit bona genti suae,* rogat ea quae *ad* pacem sunt *Jerusalem,* '*His heart* is always *uttering* to us *the good news* of you and yours, he seeks blessings for his people, *he asks for those things which are* for *the peace of* Jerusalem' (ibid. = Ps 44. 2; Lc 14. 32).

[153] See Chapter 7.

[154] *Eructavit cor meum verbum bonum dico opera mea regi lingua mea calamus scribae velociter scribentis* (Ps 44. 2). In letter 182 to Nicholas, Peter also draws a parallel between the tongue and the pen: *Nam si talis est stilus tuus, qualis est animus tuus? Si talis littera tua, qualis lingua tua?,* '(For) if such is your pen, of what sort is your mind? If such is your written mark, of what sort is your tongue?' (letter 182, p. 426).

[155] *Aut qui rex iturus committere bellum adversus alium regem non sedens prius cogitat si possit cum decem milibus occurrere ei qui cum viginti milibus venit ad se alioquin adhuc illo longe agente legationem mittens rogat ea quae pacis sunt,* '(Or) what king, about to engage in war against another king, does not first sit and consider whether with ten thousands he may meet him who is coming against him with twenty thousands? Otherwise, while he is still acting far off, sending an embassy he asks for those things which are of peace' (Lc 14. 31–2).

[156] *Sic ergo omnis ex vobis qui non renuntiat omnibus quae possidet non potest meus esse discipulus,* 'Thus, therefore, anyone of you who does not renounce everything which he possesses cannot be my disciple' (ibid., 14. 33).

[157] *Duplex vere tunc fui ..., duplex plane tunc fui in verbo,* 'Truly, I was duplicitious then ... plainly I was duplicitous then in speech' (letter 181, p. 424).

Nicholas for anything 'great',[158] thus providing an inverted echo of the opening.[159] As with the notion of petition, the language of confession is made explicit: *fateor*, 'I admit'; *da veniam*, 'grant forgiveness'; *ecce confiteor*, 'lo, I confess'.[160] As with the language of petition, however, the motif has been subverted. The confession is tied into the *topos* of openness in friendship, and converted into a demand for 'profit': 'Let my confession be of advantage. Let it be of advantage that I have not veiled the truth with the covering of falsity. Let it be of advantage that because, as it is said, between friends everything should be open, I have revealed in the presence of a friend the guile of the heart hidden in cloud.'[161] Again, the language seems to look back to an earlier stage in the correspondence. In letter 29, concerning Langres, Peter had reported the candidate as having denied that he had 'veiled his heart' with 'the mantle of the lie'.[162] Subsequently, he had offered to 'reveal to clarity' how 'the murky cloud of the lie' had tried to eclipse the 'sharp vision' of Bernard's mind.[163] Its significance there, as previously argued, lay in the Augustinian demand for spiritual perception.[164]

At first sight, Peter may seem in this letter to have mounted a double justification in the name of (practical) *amicitia* and (spiritual) *dilectio*. In fact, however, this dualism may serve to undermine the very need for petition. *Amicitia* has seemingly been reduced to enlightened self-interest, the Cistercian desire to make new converts.[165] *Dilectio*, love of God and neighbour with salvation as its goal, should, on the other hand, need no petition. The point is made explicit through Biblical allusion, as Peter suggests that the request should have brought immediate compliance: 'You have asked and you have not been heard. Why should you pour out your prayers again?'[166] According to the Gospels, 'I say to you, ask and it will

---

[158] *Respondi: Non est tale quid, non est magnum*, 'I replied: It (the purpose for which I want him) is nothing such, no great matter' (ibid.).

[159] *Nec nego tamen rem grandem ...*, 'I do not deny, however, that the matter is great ...' (ibid., p. 423).

[160] Letter 181, p. 424. In similar vein, Peter's previous words are said to have been *indignantis*, 'of one indignant', rather than *confitentis*, 'of one confessing' (the truth.) He claims to have asked himself, *Quid quod vis totiens profitereris?*, 'Why should you profess openly your wish so often?' (ibid.).

[161] *Prosit quod confessus sum. Prosit quia veritatem falsitatis tegmine non velavi. Prosit ut quia sicut dicitur, inter amicos omnia nuda, dolum nubilo pectoris tectum coram amico nudavi* (ibid.) Bernard had used this *topos* in ep. 228, to justify plain speaking: *Sed hoc dixi, ne quid clausum in mente retinerem quod ore non promerem, quod id vera recuset amicitia*, '(But) I have said this so as not to keep shut in my mind what I would not bring forth with my mouth, because this is rejected by true friendship' (Bernard, ep. 228, 1, *SBO*, VIII, p. 98).

[162] *Post quae omnia id responsi accepi, numquam se amictu mendacii cor suum mihi velasse ...* (Peter, letter 29, p. 103).

[163] *(et) quam ... perspicuam mentis vestrae aciem caligosa mendacii nubes obfundere conata sit, ad liquidum exposuissem ...* (ibid.).

[164] Augustine, *De Trinitate*, IX, VI, 10–11. See Chapter 4.

[165] This may represent a perversion of the Ciceronian assertion that *utilitas* should follow *amicitia* rather than be its cause (Cicero, *Laelius*, XIV, 51).

[166] *Rogasti nec auditus es. Quid iterum preces funderes?* (letter 181, p. 424).

be given, seek and you will find, knock and it will be opened to you.'[167] The hint is developed through direct citation. Peter claims that he wanted to reply what the man 'blind from birth' said to the Pharisees: '*I have told you already and you have heard. Why do you wish to hear again?*'[168] Catechised there as to the nature of his miraculous cure, the man's assertion is rejected in disbelief.[169] The target here may be Bernard's assertion in his previous letter that a visit to Cluny would enable him to perceive Cluniac merits *fide oculata*, 'with clear-sighted faith'.[170] Peter may be insinuating that despite such a visit, Bernard's eyes have not been opened to spiritual insight.

It is possible that the accusation of 'duplicity' which fuels this confession is to be seen as emanating from Bernard himself, perhaps via the (mis?)representation of Nicholas. Nicholas's preceding letter claims that Peter has 'challenged' and 'summoned' him *duplici ... epistola*, in a 'double', 'duplicitous' letter.[171] The letter in question is Peter's 175, as the following quotation makes clear. In this light, Peter's opening allusion to Elisha and Naaman may take on an extra dimension. Elisha's command to Naaman had been, 'Wash and you will be cleansed.'[172] James, from which the second part of the salutation to this letter is taken, makes several allusions to those who are *duplex animo*, 'double in mind'.[173] In particular, sinners are instructed to 'cleanse their hands', the double-minded to 'purify their hearts'.[174] Through his confession, Peter can claim to have cleansed himself of his duplicity.[175] The opening, accordingly, might be construed as calling upon Bernard likewise to cleanse himself of his suspicion. At the same time, the notion of duplicity can itself be set against the *oculus simplex* of charity. Peter's letter has proved the purity of his intentions. Bernard must now prove the purity of his reception. The letter concludes with a demand for acquiescence: 'Therefore let there be done for me, let there be done, what I wish.'[176] The

---

[167] *(Et) ego dico vobis petite et dabitur vobis quaerite et invenietis pulsate et aperietur vobis* (Lc 11. 9).

[168] *Respondere volui, quod caecus ab utero Pharisaeis:* Dixi vobis iam et audistis. Quid iterum vultis audire? (letter 181, p. 424 = Io 9. 27).

[169] *Maledixerunt ei et dixerunt tu discipulus illius es nos autem Mosi discipuli sumus,* 'They cursed him and said, "You are His disciple, but we are the disciples of Moses" ' (Io 9. 28); *Responderunt et dixerunt ei in peccatis natus es totus et doces nos et eiecerunt eum foras,* 'They replied to him and said, "You were wholly born in sins, and you teach us?", and they threw him out of doors' (ibid., 9. 34).

[170] Bernard, ep. 265, p. 174.

[171] *Duplici enim epistola et provocasti me et evocasti ...* (Nicholas, letter 179, p. 422).

[172] *(quanto magis quia) nunc dixit tibi lavare et mundaberis,* '(how much more because) now he has said to you, "Wash and you will be cleansed" ' (4 Rg 5. 13).

[173] *vir duplex animo inconstans in omnibus viis suis,* 'a man double in mind, inconstant in all his ways' (Iac 1. 8).

[174] *Emundate manus peccatores et purificate corda duplices animo,* 'Cleanse (your) hands, sinners, and purify (your) hearts, you double in mind' (ibid., 4. 8).

[175] Referring to the conversation at Cluny, Peter claims: *Aliud tunc corde servatum est, aliud lingua depromptum est,* 'One thing at that time was kept in my heart, another brought forth by my mouth' (letter 181, p. 424).

[176] *Fiat ergo mihi, fiat quod volo ...* (ibid., p. 425).

seeming biblical echo may call upon Bernard to follow in the steps of Christ and resign himself to 'martyrdom'.[177]

The subversion of form found in this letter seems to represent something of a departure from the more subtle networks of allusion which have marked Peter's previous letters to Bernard. The uncertainty as to whose salvation is at stake, Peter's, Bernard's, Cluniacs', Cistercians', even Nicholas's, may serve to distract attention from the issues of loyalty and stability raised in Bernard's letter. Equally, the self-accusation of 'duplicity', framed here in terms of having kept the 'real' and laudable motive secret, may represent some kind of riposte to the doubts expressed there. Whether the letter succeeded in its object must, as already stated, remain an open question. Bredero, indeed, goes so far as to imply that the accusations of fraud subsequently brought against Nicholas by Bernard were simply a pretext for his dismissal, occasioned by Bernard's dislike and distrust of his axis with Peter.[178] In terms of the correspondence as a whole, this epistolary interchange can be seen as a microcosm of the whole debate. The presence of Nicholas seems to be presented by Peter as a concrete symbol of the monastic *caritas* which he is continually demanding. Indeed, it may almost be seen as a substitute for the recantatory palinode, wiping out the bitterness of the *Apologia* and of the succeeding disputes over tithes and elections. In terms of Peter's collection, however, the effect remains unchanged. Vigorous overtures from Peter, couched in terms of communal charity and the attainment of salvation, are met by apparently blocking responses from Bernard, then followed by silence.

---

[177] *non quod ego volo sed quod tu*, 'not what I wish but what You [wish]' (Mc 14. 36); *non mea voluntas sed tua fiat*, 'let not my will but Yours be done' (Lc 22. 42).
[178] Bredero, *Bernard of Clairvaux*, pp. 246–7.

Chapter 11

An Epistolary Closure: Peter, Letter 192

Bernard's ep. 265, written in autumn 1150, is his last preserved communication to Peter. The next and final phase of the correspondence, dating to May 1152, is preserved only on Peter's side, where it provides the closure to his letter-collection. It comprises a pair of related letters, 192 to Bernard,[1] and 193 to Nicholas,[2] which can be dated through references to Peter's visit to Italy which took place between November 1151 and April 1152.[3] Both letters offer an account of this journey, with that to Bernard containing added detail relating to Peter's reception by Eugenius III and the papal Curia. More importantly, both refer to a proposed meeting between Peter and Bernard, postulated to take place either at Dijon or at Clairvaux.[4] Almost certainly, this meeting, which appears to have taken place at Cluny, concerned the problems relating to tithes between Gigny and Le Miroir.[5] In spite of an apparent *concordia* reached previously, probably during Bernard's visit to Cluny over the Christmas period of 1150,[6] renewed trouble seems to have broken out during Peter's absence in Italy, culminating in a violent attack on Le Miroir organised by ringleaders from Gigny.[7] This resulted in two papal bulls, one addressed to Humbert, archbishop of Lyons, in whose diocese both institutions lay,[8] the other to Peter and the Cluniacs,[9] demanding immediate reparation under threat of interdiction.

---

[1] Peter, letter 192, *Letters*, I, pp. 443–8.

[2] Idem, letter 193, ibid., pp. 448–50.

[3] Constable, *Letters* II, pp. 226–7. For a reconstruction of Peter's movements during this visit, see van den Eynde, 'Principaux voyages', pp. 79–84.

[4] *Occurram ... inquam servo meo ... vel apud Divionem, vel apud ipsam Clarevallem*, 'I will meet ... I say, my servant, either at Dijon or at Clairvaux itself' (letter 192, p. 448); *Da operam quaeso, ut dies colloquii inter me et dominum Clarevallensem tertia post pentecosten dominica apud Divionem si fieri potest habeatur*, 'Take pains, I ask, that the day of conference between myself and the lord of Clairvaux may take place at Dijon, if possible, on the third Sunday after Pentecost' (letter 193, p. 450).

[5] The evidence for this comes from Bernard's ep. 283 to Eugenius: *Apud Cluniacum occurrimus Gigniacensibus spe pacis ...*, 'At Cluny we met those of Gigny, in the hope of peace ...' (Bernard, ep. 283, *SBO*, VIII, p. 197). See Constable, *Letters*, II, p. 229, which revises the chronology previously given in 'Cluniac tithes.' Leclercq dates this meeting to March rather than June (ibid., n. 12). In view of the surrounding chronology, however, this seems improbable.

[6] Cf. Constable, *Letters*, II, p. 229

[7] See Constable, 'Cluniac tithes', pp. 617–24; idem, *Letters*, II, p. 229.

[8] *Nequitia illorum*, dated 5 March, 1152 (Eugenius III, ep. 99, in Brial, *RHGF*, 15, pp. 472–3 = JL 9562). There Eugenius states that the attack took place *post factam etiam inter eos per carissimum filium nostrum Bernardum Claraevallensem et Petrum Cluniacensem abbates, concordiam ...*, 'even after an agreement had been made between them, through our dearest son Bernard, abbot of Clairvaux and Peter, abbot of Cluny ...' (ibid., p. 472).

[9] *Inebriati sicut*, dated 14 March 1152 (Eugenius III, ep. 98, ibid., pp. 471–2 = JL 9563).

Letter 192 presents itself as a delayed response to a letter from Bernard.[10] The contents of this letter, however, can only be reconstructed from Peter's reply. According to this, Bernard is reported as having requested Peter to show 'clemency', and to take back into his affection his 'withdrawing sons'.[11] Peter's response nowhere makes clear in concrete terms what the offence prompting this request has been. In fact however, as Constable suggests, this missing letter was surely concerned with the attack on Le Miroir.[12] Although neither institution is mentioned by name in Peter's letter to Bernard, there is a somewhat enigmatic reference to the abbot of Le Miroir in the companion-letter to Nicholas.[13] Additionally, as will be seen, the contents of the letter to Bernard may function as an ironic commentary on the papal bull received by Peter. Moreover, the letter is permeated by biblical allusions which provide support, albeit circumstantial, for the identification. If, accordingly, the affair between Gigny and Le Miroir is accepted as forming the subject of Bernard's trigger-letter and the basis of Peter's response, it may be noted that an external attack is apparently being construed and presented here in the light of an internal revolt. Equally significant in terms of Peter's letter-collection is the fact that in the accompanying letter to Nicholas, as will be shown, journey and return are constructed in a fashion diametrically opposed to that found in the letter to Bernard.

At first sight, letter 192 appears to fall into discrete sections. The first half deals entirely with Peter's journey and reception,[14] the second, slightly longer, with Bernard's request.[15] The whole is prefaced by a 'personal' *captatio*, which pleads pressure of business as an excuse for delay,[16] while the second section is followed by a lengthy coda, which also takes its subjects from Bernard's letter.[17] The

---

[10]   *Quoniam sanctitati vestrae mihi tam dulciter tam benigne scribenti, tot diebus rescribere distuli, nolite mirari*, 'That I have put off writing back for so many days to your Sanctity writing to me so sweetly, so kindly, do not wonder' (letter 192, p. 443). Bredero's suggestion that Bernard's letter arrived before Peter's departure in November lacks any supporting evidence, and seems unlikely in the light of Peter's wording (Bredero, 'Saint Bernard in his relations', p. 342; idem, *Bernard of Clairvaux*, p. 246). The first reference to *tot diebus*, 'for so many days' is subsequently emended to *paucis ... diebus*, 'a few ... days' (ibid., p. 444).

[11]   *monet* [*textus epistolae*] *ut nunc illi qui voluerunt, sed non potuerunt aliud agere, experiantur clementiam nostram, et affectus patris filios recedentes resignet visceribus suis*, 'it [the text of the letter] advises that those who wished to do, but could not do otherwise, should now experience our clemency, and that the affection of a father should give back to his entrails his withdrawing sons' (letter 192, p. 445).

[12]   Constable, *Letters*, II, p. 227.

[13]   *De consanguineo meo, abbate Miratorii mirando et admirabili, quid dicam non invenio. Invenirem vero fortassis, nisi brevitatis studium finire me epistolam cogeret*, 'Concerning my kinsman, the wonderful and admirable/astonishing abbot of Le Miroir, I cannot find what to say. Perhaps I would find what to say, if zeal for brevity did not compel me to finish the letter' (letter 193, p. 450). As mentioned in a previous note, both terms can connote astonishment, without necessarily commanding belief or admiration. See Torrell and Bouthillier, '*Miraculum*', pp. 369–70.

[14]   Letter 192, pp. 444–5.

[15]   Ibid., pp. 445–8.

[16]   Ibid., pp. 443–4.

[17]   Ibid., p. 448.

apparent separability of the two halves, reinforced by a seemingly abrupt transition,[18] is partly redressed by formal verbal echoes. The *captatio* ends with a statement of Peter's 'debt' to Bernard.[19] The notion of 'debt' is reintroduced before the coda, forming a kind of ring-composition.[20] A similar device, based on the notion of 'sparing', encloses the second section.[21] The separability is further undermined by a series of verbal and thematic links, relating, at least in part, to these notions of debt and sparing.[22] In fact, as will be seen, the notion of separability is entirely misleading. A close examination of the *captatio* reveals the presence of a number of motifs which will determine the rest of the letter. Just as the account of visit and reception takes on a fresh significance in the light of this *captatio*, so Peter's response to Bernard's request is closely tied in to the account of the Italian visit. Central to the whole, as will be seen, is the notion of 'change'.

The opening excuse for delay in writing is couched in terms of elaborate imagery representing threats from nature: 'There had rushed upon me then by chance so great a whirlwind of business, and so great a mass of cases was suffocating me from all sides, that, not to say to write, it was scarcely allowed me then to live.'[23] What follows develops the image of a flood and links it with the return from Rome: 'With the bursting of the barrier an immense flood of waters poured out, and what the journey to Rome, accumulating little by little in my absence, had contained for some time after the manner of a standing pool, it poured forth in profusion upon my return.'[24] The explicit nature of this image suggests that the preceding use of *congeries*, 'mass', 'heap', may also connote

---

[18]   *Hortatur ... textus epistolae dulcis et sanctae ...*, 'The text of (your) sweet and holy letter exhorts me ...' (ibid., p. 445).
[19]   *Haec fuit causa, qua illi cui me totum debeo, debitum respondendi ... subtraxi*, 'This was the reason why I withheld the debt of replying ... from him to whom I owe myself wholly' (letter 192, p. 444).
[20]   *Non invenio, non sufficio. Sufficio tamen non quidem ad respondendum, sed ad rependendum tanto amori totum et integrum mei animi vel cordis affectum*, 'I cannot find, I do not suffice, not indeed to reply, but to repay to so great a friend the whole and untouched affection of my mind and heart' (ibid., p. 448).
[21]   *Ad illum [statum curiae] explicandum, quia brevis sermo non sufficit, parco litteris, sed ... cum praesens fuero non parcam verbis*, 'Because a short discourse does not suffice to unfold it [the attitude of the Curia] I spare the letter, but ... when I am present I will not spare speech' (ibid., p. 445); *Agnosco enim et vere agnosco quod dixistis, quia quantum pepercero vobis, parcam et mihi*, 'I recognise and truly recognise what you have said, that however much I spare you, I will also be sparing myself' (ibid., p. 448).
[22]   The notion of debt may find multiple applications in this letter, some of which explicitly equate it with sparing: the debt of friendship in general; Peter's debt to Bernard in particular; the forgiveness of sins, as in the petition 'let us off our debts as we have let off our debtors', *et dimitte nobis debita nostra sicut et nos dimisimus debitoribus nostris* (Mt. 6. 11); the dues remitted by the 'steward of inquity', a parable regularly interpreted in terms of the bestowing of alms (Lc 16. 1–12).
[23]   *Irruerat forte tunc tantus negotium turbo, tantaque causarum congeries me undique suffocabat, ut non dicam scribere, sed vix mihi vivere tunc liceret* (letter 192, p. 443).
[24]   *Exundabat disrupto obice immensa vis aquarum, et quas Romanum iter me absente paulatim congregans, stagni more aliquamdiu continuerat, in praesentem largissime profundebat* (ibid., pp. 434–4).

water, and seems to point towards a biblical source. According to Ecclesiasticus, 'At His (the Lord's) word, the water stood as a heap, and at the speech of his mouth, as reservoirs of water ...'[25] If so, it may seem that Peter has reversed the direction. From having been held in, the waters are said here to burst forth. The Biblical passage is celebrating the power of God, exalting both his mercy and his vengeance: 'since in His precept is approval and there is not diminution in His salvation',[26] and, again, 'His blessing has flooded as a river, and, just as the flood has inundated the dry land, so His anger will be the inheritance of the peoples who have not sought Him', that is, the Gentiles.[27] *Turbo*, 'whirlwind', 'storm', with which *congeries* is twinned here, similarly appears in a variety of Old Testament contexts signifying the wrath of God.[28]

This association with the manifestation of divine displeasure suggests that Peter is alluding here to more than the normal business of an abbot of Cluny. That he is refering to the revolt of his 'withdrawing sons' may be confirmed by two other possible Biblical references. The use here of *suffocare*, to 'stifle', 'suffocate', in a context associated with drowning, may look towards the presentation of demonic possession in the Gospels. Cast out of the man, the evil spirits are sent into a herd of swine, which is subsequently drowned.[29] At the same time, the same verb is used in another Biblical context, that of the parable of the sower, some of whose seed is said to land among 'thorns' and to be 'choked'.[30] In 193, the accompanying letter to Nicholas, Peter will contrast *spinae negotiorum*, the 'thorns of business', with *lilia gaudiorum*, the 'lilies of joys', in a context which parallels the whirlwind and flood as discussed above.[31] While this cannot in itself be held to prove that the 'withdrawing sons' are to be equated with those who initiated the attack on Le Miroir, the very choice of imagery may point in that direction. The notion of a flood as a threat to the 'fire' of fraternal *caritas* had been spelled out in Peter's earlier letter 111, where it had been linked with the disputed election at Langres and with

---

[25]   *In verbo eius (Domini) stetit aqua sicut congeries et in sermone oris eius sicut exceptoria aquarum ...* (Sir 39. 22).

[26]   *quoniam in praecepto ipsius placor fit et non est minoratio in salute illius* (ibid., 39. 23).

[27]   *Benedictio illius quasi fluvius inundavit et quomodo cataclysmus aridam inebriavit sic ira ipsius gentes quae non exquisierunt eum hereditabit* (ibid., 39. 29).

[28]   Iob 9. 17; Os 8. 7; Ier 23. 19; Is 28. 2.

[29]   *Exierunt ergo daemonia ab homine et intraverunt in porcos et impetu abiit grex per praeceps in stagnum et suffocatus est* (Lc 8. 33; Mc 5. 13, with *in mare* for *in stagnum*).

[30]   *Alia autem ceciderunt in spinas et creverunt spinae et suffocaverunt ea* (Mt 13. 7). Elsewhere in the Gospels, the symbolism is spelled out, in terms which target worldly anxieties and desires: *Quod autem in spinis cecidit hii sunt qui audierunt et a sollicitudinibus et divitiis et voluptatibus vitae euntes suffocantur et non referunt fructum*, 'That which fell among thorns is those who have heard, and going away are choked by the cares and riches and pleasures of life, and they do not bear fruit' (Lc 8. 14).

[31]   *In his constitutus ... statim post lilia gaudiorum spinas intravi negotiorum. Inundaverunt aquae super caput meum, et paene dixi parvus*, 'Set amongst these ... immediately after the lilies of joys I entered the thorns of business. *The waters flooded over my head*, and I almost *said* "little" ' (letter 193, p. 450 = Lam 3. 54). As Constable points out, the Vulgate reads *perii*, 'I have perished', for *parvus*, 'little.' If the reading here is correct, there may be an understood *sum*, 'I am'.

disputes over tithes.³² Moreover, as will be seen, the language surrounding the depiction of Eugenius may point towards an equation between the idea of divine wrath and the papal bull, presumably awaiting Peter on his return to Cluny.

The depiction of the journey is linked to what precedes by the biblical citation to which this builds up: 'Then I could deservedly cry out, *Save me God, since the waters have entered even up to my soul.*'³³ Not only does its continuation there, 'I have been thrust into the mud of the the abyss ...',³⁴ leading to the plea, 'Snatch me from the mud, that I be not imprisoned there ...,'³⁵ find a verbal echo in what follows,³⁶ the Psalm from which it is taken can be said have something of a programmatic function for the letter as a whole. It will be directly invoked on two further occasions, once in the second section,³⁷ and once in the coda.³⁸ The contexts from which these later citations are taken evoke alienation³⁹ and persecution respectively.⁴⁰ On the surface, the depiction of journey and stay charts the obverse. At its heart is a borrowing from Psalms: 'The Lord has magnified to deal with us ...'⁴¹ In the original, this is followed by the phrase, 'we have been made rejoicing'.⁴² Peter will subsequently declare, 'I found everything happy, indeed, on the way, but happier in the presence of the father.'⁴³ In fact, however, as with the previous allusion to Ecclesiasticus, Peter may seem to have inverted it. The Psalm continues 'Turn aside, Lord, our captivity, as the torrent in the south. Those who sow in tears will reap in exultation. Going, they went and wept, carrying their seeds; coming, however, they will come in exultation, carrying their

---

³² *cum nec aquae multae decimarum potuerint eum [affectum meum erga vos] exstinguere, nec impetus Lingonensium fluminum obruere(?)* (Peter, letter 111, p. 277). See Chapter 5.
³³ *Exclamare tunc merito poteram:* Salvum me fac deus, quoniam intraverunt aquae usque ad animam meam (letter 192, p. 444 = Ps 68. 2).
³⁴ *Infixus sum in limo profundi ...* (Ps 68. 3).
³⁵ *Eripe me de luto ut non infigar ...* (ibid., 68. 17).
³⁶ *Lutosas vias, quibus maxime angi, immo ... infigi verebamur ...,* 'The muddy ways, in which we greatly feared to be pressed tight, or rather ... imprisoned ...' (letter 192, p. 444). *Angere* commonly appears as a synonym for *suffocare*.
³⁷ *Mercatores ... de templo dei ... eiecit, quando discipuli de ipso dictum in psalmo recordati sunt:* Zelus domus tuae comedit me, 'He (Christ) threw out the merchants ... from the temple of God, when the disciples remembered that it had been said of Him in the Psalm: "Zeal for Your house consumes me" ' (ibid., p. 447 = Ps 68. 10; Io 2. 17).
³⁸ *Sed hoc quidem* gratis *ut psalmus ait, et salvator meminit,* 'But this indeed [the hatred of my serpents] is *for nothing,* as the Psalm says, and the Saviour remembers' (letter 192, p. 448 = Ps 68. 5; Io 15. 25).
³⁹ *Extraneus factus sum fratribus meis et peregrinus filiis matris meae quoniam zelus domus tuae comedit me,* 'I am made a stranger to my brothers and a foreigner to the sons of my mother, since zeal for your house devours me' (Ps 68. 9–10).
⁴⁰ *Multiplicati sunt super capillos capitis mei qui oderunt me gratis confortati sunt qui persecuti sunt me inimici mei iniuste quae non rapui tunc exsolvebam,* 'Those who hate me for nothing have been multiplied over the hairs of my head, my enemies who persecuted me unjustly have been strengthened, I paid then what I did not take' (Ps 68. 5).
⁴¹ Magnificavit vere Dominus facere nobiscum.. (letter 192, p. 444 = Ps 125. 3). The borrowing is not indicated by Constable.
⁴² *facti sumus laetantes* (Ps 125. 3).
⁴³ *Laeta plane in via cuncta repperi, sed laetiora apud patrem inveni* (letter 192, p. 144).

sheaves.'[44] Peter's account can be seen to go in the opposite direction. The journey to Rome is said to start and end in 'joy', while it is the return which will be marked by 'sadness' and a ruined 'harvest'.

In between comes a lengthy passage which plays on the concept of what can be termed metaphorical topography, that is, a depiction of geographical features which can be shown to have an underlying metaphorical application.[45]

> The frozen Alps themselves, and the peaks condemned to perpetual snow, almost forgot their ancient horror. The very weather which, as I learnt after our return, showed itself more importunate than usual during the winter months to our Gaul with heavy showers, with the exception only of five days, the whole time I delayed in Italy, both journeying by land and by river (for the Po detained us sailing for some days and nights), showed itself always pleasant and serene. We found the muddy ways, in which we greatly feared to be pressed tight, or rather, since all threatened it, to be imprisoned, almost stony with dryness. We rescued certain brothers, companions of our journey, men of pure and simple life, submerged in the waves, and now, even now, doomed to be extinguished, alive, so to speak, from the very jaws of death. I myself, more daring than usual, while I was trying to mount a certain bridge as a horseman, because I was weary of going on foot, as the tenacious mud sucked back the back feet of my mule, almost fell forward into a certain abyss lying beneath the same bridge. But with the strength of God adding force to the mule, suddenly I found myself together with it over the bridge, and so, apart from fear, I escaped, having suffered nothing grave. In short, in going, in returning, such not fortune but grace assiduously accompanied us, that nothing befell me, nothing befell ours, contrary to (our) wish, apart from the disappearance and death of beasts, for which God has no concern.[46]

Taken at a literal level of interpretation, this description might seem to represent, as van den Eynde claims, a celebration of a physical journey

---

[44]   *Converte Domine captivitatem nostram sicut torrens in austro qui seminant in lacrimis in exultatione metent euntes ibant et flebant portantes semina sua venientes autem venient in exultatione portantes manipulos suos* (Ps 125. 3–6).

[45]   On this concept, see Chapter 1.

[46]   *Alpes ipsae gelidae, et perpetuis nivibus condemnati scopuli, illius sui antiqui horroris paene obliti sunt. Aer ipse qui ut post reditum nostrum accepi, nostrae se Galliae, hibernis mensibus importuniorem solito nimiis imbribus praebuit, quinque solis diebus exceptis, toto quo in Italia demoratus sum tempore, tam terreno itinere, quam fluviali, nam aliquantis diebus ac noctibus, Padus nos navigantes detinuit, iocundum se semper ac serenum exhibuit. Lutosas vias, quibus maxime angi, immo cunctis id minantibus infigi verebamur, fere lapideas siccitate invenimus. Fratres quosdam itineris socios, purae ac simplicis vitae viros, fluctibus mersos, et iam iamque exstinguendos, ab ipsis ut sic loquar mortis faucibus vivos recepimus. Ipse plus solito audax, dum pontem quendam quia peditem ire pigebat, conscendere eques conarer, ultimos mulae meae pedes tenacissimo retrahente luto, in subiacentem eidem ponti quandam abyssum paene prolapsus sum. Sed dei virtute mulae vires addente, subito me cum eadem super pontem inveni, sicque praeter timorem, nihil triste passus evasi. Quid multa? Talis nos in eundo, talis in redeundo, non fortuna sed gratia assidue comitata est, ut nihil mihi, nihil nostris praeter votum contigerit, excepto defectu vel morte bestiarum, de quibus deo cura non est* (letter 192, p. 444).

successfully accomplished.[47] Even at this level, however, there is a potential contradiction, between the depiction of the roads as 'almost stony with dryness' and the 'mud' encountered by the mule. The journey seems to be constructed as a series of minor miracles, starting with the removal of the barrier of the Alps. The statement that these 'forgot their ancient horror' is reminiscent of the depiction of transalpine Gaul as found in Ammianus Marcellinus, 'shut off' by the 'elevations of mountains', always 'blocked by snowy horror'.[48] In figurative terms, the dispersal of the chill can be ascribed to the fire of *caritas*, as can the miraculous dryness in Italy. This is counterbalanced, however, by a reminder of the 'heavy rains' in France, building up, perhaps, into the 'standing pool' which Peter claims to have discovered on his return. It might be argued that the removal of one obstacle will be cancelled out by the subsequent 'bursting of the barrier' which will threaten to drown him. The potential for figurative interpretation continues into the depiction of the miraculous escapes from death, through the emphasis on 'mud' and 'abyss'. In Rabanus Maurus *lutum* as used in Psalm 68 is glossed as 'carnal pleasure',[49] *abyssus* as both the judgement of God and, more directly, hell,[50] while a mule is said to be a symbol of laziness.[51] This may suggest that rather than simply charting physical dangers, Peter is also hinting at spiritual peril, encountered but overcome, a hint which, as will be seen, is made more explicit in the letter to Nicholas.

The ambiguity is compounded by a potential layering of classical and biblical allusion. The reference to the 'frozen Alps' may recall Lucan's depiction of Julius Caesar's march on Rome.[52] There, Caesar is constantly presented as guided by *fortuna*. Peter explicitly rejects fortune in favour of *gratia*, 'divine grace'. This rejection can be linked back to an earlier ascription of the prosperity of his journey to the 'zeal' of Bernard and the 'prayers' of the

---

[47] 'Le climat, le temps, le passage des Alpes, l'état des routes, tout avait été merveilleux' (van den Eynde, 'Principaux voyages', p. 83). *Merveilleux* may in itself, however, point towards some supernatural element.

[48] *Hanc Galliarum plagam ob suggestus montium arduos et horrore nivali semper obductos orbis residui incolis antehac paene ignotam ... munimina claudunt undique natura velut arte circumdata*, 'This region of the Gauls, previously almost unknown to the inhabitants of the rest of the world on account of the elevations of mountains, lofty and always blocked with snowy horror ... is shut off by fortifications on all sides, placed around by nature as if by art' (Ammianus Marcellinus, *Res gestae*, 15. 10. 1, ed. W. Seyforth, *Rerum gestarum libri qui supersunt*, Bibliotheca Scriptorum Graecorum et Romanorum Teubneriana, 2 vol., Leipzig, 1987, I).

[49] Rabanus Maurus, *Allegoriae in sacram scripturam*, in B. Rabani Mauri, *Opera omnia*, ed. J.-P. Migne, 6. vols, *Patrologia Latina*, 112, Paris, 1852, 991.

[50] Ibid., 852–3.

[51] *Mulus est quilibet piger, ut in Psalmis:* Nolite fieri sicut equus et mulus, *id est, nolite superbi esse et pigri*, 'A mule is anyone who is lazy, as in the Psalms: *Do not become as the horse and the mule*, that is, do not be proud and lazy ' (ibid., 1003 = Ps 31. 9). This may underlie Peter's comment *(quia) peditem ire pigebat*, '(because) I was weary of going on foot'.

[52] *Iam gelidas Caesar cursu superaverat Alpes*, 'Now Caesar had overcome the frozen Alps in his course' (Lucan, *De bello civili*, I, 183, ed. D. R. Shackleton Bailey, Bibliotheca Scriptorum Graecorum et Romanorum Teubneriana, Stuttgart, 1997, p. 7).

Cistercians.[53] In turn, however, the statement may seem to be undercut by the final dismissal of the death of beasts as a matter 'for which God has no concern', appearing to invert the Biblical assertion that God cares even for the 'fall of a sparrow'.[54] The topographical features in between may seem to look towards the descent of Aeneas into the underworld, with its standing pools of Cocytus and its Stygian swamp,[55] its mud and its abyss.[56] The essentially parodic nature of such mock-epic parallels, encapsulated in Peter's self-representation as *plus solito audax*, 'more daring than usual', runs in tandem, however, with a preceding biblical allusion, which again highlights the role of Bernard and points towards a potential identification of Peter with Christ: 'Even to the letter, *the crooked was made straight* for us, *and the harsh into smooth paths.*'[57] Originating in Isaiah, this citation is applied in the New Testament to the preaching of John the Baptist, heralding the coming of 'one whose shoes I am not fit to carry'.[58] At the same time, the reference to the abyss may also conjur up the ironic question in Romans: 'Or who goes down into the abyss, that is, to call Christ back from the dead?'[59]

The interplay between biblical and classical diagnosed above seems to form part of a wider pattern which appears to explore the overlap between the spiritual and temporal authority of Eugenius. The description of the weather in Italy as always *iucundus*, 'pleasant', and *serenus*, 'bright', 'serene', can be seen to set Christian against pagan overtones. In Christian terminology, *iucunditas* is primarily associated with the joys of eternity.[60] *Serenator*, on the other hand, had been an

---

[53]   *prosperum (Dominus) fecit iter nostrum, et gratia sua, studio vestro, precibus vestrorum, duxit et reduxit incolumes ...*, '(the Lord) has made our journey prosperous, and by His grace, your zeal and the prayers of yours, has lead us and brought us back in safety ...' (letter 192, p. 444).

[54]   *Nonne duo passeres asse veneunt et unus ex illis non cadet super terram sine Patre vestro*, 'Surely two sparrows are bought for a penny and one of them will not fall upon the ground without your Father?' (Mt 10. 29).

[55]   *Anchisa generate, deum certissima proles,*
      Cocyti stagna alta vides Stygiamque paludem,
      di cuius iurare timent et fallere numen
'Son of Anchises, most certain offspring of the gods, you see the deep pools of Cocytus and the Stygian swamp, whose power the gods fear to swear by and deceive' (Virgil, *Aeneid*, 6, 322–4, Mynors, p. 237).

[56]   *Hinc via Tartarei quae fert Acherontis ad undas.*
      turbidus hic caeno vastaque voragine gurges
      aestuat atque omnem Cocyto eructat harenam
'Hence is the way which leads to the waters of Tartarean Acheron. Here seethes the whirlpool, turbulent with mud and with the vast abyss, and belches all its sand into Cocytus' (ibid., 295–7, Mynors, p. 236).

[57]   *Facta sunt nobis etiam ad litteram* prava in directa, et aspera in vias planas (letter 192, p. 144 = Is 40. 4; Lc 3. 5).

[58]   *Qui autem post me venturus est fortior me est cuius non sum dignus calciamenta portare*, 'But He who is to come after me is stronger than me, whose shoes I am not fit to carry' (Mt 3. 11).

[59]   *Aut quis descendit in abyssum hoc est Christum ex mortuis revocare* (Rm 10. 7).

[60]   *cui promittitur omnimoda iucunditas aeternorum*, 'to whom is promised all the kinds of pleasure of eternal things' (Peter, letter 10, p. 17). See Chapter 5.

epithet of Jupiter, while *Serenitas* had come to function as an imperial honorific. The terminology finds an echo in the subsequent depiction of Eugenius himself: 'While that countenance of his, in which, truly, apostolic vigour and beauty shines, would change in accordance with the variation of cases, persons, occurrences, and show itself most differently now bright, now cloudy, to some and others, to me it never changed to the contrary.'[61] On the one hand this looks towards various biblical citations which evoke the light of God's countenance.[62] The notion of changeability found here, however, may recall the Horatian image of Jupiter 'thundering' from an 'unclouded sky'.[63] It is doubled by a statement that makes explicit the twin functions of divinity to anger and mercy: 'I noted often that when I was addressing him, either in private, or in public, he would exchange the rather harsh and gloomy mien which he was frequently compelled to put on for other cases from the appearance of a judge to the grace of a father.'[64] The statement may function in two directions. Proleptically, it will provide a justification for Peter's demand in the second part of the letter that he be allowed to exchange the role of father for that of judge in relation to his 'withdrawing sons'.[65] At the same time, in conjunction with the weather imagery which introduced it, it may point back towards the 'flood' of the *captatio*. If, as suggested previously, Peter has in mind the papal bull directed against Gigny, God may be said to have turned to wrath, Jupiter to have thundered from a 'cloudless sky'.

As Bernard's prayers are said to have furthered the prosperity of the journey, so

---

[61]   *Cumque vultus ille illius in quo vere apostolicus vigor et forma relucet, pro varietate causarum, personarum, et eventuum mutaretur, et aliis atque aliis nunc iocundum, nunc nubilum discretissime sese praeberet, mihi tamen numquam in diversa mutatus est* (letter 192, p. 444).

[62]   Ps 4. 7; ibid., 43. 4; ibid., 66. 2.

[63]   *namque Diespiter*
igni corusco nubila dividens
plerumque, per purum tonantis
egit equos volucremque currum ...

'for Jupiter, usually parting the clouds with flashing fire, has driven his thundering horses and his winged chariot through an unclouded sky ...' (Horace, *Carmina*, I. 34, 5–8, ed. D. R. Shackleton Bailey, in *Q. Horati Flacci opera*, Bibliotheca Scriptorum Graecorum et Romanorum Teubneriana, 3rd ed., Stuttgart, 1995, 1–134, p. 36).
Peter will subsequently claim that he has never experienced *patrem puriorem*, a 'purer/brighter Father' (letter 192, p. 445).

[64]   *Notabam saepe austeriorem vel maestiorem quam frequenter induere aliis de causis cogebatur speciem, ipsum aut privatim aut publice me alloquente, de iudicis forma in patris gratiam commutare* (letter 192, p. 445).

[65]   *Assuetus sum pati, assuetus et indulgere ... Sed quid? Numquid ita semper? Numquid semper misericordiam Deo cantabo, et numquam iudicium?*, 'I am accustomed to endure, I am accustomed also to indulge ... What then? Shall it always be so? Shall I always sing mercy to the Lord and never judgment?' (ibid., p. 446). The last statement may offer an echo of Psalms which can be seen to reinforce the notion of 'change': *Cantate ei canticum novum bene psallite in vociferatione quia rectum est verbum Domini et omnia opera eius in fide diligit misericordiam et iudicium*, 'Sing to Him a new song, sing well to the cithera in vociferation, because the word of the Lord is upright and all His works are in faith. He loves mercy and justice' (Ps 32. 3–6).

the favour shown by Eugenius may be laid at the door of Bernard's intervention. Eugenius is said to have appeared 'such as if I had never seen him'.[66] Peter's success in obtaining his petitions is explicitly attributed to *vota*, the 'prayers', 'wishes' of Bernard.[67] This may find circumstantial support in the form of a letter of recommendation written by Bernard to Eugenius on behalf of Peter,[68] now generally accepted as relating to this visit.[69] In this letter, Bernard seemingly praises Peter for two aspects: his generosity towards the Cistercians,[70] and his introduction of reforms amongst the Cluniacs.[71] Eugenius is asked to fulfil his petitions, provided that they are made in the 'name of the Lord Jesus',[72] a proviso subsequently explained in terms of Bernard's 'fear' that Peter will ask to be released from his responsibilities as abbot.[73] It is not clear, however, that this letter is as straightforwardly laudatory as it might seem. Peter is subsequently identified through two Biblical citations as *honorabile membrum*, an 'honourable limb' of

---

[66]   *sed talis nunc apparuit, quasi numquam vidissem* (letter 192, p. 445).

[67]   *Si quid ibi vel alibi petii, aut indultum est, aut rationabiliter ita ut queri non possem negatum. Haec dicens non glorior, sed vestra vota in me per ipsum impleta declaro*, 'Whatever I sought there or elsewhere was either indulged, or so reasonably denied that I could not complain. I am not saying this in boast, but in declaration that your wishes/prayers towards me have been fulfilled through him' (ibid.).

[68]   Bernard, ep. 277, *SBO*, VIII, pp. 189–90.

[69]   See Constable, *Letters*, II, p. 226; Bredero, *Bernard of Clairvaux*, pp. 245–6; Leclercq, *SBO*, VIII, p. 189, n. 1.

[70]   *Nam, si nescitis, iste est qui manus suas* extendit ad pauperes *Ordinis nostri; iste est qui de possessionibus ecclesiae suae, quantum cum pace suorum potest, libenter et frequenter largitur ad victum*, 'For, if you do not know, he it is who *extends* his hands *to the poor* of our Order; he it is who from the possessions of his church, as much as he can with the peace of his people, willingly and frequently bestows for nourishment' (ep. 277, p. 189 = Prv 31. 20).

[71]   *Quamquam paene ab introitu suo in multis Ordinem illum meliorasse cognoscitur, verbi gratia, in observantia ieiuniorum, silentii, indumentorum pretiosorum et curiosorum*, 'Although, almost from his entry, he is known to have ameliorated that Order in many things, by the grace of the Word: in the observance of fasts, of silence, of precious and over-nice clothing' (ibid., p. 190).

[72]   *Sane si quid petierit in nomine Domini Iesu, non debet apud vos pati difficultatem*, 'Whatever indeed he petitions in the name of the lord Jesus, he should suffer no difficulty with you' (ibid., p. 189).

[73]   *Si enim petierit, quod suspicor vereorque, dimitti a regimine monasterii, quis illum noscens in nomine Iesu petere putet?*, 'For if he seeks, which I suspect and fear, to be released from the rule of the monastery, who knowing him would think that he asks in the name of Jesus?' (ibid., pp. 189–90). Bredero seems to treat this remark as indicative of genuine concern (Bredero, *Bernard of Clairvaux*, pp. 245–6). It is possible, however, that it should rather be construed as a warning. In the second half of letter 192, Peter does indeed voice what can be read as a threat in this direction: *Praeferantur, principentur, regnent, sed sine me*, 'Let them get preference, let them rule, let them reign, but without me' (letter 192, p. 447). The reference is to *filii recedentes*. A similar threat had previously been made in Peter's letter 34, also relating to tithes: *Si aliter res processerit ... aut sua mecum ecclesia retinebit, aut sine me hucusque iuste possessis carebit*, 'If the affair goes otherwise ... either the church (of Cluny) will retain what is its own with me, or without me it will be deprived of what is has justly possessed until now' (Peter, letter 34, p. 109). See Chapter 4.

Christ's body,[74] and as *vas ... in honorem*, a 'vessel (destined for) honour'.[75] The first of these is drawn from a biblical context where the limbs of the body are said to need each other, the 'more ignoble' being the 'more necessary' and receiving 'more abundant honour'.[76] The second sets the vessel destined 'for honour' against that destined 'for contumely', 'vessels of wrath' against 'vessels of mercy'.[77] The statement which precedes these, to the effect that 'grace itself absolves from debt, because necessity has been changed into inclination',[78] might be held to imply that from being merely a 'necessary limb' Peter has now been chosen as a 'vessel of mercy' for the salvation of the Cluniacs.

It seems reasonable, accordingly, to conclude that the apparently eulogistic tone of the first part of Peter's letter can be seen as offering an acknowledgement of the part played by Bernard in smoothing his path and ensuring a favourable reception in Rome.[79] At the same time, an awareness of the nature of this intervention might also help to explain the reservations expressed there. Peter dwells at length on the motif of *amicitia*. At first sight, this is unambiguously positive. Of Eugenius Peter claims: 'Never have I experienced a more faithful friend, never a more sincere brother, never a more pure father in conferences of this kind.'[80] The claim is then apparently extended to the papal Curia as a whole,'I relate succinctly how I found then the disposition of the whole Roman curia towards me and ours, as that of faithful friends, of sweetest brothers, of family members from, as far as could be

---

[74] *Honorate virum, ut vere honorabile membrum in Christi corpore*, 'Honour the man, as a truly honourable limb in the body of Christ' (ep. 277, p. 189 = I Cor 12. 23).

[75] Vas *est* in honorem, *ni fallor*, plenum gratiae et veritatis, *refertum pluribus bonis*, 'He is, if I am not mistaken, *a vessel for honour, full of grace and truth*, packed full with many good things' (ibid. = Rm 9. 21; Io 1. 14).

[76] *Sed multo magis quae videntur membra corporis infirmiora esse necessariora sunt et quae putamus ignobiliora membra esse corporis his honorem abundantiorem circumdamus*, 'But much more, the limbs of the body which seem weaker are the more necessary, and those which we think to be the more ignoble limbs of the body we surround with more abundant honour' (I Cor 12. 22–3).

[77] *An non habet potestatem figulus luti ex eadem massa facere aliud quidem vas in honorem aliud vero in contumeliam quod si volens Deus ostendere iram et notam facere potentiam suam sustinuit in multa patientia vasa irae aptata in interitum ut ostenderet divitias gloriae suae in vasa misericordiae quae praeparavit in gloriam*, 'Or does the potter of the clay not have the power to make from the same mass one vessel to honour, another to contumely? What if God wishing to display his anger and make known his power has endured in much long-suffering the vessels of wrath fit for destruction, that he might show the riches of his glory towards the vessels of mercy, which he has prepared for glory?' (Rm 9. 21–3). The context is that God 'takes pity on whom he will and hardens whom he will' (ibid., 9. 18).

[78] *Sed debito ipsa absolvit gratia, quia necessitas in voluntatem transiit* (ep. 277, p. 189).

[79] It is possible that Peter's depiction of obstacles overcome draws on a gambit from Bernard: Quis nos separabit? *Nec altitudo Alpium, nec nivium frigora, nec longitudo itineris*, 'Who will separate us? Neither the height of the Alps, nor the cold of the snows, nor the length of the journey' (ep. 277, p. 189 = Rm 8. 35). The opening question continues there *a caritate Christi*, 'from the love of Christ'.

[80] *Numquam amicum fideliorem, numquam fratrem sinceriorem, numquam patrem puriorem in huiusmodi colloquiis expertus sum* (letter 192, p. 445).

recognised, a pure and sincere heart.'[81] The self-evident *caveat*, 'as far as could be recognised', is matched by a more subtle usage in relation to Eugenius of language associated with appearance, and even with acting. The verb *se praebere*, as applied to his change of countenance, can connote to 'exhibit', 'represent'. Of the expression with which it is doubled, *speciem induere*, *species* can suggest 'outward appearance', 'look', 'semblance', while *induere* can imply to 'put on', 'assume'. Finally, Peter will claim of Eugenius in his role as 'high pontiff', 'it is new for nothing sinister to have been able to be noted in his acts, in his words, in his very bearing ...'[82] *Actus*, in the sense of 'act', 'performance', can denote the representation of a play, part or character, while *gestus* may be applied to the gesticulation of an actor.[83]

More damagingly, if Bernard is being presented as having wrought this miraculous change of affairs in Italy, it seems permissible to wonder whether he is also being targeted as bearing the responsibility for the change in the opposite direction on Peter's return. Again, there may be circumstantial evidence to point towards this. The papal bull concerning Gigny, addressed jointly to Peter and the Cluniacs, betrays a partisan verbal violence which stands in marked contrast to the graciousness attributed to Eugenius during Peter's stay. It attacks the monks of Gigny for oppression old and new, depicting their behaviour in terms of 'tyranny',[84] 'madness',[85] 'barbaric ferocity',[86] and 'despoliation of the poor'.[87] The criticism, moreover, extends beyond those accused of having committed the attack on Le Miroir on to the Cluniacs in general, and, by implication, on to Peter himself, as their head, with accusations of ingratitude,[88] and even of tacit encouragement.[89]

---

[81]   *Qualem deinde totius Romanae curiae erga me et nostra statum invenerim, succincte refero, ut amicorum fidelium, ut dulcissimorum fratrum, ut ex mero et sincero corde, quantum agnosci potuit familiarium* (ibid.).

[82]   *(sed) novum est nihil sinistri in eius actu, nihil in verbis, nihil in ipso gestu.. potuisse notari*, (letter 192, p. 445).

[83]   The section as a whole may also recall a statement in Cicero's *De officiis*, which stresses the incompatibility of the roles of friend and judge: *ponit enim personam amici, cum induit iudicis*, 'for he puts off the part of a friend, when he assumes the part of a judge' (Cicero, *De officiis*, 3. 10. 43, ed. C. Atzert, Bibliotheca Scriptorum Graecorum et Romanorum Teubneriana, Fasc. 48, Leipzig, 1963, reprinted 1985, p. 98).

[84]   *Quanta tyrannide fratres vestri de Gigniaco ... debacchati ...*, 'With what tyranny your brothers of Gigny have raged ...' (*Inebriati sicut*, Brial, *RHGF*, 15, p. 471).

[85]   *Ad eorum cohibendam insaniam ...*, 'To check their madness.. ' (ibid., p. 472).

[86]   *famulis Christi feritate barbarica trucidatis ...*, 'massacring the servants of Christ with barbaric ferocity ...' (ibid.).

[87]   *Postquam ... depraedantes pupillos, pauperes spoliarunt ...*, 'After ... robbing orphans, they despoiled the poor ...' (ibid.).

[88]   *Cluniacensis Ecclesia ... quantum ... a sede apostolica sit dilecta, quantum in necessitatibus suis adiuta, et semper ad maiora provecta, licet in oblivionem vos duxeritis ...*, 'Although you have consigned to oblivion how much the Church of Cluny ... has been loved by the Apostolic See, how much it has been helped in its times of need, and always promoted to greater ...' (ibid., p. 471).

[89]   *Quia vero et vestrorum excessus, et nostrorum miserias, dissimulanti vel potius subsannanti oculo respexistis ...*, 'Because you have looked upon both the excesses of yours and the miseries of ours with a neglectful, or rather, mocking eye ...' (ibid., p. 472).

Citing the comment of Brial, to the effect that the letter 'is redolent of the pen/style of St Bernard',[90] Constable conjectures that it was most probably the latter who supplied Eugenius with an account of the attack.[91] Certainly, Bernard would become heavily involved in the question of reparations, as demonstrated by his subsequent letter to Eugenius, reporting the failure of the meeting with Peter and representatives from Gigny.[92]

As suggested earlier, 193, the accompanying letter to Nicholas, seemingly inverts the presentation of journey and return. Rather than a series of miraculous escapes from physical danger, the former is depicted in terms of tedious and routine physical discomfort.[93] The notion of joy, previously reserved for Peter's meeting with Eugenius, is here applied to his reception at Cluny.[94] Friendship is constructed internally rather than externally through the image of the fire of *caritas*,[95] trouble, when it comes, shown as emanating from outside rather than inside.[96] Conversely, the hints of spiritual danger within Italy are developed through language which may associate Peter with Ulysses rather than Aeneas. In justification of his epistolary protest that he has not changed towards Nicholas, Peter cites Horace: 'Or perhaps you thought ... that infected by the touch of a foreign climate, changed from a man to a beast by the drugs of Circe, I had burst forth into something monstrous, although the one whom you know says, *they change climate not mind, who rush*

---

[90]   *Stilum S. Bernardi redolet haec epistula* (Brial, ibid., p. 471, n. d.).

[91]   Constable, 'Cluniac tithes', p. 618.

[92]   *Repetita est, iuxta tenorem litterarum vestrarum, damnorum resarcitio, restitutio ablatorum; sed incassum*, 'There was sought, according to the tenor of your letter, the making good of losses, the restitution of what had been taken away: but in vain' (Bernard, ep. 283, p. 197).

[93]   *Quid poteram positus in itinere scribere, qui vix poteram vivere? Vivere dico, non quod.. aliquid mihi praeter votum contigerit, sed quia integra paene semper die equitanti, media nocte edenti, valde mane surgenti, in agone continuo desudanti, quis animus ad meditandum, quae lingua ad dictandum, quae manus ad scribendum parare se poterat?*, 'Situated on the journey, what could I write, who could scarcely live? I say live, not because.. anything befell me contrary to (their) wish/prayer, but because, for one riding on horseback almost the whole day, eating in the middle of the night, rising very early in the morning, perspiring in continual struggle, what mind could prepare itself to meditate, what tongue to compose, what hand to write?' (Peter, letter 193, p. 449).

[94]   *Laeta quidem, iocunda et arridentia cuncta repperi, et praeter devotum clericorum et laicorum occursum, fratrum quod mihi magis cordi erat, tam vocis canticum quam cordis iubilum inveni. Laetebar in eis ...*, 'I found everything, indeed, joyful, pleasant and smiling, and over and beyond the devoted reception of clergy and laity, I found both the hymn of the voice and the song of joy of the heart of the brothers, which was dearer to me. I rejoiced in them ...' (ibid.).

[95]   *Mirabar vix quinque mensium absentiam meam in tantam amoris flammam ex occultis subito prodiisse, ut mirum videri posset, si quinquennii mora tantam parere potuisset*, 'I wondered that my absence of scarcely five months had suddenly sprung forth from hidden places into so great a flame of love that it could seem wonderful if a five-years delay could have begotten so much' (ibid., pp. 449–50).

[96]   *Aquae istae populi fuerunt et gentes ab Italia, Germania, Hispaniis, Anglia, ab ipsa nostra Gallia Cluniacum dirivatae ...*, 'Those waters were peoples and nations, diverted to Cluny from Italy, Germany, Spain, England and our France itself ...' (ibid. p. 450).

across the sea?'[97] The reference to Circe may point towards another, hidden Horatian allusion: 'You know the voices of the Sirens and the cups of Circe: had he drunk them with his companions, foolish and greedy, he would have been shameful and senseless under a harlot mistress, he would have lived as a filthy dog, or as a sow which loves the mire.'[98] The perils and temptations faced by Aeneas hampered him in his mission to get to Rome. Those faced by Ulysses stood in the way of his desire to return home.

The second section of letter 192, dealing with Bernard's request for 'clemency', is structured around a series of rhetorical markers that serve to signal changes in direction, and which mark a partial return to the illusion of dialogue or debate which had characterised letters 28 and 111. Bernard's petition is recapitulated through a triad of virtually synonymous exhortations,[99] purporting to emanate directly from the missing letter. Peter's response is prefaced by a formal introduction.[100] The ensuing declaration of his previous indulgence is cut short by rhetorical exclamation,[101] leading to a five-fold series of rhetorical questions[102] which insinuate the possibility of substituting judgement for mercy. Again, this is cut short, this time by an anticipated objection.[103] Seemingly accepted by Peter,[104] the objection is, in fact, progressively undermined, through the mustering of a string of biblical *exempla*. Further rhetorical exclamation[105] paves the way for a passage of heavy satire, which culminates in an opposition between 'pardon' and 'reward'. Once again, this is interrupted by an anticipated objection.[106] The ploy of seeming acceptance is repeated,[107] only to be further undercut by further hyperbolic sarcasm. Rounded off by formal closure,[108] the section will be followed, however, by a hint that Peter will, in fact, comply with Bernard's request.[109]

---

[97]   *An forte putasti ... me ... infectum peregrini aeris tactu ... Circe medicaminibus de homine bestiam factum, in monstrum aliquod erupisse, cum dicat quem nosti,* caelum non animum mutant, qui trans mare currunt? (ibid., p. 449 = Horace, *Epistles*, I, xi, 27).

[98]   *Sirenum voces et Circae pocula nosti;*
   quae si cum sociis stultus cupidusque bibisset,
   sub domina meretrice fuisset turpis et excors,
   vixisset canis immundus vel amica luto sus
(Horace, ibid., I, ii, 23–6.) If Peter has this in mind, the 'Siren voices' and the 'cups of Circe' might be thought to represent an ironic allusion to the 'enticements' of Eugenius and the papal Curia.

[99]   *Hortatur ... ne ..., monet ut ... Instat ut ...* (letter 192, p. 445).

[100]   *Ad haec ego ...,* 'To this I (reply) ...' (ibid, p. 446).

[101]   *Sed quid?,* 'What then?' (ibid.).

[102]   *Numquid ita ...? Numquid semper ...? Numquid ...? Nonne et ...? Numquid semper ...?* (ibid.).

[103]   *Sed dicet quispiam ...,* 'But someone will say ...' (ibid.).

[104]   *Verum est, inquam, verum est,* 'It is true, I say, it is true' (ibid.).

[105]   *Quorsum ista?,* 'Whither is this leading?'; *Quid ergo?,* 'What then?' (ibid., p. 447).

[106]   *Sed dicetur ...,* 'But it will be said ...' (ibid.).

[107]   *Eia,* 'Indeed' (ibid.).

[108]   *De his ita ad praesens,* '(Enough) of this for the present' (ibid., p. 448).

[109]   *Munus quod pro magno vos habiturum scripsistis, vobis concessi, donec optabili colloquio perfrui merear,* 'I have conceded to you the gift which you wrote that you would value greatly, until I may deserve to enjoy the desired colloquy' (ibid.). The opposition between spoken and written word suggests that the gift in question is the letter. The whole tenor of the section, however, points to 'clemency.'

The combative flavour of the whole approach may, perhaps, be related in part to the pressurising nature of the hortatory triad attributed to Bernard. This draws overtly on the notion of reciprocity, placing Peter's future actions into alignment with the papal reception described earlier:

> Hence the text of your sweet and holy letter exhorts that there is the opportunity and the need, not to return *evil to those requiting me*. It warns that now those who wished to, but could not, do otherwise should experience our clemency, and that the affection of a father should give back (his) withdrawing sons to his entrails. It urges that they should feel that I found rather a father than a judge in the bosom of the apostolic see, and that the sword already drawn to strike has been replaced in the sheath of mercy, and the rest after this wise.[110]

The underlying message, that divine and human mercy are inextricably linked, seems to be reinforced by hidden biblical allusion. The injunction from the Old Testament, to repay good with good, may call to mind its New Testament mirror, not to repay evil with evil.[111] The expression *recedentes filii*, 'withdrawing sons', seems to draw on Old Testament pleas for mercy in respect of transgression against God.[112] Peter's subsequent declaration, 'I have not been, I am not, nor can I be their tormentor',[113] seems to acknowledge the reminder. *Tortor*, 'tormentor', 'torturer', occurs in the Gospels in relation to the punishment of the servant whose master has let him off his own debts, but who then mistreats his indebted fellow-servant.[114]

At the same time, the parallel between Eugenius and God may also be seen as constituting a form of warning. The citation from Psalms is set there within a context which calls down the wrath of enemies if the injunction to repay 'good with good' is flouted.[115] The reference to *tempus et opus*, 'opportunity and need', which

---

[110] *Hortatur dehinc textus epistolae dulcis et sanctae, tempus et opus esse, ne reddam retribuentibus mihi mala, monet ut nunc illi qui voluerunt, sed non potuerunt aliud agere, experiantur clementiam nostram, et affectus patris filios recedentes resignet visceribus suis. Instat ut sentiant nos in gremio sedis apostolicae plus patris quam iudicis invenisse, et gladium iam ad percutiendum exertum in vaginam pietatis esse repositum, et reliqua in hunc modum* (ibid., pp. 445–6 = Ps 7. 5).

[111] *non reddentes malum pro malo vel maledictum pro maledictum sed e contrario benedicentes quia in hoc vocati estis ut benedictionem hereditate possideatis*, 'not returning evil for evil or curse for curse, but on the contrary blessing, because you have been called to this, that you should possess blessing by inheritance' (I Pt 3. 9).

[112] *Peccavimus inique fecimus impie egimus et recessimus et declinavimus a mandatis tuis ac iudiciis*, 'We have sinned unjustly, we have acted impiously, and we have withdrawn and deviated from Your mandates and judgements' (Dn 9. 5); *Tibi autem Domino Deo nostro misericordia et propitiatio quia recessimus a te*, 'Yours, Lord our God, is mercy and pardon, because we have withdrawn from you' (ibid., 9. 9).

[113] *Non fui, non sum, nec esse possum tortor eorum* (letter 192, p. 447).

[114] *et iratus dominus eius tradidit eum tortoribus quoadsque redderet universum debitum*, 'and his angry master handed him over to the torturers until he should pay back the totality of the debt' (Mt 18. 34).

[115] *Si reddidi retribuentibus mihi mala decidam merito ab inimicis meis inanis persequatur inimicus animam meam et comprehendat et conculcet in terra vitam meam ...*, 'If I have returned evil to those requiting me let me fall deservedly lifeless at the hands of my enemies. Let my enemy pursue my soul and seize it and trample my life on the ground ...' (Ps 7. 5–6).

has preceded, may look towards a New Testament allusion, which preaches 'now is the time of salvation'.[116] There it is preceded by a call for reconciliation with God.[117] Similarly, the image of the sheathed sword may point towards the Old Testament, where David is said to have averted the wrath of God through *pacifica*, 'peace offerings', whereupon, on the command of God, the angel 'sheathed the sword' which was raised to strike.[118] The accompanying papal bull sent by Eugenius to Humbert of Lyons stresses previous papal patience: 'Although, indeed, they (the monks of Gigny) had long since deserved to be cut off from the body of the Church by the apostolic axe, we have endured them up until now, believing that they would now return to the heart, and cease from the the persecution of our aforesaid sons.'[119] The peace-offerings demanded there, however, are financial, reparation for the damage that has been inflicted. If Peter is citing Bernard's words verbatim, this may suggest a coded hint on the part of the latter that Peter should himself seek reconciliation with Eugenius through compliance. Alternatively, it is possible that both wording and allusions should be seen as emanating from Peter himself.[120]

A close study of the passage that follows, seemingly asserting the right of Peter to take vengeance in despite of Bernard's petition for mercy, may reveal the presence of another technique, in the form of arrogating and turning against Bernard arguments which he himself had employed elsewhere. The image of 'sheathing the sword', taken apparently from Bernard's own letter, is twice directly placed in question: 'Shall any soldier of God always keep back *his sword from blood*? In this case, not only the King but also his soldier carries the sword in vain';[121] 'If this sword rests, if it is always hidden, if, never drawn, it is never an

---

[116] *Adiuvantes autem et exhortamur ne in vacuum gratiam Dei recipiatis ait enim tempore accepto exaudivi te et in die salutis adiuvavi te ecce nunc tempus acceptabile ecce nunc dies salutis nemini dantes ullam offensionem ut non vituperetur ministerium*, 'But helping we exhort you not to receive the grace of God in vain. For He says: "At the acceptable time I heard you and on the day of salvation I helped you." Lo, now is the acceptable time, now is the day of salvation, giving offense to no one, that the ministery be not censured' (II Cor 6. 1–4).

[117] *Obsecramus pro Christo reconciliamini Deo* ..., 'We beseech you for the sake of Christ, be reconciled to God ...' (ibid., 5. 20).

[118] *levansque David oculos suos vidit angelum Domini stantem inter terram et caelum et evaginatum gladium in manu eius et versum contra Hierusalem* ..., 'and raising his eyes, David saw an angel of the Lord standing between earth and heaven, and a drawn sword in his hand, turned against Jerusalem ...' (I Par 21. 16); *Praecepitque Dominus angelo et convertit gladium suum in vaginam*, 'And the Lord commanded the angel, and he returned his sword into the sheath' (ibid., 21. 27).

[119] *Cum vero ab Ecclesiae corpore iamdiu meruissent apostolica securi praecidi, usque modo sustinuimus, credentes eos aliquando reversuros ad cor, et a praedictorum filiorum nostrorum persecutionibus cessaturos (Nequitia illorum*, Brial, *RHGF*, 15, p. 473 = Mt 3. 10; Lc 3. 9).

[120] In contrast to letters 111 and 149, where Peter directly cites lengthy sections of Bernard's previous missives, it is noticeable that the use here of introductory verbs, *hortatur, monet, instat*, converts what follows from direct into reported speech, thus blurring the accuracy of the reportage.

[121] *Numquid semper prohibebit quilibet miles dei gladium suum a sanguine? Sic hoc, non tantum rex, sed et miles eius frustra gladium portat* (letter 192, p. 446 = Ier 48. 10).

object of terror to anyone, what will it be?'[122] Bernard had made the self-same point in relation to the temporal sword in his ep. 521, urging a new crusade, through a citation from Romans, 'they (the princes) carry a sword *without a purpose*'.[123] Peter reinforces his argument by citing the verse which precedes this: 'In vain also are read those words, known to the Christian world: *Do you wish not to fear the power (of princes)? Do good, and you will have praise from it.*'[124] In between, comes a passage which may seem to take issue with Bernard's claim that the papacy possesses both spiritual and temporal sword,[125] as expounded in his ep. 256 to Eugenius, also on the subject of crusade. The concept is introduced through anticipated objection:

> But someone will say: 'The Church does not have a sword. Christ took it away, when he said to Peter: "*Return the sword into the sheath. Everyone who receives the sword will perish by the sword.*" ' It is true, I say, it is true. The Church does not have the sword of the king, but it has the rod of the shepherd. Concerning this the apostle says: "*What do you wish? Shall I come to you in the rod or in the spirit of mercy?*" And why do I say it has the rod? Rather, it also has a sword, according to the same: "*And take up the helmet of salvation and the sword of the spirit, which is the word of God.*"[126]

At one level, the clear distinction drawn here between *gladius regis* and *gladius spiritus* may seem to undermine Bernard's claim to Eugenius, 'Both are Peter's, the one to be drawn by his command, the other by his hand, whenever it is necessary.'[127] More importantly, it was on this very passage from the Gospels, placed here in the mouth of an imaginary interlocutor, that Bernard had based his claim. This had been achieved by conflating two separate passages: 'Indeed, it was concerning the one about which it seemed to be missing that it was said to Peter: *Return your sword into the sheath.* Therefore that (sword) also was his, but not to be drawn forth by his hand.'[128] The relevant verse in Matthew runs: 'Then Jesus said to him, "Return your

---

[122] *Hic gladius si quieverit, si semper latuerit, si numquam exertus, nulli umquam terrori fuerit, quid erit?* (ibid.).

[123] sine causa gladium *(principes) portant: pellibus mortuorum animalium reconditus est, rubigini consecratus,* 'they carry a sword *without a purpose*: it is sheathed in the hides of dead beasts, consecrated to rust' (Bernard, ep. 521, p. 483 = Rm 13. 4.) See Chapter 9.

[124] *Frustra et leguntur verba illa, orbi Christiano nota:* Vis non timere potestatem? Bonum fac, et habebis laudem ex illa (letter 192, p. 446 = Rm 13. 3).

[125] Constable, *Letters*, II, p. 229; Iogna-Prat, *Ordonner et exclure*, p. 333.

[126] *Sed dicet quispiam: Ecclesia non habet gladium. Christus illum abstulit, cum Petro dixit:* Converte gladium in vaginam. Omnis qui acceperit gladium, gladio peribit. *Verum est inquam, verum est. Non habet ecclesia gladium regis, sed habet virgam pastoris. De qua apostolus:* Quid vultis? In virga veniam ad vos, an in spiritu mansuetudinis? *Et quid dico habet virgam? Immo habet et gladium, secundum eundem: Et galeam salutis assumite, et gladium spiritus quod est verbum dei* (letter 192, p. 446 = Mt 26. 52/Io 18. 11; I Cor 4. 21; Eph 6. 17).

[127] *Petri uterque est, alter suo nutu, alter sua manu, quoties necesse est, evaginandus* (Bernard, ep. 256, 1, *SBO*, VIII, p. 163).

[128] *Et quidem de quo minus videbatur, de ipso ad Petrum dictum est:* Converte gladium tuum in vaginam. *Ergo suus erat et ille, sed non sua manu utique educendus* (Bernard, ibid.). The translation of James appears to obscure the emphasis here (James, *The letters*, p. 471). The significance is brought out, however, by Jacqueline (Jacqueline, *Épiscopat et papauté*, p. 123).

sword into its place. For all who receive the sword will perish by the sword." '[129] In John, however, it is somewhat different: 'Therefore Jesus said to Peter: "Return the sword into the sheath." '[130] In essence, Bernard has followed the latter. However, he has appropriated from Matthew the possessive adjective crucial to his argument. Peter has done the opposite, retaining the second part of Matthew, but omitting the telling possessive. Not only does this, by inference, target Bernard for selective use of scripture, but it may also hark back to the blurring of Eugenius' spiritual and temporal authority as signalled in the first part of the letter.

The mustering of Biblical *exempla* which follows may again look towards Bernard. The device of *praeteritio* is employed to introduce, but semingly pass over,[131] the names of Phineus, Elijah, the Maccabees, characterised here as *diri scelerum ultores*, 'terrible avengers of wickedness'. In preference to these, Peter offers a figure, said to need no identification, but presented as embodying legitimate change from 'mercy' to 'vengeance': 'I propose that most gentle above all men who delayed on the earth. Who would not know his name? Although he was so great by virtue of mercy, he did not fear to avenge his injuries and those of God by the horrible example of death.'[132] The principle of 'change' is further illustrated through explicit references to Samuel's hacking into pieces of Agag[133] and David's smiting of his enemies, each prefaced by a *praeteritio* which emphasises their customary mercy,[134] and culminating in Christ's violent ejection of the merchants from the Temple.[135] Of these *exempla* the first, concerning the punishment for exogamous fornication inflicted by Phineus, had been memorably invoked by Bernard to press for the deposition of the Cluniac bishop-elect at Langres,[136] as well as figuring frequently elsewhere.[137] One letter in particular, addressed to Innocent, and calling for the punishment of those who had murdered Thomas, prior of St Victor,[138] may

---

[129] *Tunc ait illi Iesus converte gladium tuum in locum suum omnes enim qui acceperint gladium gladio peribunt* (Mt 26. 52). Peter is not specified here by name. The preceding reference is to *unus ex his qui erant cum Iesu*, 'one of those who were with Jesus'.

[130] *Dixit ergo Iesus Petro mitte gladium in vaginam* (Io 18. 11).

[131] *Transeo ..., praetereo ..., taceo ...*, 'I pass over ..., I omit ..., I am silent ...' (letter 192, p. 446).

[132] *Virum illum mitissimum super omnes homines qui morabantur in terra, propono. Nomen eius quis nesciat? Is cum tantus virtute mansuetudinis fuerit, Dei suasque iniurias ulcisci, horribili mortis exemplo non timuit* (ibid.).

[133] I Sm 15. 33.

[134] *Quid loquerer Samuelem pro inimicis orantem? Quid David totiens et totiens hostibus nequissimis parcentem?*, 'Why should I mention Samuel praying for his enemies? Why [should I mention] David so often sparing the most worthless enemies?' (letter 192, pp. 446–7).

[135] Mt 21. 12; Mc 11. 15; Lc 19. 45–6; Io 2. 14–16.

[136] Bernard, ep. 165, *SBO*, VII, p. 367. See Chapter 4.

[137] Bernard, ep. 178, 1, *SBO*, VII, p. 398; ep. 247, 1, *SBO*, VIII, p. 140; ep. 520, ibid., p. 481.

[138] This murder had led to the Synod of Jouarre, held probably in 1133/1134. Peter himself, in a letter to Innocent, brands this murder, together with that of the subdean Archibald of Orléans, as *execrabile facinus, puniendum flagitium, inauditum nostris saeculis scelus*, 'an execrable crime, a shameful act worthy of punishment, a wickedness unheard of in our times' (Peter, letter 17, *Letters*, I, p. 24). See Constable, *Letters*, II, p 106.

cast light on Peter's nameless examplar.[139] There, Bernard had strung together the slaying of 3,000 Israelites at the command of Moses,[140] Phineus, Matthias' slaying of an Israelite sacrificing to idols,[141] Christ in the Temple. Closing the list come the dramatic deaths of Ananias and Sapphira following their denunciation by St Peter.[142] It is this last story that Peter may have in mind.[143]

In accordance with Bernard's own arguments, therefore, Peter can lay claim to the temporal and spiritual authority of his namesake. Behind this may lie a further insinuation, that Bernard, too, appears to have 'changed', from the violent denunciations of the past to the more merciful attitude seemingly evinced by his present request, thus providing further support for Peter's right to do the same, but in the opposite direction. At the same time, the insinuations may conceal a deeper irony. In his *Apologia*, Bernard had vigorously attacked laxity masquerading as discretion: 'Such mercy is full of cruelty, by which, namely, the body is so served that the soul is murdered';[144] 'That charity destroys charity, this discretion confounds discretion.'[145] Earlier in this section Peter has made great play with his own past 'indulgence': 'Nature itself provokes me sufficiently to indulgence; the practice of indulgence itself incites me. I am accustomed to endure, I am accustomed also to indulge.'[146] The immediate context is the violence associated with the return of the former abbot of Cluny, Pons of Melgueil,[147] which, it was suggested previously, Bernard's *Apologia* may have been seen as helping to fuel.[148] *Caritas* is highlighted twice in this section of the letter, the first time by its absence,

---

[139] Bernard, ep. 158, 1, *SBO*, VII, pp. 365–7. In this letter, Bernard asks: *Atque ... quid spirituali gladio ... relinquitur, si ... nullus mutire iam audeat contra insolentiam clericorum?*, 'But ... what is left to the spiritual sword ..., if none should now dare to mutter against the insolence of clerics?' (ibid., 2, p. 366). In similar vein, Peter prefaces his examples with the question: *Et quid faciet pravorum perversitas, quos in malis suis deteriores reddet impunitas?*, 'What will the perversity of the wicked do, whom impunity will render worse in their evils?' (letter 192, p. 446).

[140] Ex 32. 25–9.

[141] I Mcc 2. 24.

[142] Act 5. 3–10.

[143] The ultimate source for this type of grouping may be Jerome. In a letter directed to a certain Riparius, Jerome justifies his renewed denunciation of Vigilantius through a string of biblical *exempla*: Phineus; Elijah's destruction of the priests of Baal; Simon the Zealot; Ananias and Sapphira; Paul's blinding of the sorcerer Elymas (Jerome, ep. 109, 3, *CSEL*, 55, p. 354). There, Peter is described as *trucidans*, 'slaying', the guilty couple.

[144] *Talis misericordia crudelitate plena est, qua videlicet ita corpori servitur, ut anima iuguletur* (Bernard, *Apo*, VIII. 16).

[145] *Ista caritas destruit caritatem, haec discretio discretionem confundit* (ibid.).

[146] *Natura ipsa satis ad indulgendum me provocat, usus ipse indulgendi me instigat. Assuetus sum pati, assuetus sum et indulgere* (letter 192, p. 446).

[147] *Declarat hoc ... de Pontiano scismate, in quod cum innumeri declinaverint, ac nefanda et in ordine monastico inaudita fecerint, numquam gladium meum, numquam mucronem, numquam frameam experti sunt, vix umquam asperum ab ore meo verbum audierunt*, 'This is shown.. by the Pontian schism: although countless deviated and did wicked deeds, unheard of in the monastic order, they never felt my sword, never my point, never my blade; scarcely ever did they hear a harsh word from my mouth' (ibid.).

[148] See Chapter 3.

the second by its presence. Peter has repeated the Pauline question, '*What do you wish? Shall I come to you in the rod or in the spirit of mercy?*'[149] In its original form, the last phrase is prefaced by the words *in caritate*, 'in charity'.[150] Subsequently, as will be seen, through anticipated objection *plena caritas*, 'full charity', will be seemingly equated with 'reward' and 'preferment'.

Certain of the *exempla* mustered by Peter may also fulfil another function, that of setting up the idea of fraudulent or inappropriate financial transaction. The deaths of Ananias and Sapphira which, it was suggested, underlie Peter's reference to the 'mildest of men', occur after they have attempted to 'cheat' the apostles of the price of a field, that is, of alms for the Church.[151] The language of commercial transaction is made explicit in his handling of Christ's ejection of the sellers from the Temple: 'He cast out with blows from the Temple of God ... the merchants trading illicitly in a place unsuitable for commercial transaction ...'[152] Setting up an implicit antithesis between spiritual and material profit, this may, again, be directly related to the conflict between Gigny and Le Miroir. The papal bulls had focused on material damage and material compensation,[153] under threat of spiritual interdiction.[154] In the satirical passage to follow, Peter can be seen to shift the emphasis on to spiritual damage. At the same time, the clemency demanded by Bernard will be distorted into the notion of material profit:

Although they have sinned much against their brothers by malign detraction, susurration, obloquy, although they have torn their flesh with canine tooth, have mangled their entrails with their own claws, have worthlessly, as I know, lacerated the body of their church in certain of its limbs, let them, if it seems beneficial to you, have pardon, let them not merit reward. ... But it will be said: It will not be full charity if it does no harm, but it will be whole if it does benefit. Very well. Willy-nilly, I will be compelled to be perfect. I will be what I had not thought, perfect, just as my heavenly Father is perfect. I will not take vengeance on my enemies, rather, I will benefit my enemies. Let them be preferred, let them rule, let them reign, but without me. How without me? Let them have dignities. Let them have, if it must be said, monastic honours from me, but not about me. Let them,

---

[149] *De qua [virga pastoris] apostolus:* Quid vultis? In virga veniam ad vos, an in spiritu mansuetudinis? (letter 192, p. 446).

[150] *Quid vultis in virga veniam ad vos an in caritate et spiritu mansuetudinis* (I Cor 4. 21).

[151] *Dixit autem Petrus Anania cur temptavit Satanas cor tuum mentiri te Spiritui Sancto et fraudare de pretio agri*, 'But Peter said: "Ananias, why has Satan tempted your heart that you lie to the Holy Spirit and defraud it of the price of the field?" ' (Act 5. 3).

[152] *Mercatores in loco mercationi incongruo illicite mercantes, de templo Dei.. verberando eiecit ...* (letter 192, p. 447).

[153] *Quocirca vobis.. mandamus.. ablata omnia restitui, damna irrogata pleniter resarciri, et de tantis malis faciatis (taliter) satisfieri (ut) ...*, 'Therefore, we order you ... to cause everything which has been removed to be restored, the losses which have been inflicted to be made good, and from such great evils (such) satisfaction to be given (that) ...' (*Inebriati sicut*, Brial, p. 472).

[154] *Si vero infra viginti dies post commonitionem tuam haec omnia effectui mancipare contempserint, nos in loco ipso et in omnibus cellis et ecclesiis eius divina extunc officia interdicimus ...*, 'But if within twenty days after your warning they have scorned to deliver all these things into execution, we interdict divine offices from that point in the place itself, and in all its cells and churches ...' (*Nequitia illorum*, ibid., p. 473).

placed outside, have both my property and even, if they deserve it, my heart, let them not encompass my side.[155]

The animal imagery with which this opens[156] recalls both Jeromian attacks on those who criticise his writing,[157] and Peter's own condemnation of detraction in letter 111.[158] At the same time, the wording may also undercut that found in the papal bull. Eugenius had repeatedly identified himself there with those of Le Miroir through the trope *viscera nostra*, 'our entrails'.[159] Peter's declaration that the malefactors have damaged *sua viscera*, 'their (own) entrails', have harmed the body *ecclesiae suae*, 'of their (own) Church', may draw attention to the fact that Cluniacs and Cistercians are, or should be, members of one Church. The primary damage, accordingly, is spiritual, a wounding of mutual *caritas*. The language of kingship through which the notion of reward is pursued

[155] *Qui licet fratribus suis maligne detrahendo, susurrando, obloquendo, multum deliquerint, licet carnes eorum dente canino laniaverint, ipsa sua viscera unguibus propriis discerpserint, corpus ecclesiae suae in quibusdam eius membris, nequiter ut ego novi laceraverint, habeant si sic vobis utile videtur veniam, non mereantur praemium. ... Sed dicetur: Non erit plena caritas si non nocuerit, sed ea erit integra si profuerit. Eia. Velim nolim, perfectus esse compellar. Ero quod non putaveram perfectus, sicut pater meus caelestis perfectus est. Non ulciscar in hostes immo benefaciam hostibus. Praeferantur, principentur, regnent, sed sine me. Sine me quomodo? Habeant dignitates. Habeant honores si dici debet monasticos a me, sed non circa me. Habeant extra positi et res meas et etiam, si merentur, cor meum, non ambiant latus meum* (letter 192, p. 447).
[156] This imagery has already been foreshadowed through a conflation of two biblical citations, with a possible hint of a third: *Multiplicabuntur* forte *iuxta Salomonem* contra *remissam manum* bestiae *agri, nec iuxta cuiusdam amici Iob verba,* pacificae erunt *illi,* '*Perhaps*, according to Solomon, *the beasts* of the field will be multiplied *against* the slack hand, nor, according to the words of a certain friend of Job, *will they be peaceful* to it' (letter 192, p. 446 = Dt 7. 22; Iob 5. 23). Both citations, in their original context, connote promises of divine protection, but the sense in each case has been marginally subverted. In the first, the significance has been inverted by the removal of a negative: Israel is promised victory over her enemies, with the *caveat* that this must happen 'gradually' and 'by degrees', 'lest the beasts of the earth be multiplied against you.' In the second, the insertion of a negative seemingly cancels out the promise of peace: 'In devastation and famine you will laugh, you will not dread the beast of the earth, but your covenant will be with the boundary stones of the regions, and the beasts of the earth will be peaceful towards you.' In addition, the expression *remissa manus*, a 'slack hand', can perhaps be traced to the New Testament, where it forms part of a justification of divine chastisement (Hbr 12. 12). All three may again look towards the role of Eugenius.
[157] *Scribis eos ... libros, quos contra Iovinianum scripsi, canino dente rodere, lacerare, convellere ...,* 'You write that they gnaw, lacerate, tear apart with canine tooth the books which I have written against Jovinianus' (Jerome, ep. 50, 1, *CSEL*, 54, p. 388).
[158] *Cur vos ipsos non iam ovino sed lupino dente mordetis? Cur detrahitis? Cur laceratis?,* 'Why do you bite one another, not now with ovine but with lupine mouth? Why do you engage in detraction? Why do you lacerate (one another)?' (Peter, letter 111, p. 290).
[159] *in viscera nostra ... debacchati,* 'raging ... against our entrails'; *visceribus vero nostris non licuit iuxta fratres vestros suum imponere domicilium,* '(but) our entrails have not been allowed to place their dwelling next to your brothers'; *Quoniam ... (nec) nos possumus nostrorum viscerum non sentire dolorem ...,* 'Since ... we cannot not feel the pain of our entrails ...' (*Inebriati sicut*, Brial, pp. 471–2).

also points in several directions. Recalling the declaration in Peter's letter 175, that he would prefer to adhere to Bernard, rather than to 'rule ... or reign elsewhere',[160] it may also adapt a Boethian disquisition on the limitations of kingship. The latter asks whether one who 'flanks his side' with a henchman, and who is 'in the hand of those who serve him', should really be considered 'powerful'.[161] The conclusion there, that it is both dangerous to wish for power and impossible to lay it down,[162] may be linked to the hint of retirement found both here and in Bernard's letter of recommendation. At the same time, the sarcasm seems to be fuelled by an underlying subversion of scripture, in the form of a *reductio ad absurdum* of the parable of the Prodigal Son. There, the father's mercy towards his errant son is expressed not only in terms of affectionate embrace,[163] but also through material reward.[164]

The interplay here between the spiritual and the temporal may hint at a confounding of values on the part of Eugenius, with spiritual damage being rated below material loss. At the same time, the section may also target Bernard himself, and through him the Cistercians. Peter had called in letters 111 and 150 for Bernard to join him in eradicating detraction. The call had seemingly remained unanswered. The language of kingship recalls various attacks by Bernard on the power and wealth of Cluny. Expressed most directly in the latter's attack during the Langres affair on Peter the Venerable and Peter of Lyons as 'strong gods of the earth', 'trusting *in their strength and* glorying *in the multitude of their riches*',[165] it can also be associated with arguments previously placed by Peter in the mouth of (unnamed) Cistercian supporters, calling for the forced alienation of tithes from Cluny.[166] The

---

[160]   *Si liceret ... maluissem ... beatitudini tuae ... adhaerere, quam vel principari inter mortales alicubi, vel regnare* (Peter, letter 175, p. 416). See Chapter 10.

[161]   *An tu ... potentem censes qui satellite latus ambit, qui.. in servientium manu situm est?* (Boethius, *De consolatione Philosophiae*, III, 5. 8, ed. C. Moreschini, Bibliotheca Scriptorum Graecorum et Romanorum Teubneriana, Munich, 2000, p. 70).

[162]   *Quae est igitur ista potentia, quam pertimescunt habentes, quam nec cum habere velis tutus sis et cum deponere cupias vitare non possis?*, 'What then is that power, which those who have it dread, such that when you wish to have it you are not safe, and when you wish to lay it down, you cannot avoid it?'(ibid., III, 5. 12, p. 70). Subsequently, Peter will cite the statement which ends this section: *Nulla.. ad nocendum efficacior pestis quam familiaris inimicus,* 'No ... *pest is more efficacious to harm than a friend (become an) enemy*' (letter 192, p. 447).

[163]   *Cum autem adhuc longe esset vidit illum pater ipsius et misericordia motus est et accurrens cecidit supra collum eius et osculatus est illum,* 'But when he was still a long way off, his father saw him and was moved with pity, and running up, he fell upon his neck and kissed him' (Lc 15. 20).

[164]   *Dixit autem pater ad servos suos cito proferte stolam primam et induite illum et date anulum in manum eius et calciamenta in pedes et adducite vitulum saginatum et occidite ...,* 'But the father said to his servants, "Go quickly, bring the foremost garment and put it on him, and place a signet ring upon his hand and shoes on his feet, and bring a fatted calf and kill it ..." ' (ibid., 15. 22–3).

[165]   Bernard, ep. 168, 1, *SBO*, VII, p. 380. See Chapter 4.

[166]   *Monstruosum praedae genus, si laborent divitibus sancti pauperes extorquere, quod pessimi divites pauperibus solebant auferre,* 'It is a monstrous kind of pillage, if holy poor men are to labour to extort from the rich, what the wicked rich were accustomed to take away from the poor' (Peter, letter 34, p. 111). See Chapter 4.

parable of the Prodigal Son may also be capable of further application through inversion, involving as it does a younger and an elder brother, the latter of whom is said to resent the preferential treatment of his wasteful sibling.[167] In letter 33 to Innocent, Peter had invoked the parallel of the elder son, Esau, deprived of his rightful inheritance through the machinations of his younger brother, Jacob, to protest against the withholding of tithes from Cluny.[168] Here, it might suggest that Le Miroir is being rewarded for an initial transgression. Likewise, the claim that Peter is called upon to imitate the 'perfection of the Father' seems to look towards two New Testament passages. In one of these, perfection is associated with loving one's enemy.[169] In the other, however, it is equated with giving one's belongings to the poor.[170]

That Peter is looking back here to the beginnings of conflict may find confirmation in what follows. He claims that he would have no concern for the world if *filii saeculi*, 'the sons of the world', so permitted: 'But because they are *more prudent than the sons of the light in their begetting*, would that I might be given the *simplicity of a dove* to avoid their wickedness, and the *prudence of a serpent* to guard against their malice.'[171] This combines two biblical allusions. The first, to the parable of the 'steward of iniquity', concerns the remission of 'debts'. Dismissed for wastefulness, the steward is said to have remitted dues which others owed to his master.[172] Rather than incurring blame, however, this action is said to have attracted praise for prudence. On the surface, this would appear to reinforce Bernard's claim that Peter, 'steward' under God, should also let others off their dues. The resonance here, however, may extend in several directions. Seemingly, it is Bernard who has asked for their forgiveness. Accordingly, it may seem that it is he who is being equated with the steward of the parable, remitting 'dues' which actually belong to Peter. More trenchantly, the reference may also allude to the Cistercian demand for reparation. The interpretation of the parable in terms of 'fraudulent alms' as condemned by Augustine,[173] giving to God what is not rightly one's own to give, seems to have underlain Peter's earlier attacks on the Cistercian withholding of tithes.[174] Once

---

[167] Lc 15. 25–32.

[168] Peter, letter 33, p. 109. See Chapter 4.

[169] *Ego autem dico vobis diligite inimicos vestros benefacite his qui oderunt vos et orate pro persequentibus et calumniantibus vos ... estote ergo vos perfecti sicut et Pater vester caelestis perfectus est*, 'But I say to you, love your enemies, and benefit those who hate you, and pray for those who persecute you and calumniate you ... Therefore be perfect, just as your heavenly Father is perfect' (Mt 5. 44–8).

[170] *Ait illi Iesus si vis perfectus esse vade vende quae habes et da pauperibus et habebis thesaurum in caelo et veni sequere me*, 'But Jesus said to him, "If you wish to be perfect, go, sell what you have and give it to the poor, and you will have treasure in heaven, and come, follow me" ' (Mt 19. 21).

[171] *Sed quia ipsi* prudentiores sunt filiis lucis in generatione sua, *utinam mihi daretur* simplicitas columbae *ad illorum vitandam nequitiam, et* serpentis prudentia *ad praecavendam malitiam* (Peter, letter 192, p. 448 = Lc 16. 8; Mt 10. 16).

[172] Lc 16. 1–7.

[173] Augustine, *Quaest. Evang.*, II, XXXIV, 1. See Chapter 4.

[174] See Chapter 4.

again, Peter may seem to be hinting that he is being forced to make good what had been fraudulently withheld in the first place.

The second allusion, drawn from Matthew, paves the way for the reappearance of animal imagery in the coda, where the 'withdrawing sons' will be presented as 'hissing serpents'. Seemingly Peter is declaring the need to match guile with guile. In so doing, however, he may also be making a final, ironic renunciation of his claim to vengeance. Just as Augustine warns against wilful misinterpretation of the parable of the steward, so Jerome warns: 'It is better for the just man to have a little simplicity, and that he seem foolish through too much patience, while he reserves vengeance for God, than, immediately avenging himself, that he exercise malice under the veil of prudence.'[175] What follows may seem, however, to undercut the premises on which Bernard's whole letter was based. Peter claims to have 'wondered' at Bernard's remarks concerning an (unnamed) sub-prior: 'I immediately met the man, and heard from him that almost everything which had been suggested to you concerning him was completely false. I feared the hissings of my serpents, lest they had whispered into your ears similar things to what they have poured forth within this year. And indeed, the greater part of the matter which your letter contains seems to have been imparted by them.'[176] If Constable's suggestion, that this refers to the otherwise unknown sub-prior of Gigny, and that Bernard's letter had presented him as bearing the brunt of the responsibility, is correct,[177] the validity of Bernard's intervention may seem to be cast into doubt. Earlier Peter had cited a 'common proverb', to the effect that 'to be deceived once is disagreeable, a second time foolish, a third time shameful'.[178] To this had been appended a citation from Ecclesiasticus: '*Let ... your* friends *be many, your counsellor, one from a thousand.*'[179] In retrospect, this may be turned against Bernard himself. Twice deceived, as the sandwiching of *vestris auribus*, 'your ears', between two verbs connoting detraction might appear to suggest,[180] his suitability as a 'counsellor' for Peter would seem to be brought into question.[181]

---

[175] *Convenit iusto parvum habere simplicitatis, et propter nimiam patientiam, dum ultionem reservat Deo, stultum videri, quam statim se vindicantem sub velamento prudentiae exercere malitiam* (Jerome, *Commentarius in Ecclesiasten*, X, 1, ed. M. Adriaen, *CCSL*, 72, Turnhout, 1959, p. 333).

[176] *Conveni statim hominem, et cuncta fere quae de eo vobis suggesta fuerant, ab ipso falsissima esse audivi. Veritus sum meorum sibilos serpentium ne similia his quae hoc anno profuderunt vestris auribus insibilassent. Et vere maior pars materiei, quam epistola vestra continet ab ipsis infusa videtur* (letter 192, p. 448).

[177] Constable, *Letters* II, p. 230. Peter will go on to claim, drawing again on Psalm 68, with which the letter opened, *Hi ... odiunt quod diligo, diligunt quod odio. Sed hoc quidem* gratis *ut psalmus ait* ..., 'These ... hate what I love, love what I hate. But this indeed is *for nothing*, as the Psalm says ...' (letter 192, p. 448).

[178] *Proverbium est etiam vulgatum: Primo falli incommodum est, secundo stultum, tertio turpe* (ibid., p. 447).

[179] *Amici.*. sint tibi multi, *consiliarius* unus de mille (ibid. = Sir 6. 6). *Amici*, 'friends', has replaced *pacifici*, 'peaceable', of the original, while 'counsellor' has shifted from plural to singular.

[180] *Veritus sum ... ne similia his quae hoc anno profuderunt vestris auribus insibilassent* (letter 192, p. 448).

[181] Subsequently, the sub-prior will be praised as *prudens*, 'prudent', *utilis*, 'useful', *necessarius*, 'necessary', *fidelis*, 'faithful'. The first epithet may look back to Peter's expressed desire for *serpentis prudentia*, the 'prudence of a serpent.'

It may be that some of the irony in this letter should be seen as being directed towards the abbot of Le Miroir. The potentially ambiguous characterisation of this man in the letter to Nicholas as *mirandus et admirabilis*, 'wonderful and astonishing',[182] might suggest that he is being presented as the ultimate source of the request for clemency. While letting the Cluniacs off their spiritual dues might, indeed, be held to provoke admiration, the concomitant refusal to rescind their material dues might rather be held worthy of astonishment. Bernard's letter to Eugenius, reporting on the unsuccessful meeting held at Cluny, estimates the damage to Le Miroir at 'more than 30,000 shillings'.[183] In the event, Peter himself would pay 17,000 shillings. The payment, however, would not go unchallenged. A subsequent papal bull issued in 1154, under Anastasius IV, Eugenius' successor, and after the death of Bernard, presents this payment as having been made under duress, and orders restitution of the money,[184] while at the same time commanding the damage inflicted on Le Miroir to be made good.[185] The final settlement, achieved in 1155, would appear to reflect this, consisting, as it does, of a repayment to Peter of 11,000 shillings. At the same time, an undertaking was made by Le Miroir to replace the lost tithes by an annual rent.[186]

Providing the closure to Peter's letter-collection, letters 192 and 193 might also be expected to provide some kind of closure to the correspondence with Bernard. In fact, the features noted above, quasi-dialogic elements, heavy sarcasm, hidden and potentially ambivalent allusion, together with reminders of previous interference, do seem to constitute a form of ring-composition with letter 28, the official opening of communication. The effect, however, is arguably less one of resolution than of the reopening of old wounds. The seeming transparency of the first half of letter 192, with its apparent praise of Eugenius, and its expressions of gratitude towards Bernard, is undermined both by irony and by a satirical highlighting of the continuing presence of detraction and the concomitant absence of mutual *caritas*, an effect enhanced by the contradictory narrative of letter 193. Rather than marking a new stage of open and intimate relations between Peter and Bernard, and heralding a brighter dawn of Cluniac–Cistercian co-operation, these letters offer a glimpse of past conflict, which can be read as threatening to cast its shadow over an uncertain future.

---

[182] Peter, letter 193, p. 450.

[183] *quippe ultra triginta millia solidorum computatio facta est amissorum* (Bernard, ep. 283, p. 197). Bernard claims there that the Cistercians were ready to remit 'much' of the losses, but that those from Gigny offered 'so little' that Peter himself thought it 'unworthy of reporting'.

[184] *iudicavimus, ut praedictus abbas de Miratorio decem et septem millia solidorum Lugdunensis monetae, quos, licet pro pace, violenter tamen ei donaveras ... restituat*, 'we have judged that the aforesaid abbot of Le Miroir should restore the 17,000 shillings of Parisian coinage which, although on behalf of peace, you (Peter) had given him under duress' (Anastasius IV, ep. 46, *Anastasii IV romani pontificis, epistolae et privilegia*, ed. J.-P. Migne, *Patrologia Latina*, 188, Paris, 1855, 1037 = JL 9866).

[185] *Postmodum vero ea quae per eosdem fratres Gigniacenses ablata sunt ... restitui faciat, damna quoque illata eidem abbati resarciri ...*, 'But afterwards he (cardinal Odo) should cause to be restored what was carried off by those same brothers of Gigny, and the damage inflicted on the same abbey to be made good ...' (ibid.).

[186] *Recueil des chartes de l'abbaye de Cluny, Collection de Documents inédits sur l'Histoire de la France*, ed. A. Bernard and A. Bruel, 6 vols, Paris, 1876–1903, V, Paris, 1894, 530–31, no. 4180. See Constable, 'Cluniac tithes', pp. 620–24.

Conclusion

The aim of this study has been not to reconstruct the actual historical relationship between Peter the Venerable and Bernard of Clairvaux, although that has inevitably played some part, but rather to deconstruct their epistolary relationship, drawing on modern notions of epistolarity as developed through the work of Doty and Altman, supported where appropriate by dictaminal precepts and by classical rhetorical practice. At the same time, an element of historicity has been applied. Contemporary documentation has been used to set the letters within their immediate historical context. Equally, there has been some attempt to relate these letters to the developing tradition of letter-writing, fuelled by classical and Christian concepts of *amicitia*, and governed by conventions pertaining to epistolary etiquette.

The underlying principle has been two-fold: to demonstrate the effect of applying the tools of contemporary literary criticism to individual letters treated as whole constructs, and to investigate the dynamics of the interplay generated by the reconstruction of an epistolary sequence. The emerging patterns of semantic usage have been argued to be intrinsic rather than extrinsic to the significance of the correspondence as a whole, the citations with which both sets of letters are studded to form part of a wider pattern of secondary allusion and borrowing. Through the adaptation and subversion of rhetorical and conventional norms, these letters have been seen to generate a multiplicity of possible readings, with a potential for ambiguity and ambivalence which reflects both the inherent dichotomy between public and private and the possibility of wider dissemination. At the same time, they have appeared to offer what may be classified as a coherent, essentially ironic sub-text. The rhetoric is both manipulative and subject to manipulation, the irony is capable of functioning as either bridge or barrier.

Specifically, it has been argued that the dominating intertext is the correspondence between Augustine and Jerome, centring on Jerome's interpretation of a contentious passage from Galatians. Offering the concept of *officiosum mendacium*, the 'dutiful lie', and raising issues of 'judaising' and hypocrisy, this disputed passage can be seen as an influential shaping mechanism behind the framework of Peter's letter 28, argued here to be a response to Bernard's critical *Apologia*. Its unacknowledged but persistent presence suggests the establishment of an equation between the Mosaic Law and the monastic *Rule*, with a concomitant polarisation, perhaps already hinted at in the *Apologia*, between Cistercians and Cluniacs as orthodox Jews and Gentiles respectively. This initial polarisation, rooted in contradictory interpretations of the nature of *caritas*, will, it has been argued, inform the epistolary exchange which follows, finding overt expression in Peter's third and final 'public' letter, 150.

It has been further argued that the earlier correspondence can be viewed as offering a kind of mirror or prism for the subsequent epistolary relationship between Peter and Bernard. In particular, Augustine's demand that Jerome write a 'palinode' and/or enter into theological debate can be seen to underlie both 111, Peter's second 'public' letter, and ep. 228 of Bernard which provides its trigger. It will be finally replaced in 150 by the more contemporary, and arguably less contentious, parallel of Peter's own correspondence with Guigo of La Chartreuse. The effect of this mirroring may be two-fold. By casting the participants in the role of saints and patristic authorities, and creating the concept of 'debate', it raises the exchange to a higher level and distracts attention from actual points of conflict. At the same time, it can be seen to influence the projected balance of power. Jerome may have refused to capitulate within the 'debate', but it was Augustine's interpretation which would carry the day. The Jeromian voice, on the other hand, lends itself to a range of 'blocking' manœuvres. Moreover, within the Peter/Bernard correspondence, the voices can be interchanged at will.

The consequent fictionalisation and distortion of the underlying 'reality' can be seen to take on a further dimension through the incorporation of the letters within a letter-collection. Although there is no conclusive evidence concerning the editorial principles applied in a process encompassing the stages of authorship, editing and collection,[1] it is generally accepted that an element of selection was involved.[2] The evidence suggests that in the case of Peter and Bernard both political and artistic considerations may have been at work. Peter's collection is prefaced by a letter from his secretary, Peter of Poitiers, which praises his literary style in extravagant terms,[3] and associates him with his predecessor Odo, the founder of Cluny, in terms which glorify abbot and institution alike.[4] Letter 193 with which the collection concludes identifies Peter with Cluny, reaffirmed as the seat of *caritas*, to the potential exclusion of Bernard and Clairvaux. The opening to Bernard's collection is formed by the rhetorically elaborate *Letter to Robert*, attacking the Cluniacs, and allegedly miraculously written in a shower of rain.[5] Subsequently, a dramatic closure would be provided by a letter addressed to Arnold of Bonneval, one of Bernard's biographers, and supposedly emanating from Bernard's death-bed.[6] If, as

---

[1]   Cf. Haseldine, 'Peter of Celle', pp. 243–4.

[2]   Haseldine, ibid., p. 242; cf. Constable, *Letters*, II, p. 10; Leclercq, 'Lettres de S. Bernard', p. 126.

[3]   It is depicted there in terms which appear to derive from the *trivium* and the *quadrivium*: three classical *auctoritates*, Plato, Aristotle and Cicero, are balanced with the 'four rivers of Paradise', Jerome, Augustine, Ambrose and Gregory (Peter of Poitiers, *Epistola ad dominum Petrum abbatem Cluniacensem*, ed. G. Constable, *Letters*, I pp. 1–2).

[4]   The abbots of Cluny are said to possess the zeal of writing, *speciali praerogativa*, 'by special prerogative', *a temporibus antiquis*, 'from ancient times' (ibid., p. 3). Odo, described as *primus ... tantae rei publicae princeps, primus tanti coenobii pater, primus tantorum in Christo filiorum genitor et nutritor*, 'the first ruler of so great a commonwealth, the first father of so great a cloister, the first begetter and sustainer of such great sons in Christ', is said to have been *gloriosus*, 'glorious', by reason of his learning and miracles, and *celeberrimus*, 'very renowned', for his writing (ibid.).

[5]   Geoffrey of Auxerre, *Fragmenta de vita et miraculis S. Bernardi*, ed. R. Lechat, Analecta Bollandiana 50 (1932), 26, p. 103. See Leclercq, *SBO*, VII, pp. ix–x.

[6]   Bernard, ep. 310, *SBO*, VIII, p. 230. See Leclercq, 'Lettres de S. Bernard', pp. 127–8; Bredero, *Bernard of Clairvaux*, pp. 104–8.

Bredero suggests, this Arnold can be identified with the abbot of Bonneval mentioned in the second letter of Peter's collection, dated by Constable to 1134/1135,[7] as desiring to retire to Cluny,[8] this letter may be viewed as presenting some kind of 'conversion'. It seems reasonable, accordingly, to view these collections, in part at least, as an exercise in self-presentation which encompasses both the letter-writer and the institution of which he is the figurehead.[9]

It was suggested in the introduction that a letter-collection can be viewed as offering a kind of extended but discontinuous narrative. Viewed in this light, the part played in each collection by the epistolary sequence which has been reconstructed here emerges somewhat differently. Principally, this is a matter of emphasis: only seven as opposed to eighteen of the letters are to be found in Bernard's official collection. Of these, only one was written by Peter. There is also, however, a question of selectivity and slanting. In Peter's collection, the three 'open' letters relating to Cluniac–Cistercian relations are prominently placed. The *apologetic* letter 28 is followed by the equally combative, and chronologically displaced, letter 29, relating to Langres. Both letter 111 and 150 are preceded by trigger-letters from Bernard. That neither is followed by a response would appear to enhance the moral authority of Peter. In contrast to this, only the first of these trigger-letters, ep. 228, appears in Bernard's official collection, where its isolation serves to disconnect it from the Cluniac–Cistercian debate. On the other hand, Peter's seemingly complimentary letter 175, requesting the visit of Nicholas, is followed in Bernard's collection by his blocking ep. 265. In the absence, however, of letter 181, Peter's vigorous and challenging return to the offensive, both letters may appear to be weakened, and the effect largely neutralised.[10]

The effect of such patterns of omission and inclusion on the two collections is profound. In Peter's collection, the concern with improving domestic monastic harmony seems to be presented as a significant and recurrent preoccupation. The shadowy presence of Bernard elsewhere in the collection may seem to shape Peter's reaction there to issues which affected the Church and western Christendom on a broader level, such as crusading, episcopal election, papal schism and even heresy. Bernard's collection, on the other hand, would appear to relegate the concerns of both Cluny and Peter to the margins of twelfth-century history. It might indeed be argued that this difference in emphasis has played some part in shaping subsequent perceptions of the relationship, with Bernard, the 'saint', frequently being seen as

---

[7] Constable, *Letters*, II, p. 97.

[8] *Abbas Bonae Vallis quae iuxta Carnotum est, cum quampluribus honestis et sapientibus viris ut asserit, Cluniacum venire disponit, si per consilium sapientiae vestrae licentiam recedendi a domino papa impetrare potuerit*, 'The abbot of Bonneval, which is near to Chartres, with, so he asserts, very many honourable and wise men, is planning to come to Cluny, if, through the counsel of your Wisdom, he is able to obtain permission to withdraw from the lord Pope' (Peter, letter 2, *Letters*, I, p. 6). See Bredero, *Bernard of Clairvaux*, p. 103.

[9] This aspect seems to be acknowledged in Leclercq's admission that the definitive version of Bernard's collection, produced after his death, might have served as a useful document for obtaining his canonisation (Leclercq, 'Lettres de S. Bernard', p. 224).

[10] Bredero, indeed, reads the inclusion of letter 175 as an attempt to disguise a subsequent rift (Bredero, *Bernard of Clairvaux*, p. 276).

its dominant and dynamic spiritual force and Peter, the 'venerable' abbot, as a more passive and pacific recipient of admonition and advice.[11] In conclusion, the question posed at the beginning of this work as to the validity of using this correspondence as historical source material may seem to find an affirmative answer, but with the *caveat* that it must be approached with considerable caution, respecting the parameters of epistolary dialogue within which it is set, and maintaining a critical scepticism with regard to its interpretation.

---

[11] 'Mais la charité de l'un s'enflamme souvent en zèle, alors que celle de l'autre se fond d'ordinaire en douceur' (Auniord, 'L'ami de saint Bernard', p. 98); 'spontanément Pierre aime Bernard et si cet amour a été parfois durement secoué, il ne demandait qu'à s'épanouir en toute confiance' (Torrell and Bouthillier, *Pierre et sa vision*, p. 101). It may find its traces also in Bredero's assertion that Peter the Venerable was seeking to improve the relationship 'if only for pragmatic reasons', defined there as the desire to enlist Bernard's help and support in promoting reforms (Bredero, *Bernard of Clairvaux*, p. 243).

Bibliography

Sources

Acta primi capituli provincialis ordinis S. Benedicti Remis A. D. 1131 habiti, ed. S. Ceglar, 'William of Saint-Thierry and his leading role at the first Chapters of the Benedictine abbots (Reims 1131, Soissons 1132)', in *William, abbot of St. Thierry, a colloquium at the abbey of St. Thierry*, trans. J. Carfantan, Cistercian Studies Series 94, Kalamazoo, 1987, 34–112, pp. 51–63.

Adalbert of Samaria, *Adalbertus Samaritanus, Praecepta dictaminum*, ed. F.-J. Schmale, Monumenta Germaniae Historica, Quellen zur Geistesgeschichte des Mittelalters III, Weimar, 1961, 28–74.

Ad C. Herennium de ratione dicendi, ed. F. Marx, *M. Tulli Ciceronis scripta quae manserunt omnia*, fasc. 1, Bibliotheca Scriptorum Graecorum et Romanorum Teubneriana, Leipzig, 1964.

Aelred of Rievaulx, *Liber de speculo caritatis*, ed. A. Hoste and C. H. Talbot, in *Aelredi Rievallensis Opera Omnia* 1, *Opera Ascetica, CCCM*, 1, Turnhout, 1971, 3–161.

Alberic of Monte Cassino, *Albericus, Breviarium de dictamine*, ed. L. Rockinger, in *Briefsteller und Formelbücher des eilften bis vierzehnten Jahrhunderts*, Quellen und Erörterungen zur bayerischen und deutschen Geschichte 9, Munich, 1863, reprinted in 2 vols, New York, 1961, I, 29–46.

Alberic of Monte Cassino, *Alberici Casinensis Flores rhetorici*, ed. D. M. Inguanez and H. M. Willard, Miscellanea Cassinense 14, Montecassino, 1938.

Alberic of Monte Cassino, *Flowers of rhetoric*, trans. J. M. Miller in *Readings in medieval rhetoric*, ed. J. M. Miller, M. H. Prosser and T. W. Benson, Bloomington, Indiana, 1973, 131–61.

Alcuin, *Alcuini sive Albini epistolae*, ed. E. Dümmler, Monumenta Germaniae Historica Epistolae IV, Aevi Karolini ii, Berlin, 1895, reprinted 1974.

Ambrose, *De officiis ministrorum*, ed., trans. and annotated by M. Testard, *Saint Ambrose, Les devoirs*, 2 vols, Paris, 1992.

Ammianus Marcellinus, *Rerum gestarum libri qui supersunt*, ed. W. Seyforth, Bibliotheca Scriptorum Graecorum et Romanorum Teubneriana, 2 vols, Leipzig, 1987.

Anastasius IV, *Anastasii IV romani pontificis, epistolae et privilegia*, ed. J.-P. Migne, *Patrologia Latina*, 188, Paris, 1855, 289–1088.

Anonymous of Bologna, *Rationes dictandi*, ed. L. Rockinger, in *Briefsteller und Formelbücher des eilften bis vierzehnten Jahrhunderts*, Quellen und Erörterungen zur bayerischen und deutschen Geschichte 9, Munich, 1863, reprinted in 2 vols, New York, 1961, I, 9–28.

Anonymous of Bologna, *The principles of letter-writing*, trans. J. J. Murphy, in

Three Medieval Rhetorical Arts, ed. J. J. Murphy, Berkeley; Los Angeles, 1971, 5–25.

Augustine, *Confessiones*, ed. L. Verheijen, *CCSL*, 27, Turnhout, 1981.

Augustine, *De doctrina christiana libri quattuor*, ed. G. M. Green, *CSEL*, 80, Vienna, 1963.

Augustine, *De Trinitate*, ed. W. J. Mountain, 2 vols, *CCSL*, 50, 50A, Turnhout, 1968.

Augustine, *Enarrationes in Psalmos*, ed. D. E. Dekkers and I. Fraipont, 3 vols, *CCSL*, 38–40, Turnhout, 1956.

Augustine, *Epistolae*, ed. A. L. Goldbacher, *CSEL*, 34/1, 34/2, 44, 57, Vienna, 1895–1911.

Augustine, *In Ioannis epistolam ad Parthos*, ed. P. Agaësse, *Commentaire de la première épître de S. Jean*, Sources chrétiennes, 75, Paris, 1961.

Augustine, *Quaestiones evangeliorum*, ed. A. Mutzenbacker, *CCSL*, 44B, Turnhout, 1980.

Augustine, *Sermones de scripturis veteris et novi testamenti*, ed. J.-P. Migne, *Patrologia Latina* 38, Paris, 1865, 23–994.

Augustine, *Sermones Frangipane*, ed. G. Morin, *Sancti Augustini sermones post Maurinos reperti, Miscellanea Agostiniana*, 1, Rome, 1930.

Benedict of Monte Cassino, *Benedicti Regula*, ed. R. Hanslik, *CSEL*, 75, Vienna, 1960.

Bernard of Clairvaux, *Apologia ad Guillelmum abbatem*, in *Sancti Bernardi Opera*, ed. J. Leclercq and H. M. Rochais, 8 vols, III, Rome, 1963, 81–108.

Bernard of Clairvaux, *Apologia*, trans. M. Casey, in *The works of Bernard of Clairvaux*, Cistercian Fathers Series 1, Spencer, Mass., 1970, 33–69.

Bernard of Clairvaux, *De consideratione ad Eugenium Papam*, in *Sancti Bernardi Opera*, ed. J. Leclercq and H. M. Rochais, 8 vols, III, Rome, 1963, 393–493.

Bernard of Clairvaux, *Epistolae*, in *Sancti Bernardi Opera*, ed. J. Leclercq and H. M. Rochais, 8 vols, VII, Rome, 1974; VIII, Rome, 1977.

Bernard of Clairvaux, *Epistolae*, ed. D. J. Mabillon and J.-P. Migne, in *Sancti Bernardi abbatis Claraevallensis opera omnia, Patrologia Latina*, 182, Paris, 1859, 67–662.

Bernard of Clairvaux, *Letters*, trans. B. S. James, *The Letters of St. Bernard of Clairvaux*, London, 1953, reprinted with introduction by B. M. Kienzle, Thrupp, Stroud, 1998.

Bernard of Clairvaux, *Letters*, trans. by H. Rochais, *Bernard de Clairvaux, Lettres*, texte latin des S. Bernardi Opera by J. Leclercq, H. Rochais and Ch. H. Talbot, intro. and notes by M. Duchet-Suchaux, Sources chrétiennes, 425, Paris, 1997.

Bernard of Clairvaux, *Liber de praecepto et dispensatione*, in *Sancti Bernardi Opera*, ed. Dom J. Leclercq and H. M. Rochais, 8 vols, III, Rome, 1963, 253–94.

Bernard of Clairvaux, *On precept and dispensation*, trans. C. Greenia, in *The works of Bernard of Clairvaux*, Cistercian Fathers Series I, Spencer, Mass., 1970, 105–50.

Bernard of Clairvaux, *Sermones per annum*, in *Sancti Bernardi Opera*, ed. J. Leclercq and H. M. Rochais, 8 vols, V, Rome, 1968.

Boethius, *De consolatione Philosophiae; Opuscula theologica*, ed. C. Moreschini, Bibliotheca Scriptorum Graecorum et Romanorum Teubneriana, Munich, 2000.

Cassian, *Collationes XXIIII*, ed. M. Petschenig, *CSEL*, 13, Vienna, 1886, reprinted 1966.

Cicero, *De officiis*, ed. C. Atzert, *M. Tulli Ciceronis, scripta quae manserunt omnia*, Bibliotheca Scriptorum Graecorum et Romanorum Teubneriana, fasc. 48, Leipzig, 1963, reprinted 1985.

Cicero, *Epistulae ad familiares, libri I–XVI*, ed. D. R. Shackleton Bailey, Bibliotheca Scriptorum Graecorum et Romanorum Teubneriana, Stuttgart, 1988.

Cicero, *Laelius de amicitia*, ed. with trans. and commentary by J. G. F. Powell, *Cicero, Laelius, on friendship & The dream of Scipio*. Warminster, England, 1990.

Cicero, *Partitiones oratoriae*, ed. A. S. Wilkins, *M. Tulli Ciceronis, Rhetorica*, 2 vols, Scriptorum Classicorum Bibliotheca Oxoniensis, 2nd ed., Oxford, 1935, II.

Demetrius, *De elocutione*, ed. L. Radermacher, Stuttgart, 1966.

Demetrius, *De elocutione*, trans. G. M. A. Grube, *A Greek critic: Demetrius on style*, Toronto, 1961.

Demetrius [of Phalerum], *Typoi epistolikoi*, ed. V. Weichert, in *Demetrius and Libanius*, Leipzig, 1910, 1–12.

Epiphanius Latinus, *Interpretatio Evangeliorum*, ed. A. Hamman, *Patrologia Latina supplementum* 3, Paris, 1964, 836–964.

Gellius, *Noctes Atticae*, ed. P. K. Marshall, 2 vols, Oxford, 1968, revised 1990.

Geoffrey of Auxerre, *Fragmenta de vita et miraculis S. Bernardi*, ed. R. Lechat, Analecta Bollandiana 50 (1932), 83–122.

Gilbert Foliot, *Gilbert Foliot and his letters*, ed. Dom. A. Morey and C. N. L. Brooke, Cambridge Studies in Medieval Life and Thought 11, Cambridge, 1965.

Gregory the Great, *Gregorii Magni, Dialogi libri IV*, ed. U. Moricca, Istituto Storico Italiano Fonti per la Storia D'Italia, Rome, 1924.

Gregory the Great, *Homiliae in Hiezechielem prophetam*, ed. M. Adriaen, *CCSL*, 142, Turnhout, 1971.

Gregory the Great, *Regula pastoralis*, ed. B. Judic, C. Morel and F. Rommel, *Grégoire le Grand, Règle pastorale*, 2 vols, Sources chrétiennes, 381–2, Paris, 1992.

Gregory the Great, *Homiliae in Evangelia*, ed. R. Etaix, *CCSL*, 141, Turnhout, 1999.

Guigo of La Chartreuse, *Epistulae Cartusianae, Frühe Kartäuserbriefe*, ed. G. Greshake, Fontes Christiani 10, Freiburg, 1992, 104–57.

Horace, *Ars poetica*, ed. D. R. Shackleton Bailey, *Q. Horati Flacci opera*, Bibliotheca Scriptorum Graecorum et Romanorum Teubneriana, 3rd ed., Stuttgart, 1995, 310–29.

Horace, *Carmina (Odes)*, ed. D. R. Shackleton Bailey, *Q. Horati Flacci opera*, Bibliotheca Scriptorum Graecorum et Romanorum Teubneriana, 3rd ed., Stuttgart, 1995, 1–134.

Horace, *Epistles*, ed. D. R. Shackleton Bailey, *Q. Horati Flacci opera*, Bibliotheca Scriptorum Graecorum et Romanorum Teubneriana, 3rd ed., Stuttgart, 1995, 251–309.

Horace, *Satires*, ed. D. R. Shackleton Bailey, *Q. Horati Flacci opera*, Bibliotheca Scriptorum Graecorum et Romanorum Teubneriana, 3rd ed., Stuttgart, 1995, 165–250.

Hrotswitha of Gandersheim, *Hrotsvithae opera*, ed. H. Homeyer, Munich, Paderborn, 1970.

Hugh of Bologna, *Hugonis Bononiensis, Rationes dictandi prosaice*, ed. L. Rockinger, in *Briefsteller und Formelbücher des eilften bis vierzehnten Jahrhunderts*, Quellen und Erörterungen zur bayerischen und deutschen Geschichte 9, Munich, 1863, reprinted in 2 vols, New York, 1961, I, 53–94.

Idung of Prüfenig, *Dialogus duorum monachorum*, ed. R. B. C. Huygens, *Studi Medievali*, 3rd series, 13.1 (1972), 307–8.

Isidore of Seville, *Isidori Hispaliensis Episcopi, Etymologiarum sive originum libri XX*, ed. W. M. Lindsay, 2 vols, Oxford, 1911, reprinted 1985.

Jerome, *Commentarius in Ecclesiasten*, ed. M. Adriaen, *CCSL*, 72, Turnhout, 1959, 250–361.

Jerome, *Commentariorum in Esaiam Libri I–XVIII*, ed. M. Adriaen, 2 vols, *CCSL*, 73–73A, Turnhout, 1963.

Jerome, *Contra Rufinum*, ed. and trans. P. Lardet, *Saint Jérôme, Apologie contre Rufin*, Sources chrétiennes, 303, Paris, 1983.

Jerome, *Epistolae*, ed. I. Hilberg, *CSEL*, 54, 55, 56/1, Vienna, 1910–18, reprinted 1996.

Jerome, *Hebraicae quaestiones in Libro Geneseos*, ed. P. de Lagarde, *CCSL*, 72, Turnhout, 1959, 1–56.

John of Salisbury, *The letters of John of Salisbury*, ed. W. J. Millor and H. E. Butler, revised C. N. L. Brooke, 2 vols, Oxford, 1955–79, reissued Oxford, 1986.

Julius Victor, *Ars rhetorica*, ed. R. Giomini and M. S. Celentano, Leipzig, 1980.

Justinian, *Digesta*, in *Corpus iuris civilis*, ed. T. Mommsen and P. Krüger, 3 vols, Berlin, 1954, I, 1–926.

Le cartulaire de Marcigny-sur-Loire (1045–1144). Essai de reconstitution d'un manuscript disparu, ed. J. Richard, Analecta Burgundica 4, Dijon, 1957.

Libanius the Sophist, *Epistolemaioi Caracteres*, ed. V. Weichert, in *Demetrius and Libanius*, Leipzig, 1919, 13–34.

Lucan, *De bello civili*, ed. D. R. Shackleton Bailey, Bibliotheca Scriptorum Graecorum et Romanorum Teubneriana, Stuttgart, 1997.

Lucretius, *De rerum natura*, ed. J. Martin, *T. Lucretius Carus De rerum natura*, Bibliotheca Scriptorum Graecorum et Romanorum Teubneriana, Leipzig, 1969.

Matthew of Albano, *Epistola Matthaei Albanensis Episcopi*, ed. S. Ceglar, 'William of Saint-Thierry and his leading role at the first Chapters of the Benedictine abbots (Reims 1131, Soissons 1132)', in *William, abbot of St. Thierry, a colloquium at the abbey of St. Thierry*, trans. J. Carfantan, Cistercian Studies Series 94, Kalamazoo, 1987, 34–112, pp. 65–82.

Nicholas of Clairvaux, *Nicolai Claraevallensis Epistolae*, ed. J.-P. Migne, *Patrologia Latina*, 196, Paris, 1880, 1593–1654.

Orderic Vitalis, *Historia ecclesiastica*, ed. and trans. M. Chibnall, *The ecclesiastical history of Orderic Vitalis*, 6 vols, Oxford, 1969–80.

Persius, *Satires, A. Persi Flacci, Saturarum liber*, ed. D. Bo, Corpus Scriptorum Latinorum Paravianum, Torino, 1969.

Peter of Celle, *Epistolae*, ed. J.-P. Migne, *Patrologia Latina* 202, Paris, 1855, 405–636.

Peter of Poitiers, *Epistola ad dominum Petrum abbatem Cluniacensem*, ed. G.

Constable, *The Letters of Peter the Venerable*, Harvard Historical Studies 78, 2 vols, Cambridge, Mass., 1967, I, 1–3.

Peter the Venerable, *Contra Petrobrusianos hereticos*, ed. J. Fearns, *CCCM*, 10, Turnhout, 1968.

Peter the Venerable, *Contra sectam Sarracenorum*, ed. R. Glei, in *Petrus Venerabilis Schriften zum Islam*, Corpus Islamo-Christianum, Series Latina, 1, Altenberge, 1985, 30–225.

Peter the Venerable, *De miraculis libri duo*, ed. D. Bouthillier, *CCCM*, 83, Turnhout, 1988.

Peter the Venerable, *Epistola de translatione sua*, ed. R. Glei, in *Petrus Venerabilis Schriften zum Islam*, Corpus Islamo-Christianum, Series Latina, 1, Altenberge, 1985, 22–8.

Peter the Venerable, *Letters*, ed. G. Constable, *The Letters of Peter the Venerable*, Harvard Historical Studies 78, 2 vols, Cambridge, Mass., 1967.

Peter the Venerable, *Statuta*, ed. G. Constable, *Corpus Consuetudinum Monasticorum*, 6, Siegburg, 1975, 19–106.

Peter the Venerable, *Summa totius haeresis Sarracenorum*, ed. R. Glei, in *Petrus Venerabilis Schriften zum Islam*, Corpus Islamo-Christianum, Series Latina, 1, Altenberge, 1985, 2–22.

Plautus, *T. Macci Plauti Comoediae*, ed. W. M. Lindsay, 2 vols, Oxford, 1904, reprinted 1946.

Quintilian, *The Minor Declamations ascribed to Quintilian*, ed. with commentary M. Winterbottom, Berlin, 1984.

Rabanus Maurus, *Allegoriae in sacram scripturam*, in B. Rabani Mauri, *Opera amnia*, ed. J.-P. Migne, 6 vols, *Patrologia Latina*, 107–12, Paris, 1864, 112, 850–1088.

Recueil des chartes de l'abbaye de Cluny, Collection de Documents inédits sur l'Histoire de la France, ed. A. Bernard and A. Bruel, 6 vols, Paris, 1876–1903.

Recueil des Historiens des Gaules et de la France. Rerum Gallicarum et Francicarum scriptores, ed. M. Bouquet et al., 24 vols, Paris, 1685–1754, new ed. vols 1–19, L. Delisle, Paris, 1869–1904.

Sallust, *Catilina*, ed. L. D. Reynolds, *C. Sallusti Crispi, Catilina, Iugurtha, historiarum fragmenta selecta*, Oxford, 1991.

Seneca the Elder, *Controversiae*, ed. L. Håkanson, *L. Annaeus Seneca Maior, Oratorum et rhetorum sententiae, divisiones, colores*, Bibliotheca Scriptorum Graecorum et Romanorum Teubneriana, Leipzig, 1989.

Statuta capitulorum generalium ordinis Cisterciensis ab anno 1116, ed. J.-M. Canivez, 8 vols, Bibliothèque de la revue d'histoire ecclésiastique 9–14, Louvain, 1933.

Suger, *Epistolae, Œuvres complètes de Suger*, ed. A. Lecoy de la Marche, Société de l'histoire de la France, Paris, 1867, 239–84.

Tertullian, *Adversus Marcionem*, ed. E. Evans, Oxford Early Christian Texts, 2 vols, Oxford, 1972.

Testamentum Porcelli, ed. F. Bücheler, in *Petronii Saturae*, Berlin, 1922, 268–9.

Virgil, *Aeneid*, ed. R. A. B. Mynors, *P. Vergili Maronis opera*, Scriptorum Classicorum Bibliotheca Oxoniensis, Oxford, 1969, reprinted with corrections 1972, 103–422.

Virgil, *Eclogues*, ed. R. A. B. Mynors, *P. Vergili Maronis opera*, Scriptorum
    Classicorum Bibliotheca Oxoniensis, Oxford, 1969, reprinted 1972, 1–28.
Virgil, *Eclogues*, ed. with commentary by T. E. Page, *P. Vergili Maronis, Bucolica
    et Georgica*, Classical Series, London, New York, 1898, reprinted 1968.
William of St Thierry, Arnold of Bonneval, Geoffrey of Auxerre, *Sancti Bernardi
    vita prima libri V*, ed. J.-P. Migne, *Patrologia Latina* 185-I, Paris, 1859, 225–372.

Secondary Works

Altman, J. G., *Epistolarity: Approaches to a Form*, Columbus, 1982.
d'Alverny, M.-T., 'Deux traductions latines du Coran au Moyen Age', *Archives
    d'Histoire Doctrinale et Littéraire du Moyen Age* 16 (1947–48), 69–131.
d'Alverny, M.-T., 'Pierre le Vénérable et la légende de Mahomet', in *A Cluny,
    Congrès scientifique: fêtes et cérémonies liturgiques en l'honneur des saints
    Abbés Odon et Odilon, 9–11 juillet 1949*, Dijon, 1950, 161–70.
Auberger, J.-B., *L'unanimité cistercienne primitive: mythe ou réalité*,
    Cîteaux–Achel, 1986.
Auniord, J., 'L'ami de Saint Bernard. Quelques textes', *Collectanea Sacri Ordinis
    Cisterciensis* 18, 1956, 88–99.
Baker, D., '*Viri religiosi* and the York election dispute', *Studies in Church
    History* 7, ed. G. J. Cuming and D. Baker, London, 1971, 87–100.
Baker, D., "San Bernardo e l'elezione di York', *Studi su S. Bernardo di Chiaravalle,
    nell' ottavo centenario della canonizzazione, Convegno internazionale certosa di
    Firenze (6–9 Novembre 1974)*, Bibliotheca Cisterciensis 6, Rome, 1975, 115–80.
Benton, J. F., 'The court of Champagne as a literary centre', *Speculum* 36 (1961),
    551–91, reprinted in Benton, *Culture, power and personality*, ed. T. N. Bisson,
    London, 1991, 3–43.
Berry, V., 'Peter the Venerable and the Crusades', in *Petrus Venerabilis,
    1156–1956: studies and texts commemorating the eighth centenary of his death*,
    ed. G. Constable and J. Kritzeck, Studia Anselmiana 40, Rome, 1956, 141–62.
Billy, D. J., 'The *Ysengrimus* and the Cistercian–Cluniac controversy', *The
    American Benedictine Review* 43 (1992), 301–28.
Bishko, C. J., 'Peter the Venerable's journey to Spain', in *Petrus Venerabilis,
    1156–1956: studies and texts commemorating the eighth centenary of his death*,
    ed. G. Constable and J. Kritzeck, Studia Anselmiana 40, Rome, 1956, 163–75.
Bligny, B., 'Les Chartreux dans la société occidentale du XIIe siecle', *Cahiers
    d'Histoire* 20 (1975), 137–66.
Bolton, B., 'The Cistercians and the aftermath of the Second Crusade', in *The
    Second Crusade and the Cistercians*, ed. M. Gervers, New York, 1992, 131–40.
Boureau, A., 'The letter-writing norm, a medieval invention', in *Correspondence:
    models of letter-writing from the Middle Ages to the Nineteenth century*, R.
    Chartier, A. Boureau and C. Dauphin, trans. C. Woodall, Cambridge, 1997,
    24–58.
Bouton, J. de la Croix, 'Bernard et l'ordre de Cluny', in *Bernard de Clairvaux,
    1953: Commission d'Histoire de l'ordre de Cîteaux*, Paris, 1953, 193–217.
Bouton, J. de la Croix and van Damme, J. B., *Les plus anciens textes de Cîteaux,*

sources, textes et notes historiques, Cîteaux, Commentarii Cistercienses Studia et Documenta 2, Achel, 1974.

Bredero, A. H., *Cluny et Cîteaux au douzième siècle: l'histoire d'une controverse monastique*, Amsterdam–Maarssen, Lille, 1985.

Bredero, A. H., 'William of Saint Thierry at the crossroads of the monastic currents of his time', in *William, abbot of St Thierry, a colloquium at the abbey of St Thierry*, trans. J. Carfantan, Cistercian Studies Series 94, Kalamazoo, Mich., 1987, 113–37.

Bredero, A. H., 'Saint Bernard in his Relations with Peter the Venerable', in *Bernardus Magister: papers presented at the nonacentenary celebration of the birth of Saint Bernard of Clairvaux, Kalamazoo, Michigan*, ed. R. Sommerfeldt, Spencer, Mass., 1992, 315–47.

Bredero, A. H., 'Saint Bernard, est il né en 1090 ou en 1091?', in *Papauté, monachisme et théories politiques. Etudes d'histoire médiévale offertes à Marcel Pacaut*, ed. P. Guichard, M.-T. Lorcin, J.-M. Poisson and M. Rubellin, 2 vols, Lyons, 1994, I, 229–41.

Bredero, A. H., *Bernard of Clairvaux, between cult and history*, Grand Rapids, Mich., 1996.

Brolis, M.-T., 'La Crociata di Pietro il Venerabile: guerra di arma o guerra di idee?', *Aevum* 61 (2) (1987), 327–54.

Brownlee, M. S., *The severed word. Ovid's Heroides and the novela sentimental*, Princeton, New Jersey, 1990.

Camargo, M., *Ars dictaminis ars dictandi*, Typologie des Sources du Moyen Age occidental 60, Turnhout, 1991.

Cassidy, E. G., ' "He who has friends can have no friend": classical and Christian perspectives on the limits to friendship', in *Friendship in medieval Europe*, ed. J. Haseldine, Thrupp, Stroud, 1999, 45–67.

Ceglar, S., 'William of Saint-Thierry and his leading role at the first Chapters of the Benedictine abbots (Reims 1131, Soissons 1132)', in *William, abbot of St Thierry, a colloquium at the abbey of St Thierry*, trans. J. Carfantan, Cistercian Studies Series 94, Kalamazoo, Mich., 1987, 34–112.

Champlin, E., 'The testament of the piglet', *Phoenix* 41 (1987), 174–83.

Cherewatuk, K., Wiethaus, V., *Dear sister: medieval women and the epistolary genre*, Philadelphia, 1993.

Clanchy, M. T., 'Abelard – knight (miles), courtier (palatinus) and man of war (vir bellator)', in *Medieval Knighthood* V, Papers from the Strawberry Hill Conference 1994, ed. S. Church and R. Harvey, Woodbridge, 1995, 101–18.

Clanchy, M. T., *Abelard, a medieval life*, Oxford, 1997.

Clausen, W., *A commentary on Virgil's Eclogues*, Oxford, 1994.

Clémencet, Dom C., *Histoire littéraire de S. Bernard, abbé de Clairvaux, et de Pierre Vénérable, abbé de Cluni*, Paris, 1773.

Coleman, J., *Ancient and Medieval Memories*, Cambridge, 1992.

Colker, M., 'Anecdota mediaevalia', *Traditio* 17 (1961), 469–82.

Constable, G., 'The Second Crusade as seen by contemporaries', *Traditio* 9 (1953), 213–79.

Constable, G., 'The letter from Peter of St John to Hato of Troyes', in *Petrus Venerabilis, 1156–1956: studies and texts commemorating the eighth centenary of his death*, ed. G. Constable and J. Kritzeck, Studia Anselmiana 40, Rome, 1956, 38–52, reprinted in Constable, *Cluniac Studies*, Variorum Reprints, London, 1980.

Constable, G., 'The disputed election at Langres in 1138', *Traditio* 13 (1957), 119–52, reprinted in Constable, *Cluniac Studies*, Variorum Reprints, London, 1980.

Constable, G., 'Cluniac tithes and the controversy between Gigny and Le Miroir', *Revue Bénédictine* 70 (1960), 591–624, reprinted in Constable, *Cluniac Studies*, Variorum Reprints, London, 1980.

Constable, G., *Monastic tithes from their origins to the twelfth century*, Cambridge Studies in Medieval Life and Thought 10, Cambridge, 1964.

Constable, G., 'A report of a lost sermon by St Bernard on the failure of the Second Crusade', in *Studies in Medieval Cistercian History presented to J. F. O'Sullivan*, Cistercian Studies Series 13, Spencer, Mass., 1971, 49–54.

Constable, G., 'The monastic policy of Peter the Venerable', in *Pierre Abélard–Pierre le Vénérable. Les courants littéraires et artistiques en occident au milieu du XIIᵉ siècle*, Colloques internationaux du Centre National de la recherche scientifique 546, Paris, 1975, 119–42.

Constable, G., 'Cluny, Cîteaux, La Chartreuse: San Bernardo e la diversità delle forme di vita religiosa nel XII secolo', in *Studi su S. Bernardo di Chiaravalle, nell'ottavo centenario della canonizzazione, Convegno internazionale certosa di Firenze (6–9 Novembre 1974)*, Bibliotheca Cisterciensis 6, Rome, 1975, 93–114.

Constable, G., 'On editing the letters of Peter the Venerable', *Quellen und Forschungen aus italienischen Archiven und Bibliotheken* 54 (1974), 483–508.

Constable, G., *Letters and Letter-Collections*, Typologie des Sources du Moyen Age occidental 17, Turnhout, 1976.

Constable, G., *The reformation of the twelfth century*, Cambridge, 1996.

Constable, G., *Love and do what you will. The Medieval History of an Augustinian precept*, Morton W. Bloomfield Lectures IV, Medieval Institute Publications, Kalamazoo, Mich., 1999.

Conybeare, C., *Paulinus noster: self and symbols in the letters of Paulinus of Nola*, Oxford, 2000.

Cowdrey, H. E. J., 'Abbot Pontius of Cluny', *Studi Gregoriani* 11 (1978), 177–298.

Cowdrey, H. E. J., ' "Quidam frater Stephanus nomine, Anglicus natione." The English background of Stephen Harding', *Revue Bénédictine* 101 (3–4) (1991), 322–40.

Deissman, G. A., *Light from the Ancient East. The New Testament Illustrated by Recently Discovered Texts of the Graeco-Roman World*, trans. L. R. M. Strachan, London, 1910.

Dimier, Dom A., 'Outrances et roueries de saint Bernard', in *Pierre Abélard–Pierre le Vénérable. Les courants littéraires et artistiques en occident au milieu du XIIe siècle*, Colloques Internationaux du Centre National de la Recherche Scientifique 546, Paris, 1975, 655–70.

Doty, W., 'The Classification of Epistolary Literature', *The Catholic Biblical Quarterly* 31 (1969), 183–99.

Drumbl, J., '*Ludus iucundus, honestus, gravis, spectabilis.* Die Metapher des *Theatrum Mundi* bei Bernhard von Clairvaux', *Aevum* 72:2 (1998), 361–74.

Duby, G., 'Un inventaire des profits de la seigneurerie clunisienne', in *Petrus Venerabilis, 1156–1956: studies and texts commemorating the eighth centenary of his death*, ed. G. Constable and J. Kritzeck, Studia Anselmiana 40, Rome, 1956, 128–40.

Duby, G., 'Le Budget de Cluny entre 1080 et 1155', in *Hommes et structures du Moyen Âge. Un recueil d'articles*, ed. G. Duby, Paris, 1973, 61–82.

Ferzoco, G., 'The origin of the Second Crusade', in *The Second Crusade and the Cistercians*, ed. M. Gervers, New York, 1992, 91–9.

Fiske, A., *Friends and friendship in the monastic tradition*, Cidoc Cuardeno 51, Cuérnavaca, Mexico, 1970.

Fiske, A., 'Alcuin and mystical friendship', *Studi Medievali* 2 (2) series 3 (1961), 551–75.

Ganz, D., ' "Mind in character": ancient and medieval ideas about the status of the autograph as an expression of personality', in *Of the making of books. Medieval manuscripts, their scribes and readers, essays presented to M. B. Parkes*, ed. P. R. Robinson and R. Zim, Aldershot, 1997, 280–99.

Garrison, M. D., 'Alcuin's world through his letters and verse', unpublished PhD thesis, Cambridge, 1995.

Goodrich, W. E., 'The limits of Friendship: A disagreement between Saint Bernard and Peter the Venerable on the role of charity in dispensation from the Rule', *Cistercian Studies* 16 (1981), 81–97.

Grabois, A., 'Le schisme de 1130 et la France', *Revue d'Histoire Ecclésiastique* 76 (1981), 594–612.

Grivot, D., 'Saint Bernard et Pierre le Vénérable', in *Saint Bernard et la recherche de Dieu*. Actes du colloque organisé par l'Institut catholique de Toulouse, 25–29 janvier, 1991, Bulletin de Littérature Ecclésiastique 93 (1992), fasc. I, 85–99.

Haseldine, J., 'Friendship and rivalry: the role of *amicitia* in twelfth-century monastic relations', *Journal of Ecclesiastical History* 44 (1993), 390–414.

Haseldine, J. P., 'A study of the letters of abbot Peter of la-Celle (c. 1115–1184)', unpublished PhD thesis, Cambridge, 1991.

Haseldine, J. P., 'Understanding the language of *amicitia*. The friendship circle of Peter of Celle (c. 1115–1183)', *Journal of Medieval History* 20 (1994), 237–60.

Holsinger, B., 'The color of salvation', in *The tongue of the Fathers. Gender and ideology in twelfth-century Latin*, ed. D. Townsend and A. Taylor, Philadelphia, 1998, 156–86.

Hutchinson, G. O., *Cicero's correspondence. A literary study*, Oxford, 1998.

Hyatte, R., *The arts of friendship: the idealisation of friendship in medieval and early renaissance literature*, Leiden, 1994.

Iogna-Prat, D., *Ordonner et exclure. Cluny et la société chrétienne face à l'hérésie, au judaïsme et à l'islam 1000–1150*, Paris, 1998.

Jaffé, P., *Regesta pontificum Romanorum*, 2nd ed., F. Kaltenbrunner, P. Ewald and S. Löwenfeld, 2 vols, Leipzig, 1885–88.

James, B. S., *Saint Bernard of Clairvaux, an essay in biography*, London, 1957.

Janson, T., *Prose rhythm in medieval Latin from the 9th to the 13th century*, Studia Latina Stockholmiensia 20, Stockholm, 1975.

Kedar, B. J., *Crusade and mission. European approaches towards Muslims*, Princeton, New Jersey, 1984.

Kneepkens, C. H., 'There is more in a Biblical quotation than meets the eye: on Peter the Venerable's letter of consolation to Heloise', *Media Latinitas, a collection of essays to mark the occasion of the retirement of L. J. Engels*, ed. R. I. A. Nip, H. van Dijk, E. M. C. van Houts, C. H. Kneepkens and G. A. A. Kortekaas, Instrumenta Patristica 28, Turnhout, 1996, 89–100.

Knight, G. R., 'Politics and pastoral care: papal schism in some letters of Peter the Venerable', *Revue Bénédictine* 109 (3–4) (1999), 359–90.

Knight, G. R., 'The language of retreat and the eremitic ideal in some letters of Peter the Venerable', *Archives d'Histoire Doctrinale et Littéraire* 63 (1996), 7–43.

Knight, G. R., 'Rhetoric and stylistics: the personalisation of convention in the letters of Peter the Venerable', unpublished PhD thesis, Reading, 1997.

Knight, G. R., 'Uses and abuses of *amicitia*: the correspondence between Peter the Venerable and Hato of Troyes', *Reading Medieval Studies* 23 (1997), 35–67.

Konstan, D., *Friendship in the classical world*, Cambridge, 1997.

Knowles, Dom D., *Saints and scholars, 25 medieval portraits*, Cambridge, 1962.

Knowles, Dom D., 'Cistercians and Cluniacs: the controversy between St Bernard and Peter the Venerable', Friends of Dr Williams' Library Ninth Lecture, London, 1955, reprinted in *The historian and character and other essays*, Cambridge, 1963, 50–75.

Knowles, Dom D., 'The case of St William of York', *Cambridge Historical Journal* 5(2) (1936), 162–77; 212–14, reprinted in Knowles, *The historian and character and other essays*, Cambridge, 1963, 76–97.

Knowles, Dom D., 'The reforming decrees of Peter the Venerable', in *Petrus Venerabilis, 1156–1956: studies and texts commemorating the eighth centenary of his death*, ed. G. Constable and J. Kritzeck, Studia Anselmiana 40, Rome, 1956, 1–20.

Kramer, S. M., 'The friend as "second self" and the theme of substitution in the letters of Bernard of Clairvaux', *Cistercian Studies Quarterly* 31:1 (1996), 21–33.

Kritzeck, J., 'De l'influence de Pierre Abélard sur Pierre le Vénérable dans ses œuvres sur l'Islam', in *Pierre Abélard–Pierre le Vénérable. Les courants littéraires et artistiques en occident au milieu du XIIe siècle*, Colloques Internationaux du Centre National de la Recherche Scientifique 546, Paris, 1975, 205–12.

Kritzeck, J., 'Peter the Venerable and the Toledan Collection', in *Petrus Venerabilis, 1156–1956: studies and texts commemorating the eighth centenary of his death*, ed. G. Constable and J. Kritzeck, Studia Anselmiana 40, Rome, 1956, 176–201.

Kritzeck, J., *Peter the Venerable and Islam*, Princeton Oriental Studies 23, Princeton, New Jersey, 1964.

Lamma, P., *Momenti di storiografia Cluniacense*, Istituto Storico Italiano per il Medio Evo: Studi Storici 42–4, Rome, 1961.

Lang, A. P., 'The Friendship between Peter the Venerable and Bernard of Clairvaux', in *Bernard of Clairvaux, Studies presented to Dom J. Leclercq*, Washington, 1973, 35–53.

Lanham, C. D., *Salutatio formulas in Latin letters to 1200: syntax, style and theory*, Munich, 1975.

Lausberg, H., *Handbook of literary rhetoric, a foundation for literary study*, trans. M. T. Bliss, A. Janson and D. E. Orton, ed. D. E. Orton and R. D. Anderson, foreword G. A. Kennedy, Leiden; Boston; Cologne, 1998.

Leclercq, Dom J., 'Le thème de la jonglerie dans les relations entre Saint Bernard, Abélard et Pierre le Vénérable', in *Pierre Abélard–Pierre le Vénérable. Les courants littéraires et artistiques en occident au milieu du XIIe siècle*, Colloques Internationaux du Centre National de la Recherche Scientifique 546, Paris, 1975, 671–84.

Leclercq, Dom J., 'Les lettres de Guillaume de Saint-Thierry à saint Bernard', *Revue Bénédictine* 79 (1969), 375–91.

Leclercq, Dom J., 'Pour l'histoire des traités de S. Bernard', in *Recueil d'études sur saint Bernard et ses écrits*, 5 vols, II, Rome, 1966, 101–30.

Leclercq, Dom J., 'Lettres de vocation à la vie monastique', *Studia Anselmiana* 37, Analecta Monastica III, Rome, 1955, 169–97.

Leclercq, Dom J., 'Aspects littéraires de l'œuvre de saint Bernard', *Cahiers de Civilisation Médiévale* 1 (1958), 425–50.

Leclercq, Dom J., 'Pierre le Vénérable et les limites du programme clunisien', *Collectanea Ordinis Cisterciensium Reformatorum* 18 (1956), 84–7.

Leclercq, Dom J., 'L'amitié dans les lettres au Moyen Age', *Revue du Moyen-Age Latin* I (1945), 391–410.

Leclercq, Dom J., 'Lettres de S. Bernard: histoire ou littérature?', in *Recueil d'études sur saint Bernard et ses écrits*, 5 vols, IV, Storia e letteratura 167, Rome, 1987, 125–225.

Leclercq, Dom J., *Pierre le Vénérable*, Abbaye St Wandrille, 1946.

Leclercq, Dom J., 'Diversification et identité dans le monachisme', *Studia Monastica* 28 (1986), 51–74.

Leclercq, Dom J. (ed.), 'Nouvelle réponse de l'ancien monachisme au manifeste de saint Bernard', *Revue Bénédictine* 67 (1957), 77–94.

Leclercq, Dom J., 'L'encyclique de saint Bernard en faveur de la croisade', *Revue Bénédictine* 81 (1971), 282–308.

Lekai, L. J., *The Cistercians, ideals and reality*, Kent, Ohio, 1977.

Lortz, J., 'Einleitung', in *Bernhard von Clairvaux, Mönch und Mystiker*, Internationaler Bernhardkongress, Mainz, 1953, Wiesbaden, 1955, IX–LVI.

Luchaire, A., *Études sur les actes de Louis VII, histoire des institutions monarchiques de la France sous les premiers capétiens (mémoires et documents)*, Paris, 1885.

Mahn, J.-B., *L'ordre cistercien et son gouvernement des origines au milieu du XIIIe siècle (1098–1265)*, Paris, 1945, 2nd ed., Paris, 1951.

Maitland, S. R., *The Dark Ages, a series of essays*, London, 1844.

Malherbe, A. J., *Ancient epistolary theory*, Society of Biblical Literature 19, Atlanta, Georgia, 1988.

Marenbon, J., *The philosophy of Peter Abelard*, Cambridge, 1997.

McEvoy, J., 'The theory of friendship in the Latin Middle Ages: hermeneutics, contextualization and the transmission and reception of ancient texts and ideas, from AD 350 to c. 1500', in *Friendship in medieval Europe*, ed. J. Haseldine, Thrupp, Stroud, 1999, 3–44.

McGuire, B. P., *The difficult saint. Bernard of Clairvaux and his tradition*, Cistercian Studies Series 126, Kalamazoo, Mich., 1991.

McGuire, B. P., *Friendship and community, the monastic experience 350–1250*, Cistercian Studies Series 95, Kalamazoo, Mich., 1988.

McLoughlin, J., '*Amicitia* in practice: John of Salisbury (c. 1120–1180) and his circle', in D. Williams (ed.), *England in the twelfth century* (Proceedings of the 1988 Harlaxton Symposium), Woodbridge, 1990, 161–81.

Mews, C. J., 'Peter Abelard', in *Authors of the Middle Ages, historical and religious writers of the Latin West*, ed. P. J. Geary, 4 vols, Aldershot, 1995, II, no. 5, 1–88.

Meyvaert, P., 'Diversity within unity: a Gregorian theme', *Heythrop Journal* 4 (1963), 141–62.

Mollat, D. and Derville, A., 'Folie de la Croix', in *Dictionnaire de spiritualité ascétique et mystique, doctrine et histoire*, founded M. Viller, F. Cavallera and J. de Guibert, continuation A. Rayez and C. Baumgartner, 16 vols, 5, fasc. 35–6, Paris, 1964, 635–50.

Moo, D. J., *The epistle to the Romans*, New International Commentary on the New Testament, ed. N. Stonehouse, F. Bruce and G. Fee, Grand Rapids; Cambridge, 1996.

Moore, R. I., *The origins of European dissent*, London, 1977, revised Oxford, 1985.

Murphy, J. J., *Rhetoric in the Middle Ages. A history of rhetorical theory from Saint Augustine to the Renaissance*, Berkeley; Los Angeles; London, 1974.

Murphy, J. J. (ed.), *Three Medieval Rhetorical Arts*, Berkeley; Los Angeles, 1971.

d'Olwer, L. N., 'Sur quelques lettres de S. Bernard, avant ou après le concile de Sens?', in *Mélanges saint Bernard*, XXIVᵉ congrès de l'association bourguignonne des sociétés savantes, Dijon, 1953, 100–108.

Oursel, R., *La dispute et la grace: Essai sur la rédemption d'Abélard*, Publications de l'Université de Dijon 19, Paris, 1959.

Oury, G., 'Idiota', in *Dictionnaire de spiritualité ascétique et mystique, doctrine et histoire*, founded M. Viller, F. Cavallera and J. de Guibert, continuation A. Rayez and C. Baumgartner, 16 vols, 7.2, fasc. 48–9, Paris, 1970, 1242–8.

Pacaut, M., *L'ordre de Cluny*, Paris, 1986.

Palumbo, P. F., *Lo Scisma del MCXXX: i precedenti, la vicenda romana e le ripercussioni europee della lotta tra Anacleto e Innocenzo II, col regesto degli atti di Anacleto II*, Rome, 1942.

Pepin, R. E., '*Amicitia iocosa*: Peter of Celle and John of Salisbury', *Florilegium* 5 (1983), 140–56.

Pétré, H., *Caritas: Étude sur le vocabulaire latin de la charité chrétienne*, Spicilegium Sacrum Lovaniense, Études et documents 42, Louvain, 1948.

Phillips, J., *Defenders of the Holy Land*, Oxford, 1996.

Piazzoni, A. M., 'Un falso problemo storiografico: Note a proposito della "amicizia" tra Pietro il Venerabile e Bernardo di Clairvaux', *Bullettino dell'Istituto Storico Italiano per il Medio Evo e Archivio Muratoriano* 89 (1980–81), 443–87.

Pignot, J.-H., *Histoire de l'ordre de Cluny depuis la fondation de l'abbaye jusqu'à la mort de Pierre-le-Vénérable*, 3 vols, Autun, 1868.

Rosenmeyer, P. A., 'Ovid's *Heroides* and *Tristia*: voices from exile', *Ramus* 26 (i) (1997), 29–56.

Rosenwein, B., *Rhinoceros bound. Cluny in the tenth century*, Philadelphia, 1982.

Rowe, J. G., 'The origins of the Second Crusade: Pope Eugenius III, Bernard of

Clairvaux and Louis VII of France', in *The Second Crusade and the Cistercians*, ed. M. Gervers, New York, 1992, 79–89.

Rudolph, C., *The 'things of greater importance': Bernard of Clairvaux's Apologia and the medieval attitude towards art*, Philadelphia, 1990.

Schmale, F.-J., *Studien zum Schisma des Jahres 1130*, Forschungen zur kirchlichen Rechtsgeschichte und zum Kirchenrecht 3, Cologne-Graz, 1961.

Seguin, A., 'Bernard et la seconde Croisade', in *Bernard de Clairvaux*, Commission d'histoire de l'ordre de Cîteaux 3, Paris, 1953, 379–409.

Siberry, E., *Criticism of crusading 1095–1274*, Oxford, 1985.

Silvestre, H., 'Diversi sed non adversi', *Recherches de théologie ancienne et médiévale* 31 (1964), 124–32.

Špidlík, T. and Vandenbroucke, F., 'Fous pour le Christ', in *Dictionnaire de spiritualité ascétique et mystique, doctrine et histoire*, founded M. Viller, F. Cavallera and J. de Guibert, continuation A. Rayez and C. Baumgartner, 16 vols, 5, fasc. 35–6, Paris, 1964, 752–70.

Stowers, S. K., *Letter Writing in Greco-Roman Antiquity*, Philadelphia, 1986.

Stowers, S. K., *A re-reading of Romans*, New Haven, London, 1994.

Stroll, M., *The Jewish pope: ideology and politics in the papal schism of 1130*, Leiden, 1987.

Talbot, C. H., 'The date and author of the *Riposte*', in *Petrus Venerabilis, 1156–1956: studies and texts commemorating the eighth centenary of his death*, ed. G. Constable and J. Kritzeck, Studia Anselmiana 40, Rome, 1956, 72–80.

Talbot, C. H., 'New documents in the case of Saint William of York', *The Cambridge Historical Journal* 10(1) (1950), 1–15.

Tellenbach, G., 'La chute de l'abbé Pons de Cluny et sa signification historique', *Annales du Midi* 76 (3–4) (1964), 355–62.

Torrell, J.-P. and Bouthillier, D., *Pierre le Vénérable et sa vision du monde. Sa vie, son œuvre. L'homme et le démon*, Spicilegium Sacrum Lovaniense, Études et documents 42, Louvain, 1986.

Torrell, J.-P., 'Une spiritualité de combat. Pierre le Vénérable et la lutte contre Satan', *Revue Thomiste* 84 (1984), 47–81.

Torrell, J.-P., 'La notion de prophétie et la méthode apologétique dans le *Contra Saracenos* de Pierre le Vénérable', *Studia Monastica* 17 (1975), 257–82.

Torrell, J.-P. and Bouthillier, D., '*Miraculum*. Une catégorie fondamentale chez Pierre le Vénérable', *Revue Thomiste* 80 (1980), 357–86, 549–66.

Vacandard, E., *Vie de Saint Bernard, abbé de Clairvaux*, 2 vols, Paris, 1927.

De Valous, G., *Le monachisme clunisien des origines au XVᵉ siècle*, 2 vols, 2nd ed., Paris, 1970.

van den Eynde, D., 'Les principaux voyages de Pierre le Vénérable', *Benedictina* 15 (1968), 58–110.

van den Eynde, D., 'Les premiers écrits de saint Bernard', in *Recueil d'études sur saint Bernard et ses écrits*, ed. Dom J. Leclercq, 5 vols, III, Rome, 1969, 343–422.

Versini, L., *Le roman épistolaire*, Paris, 1979.

von Moos, P., 'Le silence d'Héloïse', in *Pierre Abélard–Pierre le Vénérable. Les courants littéraires et artistiques en occident au milieu du XIIe siècle*, Colloques Internationaux du Centre National de la Recherche Scientifique 546, Paris, 1975, 425–68.

Walther, H., *Lateinische Sprichwörter und Sentenzen des Mittelalters*, 6 vols, Göttingen, 1963–69.

White, C., *Christian friendship in the fourth century*, Cambridge, 1992.

White, C., *The Correspondence (394–419) between Jerome and Augustine of Hippo*, Studies in Bible and Early Christianity 23, Lewiston; Queenston; Lampeter, 1990.

White, C., 'Friendship in absence – some patristic views', in *Friendship in medieval Europe*, ed. J. Haseldine, Thrupp, Stroud, 1999, 68–88.

Wiesen, D. S., *St. Jerome as a satirist, a study in Christian Latin thought and letters*, Cornell Studies in Classical Philology 34, Ithaca, New York, 1964.

Williams, W., 'Peter the Venerable, a letter to St Bernard', *Downside Review* 56 (1938), 344–53.

Wilmart, A., 'Une riposte de l'ancien monachisme au manifeste de Saint Bernard', *Revue Bénédictine* 46 (1934), 269–344.

Wollasch, J., 'Das Schisma des Abtes Pontius von Cluny', *Francia* 23/1 (1996), 31–52.

Zerbi, P., 'Intorno allo scisma di Ponzio, abbate di Cluny (1122–1126)' in *Tra Milano e Cluny, momenti di vita e cultura ecclesiastica nel secolo XII*, Italia Sacra 28, Rome, 1978.

Zerbi, P., 'Les différends doctrinaux', in *Bernard de Clairvaux. Histoire, mentalités, spiritualité*, Colloque de Lyon–Cîteaux–Dijon, Sources Chrétiennes 380, Paris, 1992, 429–58.

Zerbi, P., 'Remarques sur l'epistola 98 de Pierre le Vénérable', in *Pierre Abélard–Pierre le Vénérable. Les courants littéraires et artistiques en occident au milieu du XIIe siècle*, Colloques Internationaux du Centre National de la Recherche Scientifique 546, Paris, 1975, 215–32.

Zerbi, P., ' "In Cluniaco vestra sibi perpetuam mansionem elegit" (Petri Venerabilis Epistola 98): un momento decisivo nella vita di Abelardo dopo il concilio di Sens', in *Tra Milano e Cluny. Momenti di vita e cultura ecclesiastica nel secolo XII*, Italia Sacra 28, Rome, 1978, 373–95.

Zerbi, P., 'William of Saint Thierry and his dispute with Abelard', in *William, abbot of St. Thierry. A colloquium at the Abbey of St. Thierry*, trans. from the French by J. Carfantan, Cistercian Studies Series 94, Kalamazoo, Mich., 1987, 181–203.

Index

Abelard, Peter
  Bernard
    condemnation by 102
    reconciliation 105–6
  excommunication 103
  life 102 n.7
  and Peter 102–5
Aelred of Rievaulx 26
  De speculo caritatis 165
agape, caritas, equated 14
alterity, in Peter's letter 150 190–91
Altman, J.G., epistolarity model 8
amicitia
  in Bernard's epistle 147 173
  caritas, contrasted 13, 14, 15, 22, 110,
    117, 121
  dilectio, contrasted 245, 246, 250
  meaning 13, 14, 15, 22
  in Peter/Bernard correspondence 279
  in Peter's letter 65 59
  in Peter's letter 192 263
  philia, equated 14
  see also friendship
amicitia iocosa
  in Bernard's epistle 228 107–10
  in Bernard's epistle 387 159
  examples 16–22
  purpose 22–3, 109
Ammianus Marcellinus, *Res Gestae* 259
amor
  caritas, contrasted 13
  meaning 13
  in Peter's letter 65, 59
Anacletus (antipope)
  and Bernard 64, 70
  death 65, 73
  and Innocent II 56–7, 88, 99
Anastasius IV, Pope 277
Antioch 215
argumentation, and *caritas* 40
Arnold of Bonneval 280–81
Arnold of Brescia 103

auctoritas, ratio, interplay 30, 33, 137
Augustine, St
  De Trinitate 94
  on friendship 18
  St Jerome, correspondence
  influence on Peter/Bernard
    correspondence 23, 26, 44–56,
    59–60, 62–4, 101, 111–15, 120–23,
    160, 182, 231–2, 276, 279, 280
  Virgil, references 114

Baro, sub-deacon, legacy 174–5
Benedict, St
  Rule
    in Bernard's epistle 265 241
    and *caritas* 30, 35–7, 38, 128, 129,
      134
    in Peter's letter 28 25, 30, 33, 34,
      35–7, 41, 49, 51, 279
    in Peter's letter 29 91
    in Peter's letter 111 137, 139, 140
    in Peter's letter 150 192
Bernard of Clairvaux
  and Anacletus (antipope) 64, 70
  Apologia 31, 33, 35, 41–2, 50
    caritas in 29–30, 37, 271
    date 27
    in Peter's letter 28 26–7, 43–4, 53,
      64, 279
    in Peter's letter 111 128, 132–3
    Phariseism in 40–41
    prolepsis in 31
    St Jerome, citation 29
    structure 28–30
  De consideratione 215
  De praecepto et dispensatione 150
  Dean Falco, letter to 98
  epistle 147, 57, 64, 70–74, 97
    amicitia in 173
    biblical allusions 66, 69, 213
    date 65, 73
    language 67–8

Pauline echoes 71
and schism 65
structure 66
sub-text 65–6
syntactical devices 69–70
epistle 148, 72, 73–4
on Saint-Bertin monastery 98–9
epistle 227, 262
epistle 228, 101, 118
amicitia iocosa in 107–10
biblical allusions 110
caritas in 115
date 106
Pharisaism in 115–16
rhetorical devices 115–17, 127
silence in 115, 116, 127
epistle 265
biblical allusions 238–9
bucella 237–8
date 253
language 235–7
St Benedict's *Rule* 241
epistle 363 217
epistle 364, 209–10
biblical allusions 213
caritas in 211, 224
date 208
language 210–12
epistle 387, 155–6, 161–2
amicitia iocosa in 159
biblical allusions 162, 165–8
caritas in 162
date 201–2
language 164
purpose 177
structure 159–60
style 158–9
epistle 389, 157–8, 195–6
biblical allusions 197–9
date 202
language 196
epistle 521 221–3
Letter to Robert 280
life ix–x
Peter
correspondence, and friendship 2–3,
45–6, 51
meeting, proposed 71, 74, 110, 190,
223, 253
Peter Abelard
condemnation 102

reconciliation 105–6
on plurality 41–3
and the Second Crusade 208–9, 212
William of St Thierry, correspondence
19–20, 26, 50
Bonami, canon 88
bone vir, significance 67
Bredero, A.H., on Peter's letter 28 53–4, 55
bucella, in Bernard's epistle 265 237–8

caelia, cervisia, equated 16
caritas
agape, contrasted 14
amicitia, contrasted 13, 14, 15, 22,
110, 117, 121
amor, contrasted 13
and argumentation 40
in Bernard's *Apologia* 29–30, 37, 271
in Bernard's epistle 228 115
in Bernard's epistle 364 211, 224
in Bernard's epistle 387 162
and the Cluniacs 128–9
meaning 13, 14, 15, 22, 279
and Nicholas of Clairvaux 227
personified 32
in Peter's letter 28 30, 32–3, 35–8, 40,
54–5, 128
in Peter's letter 65 59, 64
in Peter's letter 111 101, 123–4, 129,
130, 133, 139, 143, 144, 153
in Peter's letter 149 174
in Peter's letter 150 155, 182, 184,
189, 193, 232
in Peter's letter 181 252
in Peter's letter 192 259, 271–2, 273
in Peter's letter 193 265, 280
and *rectitudo* 38
and St Benedict's *Rule* 30, 35–7, 38,
128, 129, 134
and salvation 182–3, 236
and *scandalum* 84
cervisia, caelia, contrasted 16
Cicero
on friendship 17
Laelius 17, 240, 246
Cistercians, Cluniacs
hostility 3, 25, 38, 55–6, 82–3, 96, 99,
117, 133–4, 273
and Langres, election 75
and tithes 75–6, 101, 163, 274, 275,
277

rapprochement 234
Cluniacs
  and *caritas* 128–9
  reforms 116, 193, 262
Cluniacs, Cistercians
  hostility 3, 25, 38, 55–6, 82–3, 96, 99,
    117, 133–4, 273
  and Langres, election 75
  and tithes 75–6, 101, 163, 274, 275,
    277
cohabitatio
  in Peter's letter 150, 155, 165, 172,
    195, 234
  in Peter's letter 175, 232, 233, 234
Collectio toledana 117
Crusade, Second (1147–48) 201, 212, 217
  failure 208–9, 221
  Peter on 214–15
  Pope Eugenius III on 221

Demetrius, *De elocutione* 7
dictamen, examples 4–5
dilectio 13
  amicitia, contrasted 245, 246, 250
  in Peter's letter 29, 96
  in Peter's letter 65, 59
  in Peter's letter 181, 247
dilemmas, logical, in Peter's letter 28
    37–40

epistles
  letters, distinction 3–4
  see also letter-writing; letters
epistolarity
  application 279
  discourse 1
  model xi, 8
  value 23, 158
Eugenius III, Pope x, 163, 175, 207, 262,
    268, 273, 274, 277
  Peter, meeting 253
  Peter on 263–4
  on the Second Crusade 221

Falco, Dean, Bernard, letter from 98
Fitzherbert, William, archbishop 162–3
friendship
  Cicero on 17
  definition 12–13, 15, 17
  joking *see amicitia iocosa*
  language of 10–12, 13–15, 228–9

and letter-writing 9, 16
Peter on 12–13, 15
  in Peter's letter 28 25, 45–6
  in Peter's letter 29 90
  in Peter's letter 65 57–9
  in Peter's letter 149 164–5, 171–2
  and rhetoric 2–3
  St Augustine on 18
  terminology of 13–15
  as *topos* 9–10, 45
  see also amicitia

Gigny priory
  attack on Le Miroir 253, 264–5, 272,
    277
  papal bull on 253, 264, 272
  tithes payment 76, 86, 99, 143, 243,
    253
Gilo of Tusculum 74
  Peter, correspondence 57
gloria, meaning 67, 71
Godfrey of La Roche-Vanneau 86, 205
Guigo of La Chartreuse, prior 170–71,
    280

Haimeric, cardinal 85
  Peter, correspondence 76, 77, 78, 79,
    80
Hato of Troyes, bishop 12, 155, 159, 229
Heloise 106
Henry of Blois 163
  life 19 n.136
  Peter, correspondence 20–22
Henry of France, bishop 156, 201, 202,
    224
  appointments held 206–7
history, and literature 1–2
Horace, *Epistles* 180, 233, 265–6
Hugh of Auxerre, bishop 241
Hugh II of Grenoble, bishop 175
Humbert, Archbishop of Lyons 253, 268

Innocent II, Pope
  and Anacletus 56–7, 88, 99
  Peter, correspondence 57, 76, 78–9, 80,
    102, 270, 275
  and tithes payment 76
irony, in Peter/Bernard correspondence
    279
Islam, in Peter's letter 111 117, 144–51,
    153

Italy, Peter's visit 253
iustitia, meaning 80

Jerome, St 18–19
　cited in Bernard's *Apologia* 29
　Rufinus, hostility 63–4, 135, 160
　Rusticus, correspondence 135
　St Augustine, correspondence
　　influence on Peter/Bernard
　　correspondence 23, 26, 44–56,
　　59–60, 62–4, 101, 111–15,
　　120–23, 160, 182, 231–2, 276,
　　279, 280
　Virgil references 114
John of Salisbury 16, 22
　Peter of Celle, correspondence 158–9
Jouarre, Synod of (1133/34) 270 n.138

Langres, diocese
　election 75, 86, 96–7, 99, 101, 118,
　　163, 205, 219, 256–7, 270
　investiture 87–8
language, of friendship 10–12, 13–15,
　228–9
Le Miroir abbey
　attack by Gigny 253, 264–5, 272, 277
　tithes payment 76, 77, 86, 143, 243,
　253
letter-writing
　critical approaches to 4–9
　and friendship 9, 16
　manuals 4–5, 6–7
　models 4, 6
　and rhetoric 7–8
letters
　definition 4
　epistles, distinction 3–4
　and friendship 9
　function 8
　literary, status 1
　as literary artefacts 8
　literary criticism, application of 8, 279
　and *topoi* 8, 9
　and verbal play 18–19
　see also epistles; epistolarity
literary criticism, letters, application to 8,
　279
literature, and history 1–2
Louis VII, King 87, 202, 205, 209
Lucan, *De bello civili* 259

manual labour, in Peter's letter 111
　140–41, 153
mendacium, in Peter's letter 29 90–94, 95
Molesme 86
Murdach, Henry, abbot 163

Nicholas of Clairvaux 177, 194, 199, 202,
　208, 225
　Bernard's secretary 155–6
　and *caritas* 227
　Cluny, proposed visit 227–8, 241–3,
　246–7
　Peter
　　correspondence 159, 227, 228–9,
　　253
　　friendship 228–30
　　proposed meeting 227–8

Odo, founder of Cluny 280
Orderic Vitalis 142

paraenesis 7
Persius, *Satires* 121–2
Peter of Blois 9
Peter of Celle 16, 17, 22
　John of Salisbury, correspondence
　　158–9
Peter of Lyons, archbishop 86, 88, 89, 97,
　143, 164, 274
Peter of Poitiers, Peter, correspondence
　14–15, 233, 280
Peter the Venerable
　Bernard, meeting, proposed 71, 74,
　　110, 190, 253
　Cardinal Haimeric, correspondence 76,
　　77, 78, 79, 80
　correspondence
　　amicitia in 279
　　authenticity xii
　　and friendship 2–3, 45–6, 51, 57–9
　　as historical documents 3
　　influence of Augustine/Jerome
　　correspondence 23, 26, 44–51,
　　55–6, 59–60, 62–4, 101, 110,
　　111–15, 120–23, 160, 182, 231–2,
　　276, 279, 280
　　irony in 279
　　issues reflected in ix, xi
　　as literary documents 3
　　significance 281–2
　　structure 6

on Eugenius III 263–4
Eugenius III, meeting 253
on friendship 12–13, 15
Gilo of Tusculum, correspondence 57
Henry of Blois, correspondence 20–22
Innocent II, correspondence 57, 76,
    78–9, 80, 102, 270, 275
Italy, visit 253
letter 28
    A.H. Bredero on 53–4, 55
    caritas in 30, 32–3, 35–8, 40, 54–5,
      128
    date 26–7
    friendship in 25, 45–6
    logical dilemmas in 37–40
    prolepsis in 31
    prosopopoeia in 31
    reductio ad absurdum in 34
    response to Bernard's *Apologia*
      26–7, 43–4, 53, 64, 279
    rhetorical devices 31–2, 35–6, 43–4
    ridicule, use of 34–5
    St Benedict's *Rule* 25, 30, 33, 34,
      35–7, 41, 49, 51, 279
    structure 30–31
letter 29, 88–9
    date 87
    dilectio in 96
    friendship 90
    language 87
    mendacium in 90–94, 95
    rhetorical devices 89–90
    St Benedict's *Rule* 91
    structure 87
letter 34, and schism 76–7
letter 65
    rhetorical devices 60–63, 212
    amicitia in 59
    amor in 59
    caritas in 59, 64
    friendship in 57–9
    language 57
    purpose 75
letter 73 72–3
letter 98 106
letter 111, 143
    Bernard's *Apologia* in 128, 132–3
    biblical allusions 136–7
    body language 135–6
    caritas in 101, 123–4, 128, 129,
      130, 133, 139, 143, 144, 153

    as exegesis 117–18, 168–74
    Islam in 117, 144–51, 153
    language 141–2
    and manual labour 140–41, 153
    prolepsis in 130
    prosopopoeia in 130
    purpose 139–43
    rhetorical devices 118–20, 130–32
    St Benedict's *Rule* 137, 139, 140
    silence in 122, 127
    structure 101, 117–18, 129–38
letter 145
    biblical allusions 207
    date of 201
    language 204–5
    rhetorical devices 202–4, 205–6
letter 149
    156–7, 162
    biblical allusions 171–2
    caritas in 174
    date of 179
    as exegesis 168–74
    friendship in 164–5, 171–2
    language 169–70
    purpose 177
letter 150
    alterity in 190–91
    biblical allusions 179–81, 186,
      192–3, 232
    caritas in 155, 182, 184, 189, 193,
      232
    cohabitatio in 155, 165, 172, 195,
      234
    date of 156
    language 184–8, 194, 196–7,
      229–30
    prosopopoeia in 190
    purpose 199–200
    rhetorical devices 183–4, 190–94,
      232–3
    St Benedict's *Rule* 192
    structure 179
letter 151, 229
letter 164, 201
    language 216–17
    rhetorical devices 214, 218–21
letter 175, 274
    biblical allusions 231–2
    cohabitatio in 232, 233, 234
    language 231–3
    purpose 251–2

structure 230–31
letter 181, 244
    caritas in 252
    dilectio in 247
    language 247–52
    structure 245–6
letter 192, 253
    amicitia in 263
    biblical allusions 257–8, 260,
        267–8, 270–71, 275–6
    caritas in 259, 271–2, 273
    classical allusions 259–60
    language 255–6, 260–61, 268–70,
        272–4, 277
    metaphors 258–60
    rhetorical devices 266
    structure 254–5
letter 193
    caritas in 265, 280
    classical allusions 266
life ix
Nicholas of Clairvaux
    correspondence 159, 227, 228–9,
        253
    friendship 228–30
    meeting, proposed 227–8
and Peter Abelard 102–5
Peter of Poitiers, correspondence
    14–15, 233, 280
on the Second Crusade 214–15
on tithes 76–8, 79, 80, 84–5, 97, 118
works, other
    Adversus Iudaeos 150
    Contra Petrobrusianos 150
    Contra Sarracenos 145, 150
    Epistola de translatione sua 146,
        147, 150
    Statutes 116
    *Summa totius haeresis
        Sarracenorum* 146, 150
Phariseism
    in Bernard's *Apologia* 40–41
    in Bernard's epistle 228 115–16
philia, amicitia, equated 14
Pisa, Council of (1135) 85, 189–90
plurality, Bernard on 41–3
Pons of Melgueil, return to Cluny 53, 271
Pontius, Peter's brother 242
Prodigal Son, parable 274, 275
prolepsis
    in Bernard's *Apologia* 31

in Peter's letter 28 31
in Peter's letter 111 130
prosopopoeia
    in Peter's letter 28 32
    in Peter's letter 111 130
    in Peter's letter 150 190

Rabanus Maurus 259
ratio, auctoritas, interplay 30, 33, 137
Raymond of Antioch 209
rectitudo
    and *caritas* 38
    tortitudo, contrasted 38
reductio ad absurdum, in Peter's
    correspondence 34, 81–2, 274
rhetoric
    and friendship 2–3
    and letter-writing 7–8
    types 7
ridicule, in Peter's letter 28 34–5
Rufinus, St Jerome, hostility 63–4, 135,
    160
Rusticus, St Jerome, correspondence 135

Saint-Bertin, abbot 99
Saint-Gilles, abbey 94
Saint Saturnin-du-Pont, priory 94
salvation, and *caritas* 182–3, 236
scandalum 78, 83–4
    and *caritas* 84
schism xi, 56–7, 74, 88, 99
    and Bernard's epistle 147 65
    and Peter's letter 34 76–7
Sens, Council of (1140/41) 102, 104
silence
    in Bernard's epistle 228 115, 116, 127
    in Peter's letter 111 122, 127
Stesichorus 114
'steward of injustice' parable 82, 275
Suger, abbot 221
    life 209 n.59

terminology, of friendship 13–15
Tertullian 92
tithes
    and Cistercians/Cluniacs hostility
        75–6, 83, 101, 163, 274, 275,
        277
    and Innocent II 76
    payment to Gigny priory 76, 86, 99,
        143, 243, 253

payment by Le Miroir abbey 76, 77, 86, 143, 243, 253
Peter on 76–8, 79, 80, 84–5, 97, 118
topos
  application to letters 8, 9
  friendship as 9–10, 45
tortitudo, rectitudo, contrasted 38

verbal play, and letters 18–19
Victor, Julius, *Ars rhetorica* 7, 168

Virgil
  Aeneid 114
  Eclogues 81, 114

William of Sabran 86, 94
William of St Thierry 115
  Bernard, correspondence 19–20, 26, 50
  life 19 n.135
William X, Duke 57